A SURVEY OF ACCOUNTING

Ronald J. Huefner, Ph.D., C.M.A., C.P.A.

State University of New York at Buffalo

Robert P. Derstine, Ph.D., C.P.A.

Villanova University

McGraw-Hill Publishing Company

New York   St. Louis   San Francisco   Auckland   Bogotá   Caracas
Hamburg   Lisbon   London   Madrid   Mexico   Milan
Montreal   New Delhi   Oklahoma City   Paris   San Juan
São Paulo   Singapore   Sydney   Tokyo   Toronto

This book was set in Times Roman by Publication Services.
The editor was Robert Lynch;
the cover was designed by Rafael Hernandez;
the production supervisor was Denise L. Puryear.
Project supervision was done by Publication Services.
R.R. Donnelley & Sons Company was printer and binder.

A Survey of Accounting

3 4 5 6 7 8 9 0 DOCDOC 9 2 1 0

ISBN 0-07-030822-5

LIBRARY OF CONGRESS
Library of Congress Cataloging-in-Publication Data

Huefner, Ronald J.
    A survey of accounting / Ronald J. Huefner, Robert P. Derstine.
      p.   cm.
    Includes index.
    ISBN 0-07-030822-5
    1. Accounting.   I. Derstine, Robert P.   II. Title.
HF5635.H8833 1988
657–dc19   87-30782
           CIP

To our students—past, present, and future

ABOUT THE AUTHORS

RONALD J. HUEFNER is Professor of Accounting in the School of Management at the State University of New York at Buffalo. He received his B.A. degree from Canisius College, and his MBA and Ph.D. from Cornell University. He holds the CMA and CPA certificates, and is a member of the American Institute of Certified Public Accountants, the New York State Society of Certified Public Accountants, the American Accounting Association, the National Association of Accountants, and other professional organizations. His authored and coauthored articles have appeared in *The Accounting Review*, the *Journal of Accounting Research, Management Accounting*, and other journals. He is author of *An Introduction to New York State Income Taxation* (Horton, 1983), coauthor of *Advanced Financial Accounting* (Dryden Press, 1986), and a contributor to the *Handbook of Modern Accounting*, the *Handbook of Cost Accounting*, and the *Accountant's Cost Handbook*. Professor Huefner teaches undergraduate and graduate courses in financial and managerial accounting. He has received the Chancellor's Award of the State University of New York for Excellence in Teaching.

ROBERT P. DERSTINE is Professor of Accountancy in the College of Commerce and Finance at Villanova University. He received his Bachelor's and MBA degrees from Drexel University, and his Ph.D. from the State University of New York at Buffalo. He is a CPA and a member of the American Institute of Certified Public Accountants and the Pennsylvania Institute of Certified Public Accountants. He was a staff accountant for Ernst & Whinney and for Arthur Andersen & Co. His authored and coauthored articles have appeared in various journals including the *Journal of Accountancy*, the *Journal of Accounting Research*, and *The Woman CPA*. Professor Derstine teaches undergraduate and graduate courses in financial accounting and auditing. He has received the Lindback Award for Teaching Excellence from Villanova University.

CONTENTS

CHAPTER 4: INTERNAL CONTROL AND CASH   110

CHAPTER 5: ACCOUNTING FOR SALES
AND RELATED RECEIVABLES   138

CHAPTER 6: COST OF GOODS SOLD
AND INVENTORY ACCOUNTING   173

CHAPTER 7:   DEPRECIATION AND AMORTIZATION—
PROPERTY, PLANT, EQUIPMENT, AND INTANGIBLES 207

CHAPTER 8:   ACCOUNTING FOR INTEREST EXPENSE,
BONDS PAYABLE, AND LEASES 239

CHAPTER 13: ISSUES IN FINANCIAL REPORTING   391

CHAPTER 14: INTRODUCTION TO
MANAGERIAL ACCOUNTING   423

CHAPTER 15: PRODUCT COSTING   450

CHAPTER 16: STANDARD COSTING   493

PREFACE

OBJECTIVES

The objective of this text is to provide an introductory coverage of financial and managerial accounting. Coverage is concise yet comprehensive, and provides a balanced emphasis among accounting concepts, transaction recording, understanding of financial statements, and managerial applications.

The text is designed for use in a first course in accounting for either majors or nonmajors. Upon completing the text, students should be able to understand and interpret accounting data, analyze financial statements, and use accounting information in decision analysis.

Selection of approximately 16 to 18 of the 20 chapters would typically be appropriate for a one-semester or two-quarter survey course. Use of all 20 chapters, including the various chapter appendices and/or the practice cases in the Student Resource Manual, would make the text suitable for a two-semester course.

TOPICAL COVERAGE

The text is organized into 20 chapters, 13 on financial accounting and seven on managerial accounting. Chapters 1 through 3 cover an introduction to transaction analysis, basic elements of the accounting cycle, and an introduction to financial statements. Chapter 4 discusses internal control and cash, including coverage of bank reconciliations. Chapters 5 through 10 cover the main topics of financial accounting: sales and accounts receivable; cost of goods sold and inventories; depreciation and fixed assets; interest expense and bonds payable; investments in stocks and bonds; and stockholders' equity. Throughout this coverage, emphasis is given to financial statement presentation as well as to the recording of transactions. Chapters 11 through 13 cover broader topics of financial reporting. Chapter 11 discusses the statement of cash flows. Chapter 12 presents the analysis of financial statements. Chapter 13 covers several contemporary topics in income reporting (income tax allocation, discontinued operations, extraordinary items, and changes in accounting principle), a discussion of the international aspects of accounting (primarily, accounting for import and export transactions), and inflation accounting.

In the managerial accounting section, Chapter 14 provides an overview. Subsequent chapters present product costing (both job-order and process), standard costing, budgeting, performance evaluation and control, short-term decision analysis, and capital investment analysis.

For flexibility of use, certain chapters may be omitted or resequenced. In the financial accounting coverage, Chapters 9, 12, and/or 13 could be omitted without impact on other topics. In the managerial accounting section, chapters could be covered in any sequence after Chapter 14. Any of Chapters 15 through 20 could be omitted without significant impact on other topics. Various chapter appendices are provided; these may also be omitted without impact on other topics.

SPECIAL FEATURES

The text contains a number of special features designed to enhance its ease of use and students' ability to learn:

1 Learning objectives are provided at the beginning of each chapter.

2 Computer inserts, set off for easy identification, alert the students to potential computer applications. These inserts are brief and general, and do not upset the flow of text material.

3 Chapter summaries, coordinated with the chapter learning objectives, allow students to review material with reference to the goals established earlier.

4 A list of key terms at the end of each chapter, and a glossary of over 450 terms at the end of the book, aid in becoming familiar with accounting terminology.

5 End-of-chapter assignment material includes review questions, exercises, problems, and a business decision problem. There are approximately 720 assignment items.

6 A corporate approach is introduced at the beginning of the text and maintained throughout.

7 Financial statement presentation is discussed at the end of most of the financial accounting chapters in order to illustrate clearly the impact of each topic on financial reporting.

8 Current topics—such as the cash flow statement, inflation accounting, and international aspects of accounting—are given the most up-to-date treatment.

9 Coverage of managerial accounting begins with an overview of all major aspects of managerial accounting: product costing, planning, performance evaluation and control, and decision analysis. This feature facilitates the transition from financial accounting to managerial accounting.

10 A set of actual financial statements (Goodyear Tire and Rubber Company), including many of the notes and disclosures, is also presented. Assignments based on these statements are included in the financial analysis chapter.

STUDENT SUPPORT MATERIALS

A Student Resource Manual is available, prepared by Sanford C. Gunn (State University of New York at Buffalo) and Francis E. Kearns (Rochester Institute of Technology). This manual includes a study guide that contains chapter summaries and self-test materials, working papers for selected problems, and three practice cases. The first practice case involves a concise review of the accounting cycle. The second illustrates the effects of alternative financial accounting methods on a firm's financial statements. The third case requires the preparation of a budget and a subsequent performance report comparing actual activity and costs to the budget. Necessary working papers are included.

INSTRUCTOR SUPPORT MATERIALS

A Solutions Manual is available that contains solutions to all review questions, exercises, problems, and business decision problems. Time and difficulty estimates are provided for each problem.

An Instructor's Resource Manual contains a variety of instructor aids. An instructor's guide provides: lecture notes and suggestions, a summary of assignment material organized by learning objective, and a listing of problem topics with time and difficulty estimates. A test bank contains for each chapter: 20 true-false questions, 20 multiple choice questions, and six short problems. Solutions for each test item are also provided. Check figures to problems, in a form suitable for reproduction, are given. Finally, solutions to the three practice cases are presented.

ACKNOWLEDGMENTS

Many individuals have served as reviewers during the course of the development of this manuscript. We express our appreciation for their efforts:

Clifford D. Brown, Bentley College
John A. Brozousky, California State University—Fresno
Ronald D. Burnette, Macomb Community College
David C. Burns, University of Cincinnati
Harold L. Cannon, State University of New York at Albany
Ronald C. Clute, University of Wyoming
Ted R. Compton, Ohio University
Rosalind Cronor, Virginia Polytechnic Institute and State University
James Fischer, University of Wisconsin, Whitewater
Louis Geller, Queens College, City University of New York
David Greenfield, University of California—Los Angeles
Loyd C. Heath, University of Washington
H. Peter Holzer, University of Illinois, Urbana-Champaign
George C. Holdren, University of Nebraska, Lincoln
Clair Jones, San Jose State University
Peter B. Kenyon, Humboldt State University

Larry Konrath, University of Toledo
D.L. Kleespie, University of Arizona
Thomas J. Krissek, Northeastern Illinois University
Shu S. Liao, Naval Postgraduate School
Henry Longfield, Indiana State University
Kenny L. Loquist, Western Illinois University
E. James Meddaugh, Ohio University
Anne C. Reley, American University
Mary Swanson Rolfes, Mankato State University
Fred W. Schaeberle, Western Michigan University

Professor Walter A. Parker of Central Connecticut State College reviewed all solutions to end-of-chapter assignment material.

We appreciate the services of our student assistants who aided in many of the details involved in preparing the text and the supplements: Mary Roberta Cesar, Jeanne Cribben, Ann Marie Gibbons, Mark Fuller, Mary Kay Schiesser, Michele Sciortino, and Ann Towsley. We also greatly appreciate the secretarial support provided by Nancy Carpenter, Deborah Kelsch, Marcelle Kirsch, Mary Kozin, Sharon Murawski, and Cheryl Tubisz.

We also appreciate the assistance received from Robert D. Lynch, Jim DeVoe, Kate Moran Aker, and Joan Holman of McGraw-Hill; and Dave Mason and Terri Gitler of Publication Services.

Suggestions and comments from users are encouraged.

Ronald J. Huefner
Robert P. Derstine

A
SURVEY
OF
ACCOUNTING

1

ACCOUNTING: AN INTRODUCTION

LEARNING OBJECTIVES

When you complete this chapter, you should be able to:
1 Identify several uses and users of accounting information.
2 Describe the three types of business organization and identify the two basic objectives of a business.
3 Define basic accounting terms.
4 Record accounting entries on a transaction worksheet.
5 Prepare an income statement and a balance sheet.

Accounting is the process of recording, classifying, summarizing, and reporting financial information to assist people in making decisions. There are many situations where accounting information is relevant for decisions; following are several examples:

1 The President of the United States evaluates which federal spending programs might be reduced in order to trim the budget deficit.

2 Ralph Stanley, a hospital administrator, increases the price for a private room to $450 per day due to increased costs for salaries, utilities, food, and insurance.

3 Janet Kenney, M.D., has to choose between leasing for five years or purchasing for cash a microcomputer on which to maintain her patients' medical files.

4 Sarah Lehman, loan officer for Second National Bank, has to decide whether to grant Needy Hardware Store a $300,000 bank loan.

5 George Lewis, recent winner of $500,000 in the state lottery, is trying

to select among bank savings certificates, real estate, or shares of Ford Motor Company stock for investing his winnings.

6 Members of the State Public Utilities Commission are voting on whether to approve Ready Electric Company's request for a $248,000,000 rate increase.

7 Jennifer Smith, a college student, is trying to budget her limited resources to cover tuition, room and board, textbooks, and a stereo.

8 Mark Harkness, owner of Widgets Manufacturing Company, is considering the purchase of a new machine for his factory.

9 Bert Cooke, manager of Fancy Banquet Services, is quoting a price per dinner for a wedding banquet to be held in nine months.

10 Diane Marshall, accountant for the Profito Company, recommends changing the manner in which the company values its inventory; the change is expected to reduce taxes by $30,000.

11 Gary Traynor, accountant for Seabrook Manufacturing, is preparing a report on why raw materials costs for the company's major product increased by 10 percent last month.

USERS OF ACCOUNTING INFORMATION

As can be seen from the above, virtually everyone in our complex society requires accounting information as a basis for making decisions. It is the task of accounting professionals to collect the relevant information and present it in an understandable manner. Different users expect the accounting system to provide different types of information. These users may be grouped into six categories:

1 The *owners* of the company need to know the company's performance (i.e., profits) during the past year and the company's present financial position (i.e., cash held, debts owed, and so forth). Based on this information, the owners may decide to replace the company's management, or to reward management with a bonus. An individual owner may decide to increase or decrease his or her ownership interest. As a group, the owners (or their elected representatives) may decide to reinvest profits within the firm or to distribute some portion of the profits to the owners. These and other decisions are likely to be based, at least in part, on information contained in accounting reports.

2 *Potential owners* also are interested in information relating to the financial position of the firm and the results of its past operations in order to decide whether to invest in the firm. Knowledge of past financial position and profits will aid them in estimating the company's future prospects and thus whether an investment in the company would be profitable.

3 The *management* of an organization also requires information on its financial position and results of operations. However, management needs data that are more detailed, more frequently compiled, and more up-to-date than are usually provided to others. For example, while persons outside the organization may only be interested in the cash balance at the end of the year, management needs to know daily cash balances to determine if short-term loans are needed

to cover cash shortages or if short-term investments can be made with cash surpluses. In addition, management requires data for numerous other day-to-day decisions that must be made. Typical examples include:

a What are the costs of producing this particular product? Should we drop the product? Should we increase its price?

b Should we replace an existing machine with a new one? What are the potential costs and benefits? Should we buy the new machine, or lease it?

4 *Creditors* (actual or potential) also require information concerning financial position and results of operations to aid them in deciding whether or not to extend credit. Examples range from a supplier of materials considering shipment of a large order to a customer on 30-day payment terms to a bank considering a multi-million dollar 20-year loan to finance a firm's plant expansion.

5 *Employees* require information on the company's profitability to aid in negotiations for pay increases and a profit-sharing plan in a new labor contract.

6 *Governmental agencies* require information to determine compliance with laws and regulations and to make recommendations concerning national economic and social policy. For example, an income tax return is necessary to comply with the tax laws. Information on sales to foreign countries, or on the purchase of foreign oil, may be needed to set policy concerning the balance of payment or import taxes.

Types of Business Organization

The three basic forms of business organization are: (1) proprietorships, (2) partnerships, and (3) corporations. A *proprietorship* is a business that is not incorporated and is owned by one individual. Often, the owner is also the manager of the business. Proprietorships are found almost exclusively in small businesses.

A *partnership* is an unincorporated business owned by two or more persons. Partnerships frequently are formed where the combination of talents and resources of two or more persons is needed, yet where large amounts of capital are not required. Professionals such as doctors, lawyers, and CPAs often organize as partnerships.

Corporations, unlike proprietorships and partnerships, are legal entities that have an existence separate from that of their owners (who are called stockholders). A corporation can conduct transactions in its own name—buy property, enter into contracts, pay income taxes, sue and be sued, and so forth.

While there are more proprietorships and partnerships than corporations in the United States, corporations produce a substantially greater share of the nation's goods and services. For companies needing large amounts of investment capital from a number of investors, the corporate form of organization is virtually necessary. Features of the corporate form, such as limited risk for the owners (stockholders) and ease in transferring shares of stock ownership, make the corporation an attractive structure for both large and small businesses.

Because of its dominance in our economy, accounting for corporations will be emphasized in this textbook. In most circumstances, the accounting practices followed by a proprietorship or a partnership will parallel those used by corporations.

Accounting is also important in other contexts. Local, state, and federal government bodies are a significant part of our economy and require accounting reports for both internal and external purposes. Nonprofit organizations, such as churches, hospitals, and charitable groups, also maintain accounting records and prepare financial statements. While government and nonprofit accounting are very important, coverage of these topics is beyond the scope of this text.

Business Objectives

Regardless of the form of business organization, a firm must achieve two objectives: (1) it must be *profitable* and (2) it must be *solvent*. While firms may operate at a loss for a period of time, in the long run firms must be profitable; that is, the price at which the firm sells its products or services to customers must exceed the costs incurred by the firm in running the business. In addition, firms must be solvent; they must be able to pay their debts when due. If resources are not available to pay debts when due, the firm is insolvent and creditors can force the firm into bankruptcy.

The Language of Business

Accounting often is called the *language of business* because it is a means of communicating financial and operating information concerning business activities. Compare the study of accounting to the study of a language. In learning a language, it is necessary to learn *vocabulary* (the meaning of words) and *grammar* (the structure of the language—how words fit together to communicate meaning). These same requirements apply to the study of accounting. You must learn the vocabulary of accounting—the meaning of words such as assets, revenues, retained earnings, and working capital. In addition, you must learn the structure of accounting—how the words and data fit together to convey meaning. Words have little meaning unless they are organized into proper sentences; similarly in accounting, words and numbers have little meaning unless they are organized into reports. Thus, you must understand the construction of financial statements and the interrelationships contained within them. As we proceed, you will soon be speaking the language of business.

EXTERNAL AND INTERNAL REPORTING

As noted earlier, some users of accounting information (owners, potential owners, creditors, and government agencies) are not involved directly in the management of the firm. External reporting (*financial accounting*) provides information to these parties. Because of the needs of these users, financial accounting has two essential characteristics.

First, information must be *summarized*. A firm may engage in several thousand transactions during the year. To be useful to most outside parties, this mass of data must be classified, organized, and summarized into financial statements. As a result of this summarization, the financial statements of even the largest corporations frequently cover no more than ten pages. Therefore, in studying financial accounting, considerable attention is given to the process of converting a large mass of data to summarized financial statements.

COMPUTER APPLICATION

The use of computers has greatly aided the process of recording, organizing, and summarizing large volumes of accounting data. Since the cost of computer technology has decreased over the years, even very small companies find it economically feasible to use a computer for financial accounting purposes.

Throughout this text, these brief "computer application" inserts will call attention to the many uses of the computer in accounting.

Second, financial statements for external parties must be based on *generally accepted accounting principles* (GAAP). There are thousands of business firms, each preparing financial statements. Interpretation of statements would be impossible if each firm established its own accounting principles. On the other hand, since firms are different, it is unlikely that a single set of principles could adequately serve all situations. Generally accepted accounting principles try to provide both consistency and flexibility. In those instances where flexibility is needed, alternative means of reporting may be available. Thus, the user knows the accounting principles on which the statements are based, and the firm has some flexibility in selecting accounting principles appropriate to its circumstances.

Internal reporting (*managerial accounting*) is concerned with providing information to the management of the firm to aid in planning, control, decision making, and performance evaluation. Internal reporting is usually much more detailed than external reporting. For example, where external reports present only the total cost of inventory, management may need the cost of each product type in the inventory.

COMPUTER APPLICATION

Use of the computer is very important in internal reporting. The preparation of detailed reports, along with the required calculations and analyses, can be done much more rapidly by computer than by manual methods. To be most useful to management in planning, control, decision making, and performance evaluation, such reports must be produced as quickly as possible. Speed of preparation is especially important when reports are required on a very frequent basis, such as a daily cash report.

Internal reporting also differs from external reporting in the use of accounting standards. Financial statements used by various outside parties require that common standards (generally accepted accounting principles) be followed so that all know the accounting methods being used. Common standards are much less important when reports for managers are prepared. Thus, when we study managerial accounting later in the text, there will be considerably less emphasis on generally accepted accounting principles.

Setting Accounting Principles

Currently, the task of determining acceptable accounting principles is performed primarily by the *Financial Accounting Standards Board* (FASB). The FASB is an independent body of accountants, whose statements on accounting principles are recognized by the accounting profession, industry, and government. The FASB's organizational structure, member selection, and operating procedures are purposely designed to keep the FASB independent of the various users of accounting principles.

FINANCIAL STATEMENTS

Suppose the stockholders (owners) of the Spartan Hardware Store ask the following questions:

1 What was the financial position of the business as of December 31, 1988? That is, what assets did it have? What debts did it have? Was it solvent?

2 What were the financial results of the business activities for the past year? That is, what revenues were earned and what expenses were incurred? Was the business profitable?

Financial statements aid in answering these questions. In this section, we introduce two financial statements: the *balance sheet* and the *income statement*. Two other statements—the retained earnings statement and the statement of cash flows—will be introduced in later chapters. These four statements are commonly presented in a financial report.

Balance Sheet

The financial condition of a business is reported on a statement of financial position, commonly called a *balance sheet*. The balance sheet of Spartan Hardware Store on December 31, 1988, shown in Exhibit 1-1, lists the assets of the corporation, the liabilities (debts) it owes, and the stockholders' (owners') equity in the business.

Assets *Assets* are items of value owned or controlled by the firm. On December 31, 1988, the balance sheet of Spartan Hardware Store shows three assets—cash, accounts receivable, and inventory. The $8,500 cash represents balances on hand or in bank accounts on December 31, 1988. The $6,500 accounts receivable is the amount owed to Spartan by customers who have not paid as of December 31, 1988 for items previously purchased. Accounts receivable arise

EXHIBIT 1-1
Spartan Hardware Store
Balance Sheet
December 31, 1988

Assets

Cash	$ 8,500
Accounts Receivable	6,500
Inventory	38,000
Total Assets	$53,000

Liabilities and Stockholders' Equity

Liabilities:		
Accounts Payable		$ 5,700
Bank Loan Payable		8,000
Total Liabilities		$13,700
Stockholders' Equity:		
Capital Stock	$10,000	
Retained Earnings	29,300	39,300
Total Liabilities and		
Stockholders' Equity		$53,000

when businesses sell to customers on credit, not requiring payment until some time after the sale. In general, the asset inventory represents the costs of goods being manufactured or being held for sale to customers. Spartan's inventory of $38,000 on December 31, 1988 represents the cost of hammers, nails, and other hardware in stock for future sale to customers.

In addition to the assets shown for Spartan Hardware Store, other assets commonly held by businesses include land, buildings, equipment, delivery trucks, office furniture, and investments in securities of other companies.

Liabilities and Stockholders' Equity   In addition to presenting the list of assets owned by Spartan Hardware Store, the balance sheet also indicates how the assets are financed, that is, the source of the resources used to acquire the assets. A corporation's assets are financed in one of two ways:

1 Resources provided by creditors—amounts loaned to the company in various forms, such as bank loans, mortgages, and trade credit.

2 Resources provided by the stockholders of the company—amounts directly invested when the stockholders buy shares of stock and amounts indirectly invested by the accumulation of past earnings.

A corporation's balance sheet identifies the source of assets as either amounts owed to creditors (*liabilities*) or amounts of stockholders' resources (*stockholders' equity*). This relationship between a corporation's assets and the sources of the assets is expressed by the *accounting equation*.

Assets = Liabilities + Stockholders' Equity

Since each asset must be financed either by borrowing or by resources provided by stockholders, the total of the liabilities plus the stockholders' equity must equal the total of the assets.

Spartan's balance sheet shows two liabilities: accounts payable and bank loan payable. The $5,700 accounts payable on December 31, 1988 represents amounts owed by Spartan to suppliers who have sold merchandise to Spartan on credit. Payment of this liability will be due in the next several weeks. The $8,000 bank loan payable represents the amount owed to the bank as a result of past borrowings. The due date for repaying this loan is important in evaluating Spartan's solvency, its ability to pay liabilities as they become due. If the bank loan is due in the very near future, Spartan must consider whether there will be sufficient cash on hand to make the required payments.

The stockholders' equity of $39,300 can be determined by subtracting the total liabilities ($13,700) from the total assets ($53,000). Stockholders' equity arises from both direct investment by the owners and the retention of accumulated past earnings by the corporation. Direct investment of $10,000 by Spartan stockholders is shown on the balance sheet as capital stock. The accumulated past profits of $29,300 are reported as retained earnings.

A balance sheet represents the accounting equation: assets equal liabilities plus stockholders' equity. Since assets must be financed either by creditors or by stockholders, the accounting equation (and hence the balance sheet) must always balance. In Exhibit 1-1, the $53,000 total of Spartan's liabilities plus stockholders' equity equals the $53,000 total of Spartan's assets.

Statement of Income

An *income statement* reports a firm's profitability for a period of time. To determine profit, the expenses for the period are subtracted from the revenue. This excess of total revenue over total expenses is called *net income*. In some cases, expenses may exceed revenues, resulting in a negative net income, or *net loss*. Exhibit 1-2 presents Spartan Hardware Store's income statement for the year ended December 31, 1988. Notice that the income statement reports on profitability over a period of time (the year ended December 31, 1988), while the balance sheet shows the company's financial condition at a particular time (on December 31, 1988).

EXHIBIT 1-2
Spartan Hardware Store
Statement of Income
For the Year Ended December 31, 1988

Revenue: Sales		$160,600
Expenses:		
Cost of Goods Sold	$51,000	
Rent	48,000	
Salaries	37,000	
Advertising	7,500	
Interest on Bank Loan	1,000	144,500
Net Income		$ 16,100

Revenues   *Revenue* for the Spartan Hardware Store is $160,600, the total price of items sold to customers during the year. Revenue represents the gross amount earned from the sale of merchandise before consideration of expenses. Companies earn revenue from their business activity—by selling goods or services to others; for Spartan, this activity is the sale of hardware. Revenues for other companies could include commissions earned on the sale of property by a real estate agency, patient fees earned by a dental clinic, interest earned on money deposited in bank accounts, and rent earned from leasing a building to another party. Amounts that are not earned from business activity are not revenue; for example, the proceeds of a bank loan would not represent revenue to Spartan Hardware Store.

Expenses   *Expenses* are the cost of goods and services consumed (used up) during the period in order to earn revenues. To earn its $160,600 of revenue during 1988, Spartan incurred expenses of $51,000 for the cost of the merchandise that was sold, $48,000 to rent the store building, $37,000 for salaries paid to employees, $7,500 for advertising, and $1,000 for interest on the bank loan. All these were necessary to run the business, and hence earn the revenues, during the year. Other examples of expenses include travel, utilities, insurance, and taxes.

Profitability   One use of financial statements is to evaluate the profitability of the company. Spartan had revenues of $160,600 and expenses of $144,500 during 1988, resulting in net income of $16,100. Net income could be expressed in relation to other financial measures. For example, net income was 10 percent of sales revenue ($16,100 \div $160,600 = 10\%$), and net income represented an earning of 30% on the company's assets ($16,100 \div $53,000 = 30\%$). In evaluating these results, we could compare 1988 to prior years for Spartan, and we could compare Spartan to other hardware stores. The data for 1988 might also be used to aid in predicting Spartan's future profitability.

TRANSACTION WORKSHEET

Before financial statements can be prepared, it is necessary to record the transactions of the company. The transaction worksheet is a convenient way of becoming familiar with the recording, classifying, and summarization that occur in the accounting process.

To illustrate the accounting process in a very simple environment, we will record transactions for two months for the Newton Beauty Salon, a corporation beginning its business in January, 1988.

Worksheet for January

Exhibit 1-3 shows the transaction worksheet for Newton Beauty Salon for January, 1988. Carefully read the description of each transaction below, and observe how it is recorded on the worksheet. Notice that for each entry, the accounting equation of assets = liabilities + stockholders' equity remains in balance.

EXHIBIT 1-3
Newton Beauty Salon
Transaction Worksheet
For January 1988

	Assets				=	Liabilities		+	Stockholders' equity	
Entry	Cash	Accounts receivable	Supplies inventory	Land		Accounts payable	Bank loan payable		Capital stock	Retained earnings
1. Jan. 2—direct investment by stockholders	+ $29,000								+ $29,000	
2. Jan. 12—purchased supplies on credit			+ $16,000			+ $16,000				
3. Jan. 14—purchased land for cash	− 25,000			+ $25,000						
4. Jan. 16—sold one-half of land on credit		+ $12,500		− 12,500						
5. Jan. 26—partial payment for previous purchases on credit	− 4,000					− 4,000				
6. Jan. 31—borrowed from bank	+ 18,000						+ $18,000			
January 31, 1988 balances	$18,000	$12,500	$16,000	$12,500		$12,000	$18,000		$29,000	$ −0—

Entry 1 On January 2, 1988, the Newton Beauty Salon was formed and investors purchased 1,000 shares of its capital stock for $29,000. On the transaction worksheet, this requires a $29,000 increase to the asset Cash and a $29,000 increase to the stockholders' equity Capital Stock.

Entry 2 On January 12, beauty supplies costing $16,000 were purchased on credit, with partial payments to be made beginning on January 26. The asset Supplies Inventory is increased by $16,000 and the liability Accounts Payable also is increased by $16,000.

Entry 3 On January 14, the asset Land is increased by $25,000 and the asset Cash is decreased by $25,000 to record the cash purchase of a parcel of land.

Entry 4 On January 16, when the company decided it did not need the entire parcel of land, it sold half of the property at cost ($12,500 for one-half the parcel). The buyer promised to pay the $12,500 on February 18. The asset Accounts Receivable is increased by $12,500 and the asset Land is decreased by $12,500.

Entry 5 On January 26, a $4,000 payment was made to suppliers in partial settlement of the purchases of January 12. The asset Cash is decreased by $4,000 and the liability Accounts Payable is decreased by $4,000.

Entry 6 On January 31, the company borrowed $18,000 from the bank. The asset Cash is increased by $18,000 and the liability Bank Loan Payable is increased by $18,000.

After recording these transactions on the worksheet in Exhibit 1-3, the columns are totaled. These totals are used to prepare Newton's balance sheet on January 31, 1988, which is presented in Exhibit 1-4.

EXHIBIT 1-4
Newton Beauty Salon
Balance Sheet
January 31, 1988

Assets

Cash	$18,000
Accounts Receivable	12,500
Supplies Inventory	16,000
Land	12,500
Total Assets	$59,000

Liabilities and Stockholders' Equity

Liabilities:		
Accounts Payable		$12,000
Bank Loan Payable		18,000
Total Liabilities		$30,000
Stockholders' Equity:		
Capital Stock	$29,000	
Retained Earnings	-0-	29,000
Total Liabilities and		
Stockholders' Equity		$59,000

Worksheet for February

During January, Newton Beauty Salon was organized and acquired assets, but had no revenues or expenses from its beauty salon operations. Thus we prepared no income statement for January. Business operations began in February, as reflected in the transactions listed below. Exhibit 1-5 shows the transaction worksheet for February. Again, carefully read each transaction and observe how it is recorded on the transaction worksheet.

Note that we enter the revenue and expense transactions in the retained earnings column of the worksheet. Retained earnings is the component of stockholders' equity that represents the accumulated profits of the company. When revenues are earned, the company receives assets (cash or accounts receivable), and the retained earnings component of stockholders' equity increases. When expenses are incurred, assets are reduced (or liabilities are increased) and retained earnings are also reduced. The retained earnings account thus maintains a cumulative record of the profits (revenues minus expenses) of the company.

Entry 1 On February 1, Newton paid $2,000 rent for the beauty salon for the month of February. The asset Cash is decreased by $2,000, and rent expense for February is recognized by recording a $2,000 decrease in Retained Earnings.

Entry 2 On February 18, $12,500 was received from the company which purchased the half-parcel of land on January 16. The asset Cash is increased by $12,500 and the asset Accounts Receivable is decreased by $12,500.

Entry 3 On February 20, Newton paid the bank $18,300 to repay the $18,000 loan of January 31 plus $300 for interest. The asset Cash is decreased by $18,300, the liability Bank Loan Payable is decreased by $18,000, and interest expense is recorded as a $300 decrease in Retained Earnings. Notice that this entry affected three accounts, but the equality of the accounting equation was maintained.

Entry 4 On February 23, employee salaries of $1,200 were paid. The asset Cash is decreased by $1,200 and salary expense is recorded by a $1,200 decrease in Retained Earnings.

Entry 5 On February 29, Newton recorded $7,000 revenue earned from services to customers during February. Of this revenue, $5,000 was received in cash at the time the services were rendered, and $2,000 was for services performed on credit, with payment due in March. The asset Cash is increased by $5,000, the asset Accounts Receivable is increased by $2,000, and revenue of $7,000 is recorded as an increase in Retained Earnings.

Entry 6 On February 29, Newton determined that during February $1,800 of supplies had been used out of the $16,000 inventory. The asset Supplies Inventory is decreased by $1,800 and Supplies Expense is recorded as an $1,800 decrease in Retained Earnings.

The individual entries in the retained earnings column of the transaction worksheet serve as the basis for preparing Newton's income statement for February, as shown in Exhibit 1-6. The column totals again serve as the basis for preparing the balance sheet as of February 29, 1988, which is shown in Exhibit 1-7. Note the two components of stockholders' equity on the February 29 balance sheet. The capital stock amount reflects the direct investment made by stockholders,

EXHIBIT 1-5
Newton Beauty Salon
Transaction Worksheet
For February 1988

Entry	Assets				=	Liabilities		+	Stockholders' equity		
	Cash	Accounts receivable	Supplies inventory	Land		Accounts payable	Bank loan payable		Capital stock	Retained earnings	
Beginning balances	$18,000	$12,500	$16,000	$12,500		$12,000	$18,000		$29,000	$ -0-	
1. Feb. 1—paid rent for month	– 2,000									–2,000	Rent expense
2. Feb. 18—collected amount due from sale of land on account on January 16	+ 12,500	–12,500									
3. Feb. 20—repaid bank loan plus interest	–18,300						–18,000			– 300	Interest expense
4. Feb. 23—paid February salaries	– 1,200									–1,200	Salaries expense
5. Feb. 29—recorded revenue earned for month	+ 5,000	+ 2,000								+7,000	Revenue earned
6. Feb. 29—recorded beauty supplies used during month			– 1,800							–1,800	Supplies expense
February 29, 1988 balances	$14,000	$ 2,000	$14,200	$12,500		$12,000	$ -0-		$29,000	$ 1,700	

EXHIBIT 1-6
Newton Beauty Salon
Statement of Income
For the Month Ended February 29, 1988

Revenue:		
Fees Earned from Beauty Treatments		$7,000
Expenses:		
Rent	$2,000	
Interest	300	
Salaries	1,200	
Supplies Used	1,800	5,300
Net Income		$1,700

while the retained earnings amount represents the stockholders' equity arising from accumulated profits to date.

The Ground Rules of Accounting

In recording these transactions, we had to resolve a number of questions. When do we record transactions? What amounts should be reported on financial statements? How often should financial statements be prepared? Fundamental to accounting is a set of basic concepts and rules; these underlie and provide a general rationale for specific accounting procedures. The ten basic ideas discussed below constitute a set of assumptions on which accounting is based. As you progress through the text, your understanding and appreciation of them will develop.

EXHIBIT 1-7
Newton Beauty Salon
Balance Sheet
February 29, 1988

Assets

Cash		$14,000
Accounts Receivable		2,000
Supplies Inventory		14,200
Land		12,500
Total Assets		$42,700

Liabilities and Stockholders' Equity

Liabilities:		
Accounts Payable		$12,000
Total Liabilities		$12,000
Stockholders' Equity:		
Capital Stock	$29,000	
Retained Earnings	1,700	30,700
Total Liabilities and		
Stockholders' Equity		$42,700

1 The *entity* concept. Accounting is concerned with reporting the results of business activity. The entity concept means that we focus on the business organization, not on its owners. For example, if Roger Newton is the sole owner of the corporation Newton Beauty Salon, the financial statements should show only the activity of Newton Beauty Salon (its revenues, expenses, assets, liabilities). The financial activities of Roger Newton as an individual (such as the dividends on his personal stock holdings, or the mortgage on his house) are not included in the financial statements of Newton Beauty Salon. While financial statements give information to the owners of the business, they report on the financial activities of the business entity, not on the financial activities of the owners.

2 The *going concern* concept. A basic assumption of accounting is that the firm will continue its business activity indefinitely—that the firm will retain its assets and continue its operations, rather than terminate operations and sell its assets. Thus, if the firm buys a new machine, we are interested in how long it will serve the company's production activities, rather than how much the machine would be worth if it were sold next month. If the going concern assumption cannot be justified (if, for example, the firm is on the verge of bankruptcy), then many of the normal rules of accounting may not be applicable.

3 The concept of *accounting periods*. Accounting provides information to various parties on a regular basis. The ongoing activities of the firm must be broken up into periods (months, years) so that useful financial statements can be issued. Several problems in accounting center around this requirement of periodic reporting. For example, merchandise may be sold and delivered to a customer in December, and payment received in January. The question of when (December or January) to report the sale on the financial statements must be answered.

4 The concept of the *dollar as a stable unit of measurement*. Financial information about a firm's financial condition and operations is reported in monetary terms (dollars). A basic assumption is that the dollar is approximately stable in value over long periods of time. This assumption permits us to add together costs originating in different time periods (for example, the cost of a building bought in 1957 and the cost of a building bought in 1985). The assumption of a stable dollar underlies most of what we study in accounting. However, we know that the economy often encounters periods of inflation where the value of the dollar is not stable. The stable dollar assumption has often been criticized as unrealistic; we will briefly consider the impact of inflation on accounting in Chapter 13.

5 The *realization* rule. In accounting, the term *recognize* means to record an event or transaction. To properly measure income, we must begin by asking when revenue should be recognized. The answer is that revenue should be recognized when it is *realized*. Realization means that the major activities of earning revenue, including actual sale to a customer, have been accomplished. When these major activities are completed, the revenue is recorded.

6 The *matching* rule. Once revenues are recognized, accountants match against those revenues the costs of the goods and services consumed in generating the revenues (these costs are called expenses). This matching of revenues and expenses enables the calculation of income (profit) for the period.

7 The *conservatism* concept. Estimates and judgments are often required in accounting. The attitude of conservatism suggests that these estimates and judgments be made in a spirit of caution rather than a spirit of great optimism. Thus, if a probable loss or reduction in asset value exists, it is recognized in the financial statements. But if a possible gain or increase in asset value exists, it is usually not recognized until it actually occurs (such as by sale of the asset). Conservatism has its roots in the early uses of financial statements, which were primarily for the benefit of creditors. It was in the interest of bankers and other creditors that the assets and income of a company not be overstated. Understatement, while not desirable in itself, was viewed as preferable to overstatement. Although today the use of financial statements is oriented toward investors as well as creditors, much the same aversion to overstatement exists.

8 The *objectivity* concept. Although estimates and judgments are often necessary in accounting, financial statements would have little value if they were based only on such information. To the greatest extent possible, accountants seek data that are objective—that is, can be substantiated by evidence and verified by others. The desire for objectivity is one reason that *historical* (original) *cost* is widely used in accounting as a measure of value.

9 The *materiality* concept. The concept of materiality suggests that the dollar size and significance of an item helps determine its accounting treatment. For example, since a building is expected to be useful for many years, its costs are spread over its estimated useful life in measuring income. A $10 hammer may also be useful for many years. The cost of the hammer is so small, however, that it makes no significant difference if we expense the entire cost in one year rather than spreading it over its useful life.

10 The *consistency* concept. Accounting data are often used for trend analysis. For example, to determine whether the company's sales and profits are improving, static, or deteriorating, this year's data can be compared with that of previous years. As mentioned earlier, there are many cases where alternative accounting principles exist. To ensure comparability of financial statements, the concept of consistency requires that the same principles be used from one period to the next.

These ten concepts and rules form the foundation for the accounting principles you will study throughout this text.

SUMMARY

Learning Objective 1: Identify several uses and users of accounting information.
  Accounting information is used by both internal users (management accounting) and external users (owners, potential investors, creditors, employees, and government agencies) to aid in decision making.

Learning Objective 2: Describe the three types of business organization and identify the two basic objectives of a business.
  The three types of business organization are proprietorships, partnerships, and

corporations. While proprietorships and partnerships are more numerous, corporations provide an overwhelming majority of the goods and services produced in the United States. The basic objectives of a business organization are to be profitable and solvent.

Learning Objective 3: Define basic accounting terms.

Important terms used in the chapter include: asset, liability, stockholders' equity, revenue, expense, and net income. The glossary at the back of the textbook defines these important terms.

Learning Objective 4: Record accounting entries on a transaction worksheet.

Exhibits 1-3 and 1-5 in the chapter illustrate the process of recording increases and decreases in assets, liabilities, and stockholders' equity on a transaction worksheet.

Learning Objective 5: Prepare an income statement and a balance sheet.

An income statement presents revenues, expenses, and net income for the period. Exhibits 1-2 and 1-6 in the chapter illustrate statements of income. The balance sheet shows the equality of the accounting equation (assets = liabilities + stockholders' equity) as of the end of the period. Balance sheets are shown in Exhibits 1-1, 1-4, and 1-7.

KEY TERMS

Accounting	Historical cost
Accounting concept	Income statement
Accounting equation	Inventory
Accounts payable	Liabilities
Accounts receivable	Managerial accounting
Assets	Net income
Balance sheet	Profitability
Capital stock	Retained earnings
Corporation	Revenue
Expense	Solvency
Financial accounting	Statement of income
Generally accepted accounting principles	Stockholders' equity
	Transaction worksheet

REVIEW QUESTIONS

1 In addition to the stockholders who own the company, list five other users of accounting information.

2 What are some specific questions each individual user group seeks to answer with accounting information? What accounting information is particularly relevant in each situation?

3 Describe the three basic forms of business organization.

4 A business organization must achieve two objectives to be successful. Briefly discuss the two objectives.

5 Differentiate between "financial accounting" and "managerial accounting."

6 Because of the nature of external users, financial reporting to outsiders has two essential characteristics. One is that literally thousands of transactions must be carefully classified, organized, and summarized to be useful to the needs of outside parties. Discuss the other essential characteristic of financial accounting.

7 The accounting equation for a corporation is:

$$\text{Assets} = \text{Liabilities} + \text{Stockholders' Equity}$$

Why should the equation always balance?

8 "Accounting like physics and chemistry is an exact science governed by unchanging natural laws." Comment on the preceding statement.

9 Which financial statement reports a firm's profitability for the period? Which financial statement reports the financial condition of a firm as of a particular date?

10 What are the two sources of a corporation's stockholders' equity?

11 During 1988, McDugal's Barber Shop performed 3,000 haircuts at $6.00 per haircut. Also during 1988, the barber shop borrowed $6,000 from HFS Finance Company and received $200 interest on its bank savings account. How much revenue would be shown on the statement of income for McDugal's Barber Shop for 1988? How did you implicitly define "revenue" in answering the question?

12 Johnson Company has the following assets (i.e., items of value owned by the business) on December 31, 1988:

a Cash, $40,000

b Stock in General Motors, $2,500 original cost; estimated current worth, $3,300

c Land held as an investment, $10,000 original cost; estimated current value, $13,000

How would the assets of Johnson Company be presented on a balance sheet at December 31, 1988 (i.e., at what dollar amount would each asset be shown)? What accounting rule and concepts support your answer?

13 Torson's Bakery purchased land as an investment on January 1, 1989 for $8,000. Assume that, during 1989, the country had a 16 percent rate of inflation (i.e., the value, or purchasing power of the dollar decreased). Would Torson's Bakery continue to show the investment in land at $8,000 on its December 31, 1989 balance sheet? Which basic accounting concept supports your answer?

14 Anton's Hardware Store owns 10 shares of stock in Ford Motor Company. The shares were acquired a year ago at a cost of $400. Under the concept of conservatism, if the shares decrease in value to $300 at the end of the current year:

a What gain or loss should be recognized for the year?

b At what amount should the shares of stock be shown on the balance sheet at the end of the current year?

What would be your answer to (a) and (b) if the shares of stock had increased in value to $500 at the end of the current period?

EXERCISES

E1-1 Which user group needs accounting information to help make the following decisions? The first one is done as an example.

Decision	**User group**
(a) Replace the company's management	Company owners
(b) Loan a company a large amount of money	
(c) Replace an existing machine with a new one	
(d) Determine if correct income tax was paid	
(e) Sell ownership interest in company	
(f) Increase price of a product	
(g) Ship a large order to a customer on 30-day payment terms	
(h) Discontinue production of a product	

E1-2 From the information below concerning Smith's Auto Rental Agency, calculate the corporation's net income for 1988. (Hint: You may not need to use all the information presented. You may want to review the definitions and illustrations in the chapter.)

Cash at December 31, 1988	$ 4,500
Land owned as an investment	55,800
Mortgage loan on land, balance due at December 31, 1994	35,000
Principal repayments on mortgage during 1988	2,000
Rental fees earned from customers during 1988	15,500
Interest on Smith's Auto Rental Agency, Inc.'s bank savings account for 1988	300
Cost to agency of leasing cars from Fleet Leasing Co. during 1988	6,000
Advertising for 1988	1,200
Interest on mortgage for 1988	3,000

E1-3 Using the information presented in Exercise 2 and the accounting equation (Assets = Liabilities + Stockholders' Equity), determine the stockholders' equity in Smith's Auto Rental Agency, Inc. as of December 31, 1988 (i.e., the portion of the agency's assets financed by the stockholders).

E1-4 Presented below is a balance sheet prepared for Reig's Modeling School, Incorporated on October 31, 1988. What errors can you find on the corporation's financial statement? Other than errors, are there any other items on the modeling school's statement that appear unusual?

Reig's Modeling School, Incorporated
Balance Sheet

Revenues		**Liabilities and Stockholders' Equity**	
Cash	$20,000	Charge Accounts	$ 1,000
Accounts Receivable	8,200	Mortgage on Land	18,000
Inventory	12,800	Total Liabilities	$19,000
		Salary	20,000
		Total Liabilities and	
Total Assets	$41,000	Stockholders' Equity	$39,000

E1-5 Identify the relevant accounting concept(s) that underlie(s) the accounting treatment indicated for each situation below:

1 Rental fees earned by George Smith's Car Rental Agency totaled $33,000 for the year ended December 31, 1988. Working part time during the year as a notary public, George Smith, sole owner of the agency, earned an additional $4,100. The statement of income for George Smith's Car Rental Agency shows only $33,000 in revenue.

2 Britely's Pizzaria purchased a pencil sharpener for $3.95. The entire cost of the pencil sharpener is expensed during the year of purchase even though it is expected to be used for several years.

3 Grover's Meat Markets purchased land for $12,000 in January, 1977. During the summer of 1977, a new meat market was constructed on the site. The new location proved successful. At the end of 1988, the land was estimated to have a value of $23,000 (excluding the value of the meat market). On its balance sheet at the end of 1988, Grover's Meat Markets continues to show the land at $12,000.

PROBLEMS

P1-1 *Income Statement and Balance Sheet*

Information for Peterson's Dog Clipping Service is below:

Assets	
Cash	$24,000
Accounts Receivable	15,000
Total Assets	$39,000
Liabilities	
Accounts Payable	$ 2,000
Bank Loan Payable	? 12,000
Total Liabilities	$14,000
Stockholders' Equity	$? 39,000−14,000= 25,000
Revenues	
Fees Earned	$19,000
Total Revenues	$19,000
Expenses	
Supplies Used	$ 7,000
Interest on Bank Loan	1,000
Advertising	3,000
Total Expenses	$11,000
Net Income	$? 19,000−11,000=8000

Required:

Prepare for Peterson's Dog Clipping Service an income statement for 1988 and a balance sheet as of December 31, 1988 based on the items shown above. (In preparing the financial statements for the corporation, follow the format used in the Spartan Hardware Store and Newton Beauty Salon illustrations in the chapter.)

P1-2 *Identifying Assets, Liabilities, Revenue, and Expenses*

Presented below is a summarization of information compiled about a corporation named Simpson Marriage Counseling Service:

1 $30,000 owed on December 31, 1989 to bank for mortgage on land

2 $30,000 cost of land owned as an investment

E **3** $2,000 interest incurred and paid during 1989 on mortgage loan from bank

E **4** $500 cost of brochures and pamphlets used during 1989

E **5** $3,000 advertising for 1989

R **6** $300 interest earned during 1989 on the service's bank savings account

A **7** $10,000 owed to Simpson Marriage Counseling Service by customers as of December 31, 1989

R **8** Fees for counseling services earned during 1989 totaled $16,000

A **9** $2,500 cash balance in bank savings account on December 31, 1989 (includes interest earned during year)

Required:

Classify each item listed as either: (a) asset, (b) liability, (c) revenue, or (d) expense. (Hint: You may want to review the definitions in the chapter before attempting the problem.)

P1-3 *Balance Sheet and Income Statement*

Required:

From the list of items in Problem 2, prepare for Simpson Marriage Counseling Service:

1 A balance sheet as of December 31, 1989. (Follow the format used in the Spartan Hardware Store and Newton Beauty Salon illustrations in the chapter—except that stockholders' equity should not be subdivided into a capital stock and retained earnings component.)

2 An income statement for the year ended December 31, 1989. (Follow the format used in the Spartan Hardware Store and Newton Beauty Salon illustrations in the chapter.)

P1-4 *Transaction Worksheet, Balance Sheet*

On May 1, 1988, Bob's Barber Boutique was founded. The firm, organized as a corporation, experienced the following events during May. (Actual operations didn't begin until June.)

1 On May 1, the corporation issued 10,000 shares of capital stock and received $100,000 from the stockholders who purchased the shares.

2 On May 14, grooming supplies costing $9,000 were purchased on credit. The $9,000 purchase price is to be paid in three equal installments of $3,000 on June 28, July 28, and August 28.

3 On May 15, Carter's Crewcuts Co. (another local barber shop, which had depleted their own supply of grooming supplies) asked to purchase one-ninth of Bob's grooming supplies. Bob sold the grooming supplies to Carter's Crewcut Co. on credit for exactly the same amount that they had cost Bob—that is, $1,000. Carter's Crewcut Co. promised to pay for the grooming supplies by June 8.

4 On May 31, the corporation borrowed $60,000 from the bank.

Required:

1 Prepare a transaction worksheet for May following the format of Exhibit 1-3 in the chapter.

2 Prepare a balance sheet as of May 31, 1988.

P1-5 *Transaction Worksheet, Income Statement, Balance Sheet*
Glorian Portrait Studios, Incorporated had the following balances on October 1, 1988:

Cash	$11,000
Accounts Receivable	7,000
Supplies Inventory	2,000
Accounts Payable	3,500
Capital Stock	7,500
Retained Earnings	9,000

During October, the following events occurred:

1 On October 1, paid $5,000 for rent of the studio for October.

2 On October 8, collected $1,000 from a customer whose portrait had been painted in August. The customer had purchased the portrait on credit on August 10 with 60 days to pay. (Hint: Reduce Accounts Receivable.)

3 On October 12, paid $3,500 to Ace Painting Supply House for painting supplies that had been purchased on credit on September 13 with 30 days to pay.

4 On October 20, purchased on credit painting supplies costing $6,000. Payment is due on November 19.

5 On October 31, recorded revenue for eight portraits sold during October. Each portrait had a $3,000 selling price. Six of the eight customers paid cash for their portraits. The other two customers promised to pay for their portraits in November.

6 On October 31, determined that painting supplies costing $1,200 had been used up in October in painting the portraits.

7 On October 31, paid artist $8,000 for work done during October.

Required:

1 Prepare a transaction worksheet for October. Enter the beginning balances on the worksheet and record the seven items for October. Follow the format of Exhibit 1-5 in the chapter.

2 Prepare an income statement for October.

3 Prepare a balance sheet as of October 31, 1988.

P1-6 *Transaction Worksheet, Income Statement, Balance Sheet*
Yolanda's Kitchen and Bath Remodelers had the following balances on May 1, 1988:

Cash	$29,000
Accounts Receivable	11,000
Supplies Inventory	30,000
Accounts Payable	15,000
Notes Payable	10,000
Capital Stock	25,000
Retained Earnings	20,000

During May the following events occurred:

1 On May 1, purchased $10,000 of additional remodeling supplies from Building Wholesalers, Inc. Yolanda's has 30 days before being required to pay the $10,000 amount to Building Wholesalers.

2 On May 15, paid employee $125 for work done in May.

3 On May 17, collected $1,000 from a customer for remodeling work done during April.

4 On May 19, collected cash totaling $2,900 for remodeling work performed from May 1 to May 18. Cost of remodeling supplies used from May 1 to May 18 totaled $1,000.

5 On May 20, paid $1,000 for insurance for the month of May.

6 On May 21, received $200 from a customer for remodeling work performed on May 20. Cost of remodeling supplies used on the job was $105.

7 On May 29, paid $700 for rent of the building for May.

Required:

1 Prepare a transaction worksheet for May. Enter the beginning balances on the worksheet and record the items for May. Follow the format of Exhibit 1-5 in the chapter.

2 Prepare an income statement for May.

3 Prepare a balance sheet as of May 31, 1988.

P1-7 *Matching Problem*

On the blank line preceding each item write the letter of the answer that best matches the item. (Some letters may be used more than once; some letters may not be used at all.)

    d   **1** Balance sheet
    a   **2** Expenses
    j   **3** Historical cost rule
    b   **4** Revenues
    l   **5** Solvency
    e   **6** Entity concept
    h   **7** Consistency concept
    i   **8** Liabilities
    c   **9** Potential investors and government agencies

a Cost of goods and services consumed during the period
b Gross amounts earned from activities during the period
c External users of financial statements
d Shows financial condition of firm as of a given date
e Reporting on the activities of the company, excluding the personal affairs of the owners of the company
f Presents the revenues and expenses of the firm for the period   *income statement*
g Items of value which are owned   *assets*
h Using the same accounting principles from one period to the next
i Amounts owed by firm, other than to owners
j Reporting assets at original purchase price
k Revenues exceed expenses   *net income, profit*
l Ability to pay debts owed when the debts mature

P1-8 *Matching Problem*

On the blank line preceding each item write the letter of the answer that best matches the item. (Some letters may be used more than once; some letters may not be used at all.)

_e_   **1** Financial Accounting Standards Board (FASB)

_b_   **2** Assets

_h_   **3** Going concern concept

_f_   **4** Corporation

_a_   **5** Proprietorship

_d_   **6** Assets = Liabilities + Stockholders' Equity

_j_   **7** Financial accounting

_g_   **8** Classification, organization, and summarization of accounting data

a Business entity owned by one individual

b Items of value that are owned by the firm

c Assumption that value of the dollar is essentially stable _dollar as a stable unit of measure / historical cost rule_

d The accounting equation

e The organization primarily responsible for determining acceptable accounting principles

f Legal entity that has an existence separate from that of its owners (the stockholders)

g An essential characteristic of financial accounting

h Assumption that firm will retain its assets and continue its operations, rather than stop operating and liquidate all assets

i Creditors   _liabilities_

j External reporting

Business Decision Problem

Mary Johnson has $10,000 cash to lend to either Sam's Butcher Shop or Sara's Beauty Parlour. Condensed financial statements for the two businesses show:

Sam's Butcher Shop

Revenues	$100,000
Expenses—Other than	
Interest	88,000
Income Before Interest	$ 12,000
Interest Expense	9,000
Net Income	$ 3,000

Assets

Cash	$ 15,000
Property, Plant, and Equipment	85,000
Total Assets	$100,000

Liabilities and Stockholders' Equity

Current Liabilities (due within one year)	$ 60,000
Long-term Liabilities	30,000
Total Liabilities	$ 90,000
Stockholders' Equity	10,000
Total Liabilities and Stockholders' Equity	$100,000

Sara's Beauty Parlour

Revenues	$40,000
Expenses—Other than	
Interest	37,000
Income Before Interest	$ 3,000
Interest Expense	1,000
Net Income	$ 2,000

Assets

Cash	$30,000
Property, Plant, and Equipment	20,000
Total Assets	$50,000

Liabilities and Stockholders' Equity

Current Liabilities (due within one year)	$15,000
Long-term Liabilities	5,000
Total Liabilities	$20,000
Stockholders' Equity	30,000
Total Liabilities and Stockholders' Equity	$50,000

Sam's Butcher Shop offers Mary Johnson $1,000 interest for a one-year loan. Sara's Beauty Parlour offers $900 interest for a one-year loan. Since Sam's Butcher Shop offers $100 more interest and earned $1,000 more profit ($3,000 net income vs. $2,000 net income), Mary has decided to lend the $10,000 to Sam's Butcher Shop.

Required:
Evaluate Mary's decision.

2

THE ACCOUNTING PROCESS: I

LEARNING OBJECTIVES

When you complete this chapter, you should be able to:

1 Analyze a transaction and determine the debit-credit entry to record the transaction under the accrual method of accounting.
2 Record journal entries.
3 Post journal entries to ledger accounts.
4 Prepare a trial balance.

As discussed in Chapter 1, financial statements are the end product of the accounting process. They present financial information to investors, creditors, and others to aid them in making decisions. If financial statements are to reflect the financial position of the company and the results of profit-directed activities, the accounting system must be designed to provide this information.

In Chapters 2 and 3 we study the accounting process—the means by which business transactions and other pertinent information are recorded, classified, summarized, and translated into financial statements. The accrual concept, the debit-credit recording system, journal entries, ledger postings, and the trial balance will be covered in this chapter. Chapter 3 will complete the study of the accounting process by discussing adjusting entries, the adjusted trial balance, financial statements, closing entries, special journals, subsidiary ledgers, and the after-closing trial balance. The accountant's end-of-period worksheet is presented in the appendix to Chapter 3.

While studying these two chapters keep in mind that the accounting process not only aids in financial statement construction, but also serves as the data base for billing customers, ordering goods, paying company debts, and carrying out many other essential business activities. Thus, understanding the mechanics of accounting is important for two reasons. First, financial statement preparation is based on the company's accounting records. Second, accurate and adequate accounting records facilitate company operations.

ACCRUAL ACCOUNTING

A firm earns revenue by selling a product or service. A sale may involve many steps—buying or producing a product, finding a customer, delivering the product to the customer, and collecting payment. Each of these steps may occur at a different time. When should the company record the revenue from the sale? Under *accrual accounting,* which is followed by most companies, it is argued that the critical events are that a customer has agreed to a price and taken delivery. Once this has occurred, the remaining events (such as the collection of the cash) normally follow with reasonable certainty. Because the critical events in the sales process have been completed at time of delivery, sales revenue is considered *earned,* and thus recorded, even though the cash remains to be collected.

A sale is said to be made on credit when collection of cash will not occur until after delivery. Recording a sale on credit involves an increase in the asset Accounts Receivable. For example, assume a customer purchases $400 of clothing and charges it. The credit sale would be shown on the clothing store's transaction worksheet as:

Situation	Assets		=	Liabilities		+	Stockholders' equity	
	Cash	Accounts receivable		Com- missions payable	Bank loan payable		Capital stock	Retained earnings
Sale of merchandise on credit		+400						+400 Sales

Revenue, therefore, results from selling a product or performing a service. Recording revenue produces an increase in assets and an increase in the retained earnings component of stockholders' equity. Collection of cash is not necessary in order to recognize revenue. Consider the following three situations. Which, if any, would result in the recognition of revenue?

1 The direct investment by stockholders of $10,000 cash into the corporation in exchange for additional shares of capital stock.
2 Borrowing of $50,000 from the bank.
3 The subsequent collection of $400 cash for the previously discussed sale on credit of the clothing.

All three situations increase the firm's cash, but none would be recorded as revenue. Situation 1, the direct investment by the stockholders, does increase the corporation's assets and stockholders' equity. However, the increase is not the result of selling a product or providing a service and thus does not result in revenue being recorded. The invested capital portion of stockholders' equity, not retained earnings, would be increased by the capital stock issue. Situation 2, the bank loan, increases assets and liabilities (not stockholders' equity). Again no revenue is earned since there was neither sale of a product nor provision of a service. In situation 3, the cash collection on the charge account does not generate revenue. Recall that under accrual-basis accounting, revenue was recognized when the sale was made. Recognizing revenue *again* when cash is received would result in recording the sales revenue twice.

On a transaction worksheet, the three situations discussed above would appear as:

	Assets		=	Liabilities		+	Stockholders' equity	
Situation	Cash	Accounts receivable		Com-missions payable	Bank loan payable		Capital stock	Retained earnings
1. Direct investment by stockholders	+10,000						+10,000	
2. Borrowing from bank	+50,000				+50,000			
3. Collection of pre-vious sale on credit	+ 400	−400						

Matching

Recording revenue when it is earned—when the product is sold or service rendered—is only the first of two major aspects underlying accrual accounting. It is also extremely important to record expenses in the correct time period. If the income statement is to properly measure results of operations (profitability) for the period, expenses must be recorded in the same time period that the related revenue is recorded (this is the matching rule mentioned in Chapter 1). Accrual-basis accounting records expenses when the goods and services are consumed in generating revenue, which may not be the same time that cash for the goods or services is paid. For example, assume salesclerks are paid a commission on the first Friday of January for sales they made during the month of December. The expense for commissions the salesclerks earned during December must be recorded in December since the expense relates to December sales revenue. If we assume these commissions amount to $1,430, they would be recorded in December as:

	Assets		=	Liabilities		+	Stockholders' equity	
Situation	Cash	Accounts receivable		Com-missions payable	Bank loan payable		Capital stock	Retained earnings
Commissions earned by salesclerks in December				+1,430				−1,430 Commissions expense

In January, when salesclerks are paid their December commissions, we have:

	Assets		=	Liabilities		+	Stockholders' equity	
Situation	Cash	Accounts receivable		Com- missions payable	Bank loan payable		Capital stock	Retained earnings
Payment of Decem- ber commissions	−1,430			−1,430				

In the above example, cash payment occurred *after* the expense was recorded. In other cases, goods or services may be purchased and paid for *before* they are consumed in earning revenues. For example, assume a company pays $2,400 on December 1 for a one-year insurance policy on its delivery trucks. How is the prepaid insurance cost to be accounted for? Initially, we record an asset to reflect the right (insurance coverage for the next year) owned by the company. This would be recorded as:

	Assets		=	Liabilities	+	Stockholders' equity	
Situation	Cash	Prepaid insurance				Capital stock	Retained earnings
Payment for one-year insurance policy	−2,400	+2,400					

During December, one-twelfth (or $200) of the prepaid insurance asset is used up. This $200 is a necessary cost of operating the business and earning revenue during December. To properly match the $200 insurance expense against December's revenues and reduce the prepaid insurance asset to the correct remaining balance of $2,200 on December 31, we would record:

	Assets		=	Liabilities	+	Stockholders' equity	
Situation	Cash	Prepaid insurance				Capital stock	Retained earnings
One month of insur- ance coverage is consumed		−200					−200 Insurance expense

There are many other examples where goods or services are purchased before they are consumed. Merchandise bought for resale is initially recorded as an asset (inventory), then later is charged to expense (cost of goods sold) when the merchandise is sold to customers. Buildings, equipment, and trucks are recorded as assets when purchased. These are also gradually used up over time and are charged to expense (called depreciation expense). We will discuss the procedures for recording these expenses as we proceed through the next several chapters.

Summary of Accrual Accounting

Accrual accounting is commonly used by business to record its revenues and expenses. Under this approach, revenues are recognized when they are earned— when the sale is essentially complete (usually at time of delivery). Expenses are recorded when goods and services are consumed in the process of earning revenue. Revenues minus expenses equals income. Note the distinction between the terms *revenue* and *income*. Revenue refers to the gross increase in assets and the retained earnings component of stockholders' equity resulting from a sale. Income is the net amount earned after deducting expenses. For example, if you buy a textbook for $35, the bookstore's revenue is $35, but its income, after deducting the cost of the book and all other expenses, may be only $4.

TRANSACTION ANALYSIS

The process which ends with financial statements begins with individual business transactions. A *transaction* is an exchange between parties that has financial significance (that is, it affects the firm's assets, liabilities, or owners' equity). For a transaction to occur there must be (1) at least two parties (one of which is the firm); (2) an exchange of goods, services, rights, etc., between the parties; and (3) some dollar effect on the firm's assets, liabilities, or owners' equity. Exhibit 2-1 presents six transactions for Blondine Corporation, a consulting firm. Note that for each transaction presented on Exhibit 2-1 an exchange of goods, services, or rights has occurred between Blondine Corporation and another party and that Blondine's assets, liabilities, or stockholders' equity was affected. Analysis of a transaction identifies which assets, liabilities, or components of stockholders' equity have increased or decreased. After the analysis is completed, the transaction may be recorded. Events such as the receipt of an order from a customer or the hiring of an employee are *not* accounting transactions and therefore are not recorded. While two parties have entered into an agreement, no exchange has as yet occurred, and so far there is no effect on the firm's assets, liabilities, or owners' equity.

COMPUTER APPLICATION

Transaction analysis is a very important step in the accounting process. As a result of this analysis, a decision is made as to whether an event requiring an entry has occurred, and the affected accounts are identified. Even if the accounting system is fully computerized, transaction analysis remains a largely human function; someone must decide that an entry is needed. If an error is made in transaction analysis, the error will continue through all the subsequent steps in the accounting process, and may be difficult to correct. The difficulty many people have in trying to correct a computerized billing error on a charge account is an example of how an initial error in transaction analysis can lead to continuing problems.

EXHIBIT 2-1   Analysis of Blondine's Transactions

Transaction	Parties	Exchange	Blondine Corp.
Stockholders purchased shares of stock from the corporation	Blondine	Blondine receives cash	Increases assets (Cash) Increases invested capital component of stockholders' equity (Capital Stock)
	Stockholders	Stockholders receive ownership rights to corporation	
Purchased land for cash	Blondine	Blondine receives land	Increases assets (Land) Decreases assets (Cash)
	Seller of land	Seller receives cash	
Provided consulting services for customers on account	Blondine	Blondine receives customers' promise of future payment	Increases assets (Accounts Receivable) Increases retained earning component of stockholders' equity (Revenue—Consulting Fees Earned)
	Customer	Customer receives services	
Payment made to employees for current period salaries	Blondine	Blondine receives employees' services	Decreases retained earnings component of stockholders' equity (Salaries Expense) Decreases assets (Cash)
	Employees	Employees receive cash	
Advertisement placed in newspaper with payment promised to newspaper within 30 days	Blondine	Blondine receives benefits of newspaper ad	Decreases retained earnings component of stockholders' equity (Advertising Expense) Increases liabilities (Accounts Payable)
	Newspaper	Newspaper receives promise of future cash	
Partial payment made to newspaper for previously published advertisement	Blondine	Blondine pays cash	Decreases liabilities (Accounts Payable) Decreases assets (Cash)
	Newspaper	Newspaper receives cash	

THE ACCOUNTING PROCESS

The accounting process must properly record, classify, and summarize all appropriate transactions for the period if the financial statements are to be presented fairly. Transactions are recorded as they occur (i.e., in chronological order). However, something more than a chronological list of transactions is necessary in order to have useful accounting records. If only a list of transactions were maintained, data on equipment purchased would be interspersed with data on sales, on payments of bills, and so on. Thus a necessary part of the accounting process is to maintain separate records (called *accounts*) for each asset, liability, stockholders' equity, revenue, and expense item. For example, the effects of all transactions affecting cash (and only those affecting cash) would be shown in the cash account. All transactions affecting equipment would be conveniently available in the equipment account. All transactions affecting sales would be in the sales account, and so on. Finally, before financial statements are prepared, information must be summarized. For example, for the financial statements the ending account balance for cash is needed rather than a list of all transactions affecting cash during the period.

The accounting process can be visualized as a cycle of steps that begins with business transactions, ends with financial statement preparation, and then repeats for the next reporting period. After discussing the structure of the record-keeping system, we will illustrate the accounting cycle by examining each step in detail.

THE DEBIT-CREDIT SYSTEM

In Chapter 1 a transaction worksheet featuring pluses and minuses was used as a simple tool to familiarize you with the basics of the accounting process. However, most accounting systems are based on the debit-credit recording system. Debit and credit are very important terms to learn if you are successfully going to learn the language of accounting.

Debit simply means left side. *Credit* means right side. Forget any preconceived ideas that debits are bad and credits are good or that debit means increase and credit means decrease, or vice versa. To repeat: Debit simply means left side; credit means right side. Whether a debit or credit is an increase or a decrease depends on the type of account involved.

Assets, Liabilities, Stockholders' Equity

Assets are increased by debits and decreased by credits. Liabilities and stockholders' equity are increased by credits and decreased by debits. To help remember the debit-credit increase and decrease rules, use the structure of the accounting equation as an aid:

$$\text{Assets} = \text{Liabilities} + \text{Stockholders' Equity}$$

Note that assets are shown on the left side of the accounting equation. If assets are increased, the left side of the equation increases. Thus to *increase* an *asset* requires an entry on the left side, the *debit* side, of the asset account.

Liabilities and stockholders' equity are located on the right side of the accounting equation. If liabilities or stockholders' equity are increased, the right side of the equation increases. Thus to *increase* a *liability* or *stockholders' equity* requires an entry on the right side, or *credit* side.

COMPUTER APPLICATION

From here on, we will generally use the debit-credit terminology rather than the increase-decrease terminology. There are, however, applications of the increase-decrease approach. The logic of computerized accounting systems closely parallels the transaction worksheet using increases and decreases to specific accounts, because the basic logic of computers is based on plus-minus operations. Most computerized systems use debit-credit terminology only because this language is familiar to accountants; the internal operations of the computer convert these debits and credits back into increases and decreases.

The debit-credit scheme is illustrated below using "T-accounts" (so called because the shape resembles the letter "T"). Recall that accounts are used to maintain separate records for each individual asset, liability, and stockholders' equity item. The T-account format is especially useful in emphasizing the debit-credit rules.

Assets		=	Liabilities		+	Stockholders' equity	
Cash			**Accounts payable**			**Capital stock**	
Debit	**Credit**		**Debit**	**Credit**		**Debit**	**Credit**
Increase	Decrease		Decrease	Increase		Decrease	Increase
Accounts receivable			**Bank loan payable**			**Retained earnings**	
Debit	**Credit**		**Debit**	**Credit**		**Debit**	**Credit**
Increase	Decrease		Decrease	Increase		Decrease	Increase
Land			**Salaries payable**				
Debit	**Credit**		**Debit**	**Credit**			
Increase	Decrease		Decrease	Increase			
Any other assets			**Any other liabilities**				
Debit	**Credit**		**Debit**	**Credit**			
Increase	Decrease		Decrease	Increase			

Note that the left side of every account is the debit side and the right side of every account is the credit side. Assets (on the left side of the accounting equation) are increased by debits. Liabilities and stockholders' equity (on the right side of the accounting equation) are increased by credits. For decreases, the situation reverses. Assets are decreased by credits while liabilities and stockholders' equity are reduced by debits.

Five numerical examples of the debit-credit recording method utilizing T-accounts follow. Carefully study each one to familiarize yourself with transaction analysis and the debit-credit rules.

1 *Transaction:* Equipment costing $12,000 is purchased for cash.
Analysis: The asset—equipment—has been increased. Increases in assets are recorded by debits. Therefore debit Equipment $12,000. The asset—cash—has been decreased. Decreases in assets are recorded by credits. Therefore credit Cash $12,000.
Debit-Credit Recording:

Equipment		Cash	
Debit	**Credit**	**Debit**	**Credit**
12,000			12,000

2 *Transaction:* Inventory of $11,000 is purchased from suppliers on credit.
Analysis: The asset—inventory—has been increased. Increases in assets are recorded by debits. Therefore debit Inventory $11,000. The liability—accounts payable—has been increased. Increases in liabilities are recorded by credits. Therefore credit Accounts Payable $11,000.
Debit-Credit Recording:

Inventory		Accounts payable	
Debit	**Credit**	**Debit**	**Credit**
11,000			11,000

3 *Transaction:* Stockholders purchased from the corporation 1,000 shares of capital stock for $10,000.
Analysis: The asset—cash—has been increased. Increases in assets are recorded by debits. Therefore debit Cash $10,000. The invested capital component of stockholders' equity—capital stock—has been increased. Increases in stockholders' equity are recorded by credits. Therefore credit Capital Stock $10,000.
Debit-Credit Recording:

Cash		Capital stock	
Debit	**Credit**	**Debit**	**Credit**
10,000			10,000

4 *Transaction:* Cash of $15,000 is collected from customers for sales made on credit (on account) last month.
Analysis: The asset—cash—has been increased. Increases in assets are recorded by debits. Therefore, debit Cash $15,000. The asset—accounts receivable—has been decreased. Decreases in assets are recorded by credits. Therefore, credit Accounts Receivable $15,000.
Debit-Credit Recording:

Cash		Accounts receivable	
Debit	**Credit**	**Debit**	**Credit**
15,000			15,000

5 *Transaction:* A bank loan of $21,000 is arranged, and the firm receives the cash.

Analysis: The asset—cash—has been increased. Increases in assets are recorded by debits. Therefore, debit Cash $21,000. The liability—bank loan payable—has been increased. Increases in liabilities are recorded by credits. Therefore, credit Bank Loan Payable $21,000.

Debit-Credit Recording:

Cash		Bank loan payable	
Debit	**Credit**	**Debit**	**Credit**
21,000			21,000

For each transaction, the dollar amount of the debit(s) must equal the dollar amount of the credit(s). This debit = credit equality is necessary if the accounting equation (assets = liabilities plus stockholders' equity) is to remain in balance.

Revenues, Expenses, Dividends Declared

Revenue and expense accounts follow the basic debit and credit format. The key to understanding the debit-credit usage is in understanding that revenues and expenses are temporary subaccounts of the retained earnings component of stockholders' equity. Revenue is the selling price of goods sold or services rendered during the period; it increases the retained earnings component of stockholders' equity. Since a credit to stockholders' equity signifies an increase, *revenue is recorded as a credit*. Expenses are costs of goods and services consumed during the period; they decrease the retained earnings component of stockholders' equity. Since a debit to stockholders' equity signifies a decrease, *expenses are recorded by debits*.

If a portion of the assets accumulated from profitable operations is distributed to stockholders as a dividend, rather than being retained by the corporation, a temporary retained earnings subaccount titled *dividends declared* is utilized. Dividends declared, though not an expense, also represent a decrease in the retained earnings component of stockholders' equity, and hence *dividends declared are recorded by debits*.

Five numerical examples of the debit-credit recording scheme for revenues, expenses, and dividends declared follow. In studying each one, remember that revenues are temporary retained earnings subaccounts that increase stockholders' equity while expenses and dividends declared are temporary retained earnings subaccounts that decrease stockholders' equity.

1 *Transaction:* An attorney prepared a will for $180 cash.

Analysis: The asset—cash—has been increased. Increases in assets are recorded by debits. Therefore, debit Cash $180. The retained earnings component of stockholders' equity—sales revenue—has been increased. Increases in stockholders' equity are recorded by credits. Therefore, credit Sales $180.

Debit-Credit Recording:

Cash		Sales	
Debit	**Credit**	**Debit**	**Credit**
180			180

2 *Transaction:* An appliance store sells a video cassette recorder for $500 on credit (on account).

Analysis: The asset—accounts receivable—has been increased. Increases in assets are recorded by debits. Therefore, debit Accounts Receivable $500. The retained earnings component of stockholders' equity—sales revenue—has been increased. Increases in stockholders' equity are recorded by credits. Therefore, credit Sales $500.

Debit-Credit Recording:

Accounts receivable		Sales	
Debit	**Credit**	**Debit**	**Credit**
500			500

3 *Transaction:* The appliance store removes from its stockroom a video cassette recorder that had cost the store $240 when purchased and delivers it to the customer (see 2 above).

Analysis: The retained earnings component of stockholders' equity has been decreased by the cost of the good sold. Decreases in stockholders' equity are recorded by debits. Therefore, debit Cost of Goods Sold (an expense) $240. The asset—inventory—has been decreased. Decreases in assets are recorded by credits. Therefore, credit Inventory $240.

Debit-Credit Recording:

Cost of goods sold		Inventory	
Debit	**Credit**	**Debit**	**Credit**
240			240

4 *Transaction:* Paid landlord $2,500 for rent for the month.

Analysis: The retained earnings component of stockholders' equity has been decreased by the increase in rent expense. Decreases in stockholders' equity are recorded by debits. Therefore, debit Rent Expense $2,500. The asset—cash—has been decreased. Decreases in assets are recorded by credits. Therefore, credit Cash $2,500.

Debit-Credit Recording:

Rent expense		Cash	
Debit	**Credit**	**Debit**	**Credit**
2,500			2,500

5 *Transaction:* Dividends of $6,000 were declared and paid to stockholders.

Analysis: The retained earnings component of stockholders' equity has been decreased by the dividends declared. Decreases in stockholders' equity are recorded by debits. Therefore, debit Dividends Declared $6,000. The asset—cash—has been decreased. Decreases in assets are recorded by credits. Therefore, credit Cash $6,000.

Debit-Credit Recording:

Dividends declared		Cash	
Debit	**Credit**	**Debit**	**Credit**
6,000			6,000

For each of the transactions, the debit dollar amount equaled the credit dollar amount and the accounting equation (assets = liabilities + stockholders' equity) remained in balance. The basic principles of the debit-credit system are repeated on page 38.

JOURNALS AND JOURNAL ENTRIES

Business documents provide evidence of a firm's transactions. Daily cash register tapes confirm the amount of revenue from cash sales. Invoices (bills) from suppliers for inventory items acquired on account represent evidence of the acquisition of an asset (inventory) and the creation of a liability (accounts payable). Other typical business documents include sales invoices, checks written, remittance advices accompanying cash receipts, and time cards indicating hours worked by employees.

The transactions evidenced by business documents are recorded in the firm's accounting records using the debit-credit system. *Journal entries* represent the initial recording of transactions in the accounting system. Each journal entry provides a complete record of the transaction:

1 The date of the entry
2 The account title to be debited
3 The dollar amount of the debit
4 The account title to be credited
5 The dollar amount of the credit
6 An explanation of the entry

For each entry, total debits must equal total credits. If a transaction involves more than one debit or more than one credit, it is referred to as a *compound journal entry*.

The journal entries are listed chronologically in a "book" appropriately called the *journal* or *general journal*. Since the journal contains the initial record of transactions, it is often referred to as a "book of original entry." After journal entries are recorded, we wish to summarize the effect of the transactions on each account (asset, liability, and stockholders' equity item). This is done by transferring (known as *posting*) the debit and credit amounts from the journal entries to the individual accounts (e.g., cash, accounts payable, and so on.) We first illustrate the journal entry process and later present the posting process.

Assets = **Liabilities** + **Stockholders' equity**

Asset accounts

Debit	Credit
Increase	Decrease

Liability accounts

Debit	Credit
Decrease	Increase

**(Invested capital)
Capital stock**

Debit	Credit
Decrease	Increase

Retained earnings

Debit	Credit
Decrease	Increase

Revenue accounts

Debit	Credit
	Revenue accounts are credited since revenues increase the retained earnings component of stockholders' equity

Expense accounts

Debit	Credit
Expense accounts are debited since expenses decrease the retained earnings component of stockholders' equity	

Dividends declared

Debit	Credit
Dividends declared account is debited since dividends declared decrease the retained earnings component of stockholders' equity	

Journal Entries—An Illustration

To illustrate the recording of journal entries, we shall utilize Start-Up Company. Start-Up was organized on January 2, 1988. The firm is a merchandising corporation which buys ready-made goods and resells them. Start-Up plans to prepare financial statements at the end of each month. Listed below are eleven items relating to company business during January 1988. You should read through this list to develop an understanding of what transpired during the month.

Not only will the list of items below serve as the basis for illustrating journal entries, it will also be used later in this chapter and in Chapter 3 to illustrate the remaining steps in the accounting cycle.

1 January 2. The founders of Start-Up Company invested $100,000 cash in exchange for 10,000 shares of capital stock.

2 January 3. The company purchased $24,000 of office equipment. A cash down payment of $12,000 was made with a note due in three years signed for the $12,000 balance. Interest at 10 percent per year will be paid annually. The estimated useful life of the office equipment is five years.

3 January 4. The company signed an agreement to rent warehouse, office, and showroom facilities. The agreement covered the six-month period January, 1988 through June, 1988. A cash payment of $9,000 was made, covering the entire six months' rental.

4 January 7. The company opened preliminary negotiations with Quick-Sell Realtors for the purchase of a building. The price will probably be $70,000. No contract agreement has yet been signed.

5 January 8. The company purchased inventory on account for $50,000.

6 January 15. The company paid $500 to employees for salaries earned during the first half of January.

7 January 15. The *selling price* of goods sold by the company during the first half of the month totaled $42,000 (cash sales were $16,000 and sales on account were $26,000). The *cost* of the goods sold totaled $29,000.

8 January 26. Start-Up collected $12,000 cash from the January 15 sales on account.

9 January 28. The company paid vendors $40,000 as partial payment for the inventory purchased January 8 on account.

10 January 31. The *selling price* of goods sold by the company during the second half of the month totaled $8,000 (all were cash sales). The *cost* of the goods sold was $6,000.

11 January 31. Start-Up declared and paid a dividend of $0.20 per share of capital stock.

Each item will now be analyzed and properly recorded in Start-Up Company's journal.

Item 1—The founders of Start-Up Company invested $100,000 cash in exchange for 10,000 shares of capital stock.

entry for 2 involves the date column. For the first entry, the year, month, and day were written in the date column. Since neither the year nor the month have changed by the date of the second entry, typically the year and month are not written. Only if the year or month should change, or a new journal page is started, would it be necessary to again write the year or month in the date column.

Item 3—The company signed an agreement to rent warehouse, office, and show-room facilities and paid $9,000 for the next six-months' rent.

When Start-Up signed a rental agreement on January 4 for the warehouse, office, and showroom facilities, an exchange was made:

1 The owners of the buildings received $9,000, and
2 Start-Up received the right to use the buildings for six months.

The right to use the buildings is an asset because it represents future benefit to Start-Up Company. The benefit relates to a six-month period, January through June, 1988. This benefit will not be completely consumed during the January reporting period. The cost of the asset ($9,000) is recorded by debiting an asset account entitled Prepaid Rent. As the benefit is consumed proportionately over the six months, the portion of the cost that is consumed each month will be recognized as an expense. The entry to record the partial consumption of the asset during January will be illustrated in Chapter 3. The original entry to record the January 4 exchange is:

	General journal				Page 1
Date	**Account titles and explanations**	**PR**	**Debit**		**Credit**
4	Prepaid Rent		9,000		
	Cash				9,000
	To record payment of rent for January through June, 1988 on the warehouse, office, and showroom.				

Item 4—The company opened preliminary negotiations for the purchase of a building, but no contract agreement has yet been signed.

Preliminary negotiation on the possible future purchase of a building does not constitute a transaction for recording purposes. Recall that a transaction must include an exchange of goods, services, or rights and must have a dollar effect on the firm's assets, liabilities, or stockholders' equity. In the case of negotiations, no exchange has taken place and the dollar balances of Start-Up's accounts have not changed. Thus, no journal entry is required.

Item 5—The company purchased inventory on account for $50,000.

By purchasing inventory on account, Start-Up acquired an asset (inventory) and incurred a liability (a debt of $50,000). Accounts affected are Inventory— debited for $50,000 to reflect the increase in assets, and Accounts Payable— credited for $50,000 to reflect the increase in liabilities.

General journal				Page 1
Date	**Account titles and explanations**	**PR**	**Debit**	**Credit**
8	Inventory		50,000	
	Accounts Payable			50,000
	To record purchase of inventory			
	on account.			

Note that the $50,000 is not recorded as an expense at the time of purchase. When the entries to record the sale of inventory are made (as happens on January 15 and 31), the benefit the inventory represents to Start-Up will be consumed. At that point the asset will be reduced and the cost of inventory consumed in generating revenues will be recognized as expense. *Inventory when purchased is an asset; the cost of inventory sold is an expense.*

Item 6—The company paid $500 to employees for salaries earned during the first half of January.

Salaries earned by employees are an expense to Start-Up. The $500 payment of salaries is an expense of doing business for January and a reduction of cash. Remember that expenses reduce the retained earnings component of stockholders' equity and are thus recorded as debits. Assets are decreased by credits, thus the credit to Cash.

General journal				Page 1
Date	**Account titles and explanations**	**PR**	**Debit**	**Credit**
15	Salaries Expense		500	
	Cash			500
	To record payment of salaries for			
	the first half of January.			

Item 7—The selling price of goods sold by the company during the first half of the month totaled $42,000 (cash sales of $16,000 and sales on account of $26,000). The cost of the goods sold totaled $29,000.

During the first half of January, inventory that cost $29,000 was sold for $42,000. The sale triggers *two* entries in the journal. One is the recognition of revenue, the gross amount that Start-Up earned by selling the products. The other entry relates to the expense associated with the sale, the cost of the inventory sold. The revenue entry is discussed first.

Recall that revenue, which increases the retained earnings component of stockholders' equity, is recorded by crediting. The account titled Sales Revenue or Sales is appropriate for the entry. Under accrual-basis accounting, the entire $42,000 is recognized as revenue at the time of sale. Two asset accounts are affected by the sale. Cash increased $16,000 and Accounts Receivable increased $26,000. The increases in the assets are recorded by debits. The receivables represent promises by customers to pay Start-Up in the future for goods already delivered to the customers.

General journal				Page 1
Date	**Account titles and explanations**	**PR**	**Debit**	**Credit**
15	Cash		16,000	
	Accounts Receivable		26,000	
	Sales			42,000
	To record sales revenue for first half of January.			

To make the sale, Start-Up gave up inventory which cost the firm $29,000 in exchange for $42,000 in cash and promises to pay cash. The benefits obtained by the company when it purchased the inventory have now been consumed in generating revenue. Some of the asset inventory has become an expense. The expense account Cost of Goods Sold is debited to reflect the decrease in the retained earnings component of stockholders' equity. The decrease in the asset Inventory is recorded by a credit.[2]

General journal				Page 1
Date	**Account titles and explanations**	**PR**	**Debit**	**Credit**
15	Cost of Goods Sold		29,000	
	Inventory			29,000
	To record cost of goods sold expense for the first half of January.			

Item 8—The company collected $12,000 cash from previous sales on account.

On January 26, customers paid Start-Up $12,000 of the $26,000 owed. The composition of assets changed at this receipt. Cash increased and Accounts Receivable decreased as recorded below:

General journal				Page 1
Date	**Account titles and explanations**	**PR**	**Debit**	**Credit**
26	Cash		12,000	
	Accounts Receivable			12,000
	To record collections from customers of previous sales on account.			

It is important to note that collection of cash for sales previously made on account does not represent revenue. The revenue associated with the sale was recorded at the time of sale. In the Start-Up example, revenue was recorded on January 15.

For simplicity, assume that the remaining accounts receivable are expected to be collected in full. The matter of uncollectible accounts can be ignored for Start-Up Company.

---

[2]At the time of sale, some companies make no entry to record the cost of inventory sold. Instead, at the end of the accounting period the inventory is counted and a single journal entry is made to record the ending inventory and the cost of the inventory sold for the entire period. This alternative method for recording cost of inventory sold will be discussed in Chapter 6.

Item 9—The company paid vendors $40,000 as partial payment for previous purchases of inventory on account.

Early in the month Start-Up purchased inventory on account. At that time an account payable liability account was established to reflect the balance owed to vendors. On January 28, the company paid vendors $40,000 of the total $50,000 owed. The outflow of assets (Cash) and reduction of the liability (Accounts Payable) are recorded in the journal as:

General journal				Page 1

Date	Account titles and explanations	PR	Debit	Credit
28	Accounts Payable		40,000	
	Cash			40,000
	To record payment to vendors for previous purchases on account.			

Item 10—The selling price of goods sold by the company during the second half of the month totaled $8,000 (all cash sales). The cost of the goods sold was $6,000.

The recording on January 31 of sales for the second half of January is similar to the transaction recorded on January 15 (Item 7). Two entries are prompted by a sale: the recognition of revenue and the recording of the corresponding cost of goods sold expense. Cash sales of $8,000 are journalized as:

General journal				Page 1

Date	Account titles and explanations	PR	Debit	Credit
31	Cash		8,000	
	Sales			8,000
	To record sales revenue for second half of January.			

The inventory is decreased and the cost recognized as expense in the following entry.

General journal				Page 1

Date	Account titles and explanations	PR	Debit	Credit
31	Cost of Goods Sold		6,000	
	Inventory			6,000
	To record cost of goods sold expense for second half of January.			

Item 11—The company declared and paid a dividend of $0.20 per share of capital stock.

On the last day of the month the company declared and paid $2,000 in dividends to stockholders. (The declaration was $0.20 a share and 10,000 shares were outstanding.) *Dividends are not expenses;* they are not costs incurred in the process of generating revenues. Rather, dividends represent distributions of assets, earned by profitable operations, to owners of the company. However, similar to expenses, dividends reduce the retained earnings component of stockholders' equity and thus are recorded by debits. The account Dividends Declared, a temporary retained earnings subaccount, is debited in Start-Up's journal on January 31.

General journal				Page 1
Date	**Account titles and explanations**	**PR**	**Debit**	**Credit**
31	Dividends Declared		2,000	
	Cash			2,000
	To record declaration and payment of $0.20 per share dividend on 10,000 shares of capital stock.			

LEDGERS AND THE POSTING PROCESS

The chronological ordering of journal entries facilitates the initial recording of transactions. However, users of financial data need information classified as categories, or accounts, rather than in chronological order. Therefore, records are also maintained by ledger accounts. A *ledger account* is a record of the debits, credits, and balance for each individual asset, liability, stockholders' equity, revenue, and expense item. For example, if a company begins business by receiving a $20,000 cash investment (a debit), receives an additional $10,000 cash (another debit), and spends $18,000 (a credit), the three changes in cash and the $12,000 cash balance would be shown in the ledger account for cash. Similarly, the accounts payable ledger account indicates the debits, credits, and balance for the accounts payable liability. Separate accounts also are maintained for all other items including revenues, expenses, and dividends declared. The collection of all the accounts is referred to as the general ledger.

Chart of Accounts

Accounts are listed in the general ledger in the sequence in which they appear on the financial statements. Balance sheet accounts are listed first, followed by the revenue and expense accounts. Accounts within the balance sheet are further classified following the sequence of their financial statement appearance (i.e., assets first, then liabilities, and finally stockholders' equity). For ease of identification, general ledger accounts also are assigned account numbers. The sequence of the numbers assigned to the ledger accounts parallels the classification of the accounts (e.g., 100s for assets, 200s for liabilities, and so forth). Companies with many accounts use a more sophisticated numbering system. A *chart of accounts* lists a company's ledger accounts and their assigned numbers. Start-Up Company's chart of accounts is presented in Exhibit 2-2.

EXHIBIT 2-2
Start-Up Company
Chart of Accounts

Account	Account number	Account	Account number
Cash	100	Capital Stock	300
Accounts Receivable	101	Retained Earnings	305
Inventory	102	Dividends Declared	310
Prepaid Rent	103	Sales	401
Office Equipment	140	Cost of Goods Sold	501
Accumulated Depreciation	141	Depreciation Expense	502
Accounts Payable	201	Rent Expense	503
Salaries Payable	202	Salaries Expense	504
Interest Payable	203	Interest Expense	505
Income Taxes Payable	204	Income Tax Expense	506
Long-term Note Payable	220		

COMPUTER APPLICATION

The chart of accounts is particularly important in computerized accounting systems. In entering transactions into a computerized system, accounts are always identified by number rather than by name. For example, using the account numbers in Exhibit 2-2, a collection of $1,550 on account would be entered as:

100	1,550.00
101	−1,550.00

The Posting Process

The process of transferring entries from the journal to the ledger is known as *posting.* Journal entries are posted to the ledger accounts regularly. However, it would be inefficient to post immediately after every journal entry is recorded. Normally, the entries in the journal are posted to the ledger at the end of each week or each month.

COMPUTER APPLICATION

In a computerized accounting system, posting to ledger accounts can occur as each transaction is recorded. Because posting is handled automatically by the computer, immediate posting to the ledger accounts means that two steps—recording the journal entry and posting the accounts—are handled in one operation. Many computerized accounting systems, particularly small business systems designed for microcomputers, are structured in this way. Large business systems, however, are likely to use weekly or monthly posting. While this involves two operations rather than one, there is an advantage in summarizing a large number of transactions before posting, and posting only the totals. If each transaction of a large firm were posted separately, each ledger account would become very lengthy.

Ledger accounts are of two basic types: (1) the three-column, running balance format and (2) the T-account format.

Three-Column, Running Balance Ledger Accounts The journal entry for the first transaction of Start-Up Company during January, 1988 is repeated below along with the associated three-column, running balance type of ledger accounts (i.e., debit column, credit column, and balance column). The arrows indicate the posting process (that is, the transfer of the debit and credit dollar amounts from the journal to the ledger accounts).

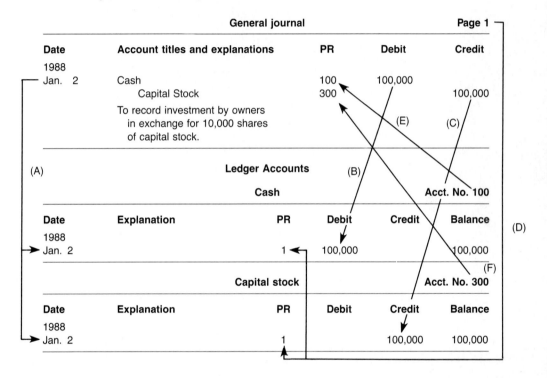

The January 2, 1988 date of the journal entry is recorded in the ledger accounts (see arrow A) to facilitate reference back to the original transaction in the journal.

The $100,000 debit to Cash in the journal entry is posted to the debit column of the Cash ledger account (arrow B). As this is the only entry so far in the cash account the balance is also $100,000. The $100,000 credit to Capital Stock in the journal entry is posted to the credit column of the Capital Stock ledger account (see arrow C). As this is the only entry in the Capital Stock account the balance is also $100,000.

Notice that the balance column in the ledger accounts is not labeled either debit or credit. The balance would be a debit balance if total amounts debited to the account exceeded total amounts credited, and vice versa for a credit balance.

Note that the column designated PR (posting reference) appears in both the journal and ledger. Notations in this column cross-reference the two records of the transaction. The entering of "1" in the PR column of the ledger accounts (see arrow D) indicates the posting is made from page 1 of the journal. Knowing the journal page from which the entry was posted is a valuable aid in attempting to locate posting errors and in obtaining more information about the entire transaction. The ledger account numbers—100 for Cash and 300 for Capital Stock—are entered in the PR column of the journal (see arrows E and F) to indicate that posting of the entry to the ledger is completed.

Care must be taken in posting the debits and credits. Common errors encountered are: entering the debit or credit in the wrong ledger account, entering a debit as a credit or vice versa, posting an entry twice, or failing to post an entry at all.

T-Accounts An alternative format to the three-column, running balance ledger account is the T-account. As illustrated earlier in the chapter when discussing the debit-credit rules, debits are recorded on the left side of the T and credits are recorded on the right side.

To illustrate usage of the T-account format of ledger accounts, the first transaction of Start-Up Company is utilized again. The journal entry after posting has been completed appears as:

	General journal			Page 1
Date	**Account titles and explanations**	**PR**	**Debit**	**Credit**
1988				
Jan. 2	Cash	100	100,000	
	Capital Stock	300		100,000
	To record investment by owners in exchange for 10,000 shares of capital stock.			

The T-accounts in the ledger after the first transaction is posted would show:

	Cash				#100		Capital stock				#300
Date	**PR**	**Debit**	**Date**	**PR**	**Credit**	**Date**	**PR**	**Debit**	**Date**	**PR**	**Credit**
1988									1988		
Jan. 2	1	100,000							Jan. 2	1	100,000

The process of posting to T-accounts is the same as the steps followed in posting to three-column, running balance ledger accounts. The only difference between the two alternative formats is that the T-account form does not provide for a running balance. To balance a T-account, perform the following steps:

1 Total all the entries in the debit column.

2 Total all the entries in the credit column.

3 Determine the difference between the two column totals (the account balance), and add this difference to the column with the smaller total.

4 Retotal the columns and double underscore the totals which should now be equal.

5 Enter the balance determined in step 3 on the opposite side of the account to which it was added in step 3.

To illustrate, Start-Up Company's T-account for Cash is presented below. All journal entries for the month have been posted and the account has been balanced. The five steps listed above are labeled on the T-account to help you follow the balancing process.

			Cash			#100
Date	PR	Debit	Date	PR	Credit	
1988			1988			
Jan. 2	1	100,000	Jan. 3	1	12,000	
15	1	16,000	4	1	9,000	
26	1	12,000	15	1	500	
31	1	8,000	28	1	40,000	
			31	1	2,000	
STEP (1)		136,000			63,500	STEP (2)
			To Balance		72,500	STEP (3)
		136,000	—STEP (4)—		136,000	
STEP (5) Balance		72,500				

Journals and Ledgers—A Recap

At this point it is helpful to examine the appearance of the formal journal and ledger accounts for Start-Up Company after January transactions have been journalized and posted. Exhibit 2-3 presents Start-Up's journal entries, and Exhibit 2-4 shows its ledger accounts. Review the journal entries in Exhibit 2-3 and T-account form of ledger postings in Exhibit 2-4.

COMPUTER APPLICATION

In a computerized accounting system, journals and ledgers have a somewhat different appearance than the manual versions illustrated in Exhibits 2-3 and 2-4. The same general logic applies, however. A journal entry must indicate the date, accounts (usually identified by number), amounts to be debited and credited, and appropriate explanatory material. A ledger account will indicate date, posting reference, debits and credits to the account, and balance. It is important to appreciate that, while the appearance of accounting records may vary, the underlying logic of the accounting system is always the same.

TRIAL BALANCE

Once transactions have been recorded in the firm's journal and posted to the ledger, a trial balance can be prepared. The *trial balance* is a list of the individual ledger accounts and their respective debit or credit balances. The trial balance lists

EXHIBIT 2-3
Start-Up's Journal Entries

	General journal			**Page 1**

Date	Account titles and explanations	PR	Debit	Credit
1988				
Jan. 2	Cash	100	100,000	
	Capital Stock	300		100,000
	To record investment by owners in exchange for 10,000 shares of capital stock.			
3	Office Equipment	140	24,000	
	Cash	100		12,000
	Long-term Note Payable	220		12,000
	To record purchase of office equipment for cash and 3-year note payable.			
4	Prepaid Rent	103	9,000	
	Cash	100		9,000
	To record payment of rent for January through June, 1988 on the warehouse, office, and showroom.			
8	Inventory	102	50,000	
	Accounts Payable	201		50,000
	To record purchase of inventory on account.			
15	Salaries Expense	504	500	
	Cash	100		500
	To record payment of salaries for the first half of January.			
15	Cash	100	16,000	
	Accounts Receivable	101	26,000	
	Sales	401		42,000
	To record sales revenue for first half of January.			
15	Cost of Goods Sold	501	29,000	
	Inventory	102		29,000
	To record cost of goods sold expense for first half of January.			
26	Cash	100	12,000	
	Accounts Receivable	101		12,000
	To record collections from customers of previous sales on account.			

EXHIBIT 2-3
(continued)

General journal   **Page 1**

Date	Account titles and explanations	PR	Debit	Credit
28	Accounts Payable	201	40,000	
	Cash	100		40,000
	To record payment to vendors for previous purchases on account.			
31	Cash	100	8,000	
	Sales	401		8,000
	To record sales revenue for second half of January.			
31	Cost of Goods Sold	501	6,000	
	Inventory	102		6,000
	To record cost of goods sold expense for second half of January.			
31	Dividends Declared	310	2,000	
	Cash	100		2,000
	To record declaration and payment of $0.20 per share dividend on 10,000 shares of capital stock.			

the accounts in the same sequence that the accounts appear in the ledger. Because the accounting system is structured to require equal dollar amounts of debits and credits for every situation, the sum of all the debit balances on the trial balance should equal the total of the credit balance accounts. The fact that the total debits on a trial balance equals the total credits does not ensure that no errors were made in the journalizing or posting steps. Failure to record a transaction in the journal or failure to post it to the ledger will not affect the equality of the debits and credits on the trial balance. Similarly, inadvertently reversing the debit-credit posting, posting an entry twice, or posting the debit or credit to the wrong account would not negate the debit-credit equality on the trial balance. Preventing such errors must depend upon controls implemented by management.

COMPUTER APPLICATION

Many of these controls are built into a computerized accounting system and operate automatically. These controls would prevent reversing of debits and credits in the posting process, double posting, or posting to the wrong account. The computer would correctly post whatever data appeared in the journal entries. Calculations of balances would be done automatically, eliminating errors from that source. Finally, the trial balance would be automatically prepared from the ledger accounts, thus eliminating errors that occur when data are manually copied from one source (the ledger) to another (the trial balance).

EXHIBIT 2-4
T-Account Ledger Accounts for Start-Up Company

Cash #100

Date	PR	Debit	Date	PR	Credit
1988			1988		
Jan. 2	1	100,000	Jan. 3	1	12,000
15	1	16,000	4	1	9,000
26	1	12,000	15	1	500
31	1	8,000	28	1	40,000
			31	1	2,000
		136,000			63,500
			To Balance		72,500
		136,000			136,000
Balance		72,500			

Accounts receivable #101

Date	PR	Debit	Date	PR	Credit
1988					
Jan. 15	1	26,000	Jan. 26	1	12,000
			To Balance		14,000
		26,000			26,000
Balance		14,000			

Inventory #102

Date	PR	Debit	Date	PR	Credit
1988			1988		
Jan. 8	1	50,000	Jan. 15	1	29,000
			31	1	6,000
		50,000			35,000
			To Balance		15,000
		50,000			50,000
Balance		15,000			

Prepaid rent #103

Date	PR	Debit	Date	PR	Credit
1988					
Jan. 4	1	9,000			

Office equipment #140

Date	PR	Debit	Date	PR	Credit
1988					
Jan. 3	1	24,000			

Accounts payable #201

Date	PR	Debit	Date	PR	Credit
1988			1988		
Jan. 28	1	40,000	Jan. 8	1	50,000
To Balance		10,000			
		50,000			50,000
			Balance		10,000

EXHIBIT 2-4 (*continued*)
T-Account Ledger Accounts for Start-Up Company

Long-term note payable   #220

Date	PR	Debit	Date	PR	Credit
			1988		
			Jan. 3	1	12,000

Capital stock   #300

Date	PR	Debit	Date	PR	Credit
			1988		
			Jan. 2	1	100,000

Dividends declared   #310

Date	PR	Debit	Date	PR	Credit
1988					
Jan. 31	1	2,000			

Sales   #401

Date	PR	Debit	Date	PR	Credit
			1988		
			Jan. 15	1	42,000
			31	1	8,000
			Balance		50,000

Cost of goods sold   #501

Date	PR	Debit	Date	PR	Credit
1988					
Jan. 15	1	29,000			
31	1	6,000			
Balance		35,000			

Salaries expense   #504

Date	PR	Debit	Date	PR	Credit
1988					
Jan. 15	1	500			

As can be seen, computerized systems prevent many errors by their built-in controls. Not all sources of error are eliminated, however. Incorrect analysis of a transaction, or failure to record it at all, can occur in a computerized system as it does in a manual system. Nonetheless, use of the computer greatly facilitates preparation of a correct trial balance.

A trial balance for Start-Up Company based on the January 31 ledger balances is shown in Exhibit 2-5. The ledger is "in balance" since both debits and credits total $172,000.

THE ACCOUNTING CYCLE REVIEWED

The accounting cycle from the creation of a business document that serves as evidence of a financial transaction to the preparation of the trial balance has been discussed. The sequential steps of the accounting cycle are outlined below. The first four steps were covered in this chapter. Steps 5 through 9 will be discussed in Chapter 3.

1 *Reviewing the business documents* that serve to indicate the occurrences of business transactions.

2 *Recording journal entries* for routine, day-to-day transactions for the period.

3 *Posting* the transactions from the journal to ledger accounts where effects of the transactions on individual assets, liabilities, and stockholders' equity accounts are summarized.

4 *Preparing a trial balance* comprised of the balances in the individual ledger accounts.

5 *Recording and posting adjusting journal entries*.

EXHIBIT 2-5
Start-Up Company
Trial Balance
January 31, 1988

	Debit	Credit
Cash	$ 72,500	
Accounts Receivable	14,000	
Inventory	15,000	
Prepaid Rent	9,000	
Office Equipment	24,000	
Accounts Payable		$ 10,000
Long-term Note Payable		12,000
Capital Stock		100,000
Dividends Declared	2,000	
Sales		50,000
Cost of Goods Sold	35,000	
Salaries Expense	500	
	$172,000	$172,000

6 *Preparing an adjusted trial balance* to verify the accounts are in balance after the adjusting entries have been posted.

7 *Preparing financial statements* that present results of operation and financial position.

8 *Recording and posting closing entries* that transfer the temporary revenue, expense, and dividends declared ledger account balances for the period to retained earnings.

9 *Preparing an after-closing trial balance* to verify the accounts are in balance after the closing entries have been posted.

COMPUTER APPLICATION

In a manual accounting system, each of these steps is a separate activity. In a computerized system, steps such as recording and posting may occur simultaneously, or one step may automatically follow another (for example, at the conclusion of posting, a trial balance might be automatically prepared).

SUMMARY

The accounting process involves the recording, classifying, and summarizing of business transactions and other pertinent information and translating it into financial statements. The accounting records also serve as the basis for performing many essential business activities—such as billing customers, ordering goods, paying debts, and so on.

Learning Objective 1: Analyze a transaction and determine the debit-credit entry to record the transaction under the accrual method of accounting.

In processing accounting data, increases or decreases are described by the terms debit and credit. Debits indicate increases in assets or decreases in liabilities or stockholders' equity. Credits indicate decreases in assets or increases in liabilities and stockholders' equity. Revenue accounts, which represent increases in the retained earnings component of stockholders' equity, are credited. Expenses and dividends declared, which reduce the retained earnings component of stockholders' equity, are debited. For each accounting entry the total debit amounts must equal the total credit amounts. Revenues are recorded when they are *earned,* which may not necessarily coincide with when the cash is collected. Expenses are *matched* against related revenue in the same time period.

Learning Objective 2: Record journal entries.

Journal entries are the initial recording of transactions in the accounting system. A journal entry involves entering in the journal the date, the account title to be debited, the dollar amount of the debit, the account title to be credited, the dollar amount of the credit, and an explanation of the entry.

Learning Objective 3: Post journal entries to ledger accounts.

A ledger account is a record of the debits, credits, and balance for each individual asset, liability, and stockholders' equity item. Posting a journal entry involves transferring the debit and credit amounts from a journal entry to the appropriate ledger accounts.

Learning Objective 4: Prepare a trial balance.

The purpose of a trial balance is to prove the equality of the debits and credits that have been posted to the general ledger. A trial balance is prepared by listing each individual ledger account and its debit or credit balance. The sum of all the debit balances should equal the total of the credit balance accounts.

KEY TERMS

Accrual accounting	Ledger account
Chart of accounts	Posting
Compound journal entry	Posting reference
Credit	T-account
Debit	Three-column, running balance
Journal	account
Journal entry	Transactions

REVIEW QUESTIONS

1 List two reasons why it is important to understand the mechanics of recording, classifying, and summarizing accounting data.

2 Define the term "revenue." Under accrual-basis accounting, when is revenue recorded?

3 Define the term "expenses." Under the matching rule, when are expenses recorded?

4 Differentiate between revenue and income.

5 What three elements must be present in order for an accountant to record a financial transaction?

6 Which of the following events are not recorded as accounting transactions: a) sell land for cash, b) send purchase order to vendor for future inventory purchase, c) collect an account receivable, d) hire employee to begin work next month?

7 Describe the debit and credit scheme as it applies to assets, liabilities, and stockholders' equity.

8 "Expense accounts have debit balances, therefore expenses are assets. Revenues have credit balances, therefore revenues are liabilities." Evaluate the preceding statements.

9 "Debits are good. Credits represent increases." Evaluate the preceding statements.

10 Are there any errors in the summarization of the debit and credit scheme that is presented below?

Stockholders' equity			Liabilities	
Dr.	**Cr.**		**Dr.**	**Cr.**
Increases	Decreases		Decreases	Increases

Assets		Revenues	
Dr.	**Cr.**	**Dr.**	**Cr.**
Increases	Decreases		Credited to increase retained earnings component of stockholders' equity

Expenses		Dividends declared	
Dr.	**Cr.**	**Dr.**	**Cr.**
Debited to decrease retained earnings component of stockholders' equity		Debited to decrease retained earnings component of stockholders' equity	

11 What is the "book of original entry"? Describe the posting process.

12 What is a ledger account? What is the difference between a three-column, running balance ledger account and a T-ledger account?

13 For each of the following accounts, indicate the type of account it is: asset, liability, permanent stockholders' equity (capital stock or retained earnings), revenue, or expense. Also indicate whether the account would have a debit or credit balance.
a Bank Loan Payable
b Cost of Goods Sold
c Sales
d Investment in Land
e Accounts Receivable
f Capital Stock

14 Among the items on Uclan Company's trial balance are: $1,974,000 cost of goods sold; $782,000 total selling, general and administrative expenses; $4,050,000 sales; and $640,000 income tax expense. Assuming these were the only income statement items on the trial balance, determine each of the following: total revenue, total expenses, and net income.

15 "The trial balance shows total debits equal to total credits; therefore, the accountant is assured that no errors have been made during the period." Evaluate the preceding statement.

16 Presented below in random sequence are the four individual steps in the traditional accounting cycle that were discussed in the chapter. Rearrange them in logical sequence by assigning each step a number from one to four (1 being the first step, 2 being the second step, and so on).
 Posting
 Journal entries
 Trial balance
 Business documents

EXERCISES

E2-1 Piecup, Inc. purchases pie trays from suppliers and then resells them to customers. A list of events during December is as follows:

1 December 2—Issued 50,000 shares of capital stock to investors in exchange for the investment of $50,000 cash.
2 December 4—Purchased 40,000 pie trays for $1 each; paid for purchase in cash.
3 December 8—Cash sale of 10,000 pie trays to a customer for $2 each.
4 December 22—Sold 25,000 pie trays to a customer for $2 each. Customer paid $30,000 cash and promised to pay the remaining $20,000 within 15 days.
5 December 24—Paid $4,000 rent for month of December.
6 December 27—Received $10,000 of the $20,000 owed by customer.
7 December 31—Paid $1,500 to employee for December salary.

Required:
1 Prepare a list of the above events that represent revenue earned for December. Indicate the dollar amount of revenue.
2 Prepare a list of the above events that represent expense for December. Indicate the dollar amount of expenses.

E2-2 Presented below in random sequence are selected accounts for Shey Company.

Salaries expense		Accounts payable		Inventories	
Dr.	Cr.	Dr.	Cr.	Dr.	Cr.

Accounts receivable		Sales		Cost of goods sold	
Dr.	Cr.	Dr.	Cr.	Dr.	Cr.

Capital stock		Retained earnings	
Dr.	Cr.	Dr.	Cr.

Required:
Indicate for each account whether an increase would be recorded by a debit or a credit and explain why (i.e., identify what type of account it is). The first one already is done as an example. Example: An increase in Salaries Expense would be recorded by a debit. Expenses decrease stockholders' equity (specifically retained earnings); stockholders' equity is decreased by debits.

E2-3 Barone, Inc. had the following occur during February, 1989:
1 February 8—Purchased $18,000 of inventory from vendors on account.
2 February 19—Sold merchandise to customers on account. The amount of the sales was $24,000.
3 February 19—Cost of merchandise sold to customers was $13,000.
4 February 26—Collected $20,000 from customers relating to February 19 sales on account.
5 February 27—Paid vendors for one-half of the inventory purchased on account on February 8.

6 February 28—Hired new employee at $800 monthly salary rate. Employee is to begin work on March 1.

Required:

Present debit and credit entries on page 23 of Barone's journal for those February events listed above that require a journal entry. Posting references need not be provided.

E2-4 The accountant for Walden Products, Inc. resigned two weeks ago, and you have been hired as a replacement. In the interim, an office clerk with no accounting training has been recording transactions. Following are the transactions which have occurred, and the entries which have been made:

1 An order for merchandise (700 units of Product 312 at $9 per unit) was received.

Accounts Receivable	6,300	
Sales		6,300

2 Merchandise costing $4,200 was purchased on account.

Inventory	4,200	
Accounts Payable		4,200

3 The goods ordered in item (1) were shipped to the customer on account.

Accounts Payable	6,300	
Sales		6,300

4 A new employee was hired to begin work on the first of next month, at a monthly salary of $800. The following was recorded at the date of hiring:

Salary Expense	800	
Salary Payable		800

5 One hundred shares of capital stock were issued for $100 per share.

Cash	10,000	
Retained Earnings		10,000

6 Collections were made from customers for goods previously sold on account.

Cash	15,200	
Sales		15,200

7 Utility bills were received and paid.

Utility Expense	1,300	
Cash		1,300

8 Cost of goods sold during the past two weeks was $3,100.

Sales	3,100	
Inventory		3,100

Required:

For each of the eight transactions, consider the journal entry that was made by Walden Products. If the entry is correct, indicate this. If the entry is incorrect, prepare the entry that should have been made. (Omit explanations for your journal entries.)

E2-5 Presented below are transactions for Mickels' Co.:

1 October 14, 1988—Paid $4,500 rent for next two years for office space.

2 October 22, 1988—Sold merchandise to customers on account. Amount of sales was $84,000.

3 October 22, 1988—Cost of merchandise sold to customers was $51,000.

4 October 31, 1988—Paid $5,000 to employees for salaries earned during October.

Required:

Prepare debit and credit entries on page 4 of Mickels' Co.'s journal for each of the transactions.

E2-6 Presented below are two journal entries from page 14 of Blanchet Company's journal:

	General journal			Page 14
Date	**Account titles and explanation**	**PR**	**Debit**	**Credit**
1989				
May 18	Cash		40,000	
	Bank Loan Payable			40,000
	To record bank borrowing. Repayment due on November 18, 1990 with interest of 8 per-cent, compounded semi-annually.			
22	Inventory		12,000	
	Cash			12,000
	To record purchase of merchandise from Abrams Manufacturing Co.			

Required:

Post the two entries to the ledger accounts provided below.

	Ledger			
	Cash			**#10**
Date		**PR**	**Debit**	**Credit**	**Balance**

	Inventory			**#12**
Date		**PR**	**Debit**	**Credit**	**Balance**

	Bank loan payable			**#22**
Date		**PR**	**Debit**	**Credit**	**Balance**

E2-7 The journal and ledger of the newly formed Skender Company are presented below:

General journal   **Page 1**

Date	Account titles and explanation	PR	Debit	Credit
1989				
Jan. 2	Capital Stock			200,000
	Cash		200,000	
	To record issuance of 200,000			
	shares of capital stock.			
1989				
Jan. 3	Equipment		3,500	
	Cash			3,500

Ledger

Cash   **#110**

Date		PR	Debit	Credit	Balance
1989					
Jan. 2		1	200,000		200,000
3		1		35,000	165,000

Capital stock   **#120**

Date		PR	Debit	Credit	Balance
1989					
Jan. 2		1		200,000	200,000

Equipment   **#130**

Date		PR	Debit	Credit	Balance
1989					
Jan. 3		1		3,500	3,500

Required:
List all errors in the journal and ledger.

E2-8 Presented below are the ledger accounts of Meyerson Company (in T-account format with date and posting reference columns omitted):

Cash   **#100**

Beg. Bal.	38,700,000	43,000,000
	60,000,000	4,000,000
	71,800,000	

Accounts receivable   **#110**

Beg. Bal.	62,300,000	71,800,000
	60,400,000	

Income taxes payable		#200
	Beg. Bal.	52,050,000
		15,000,000

Salaries payable		#210
	Beg. Bal.	–0–
		40,000,000

Capital stock		#300
	Beg. Bal.	20,000,000

Retained earnings		#310
	Beg. Bal.	28,950,000

Fees earned		#400
		120,400,000

Salaries expense		#500
43,000,000		
40,000,000		

Rent expense		#510
4,000,000		

Income tax expense		#520
15,000,000		

Required:

Present a trial balance of account balances on December 31, 1988, the end of the accounting period.

PROBLEMS

P2-1 *Account Classification*
Required:
For each account on page 63, enter an "X" in the correct column to indicate proper classification of the account, financial statement in which it appears, and whether account has debit or credit balance. The first one is already done as an example.

P2-2 *Journal Entries and Posting to Three-Column, Running Balance Ledger Accounts*
The following are selected transactions of Coder, Inc. for March, 1988:
1 March 3—Issued 1,000 shares of capital stock to stockholders for $10,000.
2 March 5—Paid $1,000 to Markville Realty for rent for the month of March.

Classification of account

Account title	Asset	Liability	Permanent stockholders' equity	Revenue	Expense	Balance sheet	Income statement	Debit	Credit
Building	X					X		X	
Investments	X					X		X	
Prepaid Rent	X					X		X	
Capital Stock			X			X			X
Wages Expense					X		X	X	
Sales				X			X		X
Administrative Expense					X		X	X	
Income Taxes Payable		X				X	X	X	X
Inventory	X					X		X	
Account Receivable	X					X		X	

Financial statement account appears on: Balance sheet, Income statement

Account balance: Debit, Credit

3 March 9—Purchased $5,000 of inventory from vendors. Made cash down payment of $2,000 and promised to pay remainder within 14 days.
4 March 19—Sold merchandise to customers for $9,000 cash.
5 March 19—The cost of the inventory sold to customers was $3,500.
6 March 23—Paid vendors remaining $3,000 owed from purchase of inventory on March 9.

Required:
1 Record the above six transactions as debit-credit journal entries in Coder's journal. Label journal page as page 1.
2 Post the six journal entries to ledger accounts. Use the three-column, running balance format of ledger accounts. Develop your own ledger account-numbering system.

P2-3 *Journal Entries and Posting to T-Accounts*
The following are selected transactions of Neilson, Inc. for May, 1989. Neilson is a small grocery store chain.
1 May 1—Issued 1,000 shares of capital stock to stockholders for $15,000.
2 May 5—Received $5,000 from First National Bank and signed a note payable for the amount.
3 May 6—Purchased $25,000 of inventory from vendors on account.
4 May 10—Recorded sales for the first ten days of May. $50,000 of sales were in cash and $7,000 were on credit. Cost of sales was $22,000.
5 May 11—Paid vendors for merchandise purchased on May 6.
6 May 15—Paid rent for the month of May, $5,000.
7 May 25—Paid $250 for utility bills for May.

Required:
1 Record the above transactions as debit-credit journal entries in Neilson's journal. Label journal page as page 1.
2 Post the journal entries to ledger accounts. Use the T-account format of ledger accounts. Develop your own ledger account-numbering system.

P2-4 *Posting to T-Accounts*
Presented below are Andersen Medical Service Co.'s journal entries for August, 1989:

General journal				Page 1
Date	**Account titles and explanation**	**PR**	**Debit**	**Credit**
1989				
Aug. 1	Cash		25,000	
	Capital Stock			25,000
	To record issuance of 10,000 shares of capital stock for $25,000.			
4	Prepaid Rent		12,000	
	Cash			12,000
	To record payment of rent for the year August, 1989 through July, 1990.			

	General journal			Page 1
Date	**Account titles and explanation**	**PR**	**Debit**	**Credit**
29	Cash		10,000	
	Accounts Receivable		8,000	
	Fees Earned			18,000
	To record revenue earned for services rendered.			
30	Salaries Expense		14,000	
	Cash			14,000
	To record employees' salaries for August.			
31	Rent Expense		1,000	
	Prepaid Rent			1,000
	To record portion of prepaid rent "used up" in August.			
31	Income Tax Expense		500	
	Income Taxes Payable			500
	To record estimated income taxes for August.			

Andersen's chart of accounts has the following ledger account numbers:

Cash	#100	Fees Earned	400
Accounts Receivable	110	Salaries Expense	510
Prepaid Rent	120	Rent Expense	520
Income Taxes Payable	200	Income Tax Expense	530
Capital Stock	300		

Required:

Prepare ledger accounts and post the August journal entries. Use the T-account format for the ledger accounts.

P2-5 *Posting to T-Accounts*

Presented below are Sincere Card Supply Co.'s journal entries for June, 1989:

	General journal			Page 1
Date	**Account titles and explanation**	**PR**	**Debit**	**Credit**
1989				
June 1	Cash		140,000	
	Capital Stock			140,000
	To record issuance of 10,000 shares of capital stock for $140,000.			
4	Inventory		35,000	
	Accounts Payable			35,000
	To record purchase of inventory on account.			
5	Prepaid Insurance		12,000	
	Cash			12,000

General journal				Page 1
Date	**Account titles and explanation**	**PR**	**Debit**	**Credit**
	To record payment of insurance for one-year coverage from June 15, 1989 to June 14, 1990.			
10	Cash		21,000	
	Accounts Receivable		10,000	
	Sales			31,000
	To record sales made for the first ten days of June.			
10	Cost of Goods Sold		7,000	
	Inventory			7,000
	To record cost of sales.			
12	Rent Expense		10,000	
	Cash			10,000
	To record payment of rent for June.			
30	Cash		20,000	
	Accounts Receivable		12,000	
	Sales			32,000
	To record sales made for the last 20 days of June.			
30	Cost of Goods Sold		14,000	
	Inventory			14,000
	To record cost of sales.			
30	Salaries Expense		7,500	
	Cash			7,500
	To record payment to employees for services provided in June.			

Sincere's chart of accounts has the following ledger numbers:

Cash	#100	Capital Stock	300
Accounts Receivable	110	Sales	400
Prepaid Insurance	120	Cost of Sales	500
Inventory	130	Rent Expense	510
Accounts Payable	210	Salary Expense	520

Required:
Prepare ledger accounts and post the June journal entries. Use the T-account format for the ledger accounts.

 P2-6 *Journal Entries and Posting to T-Accounts*
The following are selected events of Hourly Inc. during January, 1988:
1 Jan. 6—Sold merchandise inventory to customers on account. The sales price was $6,200. The cost of the inventory sold was $4,200.
2 Jan. 7—Paid in cash the unpaid salaries earned in December 1987.
3 Jan. 10—Collected from customers $3,000 from previous sales made on account.

4 Jan. 18—Purchased, on account, $2,500 of merchandise inventory.
5 Jan. 29—Hired new employee to begin work on February 1, 1988 at $750 per month.
6 Jan. 30—Forty shares of capital stock issued for $2,800 cash.

The ledger accounts, using the T-account format, are shown below with January 1, 1988 beginning balances.

Cash   #100

Date	PR	Debit	Date	PR	Credit
1/1/88 Balance		14,000			

Accounts receivable   #110

Date	PR	Debit	Date	PR	Credit
1/1/88 Balance		8,000			

Inventory   #120

Date	PR	Debit	Date	PR	Credit
1/1/88 Balance		6,000			

Accounts payable   #200

Date	PR	Debit	Date	PR	Credit
			1/1/88 Balance		3,800

Salaries payable   #210

Date	PR	Debit	Date	PR	Credit
			1/1/88 Balance		200

Capital stock   #300

Date	PR	Debit	Date	PR	Credit
			1/1/88 Balance		15,000

Retained earnings   #320

Date	PR	Debit	Date	PR	Credit
			1/1/88 Balance		9,000

Sales   #400

Date	PR	Debit	Date	PR	Credit
			1/1/88 Balance		–0–

Cost of goods sold   #500

Date	PR	Debit	Date	PR	Credit
1/1/88 Balance		–0–			

Required:

1 Prepare debit and credit journal entries for the above information. (Label journal page as #1048.)

2 Post the journal entries to the T-accounts.

P2-7 *Journal Entries and Posting to T-Accounts*

The following are selected events of Sample Inc. during January, 1989:

1 January 1—Paid $21,000 for merchandise purchased on December 15, 1988.

2 January 2—Paid $18,000 for rent for 1989.

3 January 3—Paid $1,200 for the unpaid salaries earned in December, 1988.

4 January 5—Merchandise is purchased for $21,000 cash.

5 January 10—Merchandise is sold on account. Sale price is $1,000, cost of the merchandise is $700.

6 January 15–Sample borrowed $10,000 from First National Bank. In return they signed a note payable.

The ledger accounts, using the T-account format, are shown below with the January 1, 1989 beginning balances:

Cash   **#100**

Date	PR	Debit	Date	PR	Credit
1/1/89 Balance		102,000			

Accounts receivable   **#110**

Date	PR	Debit	Date	PR	Credit
1/1/89 Balance		7,000			

Merchandise inventory   **#120**

Date	PR	Debit	Date	PR	Credit
1/1/89 Balance		12,000			

Prepaid rent   **#130**

Date	PR	Debit	Date	PR	Credit
1/1/89 Balance		–0–			

Accounts payable   **#200**

Date	PR	Debit	Date	PR	Credit
			1/1/89 Balance		21,000

Salaries payable   **#210**

Date	PR	Debit	Date	PR	Credit
			1/1/89 Balance		1,200

Notes payable   **#220**

Date	PR	Debit	Date	PR	Credit
			1/1/89 Balance		–0–

Capital stock   #410

Date	PR	Debit	Date	PR	Credit
			1/1/89 Balance		70,000

Retained earnings   #420

Date	PR	Debit	Date	PR	Credit
			1/1/89 Balance		28,800

Sales   #500

Date	PR	Debit	Date	PR	Credit
			1/1/89 Balance		–0–

Cost of goods sold   #600

Date	PR	Debit	Date	PR	Credit
1/1/89 Balance		–0–			

Required:

1 Prepare debit and credit journal entries for the above information. (Label journal page as #1000.)

2 Post the journal entries to the T-accounts.

P2-8 *Working Backward from Ledger Postings to Journal Entries*

The ledger accounts of Frazacca, Inc. at February 28, 1990 in T-account format are shown below. Beginning of the month balances have been entered and all journal entries for February have been posted.

Cash   #1000

Date	PR	Debit	Date	PR	Credit
1990			1990		
Feb. 1 Beg. Bal.		480,000	Feb. 22	18	160,000
11	18	25,000	28	18	40,000
14	18	120,000			

Accounts receivable   #1010

Date	PR	Debit	Date	PR	Credit
1990			1990		
Feb. 1 Beg. Bal.		360,000	Feb. 14	18	120,000
28	19	330,000			

Inventory   #1020

Date	PR	Debit	Date	PR	Credit
1990			1990		
Feb. 1 Beg. Bal.		610,000	Feb. 28	19	195,000
8	18	94,000			

Accounts payable #2000

Date	PR	Debit	Date	PR	Credit
1990			1990		
Feb. 22	18	160,000	Feb. 1 Beg. Bal.		212,000
			8	18	94,000

Capital stock #3000

Date	PR	Debit	Date	PR	Credit
			1990		
			Feb. 1 Beg. Bal.		900,000
			11	18	25,000

Retained earnings #3010

Date	PR	Debit	Date	PR	Credit
			1990		
			Feb. 1 Beg. Bal.		338,000

Sales #4000

Date	PR	Debit	Date	PR	Credit
			1990		
			Feb. 28	19	330,000

Cost of goods sold #5000

Date	PR	Debit	Date	PR	Credit
1990					
Feb. 28	19	195,000			

Salaries expense #5010

Date	PR	Debit	Date	PR	Credit
1990					
Feb. 28	18	40,000			

Required:

1 Recreate the February journal entries that resulted in the above ledger postings and record them in chronological order in Frazacca's journal.

2 Prepare a trial balance for Frazacca as of February 28, 1990. (You will have to determine the account balance in each account.)

P2-9 *Analyzing Incorrect Journal Entries*

Marshall Company's statement of income for the month of November, 1988 showed net income of $20,000. However, it is believed the bookkeeper incorrectly recorded some transactions. The items in question are listed below:

1 A payment of $580 for employees' salaries was recorded by debiting Delivery Truck and crediting Cash.

2 The $18,000 selling price of goods sold on account during November was recorded by debiting Sales and crediting Cash.

3 Cash payment in November of $3,000 (for payment of December insurance coverage) was recorded by debiting Insurance Expense and crediting Cash.

4 Cash payment of $12,300 to vendors for previous merchandise purchases on account was recorded by debiting Accounts Receivable and crediting Cash.

5 Cash receipt in November of $1,700 from customer from sale on account in October was recorded by debiting Cash and crediting Accounts Receivable.

6 The $1,000 dividend declared and paid during November was recorded by debiting Dividends Declared and crediting Cash.

Required:

For each of the six items in question, you are to indicate:

a Whether the bookkeeper properly recorded the transaction (write either COR-RECT or WRONG).

b Amount by which net income for November is understated or overstated because of incorrect recording by bookkeeper (indicate amount and whether understatement or overstatement—ignore income tax effect).

c Effect of error on the November 30, 1988 balance sheet (indicate accounts and amounts and whether understated or overstated—ignore income tax effect).

d What journal entry should have been made by the bookkeeper when the transaction was originally recorded (omit date and explanation from entry).

The first one is done below as an example.

Item 1:

a WRONG

b $580 overstatement of net income (due to $580 understatement of Salaries Expense).

c Delivery Truck overstated by $580 and Retained Earnings overstated by $580.

d Dr: Salaries Expense   580

    Cr: Cash   580

Business Decision Problem

Sharon Lansing is employed as a computer instructor at Northern State College. Early in 1989, she decided to write and sell a computer newsletter as a sideline business. Her newsletter is directed to owners of the popular Peach computer, and it presents information on new software, programming tips, and a question and answer column. The newsletter is published monthly, and the subscription price is $20 per year.

To begin the business, Sharon invested $1,000 of her money and borrowed $2,000 from her sister on a 9 percent loan in January 1989. She spent $1,900 to place ads in computer magazines to solicit subscriptions for The Peach Newsletter, and she bought a Peach computer for $6,000: Due to rapidly changing technology, Sharon expects the computer to last for only four years. In January, 1989, Sharon paid $390 for a one-year insurance policy on the computer.

The ads yielded 372 subscriptions. A friend of Sharon's who is an accounting student at Northern State told her that the subscription amount should be credited to a liability account, because no revenue is earned until the newsletter is delivered to subscribers. The first issue of the monthly newsletter was published in July, 1989.

At December 31, 1989, the accounting records for The Peach Newsletter, Inc. showed the following information:

	Debit	Credit
Cash in bank	$ 390	
Computer	6,000	
Prepaid insurance	390	
Loan payable		$2,000
Liability for subscriptions		7,440
Capital stock		1,000
Printing and mailing expense	1,050	
Advertising	1,900	
Computer supplies	360	
Office supplies	210	
Computer magazines and books	140	

Sharon would like to prepare financial statements for the year 1989, but is uncertain whether her records are complete. She asks your evaluation of the success of her company.

3

THE ACCOUNTING
PROCESS: II

LEARNING OBJECTIVES

When you complete this chapter, you should be able to:

1 Analyze, record, and post adjusting entries.
2 Prepare financial statements in proper form.
3 Journalize closing entries following a three-step approach.
4 Present an after-closing trial balance.

The preceding chapter presented an analysis of the principal steps in the accounting cycle. In this chapter the remaining steps—adjusting entries, adjusted trial balance, financial statements, closing entries, and after-closing trial balance—are discussed. Special journals and subsidiary ledgers are covered near the end of the chapter. The accountant's worksheet is presented in the appendix to the chapter.

ADJUSTMENTS

Amounts in the trial balance are the result of routine recording of business transactions. Business documents (such as sales invoices, cash register tapes, checks written, remittance slips accompanying cash receipts, and suppliers' bills) are the basis on which the routine sales, cash payments, cash receipts, and purchases transactions are recorded. Relying solely on business documents, however, may not provide sufficient information for preparing periodic financial statements. Adjustments may be necessary at the end of the accounting period to update the accounts. Unrecorded assets, liabilities, revenues, and expenses may exist that must be recorded if the financial statements are to be fairly presented. The accountant must examine the records and determine whether the accounts need adjusting.

Adjusting Journal Entries

Journal entries known as *adjusting entries* are commonly required at the end of a reporting period: (a) to record events that have occurred but have not yet been recorded, (b) to record a change in an item since it was originally recorded, or (c) to correct errors. Often there are no normal business documents to indicate the necessity of the adjusting entry. The accountant must rely on personal knowledge of the business and on professional accounting skills to determine the appropriate adjusting entries.

Adjusting entries are classified into five groups:

1 *Expenses incurred and not yet recorded* (such as salaries earned by employees during the current accounting period that will not be paid until the subsequent accounting period). Employees, who are paid every Friday were last paid on Friday, December 26. From December 27 to December 31, 1988 (the last day of the accounting year), the employees earned $4,250, which will be paid on Friday, January 2, 1989. The required adjusting entry for the "accrued salaries" would be:

Date	Account titles and explanation	PR	Debit	Credit
1988				
Dec. 31	Salaries Expense		4,250	
	Salaries Payable			4,250
	To record salaries earned but unpaid at December 31.			

The adjusting entry results in $4,250 expense being included in the 1988 income statement to be "matched" against the revenue generated by the employees during that period. The unpaid salaries owed to the employees will be shown as a liability on the December 31, 1988 balance sheet as a result of the credit part of the adjusting entry.

2 *Revenues earned and not yet recorded* (such as interest earned on notes receivable). If a two-month, $6,000 note with a 10 percent annual interest rate was received on December 1, 1988, then one month's interest of $50 ($6,000 × .10 × 1/12 year) would have been earned by December 31 (the last day of the accounting year). None of the interest will be received until January 31, 1989, the end of the two-month period. The required December 31 adjusting entry for the "accrued interest" earned in December would be:

Date	Account titles and explanation	PR	Debit	Credit
1988				
Dec. 31	Interest Receivable		50	
	Interest Revenue			50
	To record interest earned but not received at December 31.			

The adjusting entry records $50 interest revenue in 1988's income statement to reflect interest earned from holding the interest-bearing note during December. The debit part of the entry results in an asset appearing on the December 31, 1988 balance sheet for the interest owed to the firm on that date.

3 *Expiration of an asset* (such as the expiration of prepaid insurance or depreciation of equipment). If $12,000 had been paid on December 1, 1988 for insurance coverage for the next twelve months, $1,000 of that coverage would have been "used up" during December. If we assume that the entire $12,000 insurance premium had been debited on December 1 to the asset account Prepaid Insurance, the required adjusting entry on December 31 would be:

Date	Account titles and explanation	PR	Debit	Credit
1988				
Dec. 31	Insurance Expense		1,000	
	Prepaid Insurance *(Cash decreased)*			1,000
	To record portion of prepaid insurance "used up" in December.			

The adjusting entry records as an expense in the 1988 income statement the portion of the asset that expired during 1988. The credit part of the entry will result in a balance of $11,000 appearing as an asset in the December 31, 1988 balance sheet. The $11,000 properly represents the remaining asset—11 months prepaid insurance—that exists as of December 31.

Similar to prepaid assets (such as prepaid insurance or prepaid rent), the "benefits" obtained from the acquisition of buildings, equipment, delivery trucks, furniture and fixtures, and other long-lived tangible assets also are "used up" or consumed over more than one accounting period. A portion of the cost of these long-term property and equipment assets must be recognized as expense each period as the benefits embodied in the assets are used up in earning revenues. The process of allocating the cost of tangible long-lived plant and equipment assets to expense over the estimated useful life of the asset is called *depreciation*.

If a delivery truck was purchased for $10,800 on December 1, 1988 and it is expected all the benefits associated with the truck will be "used up" evenly over the next three years, depreciation would be $300 per month ($10,800 ÷ 36 months). The required adjusting entry on December 31, 1988 (after one month's use of the truck) would be:

Date	Account titles and explanation	PR	Debit	Credit
1988				
Dec. 31	Depreciation Expense		300	
	Accumulated Depreciation			300
	To record one month's depreciation on the delivery truck.			

The debit part of the adjusting entry results in the income statement matching of depreciation expense against December's revenue generated in part through use of the delivery truck. The $300 depreciation expense estimates the portion of the cost of the delivery truck associated with the delivery truck "benefits" used up in December.

The credit portion of the adjusting entry involves the contra asset account— Accumulated Depreciation. *Contra assets* are "minus-asset" accounts that are deducted on the balance sheet from the asset to which they relate. Accumulated depreciation would be presented as a deduction from the cost of the delivery truck as follows:

Cash		$ XX
Accounts Receivable		XX
Inventory		XX
Prepaid Insurance		XX
Delivery Truck	$10,800	
Less Accumulated		
Depreciation	300	10,500
Total Assets		$ XXX

The $10,500 is the book value (or net book value) of the delivery truck after one month.

Conceptually, the credit part of the depreciation adjusting entry could be made to the delivery truck account directly and so reduce its balance on December 31 to $10,500 and eliminate the accumulated depreciation account. However, more information is provided to the financial statement reader by using contra assets such as accumulated depreciation. A detailed discussion of plant and equipment assets and their depreciation appears in Chapter 7.

4 *Expiration of a liability* (such as a landlord earning rent which was collected in advance or a magazine publisher earning revenue for subscriptions collected in advance). If $60 for the next twelve monthly issues had been received by a magazine publisher on December 1, 1988, one-twelfth (or $5) would have been earned during December when the first issue was mailed to the subscriber. If we assume that the entire $60 subscription price had been credited on December 1 to the liability account Liability for Unearned Subscriptions, the required adjusting entry on December 31 would be:

Date	Account titles and explanation	PR	Debit	Credit
1988				
Dec. 31	Liability for Unearned Subscriptions		5	
	Subscription Revenue			5
	To record portion of subscrip-			
	tions received in advance that			
	was earned in December.			

The adjusting entry records as revenue in the 1988 income statement the $5 earned from delivery of the December, 1988 issue to the subscriber. The debit part of the entry will result in a $55 balance for the Liability for Unearned Subscriptions on the December 31, 1988 balance sheet. The $55 properly reflects the remaining liability—11 monthly issues the magazine publisher is obligated to deliver to the subscriber.

5 *Correction of an error.* Assume that on May 3, 1988, a cash payment of

$800 was debited to Supplies Expense. Later, it is discovered that the payment should have been debited to Repair Expense. The adjusting entry on December 31 to correct this error would be:

Date	Account titles and explanation	PR	Debit	Credit
1988				
Dec. 31	Repair Expense		800	
	Supplies Expense			800
	To correct classification of May 3			
	payment.			

Identifying the need for adjusting entries is a skill that will develop as your understanding of the recording and reporting functions of accounting deepens.

Start-Up Company's Adjustments

Examination of Start-Up's operating and accounting records, introduced in Chapter 2, reveals the need for five adjusting entries on January 31, 1988. Examples of other types of adjustments will be encountered in later chapters. Each of Start-Up's five adjustments is discussed below, and the adjusting journal entries are shown in Exhibit 3-1:

1 Salaries of $500 earned by Start-Up's employees during the second half of January have not been recorded because the employees have not been paid by January 31. The next payday is February 2. The cost of the salaries earned by the employees during January is an expense incurred in generating January's revenue. If January's income is to be measured properly and liabilities accurately stated on January 31, an adjustment is necessary. The adjusting entry requires a debit to Salaries Expense and a credit to Salaries Payable.

2 During January, one month's worth of the "benefits" related to the office equipment was used up in operating the business. Therefore, $400 of the $24,000 cost of the office equipment is assumed to have been consumed during January ($24,000 cost ÷ 60 month estimated useful life for the office equipment). The adjusting entry for depreciation will recognize the $400 as an expense of doing business in January by debiting Depreciation Expense and will reduce the book value of the asset accordingly by crediting the contra asset—Accumulated Depreciation.

3 One month's interest on the three-year note payable (related to the office equipment acquisition) has "accrued" during January and must be recorded through an adjusting entry. By financing through a note payable, Start Up incurs an interest cost of $100 per month ($12,000 note × 10 percent annual interest rate × 1/12). Payment of the interest will be made later, but $100 interest relates to January. The adjusting entry requires a debit to Interest Expense and a credit to Interest Payable.

4 During January, one-sixth of the prepaid rental payment made on January 4 expired. Recall that on January 4 the company paid $9,000 for warehouse, office, and showroom rent for the six-month period January, 1988 through June, 1988. The $9,000 was properly recorded as an asset (i.e., Prepaid Rent) on January 4

EXHIBIT 3-1
Adjusting Entries for Start-Up Company

General journal

Date	Account titles and explanation	PR	Debit	Credit
1988				
Jan. 31	Salaries Expense *(Cash)*		500	
	Salaries Payable			500
	To record salaries earned but unpaid at January 31.			
31	Depreciation Expense		400	
	Accumulated Depreciation			400
	To record January's depreciation on office equipment.			
31	Interest Expense		100	
	Interest Payable			100
	To record January's accrued interest on a three-year, 10 percent note.			
31	Rent Expense		1,500	
	Prepaid Rent			1,500
	To record portion of prepaid rent "used up" during January.			
31	Income Tax Expense		2,850	
	Income Taxes Payable			2,850
	To record estimated income taxes for January.			

when the rent payment in advance was made. However, by the end of January only 5 months of prepaid asset remain. A $1,500 adjustment ($9,000 prepaid rent ÷ 6 months) is necessary. The adjusting entry requires a $1,500 debit to Rent Expense to record the cost of consuming (or "using up") one month's prepayment and a $1,500 credit to Prepaid Rent to reduce the asset.

5 Unpaid corporate income taxes relating to January's income are estimated to be $2,850. Although Start-Up is not required to pay the government income taxes on January 31, the income for the month was subject to tax. Payment will be submitted later, but the expense relates to January operations. The adjusting entry required involves a debit to Income Tax Expense and a credit to Income Taxes Payable.

Adjusting entries are entered in the journal at the end of the period and posted to the ledger in the same fashion as journal entries for routine transactions.

The posting of the preceding adjusting entries will affect the balances in several of Start-Up's general ledger accounts. Prepaid Rent will be reduced from $9,000 to $7,500 and Salaries Expense will increase from $500 to $1,000. Eight new accounts that did not appear on Start-Up's trial balance in Exhibit 2-5 are created: Accumulated Depreciation, Salaries Payable, Interest Payable, Income Taxes

EXHIBIT 3-2
Start-Up Company
Adjusted Trial Balance
January 31, 1988

	Debit	Credit
Cash	$ 72,500	
Accounts Receivable	14,000	
Inventory	15,000	
Prepaid Rent	7,500	
Office Equipment	24,000	
Accumulated Depreciation		$ 400
Accounts Payable		10,000
Salaries Payable		500
Interest Payable		100
Income Taxes Payable		2,850
Long-term Note Payable		12,000
Capital Stock		100,000
Dividends Declared	2,000	
Sales		50,000
Cost of Goods Sold	35,000	
Depreciation Expense	400	
Interest Expense	100	
Rent Expense	1,500	
Salaries Expense	1,000	
Income Tax Expense	2,850	
	$175,850	$175,850

Closing entries (handwritten annotation)

Payable, Depreciation Expense, Interest Expense, Rent Expense, and Income Tax Expense.

Adjusted Trial Balance

The *adjusted trial balance* is a listing of the ledger accounts and their debit or credit balances after the adjusting entries have been posted. The purpose of the adjusted trial balance is to verify that the equality of the debits and credits has been maintained. The adjusted trial balance for Start-Up appears in Exhibit 3-2.

The adjusted trial balance is not a formal financial statement. It does serve, however, as the basis from which the formal financial statements are prepared.

FINANCIAL STATEMENTS

From the adjusted trial balance, Start-up's financial statements in Exhibits 3-3 through 3-5 were prepared. The following discussion explains the procedures and format followed in preparing the financial statements.

Statement of Income

In Exhibit 3-3, Start-Up's income statement shows Sales (or Sales Revenue) of $50,000. This represents the total selling price of products sold for January.

EXHIBIT 3-3
Start-Up Company
Statement of Income
For the Month Ended January 31, 1988

Sales		$50,000
Expenses:		
Cost of Goods Sold	$35,000	
Depreciation Expense	400	
Interest Expense	100	
Rent Expense	1,500	
Salaries Expense	1,000	38,000
Income Before Income Taxes		$12,000
Income Tax Expense		2,850
Net Income		$ 9,150
Earnings per Share		$ .92*

*.92 = $9,150 net income ÷ 10,000 shares of capital stock, rounded.

Expenses related to the sales revenue earned in January are $38,000 for cost of goods sold and other expenses, and $2,850 for income taxes. Start-Up's net income of $9,150 (the excess of revenues over total expenses) represents the increase in the retained earnings component of stockholders' equity during January from profit-directed operations.

Earnings per Share   Individual stockholders are interested in the amount of net income that pertains to their ownership interest, represented by the number of shares of stock they hold. The *earnings per share* figure expresses the company's net income on a per share basis. Earnings per share is calculated by dividing net income by the number of shares of capital stock. For Start-Up Company, dividing $9,150 net income by 10,000 shares yields $.92 earnings per share. Earnings per share is widely used as a quick and easy measure of the firm's performance. More detailed coverage of earnings per share will be presented in later chapters.

Interpreting the Income Statement   Examination of Start-Up's income statement reveals that the company's operations for January, 1988 did result in a profit. This fact alone is insufficient to appraise the company's performance. Before a creditor would decide to lend money to Start-Up or before a potential investor would decide to buy Start-Up's stock, many questions left unanswered by the January, 1988 income statement would have to be addressed. Usually, prior period financial statements are available to compare to that of the current period. However, this is Start-Up's first month in business. What are the prospects for the future? Will sales revenue, expenses, and net income vary significantly from period to period? Is $9,150 satisfactory net income for $50,000 in sales revenue? Is $9,150 an adequate return for one month on the assets invested in the business? How are other companies in the same industry doing? What are the alternative investment opportunities—how else could stockholders and creditors invest their money? How much would it cost to buy a share of Start-Up's stock? Procedures

EXHIBIT 3-4
Start-Up Company
Statement of Retained Earnings
For the Month Ended January 31, 1988

Retained Earnings, January 1, 1988	$ -0-
Plus Net Income	9,150
	$9,150
Less Dividend Declared	2,000
Retained Earnings, January 31, 1988	$7,150

used by investors and creditors to analyze financial statements and to answer questions such as the above are presented in Chapter 12—Financial Statement Analysis.

Statement of Retained Earnings

Exhibit 3-4 reconciles the beginning-of-period balance in retained earnings with the end-of-period balance. Remember that retained earnings is the portion of stockholders' equity arising from undistributed past profits. Therefore, the two items typically creating a change in the retained earnings balance are: 1) the addition of net income to the beginning balance and 2) the subtraction of dividends declared. Note that Start-Up's beginning retained earnings balance on January 1, 1988 is zero. This is because Start-Up was a new company just beginning operations on that date. After a firm's first period in business, there will be a non-zero beginning balance for retained earnings.

If a company's operations result in expenses exceeding revenues, the company has a *net loss* for the period. As might be expected, a net loss will reduce the retained earnings balance. If a company incurs substantial net losses over time, it is possible that its retained earnings balance will be negative. A negative retained earnings balance is referred to as a *deficit*.

Note the interrelationships among the financial statements. Net income, the bottom line on the income statement, appears as one of the reconciling items on the retained earnings statement. Similarly, the ending balance from the retained earnings statement will appear on the balance sheet.

Balance Sheet

Start-Up's balance sheet in Exhibit 3-5 presents the assets, liabilities, and stockholders' equity of the corporation as of January 31, 1988. This statement sometimes is called *the statement of financial position* or the *statement of financial condition*. Note that the balance sheet does not cover a *period of time* as did the income statement and the statement of retained earnings. Rather, it reflects balances on a *specified date*.

On the balance sheet, the major components (assets, liabilities, and stockholders' equity) are further classified to increase the statement's usefulness to management, investors, creditors, and other statement readers. A standardized

EXHIBIT 3-5
Start-Up Company
Balance Sheet
January 31, 1988

Assets

Current Assets:		
Cash	$ 72,500	
Accounts Receivable	14,000	
Inventory	15,000	
Prepaid Rent	7,500	$109,000
Noncurrent Assets:		
Office Equipment	$ 24,000	
Less Accumulated Depreciation	400	23,600
Total Assets		$132,600

Liabilities and Stockholders' Equity

Current Liabilities:		
Accounts Payable	$ 10,000	
Salaries Payable	500	
Interest Payable	100	
Income Taxes Payable	2,850	$ 13,450
Long-term Debt:		
Note Payable		12,000
Total Liabilities		$ 25,450
Stockholders' Equity:		
Capital Stock (10,000 shares)	$100,000	
Retained Earnings	7,150	107,150
Total Liabilities and		
Stockholders' Equity		$132,600

arrangement and sequence of items on this and other financial statements aid the user in understanding and analyzing a company and in comparing it to other companies. This standardization is not absolute. Variations in financial statement format among industries, and among firms within an industry, do exist. In many cases such variation is justified by individual firm differences requiring different financial statement presentation.

Assets   On the asset side of Start-Up's balance sheet in Exhibit 3-5, the first classification is current assets. Formally, *current assets* are defined as:

1 Cash.
2 Assets that the firm expects to *convert into cash* within one year through normal operations (e.g., accounts receivable).
3 Assets that the firm expects to *sell or consume* within one year through normal operations (e.g., inventories and prepaid rent).

Note that inventories are located below receivables in the sequence of current assets on Start-Up's balance sheet. Current assets are listed in order of liquidity or "nearness to cash." As can be seen in the operating cycle illustrated below, receivables are only one step from conversion into cash. Inventories, on the other hand, must first be sold and then the cash from the sale collected.

Operating Cycle

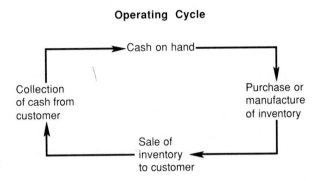

Prepaid assets are not expected to be converted into cash or sold; however, prepaids are classified as current assets since they represent expenditures already made whose benefits or services will be consumed in generating revenues during the subsequent year.

Start-Up's other asset classification is noncurrent assets. The office equipment and related contra asset accumulated depreciation are Start-Up's only noncurrent assets. Other possible noncurrent assets include: other property, plant, and equipment items, long-term investments, and intangible assets. These noncurrent assets will be discussed in subsequent chapters. Start-Up has not yet acquired any of these other noncurrent assets.

Liabilities   *Current liabilities* are defined as obligations which the firm expects to satisfy within one year. Satisfaction of current obligations involves the use of current assets or the creation of new current liabilities. Start-Up's balance sheet in Exhibit 3-5 shows four current liabilities—Accounts Payable, Salaries Payable, Interest Payable, and Income Taxes Payable.

Liabilities due more than one year from the balance sheet date are presented under the classification of long-term debt. Mortgages payable, bonds payable, and notes due more than one year in the future are frequently encountered examples of long-term debt. Start-Up's only long-term debt is the $12,000 note payable due in three years.

Stockholders' Equity   Direct investments and accumulated earnings are the two sources of stockholders' equity. Start-Up's capital stock balance of $100,000 represents the direct investment of funds by stockholders (in return for 10,000 shares of the company's capital stock). The accumulated earnings on January 31, 1988 are shown by the $7,150 retained earnings balance.

Statement of Cash Flows

A fourth financial statement showing the period's operating, investing, and financing activities on a *cash basis* is usually presented along with the income statement, retained earnings statement, and balance sheet. We will postpone coverage of this fourth statement—the statement of cash flows—until Chapter 11.

CLOSING ENTRIES

Some ledger account balances reflect only amounts accumulated during the current reporting period. Other ledger accounts reflect the cumulative balance since the origin of the firm. The cumulative nature of the balance depends on whether the account is permanent or is a temporary subaccount of retained earnings. *Permanent accounts* appear on the balance sheet. Assets, liabilities, capital stock, and retained earnings are permanent accounts. Amounts in these ledger accounts reflect the cumulative balance since the firm originated. *Temporary* retained earnings *subaccounts* appear on the statement of income and the statement of retained earnings. Categories of temporary retained earnings accounts are revenues, expenses, and dividends declared. The temporary accounts accumulate activities only for the current accounting period.

At the end of each accounting period the temporary account balances must be reduced to zero so they will be ready for the recording of revenues, expenses, and dividends for the next accounting period. The process of reducing the temporary retained earnings accounts to zero is called *closing*. In addition to closing (reducing to zero) the temporary accounts, *closing entries* also transfer the balances from the temporary accounts to the retained earnings account.

Start-Up Company's Closing Entries

To illustrate the closing entry process, recall the temporary retained earnings subaccounts appearing on Start-Up Company's adjusted trial balance.

Temporary accounts with credit balances:	
Sales	$50,000
Temporary accounts with debit balances:	
Dividend Declared	2,000
Cost of Goods Sold	35,000
Depreciation Expense	400
Interest Expense	100
Rent Expense	1,500
Salaries Expense	1,000
Income Tax Expense	2,850

Debits do not equal credits in these lists because only the temporary retained earnings accounts from the adjusted trial balance are presented. Temporary retained earnings accounts are closed in a three-step sequence.

First Step—Closing Revenue Accounts Revenues are closed by debiting the revenue accounts and crediting retained earnings. Since revenue accounts have credit balances, to reduce the revenue accounts to zero it is necessary to *debit the revenue accounts*. The credit to retained earnings increases retained earnings by the revenue earned during the period. The closing entry for Start-Up's revenue account is:

1988			
Jan. 31	Sales	50,000	
	Retained Earnings		50,000
	To close January's revenue account.		

Second Step—Closing Expense Accounts   Expense accounts have debit balances. To reduce expense accounts to zero it is necessary to *credit the expense accounts*. Retained earnings is debited, and thus reduced, for the total expenses for the period.

The closing entry for Start-Up's expense accounts is:

Jan. 31	Retained Earnings	40,850	
	Cost of Goods Sold		35,000
	Depreciation Expense		400
	Interest Expense		100
	Rent Expense		1,500
	Salaries Expense		1,000
	Income Tax Expense		2,850
	To close January's expense accounts.		40850

Step Three—Closing Dividends Declared Account   The first two steps in the closing entry process have reduced revenue and expense accounts to zero and increased the retained earnings account by the net income for the period. The final step in the closing entry process is to close out the dividends declared account and reduce retained earnings accordingly. Dividends declared (which has a debit balance) is closed by *crediting the dividends declared account* and debiting retained earnings.

Start-Up's dividends declared account is closed as follows:

Jan. 31	Retained Earnings	2,000	
	Dividends Declared		2,000
	To close January's dividends declared account.		

After the closing entries have been journalized and posted, the temporary retained earnings accounts all should have been reduced to zero in preparation for the accumulation of the next accounting period's revenues, expenses, and dividend declarations. In addition, the balance in retained earnings should be up to date through the current period. For Start-Up, the ending retained earnings balance is $7,150.

Retained Earnings, before closing	$ -0-
Addition from closing revenue	50,000
	$50,000
Reduction from closing expenses	(40,850)
	$ 9,150
Reduction from closing dividends declared	(2,000)
Retained Earnings, after closing	$ 7,150

The $7,150 balance appears on the company's balance sheet.

Closing Entries—The Income Summary Approach

An alternative procedure sometimes used in recording closing entries involves the use of an *income summary account.* When an income summary account is used, revenue and expense balances are first closed to the income summary account— rather than directly to retained earnings. After the revenues and expenses have been transferred to the income summary account, the resultant balance in the income summary account (which is the net income for the period) is closed to retained earnings. The entry to close the dividends declared account balance to retained earnings is *not* affected by the use of an income summary account. The income summary account has no entries in it during the period; it is used only as part of the closing entry process.

Regardless of whether revenue and expense account balances are closed directly to retained earnings or are first transferred to an income summary account, the end results are the same. Under both closing entry approaches, the temporary retained earnings accounts are all reduced to zero and the retained earnings balance is updated to include the current period's revenues, expenses, and dividends declared.

AFTER-CLOSING TRIAL BALANCE

The *after-closing trial balance* is a listing of the ledger accounts after the closing journal entries have been posted. The purpose of the after-closing trial balance is to test the equality of the debits and credits in the ledger after the closing entries have been posted. Since the revenue, expense, and dividends declared accounts are reduced to a zero balance during the closing process, only the balance sheet accounts (assets, liabilities, capital stock, and retained earnings) appear on the after-closing trial balance. The after-closing trial balance sometimes is called the *post-closing trial balance.*

The after-closing trial balance for Start-Up is presented in Exhibit 3-6. Note that there are no revenue, expense, or dividends declared accounts on Start-Up's after-closing trial balance and the updated, end-of-period retained earnings balance of $7,150 is shown.

EXHIBIT 3-6
Start-Up Company
After-Closing Trial Balance
January 31, 1988

	Debit	Credit
Cash	$ 72,500	
Accounts Receivable	14,000	
Inventory	15,000	
Prepaid Rent	7,500	
Office Equipment	24,000	
Accumulated Depreciation		$ 400
Accounts Payable		10,000
Salaries Payable		500
Interest Payable		100
Income Taxes Payable		2,850
Long-term Note Payable		12,000
Capital Stock		100,000
Retained Earnings		7,150
	$133,000	$133,000

ACCOUNTING PROCESS SUMMARIZED

In Chapters 2 and 3 we have discussed each of the nine steps in the accounting process:

1 Reviewing the business documents
2 Recording journal entries for routine transactions
3 Posting the journal entries to ledger accounts
4 Preparing a trial balance
5 Recording and posting adjusting journal entries
6 Preparing an adjusted trial balance
7 Preparing financial statements
8 Recording and posting closing entries
9 Preparing an after-closing trial balance

For companies that have a large volume of transactions, modifications may be found in the manner in which certain steps in the accounting process are completed. Two frequently encountered modifications are the use of special journals and subsidiary ledgers.

Special Journals

Many companies use specialized journals to make the recording process more efficient. Each *special journal* is designed to record only certain types of transactions. The most commonly used special journals are the *sales* journal, *purchases* journal, *cash receipts* journal, and *cash disbursements* journal. The types of transactions to be recorded in each of the four special journals are:

Special journal	Specific transaction to be recorded
Sales journal	Sales of goods on account
Purchases journal	Purchases of goods on account
Cash receipts journal	Receipts of cash
Cash disbursements journal	Payments of cash

Special journals can be designed to meet the special information processing requirements of any company. Regardless of the number and type of special journals in use, a company also maintains a *general journal* for all transactions that do not belong in any of the special journals.

Special journals are used to make both the initial journalizing of the transaction and the subsequent posting to general ledger accounts more efficient. Special journals significantly reduce the number of account titles and journal entry explanations that must be recorded. The posting of column totals from the special journals, rather than posting individual journal entries, also results in substantial time savings. In addition, with more than one journal, the recording process can be subdivided among several employees. Employees become specialists in handling a certain type of transaction.

Subsidiary Ledgers

Ledger accounts are used to collect and summarize financial data by categories. Separate general ledger accounts are used to serve as a record of the debits, credits, and balance for each individual asset, liability, and stockholders' equity item. Another important function of ledgers is to aid in billing and collecting from customers and in maintaining records of amounts owed and paid to vendors. For this second function, subsidiary ledgers are often used. A *subsidiary ledger* is a listing of the individual accounts that compose the main (or "control") account in the general ledger. Two common subsidiary ledgers are the accounts receivable and accounts payable subsidiary ledgers.

Accounts Receivable Subsidiary Ledger   With only a single general ledger account for accounts receivable, a company with a large number of customers who buy on account would find it extremely difficult at any particular moment to determine how much is due from an individual customer. Therefore in addition to the accounts receivable general ledger account, companies maintain an accounts receivable subsidiary ledger. The *accounts receivable subsidiary ledger* groups transactions by customer. Each individual customer account in the accounts receivable subsidiary ledger provides a complete history of the customer's purchases on account, subsequent cash collections, and balance due.

To verify that the subsidiary ledger is in balance at the end of the accounting period, it is customary to prepare a trial balance that lists the balance due from each customer. The sum of the customer account balances from the subsidiary ledger should agree with the accounts receivable control account balance in the general ledger. It is this total dollar amount due from customers that appears on the balance sheet.

Accounts Payable Subsidiary Ledger Companies maintain an accounts payable subsidiary ledger so that they can quickly determine the history of the company's business on account with an individual vendor. The *accounts payable subsidiary ledger* identifies all the firm's transactions according to vendor. The subsidiary accounts payable ledger accounts show past purchases on account, subsequent cash payments, and the current balance owed to each vendor. The sum of the subsidiary accounts equals the balance in the accounts payable general ledger account. On the balance sheet, it is this total dollar amount owed to all vendors that appears.

SUMMARY

Learning Objective 1: Analyze, record, and post adjusting entries.
Adjusting entries are frequently required at the end of the accounting period: (1) to record events that have occurred but have not yet been recorded, (2) to record a change in an item since it was originally recorded, or (3) to correct errors. Adjusting entries are needed for: (1) expenses incurred and not yet recorded, (2) revenues earned and not yet recorded, (3) expiration of an asset, (4) expiration of a liability, and (5) error corrections. Adjusting entries are recorded in the general journal and posted to the ledger in a manner identical to that followed for transaction entries.

Learning Objective 2: Prepare financial statements in proper form.
An income statement presenting revenues, expenses, net income, and earnings per share for the period was presented in Exhibit 3-3. A retained earnings statement summarizing the causes of the change in the retained earnings balance between the beginning of the period and the end of the period was shown in Exhibit 3-4. A properly classified balance sheet was shown in Exhibit 3-5.

Learning Objective 3: Journalize closing entries following a three-step approach.
At the end of the accounting period, closing entries reduce the temporary retained earnings accounts (revenues, expenses, and dividends declared) to zero and transfer the balances from the temporary accounts to retained earnings. Step one in the closing entry process requires debiting each revenue account and crediting retained earnings. Step two debits retained earnings for the total expenses for the period and credits each expense account for its individual balance. The third step requires debiting retained earnings and crediting dividends declared for the amount of the dividends declared during the period.

Learning Objective 4: Present an after-closing trial balance.
An after-closing trial balance tests the equality of the debits and credits in the ledger after the closing entries have been posted. Only permanent accounts (assets, liabilities, capital stock, and retained earnings) should appear on the after-closing trial balance.

KEY TERMS

Accountant's worksheet (Appendix)
Accounts payable subsidiary ledger
Accounts receivable subsidiary ledger
Accumulated depreciation
Adjusted trial balance
Adjusting journal entries
After-closing trial balance
Closing entries

Contra asset
Current asset
Current liability
Depreciation
Long-term debt
Permanent accounts
Special journals
Temporary accounts

APPENDIX: Accountant's Worksheet

The *worksheet*, an informal, specially designed, columnar sheet of paper, is used by the accountant at the end of the accounting period. The worksheet provides the accountant with an opportunity to test the accuracy of the end-of-period accounting work before making formal entries in the accounting records.

The worksheet is especially useful for companies with a large number of ledger accounts and numerous end-of-period adjusting entries. In such situations, even a skilled accountant can easily make errors in completing the end-of-period steps in the accounting cycle. The worksheet permits the accountant to informally complete the trial balance, adjusting entries, adjusted trial balance, and financial statements before adjusting and closing entries are formally journalized and posted in the accounting records.

By detecting and correcting errors on the preliminary, informal worksheet, the chances for errors to enter the formal accounting records are minimized. Also, once the worksheet has been satisfactorily completed, it can be used as the basis from which adjusting and closing entries are journalized and the formal financial statements are prepared.

COMPUTER APPLICATION

Electronic spreadsheets are available that computerize the accountant's traditional worksheet. A major advantage of the spreadsheet is its "what-if" power that allows the accountant to change one item on the worksheet and virtually instantaneously view the impact of the change on the entire worksheet.

To illustrate the sequence of procedures to be followed in preparing an end-of-period worksheet, the Start-Up Company example will be continued. The completed twelve-column worksheet is presented in Exhibit 3-7. The first step is to provide a proper three-line heading on the top of the worksheet. For Start-Up, the heading is:

1st line—Start-Up Company
2nd line—Worksheet

The exchange of stock for cash affected Start-Up Company by increasing its assets and increasing the invested capital component of its stockholders' equity. Remember that accounting systems are structured such that increases to assets are recorded by debits; therefore, the Cash account is debited for $100,000—the amount received. Increases to stockholders' equity are recorded as credits. Capital Stock, a stockholders' equity account, is credited for $100,000—the amount of invested capital.

In Start-Up's journal, the following journal entry is made:

General journal					Page 1
Date	**Account titles and explanations**	**PR**[1]	**Debit**		**Credit**
1988					
Jan. 2	Cash		100,000		
	Capital Stock				100,000
	To record investment by owners in exchange for 10,000 shares of capital stock.				

Note that after the date, there is a column for account titles and an explanation. The title of the account debited is written at the left margin; the title of the account credited is indented to the right. Dollar amounts of the entry are recorded in two columns. The amount debited is in the left column; the amount credited is in the right column. This format (debit on the left; credit on the right) is universal in accounting in the United States and many foreign countries. An explanation of the entry is written below the account titles.

Item 2—The company purchased office equipment costing $24,000, making a $12,000 down payment, with the balance due in three years.

Start-Up Company acquired an asset (office equipment) in exchange for another asset (cash) and a liability (the note payable). The increase in the asset Office Equipment is recorded by a debit of $24,000, and the decrease in the asset Cash is recorded by a credit of $12,000; the increase in the liability Notes Payable is also recorded by a credit of $12,000. The entry is as follows:

General journal					Page 1
Date	**Account titles and explanations**	**PR**	**Debit**		**Credit**
3	Office Equipment		24,000		
	Cash				12,000
	Long-term Note Payable				12,000
	To record the purchase of office equipment for cash and 3-year note payable.				

The only procedural difference between the journal entry for item 1 and the

[1]PR stands for posting reference, a concept covered later in the chapter.

3rd line—For the Month Ended January 31, 1988

The remaining steps followed in completion of the worksheet are systematically discussed and illustrated.

TRIAL BALANCE COLUMNS

The ledger account titles are written in the left-hand margin of the worksheet and the dollar balances are entered in the Trial Balance columns. The account titles and corresponding dollar balances are transferred directly from the ledger, after it has been posted, to the worksheet. The accounts retain their respective debit or credit balances.

In Exhibit 3-7 note that the equality of the debits and credits in the ledger is proven by totaling both Trial Balance columns to $172,000.

ADJUSTMENTS COLUMNS

Start-Up's five adjusting entries (see Exhibit 3-1) are entered in the worksheet's Adjustments columns, as shown in Exhibit 3-7. Note that each adjustment on the worksheet is indexed by placing an alphabetic notation—(a), (b), (c), (d), (e)—beside the debit and credit parts of the entry. A brief explanation of each adjustment appearing at the bottom of the worksheet is also cross-referenced to the debit and credit part of the entry. For example, the letter (a) appears before both the $500 debit to Salaries Expense and the $500 credit to Salaries Payable in the Adjustments columns. Adjustment (a) is explained at the bottom of the worksheet as "Salaries earned in January but unpaid at 1/31/88." If the adjusting entry affects an account already listed on the trial balance, the entry is recorded on that line. If the affected account is not present, the account title must be added before the entry is recorded. Note that adjusting entries required adding eight account titles below the trial balance accounts in Exhibit 3-7.

The $5,350 total of each Adjustment column proves the debit and credit equality of the adjusting entries.

ADJUSTED TRIAL BALANCE COLUMNS

The next step in preparing the worksheet involves combining the amount entered for each account in the Trial Balance columns with the amount entered (if any) for that account in the Adjustments columns. The new account balance, after considering the adjustments, is entered for each account in the appropriate Adjusted Trial Balance column. Note on Exhibit 3-7 that, since none of the adjustments affected Cash, the Cash debit balance of $72,500 appearing in the Trial Balance also appears as a $72,500 debit in the Adjusted Trial Balance. Prepaid Rent is listed as a $9,000 debit on the Trial Balance; however, due to a $1,500 credit in the Adjustments column, it is shown on the Adjusted Trial Balance as having only a $7,500 debit balance.

The Adjusted Trial Balance column totals of $175,850 provide assurance that the debit-credit equality of the accounts has been maintained.

EXHIBIT 3-7
Start-Up Company
Worksheet
For the Month Ended January 31, 1988

	Trial balance Debit	Trial balance Credit	Adjustments Debit	Adjustments Credit	Adjusted trial balance Debit	Adjusted trial balance Credit
Cash	72,500				72,500	
Accounts Receivable	14,000				14,000	
Inventory	15,000				15,000	
Prepaid Rent	9,000			(d) 1,500	7,500	
Office Equipment	24,000				24,000	
Accounts Payable		10,000				10,000
Long-term Note Payable		12,000				12,000
Capital Stock		100,000				100,000
Ret. Earn., Jan. 1, 1988		-0-				-0-
Dividends Declared	2,000				2,000	
Sales		50,000				50,000
Cost of Goods Sold	35,000				35,000	
Salaries Expense	500		(a) 500		1,000	
	172,000	172,000				
Salaries Payable				(a) 500		500
Depreciation Expense			(b) 400		400	
Accumulated Depr.				(b) 400		400
Interest Expense			(c) 100		100	
Interest Payable				(c) 100		100
Rent Expense			(d) 1,500		1,500	
Income Tax Expense			(e) 2,850		2,850	
Income Taxes Payable				(e) 2,850		2,850
			5,350	5,350	175,850	175,850

Net Income

Ret. Earn., Jan. 31, 1988

Adjustments
(a) Salaries earned in January but unpaid at 1/31/88.
(b) Depreciation for January on office equipment.
(c) Interest accrued during January on long-term note payable.
(d) Prepaid rent consumed during January.
(e) Estimated income taxes for January.

Statement of income		Statement of retained earnings		Balance sheet	
Debit	**Credit**	**Debit**	**Credit**	**Debit**	**Credit**
				72,500	
				14,000	
				15,000	
				7,500	
				24,000	
					10,000
					12,000
					100,000
			-0-		
		2,000			
	50,000				
35,000					
1,000					
					500
400					
					400
100					
					100
1,500					
2,850					
					2,850
40,850	50,000				
9,150			9,150		
50,000	50,000	2,000	9,150		
		7,150			7,150
		9,150	9,150	133,000	133,000

EXTENDING THE ADJUSTED TRIAL BALANCE

Every account balance appearing in the Adjusted Trial Balance columns is extended to one of the remaining six financial statement columns on the worksheet. Accounts with debit balances in the Adjusted Trial Balance are extended to the appropriate financial statement debit column; credit balance amounts on the Adjusted Trial Balance are treated in a similar manner.

1 Revenue and expense accounts are extended to the Statement of Income columns.

2 Beginning retained earnings and dividends declared balances are extended to the Statement of Retained Earnings columns.

3 The assets, liabilities, and capital stock account are extended to the Balance Sheet columns.

STATEMENT OF INCOME COLUMNS

After each account has been extended from the Adjusted Trial Balance to the appropriate financial statement column, the debit and credit Statement of Income columns are totaled. Usually these two columns will *not* balance. The Statement of Income credit column contains the revenue accounts for the period; the debit column lists all the expenses. Therefore, assuming revenues exceed expenses, the Statement of Income credit column total will exceed the debit column total by the net income for the period.

The debit and credit Statement of Income column totals on the worksheet are made equal by adding the net income amount to the debit column total. The amount added to the Statement of Income columns is appropriately identified as Net Income at the left margin of the worksheet. As previously seen, accounting is structured such that a debit for a certain amount must be offset by an equal amount of credits. When net income is entered in the Statement of Income debit column, a credit also must be made. Recall that net income appears on the statement of retained earnings and that net income (revenues minus expenses) increases retained earnings. Retained earnings, which is part of stockholders' equity, is increased by crediting. Therefore, on the worksheet, net income is debited to the Statement of Income columns and credited to the Statement of Retained Earnings columns.

In Exhibit 3-7, Start-Up's worksheet shows:

1 All Adjusted Trial Balance amounts have been extended to the appropriate financial statement column.

2 The Statement of Income columns have been totaled to $40,850 debits for total expenses and $50,000 credits for revenue.

3 The net income of $9,150 for the month (the $50,000 revenue less $40,850 total expenses) has been entered as a debit in the Statement of Income columns, resulting in a balance at $50,000 for both Statement of Income columns.

4 The $9,150 net income also was entered in the Statement of Retained Earnings credit column.

5 "Net Income" was written against the left margin of the worksheet to explain the $9,150 worksheet entry.

STATEMENT OF RETAINED EARNINGS COLUMNS AND BALANCE SHEET COLUMNS

Next, the debit and credit Statement of Retained Earnings columns are totaled. As was the case with the Statement of Income columns, the Statement of Retained Earnings columns very likely will *not* balance. The difference between the column totals is the retained earnings balance at the end of the period. The Statement of Retained Earnings credit column contains the retained earnings account balance as of the beginning of the period (which for Start-Up was zero since the company began operation on January 2, 1988) and the net income amount added in the previous step. The debit column consists solely of the dividends declared during the period.

The debit and credit Statement of Retained Earnings column totals are made equal by adding the retained earnings balance at the end of the year to the debit column. The amount being added to the Statement of Retained Earnings column should be appropriately explained by writing "Retained Earnings, January 31, 1988" at the left margin of the worksheet.

In addition to debiting the ending retained earnings account balance in the Statement of Retained Earnings columns, the ending retained earnings balance should be entered on the same line of the worksheet in the Balance Sheet credit column. Recall that total stockholders' equity as presented on the balance sheet includes capital stock and ending retained earnings.

Finally, total the Balance Sheet debit and credit columns on the worksheet. The column totals should balance. For a corporation, the accounting equation states: "Assets = Liabilities + Stockholders' Equity." The Balance Sheet columns on the worksheet should reflect this equality.

Exhibit 3-7 shows Start-Up's completed worksheet after:

1 The Statement of Retained Earnings columns have been totaled to $2,000 debits and $9,150 credits.

2 The retained earnings balance at the end of the period of $7,150 has been added to the Statement of Retained Earnings debit column resulting in a balance of $9,150 in both Statement of Retained Earnings columns.

3 A matching credit of $7,150 was entered in the Balance Sheet credit column.

4 "Retained Earnings, January 31, 1988" was written against the left margin of the worksheet to explain the $7,150 worksheet entry.

5 The Balance Sheet columns were totaled and balance at $133,000.

Once the worksheet has been satisfactorily completed, the adjusting entries from the Adjustments columns of the worksheet may be formally recorded in the journal. Closing entries, which transfer the revenue, expense, and dividends declared account balances for the period into the retained earnings account, also must be journalized and posted. The Statement of Income columns of the worksheet, plus the dividends declared account in the Statement of Retained

Earnings columns, conveniently provide the information for recording the closing entries.

TREATMENT OF NET LOSSES

In the Start-Up Company example, January revenues exceeded January expenses. The result was that Start-Up reported net income of $9,150 for January. It is possible, however, that a company's expenses could exceed its revenues. In such a case, the company is said to have a net loss.

When preparing a worksheet for a company with a net loss, the loss must be added to the Statement of Income *credit* column to make the Statement of Income columns equal. This credit entry is offset by a debit entry to the Statement of Retained Earnings column on the worksheet. Since net losses reduce the retained earnings component of stockholders' equity, the debit to retained earnings has the appropriate effect of reducing stockholders' equity.

RETAINED EARNINGS DEFICIT

The account Retained Earnings normally has a credit balance. If, over time, a company experiences net losses in excess of net income, Retained Earnings can have a debit balance (a deficit). When preparing a worksheet where a company has a retained earnings deficit at the end of the period, the amount of the deficit is added to the Statement of Retained Earnings credit column to make the columns equal. The offsetting debit is made to the Balance Sheet columns.

REVIEW QUESTIONS

1 Define adjusting entries. How do they differ from entries for routine business transactions?

2 List the five types of adjusting entries. Give one example of each type.

3 Marshall Co. purchased a microcomputer on January 1, 1988 for $15,000. The estimated useful life of the computer is five years. How much is the annual depreciation expense? What would be the accumulated depreciation balance for the computer on December 31, 1990?

4 On November 1, 1988, Custer Company paid $1,200 for fire insurance coverage for the next twelve months. On December 31, 1988, the end of the company's accounting year, how much of the $1,200 should be shown as insurance expense on the income statement? How much should appear as prepaid insurance (an asset) on the December 31, 1988 balance sheet?

5 What is the purpose, or objective, of the income statement, retained earnings statement, and balance sheet? In other words, what does each financial statement tell about the company?

6 Evaluate the following statement: "Accounting information solves the financial statement reader's decision-making problems."

7 Discuss the difference between the third line of the heading (the date) on the balance sheet versus the third line of the heading on both the income statement and retained earnings statement.

8 Roadway, Inc. had net income of $30,000 for 1988. There were 50,000 shares of capital stock outstanding throughout the year. What was the earnings per share for 1988?

9 Evaluate the following statement: "Net income equals retained earnings; retained earnings equals cash."

10 Discuss each of the following terms:
a Current assets (list four examples).
b Current liabilities (list three examples).
c Stockholders' equity.

11 What is the purpose of the closing entry process?

12 "In the closing entry process, revenue accounts are closed by crediting the revenue accounts. Expense and dividends declared accounts are closed by debiting them." Evaluate the preceding statements.

13 Multiple choice. The after-closing trial balance:
a Lists the debit and credit closing entries.
b Is prepared before the adjusting entries.
c Would not include any revenue or expense accounts.
d Shows the net income for the period, after income taxes.
e All of the above.

14 Presented below are the nine individual steps comprising the traditional accounting cycle listed in random sequence. Rearrange them in logical sequence by assigning each step a number from one to nine (1 being the first step, 2 being the second step, and so on).
a Posting the journal entries to ledger accounts.
b Recording and posting closing entries.
c Recording journal entries (routine business transactions).
d Preparing a trial balance.
e Preparing an after-closing trial balance.
f Preparing an adjusted trial balance.
g Preparing financial statements.
h Reviewing business documents.
i Recording and posting adjusting entries.

15 Assume Treadwell, Inc. uses a sales journal, purchases journal, cash receipts journal, cash disbursements journal, and general journal identical to those discussed in the chapter. In which journal would each of the following entries be recorded?
a Sold delivery truck for cash.
b Purchased inventory on account.
c Closed dividends declared account to retained earnings.
d Paid monthly salaries for office employees.
e Sold merchandise inventory on account.

16 G. M. Armstreak Co. currently maintains a control account for accounts receivable in the general ledger as well as a subsidiary ledger of 1,000 individual customer accounts. Management of G. M. Armstreak Co. has proposed eliminating the general ledger control account for accounts receivable and replacing it by putting the 1,000 individual customer accounts directly in the general ledger. Management is considering the proposal as a means to make the accounting system more efficient. Evaluate management's proposal.

17 (Appendix) Describe the accountant's "worksheet." What role does the worksheet play in completing the accounting cycle?

18 (Appendix) If no clerical errors have been made, which set(s) of columns on the worksheet should automatically balance without the accountant having to enter an additional balancing item? How does the accountant make equal the remaining sets of columns on the worksheet?

19 (Appendix) On Trailton's worksheet, the prepaid rent account has a $12,000 debit balance in the Trial Balance columns and a $4,000 credit entry in the Adjustments columns. What amount should be shown for prepaid rent in the Adjusted Trial Balance columns? In which financial statement column on the worksheet should the adjusted trial balance amount for prepaid rent appear?

EXERCISES

E3-1 During the month of June, 1988, Royal, Inc. had the following events occur:

1 June 1, 1988—Paid $3,000 to Ryan Realtors for rent of office space for June, July, and August. Royal debited Prepaid Rent for $3,000 and credited Cash for $3,000.

2 The June electric bill for $240 was received. Royal debited Advertising Expense and credited Accounts Payable.

3 A new secretary was hired on June 29, 1988. The secretary is to begin working on July 1 at a weekly salary of $160. No accounting entry was made by Royal.

4 Salaries earned by employees during June, 1988 but unpaid as of June 30, 1988 totaled $1,300. No accounting entry was made by Royal.

Required:
Prepare necessary adjusting entries to be made on June 30 on page 23 of Royal's journal.

E3-2 Rochmeyer Associates is a real estate agency that deals chiefly in the rental of condominiums. Transactions during 1988 included:

1 March 31—Rochmeyer charges a monthly fee to its clients. On March 31, the agency received $18,000 from three new clients to pay for their monthly fees through January, 1989. The receipt was recorded as an $18,000 debit to Cash and an $18,000 credit to Liability for Realty Fees Received.

2 July 1—Paid $1,248 for the next year's advertising in a local newspaper. The entry on July 1 was a debit to Prepaid Advertising for $1,248 and a credit to Cash for $1,248.

3 September 1—Received a 12 percent note receivable in the amount of $960,000 from the sale of condominiums at the shore. Interest will be received with the principal at the end of four years.

4 December 1—Client renewed a rental agreement in the amount of $108,000. The agreement is dated from December, 1988 through November, 1989, and no payment has been received as of December 31, 1988.

Required:
Present the adjusting entries needed on December 31, 1988 for each of the above transactions on page 85 of Rochmeyer's journal. (Note: Rochmeyer makes adjusting entries only on December 31, the last day of its accounting year. Adjustments are not made at the end of each month.)

E3-3 In September, 1988 Bonner, Tracy & Campell, CPAs, decided to open a branch office in New Vespers, PA. The following events occurred as a result of their decision:

1 November 1, 1988—Signed rental agreement and paid $78,000 for office space rental for next year.

2 November 30, 1988—Received an advance payment of $5,000 from a client in New Vespers. Payment is for preliminary work to be done in December, 1988 and final work to be done in January, 1989. One-half of the fee applies to preliminary work and the other half to final work.

3 December 31, 1988—Received a $2,800 tax bill from New Vespers Township for doing business in the area during November and December. Payment is due on February 15, 1989. No entry related to the tax bill has been recorded in 1988.

Required:

Present the original entries for transactions 1 and 2. Present all adjusting journal entries needed at December 31, 1988 to properly reflect account balances. (Note: Bonner, Tracy & Campbell makes adjusting entries only on December 31, the last day of its accounting year. Adjustments are not made at the end of each month.)

E3-4 Selected information concerning Parks, Inc. for the year ended December 31, 1988 is presented below. The information is listed in alphabetical order. The company had 100,000 shares of capital stock outstanding during the year.

Cost of Goods Sold	$32,400,000
Dividends Declared	2,500,000
Federal Income Tax Expense	1,906,500
Rent Expense	6,000,000
Retained Earnings, January 1, 1988	17,800,000
Salaries Expense	6,200,000
Sales	48,600,000

Required:

Prepare an income statement and a retained earnings statement for Parks, Inc. for 1988.

E3-5 Examine the balance sheet of Podunk, Inc. presented below. What errors, if any, are there on this statement?

Podunk, Inc.
Balance Sheet
For the Year Ended December 31, 1988

Assets			Liabilities and Stockholders' Equity			
Current Assets:			Current Liabilities:			
Accounts Payable	$ 4,000		Accounts Receivable			$ 6,000
Cash	8,000		Federal Income Tax Expense			5,000
Inventory	3,000		Total Current Liabilities			$11,000
Sales	18,000		Long-term Debt			9,000
Total Current Assets	$33,000		Total Liabilities			$20,000
Noncurrent Assets:			Stockholders' Equity:			
Property, Plant, &			Capital Stock	$30,000		
Equipment	20,000		Net Income	5,000		35,000
			Total Liabilities and			
Total Assets	$53,000		Stockholders' Equity			$55,000

E3-6   Solve each of the cases below for the missing item. Treat each case separately.

	Case A	Case B	Case C	Case D
Retained Earnings, Beginning of Year	$40,000	$ 3,000	?	($5,000) Deficit
Net Income	?	14,000	($ 2,000) Loss	(8,000) Loss
Cash Dividends, Declared	2,000	?	4,000	-0-
Retained Earnings, End of Year	58,000	12,000	16,000	?

E3-7   Listed below are thirteen items appearing on either the income statement or the balance sheet. Indicate whether the item belongs on the income statement or the balance sheet. Also properly classify the item as: current asset; noncurrent asset; current liability; long-term debt; stockholders' equity—invested capital; revenue; or expense. The first one has been completed as an example.

	Classification	Income statement or balance sheet
1. Accounts Payable	Current Liability	Balance Sheet
2. Accounts Receivable		
3. Administrative Expense		
4. Building		
5. Cash		
6. Capital Stock		
7. Cost of Goods Sold		
8. Equipment		
9. Income Tax Expense		
10. Income Taxes Payable		
11. Inventory		
12. Prepaid Insurance		
13. Sales		

E3-8   A list of the accounts on Boxtren Inc.'s Adjusted Trial Balance on December 31, 1988 is presented below. Assume all accounts have the normal debit or credit balance expected for that particular account. Note the accounts are listed in alphabetical order rather than the normal general ledger sequence.

Accounts Receivable	$ 14,000
Accumulated Depreciation	8,000
Capital Stock	10,000
Cash	26,000
Depreciation Expense	2,000
Dividends Declared	3,000
Fees Earned	118,000
Furniture & Fixtures	24,000
Income Tax Expense	12,700
Income Taxes Payable	12,700
Interest Revenue	2,000

Office Expense	16,000
Retained Earnings, January 1, 1988	8,000
Salaries Expense	61,000

Required:

Prepare closing journal entries on page 1632 of Boxtren's journal and prepare an after-closing trial balance.

E3-9 (Appendix) The Trial Balance, Adjustments, and Adjusted Trial Balance columns of Briefie's January, 1988 worksheet are presented below:

	Trial balance		Adjustments		Adjusted trial balance	
	Debit	Credit	Debit	Credit	Debit	Credit
Cash	$40,600					
Prepaid Insurance	2,400					
Capital Stock		$10,000				
Retained Earnings, January 1, 1988		5,000				
Sales		60,000				
Cost of Goods Sold	20,000					
Salaries Expense	12,000					
	$75,000	$75,000				

During January, 1988, the company consumed one-twelfth of the prepaid insurance. Salaries earned during January but unpaid at January 31 were $4,000. Income taxes are estimated to be $3,000 for January.

Required:

Complete the Adjustments and Adjusted Trial Balance columns of the worksheet.

E3-10 (Appendix) The Adjusted Trial Balance and financial statement columns of Simple Co.'s 1989 worksheet are presented below:

	Adjusted trial balance		Statement of income		Statement of retained earnings		Balance sheet	
	Debit	Credit	Debit	Credit	Debit	Credit	Debit	Credit
Cash	$ 84,000							
Accounts Payable		$ 10,000						
Capital Stock		9,000						
Retained Earnings, January 1, 1989		29,000						
Dividends Declared	6,000							
Sales		200,000						
Cost of Goods Sold	110,000							
Salaries Expense	40,000							
Income Tax Expense	8,000							
	$248,000	$248,000						

Required:
Complete the worksheet by extending the Adjusted Trial Balance amounts to the appropriate financial statement columns and properly "balance" the worksheet columns.

PROBLEMS

P3-1   *Adjusting and Closing Entries*
Briefcan Co. had the following occur during 1988:
1 On September 1, 1988 an annual insurance premium of $3,600 was paid and recorded as:

	Debit	Credit
Prepaid Insurance	3,600	
Cash		3,600

2 Supplies were purchased in December at a cost of $900. None of these supplies had been used as of December 31. The purchase was recorded as:

	Debit	Credit
Supplies Inventory	900	
Cash		900

3 Wages of $59,000 had been paid employees through December 27. From December 28 through December 31, employees earned an additional $1,500, which was to be paid January 3, 1989. The entry recorded was:

	Debit	Credit
Salaries Expense	59,000	
Cash		59,000

Required:
1 Prepare the December 31 adjusting journal entries on page 472 of Briefcan's journal.
2 Prepare the December 31 closing journal entries for the year required by the above transactions on page 473 of Briefcan's journal.

P3-2   *Determining Adjusting Entries from Trial Balance*
Presented below are both the trial balance and adjusted trial balance for Highland Company as of February 28, 1989.

	Trial balance		Adjusted trial balance	
	Debit	Credit	Debit	Credit
Cash	$ 40,000		$ 40,000	
Accounts Receivable	56,000		56,000	
Inventory of Cleaning Supplies	8,000		3,000	
Prepaid Insurance	3,000		1,900	
Prepaid Rent	14,000		12,000	
Accounts Payable		$ 18,000		$ 18,000
Salaries Payable				2,000
Bank Loan Payable		8,000		8,000

	Trial balance		Adjusted trial balance	
	Debit	Credit	Debit	Credit
Interest Payable				400
Income Taxes Payable				4,300
Capital Stock		55,000		55,000
Retained Earnings, March 1, 1988		10,000		10,000
Fees Earned		135,000		135,000
Cleaning Supplies Used Expense	26,000		31,000 √	
Salaries Expense	72,000		74,000 √	
Rent Expense	7,000		9,000 √	
Insurance Expense			1,100 √	
Interest Expense			400	
Income Tax Expense			4,300	
	$226,000	$226,000	$232,700	$232,700

Required:

Prepare the adjusting journal entries made by Highland on February 28, 1989.

P3-3 *Statement of Income*

A list of events for Beidler Company for the year ended December 31, 1988 is presented below. Some items on the list appear on the income statement.

1 To begin the company, $48,000 cash was invested by stockholders in exchange for 2,000 shares of capital stock. These were the only shares issued during the year.

2 $65,000 of inventory items for resale to customers were purchased on account.

3 Revenue from sales totaled $115,000. Cash sales were $20,000 of total. The remaining $95,000 of sales were on account.

4 The cost of goods sold in (3) above was $55,000.

5 $45,000 was paid for purchases on account in (2) above.

6 $80,000 was received for sales on account in (3) above.

7 Rent expense was $10,000 for the year and was paid in cash during 1988.

8 Salaries earned by employees during 1988 totaled $24,000. As of December 31, 1988, $2,000 of the salaries earned had not yet been paid.

9 Assume the income tax expense is $5,220. Income taxes will be paid in 1989.

Required:

Prepare Beidler's 1988 statement of income. (Hint: Before preparing Beidler's income statement, it is necessary to analyze each of the nine transactions and determine the effect, if any, the transaction has on the income statement.)

P3-4 *Balance Sheet*

Information about Splish-Splash Company on December 31, 1988 is presented below. The information is listed in alphabetical order.

Accounts Payable	$16,000,000
Accounts Receivable	12,000,000
Capital Stock	60,000,000
Cash	25,000,000
Income Taxes Payable	5,000,000

*Intangibles	2,000,000
Inventory	32,500,000
*Investment in Affiliated Companies	52,000,000
Long-term Debt	20,000,000
Notes Payable–due within one year	3,000,000
Prepaid Rent	2,500,000
Retained Earnings, December 31, 1988	(to be determined)

*List as a noncurrent asset.

Required:
Prepare a properly classified balance sheet for Splish-Splash Company at December 31, 1988.

P3-5 *Financial Statements for College Bookstore*
Listed below are the accounts and account balances for the Collegetown Book Store, Inc. The accounts appear in alphabetical order. Assume that Retained Earnings at the beginning of the year (January 1, 1988) was $85,100.

Accounts Payable	$271,300
Accounts Receivable	53,000
Salaries Payable	2,100
Accumulated Depreciation	20,800 – thru 1988
Bank Loan Payable (due Aug. 1, 1989)	27,000
Cash	46,300
Check Cashing Fees Earned	2,300
Capital Stock, 1,000 shares	238,000
Cost of Sales–Supplies	119,000
Cost of Sales–Textbooks	231,000
Depreciation Expense–Equipment	2,200 } 5,200 in 1988
Depreciation Expense–Store Fixtures	3,000
Dividends Declared	20,000
Equipment	22,000
Income Tax Expense	28,600
Income Taxes Payable	23,600
Insurance Expense	8,300
Interest Earned on Charge Accounts	1,500
Interest Expense	1,600
Inventory–Supplies	223,800
Inventory–Textbooks	284,000
Legal and Accounting Expense	2,700
Other Expenses	3,900
Payroll Tax Expense	4,500
Prepaid Rent	3,200
Rent Expense	8,400
Retained Earnings, December 31, 1988	(to be determined)
Salaries Expense	65,700
Sales–Supplies	208,000
Sales–Textbooks	317,000
Store Fixtures	60,000
Utilities Expense	5,500

Required:

1 Prepare a statement of income for the year ended December 31, 1988.

2 Prepare a statement of retained earnings for the year ended December 31, 1988.

3 Prepare a properly classified balance sheet at December 31, 1988.

P3-6 *Account Classification*

Required:

For each account listed in the table on page 106–107, enter an "X" in the correct columns to indicate proper classification of the account, financial statement(s) in which it appears, and whether the account normally has a debit or credit balance. The first one is already done as an example.

 P3-7 *Journal Entries, Ledger Accounts, Trial Balances, and Financial Statements*

A list of Henderson Company's transactions and adjustments for August, 1988 is shown below:

Transactions in August, 1988:

1 Borrowed $7,300 on August 4, 1988 from the First National Bank. Loan to be repaid October 16, 1988 with interest.

2 Paid $5,000 cash on August 6 to Wellhoney Computer Company for lease of their computer during August.

3 Paid employees $16,000 on August 24. Payment represented $3,000 for salaries earned during last week of July and $13,000 for salaries earned during period August 1 to August 24.

4 Collected $15,000 cash on August 25 from customers from sales made in June and July.

5 Purchased on August 25, $66,000 of inventory on account.

6 Paid $6,000 on August 28 to landlord for rent of building for August.

7 Sales for August totaled $127,000. ($92,000 in cash and remainder on account)

8 Cost of goods sold to customers in August was $76,000.

9 Collected $16,000 cash on August 31 from customers for previous sales on account.

10 Paid $82,000 on August 31. Payment to vendors of $72,000 for previous purchases of inventory on account, and $10,000 payment to purchase additional land to be held as an investment.

Adjustments on August 31, 1988:

a Interest expense and interest payable of $54 to be recorded for accrued interest during August on bank loan.

b Salaries earned from August 25 to August 31 of $4,000 are unpaid as of August 31.

c Corporate income tax expense is $4,589 for August.

Account titles along with account numbers and August 1, 1988 balances are:

#10	Cash	$15,000	#30	Capital Stock, 5,000 shares	$25,000
11	Accounts Receivable	32,000	31	Retained Earnings	24,000
12	Inventory	27,000	40	Sales	-0-
16	Investment in Land	10,000	50	Cost of Goods Sold	-0-

			Classification of account			
Account title	**Asset**	**Liability**	**Permanent stockholders' equity**	**Revenue**	**Expense**	**Dividends declared**
Cash	X					
Salaries Payable						
Sales						
Retained Earnings, ending balance						
Accounts Receivable						
Capital Stock						
Prepaid Rent						
Accounts Payable						
Income Tax Expense						
Dividends Declared						
Cost of Goods Sold						
Fees Earned						
Investment in Land						

20	Accounts Payable	31,600	51	Computer Lease Expense	-0-
21	Salaries Payable	3,000	52	Salaries Expense	-0-
22	Interest Payable	-0-	53	Rent Expense	-0-
23	Income Taxes Payable	400	54	Interest Expense	-0-
24	Bank Loan Payable	-0-	55	Income Tax Expense	-0-

Required:

1 Prepare journal entries for Henderson Company for the 10 transactions during August. (Label the journal page number as "page 76.")

2 Enter August 1, 1988 balances in three-column, running balance ledger accounts and post the 10 journal entries.

3 Prepare a trial balance as of August 31, 1988 for Henderson.

4 Prepare adjusting entries for Henderson's three adjustments. (Label the journal page number as "page 77.")

✳ **5** Post the adjusting journal entries to the ledger accounts.

6 Prepare an adjusted trial balance as of August 31, 1988 for Henderson.

7 Prepare three basic financial statements:

    a Statement of income

    b Statement of retained earnings

    c Balance sheet

P3-8 (Appendix) *Prepare 12-Column Worksheet*

Harmony, Incorporated's general ledger account balances, before year-end adjusting entries, are shown below:

	Debit	**Credit**
Cash	$120,000	
Accounts Receivable	85,000	
Inventory	100,000	
Prepaid Rent	18,000	
Prepaid Insurance	4,000	
Accounts Payable		$ 48,700

	Trial balance	
	Debit	**Credit**
Capital Stock		20,000
Retained Earnings, Jan. 1, 1989		8,000
Dividends Declared	18,000	
Storage Fees Earned		80,000
Rent Expense	22,000	
Salaries Expense	11,000	
	$138,000	$138,000

Other information available:

1 On December 31, 1989, a count of the office supplies was made. The count indicated $1,200 of office supplies on hand. Assume the $800 difference (the $2,000 amount shown on the trial balance minus the $1,200 of supplies on hand) represents supplies used during the year.

2 Unpaid interest of $2,600 on the note payable has not been recorded.

3 December's $2,000 unpaid rent owed to the landlord for use of the storage building has not been recorded.

4 Unpaid salaries of $1,000 for December have not been recorded.

5 Income tax estimated for 1989 is $6,300.

Required:

Prepare a 12-column worksheet similar to the one illustrated in the chapter appendix.

Business Decision Problem

Marvin Greene formed the Green Acres Landscaping Service, Inc. in April, 1988. The company provides landscaping and lawn maintenance services to homes and businesses.

In January, 1989, Marvin visited his bank to discuss a loan to buy two trucks for the business. During 1988, Marvin used an old truck which he rented from his brother-in-law. The banker requested an income statement for the year ending December 31, 1988.

While Marvin is an expert landscaper, he is not familiar with accounting. Based on his records for 1988, Marvin has prepared the following statement:

Green Acres Landscaping Service, Inc.
Statement of Profit Income
1988

Income:		
Investment in business by M. Greene	$ 6,000	
Loan from father	8,000 liability	
Received from customers	57,000	$71,000
Expenses:		
Materials and supplies	$33,000	
Salary to M. Greene	20,000	
Land for future construction of garage *(not an expense, equity)*	12,000	
Truck rental	1,000	
Insurance and other expenses	2,000	68,000
Profit for the year		$ 3,000

Before he takes this statement to the bank, Marvin requests that you review it and give him any suggestions for improving the presentation. In talking to Marvin, you learn that he has paid all his bills as of December 31, 1988, but that one of his customers still owes him $2,500 for landscaping work completed in October.

4

INTERNAL CONTROL
AND CASH

LEARNING OBJECTIVES

When you complete this chapter, you should be able to:

1 Define the objectives and principles of internal control.
2 Identify means of achieving internal control.
3 Account for a petty cash fund.
4 Prepare a bank reconciliation and record any required journal entries indicated by the reconciliation.

One area where accounting and managerial concerns coincide is an organization's internal control system. A system of internal control is essential if management is to properly conduct the organization's affairs. For example, selling a product is a major aspect of many businesses. It is crucial to the financial success of the firm that all products sold be properly billed and the bills collected. A system of internal control contains procedures designed to ensure that billing and collection are achieved with a minimum of error. It is also important that management have accurate, up-to-date information on sales so that decisions may be made on purchasing, pricing, and promotion. A system of internal control helps to ensure that accurate and timely information is available to management.

INTERNAL CONTROL OBJECTIVES

Internal control involves a firm's plan of organization and the methods and procedures it uses to accomplish several objectives:

1 Safeguard the resources of the firm against loss by fraud, waste, and inefficiency,

2 Achieve accuracy and reliability in its accounting data,

3 Encourage and measure compliance with firm policies, and

4 Evaluate the efficiency of all operations of the firm.

The first two of the broad objectives deal primarily with accounting control, while the last two deal with general managerial control. We shall focus on accounting control.

Importance of Internal Control

Internal control seeks to *prevent* errors from occurring and to *detect* errors that have occurred. Errors may be *intentional* or *unintentional*. Intentional errors result from individuals' attempts to subvert the system, often for personal gain. Unintentional errors are mistakes that result from human failure (distraction, carelessness) or from lack of understanding or training. No system of internal control can offer a total guarantee against errors, particularly in cases of collusion among employees or circumvention of the system by management. Even if it were possible to design a perfect system, the extra few benefits obtained from a perfect system would not justify the substantial extra cost of designing and implementing the system. With internal control systems, a cost-benefit analysis must be considered.

A satisfactory system of internal control has become especially necessary with the growth of large companies having hundreds, or thousands, of employees. In such situations, management finds it impossible to supervise all operations directly. In cases where a strong internal control system did not exist, this difficulty of supervision led to questionable corporate conduct, such as illegal political contributions and bribes of foreign officials. As a result of numerous examples of such conduct, the Foreign Corrupt Practices Act was passed. In addition to prohibiting certain "corrupt practices," this act requires companies to establish and monitor a system of internal control that will ensure that all transactions are properly authorized, executed, and recorded. A good internal control system will help prevent illegal payments from occurring or from being disguised in the accounting records. This is especially important in large organizations to prevent lower-level managers from making illegal payments without the awareness of top management.

COMPUTER APPLICATION

The increasing use of computers in the accounting process also requires a good system of internal control. In a computerized system, fewer people are involved, and many of the steps in processing accounting data cannot be observed. Those who have a detailed knowledge of computers often have an opportunity to manipulate the system for their personal gain. It is the role of the internal control system to minimize these opportunities and to increase the chance of detecting any manipulations that do occur.

Principles of Internal Control

For a transaction or account to be adequately controlled, four specific principles must be met. These four principles relate to: (1) authorization of transactions, (2) recording of transactions, (3) safeguarding of assets, and (4) periodic comparison of actual assets to records of those assets.

Authorizing Transactions need to be properly authorized before they are executed. For example, the principle of proper authorization would be violated if a company janitor was able to sign a contract for the company to buy a parcel of land. If internal control is adequate, a major company land purchase is not executed unless it has first been properly authorized and proper authorization for a land acquisition would not be vested with the firm's janitor.

Authorization may be general or specific. General authorization has been given when a policy on handling certain routine events has been established by management. It would be a general authorization, for example, if management directed the company's shipping department to use the firm's own delivery truck on all shipments within 50 miles of the company's plant but to use United Parcel Service for all shipments outside the 50-mile area. If management has not given general authorization that pertains to a particular situation, specific authorization is required before that transaction can be executed. For example, a major land acquisition would require management's specific authorization.

Recording Once authorized and executed, transactions must be properly recorded in accordance with generally accepted accounting principles (GAAP). That means if a $600 sale on account is authorized and executed on December 31, 1988, the internal control system must make sure the sale is properly recorded—at the correct amount ($600), in the right time period (the period ending December 31, 1988), and classified in the proper accounts (accounts receivable and sales revenue).

COMPUTER APPLICATION

In a computerized system, proper recording primarily involves the proper coding of the transaction to identify the date, amount, and account numbers. Once the transaction has been coded, the system can be relied upon to correctly process it since the system will not make errors in posting or arithmetic.

Safeguarding Internal control must provide ways of safeguarding an organization's resources. Physical safeguards such as burglar alarms and locked vaults are a way of safeguarding assets. Equally important is to limit access to an asset to only the individual having the custodial responsibility for that asset. A good example of limited access will be illustrated later in this chapter where the petty cash custodian is the only person with access to the petty cash fund. Another example of limited access to assets will be encountered in several of the managerial chapters of the text where access to the materials inventory is limited to the materials storeroom clerk.

Comparing Management is alerted to missing assets by periodic comparison of the actual quantity on hand to the quantity listed in the accounting records. By limiting access to assets (and by assigning the record-keeping responsibility over the assets to someone who does not have access to the assets), missing assets can be identified by comparing the actual assets to the recorded amount. Subsequent investigation by management of the differences should reveal the person held accountable. Bank reconciliations and petty cash fund counts are two examples presented in this chapter of periodic comparison of actual assets to records of the assets.

MEANS OF ACHIEVING INTERNAL CONTROL

Separation of Duties

The basic feature of a satisfactory internal control system is the separation of custodial and record-keeping functions. Dividing the functions among several persons provides a system of checks and balances. One individual must not have responsibility and authority to handle a transaction from beginning to end. By dividing the task among several persons, the work of each employee serves to verify the work of other employees. Thus opportunities for errors, either intentional or unintentional, to go undetected are substantially decreased.

Separation of duties becomes much more difficult to achieve in a small company. There may only be two or three employees in the entire organization. By actively involving the owner, the manager, and secretarial help, some degree of internal control can be obtained even in a small company.

Serially Numbered Documents

Another important feature of most internal control systems is the use of serial numbers on sales invoices, purchase orders, receiving reports, vouchers, checks, and many other business documents. Control is maintained by periodically accounting for and reviewing all documents issued. Since the documents have been serially numbered, it is possible to obtain assurance that all documents have been recorded in the accounting system. Preferably the sequential numbering should be done by the printing company, not by the company's own personnel.

Careful design of the documents, including provision for signing or initialing by those who have examined the document and assumed responsibility for its accuracy, also helps strengthen internal control.

Chart of Accounts and Budgets

A well-designed system of general ledger accounts can serve as an important internal control device. Separate general ledger accounts are established to accumulate amounts spent by individual departments or by specific employees. The chart of accounts is used to assist in evaluating individuals in the performance of their responsibilities. Amounts actually spent by a department or employee can be compared to amounts expected to be spent (or *budgeted* amounts). Differences between budgeted amounts and actual amounts spent by the individual department or employee may signal the need to investigate the cause of the difference and to institute corrective action.

In designing the chart of accounts to reflect separation of individual responsibility, care must be taken to assure that charges are made only for amounts which the department or individual has responsibility and authority to control. It is important that clearly defined, written statements of responsibility and authority exist and are communicated to employees.

Fidelity Bonds

Regardless of the sophistication of the internal control system, fidelity bonds providing insurance protection for the company against losses through employee dishonesty should be acquired. With fidelity bonding, if an employee steals cash or other assets from a firm, the firm obtains reimbursement for the loss from the insurance company. Not only do fidelity bonds provide insurance protection, but also the investigation of an organization's employees, which the insurance company undertakes before granting coverage, may prevent hiring persons with undesirable backgrounds.

EXAMPLES OF INTERNAL CONTROL PROCEDURES

Internal control considerations are an important factor in establishing company procedures regarding transactions. Two examples of procedures—processing a sale and handling mail receipts of cash—are examined next.

Processing a Sale

A typical sequence of steps in processing a sales transaction is listed below. Throughout the procedures, notice that different departments of the firm are involved (separation of duties). Notice also that documents are created and approvals granted at certain steps.

1 A customer's purchase order is received by the Sales Department. A document, the sales order, is prepared with several copies.
2 The sales order is sent to the Credit Department, where the customer's credit is approved. An authorized individual in the Credit Department initials the order to signify approval of credit.
3 The sales order is then sent to the Stockroom, and the items ordered are taken from stock. The Stockroom retains a copy of the order, as documentation for goods leaving its control.

4 The goods are packed and shipped by the Shipping Department. Shipping documents are prepared.

5 The sales order and shipping documents are then sent to the Billing Department, which prepares an invoice and sends it to the customer.

6 A copy of the invoice, along with the order and shipping documents, are sent to the Accounting Department, which records the sale, records the customer's account receivable, and files the supporting documents.

7 Periodically, management (or their representatives—the internal auditors) reviews the process to determine, among other things:

    a That all serially numbered documents are accounted for,

    b That necessary approvals (e.g., credit) are present and are consistent with company policies,

    c That billings are accurate as to items, quantities, prices, discounts, and so on, and

    d That complete documentation for each transaction is on file in the Accounting Department.

A flow chart that visually depicts the sequence of steps in processing a sales transaction is presented in Exhibit 4-1.

Mail Receipt of Checks

After the sales transaction discussed above, customers may send payment to the firm by mail. In designing the control procedures for cash receipts, separation of duties is again a major consideration. In particular, the person who handles the cash should be different from the person who maintains the accounting records. A typical sequence would be:

1 All incoming mail is directed to one individual (the mailroom clerk) who opens it and lists the customer's name and amount for each check received. All checks are immediately stamped with a "For Deposit Only" endorsement. The list of checks received is sent to the Accounting Department and a copy of the list is sent to the person who reconciles the bank account.

2 The Treasurer's Office receives the endorsed checks, prepares the bank deposit slip, deposits the checks, and obtains a deposit receipt from the bank. A copy of the deposit receipt is sent to the person who will reconcile the bank account.

3 The Accounting Department records the cash receipts and credits the individual customer accounts based on the list received from Step 1.

4 Monthly statements are sent to customers who have open balances. This procedure calls attention to any errors made in crediting individual customer accounts. For example, if the person who opens the mail had lost or stolen a customer's check, the customer's account would not have been reduced by the payment. When the next monthly statement was sent, the customer would complain that a payment had been made but not recorded, and the matter would be investigated.

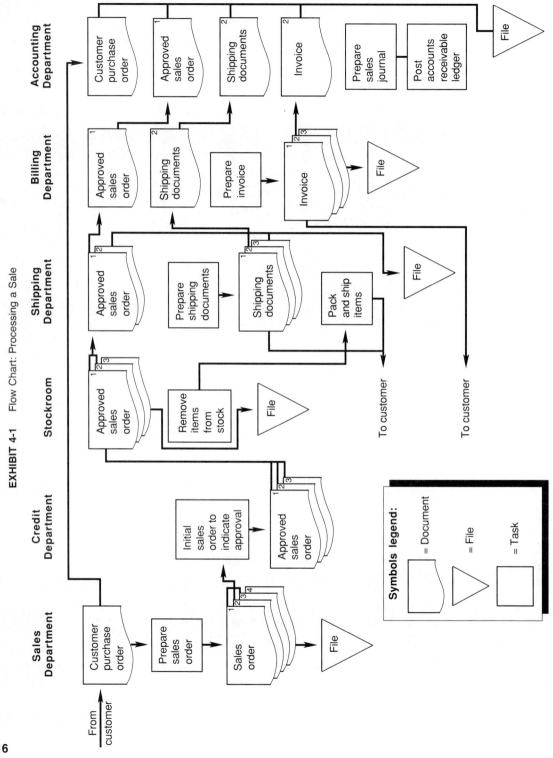

EXHIBIT 4-1   Flow Chart: Processing a Sale

116

5 A person who has not been involved in any of the above steps receives the bank statement, compares the deposit receipts obtained from the bank with the list of customer receipts, and performs the other steps involved in the bank reconciliation process.

A flow chart that visually depicts the sequence of steps in handling mail receipts of checks is depicted in Exhibit 4-2.

CASH

Most transactions involve the receipt or payment of cash. Thus, an important aspect of the accounting system is accounting for and control of cash transactions. Previous chapters discussed *accounting* for cash transactions; this chapter addresses the cash *control* part of the accounting system. Cash control involves the methods used by a company to handle cash and to verify the accounting records.

Cash is one of the assets most highly susceptible to theft. The tremendous volume of transactions flowing through the cash account offers ample opportunity for fraudulent activity. Also the nature of cash—its liquidity—makes it susceptible to theft. It's much easier to misappropriate the firm's cash than to walk off with one of its machines. Because of the high risk of theft, companies strive for good internal control over cash and cash transactions.

In accounting, the term "cash" is defined broadly. A company will typically have several forms of cash, including:

1 *Cash on hand*–coins, currency, or customer checks physically on the company's premises. A company has cash on hand because:
   a It is needed to carry on the company's business activities (e.g., change for the cash register).
   b It is needed for payment of cash expenses. (A petty cash fund, discussed in the next section, is maintained for this purpose.)
   c Money has been received by the firm but not yet deposited in the bank (e.g., collections from customers received today).
2 *Cash in bank*–money on deposit in the company's name in a bank. Included are:
   a Checking accounts.
   b Savings or time accounts. These accounts earn interest and may have to remain on deposit for a fixed period of time.
3 Other forms of cash held by the company, such as foreign currency.

Typically, the cash amounts listed above are totaled and a single amount for cash is presented on the balance sheet. Since it is the most liquid asset, cash is listed first among the current assets.

Two control procedures related to cash are the use of a petty cash fund and the bank reconciliation.

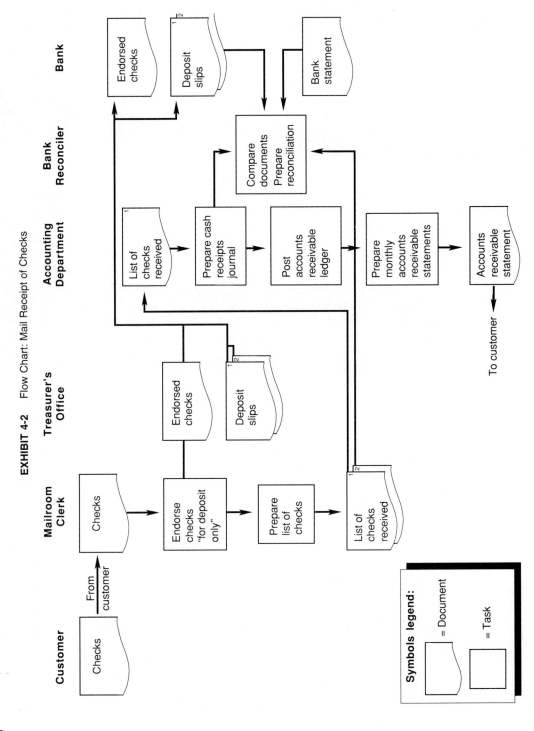

EXHIBIT 4-2 Flow Chart: Mail Receipt of Checks

118

PETTY CASH FUND

Companies should pay most of their bills by using serially prenumbered checks. The use of serially prenumbered checks, combined with a careful review and accounting for all checks issued, greatly strengthens internal control over cash disbursements. However, it is convenient to have some cash on hand to pay small bills. It is often easier for someone in the office to pay small amounts for freight charges, office supplies, maintenance supplies and the like by cash, rather than by putting these bills through the check-writing process. For this purpose, a *petty cash fund* may be established.

Establishing the Fund

The petty cash fund is established by writing a check for a given amount (e.g., $200). The check is made payable to a particular employee who will be responsible for the fund. This employee, known as the *custodian*, is instructed to cash the check and maintain the fund in a safe place, such as a locked box. The fund must be kept separate from the custodian's own cash and from other cash belonging to the company. The custodian is further instructed that at all times the fund must total the original balance, in the form of cash plus receipts for money paid out. Other instructions relating to the operation of the petty cash fund may also be given. For example, the fund is not to be used to cash checks for employees.

If a $200 petty cash fund were established on October 4, 1988, the following entry would be recorded:

1988			
Oct. 4	Petty Cash Fund	200	
	Cash		200
	To record establishment of petty cash fund.		

The account Petty Cash Fund is an asset and would be included in the classification Cash on the balance sheet.

Disbursements from the Fund

A *petty cash voucher* is normally used to maintain a record of expenditures from the petty cash fund. A voucher is a document serving as evidence for payment of a debt. When a request for payment is submitted to the custodian of the petty cash fund, a voucher is prepared showing:

1 Voucher number (these should be prenumbered, in sequential order, to aid in control)
2 Date of payment
3 Name of person or firm receiving payment
4 Amount of payment

EXHIBIT 4-3 Petty Cash Voucher

No. ___1___   Amount $ _____12.86_____

RECEIVED OF PETTY CASH

March 3   1988

For ___Eastern Truck Lines_____

Charge to ___Freight_____

delivery charges - invoice 3061

George Marshall
Received by

5 Description of goods or services
6 Signature of person receiving the cash

An example of a completed voucher is shown in Exhibit 4-3.

The completed voucher (along with any available invoice) is placed in the petty cash box, and the appropriate amount of cash is removed.[1] If we assume that the voucher in Exhibit 4-3 is the first disbursement from the $200 fund, the fund would now contain:

Cash (coin and currency)	$187.14
Voucher No. 1	12.86
Total	$200.00

Note that the petty cash fund always should total $200 in cash and paid vouchers.

Reimbursing the Fund

After a period of time, the petty cash fund will begin to get low on cash. For example, assume that on October 29, 1988, the fund contains:

Cash	$ 21.60
Vouchers No. 1–14	178.40
Total	$200.00

[1]Some companies do not use a formal petty cash voucher system. An invoice or some other type of receipt is the only record maintained to support disbursements from the petty cash fund.

It is now time to reimburse the fund. The 14 vouchers, totaling $178.40, are submitted by the petty cash custodian to the company treasurer for reimbursement. The treasurer, after reviewing the vouchers, issues a check (payable to the custodian) for $178.40 and gives it to the custodian. The treasurer then cancels the vouchers to prevent their resubmission. Upon cashing the check, the custodian again has $200 cash in the petty cash fund (the $21.60 that was in the fund, plus the $178.40 reimbursement).

Assume that the 14 vouchers are broken down as follows:

Office supplies (vouchers 2, 3, 11)	$ 60.77
Freight (vouchers 1, 5, 9, 10)	76.47
Loans to employees (vouchers 6, 12)	22.08
Postage (vouchers 4, 7, 13, 14)	11.33
Employee travel (voucher 8)	7.75
	$178.40

The journal entry to record the $178.40 petty cash fund reimbursement would be:

Oct. 29	Office Supplies Expense	60.77	
	Freight Expense	76.47	
	Employee Loans Receivable	22.08	
	Postage Expense	11.33	
	Travel Expense	7.75	
	Cash		178.40
	To record reimbursement of petty cash fund for vouchers 1–14.		

Two points should be noted concerning the reimbursement entry. First, the petty cash fund account is unaffected by the reimbursement entry. Second, the expenditures are not recorded until the fund is reimbursed. This means that unreimbursed vouchers in the petty cash box have *not* yet been recorded on the company's books.

Petty Cash Short or Over

The sum of the petty cash vouchers plus the remaining petty cash on hand should equal the established fund balance. The fund is "short" if the sum of the vouchers plus remaining petty cash is less than the fund balance. When the fund is replenished, miscellaneous expense is debited for the shortage. If the sum of the vouchers plus the remaining petty cash exceeds the fund balance, the fund is "over." Miscellaneous income is credited for an overage.[2]

To illustrate, assume in the previous example there were the same 14 petty cash vouchers totaling $178.40 but only $19.10 cash. The fund would be $2.50 short ($178.40 plus $19.10 = $197.50) of its $200 balance. The journal entry to replenish the fund would be:

[2]Some firms use an account titled Cash Short or Over instead of Miscellaneous Expense and Miscellaneous Income.

Oct. 29	Miscellaneous Expense	2.50	
	Office Supplies Expense	60.77	
	Freight Expense	76.47	
	Employee Loans Receivable	22.08	
	Postage Expense	11.33	
	Travel Expense	7.75	
	Cash		180.90

To record reimbursement of petty
cash fund for vouchers 1–14
and cash shortage of $2.50.

BANK RECONCILIATION

An important accounting procedure concerning cash is the *bank reconciliation*. As a company engages in its business transactions, it records cash receipts and cash disbursements and summarizes this information in a ledger account (Cash). Similarly, as the bank receives the company's deposits and pays the company's checks, it also summarizes the information in an account (the bank statement). On a regular basis (usually monthly), this "double record of cash"—the company's cash account and the statement provided by the bank—should be compared, and any differences reconciled.

Often there are differences between the balance in the company's cash account (*book balance*) and the balance on the bank statement (*bank balance*). There are several reasons for these differences:

1 Some transactions may have been recorded by the company, but not yet recorded by the bank, such as:
  a Checks written (and recorded) by the company which have not yet been presented to the bank for payment. These are called *outstanding checks*.
  b Money received (and recorded) by the company for deposit in the bank, but which has not yet been recorded by the bank (e.g., receipts deposited late on the last day of the month or deposits sent to the bank by mail). These are called *deposits in transit*.
2 Some transactions may have been recorded by the bank, but not yet recorded by the company. These generally involve charges by the bank. For example:
  a Bank service charges.
  b Bank charges for deposits rejected because customer checks deposited were uncollectible. These are often referred to as NSF checks (nonsufficient funds) or as "bounced checks."
  c Collection of a note receivable by bank on company's behalf.
  d Other charges or credits by the bank.
Often the company does not record (and sometimes does not even know of) these amounts until the bank statement is received early in the following month.
3 Errors may be made by either the company or the bank in recording transactions. Many companies make daily deposits (each consisting of many customer

checks) and write hundreds of checks each month. With this volume of activity, recording errors occasionally will be made.

Not all errors will be detected by the bank reconciliation process. Errors are detected only if the book recording and the bank recording *differ*. If both are wrong, the error will not show up on the bank reconciliation. Examples are paying a bill twice, or writing (and recording) a check for the wrong amount.

Mechanics of Bank Reconciliation

While several formats of bank reconciliation exist, this chapter illustrates the format designed to achieve two objectives:

1 To reconcile differences between the book balance and the bank balance, and

2 To identify any adjusting entries that should be made on the company's books.

To accomplish these objectives, two calculations are performed. We reconcile from the (existing) *book* balance to a figure called the *adjusted book balance,* as follows:

> Book balance
> $\pm$ Transactions recorded by bank but not yet recorded on books
> $\pm$ Correction of any errors made on books
> $=$ Adjusted book balance

The adjusted book balance is the amount that should be shown as cash on the company's financial statements.

We also reconcile from the (existing) *bank* balance to an *adjusted bank balance,* as follows:

> Bank balance
> $\pm$ Transactions recorded by company but not yet recorded by bank
> $\pm$ Correction of any errors made by bank
> $=$ Adjusted bank balance

If all items were identified and properly handled, the adjusted book balance will equal the adjusted bank balance. If these two are unequal, the reconciliation contains an error.

When the two steps discussed above are put into proper format, a bank reconciliation appears as shown in Exhibit 4-4.

EXHIBIT 4-4
(Company Name)
Bank Reconciliation
(Date)

Book balance (date)		$XX	Bank balance (date)			$XX
Add:			Add:			
Bank credits not yet recorded on the books	$X		Deposits in transit	$X		
Errors on books that understate book cash balance	X	X	Errors by bank that understate bank cash balance	X	X	
			$XX			$XX
Deduct:			Deduct:			
Bank charges not yet recorded on the books	$X		Outstanding checks	$X		
Errors on books that overstate book cash balance	X	X	Errors by bank that overstate bank cash balance	X	X	
Adjusted book balance		$XX	Adjusted bank balance			$XX

Example of Bank Reconciliation

Corman Corp. is preparing a bank reconciliation as of October 31, 1988. The accountant collects the following data:

1 The cash ledger account shows a balance of $12,317 on October 31, 1988.

2 The bank statement shows a balance of $15,046 on October 31, 1988.

3 A comparison of the deposits shown on the October bank statement with the cash receipts recorded on the company's books indicates that the receipts of October 30 and 31, amounting to $1,780, were deposited on October 31 but were not recorded by the bank until November 1.

4 The checks returned with the October bank statement were compared with the company's cash disbursements records. The comparison reveals that the following checks written by the company have not yet been presented to the bank for payment:

Check	#2114	$ 80.00
	2143	112.75
	2194	343.00
	2210	1,410.00
	2216	881.25
	2221	412.00
	2222	73.50
	2223	294.50
	2224	628.00
Total		$4,235.00

5 The bank statement shows an October service charge of $26. This has not yet been recorded on the books.

EXHIBIT 4-5
Corman Corp.
Bank Reconciliation
October 31, 1988

Book balance, October 31		$12,317	Bank balance, October 31	$15,046
Add:			Add:	
Error in recording			Deposits in transit	1,780
check no. 2180		450		$16,826
		$12,767	Deduct:	
Deduct:			Outstanding checks	4,235
Bank service charge	$ 26			
NSF check	150	176		
Adjusted book balance		$12,591	Adjusted bank balance	$12,591

6 A customer's check in the amount of $150 deposited October 24 was returned by the bank with the October 31 bank statement. The check was marked "uncollectible—insufficient funds." The bank charged the company's account for the amount of this check. This information has not yet been recorded on the books.

7 The checks returned with the bank statement were compared with the cash disbursements journal. the comparison indicates that check number 2180, in the amount of $2,270 (which was correct), was recorded on the books as $2,720. The check was a payment for equipment repair.

Based on the above information, the bank reconciliation shown in Exhibit 4-5 was prepared. Note that items numbered 3 and 4 above (deposits in transit and outstanding checks) appear as adjustments to the bank balance. Items numbered 5, 6, and 7 above (the unrecorded bank service charge, the customer check returned by the bank due to insufficient funds, and the error made on the books) appear as adjustments to the book balance. The error is handled on the bank reconciliation by *adding* $450 ($2,720 minus $2,270) to the book balance because the amount of recorded disbursements is too high. Note that the adjusted book balance of $12,591 equals the adjusted bank balance. Achieving this equality means that our reconciliation is complete.

Journal Entries

After Corman's bank reconciliation is completed, journal entries are necessary to adjust the cash ledger account from its balance of $12,317 on October 31, 1988, to the $12,591 adjusted book balance indicated on the bank reconciliation. The following three adjustments must be made:

1 The error in recording check number 2180 as $2,720 instead of $2,270 is corrected by increasing the cash balance and decreasing the equipment repair expense balance.

```
1988
Oct. 31      Cash                              450
                 Equipment Repair Expense               450
             To correct recording of check
               No. 2180, recorded as $2,720,
               correct amount is $2,270.
```

2 The bank service charge of $26 is recorded as:

```
31          Bank Charges Expense
               (or Miscellaneous Expense)      26
                 Cash                                   26
            To record October service charge.
```

3 The last item is the unrecorded NSF check of $150. Since the customer's check was uncollectible, the customer still owes the $150. This amount is restored to accounts receivable as follows:

```
31          Accounts Receivable               150
                 Cash                                  150
            To record return by bank of NSF check
              of Customer X.
```

After these three entries[3] are posted, the cash ledger account will have the proper balance of $12,591. If these entries were not made, the financial statements at the end of the month would be incorrect.

FINANCIAL STATEMENT PRESENTATION OF CASH

All of a company's cash accounts are generally presented as one line ("Cash") on the balance sheet. As mentioned earlier, cash includes cash on hand, the petty cash fund, checking account balances, savings account balances, and so forth. There are few problems in determining the amount to be reported on the balance sheet—cash equals the sum of the various cash account balances.

Bank Overdrafts

Sometimes a company's bank account may be *overdrawn* (i.e., has a negative balance). This means in effect that the bank has granted the company a loan by honoring checks drawn in excess of the amount on deposit.

If a bank overdraft exists at the end of a period, it should be reported as a current liability on the balance sheet.

SUMMARY

Internal control seeks to prevent errors from occurring and to detect errors which have occurred. Control procedures should be implemented only if the expected

---

[3]Note that the three entries could have been combined into a single compound entry for convenience.

benefits exceed the cost of implementing the procedures. Cash is especially vulnerable to intentional and unintentional errors and requires good internal control.

Learning Objective 1: Define the objectives and principles of internal control.

Internal control is the plans, methods, and procedures an organization uses to achieve four objectives: (1) safeguard the resources, (2) achieve accurate and reliable accounting data, (3) encourage and measure compliance with policies, and (4) evaluate the efficiency of all operations. The first two objectives deal primarily with accounting control and were emphasized in the chapter. The four principles of internal control relate to: (1) authorizing transactions, (2) recording transactions, (3) safeguarding of assets, and (4) periodic comparison of actual assets to records of those assets.

Learning Objective 2: Identify means of achieving internal control.

To help achieve internal control, organizations should: separate duties so that one individual does not handle a transaction from beginning to end, use serially numbered documents with management accounting for and reviewing all documents, design a chart of accounts and budgets that reflect separation of responsibility, and acquire fidelity bonding insurance for employees who have access to the assets.

Learning Objective 3: Account for a petty cash fund.

A petty cash fund provides a means of paying small bills without the bother of complying with the normal check-writing process. Periodic replenishment of the petty cash fund restores the cash in the fund to the established fund balance. When the petty cash fund is replenished, the expenditures indicated on the petty cash vouchers are recorded.

Learning Objective 4: Prepare a bank reconciliation and record any required journal entries indicated by the reconciliation.

A bank reconciliation accounts for differences between the cash balance reflected on the firm's books and the cash balance reported on the bank statement. The adjusted book balance must agree with the adjusted bank balance. Common items on the book part of the reconciliation are correction of any errors made on the books in recording cash receipts or cash disbursements and transactions recorded by the bank that have not yet been recorded on the books. Principal items on the bank balance part of the reconciliation are deposits in transit, outstanding checks, and bank errors. After the bank reconciliation is completed, journal entries are necessary to adjust the cash balance on the books from the existing book balance to the adjusted book balance shown on the bank reconciliation.

KEY TERMS

Bank reconciliation	NSF check
Bank service charge	Outstanding check
Deposit in transit	Petty cash fund
Fidelity bonds	Separation of duties
Internal control	Serially numbered documents

REVIEW QUESTIONS

1 Internal control is defined as a company's plan of organization and the procedures and methods used to accomplish what four basic objectives?

2 You are president of Aquarius Company. A salesperson offers you a "perfect system" of internal control specifically designed for your business. How would you respond to the salesperson's proposal?

3 George Tarus, owner of a small hardware store, believes the small size of his company makes it impossible to implement any internal control procedures. Do you agree with George's position? Explain your answer.

4 Identify and discuss the internal control principle described in the following sentences: Top-level management of Edelman's Manufacturing Co. has directed the company's purchasing department to purchase all materials to meet production requirements at the lowest available purchase price. However, acquisitions of new factory machines must be individually approved by top management.

5 Mrs. I. M. Careful, owner of Oakmont Jewelry Store, locks the store's jewels in a safe at the end of each working day. Only Mrs. Careful knows the combination to open the safe. Discuss the internal control principle illustrated in the preceding sentences.

6 Mr. J. R. Gniwe is the bookkeeper and cashier for Ewing's Drug Store. Discuss the basic feature of a satisfactory internal control system being violated.

7 Ralph's Deli makes all its cash disbursements using serially prenumbered checks. What is the advantage of using serially prenumbered checks? Do you think all of the deli's disbursements should be made by check?

8 Which of the following items would *not* be included in cash and how should each be presented on the balance sheet: petty cash, checking account, undeposited customers' checks, currency and coins on hand, an uncollectible insufficient funds check returned by the bank, and a bank overdraft?

9 What is a petty cash voucher? Describe the role played by petty cash vouchers in the operation of a petty cash fund.

10 Prepare the format of the journal entries to record: a) establishment of a petty cash fund, b) individual disbursements from the fund, and c) reimbursement of the fund.

11 It is the last day of the accounting period and Lazy Co. decides not to replenish its petty cash fund. The currency and coins remaining in the fund at year end only equal about 10 percent of the total amount of the fund. Unrcimbursed petty cash vouchers account for the remaining 90 percent of the fund balance. Will the financial statements be in error if Lazy Co. does not replenish the fund or make an adjusting entry involving the petty cash fund? Discuss.

12 What is the purpose of a bank reconciliation? Describe the "dual column" format of reconciliation illustrated in the chapter.

13 Define a deposit in transit. Define an outstanding check. What effect, if any, do a deposit in transit and outstanding checks have on a bank reconciliation?

14 What adjusting journal entries, if any, are required for deposits in transit and outstanding checks?

15 What is an uncollectible insufficient funds check? What effect, if any, would it have on a bank reconciliation?

16 What adjusting journal entry, if any, is required for an uncollectible insufficient funds check?

EXERCISES

E4-1 Internal control involves accounting controls and general managerial controls. Determine which of the following are accounting controls and which are managerial controls.

1 A basic training program is required of all new employees in order to become familiar with company rules and policies.

2 The shipping department requires two quality control checks on all products before shipment occurs.

3 An annual medical and dental examination is required of all employees.

4 One employee maintains a petty cash fund for miscellaneous expenses that arise.

5 A printing company prenumbers the firm's checks.

6 When the petty cash fund is reimbursed, the petty cash vouchers and other supporting documents are cancelled and filed.

7 Administrative and sales personnel are required to wear suit and tie; warehouse personnel are required to wear company workclothes.

E4-2 Which of the following statements involving internal control is *not* correct?

1 A system of internal control helps to ensure that timely and accurate information is available to management.

2 The only sure way to safeguard assets is to purchase quality vaults and burglar alarms.

3 By separating custodial from record-keeping functions, a system of checks and balances within an organization is implemented.

4 It is management's goal to protect an organization's resources, to have accurate and reliable accounting data, to foster compliance with the company's policies, and to evaluate the operational efficiency of the company.

E4-3 Describe internal control procedures for handling checks received from customers through the mail.

E4-4 On May 18, 1989, the Peabody Company established a $300 petty cash fund. On June 30, 1989, it was decided to reimburse the petty cash fund. The contents of the fund prior to reimbursement were:

Currency and coins	$ 80.40
Vouchers 1, 8, 10, 12—Delivery expense	34.70
Voucher 5—Loan to employee	100.00
Vouchers 2, 7, 11—Travel expense	60.72
Vouchers 3, 4, 6, 9—Postage expense	24.18
	$300.00

Present the journal entry to establish the petty cash fund and the journal entry to replenish the fund.

E4-5 The October, 1988 bank statement of Hage Corporation showed an ending balance of $1,287,618. During October, the bank incorrectly recorded a $112,500 deposit of Hugh Company into Hage Corporation's account. The bank did not detect the error until November. Also during October, the bank collected a note receivable plus interest for Hage Corporation. The face value of the note was $12,000 and the interest was $740. The bank charged a fee of $40 for a collection charge. Deposits in transit as of October 31 were $26,400. Outstanding checks on October 31 totaled $163,782. Determine the adjusted bank balance on October 31, 1988.

E4-6 Presented below is a list of items that may or may not appear on a dual column bank reconciliation. Indicate the proper treatment of each item using the following key:
A—Add to reported book balance to determine adjusted book balance
B—Subtract from reported book balance to determine adjusted book balance
C—Add to reported bank balance to determine adjusted bank balance
D—Subtract from reported bank balance to determine adjusted bank balance
X—Does not appear on bank reconciliation
The first one already is done as an example.

   C   **1** Deposits in transit.

_____ **2** Uncollectible insufficient funds check, the return of the check not yet recorded on the books.

_____ **3** Total bank deposits for the month.

_____ **4** Bank error in reducing bank account for $1,200 when check was actually for only $120. Bank error not corrected by end of the period.

_____ **5** Bank service charge for the period, not yet recorded on books.

_____ **6** Outstanding checks.

_____ **7** Book error in recording cash receipts. Receipts for $3,500 recorded as $5,300. Error not corrected by end of period.

_____ **8** Proceeds of note receivable collected by bank, not yet recorded on books.

_____ **9** Total cash disbursements per books for the period.

E4-7 Prepare a dual column bank reconciliation for May 31, 1988 based upon the following information for Goldstein Co. Also present any adjusting journal entries indicated by the bank reconciliation.

Bank balance, May 31	$13,943
Bank service charge for May	20
Book balance, May 31	10,726
Deposit in transit, May 31	1,280
Error by bookkeeper in recording check #11863. Check entered on books as $87; actual check written for $78. Check was in payment of a $78 account payable. Check cleared the bank in May.	
Uncollectible insufficient funds check charged by bank during May. No entry was made on the books during May to record the return of this NSF check.	382
Outstanding checks, May 31	4,890

E4-8 On August 31, 1989, the following information is available for Dwelling Co.:

Cash balance per bank statement	$11,629
Cash balance per ledger account	9,862
Bank service charges for August	18

check for $247 returned to company by bank on August 21 due to insufficient funds	247
Bank collected note receivable on behalf of Dwelling Co. on August 12 in the amount of $1,237	1,237
A deposit made on August 30 had not yet been recorded by bank	4,200
A number of checks written by Dwelling Co. had not been presented to the bank for payment as of August 31	4,995

Using the bank reconciliation format presented in the chapter, prepare a dual column bank reconciliation for August 31, 1989.

PROBLEMS

P4-1 *Internal Control—Separation of Duties*
The owner of Stoppe Inn has hired two individuals to handle the establishment's accounting transactions. Their duties are as follows:
Sam Letout: prepares and authorizes prenumbered checks, handles the cash disbursements journal, the general ledger, the accounts payable subsidiary ledger, and on a monthly basis reconciles the bank statement.
Sarah Takin: handles the cash receipts journal, the sales journal, the purchases journal, daily cash deposits, and keeps the accounts receivable subsidiary ledger.

Required:
In your opinion, does the assignment of duties in this way follow the objectives and principles of a proper internal control system? Explain.

P4-2 *Internal Control—Accounts Receivable/Cash Receipts*
Carol Thiel, the cashier of Dewey, Cheatum, and Howe Company, has stolen $200 from the company in the following manner:
Carol intercepted the $200 check of Customer X that was made payable to the company. Carol took the check to the bank and cashed the check by informing the bank teller that the company needed the $200 in currency and coin in order to replenish the company's petty cash fund.
To reduce the accounts receivable account to the proper amount, Carol made a journal entry debiting Cash for $200 and crediting Accounts Receivable.
The resultant $200 difference between cash per bank and cash per books was covered when Carol omitted four checks that totaled $200 from the outstanding check list when she prepared the bank reconciliation.

Required:
1 Determine whether: a) a trial balance of the general ledger accounts will be in balance, and b) the adjusted cash balance per bank will agree with the adjusted cash balance per books on Carol's bank reconciliation.
2 Briefly discuss weaknesses in Dewey, Cheatum, and Howe's internal control system over cash receipts.

P4-3 *Identifying Internal Control Strengths and Weaknesses*
The following are six independent situations:

1 After the order has been taken from the Stockroom and packed and shipped by the Shipping Department, the order is sent to the Credit Department for approval.

2 The company's internal auditor locates two checks with the number 1308 written on the blank line for the check number.

3 Because of the company's excellent internal control system and the company president's trust in key employees, the company does not have fidelity bonds on these employees.

4 Storeroom clerks count the inventory at year end and compare the quantities counted to the quantities shown on the inventory cards they maintain. The inventory cards are adjusted by the storeroom clerks to the quantities they counted.

5 The local movie theater has a ticket seller and a ticket taker. The ticket taker is required to tear each ticket purchased in half and return one-half to the customer.

6 The company requires the customer to have the cash register tape in order to return an item for a refund or exchange.

Required:
For each of the situations above, indicate the strength and/or weakness in internal control.

P4-4 *Internal Control—Cash Disbursements*

The owner of Never-Rite Company suspects that the company's bookkeeper and the company's assistant treasurer may be working together and stealing funds from the company. The bookkeeper records all of the entries on the books and writes out all the checks. The assistant treasurer provides the documentation for the disbursements, physically signs each check, and makes bank deposits. The bank reconciliation provided by the assistant treasurer is shown in Exhibit 4-6.

Additional information:

1 Check #208 was recorded incorrectly in the cash disbursements journal as $420. The correct amount of the check was $460. The check cleared the bank during August.

EXHIBIT 4-6
Never-Rite Company
Bank Reconciliation
August 31, 1988

Book balance, August 31		$18,322.05	Bank balance, August 31		$16,812.00
Add:			Add:		
Proceeds of note collected			Deposits in transit		1,085.00
by bank during August		600.00			$17,897.00
		$17,722.05			
Less:			Less:		
NSF checks:			Outstanding checks		1,095.00
	$589.00				
	246.05	$835.05			
Bank service charge		45.00			
Error in recording					
check #208		40.00	920.05		
Adjusted book balance			$16,802.00	Adjusted bank balance	$16,802.00

2 No entries were made on the books during August to record error in #1, NSF checks, bank service charges, or proceeds of note collected by bank.

3 Outstanding checks on August 31 were:

Check number	Amount
107	$456.00
112	28.29
114	414.71
207	106.00
208	290.00

$1295

4 Deposits in transit, August 31:

$247

$253 / *500*

Non-Sufficient Funds **5** NSF checks during August:

$246.05

Required:

1 Determine how much money the bookkeeper and assistant treasurer have stolen. Prepare a dual column bank reconciliation as support for your answer. The adjusted bank balance will not agree with the adjusted book balance due to the theft.

2 Indicate how the assistant treasurer's bank reconciliation concealed the theft.

P4-5 *Petty Cash Fund*

On November 14, 1988, Flintstone, Inc. established a $300 petty cash fund. On December 2, 1988, the fund was replenished. The content of the fund prior to reimbursement on December 2 was:

Currency and coin	$31.08
Postage expense	72.00
I.O.U.—company employee	50.00
Travel expense	60.00
Freight expense	81.92

On December 4, 1988, Flintstone increased the balance in its petty cash fund to $500. On December 31, 1988 (the last day of the company's accounting year) the fund was again replenished. The fund's composition on December 31 was:

Currency and coin	$102.40
Postage (of which $43.00 of stamps were still unused at December 31)	107.00
Loan to officer	200.00
Travel expense	20.10
Freight expense	70.50

Required:

Present all journal entries required for 1988 for Flintstone's petty cash fund. (Hint: If the fund is not in balance, debit Miscellaneous Expense for any shortage.)

P4-6 *Petty Cash Fund*

On June 1, 1989, Smirfs, Inc. established a $200 petty cash fund. On July 7, 1989, the fund was replenished when it contained the following items:

Transportation expense–gas	$ 17.80
Postage expense	10.00
Freight expense	15.00
Entertainment expense–lunches	23.90
Supplies expense	4.39
Currency and coin	128.91

On September 1, 1989, Smirfs, Inc. decreased the petty cash fund to $150. On December 31, 1989 (the last day of the company's accounting year), the fund was again replenished. The fund's composition on December 31 was:

Postage expense	10.00
Supplies ($50.00 of supplies were unused on 12/31/89)	77.00
Travel expense	23.00
Loan to employee	20.00
Currency and coin	15.00

Required:
Present all journal entries required for 1989 for Smirfs' petty cash fund.

P4-7 *Bank Reconciliation*
Dettita Co.'s bank balance on May 31, 1990, was $12,347.20. The general ledger cash balance on that date was $13,535.15. Cash receipts of $2,320.20 for May 31 were not received by the bank until June 3, 1990. The following items also were noted:
1 Outstanding checks (total value):

April 30	$2,340.30
May 31	2,010.25

2 Bank charges for May:

Customers' nonsufficient funds checks	$430.00
Bank service charge	125.00

3 Errors:
  a Dettita's bookkeeper recorded check #437 for $125 in the cash disbursements journal. The actual amount written on the check was $175. The check was for payment of an account payable.
  b The bank charged Dettita Co. for a check written by Dettilla Co. The check was for $273.

Required:
1 Prepare a dual column bank reconciliation for Dettita Company on May 31, 1990.
2 Prepare any adjusting entries indicated by the bank reconciliation.

P4-8 *Bank Reconciliation*
Mautz Co. maintains a checking account with the Second City State Bank. The bank statement for the month of April 1989 was as follows:

1989 date	Checks and other debits			Deposits and other credits		Balance
4-01						12,918.04
4-02				2,819.09		15,737.13
4-05	58.10	19.12				15,659.91
4-07	249.83	527.49	81.30			14,801.29
4-09	10.07	1,912.40		1,891.34		14,770.16
4-13	976.35					13,793.81
4-14	367.25 NSF					13,426.56
4-20	381.40	1,324.92	752.00	2,246.30		13,214.54
4-22	95.12					13,119.42
4-24	256.72	45.00 CF		8,200.00 CM		21,017.70
4-28	1,478.38					19,539.32
4-30	831.73	18.00 SC				18,689.59

Code: NSF—Uncollectible—insufficient funds check
     CF—Collection fee charged
     CM—Credit memo for customer's note collected (includes $200 interest)
     SC—Service charge

The activity in Mautz's cash receipts and cash disbursements records for April 1989 shows:

Cash receipts deposited:

April	1	$2,819.09
April	9	1,891.34
April	19	2,246.30
April	30	3,879.34

Cash disbursements:

Check #	Amount	Check #	Amount
2181	$ 19.12	2190	$ 95.12
2182	10.07	2191	743.15
2183	249.83	2192	1,324.92
2184	81.30	2193	381.40
2185	1,912.40	2194	944.72
2186	1,478.38	2195	256.72
2187	752.00	2196	831.73
2188	976.35	2197	1,942.35
2189	181.40	2198	587.19

The outstanding checks on the March 31, 1989 bank reconciliation were:

Check #	Amount
2156	$1,294.52
2165	58.10
2179	332.74
2180	527.49

The company's general ledger cash account shows:

Cash

April 1, Balance	10,705.19	Cash Disbursements	12,768.15
Cash Receipts	10,836.07		

Required:

1 Determine the deposits in transit on April 30, 1989.
2 Determine the outstanding checks on April 30, 1989.
3 Prepare a dual column bank reconciliation for April.
4 Present any adjusting journal entries indicated by the bank reconciliation.
5 After the adjusting journal entries are posted, what dollar balance will appear in the general ledger Cash account?
6 What amount of cash should be on the company's April 30, 1989 balance sheet?

Business Decision Problem

You have recently been hired by I. and E. Wholesalers, Inc. to analyze the internal control over cash. The president of the company believes that Randy Marsh, the company's bookkeeper and cashier, may be stealing some of the firm's cash.

Your review of the books and the bank statement on July 31, 1989 reveals:

1 Balance per the bank statement of $11,214.99 as of July 31.
2 Cash receipts for July 31 of $456.79 were not deposited until August 1.
3 Note collected by bank on July 19 for $1,247.32 has not been entered on books.
4 Outstanding checks on July 31 were: #2091 for $129.30, #2124 for $194.18, #2126 for $281.24, and #2127 for $218.41.
5 Balance per the general ledger cash account of $12,480.15 as of July 31.

Randy Marsh has prepared the following bank reconciliation following a different format than followed in the textbook.

I. and E. Wholesalers, Inc.
Bank Reconciliation
July 31, 1989

	Number	Amount	
Balance per books, July 31			$12,480.15
Add:			
Outstanding checks	2091	$ 129.30	
	2126	281.24	
	2127	218.41	528.95
			$13,009.10
Less:			
Undeposited cash receipts		$ 546.79	
Note collected by bank		1,247.32	1,794.11
Balance per bank, July 31			$11,214.99

Required:

1 Determine the amount of cash stolen by Randy Marsh by preparing a proper bank

reconciliation. Follow the format used in the textbook. Your reconciliation will not balance. The difference will be the cash shortage.

2 Examine the bank reconciliation prepared by Randy Marsh. How did he conceal the shortage on his reconciliation?

3 Discuss the major internal control weakness over cash that exists at I. and E. Wholesalers, Inc.

5

ACCOUNTING FOR SALES AND RELATED RECEIVABLES

LEARNING OBJECTIVES

When you complete this chapter, you should be able to:

1 Record sales revenue and related charges to customers.
2 Record adjustments to sales revenue.
3 Apply the direct write-off and allowance methods for bad debts.
4 Account for notes receivable and related interest.

The first step in the process of determining income must be the proper recording of revenue for the period. That is, we must be able to answer the question: What revenue did the company have during the period? The major concern in answering this question is *timing*. Consider, for example, the following sequence of events surrounding a sale:

April 23	An order is received from a customer for 1,000 units of Product X.
May 2	1,000 units of Product X are manufactured.
May 18	The product is delivered to the customer.
June 10	Full payment is received from the customer.

At which date should the company record the revenue derived from this sale? The answer is that the *revenue should be recorded when it is realized*. This statement in itself is not very helpful. We need to know what is meant by realization. *Realization* is said to occur when (1) the earning process is substantially complete, and (2) any remaining events and activities are capable of being estimated with reasonable accuracy.

The first condition for realization states that *the earning process must be substantially complete.* The major activities necessary to accomplish a sales transaction must have been performed in order for the revenue to be considered "earned." What constitutes major activities varies somewhat, depending upon the firm and the nature of its business. Remember from the discussion of accrual accounting in Chapter 2 that in most cases the critical event which must be completed is *delivery* (the transfer of the product or service to the customer). Upon delivery, the firm has completed the following activities: It has found a customer willing to buy a particular product or service; it has produced the product and delivered it to the customer (or has performed the service for the customer); and the customer has accepted it. These three activities are represented in the example above as the April 23, May 2, and May 18 events. Only payment by the customer remains. Although the remaining step of receiving payment is important, payment normally follows delivery without any major effort required by the firm. This point, however, is related to the second condition for realization.

The second condition for realization is that any remaining events and activities must be capable of *being estimated with reasonable accuracy.* In particular, this means that costs that are still to be incurred must be estimated. Such costs might include:

1 Failure of the customer to pay some or all of the amount owed. This factor, commonly known as "bad debts," can usually be estimated based on past experience. For most firms, bad debt losses are a fraction of one percent of sales.

2 The possibility that the customer might return some items as unsatisfactory or defective. Again, past experience should serve as a guide in estimating this cost, and the amount should be small relative to sales.

In most cases, the second condition for realization can also be met at time of delivery. In most business situations, bad debts and sales return are small in relation to sales and can be estimated with reasonable accuracy at time of delivery.

Note the qualification that the conditions for revenue realization are *in most cases* met at the time of delivery. There are cases where realization occurs at time of production. In other situations, realization requirements may not be met until cash is collected. These two possibilities are briefly discussed in the first appendix to this chapter.

SALES TRANSACTIONS

When a company sells goods or services, payment by the customer may take various forms:

1 The customer may pay cash at the time of sale.

2 The customer may charge the purchase to a credit card.

3 The customer may promise to pay later for the goods or services. Such a sale is said to be a *credit sale* or a *sale on account.* The customer's promise to pay is normally unwritten (*account receivable*), but sometimes is a formal, written document (*note receivable*).

Regardless of the method of payment, sales revenue is usually recognized at the time of delivery.

Cash Sales

In many cases, the customer pays for the product or service immediately upon delivery. For example, sales by a department store, a supermarket, or a hair stylist are often collected immediately. In these cases, delivery and cash collection occur at the same time.

The entry to record such sales transactions is straightforward. Assume, for example, that on September 17, the total cash sales of a meat market were $946.50. The daily sales entry, in journal entry form, would appear as follows:

Sept. 17	Cash	946.50	
	Sales		946.50
	To record cash sales.		

Since cash has been collected, the sales transaction is complete and further entries would not normally be necessary. One exception is the case where the customer later returns merchandise for a refund. The entry for sales returns is discussed later in the chapter.

Sales on Account

When cash collection does not occur until after the time of delivery, the sale is said to be *made on account*. This means that the customer has an obligation to pay in the future. Under normal circumstances, the seller debits accounts receivable, an asset account. For example, assume that a manufacturer sells $16,000 of merchandise to a retailer on October 9, with payment due in 30 days. The entry is:

Oct. 9	Accounts Receivable	16,000	
	Sales		16,000
	To record a sale on account.		

Sometimes, the customer's promise to pay takes the form of a formal written document called a *note*. In this situation, *notes receivable* instead of *accounts receivable* is the amount debited. Notes generally extend the time period allowed for payment. For this benefit, the customer normally pays interest. Accounting for notes receivable and the related interest is considered later in the chapter.

Credit Card Sales

In today's economy, many retail sales transactions are made using credit cards. While some variety of practice exists (due primarily to different arrangements by the credit card companies to pay the merchants), credit card sales are often treated much like cash sales.

Financial statement account appears on			Account balance	
Balance sheet	Statement of income	Statement of retained earnings	Debit	Credit
X			X	

	Debit	Credit
Bank Loan Payable		34,000
Capital Stock		55,000
Retained Earnings, Jan. 1, 1988		133,300
Dividends Declared	5,000	
Sales		485,000
Cost of Goods Sold	320,000	
Salaries Expense	102,000	
Interest Expense	2,000	
	$756,000	$756,000

Other information available:

1 $3,800 of prepaid rent has been consumed during 1988.

2 Prepaid insurance remaining at December 31, 1988 was $1,000.

3 Salaries earned by employees during late December but unpaid as of December 31, 1988 totaled $2,200.

4 Unrecorded interest accrued on bank loan as of December 31, 1988 was $100. *interest which has not been paid*

5 Estimated income taxes for 1988 are $18,300.

Required:

Prepare a 12-column worksheet similar to the one illustrated in the chapter appendix.

 P3-9 (Appendix) *Prepare 12-Column Worksheet*

Erie Boat Storage Co. provides winter storage facilities. The corporation's trial balance on December 31, 1989 shows:

	Trial balance	
	Debit	Credit
Cash	$ 30,000	
Accounts Receivable	55,000	
Office Supplies	2,000	
Notes Payable		$ 30,000

Many bank credit cards provide that the credit card charge slips are deposited into the seller's bank account, in much the same way as checks are deposited. Usually, the account must be at the bank which sponsors that particular credit card. The bank will increase the seller's account by the amount of the charge slips deposited less a fee (negotiated between the bank and the seller), which is generally between 3 and 6 percent.

For example, assume that on March 11 a clothing store has credit card sales of $1,070. Assume also that its credit card fee is 5 percent. The store deposits the $1,070 in charge slips. The bank will deduct the 5 percent fee ($53.50), and credit the store with a deposit of $1,016.50. The store's entry to record this transaction is:

Mar. 11	Cash	1,016.50	
	Credit Card Fee Expense	53.50	
	Sales		1,070.00
	To record credit card sales, less the applicable bank charge.		

In a few cases, credit card companies require that the seller mail in the charge slips, and then be sent a check (again, for the amount of the charge slips less the fee). Under these circumstances, the transaction is recorded as a sale on account rather than a cash sale. If this arrangement had applied in the above example, the debit for $1,016.50 would be to accounts receivable rather than cash and all other elements of the entry would remain the same. Note that this receivable is recorded as due from the credit card company, not from the individual customers.

Other Charges in Sales Transactions

In many sales transactions, the charge to the customer involves more than the price of the product or service alone. For example, a sales tax may be imposed or a freight charge may be added to the price of the product. As a result, sales transactions may involve not only credits to revenue accounts, but credits to liability or expense accounts as well.

Sales Tax   Sales taxes are imposed by governmental units (states or municipalities) on certain sales transactions. The seller acts as a collection agent by charging the tax to the customer and periodically remitting the amounts collected to the government. The amount of the sales tax is not a revenue to the seller because it does not serve to increase the owners' equity. The sales tax collected is a *liability* of the seller because the selling firm owes this amount to the government.

If on April 23 a department store makes a cash sale of merchandise in the amount of $200, on which a 6 percent sales tax applies, the proper entry is:

Apr. 23	Cash	212	
	Sales		200
	Sales Taxes Payable		12

To record a cash sale with a 6% sales
tax collected.

When the sales taxes are remitted to the government (perhaps monthly or quarterly), an entry would be made to debit sales taxes payable and credit cash.

Freight Charges Freight charges serve as an example of a charge to the customer for an additional service provided by the seller. In addition to providing a product, the seller is also shipping it to the customer's place of business. The freight charge is usually recorded as a reimbursement (reduction) of freight expense.

Sometimes the freight charge is recorded as an additional element of revenue, rather than a reduction of expense. For example, mail order companies commonly add a "postage and handling" charge to the cost of merchandise. This is often recorded as revenue.

ADJUSTMENTS TO SALES REVENUE

Recall that when sales revenue is recorded at time of delivery, the earning process is substantially complete and any remaining events and activities can be estimated with reasonable accuracy. For sales on credit, collection must still occur. If sales discounts (reductions for prompt payment) are offered, the amount received from customers may differ from the amount of sales revenue initially recorded. Some customers may return merchandise because it is defective or because in some way it does not meet their needs. A few customers may fail to pay their bills. Events such as these occur *after* the sale, and thus require *adjustments* to the amount of sales revenue previously recorded. Because these adjustments generally are a very small percentage of total sales and are somewhat predictable, they do not prevent the recording of sales revenue at time of delivery. These small adjustments are either estimated and recorded at time of sale or are recorded later.

Sales Subject to Cash Discounts

Firms selling on account may offer their customers an inducement for prompt payment. This inducement takes the form of a price reduction if payment is made within a specific period. For example, one common practice is to offer a 2 percent discount if payment is made within ten days of the invoice date. Otherwise, payment of the entire invoice price is due within 30 days of the invoice date. These terms are expressed in abbreviated form by writing "2/10, n/30", which is read as "two percent discount for payment within ten days, or net invoice amount due in thirty days."[1]

The most commonly used method of accounting for cash discounts is initially to record the sales revenue at the full invoice price, and then at the time of collection to record discounts taken as an adjustment of sales revenue.

---

[1]Strangely, in this context, "net" really means "gross."

For illustrative purposes, assume that on October 1, a firm makes two sales: $1,000 to Customer A and $1,500 to Customer B. The terms of both sales are "2/10, n/30." Customer A pays on October 10, and Customer B pays on October 28.

Entries to reflect the above events are as follows. On October 1, the total amount of the sales ($1,000 plus $1,500) is recorded.

Oct. 1	Accounts Receivable	2,500	
	Sales		2,500
	To record sales on account.		

On October 10, Customer A pays its bill. The journal entry to record Customer A's payment within the 10-day discount period would be:

Oct. 10	Cash	980	
	Sales Discount	20	
	Accounts Receivable		1,000
	To record collection within discount period.		

Since payment occurred within the 10-day discount period, the payment is $980 ($1,000 − (2% of $1,000)). We must now eliminate the $1,000 receivable (since Customer A has met its obligation) and reflect the fact that the net revenue from this transaction was $980, not the $1,000 revenue recorded on October 1. While we could debit sales for the $20 discount, it is more common to debit a separate account, *sales discounts*. This account accumulates the total amount of sales discounts taken by customers during the period. If sales revenue were debited directly, the amount of the discounts would be mixed in an account with other information (sales revenue and perhaps other adjustments like sales returns). It would then be more difficult to determine the sales discounts for the period. Therefore, separate accounts are maintained for sales discounts, sales returns, and other adjustments to sales. These accounts are referred to as *contra revenue accounts,* because they serve to offset a revenue account (in this case—sales). As will be illustrated later in the chapter, contra revenue accounts are deducted from sales revenue on the income statement.

On October 28, Customer B pays its bill. Since payment occurs after the ten-day discount period, Customer B pays the full invoice price of $1,500. The entry simply records collection of the $1,500 receivable entered on October 1.

Oct. 28	Cash	1,500	
	Accounts Receivable		1,500
	To record collection after end of discount period.		

Because sales revenue was originally recorded at gross amount, the credit to accounts receivable at time of collection must also be at gross. Notice that this is the case in both examples above.

Sales Returns

Another possible adjustment to sales revenue is the sales return. A customer may request a refund because the product received was defective or damaged, or the service was unsatisfactory. The return essentially cancels the sales revenue previously recorded. It would be reasonable to make an entry debiting sales for the amount of the return. In practice, instead of debiting sales, a separate contra revenue account *sales returns* is debited. This account accumulates the total amount of returns for the period.

To illustrate, suppose on July 8 a customer returns defective merchandise that has a selling price of $800. If the original sale was for cash, the customer will usually get a cash refund, and the following entry will be made:

July 8	Sales Returns	800	
	Cash		800
	To record refund for merchandise returned.		

If the sale was on account, and has not yet been paid for, the customer will receive a credit (reduction) to the account receivable balance, and the following entry will be made:

July 8	Sales Returns	800	
	Accounts Receivable		800
	To record credit to customer's account for returned merchandise.		

A notice is sent to the customer showing the amount of the credit to the customer's account receivable balance. This notice is called a *credit memo*.

The above example assumed that the returned goods were defective, which suggests that they were of little value to the seller, and probably could not be resold. Sometimes, however, goods are returned because they do not meet the buyer's needs. Such goods can be resold after their return. These circumstances also call for a sales return entry as illustrated above. In addition since the sale is being cancelled and the merchandise returned, a second journal entry is required to (a) restore the returned goods to inventory (debit Inventory) and (b) cancel the cost of goods sold (credit Cost of Goods Sold).

Sales Allowances

Similar to sales returns are *sales allowances,* which are price reductions granted to a customer after the sale is recorded. A common reason for an allowance is that the customer is unhappy with the merchandise and is unwilling to pay full price. The company and its customer may resolve the problem by a price reduction.

Accounting for sales allowances parallels that for sales returns. A contra revenue account (Sales Allowances) is debited, and either Cash or Accounts Receivable is credited. In a sales allowance, there is no return of merchandise, and thus no inventory/cost of goods sold entry is needed.

ACCOUNTING FOR UNCOLLECTIBLE ACCOUNTS

Another type of adjustment to sales revenue occurs when customers fail to pay their bills. The seller will make many attempts to collect, perhaps even resorting to a collection agency or court judgment. If these efforts are unsuccessful in producing payment, the seller will at some point decide that the account is *uncollectible*. Perhaps the customer has left town or is bankrupt, or there is some other reason why the seller concludes that collection will not occur. At this point, the seller *writes off* the account. Conceptually, the adjustment for uncollectible accounts (or "bad debts," as they are generally called) is an adjustment to sales revenue, because the inflow of resources anticipated (and recorded) at time of delivery will in fact not occur. Ideally, uncollectible accounts are treated as a contra revenue account, in the same manner as sales discounts, returns, and allowances. Most firms, however, treat uncollectible accounts as an *expense* (bad debt expense) rather than a contra revenue. Our discussion will follow this common practice.

Direct Write-Off Method

One simple (but not very desirable) procedure for recording uncollectible accounts is to wait until a particular customer account is deemed uncollectible and then record expense and reduce receivables. For a $110 account deemed uncollectible on November 11, the direct write-off method records the following:

Nov. 11	Bad Debt Expense	110	
	Accounts Receivable		110
	To write off an uncollectible account receivable.		

One reason why the direct write-off method is not very desirable is related to the matching rule. The matching rule emphasizes that to measure income for a period of time, it is necessary to identify and record all revenues, revenue adjustments, and expenses for that period of time. In the case of bad debts a long time usually elapses between the original sale and the point where the seller decides that the account is uncollectible. Several months—perhaps even a year to two—may be spent trying to collect the account. It is therefore likely that an account written off this year could be the result of a sale recorded last year, or even two years ago. This means that, under the direct write-off method, sales revenue is recorded in one year, while the bad debt expense might be recorded in a later year. Thus, the direct write-off method can violate the matching rule. In addition, the direct write-off method results in accounts receivable being presented on the balance sheet at their total gross amount. Receivables should be valued on the balance sheet at *net realizable value*—the amount expected to be collected. Rarely would one expect to collect one hundred percent of the gross receivables amount. By showing the gross amount for receivables, the direct write-off method results in presenting receivables on the balance sheet at an amount in excess of the proper net realizable value.

Allowance Method

A technique is needed that will record the bad debt adjustment in the same time period as the sales revenue to which it relates and will present accounts receivable at net realizable value. The *allowance method* accomplishes this by estimating the uncollectible accounts in the period of sale. Under the allowance method of accounting for bad debts, the one-step procedure illustrated above for the direct write-off method is replaced with the following two-step approach:

1 Make a periodic estimate of the amount of bad debts that can be expected from this period's sales. Record this estimate as a debit to bad debt expense with a credit to a contra asset account titled *allowance for uncollectible accounts*.

2 As specific accounts are determined to be uncollectible, write them off (i.e., eliminate them from accounts receivable) by debiting the allowance account and crediting accounts receivable, but do not again record an entry to bad debt expense.

Note the addition of a new account, Allowance for Uncollectible Accounts, to span the time between debiting the expense in step 1 and crediting the accounts receivable in step 2. Allowance for uncollectible accounts is treated as an offset (a contra account) to accounts receivable. It signifies that a reduction in the asset Accounts Receivable is expected due to uncollectibility, but the specific customer accounts (or the exact amounts) involved are not yet known. Subtracting the allowance account from accounts receivable on the balance sheet results in receivables being shown at net realizable value.

There are two procedures under the allowance method for determining the periodic estimate of bad debts. Both of these procedures—the percentage of credit sales and the percentage of accounts receivable—are illustrated below.

Allowance Method—Percentage of Credit Sales   One way of estimating bad debt expense is to estimate the *percentage of total sales on account* that will be uncollectible. Many companies estimate this percentage based on their past experience.

An example may help clarify the percentage of credit sales method. Assume that the Arbor Company began business in 1988, selling on account to a wide range of customers. During 1988, sales on account amounted to $220,000 and collections were $140,000. These were recorded as:

Accounts Receivable	220,000	
Sales		220,000
To record sales on account.		

Cash	140,000	
Accounts Receivable		140,000
To record collections on account.		

At the end of 1988, the accounts receivable balance was $80,000 ($220,000 − $140,000). The company expects to collect most of this balance in 1989, but recognizes that some customer accounts are likely to prove uncollectible. As of the end of 1988, however, no accounts had been written off as uncollectible. Under the allowance method, in order to achieve a proper matching of expense and revenues, the company must estimate what amount of its 1988 sales will be uncollectible. Assume that Arbor believes average bad debt losses will be .0075 (three-quarters of one percent) of sales on account. Arbor makes the following calculation:

$$\text{Estimated uncollectible accounts for 1988} = .0075 \times \$220,000 \text{ Sales} = \$1,650$$

The following entry is now made:

Bad Debt Expense	1,650	
Allowance for Uncollectible Accounts		1,650
To record .0075 of sales as estimated amount of uncollectible accounts.		

The debit to Bad Debt Expense is an expense, and the credit to Allowance for Uncollectible Accounts is a deduction from Accounts Receivable. In common language, the above entry says the following:

We have recorded $220,000 as sales revenue for 1988, but we think this figure should be reduced by $1,650, which is our estimate of the eventual amount of bad debts resulting from 1988 sales. This means that we expect our true revenue (inflow of assets) to be $218,350.

Similarly, our books now show accounts receivable of $80,000 but we estimate that $1,650 of that amount will never be collected.

Allowance Method—Percentage of Outstanding Receivable The *percentage of credit sales* method bases bad debts on the amount of the current period's sales that will probably prove to be uncollectible. While this approach is commonly used, it is not the only possibility. Bad debts can also be estimated by taking a *percentage of accounts receivable*. The adjustment in this case is based on estimating how much of the accounts receivable will probably prove to be uncollectible.

In basing an estimate on accounts receivable, it is logical to classify the individual customer accounts according to how many days they are past due. A customer account which has been past due for nine months is more likely to prove uncollectible than one which has been past due for fifteen days. The procedure, then, is to classify each individual customer account according to the length of time past due (this is called *aging the accounts*), and apply different percentages to the different age categories.

COMPUTER APPLICATION

Computer programs for accounts receivable systems automatically produce aging data. Dates of the sales transactions are entered when the sale is recorded. Since many systems measure the age of the account from the date when payment is *due,* rather than the date of the sale itself, it is necessary also to enter the due date (unless the due date is standard, such as 30 days after invoice date). The computer then calculates how much past due the account is (those that have not yet reached the due date are classified as "current"), and groups them into categories selected by management (such as 30–60 days past due, 61–90 days past due, and so on).

For example, assume that on December 31, 1988, Raiken Sales Company has an accounts receivable balance of $783,000. Determining how long each individual customer account is past due yields the aging analysis shown in Exhibit 5-1. Next, a percentage must be applied to each age category to reflect the risk of noncollectibility. The *older* the accounts, the higher the risk, and thus the higher the percentage. Assume that the company determined the percentages based on prior experience and carried out calculations as shown at the top of page 149:

EXHIBIT 5-1
Accounts Receivable Aging Analysis
December 31, 1988

Customer name	Totals	Current	Less than 60 days past due	60 days to 6 months past due	6 months to 1 year past due	Over 1 year past due
American Discount Stores	$ 60,000		$ 60,000			
Buffalo Dry Goods	48,000	$ 40,000		$ 8,000		
Canada Variety Stores	73,000	32,000	41,000			
Drake & Wellman	112,000	68,000	44,000			
Eastern Retailers	56,000				$56,000	
Farmersville General Store	9,000					$ 9,000
Hunt & Keller	85,000	85,000				
Lansdale Department Store	101,000	40,000	53,000	8,000		
Millicent's Boutique	14,000	14,000				
Northwest Shops	26,000		7,000	10,000		9,000
Richardson & Co.	127,000	42,000	45,000	40,000		
Xaviers Inc.	72,000			72,000		
Totals	$783,000	$321,000	$250,000	$138,000	$56,000	$18,000

Age category	Total accounts	Estimated uncollectible percentage	Allowance for uncollectible accounts
Current	$321,000	.004	$ 1,284
Less than 60 days past due	250,000	.01	2,500
60 days to 6 months past due	138,000	.03	4,140
6 months to 1 year past due	56,000	.15	8,400
Over 1 year past due	18,000	.50	9,000
Totals	$783,000		$25,324

It is important to note that the $25,324 amount computed is the desired balance for the *allowance for uncollectible accounts,* which appears on the balance sheet. This amount represents what the December 31, 1988 balance should be in the allowance for uncollectible accounts. Assume that the allowance account already has a balance of $7,500, as a result of entries prior to December 31, 1988. An entry at December 31, 1988 must bring the balance up to the calculated amount of $25,324. An entry for the difference between the calculated balance ($25,324) and the existing balance ($7,500) is needed:

Bad Debt Expense	17,824	
Allowance for Uncollectible		
Accounts		17,824
To record the charge for		
uncollectible accounts.		

Writing off Specific Accounts   Assume that in mid-1989 a customer owing $900 is declared bankrupt and Raiken writes off the account. The following entry is made:

Allowance for Uncollectible		
Accounts	900	
Accounts Receivable		900
To write off an uncollectible		
account.		

Note that under the allowance method, the write-off of a specific customer account that has proven to be uncollectible does *not* involve an entry to bad debt expense, and thus does not affect the income statement. Recall that the income effect (the debit to bad debt expense) was estimated and recorded at the end of 1988.

Recovery of Accounts Written Off   Occasionally, specific customer accounts that had been written off will actually be collected. Assume that Raiken receives a final settlement of $175 out of the $900 receivable as a result of bankruptcy proceedings. The following entries would be appropriate:

Accounts Receivable	175	
Allowance for Uncollectible		
Accounts		175

To partially reverse previous entry
writing off entire customer
account as uncollectible. That
entry has proven to be incorrect,
as $175 will be collected.

Cash	175	
Accounts Receivable		175

To record collection on customer
account received from
bankruptcy proceedings.

Note that accounts receivable is debited for $175 in the first journal entry and then credited for $175 in the second entry. While it appears simpler just to make one entry debiting cash and crediting the allowance for uncollectible accounts, this short cut, which eliminates the debit and credit to accounts receivable, is not appropriate. An entry debiting cash and crediting the allowance for uncollectible accounts would be difficult to understand. Also, the customer's account in the accounts receivable subsidiary ledger would be correct and up-to-date only if both journal entries are made; these entries restore the customer's account to the books and show that it was paid.

SALES, NOTES RECEIVABLE, AND INTEREST REVENUE

In some businesses, sales are made where payments extend over a long period of time. Long-term receivables are frequently evidenced by *notes,* reflected on the seller's books as *notes receivable.* In this situation, there is not only a sale to account for, but also long-term financing and the related interest revenue. Notes can be authorized for time periods less than one year or for extended time periods, perhaps two or three years or longer.

Simple Interest

We know from everyday experience that a dollar today is not equivalent to a dollar sometime in the future. If $1,000 is borrowed and will be repaid a year later, the amount to be repaid will be greater than $1,000. The additional amount to be repaid is the *interest* on the loan—the amount required by the lender to give up $1,000 today in exchange for the $1,000 a year later. The interest compensates the lender for:

1 Giving up the use of $1,000 for a year. (The lender could otherwise have spent it or invested it.)

2 The risk of not being repaid.

3 The risk of inflation. (The purchasing power of the $1,000 may be less a year from now than it is today.)

These three factors are commonly combined into a single *interest rate,* which is expressed as an annual percentage. In the example above, the lender might specify a 15 percent rate. At the end of the year, the total to be repaid would be $1,150 (the $1,000 originally borrowed, plus interest of 15 percent of $1,000, or $150).

Observe that interest rates are usually stated as *annual percentages.* Since the loan in the preceding example covered one year, the determination of the interest is straightforward. Multiply the amount of the loan ($1,000, often called the *principal*) by the annual interest rate (15 percent) to determine the amount of interest to be paid ($150).

For periods of time *other* than one year, multiply by the number of years or fraction of a year involved. Expressed as a formula, the computation is:

$$\text{Interest} = (\text{Principal}) \times (\text{Annual Interest Rate}) \times (\text{Number of Years or Fraction of a Year})$$

If, in the example, $1,000 had been borrowed for three months instead of a full year, the interest would be:

$$\text{Interest} = (\$1,000) \times (15\%) \times \left(\frac{3 \text{ months}}{12 \text{ months}}\right) = \$37.50$$

At the end of the three months, a total of $1,037.50 would be repaid.

The fraction of the year may be expressed in terms of months or in terms of days. When days are used, a 30-day month, 360-day year is sometimes assumed for convenience of calculation. For more exactness, a 365-day (or 366-day) year may be used. We will assume use of a 30-day month, 360-day year approach.

Interest-Bearing, Single-Payment Notes

When a company sells goods in exchange for a note receivable, revenue is earned from two sources. First, the sale of goods produces revenue. Second, the selling firm, by providing financing to the buyer, generates revenue in the form of interest. The income statement for the selling firm must show these separate classifications of revenue—sales revenue and interest revenue.

Saratoga Supply Company sells large construction equipment to contractors in exchange for notes receivable. One type of note arrangement the company uses is a note providing for payment of the principal and interest in a lump sum at the end of a specified time period. Assume a contractor buys a used road grader from Saratoga Supply on May 1, 1988 at a price of $30,000 and signs a one-year note. Interest at 18 percent is due when the note matures on May 1, 1989. The interest on the note is determined as follows:

$$\text{Interest} = (\text{Principal}) \times (\text{Annual Interest Rate}) \\ \times (\text{Number of Years or Fraction of a Year})$$

$$\$5,400 = \$30,000 \times 18\% \times 1 \text{ year}$$

On May 1, 1989 the contractor will pay $5,400 in interest plus the $30,000 principal to Saratoga Supply. Saratoga Supply records the sale on May 1, 1988 as follows:

1988			
May 1	Notes Receivable	30,000	
	Sales		30,000
	To record sale of road grader in exchange for one-year, 18% note.		

Interest revenue will be recorded as it is earned. If we assume that Saratoga Supply ends its accounting year on December 31, 1988, interest revenue of $3,600 (8/12 times $5,400 annual interest) will be recorded at year end by the following adjusting entry:

Dec. 31	Interest Receivable	3,600	
	Interest Revenue		3,600
	To record interest accrued from May 1 to Dec. 31, 1988 on $30,000, 18% note.		

On May 1, 1989, Saratoga Supply will receive a total of $35,400 cash representing $30,000 repayment of principal and $5,400 interest for one year. The preceding adjusting entry recognized $3,600 of the $5,400 interest as interest revenue (and interest receivable) in 1988. Thus only $1,800 is interest revenue to be recognized for the first four months of 1989 ($1,800 = $5,400 annual interest $\times$ 4/12).

Saratoga Supply's journal entry on May 1, 1989 to record collection of the principal and interest on the note would be:

1989			
May 1	Cash	35,400	
	Notes Receivable		30,000
	Interest Receivable		3,600
	Interest Revenue		1,800
	To record collection of $30,000 note and annual interest at 18%.		

Interest-Bearing Installment Notes

Another type of note arrangement that companies use is one providing for periodic payments of *both* interest and principal. While monthly payments are commonly employed, the following example illustrates annual payments for simplicity. Assume that on December 31, 1988, Saratoga Supply Company sells and delivers a bulldozer at a price of $38,830. The buyer signs a note agreeing to pay the $38,830 principal plus interest at 20 percent in four equal annual installments of $15,000 (the first payment is due one year later, on December 31, 1989).

The sales revenue of $38,830 is recorded at the time of delivery:

1988			
Dec. 31	Notes Receivable	38,830	
	Sales		38,830
	To record sale of bulldozer in exchange for 4-year, 20% installment note.		

On Saratoga Supply's 1988 statement of income, the $38,830 is the only revenue reported regarding this sale. Since the sale occurred on the last day of the year, no interest revenue was earned in 1988.

As each annual installment payment of $15,000 is received on the note, it is necessary to determine how much of the payment represents interest revenue and how much is a repayment of note principal. This is done as follows:

1 Calculate the amount of interest, multiplying the outstanding principal balance at the beginning of the period by the interest rate of 20 percent.

2 The remainder of the $15,000 annual payment is a principal payment.

Note that as the calculation is repeated, the interest portion of each payment gets smaller, while the principal portion of each payment gets larger. Over the life of the note, the outstanding principal balance is reduced to zero. The calculations are shown below, rounded to the nearest dollar:

Date	Interest payment (20% of principal balance)	Principal payment ($15,000 less interest payment)	Principal balance
12/31/88			$38,830
12/31/89	$ 7,766 (.20 × $38,830)	$ 7,234 ($15,000 − $7,766)	31,596
12/31/90	6,319 (.20 × $31,596)	8,681 ($15,000 − $6,319)	22,915
12/31/91	4,583 (.20 × $22,915)	10,417 ($15,000 − $4,583)	12,498
12/31/92	2,502*(.20 × $12,498)	12,498 ($15,000 − $2,502)	-0-
	$21,170	$38,830	

* $2 rounding error

The total interest of $21,170 and the principal of $38,830 equal the total payments of $60,000 ($15,000 × 4).

Once the calculation is complete, the journal entries are straightforward, as shown below (all entries are on December 31):

	1989	1990	1991	1992
Cash	15,000	15,000	15,000	15,000
Notes Receivable	7,234	8,681	10,417	12,498
Interest Revenue	7,766	6,319	4,583	2,502

To record installment
payment received and
interest earned for year.

Non-Interest-Bearing Notes

A special accounting problem arises when a note does not specify a rate of interest (or specifies an unreasonably low rate). For example, assume that on December 31, 1988 Saratoga Supply sells a dump truck in exchange for a three-year, non-interest-bearing note providing for a single payment of $25,000 on December 31, 1991. This is the only payment that Saratoga will receive. No one provides financing for free. Yet there is no explicit mention of interest in the terms of the note. Thus, *both* the true selling price *and* the three years' interest are contained in the $25,000 face value of the non-interest-bearing note. Assume that the true selling price of the dump truck is $17,795 and the remaining $7,205 of the $25,000 note represents three year's interest.[2]

Accountants typically record notes at their face value, and any "implicit" interest included in the face amount of the note is credited to unamortized discount. The unamortized discount account is a contra asset and is subtracted from the face value of the note on the balance sheet. Each year a portion of the unamortized discount is recognized as interest revenue. The amount of interest each year is determined by multiplying the carrying value of the note at the beginning of the year (face value minus unamortized discount balance) times the implicit interest rate on the note. If we assume an implicit interest rate of 12 percent on the $25,000 non-interest-bearing note received by Saratoga Supply, the determination of annual interest revenue is presented in the following table:

Date	Discount to be amortized and interest revenue (12% of carrying value of note at beginning of year)	Carrying value of note (face value minus unamortized discount on note)
12/31/88		$25,000 − $7,205 = $17,795
12/31/89	$2,135 (12% × $17,795)	25,000 − 5,070 = 19,930
12/31/90	2,392 (12% × $19,930)	25,000 − 2,678 = 22,322
12/31/91	2,678 (12% × $22,322)	25,000 − -0- = 25,000
	$7,205	

The journal entry to record the sale of the equipment and the receipt of the non-interest-bearing note would be:

[2]We will defer consideration of the techniques for calculating the true selling price of the truck and the implicit interest until a later chapter.

1988			
Dec. 31	Note Receivable	25,000	
	Unamortized Discount on		
	Note Receivable		7,205
	Sales		17,795
	To record sale of dump truck in		
	exchange for three-year,		
	non-interest-bearing note.		

Based on the table on page 154, the annual journal entries to amortize the discount and record interest revenue would be:

	1989		1990		1991	
Unamortized Discount						
on Note Receivable	2,135		2,392		2,678	
Interest Revenue		2,135		2,392		2,678
To record implicit interest						
earned on non-interest-						
bearing note.						

The journal entry on December 31, 1988 properly records sales revenue of $17,795—the true selling price of the equipment. The remaining $7,205 implicit interest included in the face value of the non-interest-bearing note is recorded as interest revenue over the three-year life of the note. The carrying value of the note (face value minus unamortized discount) is increased each year because of the decrease in the unamortized discount. At maturity, the unamortized discount is zero and the note would be shown at $25,000—its true value on that date.

Note in the above example that the accounting for the note differed from its legal form. The note specifically said "non-interest-bearing." However, accountants reflect the true economic substance of the transaction, not its legal form, and recognize the implicit interest on the note.

Dishonored Notes Receivable

If the maker of a note fails to pay the holder of the note on the maturity date, the note is said to be *dishonored*. The holder of the note still has a claim against the maker, but the note itself has expired. A typical procedure followed by the holder of a dishonored note is to transfer the note from the notes receivable account to an account titled "Dishonored Notes Receivable." However, since the maker has already failed to make payment when the note was due, there may be considerable doubt about the collectibility of the dishonored note. An adequate allowance for uncollectible notes should be established for dishonored notes (as well as notes still outstanding). An adequate allowance is needed so that the notes are presented at net realizable value (i.e., the amount actually expected to be collected).

FINANCIAL STATEMENT PRESENTATION

We have addressed the manner in which revenues from sales and interest are recorded. This section considers how these items appear on the financial statements.

Statement of Income

In a very detailed income statement gross sales revenue is shown first, followed by the various adjustments, as follows:

Sales		$1,200,000
Less:		
Sales Discounts	$15,000	
Sales Returns and Allowances	46,000	61,000
Net Sales		$1,139,000

The account Bad Debt Expense usually appears in the expense section of the income statement although it may be treated as a reduction of sales revenue. Sales discounts and sales returns and allowances are always treated as reductions of sales revenue, *not* as expenses. Most income statements are not as detailed as in the above illustration. In a more condensed form, only the $1,139,000 Net Sales would be shown. Interest revenue is usually classified as other revenues (or "other income") on the income statement.

Balance Sheet

The account on the balance sheet which is most affected by revenue accounting is accounts receivable. This asset is usually classified as a current asset, since receivables are typically due within one year. The contra asset account Allowance for Uncollectible Accounts serves to reduce the reported value of accounts receivable to a net amount that the firm actually expects to collect (i.e., net realizable value). The allowance for uncollectible accounts is shown as a deduction from accounts receivable, as follows:

Accounts Receivable	$340,000	
Less: Allowance for Uncollectible Accounts	18,000	$322,000

A shorter version of this presentation would show the allowance for uncollectible accounts parenthetically, as follows:

Accounts Receivable (net of Allowance for Uncollectible Accounts of $18,000)	$322,000

Notes receivable are presented on the balance sheet in a manner similar to accounts receivable. An allowance for uncollectible notes may be established, similar to the allowance for uncollectible accounts. If notes receivable are minor in amount, they may be combined with accounts receivable and presented on the balance sheet as accounts and notes receivable. Otherwise, a separate notes receivable line is used, either preceding or following accounts receivable.

SUMMARY

The determination of revenue earned is the starting point in the process of measuring income. This chapter has presented several topics concerning revenue, revenue adjustments, interest, and related balance sheet accounts.

Learning Objective 1: Record sales revenue and related charges to customers.

Sales revenue is normally recorded at the time goods or services are delivered to the customer. Either cash or receivables is debited, depending on the manner of customer payment. In addition to the price of the goods, related charges are recorded in different ways—as additional revenue (postage and handling charges), expense reductions (freight charges), or liabilities (sales tax).

Learning Objective 2: Record adjustments to sales revenue.

Sales are recorded at time of delivery. Events may occur after delivery that will reduce the amount of recorded revenue. Returns, allowances, cash discounts, and bad debts are four common adjustments to the sales transaction that occur after the sale.

Learning Objective 3: Apply the direct write-off and allowance methods for bad debts.

An important issue is the *timing* of recording bad debts. The direct write-off method records the bad debt expense when a specific customer account is known to be uncollectible. This usually does not occur in the same time period as the sale. Hence, the direct write-off method may violate the matching rule.

The allowance method estimates and records bad debts in the period of sale. The estimate is calculated either as a percentage of credit sales or as a percentage of accounts receivable.

While logically an adjustment of sales revenue, *bad debt expense* is usually classified as an expense item on the income statement. On the balance sheet, the *allowance for uncollectible accounts* is subtracted from accounts receivable to show the receivables at net realizable value.

Learning Objective 4: Account for notes receivable and related interest.

When a customer's promise to pay takes the form of a *note,* interest is involved. The amount of interest revenue must be calculated and recorded using the accrual basis. This process becomes more complex when the note involves several principal payments (an *installment note*) or is a non-interest-bearing note.

KEY TERMS

Aging the accounts	Discounting a note receivable
Allowance for uncollectible accounts	(Appendix)
Allowance method for uncollectible	Dishonored notes receivable
accounts	Installment notes

Bad debt expense
Cash discount
Contingent liability (Appendix)
Contra account
Direct write-off method for
   uncollectible accounts
Installment sales method (Appendix)

Interest
Maturity value (Appendix)
Non-interest-bearing note
Percentage of completion (Appendix)
Realization rule
Sales returns

APPENDIX: Revenue Recognition—Special Cases

As emphasized earlier, revenue is most commonly recorded (recognized) at the time of delivery. The point at which a product or service is delivered to (and accepted by) the customer usually satisfies the criteria that (1) the major efforts necessary to make a sale have been completed and (2) any remaining events can be predicted with reasonable accuracy. In some circumstances, however, these criteria are met at an earlier or later time. Two exceptions to the general rule of recording revenue upon delivery are recording revenue during production (*prior to* delivery) or upon collection of cash (*after* delivery).

PRODUCTION BASIS

Recording of revenue at the *time of production* is appropriate if it can be demonstrated that production is the *last significant event* the firm must accomplish in order to make a sale. There must be very little uncertainty surrounding any subsequent events, such as delivery to (and acceptance by) a customer, collection of the selling price, and generation of additional costs.

In the construction industry, work is generally done *under contract*. That is, the buyer-seller agreement is confirmed *before* production begins. The construction firm contracts to build a certain project (a commercial building, a highway, a sewer pipeline, and so on). The details of the project, including the price, are agreed upon in advance. Contrast this situation to that of merchandising and manufacturing firms where goods are purchased or produced first and then later sold to customers. In the construction industry, the contract assures sale, and the earning process is substantially complete once the construction is accomplished. Under these circumstances, it is reasonable to argue that revenue should be recorded once production is complete because all the major earnings functions have been performed.

By accepting the production basis as an appropriate way to measure revenue from construction contracts, a question of timing develops. It is not unusual for a construction project to require several years. The revenue from the project pertains to several annual reporting periods; it must be allocated appropriately to the years of construction.

The *percentage of completion method,* commonly used in the construction industry, records as annual revenue the value of production completed during the year. If, for example, half of a certain project is completed in one year, then half the revenue should be recorded on the year's income statement. The procedures for percentage of completion accounting are covered in advanced courses.

CASH COLLECTION BASIS

Recall again the criteria for recording revenue: (1) the major activities necessary to achieve a sale must have been performed and (2) any remaining acitivities must be capable of being estimated with reasonable accuracy. Normally, these criteria are met at time of delivery. In a few cases, the criteria may not be met until *the time that cash is collected*. (Assume for this discussion that cash collection occurs *after* the delivery of the product or service.)

Cash-basis accounting is acceptable only if collection is a significant (nonroutine) element in the process of making a sale, and the occurrence of collection is quite uncertain. Because this description fits very few businesses, the cash basis is rarely an appropriate way of recording revenue. Two situations where this method is appropriately employed are briefly discussed below.

Professionals who provide services on credit to the general public (doctors and dentists are prime examples) often employ cash-basis accounting on the grounds that their risk of noncollection is quite high and is difficult to estimate with reasonable accuracy. This was perhaps more of a problem in past times before the widespread development of medical insurance plans. Nonetheless, in their type of business, revenues are generally recorded when collected.

Some dealers who sell durable goods (refrigerators, automobiles, and so on) to the general public on long-term credit use cash collection as the basis of recording revenue. Perhaps the buyer will pay for the purchase in monthly installments over a period of two or three years. In this type of business, the risk of noncollection may be very high. Here a special form of cash-basis accounting, known as the *installment sales method*, is available. Generally accepted accounting principles permit the use of the installment sales method only under *very limited circumstances*. Specifically, there must be a very high degree of uncertainty that the sales price will be collected.

In many cases where goods are sold on long-term credit, the risk of noncollection *can* be estimated. For instance, an appliance store might evaluate a customer's credit history before granting credit. The store is reasonably sure of collection and would record the sales revenue in the period of delivery even though cash collection was much later.

Where the installment method is appropriate because the risk of noncollection is high and is difficult to estimate, a *portion* of sales revenue is recorded at the time each installment payment is collected.

APPENDIX: Discounting Notes Receivable

Some firms receive notes from their customers and then sell the notes to banks or finance companies. Selling a note receivable provides the firm with cash prior to the maturity date of the note. The process of selling a note is commonly called *discounting a note receivable*. The firm holding the note transfers ownership of it to the bank by endorsing the note and then delivering it to the bank. Endorsement is made when an authorized person signs the company's name on the reverse side of the note. The endorsement creates a *contingent liability* for the firm. The liability is contingent because it depends on a future event. If the maker of the note fails to pay the bank the maturity value on the due date, the contingent liability becomes a real liability for the firm that discounted the note. The bank can demand payment from the endorser (the firm) if the maker (the customer) defaults. If the maker pays the bank, the potential liability is eliminated.

PROCEEDS OF DISCOUNTED NOTE

The proceeds of a discounted note are the amount of cash received from the bank in exchange for the note. In calculating the proceeds, several steps are followed:

1 Determine the maturity value of the note. The maturity value is the amount owed by the maker on the due date. The maturity value includes the principal amount of the note plus interest from the date the note was written to the due date (assume it is a single payment note). The interest rate is stated on the note.

2 Calculate the bank's interest charge. The bank's interest rate (which may differ from the interest rate stated on the note) is applied to the maturity value of the note for the period of time from the date the note was discounted until the due date of the note. This is the period of time the bank's money is being lent.

3 Determine the cash proceeds by subtracting the bank's interest charge (Step 2) from the maturity value (Step 1).

To illustrate, consider the following situation:

On May 2, Roberts Company sells land for $100,000 and receives a 90-day, 20 percent note from the customer. The note matures on July 31.

On July 1, Roberts discounts the note at a bank. The bank's interest rate is 18 percent and is applied to the maturity value of the note for the 30 days remaining before the due date.

The cash proceeds of the note is $103,425 as calculated below:

1 Determine the maturity value of the note.

$$
\begin{aligned}
\text{Maturity Value} &= \text{Interest} + \text{Principal} \\
&= (\text{Principal} \times \text{Interest Rate} \times \text{Fraction of Year}) + \text{Principal} \\
&= (\$100,000 \times .20 \times 90/360) + \$100,000 \\
&= \$5,000 + \$100,000 \\
&= \$105,000
\end{aligned}
$$

2 Calculate the bank's interest charge.

$$\text{Bank's Interest} = \text{Maturity Value} \times \text{Bank Interest Rate} \times \text{Fraction of Year}$$
$$= \$105,000 \times .18 \times 30/360$$
$$= \$1,575$$

3 Determine the cash proceeds by subtracting the bank's interest charge from the maturity value.

$$\text{Cash Proceeds} = \$105,000 \text{ (Maturity Value)} - \$1,575 \text{ (Bank Interest)}$$
$$= \$103,425$$

A diagram of the discounting of the note would show:

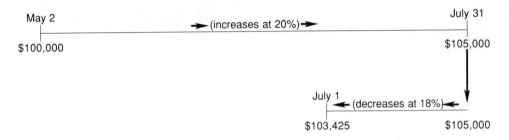

The journal entry to record the discounting of the note is:

July	1	Cash	103,425	
		Notes Receivable		100,000
		Interest Revenue		3,425
		To record cash proceeds from discounting $100,000, 90-day, 20% note at bank.		

Since the cash proceeds exceed the principal amount of the note, Roberts records the excess as interest revenue. It is possible that the cash proceeds could be less than the principal of the note. In such situations the difference would be treated as interest expense.

DISHONORING OF DISCOUNTED NOTES RECEIVABLE

If the maker of the note pays the bank on the due date, Roberts Company makes no journal entry. However, if the maker defaults and Roberts is forced to pay the maturity value to the bank, the entry by Roberts would be:

July 31	Dishonored Notes Receivable	105,000	
	Cash		105,000
	To record payment to bank for dishonored note.		

Roberts has a right to collect, from the maker who defaulted on the note, the amount that Roberts was required to pay the bank. The dishonored notes receivable account is an asset. An adequate allowance must be established for noncollectibility.

REVIEW QUESTIONS

1 Under the accrual basis of accounting, when should revenue be recognized?
2 Explain the sales terms "2/10, n/30." If the customer pays the reduced amount allowable within the discount period, what amount is still owed by the customer?
3 With terms of "1/15, n/45," a customer who fails to pay the reduced amount by the 15th day has an additional 30 days (until the 45th day) to pay the full amount. The 1 percent additional amount due for postponing payment for the 30 days represents approximately what *annual* rate of interest? (Hint: How many 30-day periods at 1 percent are there in a 360-day year?)
4 Marston Company has recorded a sale on account for 3,000 sets of pillow cases to Green's Dept. Store for $4,800. Green's Dept. Store refuses to accept the shipment from Marston because the items shipped are defective. Marston agrees the items are defective and instructs Green's Dept. Store to return them for full credit. What is the proper journal entry on Marston's books to record the customer's refusal to accept the shipment? What type of account is sales returns and where is it found on the financial statements?
5 Distinguish between the "direct write-off method" and "allowance method" for handling bad debts. Which method would you recommend? Why?
6 Squareton Co., which uses the allowance method for recording bad debts, wrote off the $320 account of George Mack, a customer whose account was deemed uncollectible. What was the journal entry to write off Mack's account? What effect will the write-off entry have on the statement of income, on total assets, on net accounts receivable?
7 If George Mack inherits a substantial sum from a long-lost aunt and decides to pay the $320 he owes Squareton Co. (which Squareton has written off as uncollectible in Question 6), what journal entries should Squareton make upon receipt of the $320?
8 Is it possible for a *debit* balance to exist temporarily in the allowance for uncollectible accounts? Explain.
9 Interim, Inc. would like an estimate of bad debts on its monthly financial statements. However, the company does not want to spend the time each month to age the individual customer accounts receivable. What alternatives are available to Interim to provide a monthly estimate of bad debts without performing an aging of the accounts receivable?
10 Vision Aid, Inc.'s aging of its accounts receivable on June 30, 1988 indicated a $24,250 balance was needed in the Allowance for Uncollectible Accounts. If the Allowance already has a credit balance of $20,750 as a result of entries prior to June 30, 1988, what journal entry would be needed on June 30? If the credit balance in the Allowance account had been $33,650, what journal entry would be needed on June 30?
11 What is "interest"? What factors are combined into a single stated interest rate?
12 Poor, Inc. borrowed $3,000 on February 1, 1988. The annual interest rate was 8 percent. If the loan is to be repaid on June 1, 1988, what is the total amount to be repaid including both principal and interest (use a 360-day year)?

13 Differentiate between an interest-bearing, single-payment note and an interest-bearing installment note.

14 Brighton Sales Co. sold a moving van on Janaury 2, 1989 for $26,645. The buyer signed a note agreeing to pay the $26,645 principal, plus interest at 9 percent annually, in five equal annual installments (beginning on December 31, 1989). The amount of each annual installment is $6,850. How much interest revenue (rounded to nearest dollar) should Brighton record in 1989, in 1990?

15 On January 2, 1988, Mandi Machine Company sold a machine to Marx, Inc. Mandi offered the following alternative terms: (a) $100,000 cash payment on January 2, 1988 or (b) two-year, non-interest-bearing $121,000 face value note maturing on December 31, 1989. If Marx elects to give Mandi the $121,000 note (rather than the $100,000 cash payment), how much sales revenue should Mandi record in 1988?

16 Which of the following accounts appear on a detailed income statement: a) allowance for uncollectible accounts, b) sales discounts, c) sales taxes payable, d) interest revenue, e) sales returns, f) notes receivable, and g) bad debt expense?

17 (Appendix) Wolfbane Construction Company began construction of a castle in Transylvania in 1855, after signing a contract with a wealthy duke. The construction is expected to take several years to complete. What method of accounting should be used to record revenue on the castle project?

18 (Appendix) What circumstances would justify use of the cash basis of recording revenue? Although it is rarely an appropriate way of recording revenue, list two situations where the cash basis is sometimes used.

19 (Appendix) What is a discounted note receivable? How are the cash proceeds of a discounted note calculated?

20 (Appendix) Describe the contingent liability that arises when a firm discounts a note receivable.

EXERCISES

E5-1 Slipshot Co.'s sales for July were composed of: a) cash sales of $8,000, b) sales on account of $106,000, and c) credit card sales of $50,000. Slipshot deposited the credit card slips into its bank account. The bank immediately credited Slipshot's account for the amount of the credit card slips less a 6 percent credit card fee. Prepare journal entries for each of the three types of sales.

E5-2 Presented below are September, 1989 sales data for Gullifties, Co.:
Sept. 4—Sale to Kellers Co. for $5,000
Sept. 5—Sale to Rex, Inc. for $2,000
Sept. 12—Kellers Co. paid amount due
Sept. 20—Rex, Inc. paid amount due
Sept. 26—Sale to Briarpatch, Inc. for $8,000
Terms of all sales are 5/10, n/30.

Required:
1 Determine how much cash was collected in September.
2 Present the revenue section of Gullifties' statement of income for the month ended September 30, 1989.
3 Calculate the approximate annual rate of interest associated with sales terms of

5/10, n/30. (Hint: how many 20-day periods at 5 percent are there in a 360-day year?)

E5-3   Lonknee Company offers terms of 2/10, n/30 on all sales on account. Present journal entries on Lonknee's books to record each of the following:
1 Sale on account for $2,000 to Marx, Inc. Sale made July 2.
2 Sale on account for $5,000 to Parker, Inc. Sale made July 3.
3 Payment of $1,960 received on July 12 from Marx, Inc.
4 On July 12 reduced by $4,000 the amount due from Parker, Inc. because most of the items shipped on July 3 were defective.
5 Received $1,000 payment on August 1 from Parker, Inc.

E5-4   Humptey's balance sheet showed the following on December 31, 1989:

Accounts Receivable	$124,800
Less: Allowance for Uncollectible Accounts	11,200

During 1990:
1 Sales on account were $1,500,000. No cash discounts are offered.
2 Humptey's used a rate of 1 percent of sales on account as an estimate of the amount of sales that probably will prove uncollectible.
3 Specific customer accounts that proved uncollectible and were written off totaled $14,400.
On December 31, 1990, the balance in accounts receivable is $140,000. Calculate: (1) cash collected from customers during 1990, (2) the bad debt expense on the 1990 statement of income, and (3) the balance in the account Allowance for Uncollectible Accounts on December 31, 1990.

E5-5   A partially completed aging of Scotch, Inc.'s accounts receivable on December 31, 1988 yields the following:

Age category	Total accounts	Estimated uncollectible percentage
Current	$400,000	1/2%
Less than 60 days past due	220,000	1%
60 days to 6 months past due	55,000	5%
Over 6 months past due	21,000	10%
	$696,000	

Complete the aging analysis and determine the balance that should be in the allowance for uncollectible accounts on December 31, 1988. If the allowance for uncollectible accounts has a $3,500 credit balance as a result of entries prior to December 31, 1988, present the journal entry to adjust the allowance account to the balance required by the aging analysis.

E5-6   Yojo Manufacturing Co. sells coal mining equipment. On January 2, 1988 the company sold two items to coal mine operators. For both sales, Yojo Manufacturing received notes. Details of the two sales were as follows:

Item sold	Sales price	Terms of note
Coal mole	$170,000	One-year, single payment note, 6% annual interest, note due on December 31.
Shaft elevator	231,145	Six-year installment note with principal and interest (at 8% annual rate) payable in six equal annual installments of $50,000 each December 31.

Required:

1 Determine for each item sold the sales revenue to be recorded by Yojo Manufacturing in 1988 and the interest revenue to be recognized on each note in 1988 and 1989. (Round all calculations to nearest dollar.)

2 Prepare journal entries for Yojo Manufacturing Co. on: 1) January 2, 1988 (date of sale) and 2) December 31, 1988 (end of first annual interest period). The company's accounting year ends December 31.

E5-7   Strochman Equipment Co. sold on December 31, 1987 a piece of equipment and received in exchange a three-year, non-interest-bearing note. The face value of the note is $13,000. The equivalent cash sales price is $9,767. Thus, as of 12/31/87 the discount on the note is $3,233 ($13,000 − $9,767). The interest rate implicit in the note is 10 percent. Complete the following table showing interest revenue for 1989 and 1990. (Round all amounts to nearest dollar.)

Date	Discount to be amortized and interest revenue (10% of carrying value of note at beginning of year)	Carrying value of note (face value minus unamortized discount on note)
12/31/87		$13,000 − $3,233 = $9,767
12/31/88	$977 (10% × $9,767)	?
12/31/89	?	?
12/31/90	?	?
Total	?	

E5-8   Presented below, in alphabetical order, are selected account balances as of June 30, 1989 for Done & Broadstreet Co. Select the appropriate accounts and prepare: a) the revenue section (in detail) of the income statement for the year ended June 30, 1989, and b) the accounts receivable section of the June 30, 1989 balance sheet.

$ 64,900	Accounts Payable
173,000	Accounts Receivable
22,000	Advertising Expense
4,800	Allowance for Uncollectible Accounts
39,250	Cash
13,200	Repairs Expense
984,000	Sales
15,500	Sales Discounts
10,000	Sales Returns
18,000	Sales Taxes Payable

E5-9 (Appendix) The following notes are discounted by Ace Company at the bank:

	Principal	Interest rate on note	Date of note	Length of note	Date discounted	Bank's rate of interest
(a)	$5,000	10%	1/2/88	45 days	2/1/88	12%
(b)	$8,000	12%	6/1/88	90 days	7/31/88	9%

Required:
1 Calculate the cash proceeds for each note. Use a 360-day year.
2 For note (a) present the journal entry made by Ace Company to record the discounting of the note. Also present the journal entry Ace would record if the maker of the note defaults and Ace must pay the maturity value to the bank on February 16, 1988.

PROBLEMS

P5-1 *Recording Cash and Credit Sales*
The Bottoms Up Beverage Co. sells cases of beer and soft drinks to customers. Customers are allowed to pay by cash, by credit card, or on account (no cash discounts). State law requires Bottoms Up Beverage to charge customers 5 percent sales tax. There is no deposit required on cases sold since plastic "throw-away" bottles are used exclusively. Sales for February 1989, *exclusive* of sales taxes were:

Cash sales	$16,000
Credit card sales	$ 2,500
Sales on account	$ 1,000

Credit card charge slips are mailed to the credit card company at the end of each month. During the following month the credit card company mails Bottoms Up Beverage a check for the amount of the charge slips less a 4 percent fee. The 4 percent fee is based on the total of sales plus sales taxes.

Required:
Prepare separate journal entries to record 1) cash sales, 2) credit card sales, and 3) sales on account. Include in each entry the sales tax.

P5-2 *Sales Discounts–Net Price Method*
The Castleman Sales Company follows a different procedure in accounting for sales discounts from the one described in the text. Anticipating that most customers will take the discount, Castleman records sales revenue initially at net price (invoice price minus discount). If a customer does not take the discount, the entry at time of collection records additional revenue under the title "Other Revenue— Lapsed Discounts."

Assume that on April 3, 1989, Castleman makes three sales, all on terms of 3/10, n/30, as follows:

Customer	Invoice price
X	$10,000
Y	15,000
Z	20,000

Customer X pays on April 8, customer Y on May 2, and customer Z on April 12.

Required:
1 Record the above transactions using the procedure described at the beginning of the problem.
2 Record the above transactions using the procedure described in the chapter.
3 What is the difference in net income between the two procedures?

 Sales, Accounts Receivable, and Uncollectible Accounts
P5-3 Real Pure Co. began operations on Janaury 1, 1988. Sales during 1988 totaled $480,000. Sixty percent of 1988's sales were on account and the remainder were cash sales. No cash discounts were offered. Real Pure has adopted the industry average of 1 percent of credit sales as its estimate of bad debts. On December 31, 1988, the Accounts Receivable balance was $40,000. No specific customer accounts were written off as uncollectible in 1988.

During 1989 sales totaled $560,000, including cash sales of $220,000. During 1989 customer accounts totaling $290,000 were collected and $2,650 of receivable were written off as uncollectible.

Required:
1 Determine the cash received from collection of accounts receivable in 1988.
2 Prepare all journal entries for both 1988 and 1989 related to sales and accounts receivable.
3 Present the accounts receivable section of Real Pure's balance sheet as of December 31, 1989.
4 Compare the bad debt expense obtained in 1988 and 1989 using the allowance method with the deduction that would have been obtained if the direct write-off method had been used by Real Pure.
5 If $500 of the accounts receivable written off by Real Pure in 1989 are subsequently collected, what are the journal entries required?

P5-4 *Accounting for Uncollectible Accounts*
Flopflip Co. uses both the percentage of sales method and the aging of accounts method of estimating bad debts. At the end of each month, for purposes of preparing monthly financial statements, Flopflip estimates bad debts for the month at 1/2 percent of net credit sales for that month. At the end of the year a detailed aging of accounts receivable is made and the allowance account adjusted accordingly.
Selected information available shows:

Accounts Receivable, December 31, 1987	$179,000
Allowance for Uncollectible Accounts,	
December 31, 1987	2,120
Sales Revenue—each month (all sales	
on account)	76,000

Sales Returns—each month	2,000
Accounts Receivable written off during 1988	3,000
Aging of accounts on December 31, 1988 indicates an Allowance balance of $2,400 is needed.	

Required:

1 Present journal entries for: a) the monthly estimate during 1988 of bad debts (present entry for only 1 month, other 11 monthly entries would be identical), b) the write-off of uncollectible accounts during 1988, and c) the December 31, 1988 adjustment of the Allowance account to the balance indicated by the aging analysis.

2 After the journal entries in part (1) are posted, what would be the balances, if determinable, in each of the following accounts: a) bad debt expense, b) allowance for uncollectible accounts, and c) accounts receivable?

P5-5 *Accounting for Notes Receivable*

1 Green Manufacturing Co. sells bulldozers to highway construction companies. On August 31, 1988, Green Manufacturing sold a bulldozer at a price of $27,000. The purchaser signed a one-year, single payment note. Interest, at 10 percent, is due at maturity.

Required:

Assuming Green Manufacturing's accounting year ends on December 31, present journal entries to record the sale, interest earned, and collection of the note and interest at maturity.

2 Koufax Car Sales, Inc. sells new and used cars. On January 2, 1989, the company sold a used Cadillac at a sales price of $15,009. The buyer paid $3,000 cash and signed an installment note agreeing to pay the $12,009 remainder, plus interest at 12 percent, in three equal annual installments of $5,000 (beginning on December 31, 1989).

Required:

Assuming Koufax Car Sales' accounting year ends on December 31, present journal entries to record the sale and receipt of the three equal annual installment payments.

P5-6 *Non-Interest-Bearing Note*

On January 2, 1988 Convos Co. sold machinery and received a three-year, non-interest-bearing note in exchange. The note had a face value of $8,005. The January 2, 1988 cash sales price of the machinery would have been $6,721. The implicit rate of interest on the note is 6 percent. Convos' accounting year ends on December 31.

Required:

1 Prepare a table showing interest earned annually. In preparing the table follow the format shown in the "Non-Interest-Bearing Notes" section of the chapter. Round all amounts to the nearest dollar.

2 Present journal entries to record the sale of the machinery, interest earned each year, and collection of the note at maturity.

P5-7 *Classification of Accounts*

Complete the chart below by placing check marks (√) in the appropriate columns for each ledger account listed. The first one is done as an example.

	Account balance							
Ledger account	Debit	Credit	Asset	Contra asset	Liability	Revenue	Contra revenue (i.e., sales adjustments)	Expense
Cash	√		√					
Freight Expense								
Sales Discounts								
Interest Revenue								
Other Revenue— Freight								
Sales								
Bad Debt Expense								
Sales Returns								
Sales Taxes Payable								
Credit Card Fee Exp.								
Accounts Receivable								
Allowance for Uncollectible Accounts								

*(Heading for the last group of columns: **Account classification**)*

P5-8 *Journal Entries, Ledger Accounts, and Financial Statements*

Crawdad Co. began operations on January 1, 1986. The company raises and sells live catfish to restaurants. General ledger accounts on January 1, 1988, arranged in alphabetical order, were:

Accounts Payable	$17,900
Accounts Receivable	38,200
Capital Stock, 2,200 shares	22,000
Cash	12,500
Inventory	40,000
Retained Earnings	50,800

During January, 1988 the following events transpired:

1 Sales of catfish to restaurants totaled $87,000. All sales were on account with terms of 2/10, n/30. In addition to the $87,000 sales, customers were billed $4,000 for freight charges on delivering the catfish to the restaurants.

2 The cost of the catfish sold was $22,000. (Debit Cost of Goods Sold and credit Inventory.)

3 Cash received from customers during January totaled $93,100. Sales discounts related to cash received from customers paying within the discount period totaled $1,520.

4 One customer was dissatisfied with the catfish received. Upon the return of the catfish, Crawdad reduced the customer's account receivable by $800. The $200 cost of the catfish was returned to inventory.

5 Crawdad paid $48,000 to Glendale Fish Hatchery for use of their facilities and delivery truck for January.

6 Salaries of $4,600 earned by Crawdad's employees during January were paid in cash.

7 Income tax expense for January was $3,800.

Required:

1 Prepare journal entries for January, 1988. Do not prepare closing entries. Treat freight charged to customers as other revenue. Label as journal page 118.

2 Open general ledger accounts using three-column, running balance format. Enter January 1, 1988 balances, and post January's journal entries from part (1). Arrange general ledger accounts in normal financial statement sequence and assign ledger account numbers as follows:

assets—100s
liabilities—200s
permanent stockholders' equity—300s
revenue—400s and
expenses—500s

3 Prepare a detailed statement of income for January, 1988.

4 Prepare a statement of retained earnings for January, 1988.

5 Prepare a balance sheet as of January 31, 1988.

P5-9   (Appendix) *Accrual Basis versus Cash Basis*

Doctor Healer, M. D., is a surgeon who specializes in tonsillectomies. Doctor Healer opened a new practice in Grove City in 1988. The following list summarizes the activities concerning Doctor Healer's new Grove City practice during 1988:

1 Doctor Healer performed 28 tonsillectomies at a standard fee of $4,000 each. One-half of the operations were covered by patients' medical insurance. The insurance companies have paid Doctor Healer for 12 of the 14 operations covered by insurance. Payment for the other two operations covered by insurance is expected early in 1989.

2 Of the remaining one-half of the operations that were not covered by insurance, nine patients have paid in full, four out of the five other patients are expected to pay in 1989, with one patient's bill believed uncollectible.

3 On January 3, 1988, Doctor Healer paid $17,000 cash to R & S Insurance Company for malpractice insurance coverage for the year.

4 Doctor Healer maintains an office and performs his operations at Central Hospital. Office rent is $20,000 per year. On January 4, 1988, Doctor Healer paid $40,000 rent covering both 1988 and 1989. Central Hospital also charges a fee of $500 per operation for use of its operating room. As of December 31, 1988, Doctor Healer still owed the hospital the operating room fee for six operations.

Required:

1 Determine Doctor Healer's income from the Grove City practice in 1988 (ignore income taxes).

2 Many physicians, dentists, and other professionals use cash-basis accounting. With cash-basis accounting, revenue is recorded when the cash is collected for the goods sold or services rendered. Expenses are recorded under cash-basis accounting when the cash payments are made. What would income from the Grove City practice be in 1988 if Doctor Healer used cash-basis accounting?

P5-10 (Appendix) *Discounting Notes Receivable*

Morton Appliance Company sells small and large appliances. For customers not paying cash, the company will accept a 90-day, single payment note. Frequently the company discounts the notes before maturity at the local bank. During the second half of 1988 the following selected transactions occurred:

1 July 1—sold a refrigerator to Carmen Johnson for $1,300. Customer signed 90-day, 10 percent note.

2 August 15—sold television to Randolph Manteeth for $900. Customer signed 90-day, 12 percent note.

3 September 14—discounted the Manteeth note at the bank. Bank's interest rate is 10 percent.

4 September 15—sold washer and dryer to Sue Foster for $1,200. Customer signed 90-day, 12 percent note.

5 September 29—Carmen Johnson paid note including interest.

6 September 30—discounted the Foster note at the bank. Bank's interest rate is 9 percent.

7 October 16—sold freezer to Mary Morris for $800. Customer signed 90-day, 12 percent note.

8 November 13—Manteeth note matured and Manteeth paid the bank the maturity value of the note.

9 December 14—Foster note matured and Foster defaulted. Morton Appliance Company paid the maturity value of the note to the bank.

Required:

1 Prepare journal entries for the above transactions.

2 Prepare an adjusting entry to record accrued interest earned as of December 31, 1988, the end of the company's accounting year. (Note: Use a 360-day year for all interest calculations.)

Business Decision Problem

Sachs Industries began operations on January 2, 1988. The company sells pianos. Three alternative payment terms are offered to customers.

1 $1,530 credit sales price with terms of 2/10; n/30, or

2 $1,500 cash price at delivery, or

3 Three-year, non-interest-bearing note with $2,000 face value.

Sachs has divided the company into geographical regions. Accounting policies have not as yet been dictated by headquarters, and the regional managers have selected their own. Accounting policies selected and other information for 1988 are summarized by geographical region in the following table:

Eastern region	**Western region**
Sales:	Sales:
1. 30 pianos sold on account (27 paid within discount period)	1. 25 pianos sold on account (22 paid within discount period)
2. 12 pianos sold for cash	2. 10 pianos sold for cash
3. 10 pianos sold on three-year, non-interest-bearing notes	3. 17 pianos sold on three-year, non-interest-bearing notes

Accounting Policies:

1. Records $1,500 sales revenue for each note sale and recognizes interest over the life of the note.

2. Estimates bad debts using the allowance method. Uses industry average of 2 percent of gross credit sales and 5 percent of the face value of note sales as estimate of bad debts expense for year.

Accounting Policies:

1. Records face value of note as sales revenue when the note is signed. Ignores implicit interest.

2. Uses direct write-off method for bad debts. During 1988, $450 of specific accounts proved uncollectible.

Assume the Eastern region earned $750 implicit interest on the notes during 1988.

Required:

1 Prepare partial income statements for 1988 for both regions using the information presented above.

2 Since each region sold a total of 52 pianos during 1988, analyze the reasons for the differing partial income statements. Discuss what impact the choice of accounting methods had on income.

3 Discuss whether future years' income statements will be affected by the accounting treatment selected by the regional managers for 1988's transactions.

6

COST OF GOODS SOLD
AND INVENTORY
ACCOUNTING

LEARNING OBJECTIVES

When you complete this chapter, you should be able to:

1   Account for the purchase of merchandise for resale.
2   Apply the gross price and net price methods for cash discounts on purchases.
3   Distinguish between periodic and perpetual inventory systems.
4   Define the specific identification, FIFO, LIFO, and weighted average methods for determining cost of goods sold and inventory.
5   Calculate cost of goods sold and inventory according to the FIFO, LIFO, and weighted average methods.
6   Calculate ending inventory by the gross profit and retail methods.
7   Apply the lower of cost or market rule to inventories.

The objective of income determination is to provide useful information to investors and creditors about how successful the business has been in increasing its wealth. The *matching* of costs with revenues is an important convention that influences many procedures used in measuring income. Chapter 5 discussed revenue accounting—the first element in the process of income determination. Through the next several chapters we will consider the other element needed to arrive at net income, the measurement of *expenses*—the costs consumed in generating revenue. That is, once the revenues for the period are identified, the expenses incurred in earning those revenues must be determined.

In most firms, the largest single expense category is the cost of providing the goods or services sold. In merchandising and manufacturing firms, the term *cost of goods sold* (or *cost of sales*) is normally used. Service firms generally use *cost of operations* in place of cost of goods sold. The particular items to be included in the cost of sales depend upon the nature of the activities by which the firm generates its revenues. These activities may be classified into three broad types:

1 Merchandising firms buy goods and resell them to others, with little or no additional processing of the goods. All wholesale and retail stores (for example, an auto parts store) fall into this category. For merchandising firms, the cost of sales consists primarily of the purchase cost of the merchandise sold during the period.

2 Manufacturing firms buy materials, and with the use of labor and machines, create new products (for example, an automobile manufacturer). For manufacturing firms, the cost of sales consists of: (a) the purchase cost of materials used in producing the items sold, (b) the cost of labor used in producing the items sold, and (c) other costs of carrying on the production activity (commonly referred to as *overhead*).

3 Service firms sell a service rather than a product. Examples include auto repair shops, accounting firms, and hospitals. For service firms, the cost of operations consists of: (a) the cost of labor used in producing the services, (b) the cost of any materials used, and (c) any other costs necessary to produce the services.

This chapter will deal primarily with the cost of sales for merchandising firms. Manufacturing and service firms are briefly covered in the appendix.

PURCHASES VS. COST OF GOODS SOLD

To determine its cost of sales for a period of time, a merchandising firm must determine the cost of the items that were *sold* during the period. Since most merchandising firms maintain inventories of goods, the cost of items *sold* during a period will be different from the cost of items *purchased* during that period. Consider, for example, a hardware store. During the year, it buys tools, paint, and other items to stock its shelves. In any given year, however, the amount of merchandise that the store *buys* is unlikely to equal the amount it *sells* to its customers.

Recall how purchases of merchandise and the cost of goods sold have been recorded in previous chapters. As purchases occurred, a debit was made to the inventory account. Then, following the recording of a sale, a cost of goods sold was determined, and an entry was made debiting cost of goods sold (an expense) and crediting inventory. This procedure of determining and recording cost of goods sold following each sales transaction is called a *perpetual inventory system*. We will first examine the perpetual inventory system, and then discuss an alternative, the periodic inventory system.

PERPETUAL INVENTORY SYSTEMS

To understand the operation of a very simple perpetual inventory system, consider the following series of transactions:

Purchases

Date	Number of units	Unit cost	Total purchase cost
January 6	2	$120	$240
10	1	135	135
20	1	140	140
27	1	170	170
		Total Purchases	$685

One unit was sold on January 11 and two units were sold on January 28. To determine cost of goods sold, we must decide which particular cost is to be associated with each sale. There are several possible methods of determining cost of goods sold; we will now consider two of these.

Specific Identification Method

It is possible that, for each sale, we can identify the *specific* units which were sold. If this is the case, we can then identify the cost of each of these items and charge it to cost of goods sold. This method is known as *specific identification*. For the data above, assume that each sale consists of the following:

January 11—sold the unit purchased for $135 on January 10
January 28—sold one of the units purchased for $120 on January 6 and the unit purchased for $140 on January 20

In T-account format, the entries to cost of goods sold would appear as follows:

Inventory				Cost of goods sold	
Jan. 6	240				
10	135				
		Jan. 11	135 →Jan. 11	135	
20	140				
27	170				
		28	120 }		
			140 }→ 28	260	
	685		395	395	
		To balance	290		
	685		685		
Balance	290				

The mechanics of specific identification are straighforward. The items that have been sold must first be identified, and then the cost of these specific items must be determined from the purchase records. Firms using this method will usually keep detailed inventory records for each product.

Specific identification of the cost of items sold requires (1) that the firm is *able* to distinguish among the items and (2) that it is *worthwhile* to do so. There are many instances where these conditions are satisfied. For example, an automobile dealer can certainly distinguish among the cars in the inventory and can identify exactly which car is sold in each transaction. A gasoline station, on the other hand, cannot distinguish one purchase of gasoline from another at the time of sale, since all purchases are mixed in the underground tank. A hardware store may be able to distinguish each hammer sold and identify its purchase cost, but because of the large volume of transactions and the number of different products handled, it is probably not worth the time needed to do this. Thus, the automobile dealer would almost certainly use the specific identification method, the gasoline station could not use this method, and the hardware store could use specific identification, but probably would not. For the gasoline station and the hardware store, some other method is needed.

First-In, First-Out Method

In cases where specific identification is not appropriate, costs are transferred from inventory to cost of goods sold in some systematic manner. One possibility is to assign costs to cost of goods sold *in the order of purchase*. This procedure is known as the *first-in, first-out (FIFO)* method. In our example, we would assume that each sale consisted of the following:

January 11—sold one of the units purchased for $120 on January 6
January 28—sold the other unit purchased for $120 on January 6 and the unit purchased on January 10 for $135

In T-account format, the entries to cost of goods sold would appear as follows:

Inventory				Cost of goods sold	
Jan. 6	240				
10	135				
		Jan. 11	120 ⟶ Jan. 11	120	
20	140				
27	170				
		28	120 }		
			135 } ⟶ 28	255	
	685		375	375	
		To balance	310		
	685		685		
Balance	310				

Note that the inventory and cost of goods sold balances differ from those obtained by using specific identification.

It is important to recognize that FIFO is an assumption about cost flow—the manner in which costs are transferred from the inventory account to the cost of goods sold account. It is not necessary that the physical flow of product to customers behave in this way. Other cost flow methods, specifically the weighted average and last-in, first-out (LIFO) methods, could also be used in a perpetual inventory system. Their application is reasonably complex, however, and will not be discussed here.

COMPUTER APPLICATION

Use of a computerized accounting system greatly facilitates the use of a perpetual inventory system. Since an entry to inventory and to cost of goods sold must be made for each sales transaction, there are many entries, and they must be made promptly. Often, the inventory/cost of goods sold entry is tied directly to recording the sale. For example, as an automobile dealer records the sale of a new car, identified by a specific code number, the entry crediting inventory and debiting cost of goods sold would automatically follow; the computer would use the code number to find the cost of that specific car. In a retail store, use of a scanning device to record the product code would similarly enable the cost of goods sold entry to follow automatically (perhaps using the FIFO method in this case). Except in cases where the number of transactions is small, a computer is necessary to maintain a perpetual inventory system.

Under a perpetual inventory, a *physical inventory*—an actual count of goods on hand—should be taken from time to time and compared to the information in the inventory account. By comparing the recorded balance of the inventory account (what should be on hand, based on recorded transactions) with the physical count (what actually is on hand), any differences will be detected and should be investigated. These differences may be due to poor record-keeping, theft of inventory, or other reasons. Comparing the actual inventory to the recorded inventory at regular intervals helps management maintain control over this important asset.

PERIODIC INVENTORY SYSTEM

The alternative to the perpetual inventory system is the *periodic inventory system*. Under this system, the cost of goods sold is determined only *at the end of the period*.

Cost of goods sold for the period is determined by considering three items of information:

1 The cost of merchandise on hand at the beginning of the period (beginning inventory)
2 The cost of merchandise bought during the period (purchases)
3 The cost of merchandise on hand at the end of the period (ending inventory)

The cost of goods sold is calculated by combining this information as follows:

```
  Beginning Inventory
+ Net Purchases
= Cost of Goods Available for Sale
- Ending Inventory
= Cost of Goods Sold
```

Thus, the cost of goods sold is determined by (1) accounting for purchases of merchandise and (2) accounting for inventory at the beginning and end of the period. Note that the subtotal of beginning inventory and purchases is called *cost of goods available for sale.* As the title suggests, this amount indicates the cost of all the merchandise that the firm had available for sale during the period. This cost must equal the cost of goods that were sold plus the cost of goods that were not sold (ending inventory).

While this system is easier to use, it does not provide as good a control over inventory as does the perpetual system. Inventory is counted and recorded only at the end of the period. Any recording errors or loss of inventory during the period will not be detected because there is no independent record of inventory to compare to the year-end count.

In discussing the periodic inventory system, we first discuss accounting for purchases of merchandise. We then consider calculation of ending inventory under several different methods.

Accounting for Purchases

There is a great deal of similarity between accounting for sales, discussed in Chapter 5, and accounting for purchases. Of course, these two activities represent two sides of the same transaction—one company sells something, another buys it. The cost of inventory purchased during the period is charged (i.e., debited) to the purchases account. At the end of the period, the purchases account will be closed by an adjusting entry, and only inventory and cost of goods sold will remain. During the period, purchases should be considered to be an asset (inventory) account.

Assume that on May 3, Coleman Variety Store, Inc. buys housewares from a local supplier. If Coleman pays cash at the time of purchase, the transaction would be recorded as:

May 3	Purchases	700	
	Cash		700
	To record purchase of housewares.		

Purchases on Account   More commonly, merchandise is purchased on account rather than for cash. In this case, the credit is made to accounts payable. If, on May 18, Coleman Variety Store buys a quantity of hardware items on account, the entry would be:

May 18	Purchases	3,000	
	Accounts Payable		3,000
	To record purchase of hardware on account.		

Freight and Other Charges   In addition to the cost of the merchandise itself, various other charges may be related to the purchase and included in the total amount of the invoice. These charges may include freight, import duties, special order charges, and the like.

Freight charges may be part of the invoice cost, or they may be paid separately to the carrier. Two accounting alternatives are possible. The easier method is to charge the freight cost to the purchases account along with the cost of the merchandise. Some firms, however, wishing to separate the freight charges, establish a freight-in account. Even if this account is used, freight costs will eventually be combined with purchases in determining the cost of goods sold.

Charges other than freight are generally combined with the cost of merchandise and debited to the purchases account.

Cash Discounts—Gross Price Method   As was the case with sales, purchases may be subject to a cash discount for prompt payment. Recall that in Chapter 5, sales subject to cash discount were recorded at the full invoice ("gross") price, and the discounts, when taken, were recorded in a separate sales discounts account.

A parallel gross price procedure may be used for purchases. That is, the full invoice price would be initially recorded in the purchases account. At time of payment, any cash discount would be recorded in a contra account, *purchase discounts*. For example, assume that on October 3, Coleman Variety Store bought toys on account. The total invoice price was $3,000 and terms were 2/10, n/30. Using the gross price method, the original purchase would be recorded as:

Oct. 3	Purchases	3,000	
	Accounts Payable		3,000
	To record purchase of toys on account.		

If payment was made on October 12 (within the discount period), the entry would be:

Oct. 12	Accounts Payable	3,000	
	Cash		2,940
	Purchase Discounts		60
	To record payment within discount period.		

If payment did not occur until October 30 (after the discount period had ended), the entry for the above transaction would be:

Oct. 30	Accounts Payable	3,000	
	Cash		3,000
	To record payment after discount period.		

Under the gross price approach, the purchases account shows the full invoice price of the merchandise. Any cash discounts taken are recorded in the purchases discount account. At the end of the period, the amount of purchases would be reduced by the amount of purchase discounts to determine the net cost of merchandise purchased during the period.

Cash Discounts—Net Price Method   In accounting for sales, the gross price method is commonly used. One reason is that the firm (the seller) does not know whether its customers will take the discount. Thus, it does not anticipate discounts, preferring to record them as they actually occur. In the case of purchases, however, the decision on taking discounts rests inside the firm (the buyer). If it is company policy to regularly take all available discounts, then it would be reasonable to adopt an accounting method that anticipates the discount. This method is known as the *net price method* and is often used in accounting for purchases.

Under the net price procedure, the $3,000 purchase discussed above would be recorded as follows. On the date of purchase (October 3), the net price (price less discount) of $2,940 would be recorded. Under the company's policy of taking all available discounts, this is the amount expected to be paid. The entry would be:

Oct. 3	Purchases	2,940	
	Accounts Payable		2,940
	To record purchase of toys on account.		

Payment on October 12 (within the discount period) would be recorded as:

Oct. 12	Accounts Payable	2,940	
	Cash		2,940
	To record payment within discount period.		

Due to oversight or temporary shortage of cash, payment occasionally may not be made within the discount period. If the invoice was paid on October 30 (after the discount period expired), the entry would be:

Oct. 30	Accounts Payable	2,940	
	Discounts Lost	60	
	Cash		3,000
	To record payment after discount period.		

The account Discounts Lost should not be viewed as an addition to inventory cost, but as a financing cost that is included in the selling, general, and administrative expenses section of the income statement. The $60 is considered a financing cost because it represents the additional amount the firm must pay for the right of delaying payment beyond the normal ten-day period.

Trade Discounts In addition to the cash discounts discussed above, other discounts may be involved in purchase transactions. One common type, particularly for merchandising companies, is the *trade discount*. For example, suppose on June 5 a college bookstore buys 100 accounting texts that have a retail price (the price which will be charged to students) of $27 each. The price from the publisher to the bookstore is usually determined by a percentage reduction (often 20%) from the retail price. This reduction is known as a trade discount. The publisher's invoice to the bookstore would show:

100 accounting texts @ $27	$2,700
Less 20% trade discount	540
Price after trade discount	$2,160

In the case of trade discounts, always record the after-discount price. Thus the bookstore would make the following entry:

June 5	Purchases	2,160	
	Accounts Payable		2,160
	To record purchase of textbooks on account.		

If additional discounts (such as *quantity discounts* given for buying a large number of units) are given, purchases are recorded in the same manner as above—at the after-discount price.

Returns and Allowances After the initial purchase transaction has been recorded, further adjustments may occur. Merchandise may prove defective and may be returned to the supplier, or a price reduction may be granted by the supplier. The supplier may accept the return of excess merchandise that a store has been unable to sell. These adjustments are recorded in a contra account called Purchase Returns and Allowances.

Assume that after recording various purchases, a firm on July 9 returns defective merchandise that had cost $600, and also receives a $75 credit from a supplier because merchandise had arrived late. Combining these two transactions results in the following entry:

July 9	Accounts Payable	675	
	Purchase Returns and Allowances		675
	To record return of merchandise ($600) and allowance from supplier ($75).		

These adjustments reduce the amounts owed to suppliers, and hence accounts payable is debited. At the end of the period, the balance in the purchase returns and allowances account (as well as any other contra purchases accounts) would be deducted from purchases to determine the net cost of merchandise bought during the period. For example:

Purchases		$8,000
Less: Purchase Discounts	$ 60	
Purchase Returns and Allowances	675	735
Net Purchases		$7,265

Characteristics of a Periodic Inventory System

A periodic inventory system has the following characteristics:

1 As goods are purchased during the period, their costs are recorded in the purchases account.

2 As goods are sold during the period, sales revenue is recorded. It is not necessary to maintain a record of which items have been sold. No attempt is made to determine the cost of the goods sold as sales occur.

3 At the end of the reporting period, a *physical inventory* is taken. That is, goods on hand are counted, and a list is prepared showing the descriptions and quantities of the goods on hand.

4 A cost is then assigned to each item on the list, using one of the several inventory costing methods described in the following sections of the chapter. In this way, the cost of the ending inventory is calculated.

5 Cost of goods sold is determined by the formula:

$$
\begin{array}{rl}
 & \text{Beginning Inventory} \\
+ & \text{Net Purchases} \\ \hline
= & \text{Cost of Goods Available for Sale} \\
- & \text{Ending Inventory} \\ \hline
= & \text{Cost of Goods Sold} \\ \hline
\end{array}
$$

Note that in a periodic system, emphasis is on the calculation of ending inventory; cost of goods sold is then determined by the formula.

Methods of Assigning Costs

Our main concern in this section is step (4) above—the assignment of cost to inventory items in a periodic system. There are several acceptable methods for making this assignment. We now consider the FIFO, LIFO, and weighted average methods of assigning cost to inventory items. Each method is acceptable under generally accepted accounting principles. However, the *consistency rule* discussed in Chapter 1 must be followed; once a particular method is adopted, it should continue to be used.

First in, First-Out Method   The first-in, first-out (FIFO) inventory method assumes that purchase costs are charged to cost of goods sold *in order of acquisition*. In other words, the cost of the first item purchased (first in) is the first cost charged to cost of goods sold (first out), and so on. Thus, the costs to be attached to the units in ending inventory under FIFO are the most recent purchase costs. In a situation where there are several different products in inventory, the FIFO analysis is applied to each product separately.

For example, Gordon's Sporting Goods is calculating its inventory cost on December 31, 1988, the end of its first year of operations. Exhibit 6-1 shows the purchases for one of the many items of merchandise which Gordon's carries— basketballs. Let's assume that Gordon's Sporting Goods does not know exactly how many basketballs have been sold during 1988. On December 31, 1988, the manager took a physical inventory (i.e., counted the quantities of each product in stock) and determined that the ending inventory included 250 basketballs.

Using the data in Exhibit 6-1, we want to determine the cost of goods sold under the FIFO method by deducting ending inventory from the cost of goods available for sale. Recall that the FIFO method charges costs to cost of goods sold in the order that they occur. In other words, to find the cost of goods sold, start

EXHIBIT 6-1
Gordon's Sporting Goods
Purchases
1988

	Basketballs		
Date	**Quantity**	**Unit cost**	**Total cost**
Jan. 5, 1988	100	$3.00	$ 300.00
Feb. 10, 1988	100	2.80	280.00
Mar. 18, 1988	200	2.95	590.00
June 3, 1988	400	3.20	1,280.00
Sept. 20, 1988	250	3.40	850.00
Nov. 6, 1988	150	3.60	540.00
Total	1,200		$3,840.00

with the *first* purchases. To find the cost of the ending inventory, it is necessary to start with the *last* purchases. To find the FIFO cost of the 250 basketballs in Gordon Sporting Goods' ending inventory, it is necessary to use the cost of the *last* 250 purchased:

Date	**Quantity**	**Unit cost**	**Total FIFO cost of ending inventory**
Nov. 6	150	$3.60	$540.00
Sept. 20	100	3.40	340.00
Total	250		$880.00

The cost of goods sold is calculated as follows:

	Basketballs
Beginning Inventory	$ -0-
Purchases (from Exhibit 6-1)	+3,840.00
Cost of Goods Available for Sale	$3,840.00
Less: Ending Inventory	− 880.00
Cost of Goods Sold	$2,960.00

Observe that this approach to calculating cost of goods sold has two advantages:

1 The company does not have to keep a record of how many units were sold during the period.

2 Calculating the cost of ending inventory, and then subtracting to find cost of goods sold, is usually less work than directly calculating the cost of goods sold for all the sales transactions during the period.

Last-in, First-out Method   The last-in, first-out (LIFO) inventory method assumes that purchase costs are charged to cost of goods sold in *the reverse order that they were purchased*. In other words, the cost of the last item purchased (last in) is the first cost charged to cost of goods sold (first out), and so on. This means that the costs associated with the ending LIFO inventory will be the earliest purchase costs.

The LIFO cost of the 250 basketballs in Gordon Sporting Goods' ending inventory is the cost of the *first* 250 purchased:

Date	Quantity	Unit cost	Total LIFO cost of ending inventory
Jan. 5	100	$3.00	$300.00
Feb. 10	100	2.80	280.00
Mar. 18	50	2.95	147.50
Total	250		$727.50

The cost of goods sold under LIFO is calculated as follows:

	Basketballs
Beginning Inventory	$ -0-
Purchases (from Exhibit 6-1)	+3,840.00
Cost of Goods Available for Sale	$3,840.00
Less: Ending Inventory	− 727.50
Cost of Goods Sold	$3,112.50

Weighted Average Method   The weighted average inventory method determines the average purchase cost and uses this figure to determine both cost of goods sold and ending inventory. This average cost is called a "weighted average" because each unit cost is multiplied (weighted) by the quantity purchased. In Exhibit 6-1, we cannot simply average the figures in the Unit Cost column, because only 100 basketballs were bought at $3.00 while 400 were bought at $3.20. The weighted average cost is defined as follows:

$$\frac{\text{Total cost of goods available (Beginning Inventory + Purchases)}}{\text{Total quantity of goods available (Beginning Inventory + Purchases)}}$$

For Gordon's Sporting Goods, the required data is available in Exhibit 6-1. The weighted average cost of basketballs is:

$$\frac{\$3,840.00}{1,200} = \$3.20$$

The cost of ending inventory for Gordon's Sporting Goods using the weighted average method is:

$$\text{Ending Inventory: } 250 \times \$3.20 = \$800.00$$

The cost of goods sold under weighted average is then:

	Basketballs
Beginning Inventory	$ -0-
Purchases (from Exhibit 6-1)	+3,840.00
Cost of Goods Available for Sale	$3,840.00
Less: Ending Inventory	− 800.00
Cost of Goods Sold	$3,040.00

COMPUTER APPLICATION

Use of the computer is helpful in applying the periodic inventory system. As purchases are recorded throughout the year, the number of units purchased and their costs can be maintained, and then used directly in applying FIFO or LIFO, or used to calculate the weighted average cost. A firm may have hundreds or even thousands of different products in its inventory; the calculations must be performed for each. Using the computer to store the information and to carry out the calculations is helpful, and also it reduces the likelihood of calculation errors.

Comparison of Methods We have defined and illustrated three methods of determining ending inventory and cost of goods sold that do not require specific identification of the items sold: the FIFO, LIFO, and weighted average methods. Each method gives a different result, as summarized in Exhibit 6-2.

Observe that, for this example, LIFO produced the highest cost of goods sold figure, FIFO the lowest, with weighted average in between. The ending inventory figures must be in the opposite direction; observe that FIFO is highest, LIFO lowest, and weighted average in between. If costs are rising throughout the period, LIFO will give the largest cost of goods sold. If costs of merchandise decline throughout the period, FIFO will give the highest cost of goods sold. In either case, weighted average will fall between FIFO and LIFO. If the pattern of costs fluctuates over the period, you cannot predict the relationship among the three methods.

You may well ask: How can there be three answers? Which one is correct? We cannot prove that one is correct and the others are not. In accounting, all three are accepted as reasonable methods. Thus, a firm may choose any one of them for its financial reporting (but once having chosen, the firm is expected to continue to use the same method each year, following the concept of *consistency*).

The objective of income determination is to seek a matching of costs and revenues. In determing cost of goods sold, therefore, we must ask: Which costing method will best achieve this matching? Three different individuals might give three different answers to this question:

EXHIBIT 6-2
Gordon's Sporting Goods
Summary of Cost of Goods Sold
and Ending Inventory
for Basketballs
1988

	FIFO	LIFO	Weighted average
Ending Inventory	$ 880.00	$ 727.50	$ 800.00
Cost of Goods Sold	2,960.00	3,112.50	3,040.00
Total Costs Accounted for	$3,840.00	$3,840.00	$3,840.00

Mr. F.: "I believe FIFO achieves the best matching. FIFO charges costs to cost of goods sold in the order in which they are purchased. This is a logical pattern to assume, and in many cases may approximate the flow of the goods themselves."

Mrs. L.: "I believe LIFO achieves the best matching. LIFO uses the most current costs to match against revenues. Since prices change over time, it is desirable to use the most recent costs to match against revenues. This eliminates the effect of price increases (inflation) on current profit and gives the truest picture of the firm's income."

Miss W.: "I believe weighted average achieves the best matching. The most reasonable approach is not to take the first or last costs, but to average all costs together. This reflects the fact that a firm's stock of merchandise is a mixture of several purchases and hence several costs."

Different firms choose different methods. If merchandise costs are regularly rising, LIFO gives the highest cost of goods sold, and hence the lowest income. Lower income means lower taxes; thus LIFO is a popular choice for income tax purposes. Firms must choose LIFO for accounting purposes if they wish to use it for tax purposes. Firms more concerned with their published financial statements than with tax savings may use FIFO during a period of rising prices. FIFO produces both a higher net income and a higher ending inventory valuation. As stated earlier, each method is acceptable in accounting. A firm may choose whichever it wishes, subject only to being consistent over time.

Effect on Subsequent Years

In the preceding sections, the illustration consisted only of current-period purchases; there were no beginning inventories. In cases where beginning inventories are present, no special problem is created. Simply treat the beginning inventory as the first "purchase" of the period.

Note that the cost of the beginning inventory depends on the inventory cost method used (specific identification, FIFO, LIFO, or weighted average). Note also that the beginning inventory may consist of more than one cost component. For example, the 1988 ending inventories for Gordon's Sporting Goods would be the beginning inventories for 1989.

The beginning inventory on January 1, 1989 would be:

Under FIFO:

150 basketballs at $3.60	$540.00
100 basketballs at 3.40	340.00
250	$880.00

Under LIFO:

100 basketballs at $3.00	$300.00
100 basketballs at 2.80	280.00
50 basketballs at 2.95	147.50
250	$727.50

Under weighted average:

250 basketballs at $3.20	$800.00

Recording the Cost of Goods Sold

Under a periodic inventory system, cost of goods sold is calculated and recorded at the end of the reporting period. Assume that on January 1, 1988, the records of Red Products, Inc. showed a beginning inventory of $53,000. During 1988, merchandise costing a total of $700,000 was purchased and recorded in the Purchases account. Thus, by the end of 1988, the records show the following balances:

Inventory	$ 53,000
Purchases	700,000

On December 31, 1988, a physical inventory is taken. Using one of the methods described in the preceding sections, the company determines its ending inventory to be $71,000 and its cost of goods sold to be $682,000. The logic of the entry to record these amounts is that the costs that presently appear in the (beginning) inventory and purchases accounts must be transferred to the cost of goods sold account or remain in the (ending) inventory account. That is:

$$\left.\begin{array}{c}\text{Beginning Inventory}\\+\\\text{Purchases}\end{array}\right\} = \left\{\begin{array}{c}\text{Cost of Goods Sold}\\+\\\text{Ending Inventory}\end{array}\right.$$

The entry needed to accomplish this transfer of costs is:

Cost of Goods Sold	682,000	
Inventory	71,000	
Inventory		53,000
Purchases		700,000

To record cost of goods sold for 1988
and ending inventory at 12/31/88.

In the entry above, the $53,000 credit removes the beginning inventory from the ledger account. The $71,000 debit establishes the correct ending inventory balance. An alternative treatment would be to debit Inventory for the $18,000 increase in the account balance.

INVENTORY DETERMINATION—ESTIMATED COST METHODS

The inventory methods discussed up to this point have been based on actual purchase costs. Once the quantity of inventory was determined, appropriate costs (under FIFO, LIFO, and so forth) were found in the purchase records and assigned to the ending inventory. Cost of goods sold was then found by subtraction.

There are also methods for estimating ending inventory and cost of goods sold that are not based on specific purchase costs. We shall briefly consider two of these: the gross profit method and the retail method.

Gross Profit Method

Under the *gross profit method,* the past relationship between sales and cost of goods sold is used to calculate an estimate of cost of goods sold for the current period. Under this approach, it is not necessary to take a physical inventory or to have perpetual inventory records. For example, assume that the statement of income of Temple Corporation showed the following for the year 1988:

Sales	$600,000
Cost of Goods Sold	− 408,000
Gross Profit	$192,000

If we express this information in percentage terms we have:

Sales	100%	
Cost of Goods Sold	− 68	($408,000 ÷ $600,000)
Gross Profit	32%	($192,000 ÷ $600,000)

Suppose now that we wish to prepare financial statements for January, 1989, but do not wish to go through all the work of taking a physical inventory. The cost of goods sold for January can be estimated by: (1) knowing the January sales and (2) assuming that the percentage relationships shown for 1988 continue to hold for January, 1989. Thus, if January sales were $55,000, the January cost of goods sold is estimated as:

$$\$55,000 \times .68 = \$37,400$$

The estimated ending inventory on January 31, 1989 can be determined by subtracting the estimated cost of goods sold from the cost of the goods available for sale. If Temple had $10,000 beginning inventory on January 1 and purchases for January totaled $40,000, the estimated ending inventory would be $12,600 ($10,000 + $40,000 − $37,400). The gross profit method is a quick, convenient approach to estimating cost of goods sold and ending inventory. It is useful in cases where a more exact determination is not needed (for example, in weekly or monthly statements for internal purposes), or not possible (for example, where records or the inventory itself have been destroyed). Because it is only an estimate, the gross profit method should not be used for annual financial statements.

Retail Method

The *retail method* is another approach to estimating the cost of ending inventory and cost of goods sold. Unlike the gross profit method, the retail method usually involves the taking of a physical inventory. When the inventory is taken, the items are counted and are valued at their *selling price*. Given the inventory at selling price (retail), we then use the relationship between cost and selling price to estimate the *cost* of the inventory.

This method is convenient for retail stores, which may have a few thousand different items on their shelves. To take the inventory, people go along the shelves, identify each item, count how many are on hand, and also write down the selling price (which often appears on the item itself). For example, a portion of the inventory of a grocery store might appear as follows:

	Quantity	Retail price	Total retail
Canned Vegetables:			
Corn	53	$.41	$ 21.73
Green Beans	80	.43	34.40
Peas	67	.40	26.80
Potatoes	112	.38	42.56
Tomatoes	77	.52	40.04
Wax Beans	91	.45	40.95
		Total	$206.48

Next, the store must know the relationship between its cost and its retail price. Assume that the store compares the cost on its purchase invoices to its current selling prices and determines that the cost of canned vegetables is 70 percent of selling price. The cost of the portion of ending inventory shown above would be:

Ending Inventory at Retail	$206.48
Percentage of Cost to Retail	× .70
Ending Inventory at Cost	$144.54

Thus, under the retail method:

1 The inventory is taken at retail price.

2 The relationship of cost to retail is determined.

3 Using the cost-to-retail relationship, the inventory is converted from retail to cost.

4 Cost of goods sold is determined by subtracting the cost of the ending inventory from the cost of goods available for sale.

INVENTORY DETERMINATION—LOWER OF COST OR MARKET VALUE

Up to this point, we have discussed the determination of the cost of ending inventory. However, the market value of inventory must also be considered. The general rule in accounting is that inventory should be reported at the *lower of cost or market.* In other words, in those cases where the market value of the ending inventory is less than the cost of the inventory, the (lower) market value figure must be used. Cases where the market value is less than cost should not be frequent, but they do occur. The concept of conservatism requires that asset values not be overstated. Thus, when the value of inventory items has declined below cost, this decline must be reflected in the financial statements.

Generally, market value means the *cost to replace,* that is, the price the firm would currently have to pay to acquire the inventory items. For example, if a store purchased radios several weeks ago at $12.00 each, but now could buy them for $10.75, the "market" is $10.75 and is lower than cost.

The lower of cost or market rule may be applied either on an item-by-item basis, or on a total inventory basis. To illustrate, assume the following inventory:

Item	Cost	Market
A	$6,000	$6,500
B	8,000	7,200
C	5,000	5,700
D	3,000	2,800

On an item-by-item basis, find the lower of the two figures for each item and total these.

Item	Cost	Market	Lower of cost or market
A	$6,000	$6,500	$ 6,000 (cost)
B	8,000	7,200	7,200 (market)
C	5,000	5,700	5,000 (cost)
D	3,000	2,800	2,800 (market)
			$21,000

The ending inventory, at lower of cost or market, would be $21,000, if we use the item-by-item approach.

On a total inventory basis, find the total cost of the inventory and also the total market value, and select the lower of these two totals. The result is:

Item	Cost	Market
A	$ 6,000	$ 6,500
B	8,000	7,200
C	5,000	5,700
D	3,000	2,800
	$22,000	$22,200

In this case, the lower total is the cost total of $22,000. Thus, the ending inventory, at lower of cost or market, would be $22,000, if we use the total inventory approach.

Note that the inventory at market value under the item-by-item approach will always be less than or equal to the value under the total approach. By whichever approach the ending inventory at lower of cost or market is determined, cost of goods sold expense would then be determined by subtracting the dollar amount of the ending inventory from the cost of goods available for sale. This means that any decline in market value of goods below their cost is reflected in the current period's income statement.

Suppose, for example, that for the year 1988 Rhoads Company had the following information:

Sales	$500,000
Purchase of Merchandise	270,000
Inventory, January 1, 1988	80,000
Inventory, December 31, 1988	110,000

The income statement would show the following:

Sales		$500,000
Cost of Goods Sold:		
Beginning Inventory	$ 80,000	
Purchases	270,000	
Cost of Goods Available for Sale	$350,000	
Less: Ending Inventory	110,000	240,000
Gross Profit		$260,000

If, however, the market value of the ending inventory had declined to $95,000, the income statement would show:

Sales		$500,000
Cost of Goods Sold:		
Beginning Inventory	$ 80,000	
Purchases	270,000	
Cost of Goods Available for Sale	$350,000	
Less: Ending Inventory	95,000	255,000
Gross Profit		$245,000

Note that the gross profit has decreased by $15,000, reflecting the $15,000 decline in the value of the ending inventory.

FINANCIAL STATEMENT PRESENTATION

Inventories represent goods on hand that eventually will be sold to customers, either directly or in the form of a product or service. The types of inventories depend upon the nature of the company's business:

1 Merchandising firms (retailers and wholesalers) have *merchandise inventory*.
2 Service firms have *materials and supplies inventory*.
3 Manufacturing firms have *raw materials inventory, work in process inventory*, and *finished goods inventory*.

The financial statements should present several items of information concerning inventories, such as:

1 The basis of valuation of inventories (cost, or lower of cost or market).
2 The particular cost method used (LIFO, FIFO, weighted average, specific identification).

3 In cases where there are several types of inventories (e.g., a manufacturing firm), the dollar amount of each type.

In each case, this information may be presented on the balance sheet itself or in the notes to the financial statements.

On the income statement, inventories enter into the determination of the cost of goods sold, as previously illustrated:

$$
\begin{array}{rl}
& \text{Beginning Inventory} \\
+ & \text{Purchases for the period (including} \\
& \quad \text{addition of freight and other} \\
& \quad \text{charges, and subtraction of} \\
& \quad \text{purchase discounts and purchase} \\
& \quad \underline{\text{returns and allowances)}} \\
= & \text{Cost of Goods Available for Sale} \\
- & \underline{\text{Ending Inventory}} \\
= & \underline{\underline{\text{Cost of Goods Sold}}}
\end{array}
$$

On some income statements, the above calculation is shown; in other cases, only a single cost of goods sold line is presented.

SUMMARY

To properly determine income, expenses incurred in generating revenue must be recorded in the same time period as the related revenue is earned. For merchandising firms, cost of goods sold is the largest expense.

Learning Objective 1: Account for the purchase of merchandise for resale.

Under the periodic inventory system, merchandise purchased for resale is recorded in a separate account called Purchases. Related charges, such as freight, are usually included in the purchases account.

Learning Objective 2: Apply the gross price and net price methods for cash discounts on purchases.

Under the gross price method, purchases are recorded at full invoice price at time of purchase. At time of payment, any cash discounts taken are credited to a contra account (purchase discounts). Under the net price method, the net (after discount) amount is recorded at time of purchase. At time of payment, any cash discounts *not* taken are debited to an expense account (discounts lost).

Learning Objective 3: Distinguish between periodic and perpetual inventory systems.

Inventories may be maintained using either a periodic or perpetual system. The periodic inventory system makes no attempt to determine cost of goods sold as sales occur during the period. A physical inventory count at the end of the period is employed to determine the ending inventory, and thus indirectly the cost of goods sold. The perpetual inventory system maintains a continuous record of inventory and cost of goods sold throughout the period, updating for each purchase or sales transaction.

Learning Objective 4: Define the specific identification, FIFO, LIFO, and weighted average methods for determining cost of goods sold and inventory.

Cost can be assigned to inventory quantities according to several acceptable methods. The four primary alternatives are: specific identification; first-in first-out (FIFO); last-in, first-out (LIFO); and weighted average. Specific identification recognizes the specific cost of each individual unit of product. FIFO assumes that the costs of the first units purchased are the first ones charged to cost of sales. LIFO assumes that the costs of the last units purchased are the first ones charged to cost of sales. Weighted average calculates an average cost of units purchased and uses this average to determine cost of sales.

Learning Objective 5: Calculate cost of goods sold and inventory according to the FIFO, LIFO, and weighted average methods.

These calculations were illustrated in the chapter. Each method produces a different inventory valuation and hence a different amount for cost of goods sold.

Learning Objective 6: Calculate ending inventory by the gross profit and retail methods.

The gross profit method and retail method are two procedures for estimating inventory and cost of goods sold. It is not necessary to take a physical inventory or maintain perpetual records in order to use the gross profit method; a physical inventory is usually employed with the retail method.

Learning Objective 7: Apply the lower of cost or market rule to inventories.

Generally, inventory should be reported at the lower of cost or market, where market usually means the cost to replace. Lower of cost or market value may be determined using either an item-by-item approach or a total inventory approach.

KEY TERMS

Cost of goods sold
Cost of operations (Appendix)
Direct labor (Appendix)
Direct materials (Appendix)
First-in, first-out method (FIFO)
Gross price method for cash discounts
Gross profit method
Indirect labor (Appendix)
Indirect materials (Appendix)
Last-in, first-out method (LIFO)
Lower of cost or market

Manufacturing overhead (Appendix)
Net price method for cash discounts
Periodic inventory system
Perpetual inventory system
Purchases account
Retail method
Schedule of cost of goods manufactured
  and sold (Appendix)
Specific identification
Weighted average method

APPENDIX: Cost of Sales and Inventory Accounting: Manufacturing and Service Firms

In the chapter, we discussed the cost of sales for merchandising firms. In this appendix, we briefly discuss cost of sales for two other types of firms— manufacturing firms and service firms.

MANUFACTURING FIRMS

Manufacturing firms use materials, labor, and machines to create products, as represented by the diagram in Exhibit 6-3. Three cost categories are used to represent the productive factors being utilized. *Direct materials* signifies the input cost of raw materials used in the production process that are identifiable in the final product. In the production of a book, for example, paper and cover materials (e.g., cloth) would be considered direct materials. Minor materials (such as ink and glue, in the case of a book) are usually considered as supplies (or *indirect materials*) rather than direct materials, and become a part of the manufacturing overhead category.

Direct labor, the second cost category, represents the cost of labor services that are directly engaged in the manufacture of the product. *Indirect labor,* such as that of production supervisors or machine repairmen, is considered a part of manufacturing overhead.

Manufacturing overhead, the third cost category, contains all other costs incurred in carrying on the manufacturing activity, such as the costs of the company's productive capacity and production support costs. By a *productive capacity,* we mean the physical facilities necessary to manufacture. Thus, there must be a factory building and equipment. The costs necessary to provide this capacity include:

Depreciation of factory building and equipment
Property taxes on factory building and equipment
Insurance on factory building and equipment
Rental of factory building and equipment

The mere presence of productive capacity is not enough. The capacity must be made operative, and the auxiliary services necessary to support production must be provided. We call these items the *production support,* which includes production related costs such as the following:

Heat, light, and power used in production
Repairs and maintenance of production facilities
Supervision of production
Supplies used in production
Indirect labor, such as material handlers and warehouse workers

EXHIBIT 6-3   Flow of Manufacturing Operations

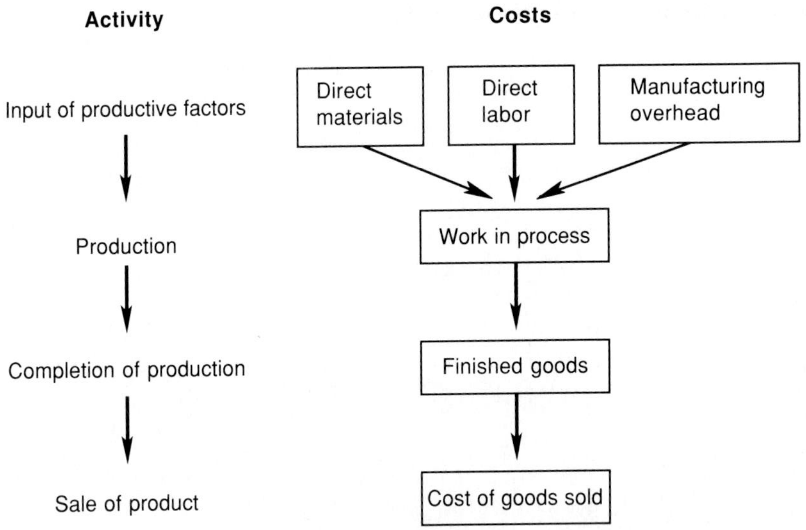

Activity   **Costs**

Input of productive factors

| Direct materials | Direct labor | Manufacturing overhead |

Production

Work in process

Completion of production

Finished goods

Sale of product

Cost of goods sold

These two sets of costs (productive capacity and production support) make up the category of manufacturing overhead, which therefore includes all production-related costs other than direct materials and direct labor.

As seen from Exhibit 6-3, the three input cost categories flow through the accounts representing the various stages of manufacturing activity. During production, direct materials, direct labor, and manufacturing overhead costs are transferred to the work in process account. When production is completed, the cost is transferred to the finished goods account. Finally, when the product is sold to customers, costs are transferred to the cost of goods sold account, which appears as an expense on the income statement.

At the beginning and end of each period, a manufacturing firm is likely to have several types of inventories: (1) direct materials for future use in production (materials inventory); (2) goods that are in the process of being manufactured, but are not yet completed (work in process inventory); and (3) goods that have been completed, but not yet been sold (finished goods inventory). These three types of inventory usually exist and must be accounted for in determining the cost of goods sold.

Financial Statement Presentation

Since many elements enter into the determination of cost of goods sold for a manufacturing firm, a separate schedule is often prepared. The *schedule of cost of goods manufactured and sold* provides the detail underlying the single cost of goods sold figure on the income statement. Exhibit 6-4 presents a typical schedule of cost of goods manufactured and sold, based on the following assumed information for the Stanford Corporation:

Direct materials:

Begin	Inventory, January 1, 1988	$19,000
	Purchases during 1988	63,000
End	Inventory, December 31, 1988	12,000
	Direct labor	78,000
	Manufacturing overhead	99,000
	Work in process:	
	Inventory, January 1, 1988	26,000
	Inventory, December 31, 1988	31,000
	Finished goods:	
	Inventory, January 1, 1988	45,000
	Inventory, December 31, 1988	39,000

SERVICE FIRMS

Service firms resemble manufacturing firms in that various inputs are combined to produce an output. However, for a service firm, the output is not a tangible product, but an intangible service. Examples of service firms include accounting and law firms, insurance companies, janitorial services, delivery services, barber and beauty shops, and hospitals.

Labor is frequently a major component of the cost of providing service. In many cases, equipment costs (depreciation, operating costs, insurance, and so on) are also significant. Materials may be an important cost in some cases, but not in others. The costs involved in providing services are very similar to the costs of manufacturing a product, namely materials, labor, and overhead. Unlike manufacturing, however, service firms have little if any inventory. An inventory of materials and supplies might exist for a service firm, but there is usually not work in process or finished goods inventory. Therefore, determining *cost of*

EXHIBIT 6-4
Stanford Corporation
Schedule of Cost of Goods Manufactured and Sold
For the Year Ended December 31, 1988

Beginning Inventory, Work in Process			$ 26,000
Current Manufacturing Costs:			
Direct Materials Used:			
Beginning Inventory	$19,000		
Purchases	63,000		
Available for Use	$82,000		
Less: Ending Inventory	12,000	$70,000	
Direct Labor		78,000	
Manufacturing Overhead		99,000	247,000
Total Manufacturing Costs in Process			$273,000
Less: Ending Inventory, Work in Process			31,000
Cost of Goods Manufactured			$242,000
Beginning Inventory, Finished Goods			45,000
Total Cost of Goods Available for Sale			$287,000
Less: Ending Inventory, Finished Goods			39,000
Cost of Goods Sold			$248,000

operations for a service firm is similar to, but simpler than, determining cost of goods sold for a manufacturing firm.

Cost of Operations

As discussed above, the cost of providing services often involves the familiar categories of materials, labor, and overhead. However, it is not necessary to segregate the accounting into these three categories. Rather, think of a single list of cost items comprising cost of operations, such as the following:

Materials and supplies used
Labor
Labor fringe benefit costs
Equipment costs (depreciation, maintenance, operating expenses, and so on)
Building costs (depreciation, property taxes, maintenance, and so on)

Other costs incurred by the firm that are not directly connected with its service activity are not included in cost of operations. Such costs as advertising, office supplies, telephone, and secretarial and sales salaries would be presented on the income statement as general and administrative expenses.

Accounting for Operating Costs

A service firm does not have the complex flow of costs of a manufacturing firm. Therefore, the accounting requirements are more straightforward. Costs may be initially recorded in descriptive accounts (e.g., supplies, depreciation of equipment, and so on). At the end of the period, costs related to operations may be reclassified into a cost of operations account, or summarized on a schedule of cost of operations.

REVIEW QUESTIONS

1 List the types of costs included in the cost of sales for each of the following three firms: Markowitz Manufacturing Company; Brenda's Lawn Care & Landscaping Service, Inc.; and Seers, Rowbuck Dept. Stores.

2 For a merchandising firm, under what circumstances would the purchases of inventory during the period be exactly equal to the cost of goods sold?

3 Differentiate between a periodic inventory system and a perpetual inventory system.

4 Elgin Store's beginning inventory was $15,000; ending inventory is $35,000 higher than the beginning inventory; and cost of goods sold for the period totals $280,000. Determine purchases for the period.

5 What does the balance in the Purchase Discounts account represent? What does the account Discounts Lost represent? Where does each account appear on the financial statements? Which account results from using the net price method of recording purchases; which results from using the gross price method?

6 Why is the net price method frequently used by the buying company in handling cash discounts, while the net price method is rarely used by the selling company?

7 UCLA's College Bookstore bought 30 copies of *Secrets to Getting a Good Grade in Accounting* from Honest Ed, Inc., a local book distributor. The retail selling price is $30, with a 15 percent trade discount allowed to college bookstores. Payment terms are 2/10, n/30. Cash discounts are to be determined on price after deducting trade discounts. At what amount should the UCLA Bookstore record the purchase if the net price method is followed; if the gross price method is followed?

8 Where does the Purchase Returns and Allowances account appear on the financial statements? What type of transactions result in entries in this account?

9 Which of the following would affect the calculation of cost of goods sold: ending inventory, purchases, beginning inventory, purchase returns and allowances, freight-in, or purchase discounts?

10 Explain how ending inventory and cost of goods sold are calculated under each of the following periodic inventory costing methods: a) specific identification, b) FIFO, c) LIFO, and d) weighted average.

11 If inventory purchase costs increase significantly during the year, which inventory costing method will yield the higher net income—FIFO or LIFO? Which method will yield the lowest income tax liability? Explain your answers.

12 Fresh Meat Packers, Inc. adopted the LIFO inventory method in 1946. If the company has continuously used LIFO since 1946, is it possible that inventory purchase costs from 1946 would be part of the current year's inventory? Would actual inventory from 1946 have to be on hand at the end of the current period?

13 Cole Coal Co. sells coal to customers from large bins maintained at the company's mine. New supplies of coal are periodically added to the top of the bins to maintain a sufficient quantity on hand. Since the last tons of coal added to the bins are the first sold, must the company use the LIFO inventory costing system?

14 B. Berry Brothers, Inc.'s beginning inventory was $28,480,000. The purchases account has a $224,080,000 balance. The year-end physical inventory indicates a $33,400,000 inventory value. Present the journal entry to record the ending inventory and cost of goods sold.

15 Quarterly, Incorporated provides its stockholders with statements of income every three months. The company does not maintain perpetual inventory records. To avoid the cost involved in taking a physical inventory every three months, how might the firm estimate its cost of goods sold and inventory values for the quarterly financial statements?

16 Write-Down Co. reduces its inventory from cost to a lower market value. What effect will the reduction of ending inventory from cost to market have on the statement of income, on the balance sheet? What accounting concept discussed in Chapter 1 is the basis for the lower of cost or market rule?

17 Dile Manufacturing Company produces sundials. What information regarding the company's inventories should be presented in the financial statements or related notes?

18 (Appendix) A manufacturing company usually has three inventories—materials, work in process, and finished goods. Describe the inventories of a typical firm that provides a service (e.g., a barber shop).

19 (Appendix) What difference would exist between: a schedule of cost of goods sold for a merchandising company, a schedule of cost of goods manufactured and sold for a manufacturing company, and a schedule of operations for a firm that provides a service?

EXERCISES

E6-1 Selected ledger account balances for Buchanon Co. on December 31, 1988 show:

Inventory, January 1, 1988	$73,400
Purchases (including $10,856	
freight charges)	684,200
Discounts Lost	1,800

The physical count of inventory at year end produces an inventory value of $64,300.

Required:
1 Is Buchanon using the net price or gross price method of recording inventory purchases?
2 Is the company following the perpetual or periodic inventory system?
3 What is the cost of goods sold for the period?
4 What is the journal entry to record the cost of goods sold and ending inventory?

E6-2 Krown, Kork, & Seal made the following inventory purchases on account and cash payments to vendors during July:
    July 2—purchase from Randell Co. Invoice price of $7,000; terms 2/10, n/30.
    July 8—purchase from Buckley Co. Invoice price of $1,200; terms 1/10, n/20.
    July 12—payment made to Randell Co.
    July 28—payment made to Buckley Co.

Required:
Record the four entries for July assuming Krown, Kork, & Seal uses the gross price method. Repeat the entries using the net price method.

E6-3 Using the following list of accounts (presented in alphabetical order), prepare the cost of goods sold section of the income statement.

Inventory, beginning of period	$312,000
Inventory, end of period	286,000
Purchase Discounts	18,000
Purchase Returns and Allowances	7,000
Purchases	1,642,000

E6-4 The Bowers Company purchased the following merchandise for resale during May. (There was no beginning inventory.)

May 5	200 units at $10 per unit	=	$2,000
10	500 units at 8 per unit	=	4,000
25	400 units at 7 per unit	=	2,800
	1,100	=	$8,800

The 200 units remaining in inventory on May 31 were specifically identified as coming from the following purchases:

From May 10th purchase	100
From May 25th purchase	100

Required:
Calculate the inventory dollar amount on May 31 and the cost of goods sold for May under each of the following inventory costing methods: (1) specific identification, (2) FIFO, (3) LIFO, and (4) weighted average. Bowers uses the *periodic* inventory system.

E6-5 Chester's Sporting Goods, Inc. was destroyed by fire on May 16, 1989. In order to receive a settlement on the fire insurance policy, the company needed to know the cost of the inventory at the date of the fire. However, this information was not directly available. Fortunately, since the company's owner, George Chester, kept most of the accounting records at his home, they were not destroyed. He is able to determine the following:

1 As of January 1, 1989, the inventory had a cost of $31,500.

2 Between January 1 and May 16, the company purchased merchandise costing a total of $92,000.

3 Chester does not know the *cost* of the items sold, but he knows that sales between January 1 and May 16 were $150,000. He also knows that, in the past, the cost of merchandise sold has averaged 60 percent of selling price (that is, an item that Chester sells for $10 would have cost the company $6 to purchase). He believes that this relationship did not change during 1989.

Required:
Estimate the cost of Chester's inventory as of May 16.

E6-6 Mattold Men's Shop uses the retail inventory method. The beginning inventory cost $119,700. The cost of the net purchases during the period was $640,300. The shop has determined that its cost is 74 percent of selling price. The ending inventory at retail selling price is $187,500. Calculate the estimated cost of the ending inventory and cost of goods sold.

E6-7 Presented below is the inventory on August 31, 1988, for Bedford Nostalgia Co.:

Item	Quantity	Unit cost	Market (unit replacement cost)
Yo-yos	10,000	$1.20	$1.10
Hula Hoops	6,000	.80	.85
Goldfish	20,000	.10	.12
Frisbees	5,000	.72	.70

Required:
Calculate the ending inventory, using the lower of cost or market rule and applying the method on: (1) an item-by-item basis and (2) a total inventory basis.

E6-8 (Appendix) Using the following information, calculate the cost of goods manufactured and the cost of goods sold for 1988.

Direct materials:	
Inventory, January 1, 1988	$ 82,000
Purchases during 1988	418,000
Inventory, December 31, 1988	70,000

Direct labor	596,000
Manufacturing overhead	718,000
Work in process:	
Inventory, January 1, 1988	86,000
Inventory, December 31, 1988	92,000
Finished goods:	
Inventory, January 1, 1988	112,000
Inventory, December 31, 1988	115,000

E6-9 (Appendix) T.D. Simpson operates Simpson's Janitorial Services, Inc. From the following list of ledger accounts taken from the company's general ledger, determine: (1) total cost of operations for the period and (2) total general and administrative expenses for the period.

Accounting and legal	$ 600
Advertising	850
Cleaning supplies used	4,810
Cost of operating truck (other than depreciation)	970
Depreciation on truck (used to transport employees and equipment)	1,200
Equipment rental (vacuum cleaners and polishers)	6,000
Liability insurance	290
Office rent	3,600
Secretarial salaries	4,370
Telephone	400
Wages of janitorial employees	14,630

PROBLEMS

P6-1 *Accounting for Purchases*

OEO Company uses the periodic inventory system. A physical inventory taken by the company's employees on June 30, 1988 yields a $3,280,000 ending inventory. On July 1, 1987, the beginning of the company's accounting year, the inventory was $2,972,000. During the year the following transactions occurred:

1 Purchases of inventory on account totaled $24,245,000.

2 Purchases of inventory returned to vendors for credit totaled $186,490.

3 Payments to vendors during the year were $23,330,000. No cash discounts are offered by the vendors.

4 Freight charges paid during the fiscal year by OEO on inventory purchased totaled $768,000. The company debits freight charges on merchandise purchased to an account titled Freight-In.

Required:

1 Prepare journal entries for the above transactions.

2 Determine the cost of goods sold for the year. (Add freight-in to purchases in your calculation.)   P.182

P6-2 *Solving for Unknown Amounts*

For each of the following independent cases, solve for the unknowns.

	Case 1	Case 2	Case 3
Beginning Inventory	$ 60,000	$ (f)	$ 52,000
Cost of Goods Sold	340,000	490,000	(h)
Ending Inventory	(a)	91,000	65,000
Gross Profit	(b)	110,000	(g)
Gross Profit Percentage	(c)	(e)	32%
Purchases	380,000	513,000	(i)
Purchase Discounts	3,000	-0-	-0-
Purchase Returns and Allowances	7,000	8,000	-0-
Sales	480,500	(d)	600,000
Sales Discounts	4,000	-0-	-0-
Sales Returns and Allowances	5,500	18,000	-0-

P6-3 *Calculating Cost of Goods Sold and Inventory Under Various Methods*

Presented below is a record of purchase transactions for Elite, Inc. during April, 1988, the firm's first month of operation:

	Units	Cost per unit	Total
Purchase, April 3	1,000	$8.50	$ 8,500
Purchase, April 5	400	8.40	3,360
Purchase, April 15	700	8.70	6,090
Purchase, April 24	500	8.85	4,425
			$22,375

During April, 1,600 units were sold.

Required:

1 Calculate the cost of the 1,000 units in inventory and the cost of goods sold for April under each of the following inventory costing methods:

a Periodic specific identification (composed of 200 units from April 3 purchase, 700 units from April 15 purchase, and 100 units from April 24 purchase)

b Periodic FIFO

c Periodic LIFO

d Periodic weighted average (round average cost to nearest four decimal places)

2 Which of the above solutions is correct? Mention the consistency concept in your answer.

P6-4 *Periodic and Perpetual Inventory Methods*

Presented below is a record of the purchase and sale transactions of Caprice Company during a recent month. All purchases and sales are on account.

Inventory, March 1—3,000 units. Cost per unit is $2.50

under FIFO, $1.00 under LIFO, and $2.00 under weighted average.

Purchase, March 4—4,000 units at $3.00 per unit.

Sale, March 9—5,000 units at selling price of $4.00 per unit.

Purchase, March 11—6,000 units at $3.50 per unit.

Sale, March 21—4,000 units at selling price of $4.00 per unit.

Required:

1 Calculate the March 31 inventory cost and cost of goods sold for March under (1) FIFO, (2) LIFO, and (3) weighted average. Assume that Caprice uses a periodic inventory system.

2 Prepare journal entries for March sales and purchases.

3 Prepare the adjusting journal entry to record cost of goods sold and ending inventory under FIFO.

4 Assume now that Caprice uses a perpetual inventory system. Calculate cost of goods sold for March and the March 31 inventory cost under FIFO.

P6-5 *Applying FIFO and LIFO*

Alexander, Inc. began operations on January 1, 1988. The company uses the *periodic* inventory system. Purchases during 1988 and 1989 were as follows:

January, 1988	1,000 units at $10	10,000
March, 1988	900 units at 10	9,000
June, 1988	1,200 units at 11	13,200
December, 1988	800 units at 13	10,400
February, 1989	1,300 units at 13	16,900
July, 1989	1,100 units at 14	15,400
December, 1989	700 units at 16	11,200

(*88* bracket for first four rows; *89* bracket for last three rows; 7000 total under units column)

Physical inventory counts show 600 units on hand as of December 31, 1988 and 700 units on hand as of December 31, 1989. Other information available:

	1988	1989
Sales	$59,500	$87,000
Sales Discounts	1,000	1,500
Sales Returns and Allowances	500	1,500
Operating Expenses (other than cost of goods sold and income taxes)	10,200	15,000
Income Tax Rate	20%	20%

Required:

1 Prepare income statements for 1988 and 1989 for both the FIFO and LIFO inventory costing methods. Include a separate schedule for the detailed calculation of cost of goods sold.

2 Answer each of the following questions regarding FIFO vs. LIFO for Alexander Inc.

a Which method produced the higher cost of goods sold expense? Why?

b Which method in 1989 best matched the most recent purchase costs against sales revenue?

c Which method yielded the higher net income? Why?

d Which method resulted in the lower income tax liability? Why? *lower income taxes*

e Which method produced inventory amounts for the year-end balance sheets that most closely approximated current replacement costs of the inventory on each December 31?

P6-6 *Estimating Inventory*

A fire early in the morning on March 1, 1988 totally destroyed the uninsured inventory of Roaster, Inc. The fire also extensively damaged the uninsured inventory of Tip Top Co. in an adjacent building. Tip Top believes it can sell its fire-damaged inventory for $18,000 salvage value.

A physical inventory of Tip Top taken at retail prices on February 29, 1988 (the end of Tip Top's accounting year) produced a $372,000 retail inventory value.

The company has determined costs are 60 percent of retail prices. Roaster, Inc., a company whose accounting year ends on December 31, has not taken a physical inventory since the $160,000 inventory taken on December 31, 1987. During 1987 sales revenue for Roaster totaled $1,200,000. The gross profit for 1987 was $300,000. Sales for the first two months of 1988 total $180,000. The Purchases account balance of Roaster on February 29, 1988 was $150,000. Percentage relationships between cost and selling prices are assumed to be the same for Roaster in 1988 as they were in 1987.

Required:
Calculate the inventory losses, at cost, suffered by Tip Top and Roaster due to the fire.

P6-7 *Lower of Cost or Market*
Presented below are selected ledger account balances of Munster, Inc. on December 31, 1988:

Freight-In	$ 4,000
Inventory, January 1, 1988	64,300
Purchases	480,000
Purchase Discounts	7,200
Purchase Returns and Allowances	3,900
Sales	735,000
Sales Returns and Allowances	11,000
Selling, General, and Administrative Expenses (including income taxes)	184,000

Details of the December 31, 1988 inventory show:

Item	Quantity	Cost	Market (replacement cost)	Cost	Market	Lower of cost or market on item-by-item basis
Little Eddie Dolls	3,500	$ 4.50	$4.95	$15750	$ 17325	$ 15750
Fester's Light Bulbs	8,000	.80	.78	6400	6240	6240
Thing-a-Phones	2,200	10.00	9.70	22,000	21,340	21,340
Grandma-ma's	4,400	3.10	3.20	13,640	14,080	13,640
Spot Burgers	5,600	.30	.25	1680	1400	1400
				59470	60385	58370

(Unit price column spans Cost and Market (replacement cost); Total inventory basis extended column spans Cost and Market)

Required:
1 Complete the above calculations of ending inventory values.
2 What is the ending inventory if the lower of cost or market rule is applied on a total inventory basis? $59470
3 What is the ending inventory if the lower of cost or market rule is applied on an item-by-item basis? $58,370
4 Prepare an income statement for Munster for 1988 assuming the lower of cost or market rule is applied on a total inventory basis.
5 Present the adjusting journal entry to record cost of goods sold and ending inventory as presented on the statement of income prepared for requirement (4). (Hint: Include a $7,200 debit to Purchase Discounts, a $3,900 debit to Purchase Returns and Allowances, and a $4,000 credit to Freight-In as part of the journal entry.)

P6-8 (Appendix) *Cost of Goods Sold for Manufacturing Firm*

Sanbor Manufacturing Company produces and sells ceramic lamps. Selected activities for the year ended June 30, 1989, are summarized below:

1 Direct materials purchased totaled $635,000.

2 The beginning direct materials inventory was $54,000. On June 30, 1989, the direct materials on hand totaled $62,000.

3 Direct labor wages earned totaled $681,000.

4 Manufacturing overhead costs incurred totaled $512,000.

5 The beginning finished goods inventory was $281,000. On June 30, 1989, the finished goods inventory totaled $239,000.

Required:

Prepare a Schedule of Cost of Goods Manufactured and Sold for the year. (Assume the ending work in process inventory is $95,000, an $18,000 decrease over the beginning work in process inventory.)

P6-9 (Appendix) *Cost of Operations for Service Firm*

Barb's Beauty Boutique served 76 customers during April, 1988. Each customer was charged a flat rate of $25, payable in cash. The Boutique maintains an inventory of shampoos, lotions, and cremes. During April, the Boutique purchased operating supplies totaling $310; $285 of the shampoos, lotions, and cremes were used. Beauticians' salaries for April, of $1,000 were paid in cash. Other costs for April were:

Depreciation on hair dryers	$120
Rent of salon	400
Salary of part-time bookkeeper	50
Advertising	80

All other costs, except depreciation, were paid in cash.

Required:

Present an income statement for April, 1988. List in detail the general and administrative expenses. Provide a supporting Schedule of Cost of Operations.

Business Decision Problem

Mary Ann Jensen is a lab technician for Wiley Pharmaceuticals. As a part-time business, she purchases expensive microscopes and resells them to members of science clubs. During 1988, the first year of this business, Mary Ann made the following purchases and sales:

January 8	Purchased two microscopes at $450 each
March 16	Purchased one microscope for $510
May 2	Sold for $700 one of the microscopes purchased on January 8
July 24	Purchased two microscopes at $580 each
September 7	Sold two microscopes for $750 each
	(purchased on March 16 and July 24)
December 28	Purchased one microscope for $610

Mary Ann knows little about accounting. She has asked your assistance in preparing financial statements and in completing the tax return for the business. Mary Ann explains that she is interested in reporting as large an income as possible on the statement of income in order to get a bank loan to expand the business. However, she would like to report the smallest taxable income possible in order to minimize her tax payments this year.

You determine that all the microscopes purchased during the year were identical. The only means of identifying one from another is by the serial number imprinted on each.

Required:
Recommend the inventory method Mary Ann should choose for financial reporting purposes and the method she should choose for income tax purposes in order to achieve her objectives (assume there is no constraint on choosing a tax method different from the accounting method).

7

DEPRECIATION AND AMORTIZATION— PROPERTY, PLANT, EQUIPMENT, AND INTANGIBLES

LEARNING OBJECTIVES

When you complete this chapter, you should be able to:

1   Account for the acquisition of property, plant, and equipment.
2   Apply the straight line, sum of years digits, declining balance, and units of production methods of depreciation.
3   Calculate partial-year depreciation.
4   Account for a change in estimated life or salvage value.
5   Calculate and record amortization of intangible assets and depletion of natural resources.
6   Calculate and record gains and losses resulting from the sale or exchange of long-lived assets.

The cost of using long-lived assets constitutes a major expense item for most firms. Many different types of long-lived assets—land, buildings, machinery, office equipment, autos and trucks, patent rights, and so forth—may be used in carrying on business operations. Because these assets are used for several years, determining the expense of using them for *one* year is a difficult accounting problem. It is not possible to directly observe and measure the consumption of a building, for example. If a supermarket spends $2,000,000 to acquire a new store, how much of this cost should be allocated to expense in the first year, the second year, and so on? The annual expense of using long-lived assets may be known as *depreciation, amortization,* or *depletion,* depending on the type of asset involved. Each of these will be discussed in subsequent sections.

DETERMINING THE COST OF PROPERTY, PLANT, AND EQUIPMENT

Under current accounting practice, virtually all transactions are recorded on the basis of *cost*. A cost signifies a sacrifice—something given up to acquire something else. Several problems may occur in determining the cost of property, plant, and equipment.

Acquisition and Installation Costs

When machinery and equipment are purchased, a question arises concerning which related costs should be associated with the item being acquired. Assume a machine with an invoice price of $36,000 is purchased. The related costs incurred include:

1 $2,160—Sales tax

2 $1,500—Freight charges (to have the machine delivered to the company's plant)

3 $730—Installation costs (to put the machine in place in the plant, provide necessary wiring, and so on)

4 $170—Testing costs (to make the machine ready for production).

The usual accounting rule is that any reasonable and necessary costs to make the machine operational should be included as part of the total cost of the machine. The logic for this rule is that the firm does not want a machine in a crate at some distant location but wants a machine which is delivered, installed, and ready to operate. Thus, the cost of the machine would be $40,560.

Invoice price of machine	$36,000
Sales tax	2,160
Freight	1,500
Installation	730
Testing	170
Cost of machine	$40,560

Bulk Purchases

Sometimes a firm may acquire several assets in one purchase transaction. This is referred to as a *bulk purchase*. For example, assume that a company buys a molding machine, a grinding machine, and a forklift from a competitor that is going out of business, paying a total of $8,000. In order to be able to calculate depreciation on each asset, the $8,000 must be divided among the three assets. This is done by using the relative market values of the three assets. Suppose that by checking market prices for used equipment or by having an appraisal, the firm estimates the market values and percentages to be:

Molding machine	$5,000	(50%)
Grinding machine	1,200	(12%)
Forklift	3,800	(38%)
Total Market Value	$10,000	(100%)

The $8,000 joint cost of the machines is then divided among the three machines based on the ratio of their market values, as follows:

Molding machine (50% of $8,000)	$4,000
Grinding machine (12% of $8,000)	960
Forklift (38% of $8,000)	3,040
Joint cost	$8,000

One type of bulk purchase that occurs very frequently is the purchase of land and building. Here the division of cost is particularly important because the building is to be depreciated, but the land is not.

Sometimes what appears to be a bulk purchase is really the purchase of only one asset. Assume that a company, seeking a site to build a new plant, buys for $180,000 a tract of land with two old houses on it. The company spends $10,000 to demolish the old houses. Lumber and other building materials salvaged from the houses are sold for $1,000. In this case none of the $180,000 purchase price is allocated to the houses. Rather the entire $180,000 purchase price plus the $9,000 net cost of demolition (a total of $189,000) should be considered cost of the land. The logic is that the company wished to buy the land on which to build a plant. The houses had no use or value to the company.

Nonmonetary Acquisitions

Property, plant, and equipment usually are acquired for cash, notes, or mortgages. However, sometimes assets are acquired in exchange for shares of stock or in exchange for other physical assets. These acquisitions are called *nonmonetary acquisitions.* Generally, nonmonetary acquisitions are recorded at the *fair market value* of the stock or assets given up. For example, if land is acquired in exchange for 100 shares of capital stock having a market value of $60 per share, the cost of the land should be recorded at $6,000 (100 shares times $60 market value).

In some cases, it may not be possible to determine the fair market value of the stock or assets given up. In this event, the fair market value of the *acquired* asset is determined and used in recording the transaction. Assume, for example, that a building is acquired in exchange for 200 shares of stock. Assume also that all the stock is owned by a few individuals and is not traded on any market. It would therefore be very difficult to determine the fair market value of the stock given up. As a substitute, the fair market value of the building acquired would be used to record the transaction.

CAPITALIZING VS. EXPENSING

A cost incurred is recorded in the accounting system when an exchange transaction occurs between two parties that results in the transfer of goods or services and the creation of an obligation for payment. The cost of the good or service obtained is initially classified as either an asset (capitalized) or an expense. Costs are *capitalized* (debited to an asset account) if it is expected that the service benefits (the revenue-generating capabilities) acquired by purchasing the item will not be entirely used up in the current period.

Costs are *expensed* at the time the transaction is initially recorded if it is expected that the service benefits will be entirely consumed in generating revenue during the current period. If net income is to be properly measured, the matching concept requires that costs consumed during the period be recorded as expenses for the period.

Judgment is required when applying the capitalize vs. expense rule to property, plant, and equipment acquisitions. One judgment to be made is that of *materiality*. Many items purchased may fit the criterion for capitalization, but their cost may be so small that whether they are capitalized or expensed has no significant effect on the financial statements. In such a case, accounting is made easier, and financial reporting is not harmed, by expensing these costs. Examples of items often expensed are small tools (e.g., hammers) and small items of office equipment (e.g, pencil sharpeners). Some firms handle the problem of materiality in the capitalize vs. expense decision by establishing a dollar cut-off. For example, the rule may be to expense any equipment items costing less than $100.

DEPRECIATION OF PROPERTY, PLANT, AND EQUIPMENT

Capitalized costs should be reviewed at the end of the accounting period to determine what portion has been consumed during the period. An adjusting entry is needed to charge (debit) to expense the portion of the cost consumed during the period. *Depreciation* is the term used to describe the periodic expensing of the portion of the cost of buildings, machinery, office equipment, and other long-lived, tangible assets consumed. It is important to remember that depreciation means the amount of the cost of these assets that is consumed (charged to expense) during a particular period of time, *not the decrease* in value of the asset. The accounting objective is the *matching* of costs and revenues for the purpose of income determination. When you see on a statement of income "Depreciation Expense ... $40,000," this is *not* saying that "the value of the company's property, plant, and equipment decreased by $40,000 this year." What it is saying is that "$40,000 of the cost of the company's property, plant, and equipment has been expensed to reflect the service benefits (or revenue-generating capabilities) consumed in earning this year's revenue."

Many people feel that the expense of using property, plant, and equipment cannot be properly measured without considering the impact of inflation. Depreciation expense based on the cost of a machine purchased ten years ago or a building purchased thirty years ago is unlikely to reflect the expense of using these assets based on today's costs. For the present, we will ignore this inflation problem; it will be discussed in Chapter 13.

Three long-lived assets commonly used in business operations are land, buildings, and equipment. For almost all purposes, land is assumed to have an *indefinite life*. No depreciation is calculated for land since land is not consumed. The only exception is when land is used for mining. In this case, the land (i.e., the natural resource deposits) is consumed in producing revenue, and thus the cost of the land is charged to expense over time. This is called *depletion,* and will be discussed later in the chapter.

Unlike land, buildings and equipment do not last indefinitely. Therefore, the cost of buildings and equipment is charged to expense over time as depreciation. Depreciation involves some estimates. Assume a company buys a machine costing $30,000, which is expected to be useful in production for several years. To determine annual depreciation expense, it must be estimated:

1 How long the machine will be used.

2 Whether, at the end of its life, it will have any remaining "salvage value" and if so, how much.

In addition, a choice must be made on which of several acceptable methods of calculating depreciation is to be used.

Estimation of Life and Salvage Value

To calculate depreciation, it is first necessary to estimate the useful life of an asset. *Useful life* means the expected period of time over which the firm expects to use the asset in its operations. In estimating the useful life, there are three factors to consider:

1 Physical considerations—buildings and equipment deteriorate over time, and thus there are physical limitations on life. For example, we might estimate that a delivery truck would have a physical life of 10 years, after which it would be so worn out that it would not be usable.

2 Economic considerations—after some period of time, an asset may have a remaining physical life, but may not be economically useful because of high maintenance costs, low productivity, technological obsolescence, and so forth. For example, we might estimate that the delivery truck has an economic life of 6 years, after which breakdowns are frequent and repair costs are high.

3 Replacement policy—for some assets a firm may establish a regular policy of replacement. For example, delivery trucks might be replaced every 4 years.

In considering these three factors for the delivery truck example, we would conclude that the estimated useful life is four years. In general, the task of estimating useful life belongs not to the accountant, but to others such as production managers or engineers.

After the useful life has been estimated, expected salvage value must be estimated. *Salvage value* means the expected value of the asset at the end of its useful life. Because salvage value is difficult to estimate, it is often estimated as a small amount and is sometimes ignored entirely. In a few cases, expected salvage value may be large. For example, if a company buys a $25,000 luxury automobile for use by its president and replaces it every two years, the salvage value of the two-year old luxury car may be over $10,000. In most cases, however, salvage values are small.

Methods of Depreciation

The accounting objective of depreciation is the matching of costs and revenues. The desire is to allocate the cost of depreciable assets to expense in a way that approximately represents the consumption of the service benefits of those assets in generating revenues. Since this process of consumption is virtually impossible to observe, several systematic methods of determining annual depreciation are used as an approximation of the (unknown) actual consumption. Four depreciation methods commonly used in accounting will be discussed.

Straight Line Method The simplest method of depreciation is the *straight line* method. Under this procedure, an equal amount of depreciation expense is charged for each year of the asset's life. To determine the annual depreciation charge, divide the *cost to be depreciated* (original cost minus salvage value) by the estimated life of the asset. Thus, the formula is:

$$\text{Depreciation Expense (straight line)} = \frac{\text{Cost} - \text{Salvage Value}}{\text{Estimated Life}}$$

For example, suppose Houser Corp. acquires a new machine costing $29,000. It is estimated to have a life of 8 years and a salvage value of $2,000. Annual depreciation expense would be:

$$\frac{\text{Cost} - \text{Salvage Value}}{\text{Estimated Life}} = \frac{\$29,000 - \$2,000}{8 \text{ years}}$$

$$= \frac{\$27,000}{8}$$

$$= \$3,375$$

In other words, the rate of depreciation is 12.5 percent (1/8) per year. Each year for 8 years, Houser Corp. would record $3,375 of depreciation expense as follows:

Depreciation Expense	3,375	
Accumulated Depreciation		3,375

To record depreciation for the year.

Sum of Years Digits Method A second method of depreciation is known as the *sum of years digits* method. Under this procedure, a decreasing amount of depreciation is charged for each successive year of the asset's life. To achieve this decreasing pattern of depreciation charges, the formula becomes more complex:

$$\begin{array}{l} \text{Depreciation Expense} \\ \text{(sum of years digits)} \end{array} = \frac{\text{Remaining Life}}{\text{Sum of Digits of Years of Life}} \times (\text{Cost} - \text{Salvage Value})$$

Two components of the formula require explanation. The "remaining life" component means the number of years of estimated asset life that currently remain, including the current year. For an asset with a five-year estimated life, remaining life would be 5 in the first year, 4 in the second year, 3 in the third year, and so on. The denominator in the above formula, the "sum of digits of years of life," means that the numbers 1, 2, 3, up to and including the estimated life are added. For an asset with a five-year life, add $1 + 2 + 3 + 4 + 5$, getting a total of 15, which becomes the denominator of the formula. There is a quick rule for getting the total of the first n digits, which is:

$$\text{sum of digits 1 through n} = \frac{n \times (n + 1)}{2}$$

$$\text{sum of digits 1 through 5} = \frac{5 \times 6}{2} = \frac{30}{2} = 15$$

For Houser Corp.'s new machine with its $29,000 cost, $2,000 salvage value, and eight-year life, sum of years digits depreciation for the first year would be:

$$\frac{\text{Remaining life}}{\text{Sum of digits of years of life}} \times (\text{Cost} - \text{Salvage value})$$

$$= (8/36) \times (\$29,000 - \$2,000)$$
$$= (8/36) \times \$27,000$$
$$= \$6,000$$

For the second year:

$$= (7/36) \times \$27,000$$
$$= \$5,250$$

Continuing this process for 8 years yields:

Year	(Cost − Salvage value) ×		Remaining life Sum of digits of years of life	Depreciation expense
1	($29,000−$2,000)	×	8/36	$ 6,000
2	($29,000−$2,000)	×	7/36	5,250
3	($29,000−$2,000)	×	6/36	4,500
4	($29,000−$2,000)	×	5/36	3,750
5	($29,000−$2,000)	×	4/36	3,000
6	($29,000−$2,000)	×	3/36	2,250
7	($29,000−$2,000)	×	2/36	1,500
8	($29,000−$2,000)	×	1/36	750
				$27,000

Observe that over the eight years, the total of the depreciation charges equals the $27,000 cost to be depreciated. Observe also that the depreciation expense decreases each year by a *constant dollar* amount (in this example $750).

Declining Balance Method   A third common method of depreciation is known as the *declining balance* method. Like the sum of years digits method, the declining balance method charges a decreasing amount of depreciation for each successive year of the asset's life. The sum of years digits method achieved this by applying a *decreasing rate* (remaining life/sum of years digits) to a *constant base* (cost − salvage value). The declining balance method reverses this process, applying a *constant rate* (such as twice the straight line rate) to a *decreasing base* (cost − accumulated depreciation). The declining balance formula, using twice the straight line rate, is:

$$\text{Depreciation Expense} = \frac{2}{\text{Estimated Life}} \times (\text{Cost} - \text{Accumulated Depreciation})$$

Note that salvage value does not appear in the formula for the declining balance method. Under declining balance depreciation, salvage value is not considered until near the end of the asset's life. This will be illustrated shortly. Note also that the rate shown in the above formula is twice the straight line rate (2 ÷ estimated life). This is often referred to as *double declining balance* or *200% declining balance* depreciation.

Continuing the Houser Corp. example (cost $29,000, life 8 years, salvage value $2,000), we will calculate 200% declining balance depreciation. The double declining balance depreciation rate is 25 percent or 2/8 (twice the 12.5% or 1/8 straight line rate). As a first step, we will ignore salvage value entirely.

Year	Cost minus accumulated depreciation	×	200% of straight line rate	=	Depreciation
1	$29,000.00		25%		$ 7,250.00
2	21,750.00		25		5,437.50
3	16,312.50		25		4,078.13
4	12,234.37		25		3,058.59
5	9,175.78		25		2,293.95
6	6,881.83		25		1,720.46
7	5,161.37		25		1,290.34
8	3,871.03		25		967.76
					$26,096.73

Observe that this formula, by taking a fraction of the undepreciated cost each year, will always leave some amount of undepreciated cost at the end of the estimated life. If this remaining amount happens to be equal (or very close to) the estimated salvage value, there is no problem. If the remaining amount does not approximate the salvage value, then the method must be adjusted. The specific adjustments to be made are covered in advanced courses. We will only note that (1) depreciation must stop when the salvage value is reached and (2) this adjustment is accomplished by a switch to the straight line method in the last years of the asset's life.

The rate used in declining balance depreciation need not be twice the straight line rate; other multiples may be used. Another common rate is one and one-half times the straight line rate (called *150 percent declining balance*).

In our example, the rate would be 18.75 percent (150 percent times 12.5 percent). Ignoring salvage value, annual depreciation is:

Year	Cost minus accumulated depreciation	×	150% of straight line rate	=	Depreciation
1	$29,000.00		18.75%		$ 5,437.50
2	23,562.50		18.75		4,417.97
3	19,144.53		18.75		3,589.60
4	15,554.93		18.75		2,916.55
5	12,638.38		18.75		2,369.70
6	10,268.68		18.75		1,925.38
7	8,343.30		18.75		1,564.37
8	6,778.93		18.75		1,271.05
					$23,492.12

Again, adjustment would be required to get the total depreciation to work out to $27,000 (cost minus salvage value).

Units of Production Method   The final depreciation method to be considered is the units of production method. Under this method, an estimate is made of the asset's life, not in years, but in some units of usage. For example, it is possible to use hours of operation (airplane engines, construction equipment), miles driven (rental cars, taxicabs), units manufactured (molds, dies), or days used (motel furniture) as the basis for estimating asset life. A rate per unit of use is calculated and then this rate is multiplied by the actual usage each year to determine annual depreciation expense.

To illustrate, assume that the Houser Corp. estimates the life of its machine to be 10,000 hours of productive use (rather than 8 years as used previously). The depreciation rate is:

$$\text{Rate per Unit} = \frac{\text{Cost} - \text{Salvage Value}}{\text{Estimated Life (units)}}$$

$$\text{Rate per Hour} = \frac{\$29,000 - \$2,000}{10,000 \text{ hours}} = \$2.70$$

Assume that in year 1, the machine is used 1,300 hours. Depreciation for year 1 would be:

$$\text{Annual Depreciation} = \text{Usage} \times \text{Rate per Unit}$$
$$\text{Year 1 Depreciation} = 1,300 \text{ hours} \times \$2.70$$
$$= \$3,510$$

Later years would be calculated in the same manner. Note that under this method, the depreciation expense is likely to fluctuate from year to year. The asset is fully depreciated when accumulated depreciation reaches $27,000 (i.e., when the life of 10,000 hours has been reached).

COMPUTER APPLICATION

The depreciation formulas presented above are easily programmed for computer application. A firm may have several thousand depreciable assets. Using the computer for these repetitive calculations saves time and reduces the chances of making calculation errors.

Tax Methods of Depreciation

Income tax law allows depreciation as a deduction in computing taxable income. Tax methods of depreciation, while following the same general logic as the accounting methods discussed above, often contain provisions to simplify their use. For example, salvage values may be ignored, and only certain specified asset lives may be allowed. To encourage investment in depreciable assets, tax law often allows a shorter life than the expected useful life determined for accounting purposes; this provides a quicker tax recovery of the investment. Because tax methods are subject to frequent legislative changes, we will not discuss them in detail here.

Partial-Year Depreciation

In the preceding illustrations, it was assumed that assets were acquired at the beginning of the year, and a full year's depreciation was calculated. Realistically, it can be expected that assets will be acquired at various times throughout the year. In making depreciation calculations, partial-year depreciation must be calculated for assets acquired during the year. This is usually done by counting how many months the asset was owned during the year (anything owned over one-half month is counted as a full month). For example, if an asset was acquired on May 7, 1987, eight months' depreciation would be taken for the year 1987. The full-year depreciation is multiplied by 8/12 to get the 1987 depreciation. If an asset was acquired on May 22, seven months' depreciation would be taken.

Note that the first and last years of the asset's life will be affected. Assume an asset costing $9,600 (estimated life 4 years, no salvage value) was acquired August 10, 1988. Depreciation each year, using straight line, would be:

Year		Depreciation expense
1988	(5/12 × $2,400)	$1,000
1989		2,400
1990		2,400
1991		2,400
1992	(7/12 × $2,400)	1,400
		$9,600

Note that to get four years' (48 months) depreciation, seven months' depreciation in 1992 is required.

Declining balance depreciation is handled in the same manner. If the asset described above were depreciated using 200 percent declining balance depreciation, the depreciation rate would be 50 percent (200 percent × the straight line rate of 25 percent). Depreciation each year would be:

Year	Cost minus accumulated depreciation	×	200% of straight line rate	×	Partial year adjustment	=	Depreciation
1988	$9,600.00		50%		5/12		$2,000.00
1989	7,600.00		50				3,800.00
1990	3,800.00		50				1,900.00
1991	1,900.00		50				950.00
1992	950.00		50		7/12		277.08
							$8,927.08

Notice that, as is common with declining balance depreciation, an implied salvage value remains of $672.92 (= $9,600.00 − $8,927.08). As mentioned earlier, adjustment techniques are available to make the salvage value come out to any figure desired. Partial-year adjustments become more complex when sum of the years digits depreciation is used. We leave this topic for advanced courses.

Firms sometimes use simpler partial-year depreciation policies instead of the nearest-full-month procedure described above. One common policy is always to use a half-year's depreciation in the year the asset is acquired, and a half-year in the year the asset reaches its estimated life (or the year of disposition, if earlier). Another common policy is to take a full year's depreciation in the year of acquisition, and no depreciation in the year of retirement. While the nearest-full-month procedure is preferable, these other policies may be acceptable on the basis of *materiality*. That is, the difference between using the correct procedure (nearest-full-month) and some other procedure may not have any significant impact on the financial statements.

Choice of Methods

The objective of depreciation calculations is to provide an annual expense of using property, plant, and equipment. Because it is impossible to observe directly how much of the asset cost has been consumed in a given year, accountants have developed the practice of using one of several systematic rules to calculate depreciation. Ideally, it should first be asked what pattern of depreciation is appropriate to a particular asset. The straight line method would be logical when it is believed that the asset produces roughly constant service (i.e., constant contribution to generating revenue) over its life. One of the accelerated methods (sum of years digits or declining balance) would be logical when it is believed that the asset's contribution towards generating revenue declines over time because it becomes less efficient or more costly to use and maintain as it ages. Finally, the units of production method would be logical when it is believed that the life of a particular asset depends heavily on the extent to which it is used, rather than the passage of time. Unfortunately, such analysis is not always used in selecting a depreciation method. Many firms choose depreciation methods on the basis of their effect on reported income.

COMPUTER APPLICATION

If impact on reported income is used as a criterion in the selection of depreciation methods, use of computer models helps to estimate quickly the impact of different choices. Either an electronic speadsheet program or a financial modeling program may be useful for this purpose.

Revision of Depreciation

Depreciation calculations involve *estimates* of asset life and salvage value. As time passes, previous estimates may be revised based on new information or changed conditions. For example, an estimate of life for a machine may be reduced because it has had extensive use or because newly introduced models have made the machine technically obsolete. The process of revising estimates because of new circumstances is an on-going part of accounting. We assume that estimates were reasonable when originally made, and past accounting entries based on these estimates should not be changed because of new information or changed conditions. Changes in estimates are therefore handled prospectively — revisions are made only for current and future effects.

An example will demonstrate the correct method of accounting for depreciation when a revision in estimated life and salvage value occurs. Assume the following:

1 A machine is purchased for $18,000 on January 2, 1985.

2 At time of purchase the estimated life and salvage value for the machine are expected to be 8 years and $2,000 respectively.

3 The company uses the straight line depreciation method and for 1985, 1986, and 1987 records annual depreciation expense of $2,000 [($18,000 − $2,000) ÷ 8 years]. Thus, the accumulated depreciation as of December 31, 1987 is $6,000.

4 Before the journal entry for depreciation is recorded for the year ended December 31, 1988, it is decided to revise the estimated life of the machine to a total of ten years from date of purchase. Also, the estimated salvage value is revised to $1,000.

The change in estimates is accounted for by revising the annual depreciation expense beginning in the year of the change (i.e., 1988). For 1988, and the remainder of the machine's revised life, the depreciation expense annually will be $1,571.43.

$$\text{Revised depreciation expense} = \frac{\$11,000 \text{ remaining depreciable amount}}{7 \text{ years remaining revised life}}$$

$$= \$1,571.43$$

The \$11,000 remaining depreciable amount is calculated as follows:

\$18,000	Cost
−1,000	Revised estimated salvage value
−6,000	Depreciation accumulated prior to change in estimated life
\$11,000	Remaining depreciable amount

The 7 years remaining revised life is determined by subtracting the three years elapsed since the machine was purchased from the revised total estimated life of ten years. In general, to calculate depreciation expense after a revision of life or salvage value has occurred, the formula is:

$$\frac{\text{Revised Depreciation}}{\text{Expense}} = \frac{\text{Remaining Book Value} - \text{Revised Salvage Value}}{\text{Remaining Revised Life}}$$

AMORTIZATION OF INTANGIBLE ASSETS

Intangible assets are long-lived, nonphysical assets owned by the firm. Often, these assets are legal or economic rights. Examples include:

1 Patents—legal rights to inventions, product designs, or manufacturing processes

2 Copyrights—legal rights to literary and artistic works

3 Trademarks—legal rights to product names and symbols

4 Franchises—contractual rights to carry on certain business operations in a particular area

5 Goodwill—economic rights to the established earning power of an acquired business

6 Leasehold improvements—improvements made to property being used under the contractual right of a lease agreement.

Intangible assets are recorded at cost. Often, intangibles are acquired by purchase. Sometimes, however, they may be produced within the firm. For example, a firm may undertake study and testing to develop an effective trademark for its product (a name, symbol, or slogan). The costs involved in developing the trademark, along with the costs involved in achieving trademark protection, would be capitalized.

Goodwill is recognized as an asset only when it is purchased. When a business is acquired, the price paid may exceed the fair market value of the individual assets acquired net of any liabilities assumed. This excess is paid for the fact that there is an existing business organization with trained employees, established customers, and so forth. This part of the purchase price is recorded as goodwill. We should note that internal development of employees (e.g., training programs) and customers (e.g., advertising) are not capitalized as goodwill, but are expensed immediately. Thus, goodwill is recorded only when *purchased*.

Not all intangible benefits are capitalized. Firms routinely carry on research and development activities to improve their products or manufacturing methods, or to develop new products. These research and development costs are expensed as incurred, not capitalized as assets. Similarly, a firm may engage in advertising to build consumer recognition and acceptance of its product. While these costs may indeed have future benefits, they are normally not capitalized.

The practice of expensing research and development, advertising, training, and similar costs results from difficulties encountered if these costs are capitalized. First, it is difficult to determine whether these costs have future benefit to the firm (this characteristic must be present if we are to consider these costs to be *assets*). If they are assets, it is difficult to estimate a useful life. Faced with these difficulties, accountants adopted a rule of expensing these costs.

All intangible assets should be charged to expense over their estimated useful life. This process is known as *amortization*. Amortization accounting is the same as depreciation accounting, with the following exceptions.

1 We use the term "amortization" instead of the term "depreciation."
2 Only the straight line method is used.
3 The credit in an amortization entry is generally made directly to the asset, rather than to an accumulated amortization account.

Often it is difficult to estimate a useful life for intangible assets because their consumption over time is hard to observe. A somewhat arbitrary life may have to be chosen. Accounting principles require that the life chosen not exceed 40 years.

Assume that on January 3, 1988, the Michelle Corporation buys patent rights to a new invention for $150,000. The company will produce and market this invention, and expects that it will be salable for ten years, after which it will be replaced by newer inventions. At time of purchase, Michelle would record:

1988			
Jan. 3	Patents	150,000	
	Cash		150,000
	To record purchase of patent rights.		

At the end of one year, the expense of using the patent would be recorded as:

Dec. 31	Amortization Expense	15,000	
	Patents		15,000
	To record amortization for the year.		

A similar amortization entry would be made in each of the next nine years.

DEPLETION OF NATURAL RESOURCES

Natural resources means land from which minerals of some kind (e.g., coal, oil, silver, gravel) are extracted by mining, drilling, excavation, and so forth.

Recall that we have treated land as a nondepreciable asset. The reason is that, for most uses, land has an unlimited life. When land is used for the extraction of natural resources, however, its life is definitely limited. Therefore, it is reasonable to match the cost of the land consumed against revenues generated. The cost of the land less any salvage value must be expensed over time. Again, this process is the same as depreciation, except that:

1 The term "depletion" is used rather than "depreciation" or "amortization."
2 Only the units of production method is used.

Assume that Wildcat Oil Co. purchases a tract of land for $3,000,000. Preliminary exploration had indicated the presence of oil reserves beneath the land. Further exploration and testing leads to the estimate that there are 8 million barrels of recoverable oil. As oil is produced, depletion of the land would be determined as follows:

Cost of land	$3,000,000
Less: Salvage value of land	
after extraction of oil	120,000
Cost to be depleted	$2,880,000

Depletion is calculated as follows:

$$\text{Depletion per Barrel} = \frac{\text{Cost to be Depleted}}{\text{Estimated Oil Reserves}}$$

$$= \frac{\$2,880,000}{8,000,000 \text{ barrels}}$$

$$= \$.36 \text{ per barrel}$$

Assume that in 1988, 850,000 barrels of oil are produced and sold. Depletion would be $306,000 (850,000 × $.36), and would be recorded as:

1988			
Dec. 31	Depletion Expense	306,000	
	Accumulated Depletion		306,000
	To record depletion for the year.		

If the oil had been stored in inventory rather than being sold during the current period, the amount calculated as depletion would be capitalized as inventory cost, until the oil was sold.

SALE OF PROPERTY, PLANT, AND EQUIPMENT

A firm acquires property, plant, and equipment assets for the purpose of using them in its operations over a period of years. Sometimes a firm will decide to sell one of these assets, perhaps because it is no longer needed or is too old to continue to maintain, or the firm is replacing it with a better asset.

When a sale occurs, the impact on income must be determined. This impact is determined by comparing the selling price with the undepreciated cost (or "book value") of the asset at time of sale. The difference between these two numbers is the *gain* or *loss* on the sale. Thus:

$$
\begin{array}{l}
\text{Selling price of asset} \\
-\ \text{Undepreciated cost at time of sale} \\
\text{(Original cost of asset} - \\
\underline{\text{accumulated depreciation)}} \\
=\ \underline{\text{Gain or Loss}}
\end{array}
$$

Assume that Wallin Mfg. Co. purchased a machine on July 1, 1985 at a cost of $95,000. It was estimated to have a ten-year life and salvage value of $5,000, and straight line depreciation was used. Assume that the machine was sold on October 1, 1989, for $65,000. The depreciation taken on this machine would be:

1985 (six months)	$ 4,500
1986	9,000
1987	9,000
1988	9,000
1989 (nine months)	6,750
Total Depreciation to October 1, 1989	$38,250

Notice that, before the gain or loss on the sale is calculated and recorded, depreciation expense up to the date of sale must be recognized. Thus on October 1, we record:

1989			
Oct. 1	Depreciation Expense	6,750	
	Accumulated Depreciation		6,750
	To record depreciation to date of sale of machine.		

The gain on the sale is $8,250, determined as follows:

Selling price		$65,000
Book value:		
Original cost	$95,000	
Accumulated depreciation	− 38,250	56,750
Gain on sale		$ 8,250

To record this transaction, make an entry that:

1 Records the receipt of $65,000 of cash

2 Removes the cost of the asset ($95,000) and the accumulated depreciation ($38,250) from the accounts

3 Records the gain or loss ($8,250 gain).

The entry needed to accomplish these three steps is:

1989			
Oct. 1	Cash	65,000	
	Accumulated Depreciation	38,250	
	Equipment		95,000
	Gain on Sale of Equipment		8,250
	To record sale of used equipment.		

In reporting a gain or loss on the income statement, only the *net figure* is shown. Thus, in the above example, the 1989 income statement would show:

Gain on Sale of Equipment   8,250

The $65,000 selling price and the $56,750 undepreciated cost would not be shown on the income statement.

EXCHANGES OF PROPERTY, PLANT, AND EQUIPMENT

A firm may exchange one asset for another. Here the general rule is that fair market value of the asset given up in the exchange is used to record the asset acquired and to determine any gain or loss. By following this rule, an exchange of asset A for asset B is treated in the same way as if asset A were sold for cash and then asset B were purchased. There is, however, one important exception to this rule. If the transaction involves a gain on the exchange of similar productive assets, then book value (rather than fair market value) is used to record the asset acquired, and the gain is not recognized. This treatment is followed because exchanges of similar assets (such as a trade-in of one truck on another) that indicate a gain are considered to be a single interrelated transaction, rather than the equivalent of two transactions (sale and purchase).

Exhibit 7-1 summarizes the rules for recording property, plant, and equipment exchanges. Note on Exhibit 7-1 that losses on *all* exchanges, whether dissimilar or similar assets are involved, are recorded. However, only gains on the exchange of dissimilar assets are recorded—gains on the exchange of similar assets are not recorded.

Exchange of Dissimilar Assets

First, assume that on August 18, 1988, Company A gives up a piece of land having a book value of $6,000 and a fair market value of $10,000 in exchange for a machine. This is *not* an exchange of *similar* productive assets (land for machine). Fair market value would be used to record the new asset and gain or loss would be recorded. The machine is recorded at its $10,000 cost (the market value of the land given up to acquire it); the machine must be worth approximately $10,000, or one of the two parties would not have agreed to make this exchange. A gain of $4,000 is recognized on the disposition of the land

EXHIBIT 7-1   Property, Plant, and Equipment Exchanges

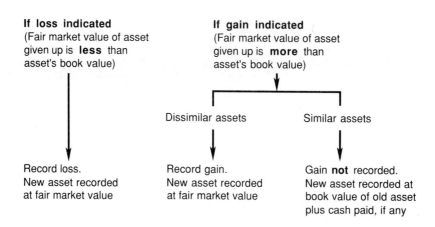

($10,000 value received minus the $6,000 cost of the land). Thus, the entry to record the transaction is:

1988			
Aug. 18	Machine	10,000	
	Land		6,000
	Gain on Disposition of Land		4,000
	To record cost of machine acquired in exchange for land having a cost of $6,000 and a fair market value of $10,000.		

The same procedure is followed in the case of a loss on the exchange of dissimilar assets.

Exchange of Similar Assets—Gain Situation

Now assume that on November 3, 1988, Company B gives up one machine having an original cost of $10,000, accumulated depreciation of $6,000 (hence a book value of $4,000) and a fair market value of $5,500, in exchange for a smaller but similar machine. This is an exchange of *similar* productive assets (machine for similar machine). The new machine would be recorded at $4,000 (the book value of the machine given up) and the $1,500 gain ($5,500 value received minus $4,000 book value) would not be recognized. The entry to record the exchange is:

1988			
Nov. 3	Machine (new)	4,000	
	Accumulated Depreciation	6,000	

original cost of $4,900 and now has a book value of $1,800). The truck dealer offers West's Market a $3,000 trade-in allowance (therefore the cash payment is $4,000). To get the new truck in this gain situation ($3,000 estimated fair market value received is more than $1,800 book value of the old truck), West is giving up two things: $4,000 cash and the old truck with a book value of $1,800. Thus it can be said that the new truck cost West $5,800. Record this transaction as follows:

1989			
Jan. 4	Truck (new)	5,800	
	Accumulated Depreciation	3,100	
	Truck (old)		4,900
	Cash		4,000
	To record purchase of new truck		
	and trade-in of old truck.		

This entry removes the cost ($4,900) and accumulated depreciation ($3,100) on the old truck and charges the $1,800 book value of the old truck plus the $4,000 cash paid as the cost of the new truck. No gain appears in the entry.

In a few cases, the exchange of similar assets may involve the *receipt* of cash. In this event, the recognition of gain or loss becomes more complex. This topic is left for advanced courses.

FINANCIAL STATEMENT PRESENTATION

We have discussed the acquisition, depreciation, and disposition of property, plant, and equipment; intangibles; and natural resources. We now consider the presentation of these items on financial statements.

Statement of Income

Depending on the level of detail in the income statement, depreciation expense (along with amortization expense and depletion expense) might appear as a separate line in the expense section. In some statements of income, depreciation expense does not appear as a separate item. Rather, it may be included within another title, such as cost of goods sold (especially in a manufacturing firm), operating expenses, or selling, general, and administrative expenses.

Gains and losses from the disposition of property, plant, and equipment typically are presented in the *other revenues* section of the income statement (losses appear as negative amounts).

Balance Sheet

The property, plant, and equipment section generally follows current assets on the balance sheet. (If an investments section exists, as will be discussed in Chapter 9, property, plant, and equipment follows the investments section.)

Land, buildings, and equipment are often listed separately. The contra asset account *Accumulated Depreciation* indicates the total amount of building and equipment cost consumed to date and is shown as a deduction, as follows:

Property, Plant, and Equipment:			
Land			$100,000
Buildings	$700,000		
Equipment	550,000	$1,250,000	
Less: Accumulated Depreciation		425,000	825,000
			$925,000

Alternatively, a shorter version might be used, which shows the property, plant, and equipment *net* of the subtraction of accumulated depreciation.

Property, Plant, and Equipment, net	$925,000

In such a case, the details shown in the previous example would be presented in the notes to the financial statements.

Natural resources (which are primarily land costs) are usually included under the property, plant, and equipment heading. If natural resources are present, the accumulated depreciation title changes to accumulated depreciation and depletion.

Intangible assets are commonly presented in the *other assets* section of the balance sheet, which follows the property, plant, and equipment section. Intangible assets are generally presented *net* of accumulated amortization. Typical presentation would be:

Other assets:	
Patents, net	$75,000

SUMMARY

Learning Objective 1: Account for the acquisition of property, plant, and equipment.

All costs related to the acquisition of property, plant, and equipment should be capitalized, including costs of delivery and installation. If several assets are acquired in a single transaction, an allocation of the total purchase price is required.

Learning Objective 2: Apply the straight line, sum of years digits, declining balance, and units of production methods of depreciation.

Under the matching concept, the cost (less salvage value) of buildings and equipment is charged to depreciation expense over the asset's estimated useful life. Physical considerations, economic considerations, and replacement policy are factors affecting estimated useful life and salvage value. Depreciation is not intended to approximate decreases in the market value of the asset. Four commonly used depreciation methods are straight line, sum of years digits, declining balance, and units of production.

Learning Objective 3: Calculate partial-year depreciation.

When a depreciable asset is purchased during the year, depreciation should be calculated to the nearest full month. Some firms use simpler policies on the grounds that no material difference results.

Learning Objective 4: Account for a change in estimated life or salvage value.

Changes in the estimated life or salvage value of a depreciable asset are accounted for prospectively. A revised amount for depreciation expense is recorded for current and future years. The new depreciation amount is determined by dividing the asset's remaining depreciable cost by the remaining revised life.

Learning Objective 5: Calculate and record amortization of intangible assets and depletion of natural resources.

When dealing with intangible assets, amortization is the term used instead of depreciation. Depletion is the correct terminology for natural resources. Amortization is calculated by the straight line method, and depletion by the units of production method.

Learning Objective 6: Calculate and record gains and losses resulting from the sale or exchange of long-lived assets.

Upon sale of a long-lived asset, an entry is required to record the cash received, remove the cost and accumulated depreciation of the asset sold from the accounts, and recognize the gain or loss on the sale. Trading of one asset for a similar asset does not result in any gain being recorded, although a loss would be recorded. Exchanging nonsimilar assets results in recording of either gain or loss, as appropriate.

KEY TERMS

Amortization	Salvage value
Capitalize	Straight line method
Declining balance method	Sum of years digits method
Depletion	Units of production method
Depreciation	Useful life

REVIEW QUESTIONS

1 Welham Manufacturing Co. purchased a new sanding machine on March 8, 1988 for $43,500. In addition, the following costs were incurred:
   a Sales tax of 6 percent on $43,500 invoice price.
   b Freight charges for delivery of $1,200.
   c Wiring and other installation costs of $2,640.
   d $1,800 cost of uninsured damage to receiving dock when machine fell off forklift truck.
   Determine the dollar amount that Welham should capitalize as the cost of the sanding machine.

2 Flett, Inc. makes a bargain purchase for $1,000,000 of a plot of land with a small warehouse on it. The appraisal values are: land $900,000 and warehouse

$300,000. How should the $1,000,000 cost be allocated between the land and the building? If Flett planned to demolish the warehouse in order to construct a new office building, how would the $1,000,000 cost be allocated?

3 Spruce Co. acquires land in exchange for 500 shares of Spruce's capital stock. How should the cost of the land be determined?

4 If the decision is made to capitalize the cost of a machine (i.e., add the cost to an asset account) when the machine is purchased, then that cost can never become an expense. Evaluate the preceding statement.

5 On May 1, 1988, Perfecto Company purchased an automatic coffee pot for use in its office. The company estimates the useful life of the coffee pot to be five years, and decides to capitalize and then depreciate its $24.95 cost using double declining balance depreciation. While Perfecto's action is theoretically justified, what practical alternative exists to account for the cost of the coffee pot? What accounting concept underlies the practical alternative?

6 Searfoss, Inc. incorrectly expenses the cost of a refrigeration unit added to the company's delivery truck. What will be the effects of this error on the financial statements? Ignore income taxes.

7 What is the purpose of depreciation? What is depreciation *not* intended to accomplish?

8 Myriad, Inc. purchased a building on January 2, 1986 for $130,000. The estimated life of the building is forty years. The estimated salvage value is $10,000. Myriad uses straight line depreciation. How much will the building be worth on January 2, 1990?

9 How is depreciation expense calculated under each of the following depreciation methods: straight line, sum of years digits, double declining balance, and units of production?

10 Which depreciation method logically would be most appropriate for a particular asset whose useful life is mainly dependent on the extent to which the asset is used? Which methods would be theoretically superior for a particular asset whose service benefits provided decline over its estimated life? Which method would be the logical choice if the service benefits provided by the asset are roughly constant over the asset's life, regardless of use?

11 What factors should be considered in determining the estimated life of a particular asset?

12 Proudville Co. decides to depreciate its new building over an estimated useful life of thirty-five years. If the company chooses the sum of years digits depreciation method, what will be the denominator (i.e., the sum of digits of years of life) in the depreciation formula?

13 If your objective is to maximize reported net income in the next few years, which depreciation methods on a practical basis should *not* be selected for current plant and equipment acquisitions?

14 Palmer Co.'s net income is reported at $538,164,928.31. Is the reported net income an exact measurement of the true income for the period? Discuss.

15 Discuss how a change in accounting estimate is handled. Use a change in the estimated life of a delivery truck as the basis for your discussion.

16 Differentiate among the following three terms: depreciation, amortization, and depletion.

17 "Calculation of depletion is a procedure similar to the units of production depreciation method." Evaluate the preceding statement.

18 "Trading in an old long-lived asset on a similar one could result in the recording of a loss but never results in the recording of a gain. However, the sale of an old long-lived asset could create either an accounting gain or loss." Evaluate the preceding statements.

19 "In the exchange of one asset for another, the fair market value of the asset given up is used to record the asset acquired and to determine any gain or loss to be recognized on the asset exchanged." Evaluate the preceding statement.

EXERCISES

E7-1 Dorway, Inc. acquired land and a warehouse building for $120,000 cash on January 2, 1988. The $120,000 cost was allocated as follows: $55,000 for the land and $65,000 for the building. The warehouse is expected to be sold for $15,000 at the end of its useful life. Also on January 2, 1988, Dorway purchased on account a $10,000 machine for use in the factory. In addition, a freight charge of $80 and state sales tax of $500 were paid in cash by Dorway on the purchase of the machine. The machine has an expected useful life of eight years. Selected general ledger accounts for Dorway for 1988 are presented below:

Land

1/2/88	55,000		

Accumulated depreciation—land

		12/31/88	2,750

Warehouse building

1/2/88	65,000		

Accumulated depreciation—warehouse building

		12/31/88	2,500

Equipment—factory machine

1/2/88	10,000		

Accumulated depreciation—factory machine

		12/31/88	1,000

Freight expense

1/2/88	80		

Sales tax expense

1/2/88	500		

Required:

1 Examine the general ledger accounts. What error(s), if any, were made by Dorway?

2 What is the estimated useful life of the warehouse building? (Assume that the accumulated depreciation-warehouse building account is correct, given the amount of asset cost recorded.)

3 What is the estimated salvage value of the machine after eight years? (Assume the accumulated depreciation-factory machine account is correct, given the amount of asset cost recorded.)

E7-2 Wolinsky, Inc. purchased a grinding machine on January 3, 1986 for $45,000. The machine had an estimated salvage value of $6,000 and an estimated life of three years. Wolinsky uses straight line depreciation. Wolinsky's bookkeeper incorrectly charged the entire $45,000 cost of the machine to repairs expense in 1986. Ignoring income taxes, indicate the effects of the error on the income statements and balance sheets for 1986, 1987, and 1988.

E7-3 Fly-by-Night Realty Co. purchases a tract of land for $600,000. The tract is subdivided into three sections with the following appraisal values: Tract—$210,000, Tract B—$350,000, and Tract C—$140,000. During the year Tract A is sold for $220,000 and one-half of Tract B is sold for $180,000. Determine sales revenue, cost of sales, gross profit, and the cost of the remaining unsold land.

E7-4 Fickle, Inc. is trying to decide which depreciation method to select for the new delivery truck the company has just acquired. The truck cost $16,000, has an estimated life of four years, and an estimated salvage value of $1,000. Calculate depreciation for each of the four years for the following three depreciation methods: straight line, sum of years digits, and 200% declining balance. What factors should Fickle consider in selecting amoung the alternative depreciation methods available?

E7-5 In January, 1988, the Hartley Company acquired several plant and equipment assets. Information concerning these assets is presented below. Determine for each asset the amount of depreciation for 1988 and 1989.

1 Building, cost $138,000, expected life forty years, estimated salvage value $18,000. Straight line depreciation is to be used.

2 Machine, cost $27,000, expected life six years, estimated salvage value $1,000. 150% declining balance depreciation is to be used.

3 Automobile, cost $4,100, expected life four years, estimated salvage value $1,100. Sum of years digits depreciation is to be used.

4 Moving van, cost $90,000, estimated useful life of 300,000 miles, estimated salvage value $12,000. Units of production depreciation method to be used. Miles actually driven: 1988 = 58,000 miles, 1989 = 72,500 miles.

E7-6 On July 1, 1985, Tee Co. purchased a machine for $11,000. The estimated salvage value was $1,000 and the estimated life was five years. The company uses straight line depreciation, and their accounting year ends on December 31. On December 31, 1988, before the depreciation entry is recorded, the company revises the estimated life of the machine to a total of seven years. Calculate depreciation expense for each year 1985 through 1992.

E7-7 T & B Coal Company on January 2, 1988 began mining their East Ridge tract. The East Ridge tract was purchased for $12,500,000. Geologists estimate the tract contains 2,000,000 tons of coal. The salvage value of the tract after mining operations are completed is estimated at $500,000. A coal-washing machine purchased by the company for use at the East Ridge tract cost $400,000. The Company decides to use the units of production method of depreciation for the machine. The estimated life of the machine is 2,000,000 tons with a zero salvage value. During 1988 the Company mined and sold 200,000 tons of coal from the East Ridge Tract. Present journal entries to record:

1 Depletion for 1988.

2 Depreciation of the coal-washing machine for 1988.

E7-8 Shilling Co. acquired a wire-baling machine on May 1, 1984 for $23,000. The machine was estimated to have a life of seven years and a salvage value of $2,000. The machine was depreciated using the straight line method. The Company's policy is to compute depreciation for each month the asset is owned during the year. On April 1, 1988 (after owning the machine for 3 years and 11 months), Shilling sells the wire-baling machine for $12,500 cash.

1 Present the journal entry to record the sale.

2 Present the required journal entry if the sales price had been $9,000, instead of $12,500.

3 Assume Shilling instead of selling the wire-baling machine, trades it along with $15,000 cash for a new machine with a $30,000 list price. Present the journal entry to record the trade-in.

E7-9 Present journal entries to record the exchange of the following *dissimilar* assets.

1 Inventory costing $18,000, and with a market price of $26,000, is exchanged for a machine with a list price of $28,000.

2 A machine which cost $160,000 and had a fair market value of $62,000 is exchanged for a tract of land appraised at $62,000. There is $92,000 accumulated depreciation associated with the machine when it is exchanged.

E7-10 Present journal entries to record the exchange of the following *similar* assets.

1 Land costing $195,000, and with a market value of $250,000, is exchanged along with $30,000 cash for another tract of land that is located closer to the business.

2 A photocopy machine worth $17,000, and with a book value of $20,000 ($80,000 cost less $60,000 accumulated depreciation), is traded along with $89,000 cash for a new photocopier.

PROBLEMS

P7-1 *Acquisition of Property, Plant, and Equipment*

Rivers, CPA, is the auditor for a manufacturing company with a balance sheet that includes the caption "Property, Plant, and Equipment." Rivers has been asked by the company's management if adjusting entries are required for the following material items that have been included in or excluded from "Property, Plant, & Equipment."

1 A tract of land was acquired during the year. The land is to be the site of the company's new headquarters, which will be constructed later in the year.

Adjustment should include installation cost

Commissions were paid to the real estate agent used to acquire the land, and expenditures were made to relocate the previous owner's equipment. These commissions and expenditures were expensed and are excluded from Property, Plant, & Equipment.

No adjustment

2 Clearing costs were incurred to make the land ready for construction. These costs <u>were included</u> in Property, Plant, & Equipment.

An adjustment should be made under Land account title

3 During the land clearing process, timber and gravel were recovered and sold. The proceeds from the sale were recorded as other income and are excluded from Property, Plant, & Equipment.

Do nothing No Adjustment

4 A group of machines was purchased. The cost of the machines, freight costs, and unloading charges were capitalized and are included in Property, Plant, & Equipment.

Required:

1 Describe the general characteristics of assets, such as land, buildings, improvements, machinery, equipment, fixtures, and so on, that should normally be classified as Property, Plant, & Equipment.

2 Indicate whether each of the above items numbered 1 to 4 requires an adjusting entry and explain why such adjustments are required or not required. Organize your answer as follows:

Item number	Is adjustment required? Yes or No	Reasons why adjustment is required or not required

(AICPA Adapted)

P7-2 *Bulk Purchases*

Mountain Developers, Inc. purchased a parcel of land in the Red Mountains for $520,000. An additional $180,000 was spent on the unimproved land to develop it and subdivide it into 64 lots for vacation homes. The types and number of lots developed were as follows:

Type	Number of lots developed
Lakeview	30
Stream Frontage	10
Deep Woods	24

The selling prices for the various types of lots were set at: $15,000 for Lakeview, $12,000 for Stream Frontage, and $7,500 for Deep Woods. To date, Mountain Developers have sold 18 Lakeview lots, 7 Stream Frontage lots, and 2 Deep Woods lots.

Required:

1 Allocate the bulk purchase cost of the tract of land and the additional development costs among the three types of lots. Use the relative market values of the total lots in each type as a basis for allocation. Compute a cost per lot for each type of lot.

2 Determine sales revenue, cost of sales, and gross profit realized to date on sales of lots from this parcel of land.

P7-3 *Recording Property, Plant, and Equipment Transactions*

Flour Co. had the following selected transactions and adjustments during 1988. The company uses the straight line depreciation method. Flour has adopted a policy of expensing tools and equipment parts costing less than $100.

1 January 2—acquired land and a store building. The land cost $10,000 and the building cost $50,000. The estimated useful life of the building is 40 years, after which it will have an estimated value of zero. Flour made a $20,000 cash down payment and signed a note payable for the remaining amount. The note is to be paid off in 20 equal semiannual installments of $3,210. The $3,210 installments include 10 percent annual interest (i.e., 5 percent semiannual interest rate).

2 January 3—purchased store fixtures and equipment for $12,000 cash. The estimated useful life of the store fixtures and equipment is 12 years. After 12 years the estimated value of the fixtures and equipment will be $2,400.

3 March 5—purchased on account a delivery truck for $9,000. The estimated useful life of the truck is four years. At the end of the four years it is estimated that the truck will be sold for $1,000.

4 May 23—purchased land and a warehouse building for $680,000 cash. Appraisal values are: land $144,000 and warehouse building $576,000. The estimated useful life and salvage value for the building are 25 years and $19,000 respectively.

5 June 30—paid first semiannual installment of $3,210 on note payable.

6 August 8—purchased on account for $80 a set of wrenches and other shop tools. The estimated useful life is three years with no salvage value.

7 October 2—acquired a sanding machine in exchange for 3,000 shares of Flour's capital stock. The stock has a fair market value of $7.50 per share. The sanding machine has an estimated useful life of ten and one-half years and an estimated salvage value of $2,040.

8 October 4—paid $160 cash to Motor Freight, Inc. to have the sanding machine delivered.

9 October 5—paid $380 cash to Brantford Electricians to install the sanding machine.

10 December 31—purchased for $7,000 cash five forklift trucks to be used next year. The estimated useful life of the forklifts is five years. After five years the forklifts are expected to be worth $500 each.

11 December 31—paid second semiannual installment of $3,210 on note payable.

12 December 31—recorded depreciation entries for the year.

Required:

Prepare journal entries for the items listed above.

P7-4 *Depreciation Under Various Methods*

Brandywine Historical Society purchased a new building on January 2, 1987. The building cost $90,000, has an estimated life of 25 years, and an estimated salvage value of $30,000.

Required:

Prepare schedules showing depreciation expense, accumulated depreciation at the end of the year, and book value at the end of the year for the first four years of the building's life. Prepare a separate schedule for: 1) straight line depreciation,

2) sum of years digits depreciation, and 3) 150% declining balance depreciation. Round depreciation amounts to nearest dollar. Use the following format for your schedules.

Year	Depreciation expense	Accumulated depreciation, end of year	Book value, end of year
1987			
1988			
1989			
1990			

P7-5 *Depreciation Under Various Methods*

Selecto Company is trying to choose a depreciation method for a recent new equipment purchase. The equipment cost of $60,000 is to be depreciated over its estimated life of four years, or 14,062 units of output. The estimated salvage value is $3,750. The company's income tax rate is 40 percent.

Required:

1 For *each* of the four depreciation methods [a) straight line, b) sum of years digits, c) double declining balance, and d) units of production], complete the schedule below.

	Year 1	Year 2	Year 3	Year 4	Total
Income Before Depreciation and Income Taxes	$130,000	$140,000	$150,000	$160,000	$580,000
Depreciation Expense					
Income Before Income Taxes	$	$	$	$	$
Income Tax Expense (40%)					
Net Income	$	$	$	$	$
Accumulated Depreciation	$	$	$	$	
Book Value	$	$	$	$	

For the units of production method, assume units produced are: 5,000 in Year 1; 3,062 in Year 2; 2,500 in Year 3; and 3,500 in Year 4.

2 Evaluate the net income pattern produced by each depreciation method. Which method is the best for financial statement purposes? Discuss.

P7-6 *Partial-Year Depreciation*

On October 1, 1986, Young, Inc. purchased a machine costing $280,000. The machine cost $5,000 to be transported to Young and $5,000 to be installed. Both of these costs were paid by the firm. The estimated useful life of the machine is ten years and the salvage value is $20,000. Round depreciation amounts to the nearest dollar.

Required:

Prepare the following schedule, which compares the different depreciation methods.

Method	Depreciation expense for 1986	Depreciation expense for 1987	Depreciation expense for 1988	Book value 12/31/88
Straight line				
Double declining balance				

P7-7 *Depletion and Depreciation*

The Onteareo Power & Light company purchased a large tract of land believed to contain rich oil deposits. The land cost $4,800,000. Test wells and a geological survey estimate 1,536,000 barrels of oil will be obtained from the tract. The estimated salvage value of the land after drilling operations cease is $192,000. Oil drilling equipment purchased for the tract cost $3,100,000. The estimated life of the oil drilling equipment is five years, with an estimated salvage value of $300,000. The oil wells are expected to produce oil for over twelve years. Onteareo Power & Light uses the double declining balance method of depreciation for the oil drilling equipment.

Required:

1 Calculate the depletion rate per barrel.

2 If 180,000 barrels are produced in the first year, what is the depletion amount for the year? If 160,000 of the 180,000 barrels are sold during that year (the remaining 20,000 barrels are in inventory at the end of the year), how much of the depletion amount would be in cost of sales and how much would be in inventory?

3 Prepare a depreciation schedule for the oil drilling equipment. Use the following format for your schedule:

Year	Cost minus accumulated depreciation, as of beginning of the year	Double declining balance depreciation rate	Depreciation expense
1			$
2			
3			
4			
5			
		Total	$

4 Assume Onteareo Power & Light at the end of the fourth year decides to replace the oil drilling equipment with technically superior new equipment. Two options available are: 1) sell the old drilling equipment to another drilling company for $526,000 and then purchase the new equipment for $4,900,000 or 2) trade in the old drilling equipment along with $4,374,000 cash to acquire the new equipment. Year 4 has been a poor year for Onteareo Power & Light. Earnings are lower than in previous years. To improve reported earnings, decide whether the old drilling equipment should be sold or traded in. Explain your decision. What effect, if any, will your decision have on reported earnings in subsequent years? Ignore tax effects in your discussion.

P7-8 *Acquisitions and Dispositions*

Required:
For each independent case presented below determine: a) the cost to be recorded for the asset acquired and b) the gain or loss, if any, to be recognized.

Case 1
On January 2, 1989, Wilbur Delivery Company traded in an old delivery truck for a newer model. Data relative to the old and new trucks follow:

Old Truck:	
Original cost	$ 8,000
Accumulated depreciation	6,000
New Truck:	
List price	10,000
Cash price without trade-in	9,000
Cash price with trade-in	7,800

(AICPA Adapted)

Case 2
On December 1, 1988, Hobart Company acquired a new rail-splitting machine in exchange for an old rail-splitting machine. The old machine was purchased for $7,000 and had a book value of $2,800. On the date of the exchange the old machine had a market value of $3,000. In addition, Hobart paid $3,500 cash for the new machine, which had a list price of $8,000.

(AICPA Adapted)

Case 3
An old machine with a book value of $18,000 (originally costing $44,000) was exchanged along with $78,000 cash for a new cabin cruiser. The old machine had a market value of $28,000 at the time of the trade-in. The list price of the boat is $110,000.

Case 4
On June 30, 1988, Posute Co. exchanged a warehouse building for a tract of land. The land had a fair market value of $460,000. The warehouse building had been acquired two years earlier on July 1, 1986 for $500,000. It was being depreciated over 40 years using straight line depreciation and an estimated salvage value of $20,000. The fair market value of the warehouse building cannot be determined.

P7-9 *Sales and Exchanges*
During 1988 O'Mara Company had the following sales and trade-ins for its long-lived assets:
1 January 2—an item of equipment that had cost $25,000 when purchased on January 2, 1982 (six years ago) was traded in on a new piece of equipment. The list price of the new equipment was $60,000. A trade-in allowance of $15,000 is allowed for the old equipment, even though the book value of the old equipment is only $7,000.
2 January 2—a machine purchased early in January of 1984 (four years ago) for $80,000 was sold for $47,000. Depreciation of $9,000 per year on the machine had been taken.

3 July 1—a new truck was acquired in trade for an old truck that had been purchased for $16,000 on March 1, 1981 (seven years, four months ago). The old truck was being depreciated over an estimated life of 10 years using straight line depreciation and an estimated $1,000 salvage value. O'Mara paid $14,000 cash, plus the old truck, to obtain the new truck. The list price of the new truck was $21,000. Assume six months' depreciation for 1988 has been recorded.

4 December 31—an automobile that had cost $7,000 when purchased on January 3, 1986 (three years ago) was sold for $1,100. The automobile was being depreciated over an estimated life of four years using the sum of years digits depreciation method. The salvage value had been estimated at $1,000. Assume depreciation for 1988 has been recorded.

Required:
Prepare journal entries to record the above transactions.

Business Decision Problem

Jane Crosson is Cedar, Inc.'s tax advisor. Cedar is a small, family-owned company. The company's primary objective for the current year, 1988, is to minimize income taxes. For each of the following situations, Jane is trying to select the alternative that will minimize current income taxes. Cedar's tax rate is 40 percent.

1 A new machine was acquired for $100,000 on July 1, 1988. The machine has an estimated useful life of twelve years. *Alternatives:* Accelerated depreciation, or straight line depreciation over twelve-year estimated useful life.

2 A machine purchased in 1978 for $45,000 with a zero estimated salvage value became fully depreciated during 1987. The machine is still functioning. Cedar has been offered $22,000 cash for the old machine. *Alternatives:* Continue during 1988 to use the fully depreciated machine or sell it for $22,000 cash.

3 The president's old car, which has a book value on Cedar's accounting records of $8,000, is to be replaced with a new car that has a list price of $18,000. *Alternatives:* Trade the old car, plus $7,000 cash, for the new car or sell the old car to a used car dealer for $11,000 and then purchase for $18,000 cash the new car.

Required:
In light of the objective of minimizing current year's income taxes, select for each situation the alternative that Jane should choose. Provide calculations and reasoning for your answers. Include in your discussions the effects of your recommendations on future years' income taxes.

8

ACCOUNTING FOR INTEREST EXPENSE, BONDS PAYABLE, AND LEASES

LEARNING OBJECTIVES

When you complete this chapter, you should be able to:

1 Discuss the advantages and disadvantages of bond financing.
2 Record the issuance and retirement of bonds.
3 Record bond interest expense and the associated amortization of discount or premium.
4 Distinguish between the concepts of present value and future value, and single amount and annuity.
5 Perform time-value-of-money calculations using present value and future value tables.
6 Calculate the issue price of a bond.

It is critical to a firm's success to consider the cost of financing business operations. In order to acquire and maintain the assets necessary to conduct its business, a firm requires financing. The main sources of financing for a corporation are:

1 Capital invested by stockholders who purchased shares of stock from the corporation.
2 Earnings that have been retained in the firm, rather than distributed to stockholders.
3 Debt of various forms.

Each of these forms of financing has its cost. The cost for invested capital takes the form of issuance of shares of stock, which in turn could require the payment of dividends. As noted in previous chapters, dividends are *not* considered as an expense in the determination of net income. Dividends are a distribution of net income to the owners of the firm. Hence, dividends are shown on the statement of retained earnings, not on the income statement. When retained earnings are used as a means of financing, no direct payment is involved. The costs here are indirect, in the sense that the assets generated by profitable operations could have been distributed as dividends to owners. The only source of financing whose cost appears on the income statement is debt. Long-term debt financing of substantial amounts often takes the form of a bond issue.

BONDS

A *bond* represents a legal obligation on the part of the issuer to make certain payments to the bondholder. These payments are of two types:

1 Interest payments that are made periodically (usually annually or semiannually). The payments are defined as a percentage (called the *coupon rate*) of the *face value* of the bond.

2 Principal payment, which is usually paid in a single amount at the end of a specified period (the *maturity date*). The payment is equal to the face value of the bond.

For example, suppose Smith, Inc. issues a bond described as follows: "7 percent, $1,000 bond, interest payable semiannually on January 1 and July 1, maturing January 1, 1998." The payments that would be made to the bondholder are:

1 Interest payments, calculated at the 7 percent coupon interest rate times the $1,000 face value, or $70. Since interest rates are always stated in annual terms, this means the corporation will pay $70 interest per year. The description above says that interest is payable semiannually; thus $35 is paid on January 1 and $35 on July 1 of each year.

2 Principal payment of the $1,000 face value of the bond. Smith, Inc. will pay this to the bondholder on January 1, 1998 when the bond matures.

Issuing Bonds Rather than Stock—Advantages and Disadvantages

There are several differences between bond financing and stock financing. Bondholders are creditors, not owners. Therefore, bondholders do not vote or share in dividend distributions or asset growth. The company issuing the bonds guarantees only that the bondholders will receive the specified cash interest payments and the face amount at maturity. In addition, the interest payments that are made to the bondholders are deductible by the issuing corporation in computing its income tax. For example, a company in the 34 percent tax bracket, which has a 9 percent bond issue outstanding, is incurring an after-tax interest cost on the bonds of only 5.94 percent [$9\% - (9\% \times 34\%)$]. Dividends that might be paid if financing were obtained from issuing stock are *not* deductible expenses. Thus the after-tax interest cost for financing a 9 percent bond issue may be lower than a 6 percent dividend cost associated with issuing shares of stock.

Using borrowed funds also offers the stockholders the financial advantage of *leverage*. If the after-tax rate of return earned on borrowed funds exceeds the after-tax interest cost of borrowing the funds, the excess accrues to the owners (stockholders) of the company. Simply stated, "If you can earn more on borrowed funds than it cost to borrow the funds, you come out ahead." Chapter 12 on Financial Statement Analysis contains a detailed discussion and illustration of leverage.

On the negative side, interest (unlike dividends) must be paid. Whether the firm has been profitable or not, and regardless of the firm's cash position, interest payments must be made. If the payments are not made when due, the trustee acting on behalf of all the bondholders can force the company to sell its assets in order to raise the necessary cash. Also, bonds must be repaid at maturity. Stock, on the other hand, usually has an unlimited life. In addition, the leverage advantage previously cited can prove a disadvantage. If the after-tax rate of return earned on the borrowed money is less than the after-tax bond interest cost, then financing through bonds will reduce the stockholders' rate of return.

The decision whether to obtain long-term financing through bonds or stock is a complex decision. Some of the factors have been discussed in the preceding paragraphs. Conditions in the bond and stock markets at the time long-range financing is being contemplated play a key role in the decision.

ACCOUNTING FOR BONDS PAYABLE AND INTEREST EXPENSE

Several events may occur which complicate the recognition of interest expense: interest payment dates may not correspond with the end of the corporation's reporting period; bonds may be issued between interest payment dates; or bonds may be issued at a discount or premium (a price lower or higher than face value). Accounting for interest expense under each of these circumstances will be discussed.

Issuance at Face Value on Interest Date

The simplest case is the issuance of bonds on an interest payment date for a price exactly equal to the face value. Consider the following bond issue for Dynatron Co.:

Bonds issued—$50,000 face value
Coupon interest rate—7 percent, payable semiannually
Issue price—$50,000
Dates of interest payment—May 1 and November 1
Date bonds issued—May 2, 1988
Maturity date of bonds—November 1, 1989

If Dynatron Co.'s accounting year ends on December 31, the appropriate entries to record the issuance of the bonds, the interest expense, and the payment of the face amount at maturity are shown in Exhibit 8-1. Since the end of Dynatron's accounting year on December 31 does not coincide with a semiannual interest payment date, an adjusting entry of $583 is necessary to record the interest expense for November and December of 1988. For the May, 1989 cash payment, only four-sixths ($1,167) of the cash paid on May 1 is recorded as expense for

EXHIBIT 8-1
Journal Entries Related to Dynatron Co.'s Bonds

			Debit	Credit
1988				
May 2	Cash		50,000	
	Bonds Payable			50,000
	To record issuance of 7%, $50,000 face value bonds. Interest payments semiannually on May 1 and Nov. 1. Bonds mature on Nov. 1, 1989.			
Nov. 1	Interest Expense		1,750	
	Cash			1,750
	To record semiannual interest expense incurred and paid ($50,000 × 7% × 6/12 = $1,750).			
Dec. 31	Interest Expense		583	
	Interest Payable			583
	To record 2 months (Nov. and Dec. 1988) bond interest expense incurred but not yet paid ($50,000 × 7% × 2/12 = $583).			
1989				
May 1	Interest Expense		1,167	
	Interest Payable		583	
	Cash			1,750
	To record semiannual interest payment on bonds. Four months (Jan. through April 1989) is current period expense ($50,000 × 7% × 4/12 = $1,167). Remainder (Nov. and Dec. 1988) represents payment of Interest Payable.			
Nov. 1	Interest Expense		1,750	
	Cash			1,750
	To record semiannual interest expense incurred and paid ($50,000 × 7% × 6/12 = $1,750).			
Nov. 1	Bonds Payable		50,000	
	Cash			50,000
	To record payment of face value of bonds upon maturity.			

1989 (that is the interest for the first four months of 1989). The remaining two-sixths ($583) represents payment of interest owed for November and December of 1988—and already recorded as expense in 1988 through the December 31, 1988 adjusting entry. At maturity on November 1, 1989, in addition to payment of the final semiannual interest, the payment of the $50,000 face value of the bonds must be recorded. The Bonds Payable liability account is debited, since this liability no longer exists.

Issuance Between Interest Dates

A full six months' interest is due to whomever owns the bonds on each interest payment date. Modify the preceding illustration to assume that Dynatron Co. issued the bonds on October 1, 1988 (instead of May 2, 1988). On November 1, 1988, a semiannual interest payment is due (which covers the six months from May 1, 1988 to October 31, 1988). Dynatron will pay a full six months' interest on November 1 despite the fact that the bonds will have been outstanding for only one month. To overcome this inequitable situation, Dynatron will charge the buyer of the bonds for accrued bond interest when the bonds are issued.

The total amount to be received by Dynatron is shown below:

Face value	$50,000
Accrued interest ($50,000 × 7% × 5/12)	+ 1,458
Total amount received	$51,458

In recording this transaction, Dynatron would record the $50,000 face value as bonds payable and $1,458 as interest payable. The entry to record the issuance of the bonds on October 1, 1988, would be:

1988				
Oct. 1	Cash	51,458		
	Bonds Payable		50,000	
	Interest Payable		1,458	

To record issuance of $50,000,
7% bonds at face value
plus 5 months' accrued interest.

When the $1,750 interest payment (representing six months' interest) is paid on November 1, only $292 is recorded as interest expense since Dynatron has only incurred one month's interest cost. The remaining $1,458, reflecting repayment of the accrued interest received by Dynatron when it issued the bond, is debited to Interest Payable. The entry on November 1, 1988, the first interest payment date, would be:

1988			
Nov. 1	Interest Expense	292	
	Interest Payable	1,458	
	Cash		1,750

> To record semiannual interest
> payment on bonds. One month's
> interest expense (October) was
> incurred ($50,000 × 7% × 1/12
> = $292). Remainder is
> repayment of accrued interest
> received when bonds were
> issued.

Entries after November 1, 1988 would be the same as in Exhibit 8-1.

Issuance at a Discount or Premium

Bonds often trade in the market at a price different from their face value, depending on their risk and their coupon interest rates. Bonds selling at less than face value are selling at a *discount*. Bonds selling at greater than face value are selling at a *premium*. Bond selling prices are adjusted by the market to equalize the differences that exist in stated coupon interest rates among different bonds. For example, bonds issued in the 1930's had interest rates of 2 to 3 percent. Some of these bonds are currently still outstanding. Recent bond issues (with a similar risk of default) have offered stated coupon interest rates of 10 percent and higher. Once issued, it is impossible to change a bond's coupon interest rate. To generate a demand for the old 2 or 3 percent bonds, it is necessary to lower the selling price for these old bonds (i.e., sell them at a discount) until the "effective yield" on the old bonds is increased to the current interest rate in the bond market for new bond issues.

Assume that on January 2, 1988 Michigan Manufacturing Corporation issues $1,000,000, 6 percent bonds, maturing in five years with interest payable annually on December 31. If the market rate of interest is 9 percent when the bonds are issued, Michigan Manufacturing would receive $883,280 proceeds. (The method used to determine the proceeds from issuance of a bond will be illustrated later in the chapter.)

The journal entry to record the issuance of the bonds requires debiting Cash for the proceeds, debiting Discount on Bonds Payable for the amount of the discount, and crediting the face amount to Bonds Payable. For Michigan Manufacturing the entry would be:

```
1988
Jan.  2      Cash                              883,280
             Discount on Bonds Payable         116,720
                Bonds Payable                              1,000,000
             To record issuance of 6%,
             5-year bonds.
```

The discount on bonds payable is a *contra liability* account that is shown as a deduction from bonds payable on the balance sheet. The face value of the bonds minus the unamortized discount is known as the *net carrying value* of the bonds.

Discount—Straight Line Amortization   Interest expense on bonds is a function of (1) the periodic cash interest payments (coupon interest rate × face value), and (2) the amortization of bond discount or premium. For the Michigan Manufacturing example, each year the company would record as interest expense the sum of:

1 The $60,000 cash interest payment ($60,000 = $1,000,000 × 6%), plus
2 A portion of the $116,720 discount. (The difference between the $883,280 received upon issuance of the bonds and the $1,000,000 face value which will be paid at maturity.)

The discount could be amortized in either of two ways. We consider straight line amortization here; effective interest amortization will be discussed later in the chapter. Under the *straight line method of amortization,* the discount would be divided equally over the five-year life of the bonds.

For Michigan Manufacturing, the annual straight line discount amortization would be $23,344 ($116,720 discount ÷ 5-year life of bonds). Under this method of discount amortization, the annual journal entry to record the interest payment and amortization would be:

Dec. 31	Interest Expense	83,344	
	Discount on Bonds Payable		23,344
	Cash		60,000
	To record annual cash interest payment on 5-year, 6% bonds with straight line amortization of discount.		

Over the five-year life of the bonds, total interest expense is $416,720, consisting of $300,000 in cash interest payments plus $116,720 in amortization of bond discount.

As the bond discount is amortized, the Discount on Bonds Payable account is reduced. Thus, the net carrying value of the bond liability increases each year, reaching face value at maturity. This is shown below:

Date	Bonds payable	Discount on bonds payable	Net carrying value
Jan. 2, 1988	$1,000,000	$116,720	$ 883,280
Dec. 31, 1988	1,000,000	93,376	906,624
Dec. 31, 1989	1,000,000	70,032	929,968
Dec. 31, 1990	1,000,000	46,688	953,312
Dec. 31, 1991	1,000,000	23,344	976,656
Dec. 31, 1992	1,000,000	-0-	1,000,000

Premium—Straight Line Amortization   If the market rate of interest had been 5 percent on January 2, 1988, when Michigan Manufacturing issued the $1,000,000, 6 percent bonds, the cash proceeds would have been $1,043,300. The $43,300 excess of cash proceeds over face amount is credited to a *premium on bonds payable* account. The journal entry to record the issuance would be:

```
1988
Jan.  2        Cash                              1,043,300
                  Bonds Payable                              1,000,000
                  Premium on Bonds Payable                      43,300

               To record issuance of 6%,
               5-year bonds.
```

The premium on bonds payable is shown as an addition to bonds payable on the balance sheet. The net carrying value of the bonds equals the face amount of the bonds plus the unamortized premium.

For Michigan Manufacturing, the annual straight line amortization of the premium would be $8,660 ($43,300 premium ÷ 5-year life of bonds). The annual journal entry to record the interest payment and premium amortization would be:

```
Dec. 31        Interest Expense                   51,340
               Premium on Bonds Payable            8,660
                  Cash                                        60,000

               To record annual cash interest
               payment on 5-year, 6% bonds
               with straight line amortization
               of premium.
```

Note that amortization of bond premium results in interest expense being lower than the cash interest payment. Recall that Michigan Manufacturing received $1,043,300 at issuance, but will repay only $1,000,000 at maturity. The extra $43,300 received by Michigan Manufacturing offsets its future interest costs. Over the five-year life of the bonds, total interest expense is $256,700 ($300,000 cash payment minus $43,300 premium amortization).

As the bond premium is amortized, the Premium on Bonds Payable account is reduced. The net carrying value of the bond liability, therefore, also is reduced each year. At maturity the premium account will have been reduced to zero and the net carrying value will equal the face value. For Michigan Manufacturing's premium example:

Date	Bonds payable	Premium on bonds payable	Net carrying value
Jan. 2, 1988	$1,000,000	$43,300	$1,043,300
Dec. 31, 1988	1,000,000	34,640	1,034,640
Dec. 31, 1989	1,000,000	25,980	1,025,980
Dec. 31, 1990	1,000,000	17,320	1,017,320
Dec. 31, 1991	1,000,000	8,660	1,008,660
Dec. 31, 1992	1,000,000	-0-	1,000,000

Year-End Adjustment   Frequently a company's accounting period does not coincide with an interest payment date. As noted earlier in the chapter, this requires an adjusting entry to accrue the interest payable. If the bonds were issued at a discount or premium, the adjusting entry must include discount or premium amortization.

To illustrate, assume Bends, Inc. issued $1,000,000 of 9 percent, ten-year bonds on October 1, 1988 for $1,040,000. Interest payment dates are April 1 and October 1. Bends' accounting year ends on December 31. The first interest payment will not occur until April 1, 1989. However, on December 31, 1988, Bends must recognize three months' interest expense and premium amortization for the period October 1 through December 31. The year-end adjusting entry would be:

1988			
Dec. 31	Interest Expense	21,500	
	Premium on Bonds Payable	1,000	
	Interest Payable		22,500
	To record 3 months' accrued bond interest ($1,000,000 × 9% × 3/12) and straight line amortization of 3 months' premium (($40,000 ÷ 10 years) × 3/12).		

If the bonds were issued at a discount, rather than a premium, the adjusting entry would credit Discount on Bonds Payable for three months' amortization.

Retirement of Bonds Payable

Retirement of bonds prior to maturity requires removal of the face value of the bonds retired from the bonds payable account. Any unamortized discount or premium related to the bonds being retired also must be eliminated from the accounts. The difference between the net carrying value of the bonds being retired and the cost of retiring the bonds is treated as a gain or loss on the income statement. According to generally accepted principles this gain or loss must be shown as an extraordinary item. For example, assume that on December 31, 1988, Yodel Co.'s long-term debt showed:

Bonds Payable	$10,000,000
Less: Unamortized Discount on	
Bonds Payable	50,000
Net Carrying Value	$ 9,950,000

If one-half of the bond issue is repurchased on January 2, 1989 for $4,750,000 and retired, the journal entry to record the bond repurchase and retirement would be:

1989			
Jan. 2	Bonds Payable	5,000,000	
	Cash		4,750,000
	Discount on Bonds Payable		25,000
	Extraordinary Gain from		
	Retirement of Bonds		
	Payable		225,000
	To record repurchase and		

retirement of one-half of
bonds payable.

Since one-half of the bonds outstanding were retired, one-half of the face value ($5,000,000 = 1/2 × $10,000,000) and one-half the unamortized discount on the bonds ($25,000 = 1/2 × $50,000) are eliminated. The difference between the $4,975,000 net carrying value of the bonds retired and the $4,750,000 repurchase cost is the extraordinary gain on the retirement. The presentation of extraordinary gains or losses on the income statement is discussed in Chapter 13.

TIME VALUE OF MONEY

The preceding sections have assumed straight line amortization of discount and premium. Before considering the alternative method—effective interest amortization—some additional procedures involving interest calculations must be introduced.

Simple and Compound Interest

Interest rates are typically quoted in *annual* terms. If a period shorter than a year is involved, the rate must be adjusted accordingly. For example, if a company borrows $100,000 at 15 percent interest for 60 days, the amount of interest (assuming it is based on a 360-day year) would be:

$$\text{Interest} = \$100,000 \times 15\% \times (60/360)$$
$$= \$2,500$$

In effect, the interest rate for 60 days is 2.5 percent (15% × (60/360)).

This procedure is known as *simple interest*. Its use is encountered occasionally, as in the notes receivable discussion in Chapter 5. Much more frequently, however, a procedure known as *compound interest* will be employed. Under compound interest procedures, a new balance would be determined at the start of each time period, and interest would be calculated on that balance. If $1,000 is borrowed for three years at 10 percent, compounded annually, interest for the first year would be:

$$\text{Interest} = \$1,000 \times 10\%$$
$$= \$100$$

Assume no payments are made until the end of the three-year period. At the end of the first year, $1,100 is owed ($1,000 principal plus $100 interest for the first year). Interest for the second year will be calculated on the total obligation of $1,100. Thus interest for the second year would be:

$$\text{Interest} = \$1,100 \times 10\%$$
$$= \$110$$

When we add this $110 to the debt, at the end of the second year the amount owed is $1,210. Interest for the third year will be based on this new total amount.

$$\text{Interest} = \$1,210 \times 10\%$$
$$= \$121$$

Thus, interest for the third year is $121. A total of $1,331 is now owed; this is the total amount to be repaid at the end of the three-year loan. The following table summarizes this information:

Year	Balance beginning of year	Interest at 10%	Balance end of year
1	$1,000	$100	$1,100
2	1,100	110	1,210
3	1,210	121	1,331

The foregoing example is illustrative of a time-value-of-money problem. There are numerous applications of such techniques in accounting. The following section will expand your familiarity with several time-value-of-money relationships.

Present and Future Value of a Single Amount

In considering the various time-value-of-money relationships, a useful and familiar illustration is the bank savings account. Let us consider the possible questions that might arise in connection with deposits in such an account:

1 If a company deposits $1,000 now and the interest rate is 6 percent, compounded annually, how much will it have in five years?

2 If a company would like to have $3,000 in ten years and the interest rate is 6 percent, compounded annually, how much must it deposit now?

3 If a company deposits $1,960 now and the interest rate is 5 percent, compounded annually, how long will it take to have $2,500?

4 If a company deposits $4,000 now and wishes to have $6,515 at the end of five years, what rate of interest, compounded semiannually, must it earn?

Further questions may be asked, but we shall first consider the above set. Note that all of the above questions involve a single amount of money to be deposited *now* (a *present value*), an amount of money to be accumulated as of some *later time* (a *future value*), a number of time periods (interest periods) between the present value and the future value, and the rate at which interest will accumulate, on a compounded basis. Thus, each question above involves four items of information. Three of these are known, and the fourth is to be determined.

Future Value of a Single Amount   In Question 1 above, the items known are: the amount of money involved now ($1,000, the present value), the number of interest periods (five years), and the interest rate per period (6 percent). The item to be determined is the future value—the amount that will exist in the account after five years. Determining a future value from a known present value is called *compounding*.

The compounding formula to determine a future value from a known present value is:

$$F = P \times (\text{future value factor, n periods, r percent})$$

where F denotes future value, P denotes present value, n is the number of interest periods, and r is the interest rate per interest period.

Table I in Appendix A (at the back of the book), entitled "Future Value of $1," contains the information required to determine the *future value factor* (or *compounding factor*). The columns of the table represent different interest rates, while the rows represent different numbers of time periods. For Question 1, look at the intersection of the 6 percent column with the five periods row, and find a factor of 1.3382. The future value factor is then multiplied by P (the known present value) to determine F (the unknown future value). Question 1 (If a company deposits $1,000 now and the interest rate is 6 percent, compounded annually, how much will it have in five years?) may now be stated as:

$$
\begin{aligned}
F &= P \times (\text{future value factor, 5 periods, 6 percent}) \\
&= \$1,000 \times 1.3382 \\
&= \$1,338.20
\end{aligned}
$$

Thus, $1,000 deposited now will grow to $1,338.20 five years from now if the interest rate is 6 percent, compounded annually.

Present Value of a Single Amount   In Question 2, we know the future value ($3,000), the number of interest periods (ten years), and the interest rate per period (6 percent), and we wish to find the present value. This is the reverse of the problem encountered in Question 1. In Question 1, the calculation moved forward in time, from a known present value to an unknown future value. In Question 2, the calculation moves backward in time, from a known future value to an unknown present value. This process is known as *discounting*.

The discounting formula to determine the present value from a known future value is stated as:

$$P = F \times (\text{present value factor, n periods, r percent})$$

Table II in Appendix A, entitled "Present Value of $1," contains *present value factors* (or *discounting factors*). Again, columns represent different interest rates, and rows represent different numbers of time periods. For Question 2, look at the intersection of the 6 percent column and ten periods row and find a present value factor of .5584. The present value factor is then multiplied by F (the known future value) to determine P (the unknown present value).

The answer to Question 2 (If a company wants to have $3,000 in ten years with interest compounded at 6 percent annually, how much must it deposit now?) may now be stated as:

$$P = F \times \text{(present value factor, 10 periods, 6 percent)}$$
$$= \$3,000 \times .5584$$
$$= \$1,675.20$$

Thus $1,675.20 deposited now will grow to $3,000 ten years from now if the interest rate is 6 percent, compounded annually.

Finding Interest Rate and Number of Periods   The two relationships (future value of a single amount, and present value of a single amount) and the corresponding tables can be used to solve other problems, such as those posed in Questions 3 and 4. In Question 3, we know the present value ($1,960), the future value ($2,500), the interest rate per period (5 percent) but not the number of periods. Solve for the factor and then search the appropriate table to determine n.

Suppose the present value relationship is used:

$$P = F \times \text{(present value factor, n periods, r percent)}$$

Substituting the known values yields:

$$\$1,960 = \$2,500 \times \text{(present value factor, n periods, 5 percent)}$$

Solving for the present value factor gives:

$$\text{(Present value factor, n periods, 5 percent)} = \$1,960 \div \$2,500$$
$$= .784$$

Looking at the 5 percent column in Table II, note that the factor for five years is .7835. Thus, the answer to the problem is that it will take approximately five years for $1,960 to grow to $2,500 if the interest rate is 5 percent, compounded annually.

In Questions 1 through 3, interest was compounded annually. In other problems, interest may be compounded *semiannually* or *quarterly*. Note that Tables I and II are defined in terms of numbers of periods. When interest is compounded annually, the length of the period is one year. If interest is compounded semiannually, the length of the period will be six months. If interest is compounded quarterly, the length of the period will be three months. In using the tables, there is a basic rule to remember: *The period may be of any length: adjust the interest rate so as to correspond with the length of the period.* Recall that interest rates are usually stated in annual terms. Thus, if there are semiannual interest periods, divide the annual interest rate by two to get the rate per semiannual period. If there are quarterly interest periods, divide the annual interest rate by four to get the rate per quarterly period.

In solving Question 4, we know the present value ($4,000), the future value ($6,515), the number of years (5), but not the interest rate. Since interest is compounded semiannually, we formulate the problem using ten interest periods.

$$P = F \times \text{(present value factor, n periods, r percent)}$$

$$\$4,000 = \$6,515 \times \text{(present value factor, 10 periods, r percent)}$$

$$\text{(Present value factor, 10 periods, r percent)} = \$4,000 \div \$6,515$$
$$= .6139$$

In Table II, look across the ten-period row. A factor of .6139 appears in the 5 percent column. Thus the *semiannual* interest rate is 5 percent. Since interest rates are stated on an annual basis, the answer to Question 4 should be stated as 10 percent, compounded semiannually.

These four questions have illustrated the basic calculations that can be made using tables for the Future Value of $1 and the Present Value of $1. These problems involved "single sums," that is, a single dollar amount to be compounded or discounted. Since more complex situations involving a series of cash flows may be encountered, it is useful to consider the case of annuities.

Present Value of an Annuity

An *annuity* (often called an "ordinary annuity") is defined as a series of equal cash flows occurring at the end of *each* of a sequence of time periods. For example, a three-year auto loan requiring monthly payments of $143 is a 36-period annuity with payments of $143. Since many problems in accounting possess this characteristic of equal periodic cash flows, annuity relationships are very useful. Most accounting applications involve present value of annuity relationships. Therefore, although future value of an annuity calculations can be made and future value of annuity tables exist, for annuities we will discuss only present value.

To illustrate present value of an annuity calculations, we will again use the illustration of the bank savings account and formulate some additional questions:

5 If a company wishes to withdraw $800 from its account at the end of *each* of the next four years, how much must it have in the account now, assuming it earns 5 percent compounded annually?

6 A company has $7,500 in its account, earning 7 percent compounded annually, to be spent during four years of a special advertising campaign. The campaign will begin at the end of this year. How much can the company withdraw at the end of *each* of the next four years?

7 If a company wants to withdraw $2,000 at the end of *each* of the next 16 years and currently has $20,212 on deposit, what rate of interest, compounded annually, must it earn?

8 If a company withdraws $1,000 at the end of *each* year and the interest rate is 8 percent, compounded annually, how long will it take to spend the present balance of $10,200?

Question 5 (and any other present value of annuity problem) could be answered by repeated use of the present value of a single-sum table. Four annual withdrawals of $800 will be made. We wish to determine the present balance required in the account, if the account earns 5 percent compounded annually. The present value of each withdrawal can be calculated and added to determine the present balance required in the account. The first $800 will be discounted for one year, the second for two years, and so forth. If we use a 5 percent interest rate and apply Table II four times, we get the following:

$$
\begin{array}{rcr}
\$800 \times .9524 &=& \$\ 761.92 \\
800 \times .9070 &=& 725.60 \\
800 \times .8638 &=& 691.04 \\
800 \times .8227 &=& \underline{658.16} \\
&& \$2,836.72
\end{array}
$$

To simplify the calculations, annuity tables exist. Observe from the above illustration that the answer could be determined by adding the four present value factors and multiplying the sum by $800.

$$
\begin{array}{l}
.9524 \\
.9070 \\
.8638 \\
\underline{.8227} \\
3.5459 \times \$800 = \$2,836.72
\end{array}
$$

Table III in Appendix A, entitled "Present Value of an Annuity of $1," does exactly this. Look in Table III for the present value factor for an annuity of four periods at 5 percent. The factor is 3.5460, which is equal to the sum shown above (except for difference due to rounding in the tables). Thus, Table III is used in the same way as Table II, except that Table III applies to problems involving the present value of annuities while Table II applies to problems involving the present value of a single future amount.

The discounting formula to determine the present value of an annuity is stated as:

$$P_A = A \times (\text{present value of annuity factor, n periods, r percent})$$

We use P_A to designate the present value of an annuity and A represents the periodic cash flow. The answer to Question 5 can be determined using the formula as follows:

$$P_A = A \times (\text{present value of annuity factor, 4 periods, 5 percent})$$

$$= \$800 \times 3.5460$$
$$= \$2,836.80$$

Thus, if $2,836.80 is in the bank now and the account earns 5 percent compounded annually, $800 could be withdrawn at the end of each of the next four years (with the account balance reduced to zero at the end of the fourth year). The following table demonstrates that this in fact occurs:

Year	Balance at beginning of year	Interest earned (5%)	Amount withdrawn	Balance at end of year
1	$2,836.80	$141.84	$800.00	$2,178.64
2	2,178.64	108.93	800.00	1,487.57
3	1,487.57	74.38	800.00	761.95
4	761.95	38.05	800.00	-0-

Question 6 requires a similar formulation, except that we are looking for the annuity amount. We know the present balance ($7,500), the interest rate per period (7 percent), and the number of interest periods (four years).

$$P_A = A \times \text{(present value of annuity factor, 4 periods, 7 percent)}$$
$$\$7,500 = A \times 3.3872$$
$$A = \$7,500 \div 3.3872$$
$$= \$2,214.22$$

Thus, with $7,500 now in an account, earning 7 percent compounded annually, $2,214 can be withdrawn from the account at the end of each of the next four years.

Finding Interest Rate and Number of Periods   Questions 7 and 8 require finding the interest rate and number of time periods, respectively. As before, this is not done directly. Rather, the required present value of an annuity factor is computed, and then Table III is searched to find the corresponding number of periods or interest rate. In Question 7, we know the present value of the annuity ($20,212), the annual withdrawal ($2,000), and the number of interest periods (16). We wish to find the interest rate. The problem is formulated as follows:

$$P_A = A \times \text{(present value of annuity factor, 16 periods, r percent)}$$
$$\$20,212 = \$2,000 \times \text{(present value of annuity factor)}$$
$$\text{Factor} = \$20,212 \div \$2,000$$
$$= 10.1060$$

Searching the 16-period row of Table III, note the factor 10.1059 appears in the 6 percent column. Thus, 6 percent compounded annually must be earned if the $20,212 current investment is to be subject to withdrawals of $2,000 per year for 16 years.

In Question 8, we know the present value of the annuity ($10,200), the annual withdrawal ($1,000), and the interest rate (8 percent compounded annually). To solve for the number of interest periods, the problem should be formulated as:

$$P_A = A \times \text{(present value of annuity factor, n periods, 8 percent)}$$
$$\$10,200 = \$1,000 \times \text{(present value of annuity factor)}$$
$$\text{Factor} = \$10,200 \div \$1,000$$
$$= 10.2$$

Searching the 8 percent column of Table III, we find a factor of 10.2007 for 22 periods. Thus, $1,000 can be withdrawn annually for 22 years, if the present account balance is $10,200 earning 8 percent, compounded annually.

Approaches to Problem Solving

Problems involving time-value-of-money relationships are not difficult to solve. Typically, all elements of the problem are known except one, which must be determined. The following steps may prove helpful in approaching the problem:

1 Does the problem involve a single sum or an annuity? This answer tells us whether to use Tables I and II (involving future and present values of $1) or Table III (involving present values of an annuity of $1).

2 What is the unknown in the problem? We may have to find a present value, a future value, the amount of the annuity payments, the number of time periods, or the interest rate.

3 In view of the answers to (1) and (2), select the appropriate formulation of the problem. If, for example, we are trying to find the amount of annuity payments and we know the present value available, we should formulate the problem in terms of the present value of an annuity relationship. Sometimes alternative formulations will be available. If, for example, we know both the present value and future value of a single sum and wish to find the interest rate, it does not matter if we formulate the problem using the present value relationship or the future value relationship.

4 Remember that the length of the time period need not always be one year. Rather, it should be the length of time between compounding dates. Thus, if a problem states that interest is compounded quarterly, we should use quarters (three months) as the time period. Interest rates are always quoted in annual terms and must be adjusted to fit the length of the period. For example, "6 percent compounded quarterly" means we should use quarters as the period and 1.5 percent as the quarterly rate.

A useful aid in solving problems, especially more complex ones, is the *time line*. It gives a visual image of what is known and what operations must be performed to solve the problem. Suppose, for example, we must determine the amount to which $1,000 will accumulate at the end of four years, with interest at 8 percent, compounded annually. The time line is:

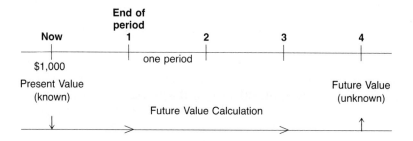

Or, if we must determine the present value of a three-year annuity of $600, the time line would be:

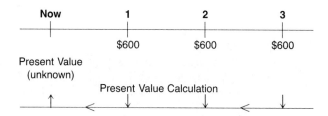

The use of the time-line technique is recommended in solving problems. The data and requirements of a problem are easier to understand when they can be readily visualized.

COMPUTER APPLICATION

Pocket calculators are available to solve time-value-of-money problems. The user merely has to determine the type of problem (present value, future value, single sum, annuity) and enter the known elements. Using built-in formulas and tables, the calculator quickly solves for the unknown.

APPLICATIONS OF TIME-VALUE-OF-MONEY TECHNIQUES

The time-value-of-money techniques presented in the preceding section have numerous applications in accounting. We now discuss some applications for bonds.

Determining Market Prices for Bonds

The market price for a bond is determined by calculating the present value of the future cash flows associated with the bond. The discount rate to be used in the present value calculations is the current market rate of interest being earned on bonds of a similar credit rating. Market interest rates fluctuate over time. Bond prices fluctuate inversely with changes in market interest rates. Only if the market rate of interest happened to be the same as the coupon rate of interest would the bond sell at face.

To illustrate, consider a $1,000 face value bond, 8 percent coupon rate of interest, maturing in five years. If interest is paid semiannually, the future cash receipt to an investor would be:

If the current market rate of interest on other bonds of similar riskiness is 10 percent, the above bond must also be priced to yield an effective interest rate of 10 percent. A 10 percent yield is built into the bond investment by using 10 percent (5 percent, semiannually) as the discount rate to be applied to the future cash payments. Using the present value techniques and tables yields:

Present value of $1,000 face amount to be paid in five years:

$$P = F \times \text{(present value factor, 10 periods, 5 percent)}$$
$$= \$1,000 \times .6139$$
$$= \$613.90$$

Present value of semiannual interest of $40:

$$P_A = A \times \text{(present value of annuity factor, 10 periods, 5 percent)}$$
$$= \$40 \times 7.7217$$
$$= \$308.87$$

$$\text{Market price of bond} = \$922.77 \ (\$613.90 + \$308.87)$$

The corporation issuing the bond for $922.77, and paying $40 cash interest every six months plus $1,000 at maturity, would incur a 10 percent effective interest cost.

When the market rate of interest is higher than the coupon interest rate (as in the preceding example), the bonds will sell at a *discount* (that is, face exceeds market price). If the market rate of interest is less than the coupon interest rate, the bonds will sell at a *premium* (i.e., market price exceeds face value). The greater the interest rate differential, and the longer the time to maturity, the bigger the discount or premium.

Bond Interest Expense—Effective Interest Method

Earlier in the chapter, we illustrated the straight line method of amortizing discount or premium on bonds payable. We now consider the *effective interest method of amortization*. Under this method, the total bond interest expense each period is a *constant percentage* of the net carrying value of the bonds. The particular percentage used is the market rate of interest implicit in the original issuance price of the bonds.

Amortization of Discount   To illustrate the effective interest method of amortization, the following data for Michigan Manufacturing will be used:

Bonds issued – $1,000,000 face value
Coupon interest rate – 6 percent, payable annually on December 31
Issue price – $883,280
Market rate of interest on date bonds are issued – 9 percent
Date bonds issued – January 2, 1988
Maturity date of bonds – December 31, 1992

The journal entry to record issuance of the bonds would be:

1988			
Jan. 2	Cash	883,280	
	Discount on Bonds Payable	116,720	
	Bonds Payable		1,000,000
	To record issuance of 6%,		
	5-year bonds.		

The discount of $116,720 is to be amortized over the five-year life of the bonds. The process of effective interest amortization may be described as follows:

	Net carrying value of bonds at beginning of period (the face value of the bonds, minus the unamortized discount or plus the unamortized premium)
Times:	Market interest rate (at the date on which the bonds were issued)
Equals:	Total bond interest expense for period
Less:	Interest paid in cash (face value × coupon interest rate)
Equals:	Amount of discount (or premium) to be amortized this period

It is convenient to carry out this calculation process in the form of an *amortization table,* with one column for each step described above. The amortization table for the $1,000,000, 6 percent, five-year bonds issued by Michigan Manufacturing is shown in Exhibit 8-2. Note in the exhibit that under the effective interest method:

1 The net carrying value of bonds is increased, by discount amortization, to the $1,000,000 face value by maturity. The dollar increase each period, however, is not a constant amount as it is under the straight line amortization method.

2 The total bond interest expense recognized each period is a constant 9 percent of the net carrying value of the bonds at the beginning of each period. As the net carrying value of the bonds increases each period, the dollar amount of total bond interest expense must increase proportionally to maintain the constant 9 percent effective interest rate.

3 The cash interest paid each period is unaffected by the choice of method used to amortize discount.

Machine (old)		10,000

To record cost of new machine, and
to remove cost and accumulated
depreciation of old machine
from books.

Exchange of Similar Assets—Loss Situation

If an exchange of similar assets, or dissimilar assets, involves a loss (that is, if the fair market value of the asset given up is *less* than the book value), then under the concept of conservatism the loss must be recognized, and the new asset must be recorded at fair market value. In the Company B example above, assume that the fair market value of the asset given up was only $3,300 (rather than $5,500). We must assume that, for both parties to agree to this exchange, the new asset must only be worth about $3,300. The $700 loss ($3,300 value received minus $4,000 book value) must be recognized, and the new asset must be recorded at $3,300. The entry would be:

1988			
Nov. 3	Machine (new)	3,300	
	Accumulated Depreciation	6,000	
	Loss on Disposition of Machine	700	
	Machine (old)		10,000

To record cost of new machine and
loss on machine exchanged,
and to remove cost and
accumulated depreciation of
old machine from books.

Trade-ins

A common form in which the exchange of similar assets occurs is the *trade-in*. Cash plus an old asset are given up to acquire a new similar asset. In a gain situation (i.e., value received is more than book value) the book value of the asset traded in plus the amount of cash paid determines the cost of the new asset and the gain determined on the trade would not be recorded. If, based on an estimate of the value received for the trade-in, a *loss* is evident (i.e, the value received is less than book value), the loss must be recognized and the new asset would be recorded at fair market value. Although the fair market value of the old asset being traded theoretically should be obtained by determining the price at which the old asset could be sold, the trade-in allowance granted often is used as a substitute. As a result of inflated list prices, the trade-in allowance probably exceeds the realistic selling price of the old asset. However, as long as the difference is not material, accountants frequently use trade-in allowances as indicators of the fair market value of the asset traded.

Assume that on January 4, 1989, West's Market is buying a new delivery truck with a list price of $7,000. It will trade in its old truck (which had an

EXHIBIT 8-2
Michigan Manufacturing Corp.
Bond Discount Amortization Table
Effective Interest Method

Year	(A) Net carrying value of bonds, beginning of period	(B) Total bond interest expense for period (9% × Col. (A))	(C) Interest paid in cash	(B) − (C) Discount to be amortized
1988	$883,280	$ 79,495	$ 60,000	$ 19,495
1989	902,775	81,250	60,000	21,250
1990	924,025	83,162	60,000	23,162
1991	947,187	85,247	60,000	25,247
1992	972,434**	87,566*	60,000	27,566**
		$416,720	$300,000	$116,720

*$47 rounding error
**$972,434 beginning balance plus $27,566 discount amortization equals $1,000,000 as of December 31, 1992.

4 The discount to be amortized each period, under the effective interest method, is the total bond interest expense needed for a 9 percent effective cost less the cash interest payment. The amount of discount amortized increases each period under the effective interest method.

At the end of 1988, Michigan Manufacturing would record interest expense as follows. The amounts are taken from the amortization table in Exhibit 8-2.

```
1988
Dec. 31      Interest Expense                    79,495
                 Discount on Bonds Payable                  19,495
                 Cash                                       60,000

             To record annual cash interest
             payment on 5-year, 6 percent
             bonds with effective interest
             amortization of discount.
```

At the end of 1989, the entry would be:

```
1989
Dec. 31      Interest Expense                    81,250
                 Discount on Bonds Payable                  21,250
                 Cash                                       60,000

             To record annual cash interest
             payment on 5-year, 6 percent
             bonds with effective interest
             amortization of discount.
```

Similar entries would be made at the end of the remaining three years using the amounts on the amortization table. The effective interest method results in a total of $416,720 of interest expense being recorded over the five years with the entire $116,720 of discount being amortized to interest expense. Recall the straight line method also resulted in $416,720 of interest expense being recorded and the entire discount of $116,720 being amortized. The amortization methods differ in that:

1 The straight line method recognized a *constant dollar amount* ($83,344 for Michigan Manufacturing) of interest expense each period.

2 The effective interest method records interest expense that is a *constant percentage* (9 percent for Michigan Manufacturing) of the net carrying value of the bonds at the beginning of each period.

The effective interest amortization method is preferred because it more accurately calculates interest expense as a percentage of the net carrying value of the liability. However, in cases where the difference between straight line and effective interest amortization amounts is minimal, the straight line method is frequently used.

Amortization of Premium   If Michigan Manufacturing issued the $1,000,000, 6 percent bonds for $1,043,300, the effective interest rate would be 5 percent. Exhibit 8-3 presents a table for effective interest amortization of the $43,300 premium. At the end of 1988, Michigan Manufacturing's journal entry for interest would be:

```
1988
Dec. 31    Interest Expense                52,165
           Premium on Bonds Payable         7,835
               Cash                                   60,000

           To record annual cash interest
           payment on 5-year, 6 percent
           bonds with effective interest
           amortization of premium.
```

Similar entries would be made at the end of the remaining four years using the amortization table.

EXHIBIT 8-3
Michigan Manufacturing Corp.
Bond Premium Amortization Table
Effective Interest Method

Year	(A) Net carrying value of bonds, beginning of period	(B) Total bond interest expense for period (5% × Col. (A))	(C) Interest paid in cash	(C) − (B) Premium to be amortized
1988	$1,043,300	$ 52,165	$ 60,000	$ 7,835
1989	1,035,465	51,773	60,000	8,227
1990	1,027,238	51,362	60,000	8,638
1991	1,018,600	50,930	60,000	9,070
1992	1,009,530**	50,470*	60,000	9,530**
		$256,700	$300,000	$43,300

*$6 rounding error
**$1,009,530 beginning balance less $9,530 premium amortization equals $1,000,000 as of December 31, 1992.

COMPUTER APPLICATION

Computer programs are available to prepare bond amortization tables. Input to the computer would be the issuance price of the bonds, face value, market rate of interest when the bonds were issued, and coupon (cash) interest rate. The computer calculates for each interest period the interest expense, cash interest payment, discount or premium amortization, and net carrying value of the bonds.

FINANCIAL STATEMENT PRESENTATION

The partial balance sheet shown below illustrates the presentation of the liabilities discussed in this chapter. Bonds payable and the related discount or premium are presented as long-term debt. Lease payables (which are discussed in the Appendix) are also shown as long-term debt. If a portion of the debt was due within one year, that portion would be shown on the balance sheet among the current liabilities.

Partial Balance Sheet

Long-term Debt:		
8% Bond Payable	$500,000	
Less Unamortized Bond Discount	12,000	$ 488,000
12% Bonds Payable	$700,000	
Plus Unamortized Bond Premium	18,000	718,000
Leases Payable		184,000
Total Long-term Debt		$1,390,000

For leases payable only the net carrying value is shown on the balance sheet. For bonds payable the face value and unamortized discount on premium also is presented.

SUMMARY

Learning Objective 1: Discuss the advantages and disadvantages of bond financing.

Raising capital by issuing bonds rather than stock has several advantages: few rights (voting, sharing in asset growth, and so on) are given up, and interest payments are tax deductible. However, interest payments and principal payments must be made when due.

Learning Objective 2: Record the issuance and retirement of bonds.

Bonds payable are recorded at face amount; any discount or premium is recorded in a separate account. Retirements of bonds require that the face value of the bonds retired be eliminated, the related unamortized discount or premium be written off, and a gain or loss calculated.

Learning Objective 3: Record bond interest expense and the associated amortization of discount or premium.

Amortization of discount or premium is included in interest expense. Bond interest expense equals cash interest paid plus amortization of discount (or minus amortization of premium). Two methods of amortization exist: straight line and effective interest.

Learning Objective 4: Distinguish between the concepts of present value and future value, and single amount and annuity.

These concepts are central to time-value-of-money calculations. A present value is calculated *prior to* one or more cash flows by *discounting*. A future value is calculated *subsequent to* one or more cash flows by *compounding*. If a single cash flow exists, it is referred to as a single amount. A series of equal cash flows, occurring at regular intervals, is called an *annuity*.

Learning Objective 5: Perform time-value-of-money calculations using present value and future value tables.

Present value and future value tables are an aid in solving time-value-of-money problems. Routine problems include finding a present or future value, annuity amount, interest rate, or the number of interest periods.

Learning Objective 6: Calculate the issue price of a bond.

The issue price of a bond is calculated by finding the present value of the cash flows associated with it. The principal constitutes a single amount, while the series of interest payments constitutes an annuity. Both are discounted using the market interest rate.

KEY TERMS

Amortization table	Effective interest method of
Annuity	amortization
Bonds	Future value
Capitalized lease (Appendix)	Operating lease (Appendix)
Compounding	Premium
Contra liability	Present value
Discount	Retirement of bonds
Discounting	Straight line method of amortization

APPENDIX: Leasing—A Hidden Element of Interest Expense

Leasing is an alternative to purchasing machinery, equipment, and buildings. The discussion in this section will use equipment as the leased item; identical considerations apply to machinery, buildings, and other items. Under a lease, the equipment is owned by another party (the "lessor"), but the company (the "lessee") uses the equipment under terms of an agreement specifying the period of use and the amount to be paid. There are several reasons why a company may prefer to lease equipment rather than buy it:

1 The company does not have to come up with the cash necessary for a lump-sum purchase price.

2 The interest cost implicit in the lease payments may be lower than the cost of borrowing money to finance a purchase.

3 The company may need the services of the equipment for only a short period of time.

Assume that the Michelle Corporation on January 2, 1989 leases equipment for five years at $3,800 per year. How should the cost of leasing this equipment be recognized? There are two possibilities:

1 To *capitalize the lease* (i.e., treat the lease arrangement as being substantially the same as a purchase of the equipment). The implied purchase price is determined and recorded as an asset and then depreciated. The implied purchase price is also recorded as a long-term debt (lease payable). Each periodic lease payment is viewed as containing an interest element.

2 To treat the lease as an *operating lease* (i.e., to record $3,800 of lease expense per year).

ACCOUNTING FOR CAPITALIZED LEASES

Accounting procedures specify that a lease must be capitalized if it meets any one of the following criteria:

1 Ownership of the equipment is transferred to the lessee at the end of the lease term.

2 The lessee has the right to buy the equipment (during or at the end of the lease term) for a price substantially below the market value of the equipment.

3 The lease term runs for 75 percent or more of the expected useful life of the equipment.

4 The present value of the payments that the lessee will make over the term of the lease is 90 percent or more of the current selling price of the equipment.

If any one of these four criteria is met, the *lessee* is viewed as the *effective* owner of the equipment (even though not the *legal* owner) because many of the risks and rewards of ownership have passed from the lessor to the lessee. A *capitalized lease* indicates that the *substance* of the transaction is the acquisition of an asset together with long-term financing.

Assuming Michelle's lease meets one of the criteria for capitalization, we proceed as follows:

1 Using the present value techniques *capitalize* (find the present value of) the lease payments of $3,800 per year. To do this, an interest rate is needed. Assuming the lease is to be capitalized at 10 percent yields:

$$P_A = A \times \text{(present value of annuity factor, 5 periods, 10 percent)}$$
$$= \$3,800 \times 3.7908$$
$$= \$14,405$$

2 Record the capitalized value in the same manner as the purchase of equipment on credit would be recorded. Both an asset and a liability would be recorded for the capitalized value of the lease payments.

```
1989
Jan.  2       Equipment                        14,405
                  Lease Payable                              14,405

              To record present value
                of capitalized lease.
```

3 Depreciate the equipment. If the straight line method is used with a five-year life, the annual depreciation entry would be:

```
Dec. 31       Depreciation Expense              2,881
                  Accumulated Depreciation
                    —Equipment                              2,881

              To record annual depreciation on
                capitalized equipment lease.
```

4 Record the annual lease payments of $3,800. The Lease Payable account must be reduced by the "principal" repayment and the "interest" must be recorded as an expense.

To determine the interest expense on a five-year debt of $14,405, with payment of $3,800 per year, the following calculations are made:

Year	(A) Liability balance, beginning of year	(B) Interest (10% × (A))	(C) Lease payment	(C)−(B) Repayment of principal
1989	$14,405.00	$1,440.50	$ 3,800	$ 2,359.50
1990	12,045.50	1,204.55	3,800	2,595.45
1991	9,450.05	945.00	3,800	2,855.00
1992	6,595.05	659.50	3,800	3,140.50
1993	3,454.55	345.45	3,800	3,454.55
		$4,595.00	$19,000	$14,405.00

To record the $3,800 payment at the end of 1989, the entry would be:

```
1989
Dec. 31       Lease Payable                     2,359.50
              Interest Expense                  1,440.50
                  Cash                                      3,800.00

              To record lease payment for 1989.
```

Subsequent years' journal entries would involve the same accounts as the first year. The dollar amounts would be based on the preceding calculations.

ACCOUNTING FOR OPERATING LEASES

If a lease does not meet one of the four capitalization criteria, the lease is classified as an operating lease. The accounting for an operating lease is quite straightforward. No asset or liability is recorded on the lessee's books. The lessee records the periodic lease payments as lease expense (or some similar title such as machinery rental expense). For example, if Michelle's lease was treated as an operating lease, the journal entry for each annual lease payment would be:

Dec. 31	Lease Expense	3,800	
	Cash		3,800
	To record lease payment.		

As with any expense that occurs continuously over time, an end-of-period accrual may be required.

REVIEW QUESTIONS

1 Poorboy Co. is desperately in need of additional funds. The company can issue stock with an 8 percent dividend rate or 12 percent bonds. The company is in the 34 percent tax bracket. Determine the after-tax cost for both the dividend on the stock and the interest on the bonds.

2 Trainer Co. issues bonds at a premium. Will the interest expense each year be greater than, equal to, or less than the cash interest paid?

3 Zambelli, Inc. issued $5,000,000 of 25-year, 9 percent bonds on March 1, 1988. The bonds were issued at face amount plus accrued interest of $75,000. The bonds pay interest annually on December 31. How much cash interest will be paid on December 31, 1988? What will be the interest expense recorded for 1988?

4 Wilco Company issued on January 2, 1989 a $2,000,000, 8 percent, ten-year bond issue for $1,940,000. The bonds pay interest semiannually on January 1 and July 1. Assume Wilco's accounting year ends on December 31 and the company amortizes bond discount using the straight line method. Determine the effects of the bond issue on the 1989 income statement and on the December 31, 1989 balance sheet.

5 Overnout, Inc. issued on November 1, 1988 a $10,000,000, 9 percent, 20-year bond issue at face, plus $75,000 accrued interest. The bonds pay interest semiannually on October 1 and April 1. The company's accounting year ends on December 31. Present the proper journal entries for November 1, 1988; December 31, 1988; and April 1, 1989 (the first interest payment date).

6 On March 8, 1988 Xtra, Inc. repurchased and retired 40 percent of its $8,000,000 outstanding bonds payable. The bonds were repurchased for $3,264,000. Unamortized discount on the total bonds payable on March 8, 1988 was $400,000. Calculate the gain or loss on the bond retirement. How would the gain or loss be shown on the company's income statement?

7 Differentiate between simple interest and compound interest.

8 If a person invests $3,000 at 8 percent interest for three years, how much total interest accumulates if: a) the simple interest method is employed, b) the compound interest method is used?

9 To determine the future value of a single present amount, what items of information are needed?

10 To determine the present value of a single future amount, what items of information are needed?

11 A company borrows money for six years and the annual interest rate is stated as 8 percent compounded semiannually. How many interest periods (n) will there be? What is the rate of interest (r) per interest period?

12 Define an "annuity."

13 List the appropriate formulas to calculate:
a Future value of a single present amount
b Present value of a single amount in the future
c Present value of an annuity

14 Brendell Corporation just obtained a $40,000 bank loan. Interest is 8 percent compounded annually. The loan is to be repaid with interest in equal yearly installments over the next 20 years. The first yearly installment is due one year from now. Which of the three formulas listed in Question 13 above should be used to find the amount of the yearly installment payment? Solve for the annual installment payment.

15 On January 2, 1987 the Farview Corp. issues $1,000,000 face value, 6 percent, ten-year bonds for $946,000. The bonds pay interest annually on December 31. What will be the total interest expense over the life of the bonds if the straight line amortization method is used to amortize the discount? What will be the total interest expense over the life of the bonds if the effective interest method is used?

16 Evaluate the following statement: "The market price of a $1,000 face value bond due in ten years, with 8 percent interest payable semiannually, is equal to the sum of the face amount of the bond and the periodic interest payments."

17 A $1,000 face value bond is issued when the market rate of interest on similar bonds is 10 percent. The bond matures in 20 years and pays 9 percent interest payable semiannually. Calculate the market price of the bond when it is issued.

18 Rodgers Co. issued bonds at a premium. This would indicate:
a The coupon rate of interest exceeded the current market rate of interest.
b The coupon rate of interest was less than the current market rate of interest.
c The bonds are non-interest bearing.
d The coupon rate of interest coincides with the current market rate of interest.

(AICPA Adapted)

19 (Appendix) Indicate whether each of the following statements is TRUE or FALSE. If false, indicate why the statement is false.
a The company using an asset that is owned by another party under terms of an agreement specifying the period of use and amount to be paid is known as the lessor.
b When a lease is capitalized, both an asset and a liability would be recorded for the present value of the lease payments.
c Whenever a lease is capitalized, the total expense deductions over the life of the lease will always be more than would be deducted if the lease is not capitalized.

d For a capitalized lease, the portion of each lease payment considered interest expense decreases over the life of the lease.

EXERCISES

E8-1   On October 1, 1988, Mid-Scream, Inc. issued $10,000,000 face value, 11 percent bonds for $10,415,520, plus accrued interest. The bonds pay interest semiannually on July 31 and January 31, and mature on January 31, 1994 (i.e., five years and four months from date of issue). The company uses the straight line method of amortizing bond discount or premium. What was the market rate of interest on the date the bonds were issued: 10 percent, 11 percent, or 12 percent? Also present all journal entries for 1988, the year the bonds were issued.

E8-2   On November 1, 1989, Casely, Inc. issued $5,000,000 of 10 percent bonds that mature on July 31, 1997 (seven years and nine months after date of issue). The bonds pay interest semiannually on January 31 and July 31. Casely's accounting year ends on December 31, and the company uses the straight line method of amortizing any bond discount or bond premium. Assume the bonds are sold for $5,150,000, plus three months' accrued interest of $125,000. Present journal entries for: 1) sale of the bonds on November 1, 1989; 2) necessary adjustments on December 31, 1989; and 3) the first semiannual cash interest payment on January 31, 1990. Round all amounts to nearest dollar.

E8-3   Orville, Inc. issued $9,000,000 face value, 7 percent, ten-year bonds on December 31, 1986 for $9,180,000. The company amortizes bond discount or premium using the straight line method. On January 2, 1990, the company repurchased for $6,552,000 and retired 70 percent of the bonds. Present journal entry to record the repurchase and retirement on January 2, 1990.

E8-4   Thrifty Co. has $13,515 to invest today at an 8 percent compound annual interest rate. Thrifty wants the investment to grow to $50,000 in order to be able to pay off the $50,000 maturity value of a bond issue that will mature in the future. For Thrifty to accomplish its investment objective, what additional information must be determined? Using the formulas in the textbook, calculate the missing information.

E8-5   Rancid, Inc. would like to set up a fund that will enable the company to pay a pension to the company's retiring president, Mrs. Moneypenny. The pension plan is designed to pay $10,000 each on Mrs. Moneypenny's 66th, 67th, and 68th birthdays. Today is Mrs. Moneypenny's 65th birthday. Present a time-line diagram of the problem. How much must Rancid invest today if the company can earn 8 percent interest compounded annually on its investment?

E8-6   Assume that Table III (present value of an annuity of $1) is not available to you. Solve E8-5 using Table II (present value of $1).

E8-7   Brannigan Company issued $1,000,000 face value, 7 percent, 20-year bonds on

July 1, 1988. The bonds pay interest semiannually on June 30 and December 31. The bonds were sold when the market rate of interest was 8 percent. Calculate the issuance price of the bonds and present the journal entry to record issuance of the bonds. Also indicate how the bond issue would be presented on the December 31, 1988 balance sheet if the effective interest method of amortization is used.

E8-8   On January 2, 1988, Courrier, Inc. issued $10,000,000 face value bonds. The bonds due in five years have a 7 percent coupon interest rate payable annually each December 31. Because the market rate of interest on January 2, 1988 for similar bonds is 8 percent, Courrier only received $9,600,890 for its bond issue. Present journal entries to record: a) issuance of the bonds and (b) the December 31, 1988 annual interest payment and discount amortization under:

1 The straight line method of amortizing bond discount. (Round all amounts to nearest dollar.)

2 The effective interest method. (Round all amounts to the nearest dollar.)

Also indicate how the bond issue would be presented on the December 31, 1988 balance sheet.

E8-9   (Appendix) Fortunato Co. leases, rather than buys, most of its long-lived assets. On January 2, 1988, the company signed a lease for use of office furniture for the next seven years. The annual lease payment due each December 31 is $5,000. Assume the lease meets the circumstances requiring capitalization of the lease. With an 8 percent interest rate, the capitalized value of the lease is $26,032. The capitalized asset is to be depreciated over seven years using the straight line depreciation method. Present journal entries to record:

1 Capitalization of the lease on January 2, 1988

2 The lease payment on December 31, 1988

3 The depreciation entry for 1988.

(Round all amounts to nearest dollar.) Also discuss which account(s) would appear on Fortunato's 1988 financial statements as a result of capitalizing the lease.

PROBLEMS

P8-1   *Accounting for Issuance and Retirement of Bonds*

During 1988, IOU Co. had the following issuances and retirements of bonds payable.

1 January 2, 1988—issued $80,000,000 face value, 8 percent, 12-year bonds for $68,963,520. The bonds pay interest semiannually on January 1 and July 1. The market rate of interest on January 2, 1988 was 10 percent. IOU elects to use the straight line method of amortizing any bond discount or bond premium on this issue.

2 May 1, 1988—issued $5,000,000 face value, 9 percent, ten-year bonds for $5,200,000, plus accrued interest. The bonds pay interest annually on December 31. IOU elects to use straight line amortization of any bond discount or premium on this bond issue. (Hint: Total amortization period is nine years, eight months.)

3 December 31, 1988—repurchased for $56,700,000 and retired 60 percent of a $90,000,000 face value, 12 percent outstanding bond issue. The bonds had originally been issued for $91,800,000. As of December 31, 1988, six years of the 20-year life of the bonds had expired. Assume that all journal entries for interest and premium amortization using the straight line method for this bond issue already have been properly recorded for 1988.

Required:

1 Prepare all required journal entries for 1988 related to the bond issues. IOU's accounting year ends on December 31. (Round all amounts to nearest dollar.)

2 Present the Long-term Debt section of the December 31, 1988 balance sheet.

P8-2 *Time-Value-of-Money Exercises*

Solve for the unknown in each of the following:

1 Find the present value of $12,000 to be received at the end of 9.5 years. The interest rate is 8 percent, compounded semiannually.

2 Find the number of years it will take a deposit of $4,000 to grow to $7,492 if the interest rate is 16 percent, compounded quarterly.

3 Find the annuity amount that can be withdrawn from a bank savings account at the end of each of the next 20 six-month periods. The interest rate is 8 percent, compounded semiannually. There is currently $35,000 in the savings account.

4 Find the rate of interest, compounded quarterly, if a $2,000 loan is to be repaid with interest compounded quarterly, in 12 equal quarterly installments of $189.12. The first of the 12 quarterly installments is due in three months.

P8-3 *Time-Value-of-Money Calculations*

1 Bordon, Inc. borrowed $12,290. The loan is to be repaid in ten equal annual installments with interest at 10 percent, compounded annually. Calculate the annual payments.

2 An investor wants to have $20,000 at the end of ten years. If he invests $4,944 today, what rate of interest, compounded annually, must be earned?

3 Greenstreet's Bookstore borrowed $30,000 from First Finance Company. The loan is to be repaid in semiannual installments of $2,968.55. The finance company's interest rate is 12 percent, compounded semiannually. How many semiannual installments must Greenstreet's Bookstore pay?

P8-4 *Annuity Calculations*

On September 1, 1988, Brightbill Company awarded Kramer University a lump sum of $22,000. The University decided the money would be used to finance the college education of a student entering the school in September 1989 and invested the $22,000 to earn 6 percent interest compounded annually.

Required:

1 What equal amount will Kramer University be able to withdraw at the end of each of the next four fiscal years (first withdrawal on September 1, 1989) so that the funds invested will be reduced to zero after the fourth annual withdrawal? (Round your answer to the nearest dollar.)

2 Prove your answer to part (1) by completing a table similar to the one in the "Present Value of Annuity" section of the chapter. (Round all amounts to nearest dollar.)

P8-5 *Accounting for Bond Interest*

Solve the specific requirements for the following three cases involving bond interest expense.

Case 1

Tricky, Inc. uses the effective interest method to amortize bond discount or bond premium. On December 31, 1988 the company issued $1,000,000 of 8 percent, ten-year bonds. The bonds pay interest semiannually on May 1 and November 1. The bonds were issued at par (i.e., face amount), plus two months' accrued interest of $13,333. The company's accounting year ends on December 31.

Required:

1 Present the journal entry to record the sale of the bonds on December 31, 1988.
2 Present the journal entries for the May 1, 1989 and November 1, 1989 interest payments.

Case 2

On January 2, 1988 Calo Co. issued 9 percent, five-year bonds. The bonds had a face value of $100,000, but were sold for $96,138. The current market rate of interest on the date the bonds were sold was 10 percent. The bonds pay interest semiannually on June 30 and December 31.

Required:

1 Calculate total interest expense to be recorded for 1988 using the effective interest method of amortizing bond discount or bond premium. Round amounts to nearest dollar.
2 Calculate total cash paid to bondholders for interest in 1988.
3 Determine the net balance of the bonds payable liability (i.e., the net carrying value of the bonds) at December 31, 1988.

Case 3

On January 1, 1989 Middle Company issued $200,000 face value, 12 percent, ten-year bonds. Since the current market rate of interest on January 1, 1989 was only 10 percent, the bonds were sold at a premium. The bonds pay interest annually on December 31, which is the end of the company's accounting year.

Required:

1 Calculate the issuance price of the bonds and the amount of the bond premium. Round to nearest dollar.
2 Present the journal entry required on December 31, 1989, the first interest payment date, assuming the straight line method of amortizing bond premium is used.
3 Present the journal entry required on December 31, 1989, the first interest payment date, assuming the effective interest method is used to amortize the bond premium.

P8-6 *Bonds Payable: Effective Interest and Straight Line Amortization*

California Industrial Services, Inc. issued $3,000,000 of four-year bonds on January 2, 1988. The bonds pay a 6 percent cash interest annually on December 31. Since the current market rate of interest when the bonds were issued was 8 percent, California Industrial Services received only $2,801,178 upon issuance of the bonds.

Required:

1 Prepare a bond amortization table for California Industrial Services bonds. Use

the effective interest method of amortizing bond discount. Follow the format of Exhibit 8-2 in the chapter. Round amounts to nearest dollar.

2 Present the required journal entries to record the issuance of the bonds and the first two annual interest payments using effective interest amortization.

3 If California Industrial Services uses the straight line method to amortize bond discount:

a Determine the total cash interest payments to be made over the life of the bonds.

b Determine the total interest expense to be recorded over the life of the bonds.

c Determine the annual interest expense to be recorded.

P8-7 (Appendix) *Lease Accounting*

On January 2, 1988, Taylor Co. signed a 12-year lease agreement for factory machines. The terms of the lease require Taylor to make $50,000 lease payments annually each December 31. The lease arrangement is substantially the same as a purchase of the machines. Therefore, Taylor properly capitalizes the lease and depreciates the capitalized asset over its estimated useful life of nine years, using a zero salvage value estimate and the straight line depreciation method. Taylor uses a 9 percent interest rate to find the capitalized value of the lease.

Required:

1 Calculate the capitalized value of the lease.

2 Present the journal entry required on January 2, 1988 to record the capitalized value of the lease.

3 Present the journal entries on December 31, 1988 to record the first annual lease payment and depreciation for 1988. Round all amounts to nearest dollar.

4 Present the journal entries on December 31, 1989 to record the second annual lease payment and depreciation for 1989. Round all amounts to nearest dollar.

5 For the 12-year life of the lease, calculate:

a Total expenses related to the capitalized lease that will have been deducted on the company's income statements.

b Total expenses for the 12 years that would have been deducted on the company's income statements if the lease had been treated as an operating lease.

Business Decision Problem

Pantella, Inc. is experiencing cash shortages. The company is struggling to meet debt payments as they become due. To help alleviate the situation, Patella is considering raising additional funds by either: 1) issuing at face, $500,000 of 12 percent, ten-year bonds paying interest semiannually on June 30 and December 31, or 2) issuing 100,000 shares of capital stock at $5 per share.

Pantella's income tax rate is 40 percent. The company believes it can earn a 15 percent return on the additional $500,000 of invested funds.

Required:

Analyze the advantages and disadvantages of the two alternative methods of raising cash. Include in your analysis a discussion of reported earnings, taxes, and cash flows.

INCOME FROM INVESTMENT IN STOCKS AND BONDS

LEARNING OBJECTIVES

When you complete this chapter, you should be able to:

1 Account for transactions involving short-term investments in marketable equity securities.
2 Distinguish among the cost, lower of cost or market, and equity methods of accounting for long-term investment in stock.
3 Record the acquisition of long-term bond investments.
4 Record bond interest revenue and the associated amortization of discount or premium.

Companies frequently invest in stocks and bonds issued by other companies or in bonds issued by governments. There are many reasons for investment, ranging from a desire to earn a return on excess cash that may temporarily exist to the desire to have a controlling ownership interest in another company. Whatever the reason for investment in securities, income is produced that must be recorded.

This chapter discusses accounting for the acquisition, ownership, and disposition of securities. Accounting differences among various types of investment will be emphasized.

SHORT-TERM INVESTMENT IN MARKETABLE SECURITIES

One form of short-term investment of excess cash is the purchase of securities of other companies. Such securities may be either *equity securities* (stock of other companies) or *debt securities* (corporate or government bonds). The investment is classified as Marketable Securities and presented in the current assets section of the balance sheet if:

1 The securities are *marketable* (i.e., there is a readily available means of buying and selling the securities on a stock exchange or "over the counter"), and

2 It is the company's intention to hold these securities as a *temporary* investment of excess cash.

Investments in securities which are not readily marketable or which the company intends to hold for a long period of time are not classified as current assets. They are known as *long-term investments*. Long-term investments in equity securities and in bonds are discussed later in the chapter.

Accounting for Investment in Marketable Equity Securities

The accounting rules for short-term investment in marketable equity securities may be summarized as follows:

1 Purchases of marketable equity securities are recorded at *cost*.

2 Each time a balance sheet is prepared, the total cost and total market value of all marketable equity securities classified as current assets must be determined.

    a If total cost is *less* than total market value, the marketable equity securities are reported at *cost*.

    b If total cost *exceeds* total market value, the marketable equity securities are reported at *market,* and the amount of the write-down is shown as a loss on the income statement.

3 If marketable equity securities which have previously been written down increase in value, the increase may be recognized so long as the amount reported on the balance sheet does not exceed the original cost. This "recovery of loss" is shown on the income statement.

Effect of Changes in Market Value   Assume that on September 7, 1988, Bauer Corporation makes a temporary investment in the stock of the following three companies:

Company	Cost
Andersen, Inc.	$15,000
Bach Brothers Co.	20,000
Connelly Incorporated	22,000
	$57,000

The journal entry to record the purchase would be:

1988			
Sept. 7	Marketable Equity Securities	57,000	
	Cash		57,000
	To record short-term investment.		

On September 30, 1988, financial statements are to be prepared. Market values on September 30 are:

Company	Market value
Andersen, Inc.	$16,000
Bach Brothers Co.	18,000
Connelly Incorporated	21,000
	$55,000

Since total market value of $55,000 is less than the $57,000 total cost, a $2,000 write-down should be recorded as follows:

Sept. 30	Unrealized Loss on Marketable		
	Equity Securities	2,000	
	Allowance for Unrealized Loss		2,000

To record write down of investment in marketable equity securities from total cost of $57,000 to total market value of $55,000.

The September 30 balance sheet would show the Allowance for Unrealized Loss account as a contra asset in the current asset section:

Marketable Equity Securities, at cost	$57,000	
Less: Allowance for Unrealized Loss	2,000	$55,000

An alternative, shorter presentation would be:

Marketable Equity Securities, at market (cost $57,000)	$55,000

The Unrealized Loss Account would appear on the income statement as:

Unrealized Loss on Marketable Equity Securities	$2,000

On October 31, 1988, financial statements are again being prepared. Assume that market values on October 31 are:

Company	Market value
Andersen, Inc.	$15,400
Bach Brothers Co.	17,000
Connelly Incorporated	24,000
	$56,400

Market value has increased by $1,400 since September 30 (when market value was $55,000), but is still less than original cost ($57,000). This $1,400 increase is considered a partial recovery of the $2,000 loss recognized last month. The journal entry is:

Oct. 31	Allowance for Unrealized Loss	1,400	
	Recovery of Unrealized Loss		
	on Marketable Equity		
	Securities		1,400
	To record partial recovery of		
	previously recognized		
	unrealized loss on marketable		
	equity securities.		

On October 31, the current asset section of the balance sheet would show:

| Marketable Equity Securities, at cost | $57,000 | |
| Less: Allowance for Unrealized Loss | 600 | $56,400 |

The income statement for October would show the $1,400 recovery as an increase in income:

| Recovery of Unrealized Loss on | |
| Marketable Equity Securities | $1,400 |

Thus, decreases in market value below original cost and subsequent recoveries are recognized. However, because of the conservatism concept, any increase in market value above original cost is *not* recognized. If in November, the total market value of the securities climbed to $59,000, the entry would recognize only $600 of loss recovery (from the $56,400 market value on October 31 to the original cost of $57,000). The November 30 balance sheet would show:

| Marketable Equity Securities, at cost | $57,000 |

and the income statement for the month of November would show:

| Recovery of Unrealized Loss on | |
| Marketable Equity Securities | $600 |

Income from Investment in Marketable Equity Securities   In addition to the treatment of losses and loss recoveries discussed above, income from short-term investment in marketable equity securities in the form of *dividends* must be considered. Unlike interest, dividends do not accrue continuously over time. Dividend revenue is not recognized until a dividend declaration occurs. Typically, the declaration of the dividend precedes the actual payment by several weeks.

Assume that on October 13, 1988, Andersen, Inc. declares a dividend of $.75 per share, payable October 28, 1988. Bauer Corporation, holder of 2,000 shares of Andersen stock, would record the following:

1988			
Oct. 13	Dividends Receivable	1,500	
	Dividend Revenue		1,500
	To record dividend declared		

by Andersen, Inc.

28	Cash	1,500	
	Dividends Receivable		1,500
	To record receipt of dividend from Andersen, Inc.		

Although the above procedure of accruing the dividend on the date of declaration theoretically is correct, many companies follow the practical alternative of making no entry until the cash dividend is actually received. If Bauer followed this practical alternative, the only entry to record would be:

Oct. 28	Cash	1,500	
	Dividend Revenue		1,500
	To record receipt of dividend from Andersen, Inc.		

If this second alternative is followed, an adjusting entry would be needed at the end of the accounting period to record any dividend that had been declared but not yet received.

Sale of Marketable Equity Securities   When short-term investments in marketable equity securities are converted back into cash, the income statement shows the gain or loss on the sale. A gain is recognized if the selling price exceeds the cost previously paid to purchase the securities. If the selling price is less than acquisition cost, the sale would result in a loss. The following example illustrates the calculation of gain or loss on the sale of marketable equity securities and the related journal entry.

Assume that on March 20, 1988 Marshall Corporation sells 100 shares of Byron, Inc.'s stock for $9,200. This stock had been purchased seven months earlier for $7,000. The journal entry to record the $2,200 gain is:

1988			
Mar. 20	Cash	9,200	
	Marketable Equity Securities		7,000
	Gain on Sale of Securities		2,200
	To record gain on sale of 100 shares of Byron, Inc. stock.		

If the stock had been sold for $6,300, there would be a loss of $700. The entry would be:

Mar. 20	Cash	6,300	
	Loss on Sale of Securities	700	
	Marketable Equity Securities		7,000
	To record loss on sale of 100 shares of Byron, Inc. stock.		

Note that the Allowance for Unrealized Loss account is not involved in the entry for the sale of marketable equity securities. The allowance account is considered only at the end of the accounting period when the total cost of the marketable equity securities owned on that date is compared to the total market value.

Accounting for Temporary Investment in Marketable Debt Securities

Debt securities (corporate or government bonds) are another category of marketable securities. When acquired, they are recorded at cost. Cost may continue to be used as the basis for presenting these securities on the balance sheet. For example, if a company temporarily invests $60,000 in corporate bonds, the current assets section of its balance sheet would show:

Marketable Debt Securities, at cost	$60,000

Another acceptable method of valuing a temporary investment in marketable debt securities is to use the *lower of cost or market* method previously illustrated for temporary investments in marketable equity securities. Thus, if at the date of the financial statements, the market value of the above bonds had dropped to $58,700, the balance sheet would show:

Marketable Debt Securities, at cost	$60,000	
Less: Allowance for Unrealized Loss	1,300	$58,700

The decrease of $1,300 would also be shown as an unrealized loss on the income statement. If, however, the market value had risen to $61,000, the bonds would continue to be reported at the $60,000 cost.

Income from marketable debt securities take the form of *interest*. Interest is usually recorded when the cash is received. However, since interest revenue is earned continuously over time, an end-of-period adjusting entry is often required. Accounting for sales of marketable debt securities is the same as the accounting for sale of marketable equity securities discussed earlier in the chapter.

LONG-TERM INVESTMENT IN STOCK

In the preceding section, we discussed the current asset Marketable Securities. Securities were included in this category if they met both of two conditions:

1 They had to be *marketable,* meaning that a readily available means of buying and selling (such as a stock exchange or over-the-counter market) had to exist, and

2 It had to be the company's intention to hold these securities as a *temporary* investment of excess cash.

A company may also own equity securities (stock in other companies) that fail to meet one or both of these conditions. It may own securities that are not regularly traded (and hence are not marketable). It may own securities that it intends to hold for a long period of time, either as an income-producing asset, or for reasons of maintaining a significant ownership interest in another company. Securities such as these would be presented on the balance sheet as long-term investments. This category typically follows the current assets section.

Several different accounting methods are employed for long-term investments in stock:

The *cost* method
The *lower of cost or market* method
The *equity* method

Three factors will be important in deciding which accounting method to apply to a particular long-term investment situation. These three factors are:

1 Marketability—whether or not a ready means of buying and selling exists
2 Type of security—whether stock or bonds
3 Extent of ownership—what percentage of Company B's stock is owned by Company A. If the percentage owned is large (usually defined as 20 percent or more), then A is said to have a *significant interest* in B.

The Cost Method

The *cost* method is used for long-term investments that are:

1 Investments in stock when:
   a The percentage owned is not significant (less than 20 percent), and
   b The securities are not marketable
2 Investments in bonds (discussed later in the chapter)

Under the cost method, the investments are always presented *at cost* on the balance sheet. On the income statement, only the interest or dividend revenue would appear.

To illustrate, assume that on March 8, 1988, Rich Corp. buys for $10,000 shares of stock of Unknown, Inc. This investment represents 5 percent of the total stock of Unknown, Inc. Unknown's stock is not traded on any stock exchange (or over-the-counter market), and thus is considered nonmarketable. The purchase would be recorded as:

```
1988
Mar.  8      Long-term Investment—Unknown,
                Inc. Stock                    10,000
                   Cash                                    10,000
             To record purchase of stock
             of Unknown, Inc.
```

Assume that on November 23, 1988, Unknown declares and pays a dividend. Rich

Corp. receives $120 on the shares it owns. This transaction would be recorded as:

Nov. 23	Cash	120	
	Dividend Revenue		120
	To record dividend received on investment in Unknown, Inc., stock.		

At the end of the year, the balance sheet would show:

Long-term Investments, at cost	$10,000

Note that, since Unknown's stock is not traded, we would have no reliable way of determining market value. Thus, cost is really the only choice available to report this asset.

The Lower of Cost or Market Method

The *lower of cost or market* method is used for long-term investments when:

1 The investments are *equity* securities
2 The securities are marketable
3 The percentage owned is not significant (less than 20 percent)

Under the lower of cost or market method, the investments are presented on the balance sheet at either total cost or total market value, whichever is lower. On the income statement, we again find only the dividends earned.

There is an important difference between the lower of cost or market method used for long-term stock investments, and the lower of cost or market method for temporary marketable equity securities discussed earlier. For temporary investments, market losses (and subsequent recoveries) were reported on the income statement. For long-term investments, this is not the case. Accumulated market losses (reduced by subsequent recoveries) are shown as a negative item in the stockholders' equity section of the balance sheet.

To illustrate, assume that on June 7, 1988, Southeastern Co. buys 2,000 shares of stock of Famous, Inc. for $25,000. The stock is traded on major stock exchanges. This investment represents less than 1 percent of the total shares of Famous, Inc. stock. At the end of the year, the market value of the long-term investment in Famous, Inc.'s stock had fallen to $24,000. This loss would be recorded as:

1988			
Dec. 31	Unrealized Loss on Noncurrent Marketable Equity Securities	1,000	
	Allowance for Unrealized Loss		1,000
	To record decrease in market value		

of Famous, Inc. stock from cost of $25,000 to market value of $24,000.

The asset side of the balance sheet would show:

Long-term Investments, at cost	$25,000	
Less: Allowance for Unrealized Loss	1,000	$24,000

The stockholders' equity section of Southeastern's balance sheet would show:

Capital Stock	$30,000
Retained Earnings	67,000
	$97,000
Unrealized Loss on Noncurrent Marketable Equity Securities	(1,000)
Total Stockholders' Equity	$96,000

If, by the end of the following year, the market value of Southeastern Co.'s investment in Famous, Inc. stock has risen to $24,350, the $350 recovery would be recognized by decreasing both the contra asset (Allowance for Unrealized Loss) and contra stockholders' equity (Unrealized Loss on Noncurrent Marketable Equity Securities) accounts. Note that there would be no effect on the income statement for this recovery, just as there was no effect for the decrease in market value in the preceding year. Note also that the Long-term Investment account cannot be reported at more than the original cost of $25,000 (and similarly, the Unrealized Loss account cannot be decreased below zero). Thus, the lower of cost or market method for *noncurrent* marketable equity securities accumulates the net market loss as a component of stockholders' equity on the balance sheet, while for *current* marketable equity securities we report losses (and subsequent recoveries) on the income statement.

The Equity Method

The *equity* method is used for long-term investments when:

1 The investments are stock
2 A significant interest is owned (20 percent or more)

To describe the basics of the equity method, we will follow through several steps of an illustration. Assume that on January 12, 1988, Thompson, Inc. buys 40 percent of the stock of Small Corporation for $300,000. We say that Thompson has a "significant interest" in Small. Owning 40 percent of the stock probably makes Thompson the largest stockholder and therefore gives Thompson considerable influence over the management of Small Corporation.

We record the purchase of the stock at cost:

1988	
Jan. 12	Long-term Investment—Small

Corp. Stock	300,000	
Cash		300,000

To record purchase of 40% of
stock of Small Corp.

Assume that during 1988, Small pays no dividends and has net income of $110,000. What will Thompson report as income from its investment? Because of its significant interest, Thompson is assumed to have considerable influence over dividend declarations by Small. We conclude that Thompson could therefore cause as much of Small's income as desired to be distributed as dividends, and hence it makes no practical difference whether or not dividends have actually been declared. As a result, we count as Thompson's income for 1988 its 40 percent share of Small's net income, or $44,000 (40% of $110,000). Since the income was not distributed as dividends, we add it to Thompson's investment. (This is analogous to having $300,000 in the bank and earning interest of $44,000. If the interest is not withdrawn, the bank account goes up to $344,000.) The entry is:

Dec. 31	Long-term Investment—Small		
	Corp. Stock	44,000	
	Income from Equity Investment		44,000

To record as income 40% of the
$110,000 net income of Small
Corp.

Thompson's balance sheet on December 31, 1988 would show:

Long-term Investment (at equity) $344,000

The income statement would show:

Income from Equity Investment $44,000

Because Thompson has included in income its entire 40 percent share of Small's net income, Thompson cannot again record income when Small's earnings are distributed as dividends. When Thompson receives dividends from Small, we record this as a reduction of Thompson's investment.

Assume that during 1989, Small has net income of $120,000 and pays dividends on December 31 of $50,000. Thompson's entries would be:

1989			
Dec. 31	Long-term Investment—Small		
	Corp. Stock	48,000	
	Income from Equity Investment		48,000

To record as income 40% of the
$120,000 net income of Small
Corp.

31	Cash	20,000	
	Long-term Investment—Small		

<table>
<tr><td>Corp. Stock</td><td>20,000</td></tr>
</table>

To record receipt of dividend from
Small Corp. (40% of $50,000).

On December 31, 1989, Thompson's balance sheet would show:

| Long-term Investment (at equity) | $372,000 |

The above balance is determined as:

Balance on December 31, 1988	$344,000
Plus: 40% of 1989 income	48,000
Less: 40% of dividends	(20,000)
Balance at December 31, 1989	$372,000

Thompson's 1989 income statement would show:

| Income from Equity Investment | $48,000 |

Note again that the dividends received during 1989 are *not* reported as income.

LONG-TERM INVESTMENT IN BONDS

In discussing long-term investment in stock in the preceding section, two investment motives were identified: generation of revenue and maintaining a significant ownership interest in another company. In the case of long-term investment in bonds, only the first motive—revenue generation—exists; bond investment does not involve ownership rights in another company.

Long-term investment in bonds produces a reasonably stable flow of revenue, as interest rates are fixed and the risk of non-payment of interest is minimal. If bonds are held to maturity, there is usually little prospect of a gain or loss; the principal amount is fixed, and default is rare. If bonds are sold prior to maturity, however, gains or losses may occur. As interest rates change, market prices of bonds change. A sale of a bond investment at market price may result in proceeds that are more, or less, than book value.

Accounting for Bonds Acquired at a Discount

In the preceding chapter, we saw how market interest rates determine the price of bonds. This calculation applies to both the price at the time of issuance and to subsequent market prices. As interest rates change, bond prices change. Bond prices rise if interest rates decline, and fall if interest rates increase.

To invest in bonds, a company may purchase bonds directly from the issuing company, or it may purchase bonds on the market from other investors. Accounting for the investment is unaffected by the source of purchase.

Assume that bonds with a face value of $100,000 are acquired by Norman Co. for $95,086 on June 30, 1988 (an interest payment date and the end of the company's fiscal year). Maturity date is July 1, 1994, and the coupon interest rate is 5 percent (payable annually). The total revenue which Norman Co. will earn consists of two elements:

1 Six annual interest payments of $5,000 (5 percent times $100,000)
2 The $4,914 discount—the difference between the $95,086 invested and the $100,000 which will be received at maturity.

The entry to record the acquisition would be:

1988			
June 30	Long-term Investment—Bonds	95,086	
	Cash		95,086
	To record purchase of $100,000,		
	5% bonds at a discount.		

Note that the $95,086 investment account balance reflects the face value of the bonds ($100,000) less the discount ($4,914). Bond investments are recorded at *net,* while bond liabilities (discussed in the preceding chapter) are recorded at face value with a separate account for the discount.

Although the $4,914 of discount will not be received until July 1, 1994, it is considered as being *earned* over the entire six-year remaining life of the bonds. Each year, a portion of the $4,914 must be recognized as revenue by amortizing the discount. As the discount is amortized, debits will be made to the investment account, gradually bringing the balance to the $100,000 maturity value. As was the case for bonds payable, two methods of amortization exist: straight line and effective interest.

Straight Line Amortization   One approach is to amortize the discount on a straight line basis; that is, recognize the $4,914 equally over six years ($819 per year). On each interest date (starting on June 30, 1989 and ending on June 30, 1994), the following entry would be recorded:

June 30	Cash	5,000	
	Long-term Investment—Bonds	819	
	Interest Revenue		5,819
	To record receipt of $5,000 annual		
	interest, plus straight line		
	amortization of discount.		

This entry reflects the $5,000 interest payment that is received (and earned), plus the earning of one-sixth of the additional $4,914 that will be received at maturity. Note that after the above entry has been made for six years, the investment account will show a balance of $100,000. The entry recording the receipt of the face value will then simply be:

```
1994
July   1      Cash                                100,000
              Long-term Investment—Bonds                      100,000
              To record at maturity the receipt
              of the face value of the bond
              investment.
```

Effective Interest Amortization   Under the effective interest method of amortization, the total bond interest revenue each period is a *constant percentage* of the balance of the long-term investment in bonds account. The particular percentage used is the market rate of interest implicit in the original purchase price of the bonds.

To illustrate the effective interest method of amortization, the same data used for the straight line amortization example will be used again:

> Face value of bonds, $100,000
> Coupon interest rate is 5 percent
>   (payable annually on June 30)
> Bonds purchased on June 30, 1988
>   for $95,086 (when the current market
>   interest rate was 6 percent)
> Maturity date is July 1, 1994 (six years
>   from date of purchase)

Again, the long-term investment in bonds account would be debited for the $95,086 purchase price. The discount of $4,914 ($100,000 face value less $95,086 price paid) is to be amortized over the six-year life of the bond. The process of effective interest amortization can be described as follows:

```
              Investment in Bonds balance at beginning of period
Times:        Market interest rate when bonds were originally purchased
Equals:       Total bond interest revenue for the period
Less:         Interest received in cash (face value × coupon interest rate)
Equals:       Amount of discount (or premium) to be amortized
              this period. This amount is added to (or in the case
              of a premium, subtracted from) the Investment in Bonds
              balance, creating a new balance for the next period's
              computation.
```

The effective interest amortization schedule for Norman's investment in bonds is presented in Exhibit 9-1. The entry on June 30, 1989 would be:

```
1989
June 30       Cash                                5,000
              Long-term Investment—Bonds           705
                  Interest Revenue                            5,705
              To record receipt of $5,000 cash
              interest and effective interest
              amortization of discount.
```

EXHIBIT 9-1
Bond Discount Amortization
Effective Interest Method

Period ended	(A) Investment in bonds balance, beginning of period	(B) Total bond interest revenue for period (6% × Col. (A))	(C) Interest received in cash	(B)−(C) Discount to be amortized
6-30-89	$95,086	$ 5,705	$ 5,000	$ 705
6-30-90	95,791	5,747	5,000	747
6-30-91	96,538	5,792	5,000	792
6-30-92	97,330	5,840	5,000	840
6-30-93	98,170	5,890	5,000	890
6-30-94	99,060**	5,940*	5,000	940**
		$34,914	$30,000	$4,914

*$4 rounding error
**$99,060 beginning balance plus $940 discount amortization equals $100,000 balance in Investment in Bonds account on 7-1-94 maturity date.

A similar entry would be made in each subsequent year, using the numbers from the amortization table. After six years, the investment account would show a balance of $100,000.

Note that under both methods of amortization (straight line and effective interest): a) the balance in the investment account is $100,000 at maturity, b) total interest revenue recorded over the six-year period is $34,914, c) total cash interest received over the six-year period is $30,000, and d) the total discount amortized over the six-year period is $4,914. It is the *timing* of the recognition of the discount that is affected by the choice between the straight line and effective interest methods of amortization. The effective interest method is preferred because the interest revenue recognized each period is a constant percentage of the beginning balance in the investment account. Under generally accepted accounting principles, the effective interest method is required except in cases where the straight line method produces substantially similar results.

Accounting for Bonds Acquired at a Premium

Accounting for bonds issued at a premium parallels that for the discount case. The investment is initially recorded at purchase price, and the premium must be amortized over the remaining life of the bonds. Existence of a premium means that the acquisition price exceeds the face value. Amortization of the premium will result in a reduction of the investment account and a reduction of interest revenue.

Assume that on January 1, 1989, $200,000 face value, 12 percent bonds were acquired for $207,092. This price reflects a market interest rate of 10 percent. The bonds pay interest semiannually on June 30 and December 31, and mature on December 31, 1990. The acquisition would be recorded as:

```
1989
Jan.  1     Long-term Investment—Bonds      207,092
                Cash                                        207,092
            To record purchase of $200,000,
            12 percent bonds at a premium.
```

The total revenue earned on these bonds will be the semiannual interest payments less the $7,092 premium. The company invested $207,092, but will receive only $200,000 at maturity.

Two methods of premium amortization exist: straight line and effective interest.

Straight Line Amortization   Under the straight line method, the premium is amortized in equal amounts over the remaining life of the bond. Since interest is received semiannually, we express the remaining two-year life as four semiannual periods; $1,773 of premium ($7,092 ÷ 4) will be amortized each period. The entry for June 30, 1989 (the end of the first semiannual period) would be:

```
June 30     Cash                                 12,000
                Long-term Investment—Bonds                1,773
                Interest Revenue                          10,227
            To record receipt of $12,000
            semiannual interest, and
            straight line amortization
            of premium.
```

The same entry would be made for each subsequent semiannual period.

Effective Interest Amortization   To calculate effective interest amortization of the premium, an amortization table is constructed, as shown in Exhibit 9-2.

EXHIBIT 9-2
Bond Premium Amortization
Effective Interest Method

Period ended	(A) Investment in bonds balance, beginning of period	(B) Total bond interest revenue for period (5% × Col. (A))	(C) Interest received in cash	(C)−(B) Premium to be amortized
6-30-89	$207,092	$10,355	$12,000	$1,645
12-31-89	205,447	10,272	12,000	1,728
6-30-90	203,719	10,186	12,000	1,814
12-31-90	201,905*	10,095	12,000	1,905*
		$40,908	$48,000	$7,092

*$201,905 beginning balance minus $1,905 premium amortization equals $200,000 balance in Investment in Bonds account on 12-31-90 maturity date.

The entry for the first semiannual period would be:

June 30	Cash		12,000	
	Long-term Investment—Bonds			1,645
	Interest Revenue			10,355

To record receipt of $12,000
semiannual interest, and
effective interest
amortization of premium.

A similar entry would be made for each subsequent period, using the numbers from the amortization table.

Entries Between Interest Dates

Other aspects of accounting for long-term bond investments parallel the discussion of bonds payable in Chapter 8. The following example illustrates the purchase of bonds between interest payment dates and the required adjustments when the bond investor's accounting year end does not coincide with an interest payment date. Assume Johnson Company purchases the following bonds of Niatross, Inc. on August 1, 1988:

Bonds acquired—$500,000 face value
Coupon interest rate—10 percent, payable semiannually on April 1 and October 1
Purchase price—$439,000 plus $16,667 accrued interest
Market rate of interest on date bonds purchased—12 percent
Maturity date of bonds—October 1, 1998

Since the August 1, 1988 bond investment occurs between interest dates, Johnson Company must pay the previous bondholder for accrued interest since April 1, 1988—the last interest payment date. The $16,667 accrued interest ($500,000 × 10% × 4/12) is not recorded as part of the cost of the bond investment, but as interest receivable.

1988				
Aug. 1	Long-term Investment—Bonds		439,000	
	Interest Receivable		16,667	
	Cash			455,667

To record purchase of $500,000
face value bonds for $439,000
plus four months' accrued
interest.

The six months' interest of $25,000 received by Johnson Company on October 1, 1988 represents collection of the $16,667 accrued interest paid to the previous bondholder plus $8,333 interest earned for August and September. The journal entry would be:

Oct. 1	Cash		25,000	
	Interest Receivable			16,667

	Interest Revenue		8,333
	To record receipt of first six months' interest.		

Also on October 1, a portion of the $61,000 discount ($500,000 face value less $439,000 purchase price) is amortized. If Johnson Company uses the straight line method, monthly discount amortization would be $500 ($61,000 discount ÷ 122 months from date of purchase of bonds to maturity). The journal entry to record discount amortization from August 1 to October 1 would be:

Oct. 1	Long-term Investment—Bonds	1,000	
	Interest Revenue		1,000
	To record two months' discount amortization using the straight line method (2 months × $500 = $1,000).		

Since Johnson's accounting year ends on December 31, the following adjusting entries are required to record interest earned and discount amortized for the three-month period from October 1 to December 31:

Dec. 31	Interest Receivable	12,500	
	Interest Revenue		12,500
	To record interest earned since October 1 but not yet received ($500,000 × 10% × 3/12 = $12,500).		
31	Long-term Investment—Bonds	1,500	
	Interest Revenue		1,500
	To record three months' discount amortization using the straight line method (3 months × $500 = $1,500).		

Sale of Bond Investments

A gain or loss is recognized on the sale of a long-term bond investment before maturity. If the book value of the investment is less than the sales price of the bond, a gain results. A loss is recorded if the book value is greater than the sales price.

Assume that on April 1, 1991 (an interest payment date), Johnson Company sells its long-term investment in Niatross' bonds for $470,000. If the balance in the investment account was $455,000, the entry to record the sale would be:

1991			
April 1	Cash	470,000	
	Long-term Investment—Bonds		455,000

<table>
<tr><td>Gain on Sale of Long-term
Bond Investment</td><td>15,000</td></tr>
<tr><td>To record gain on sale of investment
in Niatross' bonds.</td><td></td></tr>
</table>

Frequently, the sale of the bond investment does not coincide with an interest payment date. In those situations it is necessary first to accrue interest revenue and update discount or premium amortization before recording sale of the bond investment.

FINANCIAL STATEMENT PRESENTATION

Short-term investments are presented in the current assets section of the balance sheet. Long-term investments are presented in an investments section, which usually appears between current assets and property, plant, and equipment. Three methods of valuation are used—cost, lower of cost or market, and equity. Exhibit 9-3 summarizes the appropriate valuation method for each type of investment.

The income statement would show dividend revenue, interest revenue, and income from equity-method investments. Unrealized losses when market value is below cost appears on the income statement for short-term investments, but

EXHIBIT 9-3 SUMMARY OF ACCOUNTING METHODS FOR INVESTMENTS

Type of investment	Balance sheet: Investments valued at	Income statement
Short–term: Marketable Equity Securities	Lower of cost or market	Dividend revenue Unrealized loss (and recoveries of loss) on marketable equity securities
Marketable Debt Securities	Cost, or Lower of cost or market	Interest revenue Unrealized loss (and recoveries of loss) on marketable debt securities (if lower of cost or market is used)
Long–term: Stock: Less than 20% ownership and nonmarketable	Cost	Dividend revenue
Less than 20% ownership and marketable	Lower of cost or market	Dividend revenue*
Ownership of 20% or more	Equity	Income from equity investment (share of net income of investee)
Bonds	Cost adjusted for amortization to date of premium or discount	Interest revenue

*Unrealized loss (and subsequent recovery of loss) resulting from writing down to market is shown as a negative stockholders' equity item and is *not* presented on the income statement.

not for long-term investments. Treatment of these items is also summarized in Exhibit 9-3.

SUMMARY

Learning Objective 1: Account for transactions involving short-term investments in marketable equity securities.

A company may temporarily invest excess cash in stock of other companies. Purchases are initially recorded at cost. On subsequent balance sheets, marketable equity securities are presented at lower of total cost or total market value. Write-downs to market are shown as unrealized losses on the income statement. When marketable equity securities are sold, the gain or loss is computed by comparing selling price to the original cost of the securities.

Learning Objective 2: Distinguish among the cost, lower of cost or market, and equity methods of accounting for long-term investment in stock.

The cost method is used when ownership is less than 20 percent and the stocks are not readily marketable. The investment account is presented at cost on the balance sheet and only dividend revenue appears on the income statement. Ownership of less than 20 percent of a readily marketable stock is accounted for by the lower of cost or market. Unrealized losses from writing down to market are shown as a negative stockholders' equity item—they are not deducted on the income statement. The equity method is used for stock investments greater than 20 percent. The investment account and income are adjusted to reflect the owner's share of the investee's earnings. Dividends received are not recorded as revenue but reduce the investment account.

Learning Objective 3: Record the acquisition of long-term bond investments.

Bonds purchased for long-term investment are recorded at cost. If the cost does not equal the face value, there is a discount or premium that must be amortized. If bonds are acquired between interest dates, accrued interest is paid in addition to the purchase price and must be recorded as interest receivable.

Learning Objective 4: Record bond interest revenue and the associated amortization of discount or premium.

Amortization of discount or premium is included in interest revenue. Bond interest revenue equals cash received plus amortization of discount (or minus amortization of premium). Two methods of amortization exist, straight line and effective interest.

KEY TERMS

Allowance for unrealized loss
Cost method
Equity method
Long-term investments
Lower of cost or market

Marketable debt securities
Marketable equity securities
Short-term investments
Unrealized loss

REVIEW QUESTIONS

1 Mortin, Inc. acquired 1,000 shares of Tulton, Inc.'s stock for $18,000 on January 9, 1988 as a short-term investment. Four months later on May 9, Mortin sold the 1,000 shares for $21,500. What are the journal entries to record the purchase and the sale of the stock? How would the sale be shown on the company's income statement?

2 Based upon the lower of total cost or total market rule, at what amount should the following portfolio of marketable equity securities be valued?

Security owned	Cost	Market
Company Bee	$10,000	$14,000
Company See	21,000	18,000

3 Evaluate the following statements: "The lower of cost or market rule for marketable equity securities yields inconsistent results. Unrealized losses from recognizing write downs to lower market values are recorded, but unrealized gains from increases in market value above cost are not recorded."

4 What is the accounting concept that underlies the lower of cost or market rule?

5 Discuss the proper accounting treatment for temporary investments in marketable debt securities.

6 Stouffer, Inc. invests in the securities of other companies. What factors surrounding the investments would lead Stouffer to classify them as long-term investments, rather than current assets?

7 What are the three possible valuation methods for a long-term investment in stock? Under what circumstances is each appropriate?

8 Avel Co. owns 2,500 of the 10,000 shares of Lino, Inc's stock. The stock is highly marketable. If Lino declares and pays a $1.50 cash dividend per share, how much dividend income should be recorded by Avel?

9 If Avel Co. owned only 1,000 shares of Lino, Inc.'s stock (see Question 8 above), how much dividend income should be recorded by Avel?

10 Ralston Co. owns less than 20 percent of the stock of Bevan, Inc. Bevan's shares are readily marketable. Ralston values its investment in Bevan's stock at lower of cost or market. Describe the differences that would result in accounting for the lower of cost or market adjustment if: a) the investment is classified as a current asset versus b) the investment is considered long-term.

11 Under the equity method of accounting for investments, an investor recognizes its share of the investee's earnings in the period in which the:
a Investor sells the investment
b Investee declares a dividend
c Investee pays a dividend
d Earnings are reported by the investee in its financial statements.

(AICPA Adapted)

12 Arizini, Inc. owns 35 percent of the shares of Bates Co. During 1988, Bates earned net income of $180,000 and paid cash dividends of $28,000. Arizini incorrectly used the cost method to record these transactions rather than the correct method—the equity method. As a result of its error, indicate the effects on Arizini's investment in Bates Co. stock account, net income, and retained earnings.

13 On September 30, 1988 Bremser, Inc. purchased as an investment 9 percent corporate bonds paying interest semiannually on November 30 and May 31.

Bremser purchased the bonds from another investor at the $80,000 face value plus accrued interest. Compute the amount of accrued interest. Why must Bremser pay the accrued interest to the previous owner of the bonds?

14   Other than due to accrued interest, why do bonds often trade in the market at a price different than their face value? Include a definition of bond discount and bond premium in your answer.

15   On January 3, 1988, Zeron, Inc. invested $950 to purchase an 8 percent, $1,000 bond that pays interest annually on December 31. The bond matures on December 31, 1993. What is: the face value of the bond, the market price, the annual coupon interest rate, the maturity date, and the bond discount or premium?

16   For a company purchasing an investment in bonds at a discount, what effect will the choice between straight line and effective interest amortization have on annual interest revenue? Assuming the bonds pay interest annually, explain how annual interest revenue would be determined under both amortization methods.

17   Capaleto Co. purchased $5,000 face value, 9 percent bonds of Fly by Night, Inc. on an interest payment date for $4,692.57. The bonds pay interest annually and mature in ten years. Is the current market rate of interest implicit in determining the $4,692.57 current selling price of the bonds: a) 8 percent, b) 9 percent, or c) 10 percent?

EXERCISES

E9-1   Fandango, Inc. acquired a portfolio of marketable equity securities during 1985. The securities are classified as current assets. Fandango prepares financial statements annually on December 31. Total cost and total market value of the portfolio at year end for the last four years were as follows:

	Total cost	Total market value
December 31, 1985	$21,000	$22,400
December 31, 1986	21,000	19,600
December 31, 1987	21,000	22,100
December 31, 1988	21,000	21,200

At what dollar amount should the portfolio of marketable equity securities be shown at each year end? What adjusting journal entry is needed each year to obtain the correct valuation?

E9-2   On February 9, 1988, Bakrupt Co. purchased the following securities as short-term investments:

Company	Number of shares	Cost per share
Jacobus Co.	100	$20
Prendergast, Inc.	200	25
Malloy Co.	150	15

The securities are considered marketable equity securities. On October 11, 1988 the 100 shares of Jacobus Co. stock were sold for $23 per share. Market values per share on December 31, 1988 were: Jacobus, $24.50; Prendergast, Inc., $23; and Malloy Co., $16.

Required:
Present journal entries to record: 1) the purchase of the securities on February 9, 2) the sale of the Jacobus Co. shares on October 11, and 3) any adjusting entry needed on December 31 to value the securities at lower of cost or market. December 31 is the last day of the company's accounting year.

E9-3   As a short-term investment, Marzo, Inc. purchased on November 1, 1988, corporate bonds of Shedder Co. The bonds were purchased at their face value of $50,000. The bonds pay interest at 6 percent (3 percent on April 30 and 3 percent on October 31). On December 31, 1988 (the last day of Marzo's accounting year), the market value of the Shedder bonds is $48,670. Discuss the effects on the financial statements for 1988 if Marzo elects to value its temporary investment in marketable debt securities at lower of cost or market. Alternatively, how would the financial statements differ if Marzo elects to use the cost method?

E9-4   On January 2, 1988 Favel, Inc. purchased for $80,000 a 9 percent, long-term interest in the stock of Edwards Co. The stock of Edwards is nonmarketable. During 1988, Edwards earned net income of $120,000 and paid cash dividends of $108,000. Present all journal entries related to the investment in Edward's stock to be recorded on Favel's books during 1988. On December 31, 1988, illustrate how the investment would be shown on Favel's balance sheet.

E9-5   On June 30, 1988 Callender, Inc. purchased for $28,000 a 14 percent interest in the 10,000 shares of Martin Co. stock. Martin's stock is readily marketable. During 1988, Martin earned net income of $48,000 and paid cash dividends totaling $30,000. Callender received $2,100 of the total dividends. Callender considers its investment in Martin to be a long-term investment. On December 31, 1988, the last day of each company's accounting year, Martin's stock had a market value of $18 per share.

Required:
1 At what amount should Callender report its investment in Martin on December 31, 1988? How much income should Callender report in 1988 as a result of its investment?
2 If the stock were not marketable (i.e., no year-end market value could be estimated), at what amount should the investment be reported? How much income would be reported?

E9-6   Investor, Inc. on January 2, 1989 pays $200,000 for a 40 percent interest in the 1,000,000 shares of stock of Investee Co. During 1989, Investee Co. earns net income of $460,000 and pays cash dividends of $280,000. Present all journal entries related to the investment in Investee's stock to be recorded on Investor's books during 1989. Illustrate how the investment account would appear on Investor's December 31, 1989 balance sheet.

E9-7   On February 1, 1988 Rover, Inc. bought 200 of Bow Wow Biscuit Co.'s 10 percent bonds as a long-term investment. The bonds were acquired at face value of $1,000 per bond. The bonds pay interest semiannually on July 31 and January 31. Maturity date is July 31, 1995. If Rover's accounting year ends on December 31, present journal entries required for 1988 (the year of acquisition of the bonds).

E9-8 As a long-term investment, Washington Co. purchased on November 30, 1988 some 6 percent bonds of Yorktown, Inc. The Yorktown bonds pay interest semi-annually on October 31 and April 30. Washington acquired the bonds from another investor at the $100,000 face value plus accrued interest. Assuming Washington's accounting year ends on December 31: 1) present the journal entry to record the purchase of the bonds on November 30, 1988, 2) determine interest revenue to be recognized for 1988, and 3) present the journal entry to record the April 30, 1989 cash interest received.

E9-9 On January 1, 1988, Strong-Arm, Inc. acquired as a long-term investment bonds with a face value of $2,000,000 for $1,960,000. The bonds have a 3 percent coupon rate of interest payable annually on December 31. The bonds mature four years later on December 31, 1991. 1) If Strong-Arm uses straight line amortization of bond discount or premium, what is the amount to be recognized annually as interest revenue? 2) If the bonds had been purchased for $2,100,000, what would have been the annual interest revenue using straight line amortization? 3) What will be the journal entry to record the receipt of the face value at maturity if the bonds are acquired for $1,960,000?; for $2,100,000?

E9-10 Hexon Corp. acquires $10,000 face value, 8 percent bonds of Borrower, Inc. on January 2, 1988 for $10,700. The market rate of interest on the date of purchase is 7 percent. The bonds pay interest annually on December 31, which is the end of Hexon's accounting year. The bonds mature in ten years. Determine interest revenue for 1988 and 1989 using 1) straight line amortization, and 2) effective interest amortization.

PROBLEMS

P9-1 *Accounting for Marketable Equity Securities*
Quayle Corp. invests excess cash in temporary investments. The company's accounting year ends on December 31. The following information is available concerning Quayle's temporary investments in marketable equity securities during 1988:
1 September 29—Purchased the following:

Securities	Number of shares	Total cost
Ace stock	400	$12,000
Bailey stock	50	5,000
Carson stock	100	1,200

2 November 8—Received cash dividends of $480 on investment in Carson stock.
3 December 12—Sold one-half (200 shares) of Ace stock for $28 per share.
4 December 31—Market value per share: Ace stock $27, Bailey stock $98, and Carson stock $12.50.

Required:

Present the journal entries required for the above information.

P9-2 *Accounts Affected by Equity Method*

Hawkes Systems, Inc., a chemical processing company, has been operating profitably for many years. On March 1, 1988, Hawkes purchased 50,000 shares of Diversified Insurance Company stock for $2,000,000. The 50,000 shares represented 25 percent of Diversified's stock. Both Hawkes and Diversified operate on a fiscal year ending August 31.

For the fiscal year ended August 31, 1988, Diversified reported net income of $800,000 earned evenly throughout the year. In November, 1987, February, 1988, May, 1988 and August, 1988, Diversified paid its regular quarterly cash dividend of $100,000.

Required:

For the fiscal year ended August 31, 1988, how did the net income reported and dividends paid by Diversified affect the accounts of Hawkes? Indicate each account affected, the amount of the increase or decrease in the account, and explain the reason for the change in the account balance. Organize your answer in the following format:

Account name	Amount of increase or decrease	Reason for change in account balance

(AICPA Adapted)

P9-3 *Financial Statement Effects of Various Long-term Stock Investments*

Time Set Company's accounting year ends on December 31, 1988. During 1988 the company purchased the following securities as investments:

1 100 shares of the 1,749,300 shares of stock of TT&A, Inc. The purchase price was $6,250. The shares are highly marketable and Time Set's management does not intend to sell the shares in the near future.

2 4,800 shares of the 12,000 outstanding shares of Turner Co. The purchase price was $72,000. The shares are highly marketable, but Time Set's management acquired the shares of Turner Co. to obtain a significant interest and does not intend to sell the shares in the near future. The 4,800 shares were purchased on July 1.

3 50 shares of Cauley Co.'s nonmarketable stock. The purchase price was $4,960.

4 200 shares of the 1,807,155 shares of BMI Corp. The purchase price was $2,700. The shares are highly marketable, but Time Set's management intends to hold the shares of BMI as a long-term investment.

Additional information available shows:

	Income for 1988 (earned evenly throughout the year)	Cash dividends paid in 1988 while securities were owned by Time Set Company	Market value per share on December 31, 1988
TT&A, Inc.	$ 3,898,000	$1.40 per share	$60.00
Turner Co.	24,000	$16,000 total	16.50
Cauley Co.	11,491,000	$7.00 per share	Nonmarketable
BMI Corp.	19,391,684	$6.50 per share	12.50

Required:

1 State how each of the four investments should be presented on Time Set's December 31, 1988 balance sheet. Include a calculation of the dollar amount at which each investment would be shown.

2 Determine the effect(s) each investment would have on the company's 1988 income statement. Include a determination of the dollar effects.

P9-4 *Accounting for Investment in Bonds*

As a long-term investment, the Boul Weebel Co. acquired bonds with a face value of $400,000 on January 2, 1988 for $390,000. The coupon interest rate is 8 percent payable annually on December 31. The bonds mature in five years on December 31, 1992. The company's accounting year ends on December 31, and the company uses the straight line method of amortizing bond premium or discount.

Required:

1 Present journal entries for: a) acquisition of the bonds, b) annual interest revenue earned, and c) receipt of the face value at maturity.

2 Calculate the balance in the long-term investment in bonds account on January 1, 1990.

3 Assuming the bonds were acquired at a $15,000 *premium*, present the three journal entries requested in requirement (1) above.

4 Explain why someone would be willing to pay $415,000 for bonds with a face value of only $400,000.

P9-5 *Accounting for Investments in Bonds*

Investo, Inc. has the following portfolio of long-term bond investments on July 1, 1987, the first day of the company's fiscal year:

1 Zipper Co. 9 percent bonds, $100,000 face value, acquired on May 15, 1987 at face plus accrued interest. Bonds pay interest semiannually on March 1 and September 1, and mature on March 1, 1989.

2 Countsid Co. 7 percent bonds, $50,000 face value, acquired on July 1, 1982 for $47,600. Bonds pay interest annually on June 30 and mature on June 30, 1988.

On January 2, 1988, Investo acquires at face, $60,000 of 8 percent Realtoy Company bonds. The bonds pay interest semiannually on December 31 and June 30, and mature on December 31, 1989. Assume Investo's journal entries through June 30, 1987 have been correctly recorded. Investo amortizes bond premium or discount using the straight line method.

Required:

1 Prepare all journal entries for Investo's long-term bond investments for the fiscal year July 1, 1987 through June 30, 1988.

2 Determine the dollar balance on June 30, 1988 in: a) the long-term investment in bonds account, b) the interest receivable account, and c) the interest revenue account.

P9-6 *Accounting for Investment in Bonds*

Formden Company acquired $1,000,000 face value, 8 percent bonds of Byrne Co. on January 2, 1988 at a price of $1,230,000. The market rate of interest at date of purchase was 6 percent. The bonds pay interest semiannually on June 30 and December 31.

Required:

1 Prepare a bond amortization table for the first four *semiannual* interest periods assuming Formden uses the effective interest method of amortizing the bond premium. Use the general format of Exhibit 9-2 in the chapter. Round all amounts to nearest dollar.

2 Present journal entries for 1988 (i.e., January 2, 1988 acquisition of bonds and the June 30, 1988 and December 31, 1988 interest entries).

3 What additional information would be required in order to use the straight line amortization method?

P9-7 *Comparison of Amortization Methods for Bond Investments*

On January 2, 1988, both Smith Co. and Jones Co. made identical purchases of $100,000 face value, 6 percent Johnson Company bonds for $95,900. The market rate of interest at date of purchase was 7 percent. The bonds mature in five years on December 31, 1992. Smith elects to amortize bond discount or premium using the straight line method. Jones chooses the effective interest method.

Required:

1 Assuming the bonds pay interest annually on December 31 (the end of both companies' accounting years), determine for *both* Smith and Jones:

  a The amount to be recorded in the long-term investment in bonds account on January 2, 1988, the date of purchase.
  b The amount of cash interest to be received each year.
  c The total cash interest to be received over the five years.
  d The total bond discount or premium to be amortized over the five years.
  e The total interest revenue to be recorded over the five years.
  f The balance in the long-term investment in bonds account just prior to the receipt of the maturity repayment.

2 Discuss what differences will exist between the accounting records of Smith and Jones due to the choice of different methods of amortizing bond discount or premium.

3 Present journal entries for *both* Smith Co. and Jones Co. on: a) the date of purchase of the bonds; b) December 31, 1988, the first annual interest payment date; and c) December 31, 1989, the second annual interest payment date.

Business Decision Problem

On January 2, 1988, you are appointed chief accountant of Albiner, Inc. The appointment is only for one year. On December 31, 1988, you will reach the age of 30 and plan to retire. Your employment agreement with Albiner states you are to receive a salary of $60,000 for the year plus a bonus of 25 percent of net income for 1988.

Your objective is to maximize the amount of your bonus. Assuming you have the authority to make the decision, how would you elect to account for each of the following investments in stocks and bonds? Explain your choices by indicating the impact on net income (ignore tax effects).

1 Albiner purchased 20,000 shares of Centon's stock for $6.00 per share on May 1, 1988. As of December 31, 1988, the market value has decreased to $5.00 per share. Would you claim management's intent is to hold these securities as a short-term (temporary) investment of excess cash or as a long-term investment?

2 Albiner purchased for $100,000 corporate bonds of Midas, Inc. on June 1,1988. The bonds are intended to be a temporary investment in marketable debt securities. As of December 31, 1988, the market value of the bonds has dropped to $92,000. Would you elect to use the cost method or the lower of cost or market method to value the temporary investment in marketable debt securities?

3 Albiner on July 1, 1988 purchased 1,000 shares (a 20 percent interest) in Fredonia Co's stock for $18 per share. During the second half of 1988, Fredonia earned net income of $110,000 and paid cash dividends of $30,000. Would you elect to use the cost method or the equity method to account for the long-term investment in Fredonia's stock?

4 Albiner purchased $1,000,000 of Chothton, Inc.'s 10 percent, ten-year bonds on July 1, 1988, as a long-term bond investment. The bonds pay interest semiannually on December 31 and June 30. The bonds were purchased for $885,295. The current market rate of interest on July 1, 1988, was 12 percent. Would you elect to amortize the discount by use of straight line amortization or use of the effective interest method of amortization?

10

STOCKHOLDERS' EQUITY

LEARNING OBJECTIVES

When you complete this chapter, you should be able to:

1 Describe the characteristics of the corporate form of organization.
2 Record the issuance, reacquisition, and reissue of stock.
3 Describe the various possible types of preferred stock.
4 Describe and record cash dividends.
5 Distinguish between the accounting procedures for a stock dividend and a stock split.
6 Prepare a statement of retained earnings.

In this chapter, we examine in more detail the corporate form of business and accounting for the stockholders' equity of a corporation. Recall that stockholders' equity is the portion of total assets financed by the stockholders of the company. This equity consists of invested capital (capital stock and paid-in capital accounts) and undistributed profits (retained earnings).

Corporations are legal entities that have an existence separate from that of their owners (i.e., stockholders). A corporation can in its own name own property, enter into contracts, sue and be sued, and engage in any other business transactions permitted by the corporate charter. In Exhibit 10-1 the organization and other characteristics of a corporation are highlighted.

COMMON STOCK

Ownership in a corporation is evidenced by shares of stock. If you own shares of stock in a corporation, you are a stockholder, or part-owner of the company.

EXHIBIT 10-1 CORPORATE CHARACTERISTICS

Term	Definition or description
Articles of incorporation (or charter)	Specifies the powers and restrictions imposed by the state in which the company incorporates.
Board of directors	Responsible for promoting and protecting stockholders' interests. The Board determines corporate goals and strategies, approves major contracts, authorizes dividends, and evaluates corporate officers' performance.
Corporate officers	Responsible for day-to-day management of corporate affairs. Typical corporate officers are the president; vice-presidents of specific areas such as sales, personnel, and production; treasurer; controller; and secretary.
Double taxation	Disadvantage of corporate form of organization. Corporate income is taxed when earned by the corporation. In addition, if corporations distribute cash dividends, the stockholders receiving the dividends must pay income taxes on the dividends received.
Limited liability	Creditors of a corporation have a claim against the corporate assets, but do not have a claim against the stockholders' personal assets. The maximum amount a stockholder can lose if the corporation fails is his or her investment in the corporation.

The corporation owns the assets and is responsible for the liabilities of the company; the stockholders own the corporation. Stockholders do not personally own individual assets, nor are the stockholders individually liable for specific liabilities. Some corporations issue two classes of capital stock: common and preferred. In this section of the chapter we will discuss *common stock,* the residual ownership interest. Preferred stock, which has certain special rights, will be discussed later in the chapter. Every corporation issues common stock; it may or may not issue preferred stock.

Common Stockholder Rights

A common stockholder has the following basic rights:

1 To participate in stockholder votes. The common stockholders are entitled to vote on important corporate matters such as election of the board of directors, incurrence of significant debts, mergers and acquisitions, and the establishment of profit-sharing plans. Each share of common stock is usually entitled to one vote. Few stockholders usually attend the annual stockholders' meeting and personally vote. Existing management, as well as dissenting groups, attempt to solicit the right to cast the votes of stockholders not planning to attend the stockholders' meeting. This method of absentee voting is called *voting by proxy.*

2 To receive a proportionate share of dividends that have been declared by the corporation's board of directors. Note this right does not guarantee annual dividends to stockholders. If the board of directors does not declare any dividends, there are no dividends to be shared proportionately by the stockholders.

3 To receive a proportionate share of the assets if the corporation liquidates. However, all creditors must be paid in full before remaining assets are distributed to the stockholders.

4 To purchase a percentage of additional shares of common stock issued by the corporation. The percentage of the new shares to which a stockholder has first option to buy is determined by the proportion of the outstanding shares currently owned. For example, if a stockholder owns 100 of the 500 common shares currently outstanding, the stockholder would be entitled to an opportunity to purchase 20 percent of any additional common shares issued. This *preemptive right* is not applicable in some states or in those situations where the stockholders have waived the right.

AUTHORIZATION AND ISSUANCE OF COMMON STOCK

The corporate charter specifies the maximum number of shares that can be issued and the par value, if any, per share. Usually corporations seek authorization for many more shares than they initially plan to issue. Thus, most corporations have a pool of authorized but unissued shares available to sell when additional funds are needed. The unissued shares are *not* assets. They merely represent the opportunity to obtain cash or other assets through the future issuance of the shares.

Issuance of Common Stock with a Par Value

The *par value* of a share of stock is an amount printed directly on the stock certificate. Par value is selected by the organizers of the corporation and is *not* intended to indicate the market value (or selling price) of a share of stock.

The significance of par value is two-fold: 1) the par value is the amount credited to the common stock account when shares are issued and 2) in many states the par value represents the legal capital of the corporation. *Legal capital* is the minimum amount of total stockholders' equity that must be kept in the corporation. The legal capital can be reduced only if operating losses are incurred or a liquidating dividend is approved by a vote of the stockholders. Since corporate stockholders have the advantage of limited liability, the minimum legal capital requirement is designed to maintain some owners' investment and thus serve as a cushion to cover creditors' claims.

Whenever common stock is issued by a corporation, the par value is credited to the common stock account. If Bridgeport, Incorporated issues 500 shares of its $1 par value common stock on July 1, 1988, for $1 per share, the journal entry is:

1988				
July	1	Cash	500	
		Common Stock		500

To record the issuance of
500 shares of $1 par value
common stock at $1.

However, in most cases, the issue price of common stock exceeds its par value. The excess amount received over par is credited to a *paid-in capital* account. For example, assume Bridgeport issues 1,000 shares of its $1 par value common stock on August 8, 1988 at $5 per share. The journal entry on the company's books would be:

Aug. 8	Cash	5,000	
	Common Stock		1,000
	Paid-in Capital in Excess of Par		4,000

To record the issuance of
1,000 shares of $1 par value
common stock at $5.

Both the common stock and paid-in capital in excess of par are part of the invested capital of the corporation.

If shares were issued at less than par, a discount on common stock account would be debited for the excess of par value over the selling price. However, since the stockholders acquiring the shares would be personally liable for the discounts, the issuance of stock at a discount is virtually nonexistent. To avoid discounts on issuance of stock, corporations select an arbitrarily low par value. Par values of $1, $.10, or even $.01 are frequently encountered for common stock.

Issuance of No Par Common Stock

In recent years an increasing number of corporations have been issuing common stock that has no par value. If the corporation's board of directors has arbitrarily established a *stated value* per share for the no par stock, then the stated value is credited to the common stock account when the shares are issued. For example, if on April 3, 1989, Ventura, Inc. issues 500 shares of no par common stock (with a stated value of $5 per share) for $20 per share, the journal entry would be:

1989			
April 3	Cash	10,000	
	Common Stock		2,500
	Paid-in Capital in Excess of Stated Value		7,500

To record the issuance of
500 shares of no par common
stock at $20 per share, stated
value per share set at $5.

If the stock has no par value and the board of directors has not established a stated value, the entire issuance price should be credited to the common stock account. If, in the previous example, Ventura had not established any stated value for their no par common stock, the journal entry for the issuance of the 500 shares at $20 per share would have been:

April 3	Cash	10,000	
	Common Stock		10,000
	To record the issuance of		
	500 shares of no par,		
	no stated value common		
	stock, issued at $20		
	per share.		

Issuance of Common Stock for Assets Other than Cash

Occasionally investors may contribute non-cash assets to a corporation in exchange for shares of stock. In the absence of cash, it may be difficult to determine the dollar amounts for the journal entry. The non-cash assets contributed should be recorded at their *fair market value* or at the current *market value* of the shares issued, whichever is more readily determinable. Par value is not to be considered as an indicator of market value.

For example, study the following two cases:

1. An investor transfers 30 acres of land to Renninger, Inc. on September 16, 1988 in exchange for 100 shares of Renninger's $10 par value common stock. A similar parcel of adjacent land recently sold for $200 an acre. Renninger, Inc. is a family-owned corporation. There has not been any recent trading of the company's common stock to indicate its market value.

The $6,000 fair market of the land contributed (30 acres at $200 per acre) is more readily determinable than the current market value of the common stock issued. The journal entry on Renninger's books would be:

1988			
Sept. 16	Land	6,000	
	Common Stock		1,000
	Paid-in Capital in Excess		
	of Par		5,000
	To record the issuance of 100		
	shares of $10 par value		
	common stock in exchange		
	for 30 acres of land		
	valued at $200 per acre.		

2. An investor transfers ownership of a patent to RVN Corp. on February 21, 1989 in exchange for 1,000 shares of RVN's $8 par value common stock. The patent is for a new, untried plastic-compounding process. A recent trade of approximately 1,000 shares of RVN's common stock was made at $30 per share.

In this second situation, the fair market value of the asset contributed (the patent) is not readily determinable. However, the $30,000 current market value of the shares issued (1,000 shares at $30) is known and thus is used to value the transaction. The journal entry to record issuance of 1,000 shares in exchange for the patent would be:

1989			
Feb. 21	Patent	30,000	
	Common Stock		8,000
	Paid-in Capital in Excess of Par		22,000
	To record issuance of 1,000 shares of $8 par value common stock for a patent. The current market price of $30 per share is used to value the patent.		

TREASURY STOCK

Corporations occasionally repurchase shares of their own stock from stockholders. The effect of the stock reacquisition is to reduce both the corporation's assets and stockholders' equity. Corporate management may reacquire the stock because it believes the shares are currently undervalued by the market. Thus, management's strategy is to reacquire the shares at their current undervalued price and reissue them in the future when the market price has increased. Reacquisition may also reduce the chances of a "takeover" of the company by investors (often called "raiders") who also believe that the company is undervalued. In addition, corporations sometimes reacquire their own stock to have shares available to acquire other companies, or to distribute to officers as a stock bonus or as part of a stock option plan. All authorized shares may have been issued by the corporation. With no remaining unissued shares available, reacquisition of shares already issued is one way of obtaining the needed shares.

Treasury stock is the term given to shares of a corporation's own stock that have been issued, reacquired, and not formally retired. Treasury stock is *not* an asset. A corporation cannot own part of itself. The cost of the treasury stock is a reduction in stockholders' equity. The treasury stock shares, like unissued stock, merely represent a possible future source of additional funds. Treasury shares are still considered issued, but they are no longer outstanding. The shares of treasury stock do not vote or receive dividends.

Purchase of Treasury Stock

Treasury stock is recorded at cost in an account titled Treasury Stock. For example, if Clone, Inc. repurchases 100 shares of its $5 par value common stock on March 18, 1988 at the current market price of $12 per share, the journal entry would be:

1988		
Mar. 18	Treasury Stock	1,200

Cash		1,200

To record purchase of 100 shares
of treasury stock at cost of $12
per share.

The treasury stock account balance of $1,200 would be shown as a deduction in the stockholders' equity section of the balance sheet. Note that neither the stock's par value nor the original issuance price affects the reacquisition journal entry. Similarly, the reacquisition entry does not affect the common stock or paid-in capital accounts.

Reissue of Treasury Stock

The treasury shares could be reissued at: 1) the same price at which they were acquired, 2) more than the acquisition price, or 3) less than the acquisition price. In all three instances, Cash would be debited for the reissue price and the Treasury Stock account would be credited for the *cost* of the treasury stock shares that are being reissued. The remaining part(s) of the journal entry to record the reissuance of the treasury stock, however, will depend on the relationship between reissue price and acquisition cost.

Reissue at Cost Assume Clone, Inc. on September 9, 1988 reissues 50 shares of its treasury stock for $12 per share. (Recall the company had acquired 100 of its shares at a cost of $12 per share.) The journal entry would be:

Sept. 9	Cash	600	
	Treasury Stock		600

To record reissue of 50 treasury
shares, which cost $12 per share,
for $12 per share.

The effect of the entry is to increase corporate assets and increase stockholders' equity (by reducing the Treasury Stock account) by $600.

Reissue at a Price Above Cost If Clone reissues 20 additional treasury shares at $16 per share on October 27, 1988, the required journal entry is:

Oct. 27	Cash	320	
	Treasury Stock		240
	Paid-in Capital from Treasury Stock		
	Transactions		80

To record reissue of 20 treasury
shares, which cost $12 per share,
for $16 per share.

Note that the excess of the reissuance price over the cost of the treasury shares is credited to a paid-in capital account—it is not recorded as a gain. A corporation does not realize gains or losses when buying or selling its own stock. The $80 Paid-in Capital account would appear as part of stockholders' equity on the balance sheet. The transaction would not affect the income statement.

Reissue at a Price Below Cost   Although the method of recording the journal entry may vary depending on the laws of the particular state in which the firm is incorporated, the common procedure for handling the excess of the cost of treasury shares over reissue price is: 1) debit Paid-in Capital accounts for the excess and 2) if there are no Paid-in Capital accounts (or their balance is insufficient to cover the entire excess), the Retained Earnings account is debited. For example, assume Clone on December 14, 1988 reissues the remaining 30 shares of its treasury stock for only $7 per share. There is a $150 excess of cost over reissue price to be included in the journal entry ([$12 cost – $7 reissue price] × 30 shares). If we assume Clone's only paid-in capital account is the $80 account balance from the treasury stock sale on October 27, 1988, the journal entry for the reissuance of 30 treasury shares at $7 per share would be:

Dec. 14	Cash	210	
	Paid-in Capital from Treasury Stock		
	Transactions	80	
	Retained Earnings	70	
	Treasury Stock		360

To record reissue of 30 treasury shares, which cost $12 per share, for $7 per share.

Note that in all the above transactions, the Treasury Stock account reflects the *cost* of the treasury shares owned. The Treasury Stock account is debited with the cost of the treasury shares when acquired regardless of their par value. When they are reissued, the cost of the reissued treasury shares is eliminated from the Treasury Stock account—regardless of reissue price or par value.

Transactions Among Individual Investors

In all the previous transactions and entries in the chapter, a corporation was issuing or reacquiring stock from its stockholders. As a result, the corporation's assets and stockholders' equity were directly affected. However, once issued by a corporation, the shares of stock may subsequently be traded many times among investors at the then current market price. These subsequent purchases and sales of the corporation's stock among investors do *not* affect the corporation's assets or stockholders' equity. Therefore, the corporation makes no journal entry for these transactions among investors. The corporation's list of current stockholders, however, would need to be updated.

PREFERRED STOCK

In addition to issuing common stock, some corporations also issue shares of preferred stock. *Preferred stock* usually has preference over common stock in receiving dividends and in receipt of assets when the corporation is liquidated. On the other hand, the amount of the preferred dividends and asset liquidation share is limited and the preferred stockholders rarely get the right to vote. In essence, preferred stock possesses many of the features of debt rather than equity.

However, preferred stock is considered owners' equity and should be shown in the stockholders' equity section of the balance sheet.

Consider Hilie Corporation's stockholders' equity, which includes preferred stock as well as common:

6% Preferred Stock, $100 par value, 500,000 shares authorized, 200,000 shares issued and outstanding

Common Stock, $1 par value, 2,500,000 shares authorized, 800,000 shares issued and outstanding

If Hilie had sold the 200,000 shares of preferred stock at par on January 2, 1987, the journal entry to record the issuance would have been:

```
1987
Jan. 2      Cash                          20,000,000
                 Preferred Stock                        20,000,000
            To record the issuance at par of
            200,000 shares of $100 par
            value, 6% preferred stock.
```

The "6%" designation on the preferred stock indicates the preferred dividend rate as a percent of par value. Thus, for Hilie Corporation the preferred dividends are $6 per share (6% × $100 par), or a total of $1,200,000 annually for the 200,000 shares outstanding.

As was the case with common stock, preferred stockholders are not legally entitled to receive dividends until the dividends are declared by the board of directors. However, if the board of directors does declare dividends, the preferred stockholders must receive their dividends in full before common stockholders are entitled to any dividends. Thus, for Hilie Corporation, $1,200,000 of dividends must be distributed to the preferred stockholders in a given year before common stockholders are entitled to any dividends.

Not only do preferred stockholders have a preference to dividends, they may also have a preference in the asset distribution when the corporation is liquidated. The sequence of distribution would be: creditors first, preferred stockholders next, and common stockholders last. The amount to be distributed to preferred stockholders at liquidation is usually the par value of the preferred shares. Sometimes a liquidation value slightly greater than par value is specified.

Journal entries for the issuance of preferred stock, repurchase of preferred stock, and the declaration and payment of preferred dividends parallel those for common stock. Special characteristics (cumulative, participating, callable, and convertible) of preferred stock issues are discussed in the remainder of this section of the chapter.

Cumulative Preferred Stock

If the board of directors fails to declare preferred dividends for a *noncumulative* preferred stock, that year's preferred dividends are lost forever. Thus, as an inducement to get investors to purchase preferred shares, most preferred stock is *cumulative*. If the board of directors fails to declare preferred dividends for a cumulative preferred stock, the omitted preferred dividends accumulate. The accumulated preferred dividends that have been omitted (referred to as preferred *dividends in arrears*) must be paid in full in the future before any dividends can be paid to common stockholders.

For example, assume Hilie Corporation's 6 percent, $100 par value preferred stock is cumulative. The corporation's board of directors declared no preferred dividends during 1987 or 1988 on the 200,000 shares outstanding. If the corporation has $7,000,000 in total to distribute as dividends in 1989, the dividends would have to be distributed as follows:

1st—Preferred dividends in arrears for 1987 and 1988 (6% × $100 par × 200,000 shares outstanding × 2 years) =	$2,400,000
2nd—Preferred dividends for current year (1989) (6% × $100 par × 200,000 shares outstanding) =	1,200,000
3rd—Remainder to common stockholders =	3,400,000
Total dividends distributed in 1989	$7,000,000

Thus, with the cumulative feature, the preferred stockholders receive $3,600,000 ($2,400,000 + $1,200,000) of the 1989 dividend distribution. If the preferred stock had been noncumulative, the preferred stockholders would have received only the current year's dividend of $1,200,000. The prior years' preferred dividends would have been lost if the preferred stock were noncumulative.

Dividends in arrears on cumulative preferred stock are not liabilities. Dividends do not become liabilities until the dividends are formally declared by the board of directors. However, the existence and amount of preferred dividends in arrears must be disclosed in the stockholders' equity section of the balance sheet or in the notes that accompany the financial statements.

Participating Preferred Stock

Investors in *participating preferred stock* have the opportunity to receive dividends in excess of the basic preferred dividend rate. The actual portion of the additional dividends to be distributed to the preferred stockholders would depend upon the terms of the particular preferred stock. While cumulative preferred stock is very common, participating preferred stock is relatively rare.

Callable Preferred Stock

Callable preferred stock means the issuing corporation has the option to call (i.e., redeem) the preferred stock at a specified price. The call price, or redemption price, is usually slightly above the par value of the stock. The call provision works to the benefit of the corporation. While still outstanding, the callable preferred stock provides the corporation with needed capital at a fixed dividend rate without the granting of voting power to the preferred stockholders. When the corporation no longer is in need of preferred stockholders' capital and wishes to eliminate the preferred stockholders' equity and resultant dividend requirement, the corporation merely exercises the call option. The preferred stockholders have no choice but to surrender their preferred stock certificates in exchange for the prespecified call price.

Convertible Preferred Stock

Investors in *convertible preferred stock* have the option of converting their preferred shares into common stock shares at a predetermined exchange rate. Convertible preferred stock offers investors the best of both worlds. If the company prospers, cash dividends and market price per share for the common stock should increase. The convertible preferred stockholders can share in the common stock's market price and cash dividend growth by converting their preferred shares into common stock. If the company does not prosper and there is little or no improvement (or even a decrease) in the return earned by the company's common stockholders, the convertible preferred stockholders maintain their preferred shares with the preference to dividends.

RETAINED EARNINGS

The stockholders' equity section of the balance sheet reveals two sources of a company's assets provided by owners—invested capital and retained earnings. The retained earnings component measures the cumulative increase in net assets (total assets minus total liabilities) earned by the company's profitable operations since it was formed. Each year, company net assets and retained earnings increase by the amount of net income. Both assets and retained earnings decrease by the distribution of company assets to stockholders in the form of dividends. Retained earnings represents total net income (minus any net losses) minus total dividends since the firm began operations. These changes are detailed on a *statement of retained earnings;* an illustration of this statement is presented in Exhibit 10-2.

Exhibit 10-2 shows five items. Net income has been covered extensively in previous chapters. The other adjustment to retained earnings illustrated in Exhibit 10-2 (arising from the reissue of treasury stock) was covered earlier in this chapter. Prior period adjustments, dividends, and appropriations of retained earnings will be discussed in subsequent sections of this chapter. Other adjustments to retained earnings are rare and will not be discussed further.

Prior Period Adjustments

Prior period adjustments are corrections of the income of a previous period. At the end of each year, net income is closed to retained earnings. If, at some

EXHIBIT 10-2
Sample Company
Statement of Retained Earnings
For the Year Ended December 31, 1988

Unappropriated Retained Earnings:		
Retained Earnings, January 1, 1988		$3,608,320
Less: Prior Period Adjustment for		
correction of 1985 net income		20,000
Beginning Balance as Adjusted		$3,588,320
Plus: Net Income for 1988		108,300
		$3,696,620
Less: Dividends	$70,000	
Other Adjustment—cost in		
excess of reissue price for		
treasury stock	8,500	78,500
Retained Earnings, December 31, 1988		$3,618,120
Appropriated Retained Earnings—for		
future plant expansion		1,600,000
Total Retained Earnings, December 31, 1988		$5,218,120

subsequent date, a change in prior period net income is made, an entry must be made to retained earnings.

Assume that in 1988, it is discovered that $10,000 of goodwill amortization was not recorded in 1985. To correct this error, the additional expense of $10,000 should be recorded as a correction of 1985 income (not as an additional expense for 1988). Since 1985 net income has been closed to retained earnings, the correction is recorded in 1988 by reducing the beginning of the year retained earnings balance. The 1988 entry would be:

Retained Earnings	10,000	
Goodwill		10,000
To correct 1985 net income for		
omission of goodwill amortization.		

Dividends

Dividends are distributions of company assets, earned by profitable operations, to the stockholders of the corporation. The most common form of distribution is cash. Sometimes, however, the dividend takes the form of a stock dividend—additional shares of the company's own stock. A stock dividend does not reduce the company's assets or total stockholders' equity.

Dividends are not guaranteed. The board of directors must decide each year if dividends will be paid and if so, what the amount will be. Even though many corporations have paid dividends continuously for years, there is no guarantee of future dividends.

Cash Dividends Other than by selling their shares of stock at a profit, cash dividends represents the principal form by which stockholders earn a return on their investment. Securities with good prospects of making regular, substantial cash dividend payments are prized investments for those investors desiring a high current return.

In determining a corporation's cash dividend policy, the board of directors must consider not only the availability of cash to make the payment, but also the availability of retained earnings. Both cash and retained earnings are reduced by the declaration and payment of a cash dividend. Availability of a large cash balance does not necessarily mean the corporation has undistributed earnings, nor does a large retained earnings ensure availability of cash. Consider the following balance sheet:

Assets

Cash	$ 10,000
Accounts Receivable	20,000
Inventory	30,000
Property, Plant, and Equipment	140,000
Total Assets	$200,000

Liabilities and Stockholders' Equity

Liabilities:		
Accounts Payable		$ 25,000
Stockholders' Equity:		
Common Stock	$110,000	
Retained Earnings	65,000	175,000
Total Liabilities & Stockholders' Equity		$200,000

The statement is in balance, but the cash balance is not equal to the retained earnings balance. They differ because some transactions affect retained earnings but not cash (e.g., depreciation expense), while others affect cash but not retained earnings (e.g., a bank loan). Therefore, do not expect retained earnings to equal the cash balance. Although there is $65,000 of retained earnings (accumulated net income which has not been distributed to stockholders), only $10,000 of cash is currently on hand.

Dividend Dates　Three significant dates are involved with a cash dividend: the declaration date, the record date, and the payment date.

The *declaration date* is the date on which the dividend is formally declared by the board of directors. Once declared, the dividend is a legal liability of the corporation and hence must be recorded. The record date usually follows the declaration date by several weeks. Those persons listed on the corporation's records as owning the stock on the *record date* are the individuals who are entitled to receive the dividend, even if they should sell the stock before the payment date. The *payment date* is the date the dividend is distributed in cash. For example, assume that a corporation declares, on December 30, 1988, a $10,000 cash dividend, payable on January 31, 1989 to stockholders of record as of January 20. The entries would be:

Declaration Date
　Dec. 30, 1988　　　Cash Dividends Declared　　　　　10,000

Cash Dividends Payable		10,000

To record the declaration
of a cash dividend.

Record Date
    Jan. 20, 1989   No journal entry

Payment Date
    Jan. 31, 1989

Cash Dividends Payable	10,000	
Cash		10,000

To record payment of
cash dividend.

The entry on December 30 reduces retained earnings (via the cash dividends declared account) and records a current liability for the dividend obligation. Some companies do not use the separate cash dividends declared account, but debit the dividend declaration directly to retained earnings.

Stock Dividends *Stock dividends* represent a proportionate distribution of additional shares of a corporation's own stock to the company's current stockholders. The shares are free; the current stockholders do not pay the corporation for these shares. Before concluding that the stockholders have truly benefitted from a stock dividend, however, consider each of the following questions:

1 Have the assets, liabilities, or total stockholders' equity of the corporation been affected by the stock dividend?

2 Has the percentage ownership of the stockholders been altered as a result of the stock dividend?

3 Should the *total* market value of each stockholder's investment be expected to change as a result of the stock dividend?

The answer to each question is no. A stock dividend has no effect on the company's assets, liabilities, or total stockholders' equity. As will be shown in a later journal entry, the only accounting effect is to transfer some of the retained earnings amount to common stock and paid-in capital accounts. While the number of shares owned by each stockholder does increase as a result of a stock dividend, so does the total number of outstanding shares. Thus, percentage ownership for each stockholder remains unchanged. Similarly, the total value of each stockholder's investment theoretically is not affected. Corporate assets and liabilities are unchanged; therefore, the total worth (total market value of the shares outstanding) of the corporation should not be affected by the stock dividend. The size of the total "pie" is unchanged; however, the pie is now divided into more but smaller pieces (i.e., more shares of stock). Theoretically the market price per share of the stock should decrease as a result of the stock dividend. The increased number of shares owned after the stock dividend multiplied by a lower market price for each share should yield the same total investment value for each stockholder as before the stock dividend.

In light of the negative answers to the three preceding questions, the follow-up inquiry would seem to be: Why then would a corporation declare and distribute a stock dividend? In the absence of available funds for a cash dividend, a stock dividend does allow the corporation to claim it has declared a dividend. Thus, a corporation, even though not having sufficient cash for a cash dividend, could claim it "paid" a dividend by merely declaring and distributing a stock dividend. Also, the receipt of additional shares of stock from a stock dividend (without requiring the investment of any additional funds) may deceive some stockholders into believing they have received something of value. Further complicating the situation is the fact that the market price of the stock does not always decrease in proportion to the increased number of shares created by a stock dividend. If the market price per share does not decrease proportionately, the total value of each stockholder's investment will be greater after the stock dividend than it was before the stock dividend. Thus, it can be argued that it is possible for stockholders to obtain a real benefit from a stock dividend.

Accounting for Stock Dividends   The declaration and distribution of a stock dividend involves a capitalization of retained earnings. A portion of the retained earnings account balance is transferred to invested capital (i.e., the capital stock account and possibly a paid-in capital account).

For small stock dividends (less than 25 percent), the stock's market value per share is used to determine the amount of retained earnings to capitalize (for large stock dividends, the par value is used). Market value is used on the assumption that there will be little effect on the market price per share as a result of the stock dividend, even though theoretically the price should adjust proportionately.

Assume that on December 12, 1988, the following stockholders' equity existed:

Common Stock, $1 par value, 1,000,000 shares authorized, 400,000 issued and outstanding	$ 400,000
Paid-in Capital in Excess of Par	832,000
Retained Earnings	1,428,000
Total Stockholders' Equity	$2,660,000

A 5 percent stock dividend is declared and distributed on December 13. On that date, the market price of the company's common stock is $3 per share. The journal entry to record the stock dividend would be:

1988			
Dec. 13	Stock Dividends Declared	60,000	
	Common Stock		20,000
	Paid-in Capital from Stock		
	Dividends		40,000
	To record 5 percent stock dividend (20,000 shares) on $1 par value common stock, recorded at $3 per share market value.		

Notice the stock dividends declared account (which will be closed into retained earnings at the end of the accounting period) was debited with the $60,000 *market value* of the 5 percent stock dividend. The $20,000 *par value* of the stock dividend was credited to the common stock account. The paid-in capital account was increased by the $40,000 excess of market value over par value. In essence, accounting for the stock dividend capitalizes (transfers) $60,000 of retained earnings to invested capital (common stock and paid-in capital).

If a balance sheet is prepared following the dividend distribution, the stockholders' equity section would appear as follows:

Common Stock, $1 par value, 1,000,000 shares	
authorized, 420,000 issued and outstanding	$ 420,000
Paid-in Capital in Excess of Par	832,000
Paid-in Capital from Stock Dividends	40,000
Retained Earnings	1,368,000
Total Stockholders' Equity	$2,660,000

Observe that the total stockholders' equity did not change as a result of the stock dividend.

Stock Splits

A stock split is similar in impact to a stock dividend. Additional shares are received free by the current stockholders. For example, with a 2 for 1 stock split, each stockholder would own twice as many shares after the split as before the split. A *stock split,* unlike a stock dividend, requires a reduction in the par value or stated value in proportion to the increase in the number of shares outstanding. Thus a 2 for 1 stock split would halve the par value while doubling the outstanding shares.

Consider a corporation with 10,000 shares of $20 par value common stock outstanding. After a 2 for 1 split, the corporation would have 20,000 shares of $10 par value stock outstanding. Both before and after the split, the balance in the common stock account would be $200,000 (10,000 shares × $20 par value or 20,000 shares × $10 par value). No account balance is affected by a stock split. Therefore, *no journal entry is needed for a stock split.* A memorandum notation in the common stock account should be made to indicate the change in the number of shares and the new par value.

The primary purpose of stock splits, as well as large stock dividends, is to significantly lower the market price per share of a company's stock. A lower market price per share makes the stock more attractive to a larger group of potential investors. The commission rate charged by a stockbroker is less when stock is purchased in "round lots" of 100 shares. Purchase of less than 100 shares burdens the investor with a higher commission rate. Thus, stock splits, by reducing the market price per share, make it easier for investors with limited funds to make round lot purchases.

As was the case with stock dividends, theoretically the current stockholders should not benefit from a stock split. However, frequently the market price decrease is not proportionate to the increase in the number of shares outstanding. Thus, a stock selling for $100 prior to a 2 for 1 stock split may trade after the split for slightly more than its theoretical $50 market price. The increased demand by investors for the now lower priced security is a possible reason for this frequently observed occurrence.

Appropriated Retained Earnings

Retained earnings available for dividends rarely equals total retained earnings. A portion of retained earnings may be unavailable for dividends because of legal restrictions or voluntary limitations. Bank loan agreements or the requirements of a bond issue may place a limit on dividend distributions. Such restrictions are designed to conserve cash required for the company's operating needs and debt payments. In addition, the board of directors may voluntarily elect to restrict the amount of retained earnings available for dividends because cash is needed for other business purposes, such as future asset investments.

Frequently, these restrictions on retained earnings are not formally recorded and may not even be disclosed in the financial statements. In cases where the restriction is recorded, it is called an appropriation of retained earnings. Appropriated retained earnings is a part of total retained earnings and would be presented in the stockholders' equity section of a balance sheet as follows:

Retained Earnings:		
Appropriated for Plant Expansion	$500,000	
Unappropriated	308,000	$808,000

The above presentation tells the reader that the company has decided that at least $500,000 of its $808,000 retained earnings will not be distributed as dividends because the company plans to spend resources on plant expansion.

An alternative approach is to disclose the restriction in the notes to the financial statements. This approach allows a more direct and thorough discussion of the restriction, and reduces confusion over the significance and meaning of an appropriated retained earnings amount.

FINANCIAL STATEMENT PRESENTATION

The final section of this chapter presents a comprehensive income statement (Exhibit 10-3) and a comprehensive balance sheet (Exhibit 10-4). These financial statements include most of the accounts discussed in Chapters 1 through 10. They are presented at this stage of the text in order 1) to review the financial statement impact of topics already discussed and 2) to set the stage for the remaining three financial accounting chapters—"Statement of Cash Flows" (Chapter 11), "Financial Statement Analysis" (Chapter 12), and "Issues in Financial Reporting" (Chapter 13).

Note in particular the detailed description of each capital stock issue in the stockholders' equity section of the balance sheet. Included in each description is an indication of the number of shares authorized, issued, and outstanding. Consider the case of the common stock. The state in which Sample Co. is chartered has *authorized* the corporation to issue a maximum of 450,000 shares. As of December 31, 1988, Sample has *issued* 180,000 shares. Since 12,000 of

EXHIBIT 10-3
Sample Co.
Statement of Income
For the Year Ended December 31,1988

Sales Revenue			$1,455,000
Less: Sales Discounts		$ 40,000	
Sales Returns and Allowances		60,000	100,000
Net Sales			$1,355,000
Cost of Goods Sold:			
Beginning Inventory		$ 920,000	
Purchases	$1,115,000		
Less: Purchase Discounts	35,000		
Purchase Returns	45,000	1,035,000	
Cost of Goods Available for Sale		$1,955,000	
Ending Inventory		1,400,000	555,000
Gross Profit			$ 800,000
Other Expenses:			
Amortization–Patents		$ 10,000	
Bad Debts		4,650	
Depreciation		56,400	
Interest		361,200	
Office Supplies		4,150	
Rent		6,000	
Repairs		13,700	
Salaries		44,050	500,150
Operating Income			$ 299,850
Other Revenues, Gains, and Losses:			
Dividend Revenue		$ 7,500	
Gain on Sale of Equipment		13,000	
Gain on Sale of Marketable Equity Securities		1,100	
Income from Equity Method Investments		110,600	
Unrealized Loss on Marketable Equity Securities		(84,500)	47,700
Income Before Income Taxes			$ 347,550
Income Tax Expense			75,000
Net Income			$ 272,550
Earnings Per Share			$ 1.62

EXHIBIT 10-4
Sample Co.
Balance Sheet
December 31,1988

Assets

Current Assets:		
Cash		$ 485,000
Marketable Equity Securities	$ 2,149,000	
Less: Allowance for Unrealized Losses	129,500	2,019,500
Accounts Receivable	$ 1,117,300	
Less: Allowance for Uncollectible Accounts	11,680	1,105,620
Inventories (at lower of FIFO cost or market)		1,400,000
Prepaid Rent		60,000
Total Current Assets		$ 5,070,120

EXHIBIT 10-4
(*continued*)

Long-term Equity Investments			2,085,500
Property, Plant, and Equipment:			
Land		$ 3,655,000	
Buildings and Equipment	$12,463,700		
Less: Accumulated Depreciation	2,019,200	10,444,500	14,099,500
Intangible Assets—Patents (net of amortization)			100,000
Total Assets			$21,355,120

Liabilities and Stockholders' Equity

Current Liabilities:			
Accounts Payable			$ 3,912,490
Notes Payable			140,160
Income Taxes Payable			75,000
Current Portion of Long-term Debt			500,000
Dividends Payable			22,350
Total Current Liabilities			$ 4,650,000
Long-term Debt:			
Bonds Payable		$10,000,000	
Less: Unamortized Discount on Bonds		750,000	9,250,000
Total Liabilities			$13,900,000
Stockholders' Equity:			
Capital Stock:			
8% Cumulative Preferred Stock, $100 par value, callable at $104, dividends in arrears of $128,000, 50,000 shares authorized, 11,000 shares issued and outstanding		$ 1,100,000	
5% Convertible Preferred Stock, $100 par value, each share convertible into four common shares, 10,000 shares authorized, 2,000 shares issued and outstanding		200,000	
Common Stock, no par value, $1.50 stated value, 450,000 shares authorized, 180,000 shares issued of which 12,000 are in the treasury		270,000	
Paid-in Capital Accounts:*		$ 1,570,000	
Paid-in Capital in Excess of Par— on 8% Cumulative Preferred Stock		28,000	
Paid-in Capital in Excess of Stated Value— on Common Stock		560,400	
Paid-in Capital from Treasury Stock Transactions— on Common Stock		18,600	
Paid-in Capital from Stock Dividends— on Common Stock		108,000	
Total Invested Capital		$ 2,285,000	
Retained Earnings:			
Appropriated for Future Plant Expansion	$ 1,600,000		
Unappropriated	3,618,120	5,218,120	
		$ 7,503,120	
Less: Cost of 12,000 Shares of Common Stock Held in Treasury		48,000	7,455,120
Total Liabilities and Stockholders' Equity			$21,355,120

*Instead of listing all the individual paid-in capital accounts, frequently only a total paid-in capital for each class of capital stock is presented.

these issued shares have been reacquired and are being held as treasury stock at December 31, 1988, 168,000 shares are said to be *outstanding*.

Note also (1) the various types of paid-in capital accounts, (2) the appropriation of part of retained earnings, and (3) the deduction of the cost of the treasury stock.

SUMMARY

Learning Objective 1: Describe the characteristics of the corporate form of organization.

Corporations are separate legal entities that offer the advantage of limited liability. Stockholders govern a corporation through a board of directors, which in turn selects the officers to carry on day-to-day activities. Double taxation of corporate income is a negative characteristic of the corporate form.

Learning Objective 2: Record the issuance, reacquisition, and reissue of stock.

The par value of a share of stock is a purely arbitrary amount that is not an indication of the market value of the stock. The par value is credited to the capital stock account when stock is issued. Amounts received in excess of par value by a corporation when issuing shares are credited to a paid-in capital account. Other possible sources of paid-in capital include stock dividends and reissuance of treasury stock.

Learning Objective 3: Describe the various possible types of preferred stock.

Preferred stock may be *cumulative* (undeclared dividends accumulate rather than lapse), *participating* (sharing in dividends beyond the specified rate), *callable* (redeemable at the company's option), or *convertible* into other securities (at the stockholder's option).

Learning Objective 4: Describe and record cash dividends.

Cash dividends are distributions of the company's assets, earned by profitable operations, to the stockholders. Cash dividends are not guaranteed. Once declared, however, cash dividends become a legal liability of the corporation. Availability of cash to pay the dividends is a key factor in the decision to pay dividends. On the declaration date, retained earnings is reduced and a liability is recorded. On the payment date, the liability is satisfied by the payment of cash.

Learning Objective 5: Distinguish between the accounting procedures for a stock dividend and a stock split.

Stock dividends are a proportionate distribution of additional shares of a company's own stock. The accounting entry for a stock dividend capitalizes retained earnings. A stock split also affects the number of shares outstanding but requires no accounting entry.

Learning Objective 6: Prepare a statement of retained earnings.

The statement of retained earnings explains the change in the retained earnings balance during the period. Typical items presented on the statement of retained earnings include: net income, dividends declared, and prior period adjustments.

KEY TERMS

Appropriated retained earnings
Board of directors
Cash dividends
Common stock
Corporate charter
Corporations
Cumulative preferred stock
Dividends in arrears

Legal capital
Par value
Preferred stock
Prior period adjustment
Stated value
Stock dividend
Stock split
Treasury stock

REVIEW QUESTIONS

1 Differentiate between the role played by the board of directors and the role played by the officers in managing a corporation.

2 As a stockholder, which corporate characteristic would you consider advantageous? Which corporate characteristic would you consider disadvantageous?

3 The right to vote is one of four basic rights granted to common stockholders. What does voting by proxy mean? What are the other three rights of the common stockholders? In what manner do the rights of preferred stockholders differ from the rights of common stockholders?

4 The par value of a share of stock is an amount that affects the amount credited to the capital stock account when shares are issued. Why is the par value of common stock usually set at a relatively *low* arbitrary amount rather than a high one?

5 Compare and contrast the following three terms: par value, stated value, and market value.

6 Mary Jones sold her secret process for tripling the mileage obtainable from a gallon of gasoline to Mammouth Oil Corp. in exchange for 50,000 shares of the company's $3 par value common stock. How should Mammouth Oil determine the dollar amounts for the journal entry to record the issuance of its stock in exchange for the secret process?

7 Define treasury stock. At what amount (par value, original issuance price, or repurchase cost) should treasury stock be recorded? Is treasury stock an asset?

8 Lively Corporation reacquired 100,000 shares of its $5 par value common stock at a cost of $8 per share. What is the journal entry to record the purchase of the treasury shares? If the company reissues 50,000 shares of the treasury stock at $14 per share, what amount of gain should be reported on the income statement?

(AICPA Adapted)

9 Marty Weinen sold his 500 shares of $10 par value shares of Blueton, Inc. to Dianne Prince for $60 per share. What journal entry is required by Blueton?

10 Preferred stock has a preference over common stock in the receipt of dividends. Does this mean preferred stockholders are guaranteed their annual dividends?

11 Needy, Inc. plans to issue a 9 percent preferred stock with a $100 par value per share. The company plans to sell the issue for its $100 par value. As corporate treasurer, you would rather see a lower basic dividend rate than 9 percent. Adding which of the following features to the preferred stock might encourage investors to accept a lower basic dividend rate: 1) callability, 2) convertibility, 3) cumulative dividends, 4) participating dividends?

12   Belton, Inc. has 1,000 shares of a 7 percent, $100 par value, preferred stock issue outstanding. No dividends have been declared for the current year or the preceding two years. Before common stockholders can receive any dividends for the current year, how much must be paid first to the preferred stockholders? Assume the preferred stock is cumulative. Would your answer differ if the preferred stock was noncumulative?

13   Differentiate between a callable preferred stock and a convertible preferred stock. Which feature, callability or convertibility, is advantageous to the preferred stockholder?

14   In 1988, Errare, Inc. discovered it had failed to record $55,000 amortization of goodwill in 1986. What effect would the correction of this error have on the 1988 financial statements?

15   What are the three important dates associated with a cash dividend? Explain the significance of each date. Describe the journal entry required, if any, on each date.

16   Myers Corp.'s retained earnings totals $11,000,000. Is it likely that the board of directors will declare an $11,000,000 cash dividend? Discuss.

17   Define the term stock dividend. Which of the following occurs as the result of a stock dividend: number of shares outstanding increases, total stockholders' equity increases, par value per share is decreased, retained earnings is decreased?

18   Andrews Corporation declared a stock dividend of 5,000 shares when the par value was $1 per share and the market value was $4 per share. If the 5,000 shares represent a 10 percent stock dividend, what is the effect of the stock dividend on total stockholders' equity?

(AICPA Adapted)

19   What is the purpose of a stock split? How does the accounting entry for a stock split differ from that of a stock dividend?

20   Why would a company appropriate a portion of its retained earnings? Describe the financial statement presentation of appropriated retained earnings.

EXERCISES

E10-1   Company P issued 1,000 shares of its $10 par value common stock for $25 per share. Company S issued 1,000 shares of its no par common stock for $25 per share. Company S's stock has a $12 stated value per share. Company N issued 1,000 shares of its no par (and no stated value) common stock for $25 per share. What is the amount of invested capital created for each company as a result of the stock issues? Present the journal entries to record each company's stock issue.

E10-2   On January 1, 1989, Four-C Kola Company's stockholders' equity appeared as follows:

Common Stock, $.10 par value, 750,000 shares authorized, 100,000 shares issued and outstanding	$ 10,000
Paid-in Capital in Excess of Par	324,000
Retained Earnings	412,000
Total Stockholders' Equity	$746,000

During 1989 the following common stock transactions occurred:

1 April 18—Four-C Kola acquired the secret ingredients for a new watermelon-flavored soft drink by issuing 5,000 shares of its common stock. At the time the market price per share was $3.50. (Debit an asset account titled Secret Process.)

2 November 30—Company issued 3,000 shares of its common stock for $4.00 per share.

3 December 8—Company issued 10,000 shares of its common stock for $3.80 per share.

Prepare journal entries for the above transactions. Assume net income was $46,000 for 1989 and there are no other transactions affecting stockholders' equity other than those described. Present the stockholders' equity section of the company's December 31, 1989 balance sheet.

E10-3 Tree Surgeons, Inc. began business on January 2, 1988 with the issuance of 30,000 shares of $1.50 par value common stock. The shares were sold for $6.00 per share. A total of 500,000 shares are authorized. During 1988 the company entered into the following treasury stock transactions:

    May 6—Acquired 5,000 treasury stock shares at $5.00 per share.

    June 27—Reissued 2,000 of the shares at $4.00 per share.

    October 3—Reissued 1,500 of the shares at $7.00 per share.

Assume net income for the year was $90,000 and there are no other transactions affecting stockholders' equity other than those described. Present the stockholders' equity section of Tree Surgeons' balance sheet on December 31, 1988.

E10-4 The Shamus Company was organized on January 2, 1988 and issued the following stock:

1 200,000 shares of $5 par value common stock at $12 per share

2 50,000 shares of $100 par value, 4 percent cumulative, nonparticipating preferred stock at $100 per share

Net income for 1988 was $220,000 and cash dividends paid in 1988 totaled $160,000. Net income for 1989 was $920,000 and cash dividends paid in 1989 totaled $570,000. Determine for 1988 and 1989 the dividends paid to the preferred stockholders and to the common stockholders, respectively.

(AICPA Adapted)

E10-5 On December 19, 1988, Warsau Co. declared a $2.50 per share cash dividend on its 10,000 shares of common stock. The dividend is payable January 18, 1989 to stockholders of record as of January 8. Present journal entries required, if any, on the declaration date, record date, and payment date. In which year would the dividend affect Warsau's income statement?

E10-6 Present journal entries for the 1988 transactions described below:

1 June 30—Declared $8,000 cash dividend on common stock.

2 August 15—Paid cash dividend previously declared.

3 November 8—Declared and distributed a 10 percent stock dividend on the 185,000 shares of $2 par value common shares outstanding. Market value per share is $8.

4 December 28—Declared a 3 for 1 stock split on the common stock.

E10-7 From the list of transactions presented below, indicate those which would (or could) result in a change in the retained earnings account balance. If a transaction would affect retained earnings only under certain circumstances, specify those circumstances.

1 Declaration of cash dividends
2 Purchase of treasury stock
3 Payment of previously declared cash dividends
4 Reissue of treasury stock at price greater than cost
5 Reissue of treasury stock at price less than cost
6 Issuance of common stock at a price greater than par
7 Declaration and distribution of stock dividends
8 Correction of prior period error
9 Appropriation of retained earnings

E10-8 For each account title listed below, indicate how the account is presented on the financial statements. The first one already is done as an example.

1 Correction of Prior Period Error—is a prior period adjustment to the beginning retained earnings balance on the statement of retained earnings
2 Cash Dividends Payable
3 Paid-in Capital from Treasury Stock Transactions
4 Preferred Stock
5 Appropriated Retained Earnings—for Plant Expansion
6 Treasury Stock
7 Common Stock

PROBLEMS

P10-1 *Record Equity Transactions*

At December 31, 1987, the stockholders' equity section of Baker Co.'s balance sheet appeared as follows:

Common Stock, $10 par value, 10,000 shares authorized, 6,500 shares issued and outstanding	$ 65,000
Paid-in Capital in Excess of Par	28,000
Retained Earnings	32,000
Total Stockholders' Equity	$125,000

During 1988 the following transactions occurred:

1 On March 3, 2,000 shares of common stock were issued at $18 per share.
2 On June 8, 100 shares were reacquired as treasury stock at a cost of $21 per share.
3 On December 18, a cash dividend of $1 per share was declared on the common shares.

Required:

1 Present journal entries for the three 1988 transactions.
2 Prepare the stockholders' equity section of Baker's December 31, 1988 balance sheet. Assume net income for 1988 was $24,000.

P10-2 *Record Equity Transactions*

The stockholders' equity section of Wright, Inc.'s balance sheet on December 31, 1988 follows:

Common Stock, $10 par value, 500,000
   shares authorized, 90,000 shares issued
   of which 1,210 are held in the treasury $ 900,000
Retained Earnings   435,939
                            $1,335,939

Less cost of 1,210 shares of common stock
   held in treasury   (36,300)
Total Stockholders' Equity $1,299,639

The following transactions affecting stockholders' equity occurred during 1989:

1 On January 15, 650 shares of the treasury stock were reissued for $20 per share. The 1,210 shares of treasury stock on hand at December 31, 1988 were purchased in 1988 for $30 per share.

2 On July 3, the remaining shares of treasury stock were reissued for $32 per share.

3 On August 26, the company declared and distributed a 5 percent stock dividend. Market value per share is $35.

4 On November 8, the company issued 1,200 shares of common stock at a price of $38 per share.

5 On December 19, the company reacquired 1,000 shares of treasury stock at a cost of $34 per share.

Required:

1 Prepare journal entries for the above transactions.

2 Present the December 31, 1989 stockholders' equity section of Wright's balance sheet. Assume net income totaled $60,000 for 1989.

(AICPA Adapted)

P10-3 *Record Equity Transactions*

On January 2, 1988, Disco Corp. was organized. The charter authorizes the issuance of 400,000 shares of $10 par value common stock and 50,000 shares of $100 par value, 6 percent, cumulative preferred stock. The preferred stock is callable at $103. During 1988 the following transactions occurred:

1 January 2—Issued 20,000 shares of $10 par value common stock for $28 per share.

2 February 2—Issued 5,000 shares of $100 par value, 6 percent, cumulative preferred stock for $101 per share.

3 March 11—Issued 7,000 shares of $10 par value common stock for $25 per share.

4 September 8—Declared and distributed a 5 percent stock dividend on common stock. Current market price per share of common is $30.

5 November 3—Appropriated $48,000 of retained earnings for future equipment purchases. (Hint: debit Retained Earnings and credit Appropriated Retained Earnings for Equipment Purchases.)

6 December 16—Declared 6 percent annual cash dividend on preferred stock. Dividend to be paid January 15, 1989.

7 December 18—Declared $6,000 cash dividend on common stock. Dividend to be paid January 20, 1989.
8 December 29—Issued 3,000 shares of $10 par value common stock at $30 per share.

Required:
1 Prepare journal entries to record the above transactions.
2 Present the stockholders' equity section of the December 31, 1988 balance sheet. Assume net income was $180,000 for 1988.

P10-4   *Interpret Stockholders' Equity Section*
Presented below is the stockholders' equity section of MGA, Inc.'s balance sheet:

8% Cumulative Preferred Stock, par value $100 per share, 1,000 shares authorized, ? shares issued and outstanding	$ 20,000
Common Stock, par value $20 per share, 10,000 shares authorized, ? shares issued and outstanding	20,000
	$ 40,000
Paid-in Capital in Excess of Par:	
Preferred Stock	500
Common Stock	42,000
	$ 82,500
Retained Earnings	105,500
Total Stockholders' Equity	$188,000

Required:
1 Calculate the number of preferred shares issued and the average issuance price per share.
2 Calculate the number of common shares issued and the average issuance price per share.
3 For each of the transactions below, indicate the dollar change in *total stockholders' equity*. (Indicate amount and whether increase or decrease.) Assume the events are sequential (e.g., in answering b, consider the effects of a, and so on).
  a Purchased 50 shares of common stock for the treasury at a cost of $80 per share.
  b Reissued 10 shares of the common stock shares held in treasury for $95 each.
  c Declared cash dividends of $1 per share on the common stock.
  d Declared and distributed to the common stockholders a 10 percent stock dividend. The market value per share for the common is $98.

P10-5   *Matching Problem: Stockholders' Equity Terminology*
On the blank line preceding each description below, place the letter of the term *best* matching the description presented. No item is to be used more than once.
  _____ 1 Allows stockholders to maintain percentage ownership by purchasing additional shares of common stock issued by the corporation
  _____ 2 Part of total retained earnings
  _____ 3 Amount selected by organizers of corporation and printed directly on stock certificates
  _____ 4 Dividends to preferred stockholders in excess of basic preferred rate

_____ **5** Requires disclosure, but not a liability until declared by board of directors

_____ **6** Day-to-day management

_____ **7** Adjustment to beginning balance of retained earnings

_____ **8** Deducted from total stockholders' equity

_____ **9** Advantage of corporate form of organization

_____ **10** Current liability

_____ **11** Disadvantage of corporate form of organization

a Appropriated retained earnings

b Board of directors

c Callable preferred stock

d Nonparticipating preferred

e Corporate charter

f Dividends in arrears

g Cash dividends payable

h Double taxation

i Limited liability

j Officers

k Par value

l Participating preferred stock

m Basic right of common stockholders

n Accounting error discovered relating to a prior period

o Stock split

p Cost of treasury stock

P10-6 _Stock Dividends_

Each of the following cases involves stock dividends. Solve for the particular requirements of each case. Treat each case independently.

Case 1

The board of directors of Roof Corporation, whose $80 par value common stock is currently selling at $100 per share, have decided to issue a stock dividend. Roof has 200,000 shares of common stock currently issued and outstanding. The company wishes to declare a stock dividend of less than 20 percent that will result in the capitalization of $1,600,000 of the retained earnings account balance.

Required:

What percentage stock dividend should the board of directors declare to accomplish their objective?

(AICPA Adapted)

Case 2

On January 2, 1988, Wilson, Inc. declared and distributed a 5 percent stock dividend on its common stock when the market value was $15 per share. Stockholders' equity before the stock dividend was declared consisted of:

Common Stock, $10 par value, 200,000 shares authorized, 100,000 shares issued and outstanding	$1,000,000
Paid-in Capital in Excess of Par	150,000
	$1,150,000

Retained Earnings	700,000
Total Stockholders' Equity	$1,850,000

Required:
Determine the effect of the 5 percent stock dividend on retained earnings and on total stockholders' equity.

(AICPA Adapted)

P10-7   *Effect of Transactions on Liabilities and Stockholders' Equity*
For each transaction presented below, indicate whether it will increase, decrease, or have no effect on the item named in each column. The first one is done as an example.

Transaction	Total liabilities	Number of shares outstanding	Common stock account	Paid-in capital accounts	Dividends declared (retained earnings)	Total stockholders' equity
Declared a cash dividend	Increase	No effect	No effect	No effect	Decrease	Decrease
Paid the cash dividend						
Declared and distributed a 5 percent stock dividend when market price exceeded par						
Declared and distributed a 3 for 1 stock split						
Purchased 100 shares of treasury stock						
Reissued treasury shares at a price greater than cost						

P10-8   *Prepare a Statement of Retained Earnings*
The retained earnings balance for Stoecker, Inc. on January 1, 1988 was $48,980,000. During 1988, the company:
1 Declared $2,500,000 cash dividends on preferred stock. At December 31, 1988, $300,000 of these dividends were unpaid.
2 Declared and paid a cash dividend of $83,600 on the common stock.
3 Corrected a previous year's error by recording $180,000 of interest earned in 1987 on the company's investment in municipal bonds. The company's accountant had failed to record the interest in 1987; there is no income tax effect.
4 Earned net income of $2,840,000.

Required:

Prepare a statement of retained earnings for Stoecker, Inc. for 1988.

P10-9 *Journal Entries and Statement of Retained Earnings*

The retained earnings balance for Mural, Inc. on January 1, 1988 was $14,980,000. During the year, the following occurred:

1 March 8—Declared a $1,500,000 cash dividend on the common stock, payable April 14 to stockholders of record as of April 8.

2 April 14—Paid the dividend declared on March 8.

3 September 8—Corrected a previous year's error by recording $640,000 of goodwill amortization that was inadvertently omitted in 1987. There is no income tax effect.

Required:

1 Present journal entries to record the above transactions.

2 Prepare a statement of retained earnings for 1988; assume net income of $4,550,000 for the year.

Business Decision Problem

Walter Klondike and several associates are seriously considering opening a new business; they have come to you for advice.

Required:

Respond to each of the questions they have asked:

1 What are the primary advantage and primary disadvantage of organizing the business in the form of a corporation?

2 If preferred stock is issued, what features or characteristics (other than the basic dividend rate and liquidation rights) should we consider making a part of the preferred stock issue?

11

STATEMENT OF
CASH FLOWS

LEARNING OBJECTIVES

When you complete this chapter, you should be able to:

1 Identify and calculate cash flows from operating activities.
2 Identify and calculate cash flows from investing activities.
3 Identify and calculate cash flows from financing activities.
4 Prepare the statement of cash flows in good form.

Any firm engages in a number of financing and investing activities that are not evident by examining that firm's income statement, balance sheet, or retained earnings statement. For example, financial statement readers may want to know:

What happened to profits that were earned during the period?
Why weren't dividend payments larger?
How can dividends be paid in excess of earnings, or even in the presence of a loss?
Why is cash down, while profits are up, or vice versa?
What became of the proceeds from the issuance of capital stock or bonds, or from the sale of noncurrent assets?
How was the acquisition of noncurrent assets financed?
From where did the funds come to retire debt or acquire treasury stock?

Current owners of the business, potential investors, creditors, management, and others seek answers to some or all of the above questions. Since the answers will not be directly provided on any of the three aforementioned financial statements, a fourth statement—*the statement of cash flows*—is used. This statement is considered to be a basic financial statement that must be presented whenever annual financial statements are issued. It is not intended to replace the income statement, balance sheet, or statement of retained earnings, but rather to supplement these statements with additional information about the firm's operating, investing, and financing activities.[1]

The statement of cash flows can assist in providing answers to the preceding questions. Creditors should be aided in appraising the ability of the firm to repay its debts, and comparative statements over several years should help the reader obtain insights into the firm's dividend policy, financing methods, and investment strategy.

Throughout our study of accounting, we have focused on the accrual method as the means of presenting financial information. The accrual basis reflected transactions that had occurred in a given time period, even though the related cash receipt or payment had not yet been made. This approach is considered best for the measurement of income and financial position. However, information on cash flows is also useful. Cash is the medium of exchange for virtually all business transactions—the lifeblood of the firm; knowing where it comes from, where it goes, and how much remains is essential to understanding the activities of the firm. Cash is a measure familiar to all. It is no surprise that many people measure the firm's activities in terms of the amounts of cash that enter and leave the firm. Thus, we present cash transactions, rather than accrual-basis transactions, on the statement of cash flows.

The term *cash* includes cash on hand, cash in the bank (checking accounts, time accounts, certificates of deposit, and so on), and other short-term, highly liquid investments such as Treasury bills, money market funds, and commercial paper (short-term notes issued by corporations). Because some short-term investments are included in the definition of cash for the statement of cash flows, the term *cash and cash equivalents* is often used.

OPERATING, INVESTING, AND FINANCING ACTIVITIES

In describing the changes in cash that have occurred during the period, we divide the firm's activities into three major categories: operating, investing, and financing.

Operating activities are the income-producing activities of the firm—the sale and delivery of goods and services to customers. Cash is produced by collections from customers and is used for payments to suppliers (inventory purchases, insurance, supplies, and other operating costs), employees (labor costs), and government (taxes). Also included as an operating inflow is the interest or divi-

---

[1]This chapter reflects the tentative position of the FASB at the time of writing. A final statement had not yet been issued.

dends received on investments. Interest expense on long-term debt is an operating outflow.

Investing activities relate to the inflow and outflow of cash resulting from the purchase or sale of investments; property, plant, and equipment; and other nonoperating assets. The cost of purchasing these assets constitutes an outflow of cash, while the proceeds from selling these assets constitutes an inflow. Lending money is an investing outflow, and collecting repayment of loans is an investing inflow.

Financing activities relate to the inflow and outflow of cash resulting from debt and equity transactions. These transactions include the issuance and retirement/repayment of long-term debt, the issuance and retirement/repurchase of the company's stock, and the payment of cash dividends.

Format of the Statement of Cash Flows

The specific format of the statement of cash flows is subject to some variation, but typically has the following structure:

Cash Flows from Operating Activities
Inflows and outflows from operating activities, leading to "net cash flow from operating activities"

Cash Flows from Investing Activities
Inflows and outflows from investing activities, listed separately, leading to "net cash flow from investing activities"

Cash Flows from Financing Activities
Inflows and outflows from financing activities, listed separately and grouped by type (e.g., all long-term debt transactions together), leading to "net cash flow from financing activities"

Net Increase (Decrease) in Cash

An illustration of the format is given in Exhibit 11-1.

PREPARING THE STATEMENT OF CASH FLOWS

A typical firm has thousands of cash transactions each year; it is not feasible to analyze the nature of each cash transaction in order to prepare a statement of cash flows. It is more efficient to work from recorded accounting data—a trial balance or a set of financial statements. These records, however, are maintained on the accrual basis; it is necessary to convert this accrual information to cash information in order to prepare the statement of cash flows.

In the following sections, we focus on analyzing each of the three categories of activity—operating, investing, and financing. Specific transactions falling into each category are identified, and the process of converting from accrual to cash is illustrated. To facilitate the discussion, we use the Rodgers Co. example.

EXHIBIT 11-1
Sample Company
Statement of Cash Flows
For the Year Ended December 31, 1988

Cash Flows from Operating Activities:

Cash received from customers	$300,000	
Cash received from interest and dividends	10,000	
Cash provided by operating activities		$310,000
Cash paid to suppliers	$125,000	
Cash paid to employees	100,000	
Cash paid for operating expenses	20,000	
Cash paid for interest	18,000	
Cash paid for income taxes	12,000	
Cash used by operating activities		275,000
Net cash flow provided by operating activities		$ 35,000
Cash Flows from Investing Activities:		
Sale of investment in securities	$ 84,000	
Purchase of land, buildings, and equipment	(130,000)	
Net cash flow used for investing activities		(46,000)
Cash Flows from Financing Activities:		
Proceeds of bank loan	$ 80,000	
Proceeds of issuance of common stock	44,000	
Purchase of treasury stock	(30,000)	
Dividends paid	(25,000)	
Net cash flow provided by financing activities		69,000
Net Increase (Decrease) in Cash		$ 58,000

The income statement for Rodgers Co. for the fiscal year ended September 30, 1988 is shown below:

Rodgers Co.
Income Statement
For the Year Ended September 30, 1988

Revenues:		
Net Sales		$600,000
Gain on Sale of Land		40,000
Total Revenue		$640,000
Expenses:		
Cost of Goods Sold	$165,000	
Salaries Expense	65,000	
Depreciation Expense	25,000	
Insurance Expense	5,000	
Loss on Sale of Truck	3,000	
Income Tax Expense	172,000	435,000
Net Income		$205,000

Comparative balance sheets for Rodgers are as follows:

Rodgers Co.
Balance Sheets
September 30,

	1987	1988	Increase (Decrease)
Cash	$ 92,000	$ 52,000	$ (40,000)
Accounts Receivable	100,000	130,000	30,000
Marketable Securities	33,000	38,000	5,000
Inventories	75,000	82,000	7,000
Prepaid Insurance	8,000	3,000	(5,000)
Land	165,000	95,000	(70,000)
Buildings	100,000	230,000	130,000
Accumulated Depreciation— Buildings	(52,000)	(74,000)	22,000
Delivery Trucks	30,000	21,000	(9,000)
Accumulated Depreciation— Trucks	(18,000)	(17,000)	(1,000)
	$533,000	$560,000	
Accounts Payable	$ 15,000	$ 20,000	5,000
Salaries Payable	18,000	15,000	(3,000)
Income Taxes Payable	35,000	15,000	(20,000)
Bonds Payable	250,000	-0-	(250,000)
Common Stock, $10 par value	60,000	140,000	80,000
Paid-in Capital in Excess of Par	28,000	68,000	40,000
Retained Earnings	127,000	302,000	175,000
	$533,000	$560,000	

The following information about Rodgers' transactions for the year is assumed:

1 The proceeds from the land sale were $110,000.

2 A delivery truck was sold for $2,000. The truck cost $9,000 when originally purchased and had a book value of $5,000 when sold (i.e., the accumulated depreciation on the truck was $4,000 at the time it was sold).

3 Buildings were purchased at a cost of $130,000.

4 $250,000 of bonds payable were retired at face.

5 8,000 shares of common stock were issued at $15 per share.

6 Other than net income, the only item affecting retained earnings was $30,000 cash dividends declared and paid.

7 $3,000 of the depreciation expense for the year is for the delivery truck, the remainder is for the building.

Cash Flow from Operating Activities

Operating activities involve the production and sale of goods and services to customers. Such activities generate cash by collections from customers. Cash generated by interest and dividends on investments is also included in operating activities. Cash is spent in carrying on operations—payments are made for merchandise, supplies, labor, repairs, rent, insurance, interest on debt, taxes, and other costs necessary to carry on business activity.

The income statement also reports on business operations, and, thus, it is a good place to look for information on operating activities. There are two main differences, however, between the income statement and the cash flow from operating activities section of the statement of cash flows. First, not everything on the income statement represents an operating activity. Gains or losses from the sale of assets (investments, machinery, and so forth) appear on the income statement; such sales are considered investment activities. In using the income statement to identify operating activities, items such as these must be ignored. Second, the income statement is based on accrual accounting; cash flows are needed for the statement of cash flows. Hence accrual amounts must be converted to cash amounts. In using the Rodgers income statement to develop cash flow from operating activities, we must be aware of these two differences. We consider each item on the income statement, first to determine if it is an operating item, and if so, to convert it into cash.

Net Sales Converted to Cash Received from Customers   Net sales are converted into cash received from customers through use of the maximum-cash-received technique. To determine cash receipts from customers: 1) add the current period net sales to the accounts receivable balance at the beginning of the period to determine the maximum amount of cash that could have been received, then 2) subtract the ending accounts receivable balance (the amount not yet collected) to find cash received from customers during the current period. For Rodgers, the maximum cash received technique shows:

	$600,000	Net sales during the current period
Step 1	+ 100,000	Beginning accounts receivable balance
	$700,000	Maximum cash receipts from customers
Step 2	− 130,000	Ending accounts receivable balance
	$570,000	Cash received from customers during the period

Condensing the calculation to work with only the net change in accounts receivable during the year yields the following:

Cash Received from Customers = Net Sales plus the
Decrease (or minus the
Increase) in Accounts
Receivable

Gain on Sale of Land   While the land sale did result in an increase in cash, the transaction is not part of normal operations; sale of land is considered an investing activity. The entire $110,000 proceeds from the land sale will be shown in the cash flow from investing activities section of the statement of cash flows.

Cost of Goods Sold Converted to Cash Paid for Inventory   The conversion of cost of goods sold expense to cash paid for inventory acquisitions involves adjusting cost of goods sold for changes in two current accounts (inventory and accounts payable). Using a maximum-cash-paid technique, the cash paid out is determined after the current period's inventory purchases have been calculated. For Rodgers, current purchases are calculated as follows:

$165,000	Cost of goods sold during the current period
+ 82,000	Ending inventory balance
$247,000	Maximum purchases during current period
− 75,000	Beginning inventory balance available
$172,000	Current period's inventory purchases

Once the current period's inventory purchases are known, the cash paid out is determined by: 1) adding current period's purchases to accounts payable at the beginning of the period to determine the maximum amount of cash that could have been paid to inventory suppliers, then 2) subtracting the ending accounts payable balance (the amount still owed) to find cash paid out this period for inventory purchases. For Rodgers Co.:

	$172,000	Current period's inventory purchases (see above)
Step 1	+ 15,000	Beginning accounts payable balance
	$187,000	Maximum cash payments to inventory suppliers
Step 2	− 20,000	Ending accounts payable balance
	$167,000	Cash paid to inventory suppliers this period

Condensing the calculations to work with only the changes in the inventory and accounts payable accounts produces the following:

Cash Paid for Inventory = Cost of Goods Sold plus the Increase
(or minus the Decrease) in Inventory,
plus the Decrease (or minus the Increase)
in Accounts Payable

Salaries Expense and Income Tax Expense Converted to Cash Paid   To convert Rodgers' salaries expense and income tax expense to cash payments, we must analyze changes in the related liability accounts (i.e., salaries payable and income taxes payable). Using the maximum-cash-paid technique: 1) the expense amount is added to the beginning liability amount to determine the maximum amount of cash that could have been paid out, then 2) the ending liability balance (the amount still owed) is subtracted to find cash paid this period. For Rodgers Co.:

	$65,000	Salaries expense
Step 1	+ 18,000	Beginning salaries payable balance
	$83,000	Maximum cash payments to employees
Step 2	− 15,000	Ending salaries payable balance
	$68,000	Cash paid to employees this period

	$172,000	Income tax expense
Step 1	+ 35,000	Beginning income taxes payable balance
	$207,000	Maximum cash paid for taxes
Step 2	− 15,000	Ending income taxes payable balance
	$192,000	Cash paid for income taxes this period

In condensed form, the calculation where a related liability account is involved is:

$$\text{Cash Paid for Expense} = \text{Expense plus the Decrease}$$
$$\text{(or minus the Increase)}$$
$$\text{in Related Liability}$$

Depreciation Expense   Depreciation expense involves neither a cash inflow nor outflow. Thus, although depreciation expense reduces net income, the depreciation amount is not considered in determining cash flow from operating activities. Consider Rodgers' depreciation entry:

Depreciation expense	25,000	
Accumulated depreciation		25,000
To record depreciation expense		
for the year.		

The entry debiting depreciation expense and crediting accumulated depreciation neither increases nor decreases cash.

Insurance Expense Converted to Cash Paid   To determine the amount of cash spent for insurance coverage during the current period, we must examine the prepaid insurance account in conjunction with insurance expense reported in the income statement. Using the maximum-cash-paid technique, we calculate cash paid this period for insurance by 1) adding the current period insurance expense to the ending prepaid insurance asset balance to determine maximum cash that could have been paid for insurance, then 2) subtracting the beginning prepaid insurance balance that was available to find cash actually paid this period for insurance. For Rodgers Co.:

	$5,000	Insurance expense
Step 1	+3,000	Ending prepaid insurance balance
	$8,000	Maximum cash payments for insurance
Step 2	−8,000	Beginning prepaid insurance balance available
	$ -0-	Cash paid this period for insurance

For Rodgers, no cash was expended during the year for insurance. The entire $5,000 insurance expense resulted from using up some of the prepaid insurance existing at the beginning of the year.

Condensing the calculation of cash paid out when there is a related prepaid asset account yields:

$$\text{Cash Paid for Expense} = \text{Expense plus the Increase}$$
$$\text{(or minus the Decrease)}$$
$$\text{in Related Prepaid Asset}$$

Loss on Sale of Truck   The truck sale, although resulting in a loss, actually increased cash. However, the truck sale is not part of normal operations; it is considered an investing activity. The $2,000 proceeds from the truck sale will appear in the cash flow from investing activities section of the statement of cash flows.

Net Cash Flow from Operating Activities   The preceding analyses may be summarized by the following worksheet:

Item	Accrual basis income statement	Adjustment or elimination	Cash flow from operations
Net Sales	$600,000	Less $30,000 increase in Accounts Receivable	$570,000
Gain on Sale of Land	40,000	Represents investing, not operating, activity	-0-
Cost of Goods Sold	(165,000)	Plus $7,000 increase in Inventory, less $5,000 increase in Accounts Payable	(167,000)
Salaries Expense	(65,000)	Plus $3,000 decrease in Salaries Payable	(68,000)
Depreciation Expense	(25,000)	Not a cash outlay	-0-
Insurance Expense	(5,000)	Less $5,000 decrease in Prepaid Insurance	-0-
Loss on Sale of Truck	(3,000)	Represents investing, not operating, activity	-0-
Income Tax Expense	(172,000)	Plus $20,000 decrease in Income Taxes Payable	(192,000)
Net Income	$205,000	Net cash flow provided by operating activities	$143,000

The presentation of this information on Rodgers' formal statement of cash flows would appear as follows:

Cash Flows from Operating Activities:		
Cash received from customers		$570,000
Cash provided by operating activities		$570,000
Cash paid to suppliers for inventory	$167,000	
Cash paid to employees	68,000	
Cash paid for income taxes	192,000	
Cash used for operating activities		427,000
Net cash flow provided by operating activities		$143,000

Cash Flow from Investing Activities

Investing activities include:

Lending money
Collecting the repayment of loans made
Acquiring investments in securities (other than those that are "cash equivalents")
Selling investments in securities
Acquiring property, plant, equipment, and intangible assets
Selling property, plant, equipment, and intangible assets

These activities are identified by analyzing income statement transactions and by analyzing the changes that have occurred in relevant balance sheet accounts. The presence of gains and losses on the income statement is often a signal that a sale of assets (an investing activity) has occurred. Recall from the list of other information for Rodgers presented earlier that there were two sales of property, plant, and equipment during the year. The journal entries for each sale would have been:

Cash	110,000	
Gain on Sale of Land		40,000
Land		70,000
Cash	2,000	
Accumulated Depreciation—Trucks	4,000	
Loss on Sale of Truck	3,000	
Delivery Trucks		9,000

The $40,000 gain and $3,000 loss on the income statement were eliminated in the calculation of net cash flow provided by operating activities. The $112,000 cash proceeds ($110,000 + $2,000) will appear as part of cash flow from investing activities. Note that the relevant number is the amount of cash flow, not the gain or loss on the transaction.

Acquisitions of assets are not evident from the income statement. To identify these investing activities, we must analyze the changes in relevant balance sheet accounts during the year. In the Rodgers example, account balances for marketable securities, property, plant, and equipment changed as follows during the year ended September 30, 1988:

Marketable securities	$ 5,000	increase
Land	70,000	decrease
Buildings	130,000	increase
Delivery trucks	9,000	decrease

The decreases in land and delivery trucks signified sales of these assets; these transactions have already been identified by the analysis of the income statement. Recall that the proceeds from the sale of the land were $110,000, and the proceeds from the sale of the truck were $2,000. The increases in marketable securities and buildings signify purchases of these assets; these transactions are also reflected as cash flows from investing activities. Rodgers' statement of cash flows would show:

Cash Flows from Investing Activities:	
Purchase of building	$(130,000)
Proceeds from disposals of land and delivery truck	112,000
Purchase of marketable securities	(5,000)
Net cash flow used by investing activities	$ (23,000)

In this example, the change in each account balance was explained by a single transaction. In other cases, both purchases and sales may be present for a single account. For example, machinery and equipment may show an increase of $10,000. This might be explained by (1) a $22,000 purchase and (2) a sale (with a cost retirement of $12,000) yielding proceeds of $9,000. Both the $22,000 purchase and the $9,000 proceeds would be shown on the statement of cash flows; they would not be netted. Careful analysis of transactions is needed in order to identify the investing activities that have occurred.

Cash Flow from Financing Activities

Financing activities include:

Obtaining resources from stockholders (e.g., issuing stock)
Returning resources to stockholders (e.g., purchasing treasury stock)
Paying cash dividends to stockholders
Proceeds from borrowing (e.g., bank loans, bonds payable)
Repaying amounts borrowed

These activities are identified by analyzing the changes that have occurred in relevant balance sheet accounts.

In the Rodgers Co. example, analysis of changes in nonoperating liability accounts, and in stockholder equity accounts, shows the following:

Bonds payable	$250,000 decrease
Common stock	80,000 increase
Paid-in capital in excess of par	40,000 increase
Retained earnings	175,000 increase

From this analysis and the list of other information for Rodgers presented earlier, three financing transactions are evident: retirement of bonds ($250,000), issuance of common stock ($120,000), and the payment of dividends ($30,000). Observe that the change in the retained earnings account was an increase of $175,000. This change is explained as a $205,000 increase (net income) and a $30,000 decrease (dividends). All items reflected in the $205,000 net income amount have already been accounted for in determining cash flow from operating activities and investing activities; only the $30,000 of dividends remains to be presented as a financing activity.

Rodgers' statement of cash flows would show the following items for financing activities:

Cash Flows from Financing Activities:	
Repayment of long-term bonds	$(250,000)
Proceeds from issuing common stock	120,000
Dividends paid	(30,000)
Net cash flow used by financing activities	$(160,000)

The Statement of Cash Flows

Combining the three sections of the statement developed above, Exhibit 11-2 presents the statement of cash flows for Rodgers Co. This statement explains the $40,000 decrease in Rodgers' cash balance during the year ended September 30, 1988.

ANALYZING THE CASH FLOW STATEMENT

Carefully examine Rodgers' statement of cash flows in Exhibit 11-2. How would you interpret the statement? As indicated on the bottom line of the statement, there was a $40,000 net *decrease* in cash for the year. Is Rodgers facing a liquidity crisis? Will the firm be able to pay creditors in the future? Will stockholders continue to receive $30,000 in annual dividends? Does the $40,000 decrease in

EXHIBIT 11-2
Rodgers Co.
Statement of Cash Flows
For the Year Ended September 30, 1988

Cash Flows from Operating Activities:		
Cash received from customers		$ 570,000
Cash provided by operating activities		$ 570,000
Cash paid to suppliers for inventory	$ 167,000	
Cash paid to employees	68,000	
Cash paid for income taxes	192,000	
Cash used for operating activities		427,000
Net cash flow provided by operating activities		$ 143,000
Cash Flows from Investing Activities:		
Purchase of building	$(130,000)	
Proceeds from disposals of land and		
delivery truck	112,000	
Purchase of marketable securities	(5,000)	
Net cash flow used by investing activities		(23,000)
Cash Flows from Financing Activities:		
Repayment of long-term bonds	$(250,000)	
Proceeds from issuing common stock	120,000	
Dividends paid	(30,000)	
Net cash flow used by financing activities		(160,000)
Net Increase (Decrease) in Cash		$ (40,000)

cash indicate Rodgers' management has done a poor job of managing the firm's cash?

Rodgers' statement of cash flows indicates management has done a good job of managing the cash position. The net cash flow provided by operations (the source of cash most likely to be repeated in future years) is a positive $143,000. Management may not be able in future years to raise cash, as they did this year, by selling land and issuing common stock. However, the major nonoperating uses of cash (purchase of building and repayment of bonds payable) are also unlikely to continue. Specifically, Rodgers has retired all its long-term debt this year. The outlook for a substantial increase in cash next year is very good.

Reconciling Net Income to Cash Flow from Operations

In developing the statement of cash flows in the Rodgers example, cash flow from operating activities was calculated by analyzing each item on the income statement, determining whether it represented an operating activity, and if so, converting it from an accrual measure to a cash flow. This process is called the *direct method* of calculating cash from operating activities. The resulting presentation of cash flow from operating activities is easy to understand because it shows the specific cash inflows and cash outflows related to the firm's operations.

When the direct method is used, it is also useful to present a reconciliation that shows the relationship between the net income figure presented on the firm's income statement and the cash flow from operating activities figure presented on the statement of cash flows. This reconciliation begins with the net income figure, removes items that do not represent operating activities (e.g., gains and losses on sales of assets), removes items that do not represent cash flows at all (e.g., depreciation expense), and adjusts for changes in those balance sheet accounts that reflect operating transactions (accounts receivable, inventories, prepaid items, accounts payable, and accrued liabilities). The reconciliation below for Rodgers Co. illustrates this *indirect method*:

Rodgers Co.
Reconciliation of Net Income
to Cash Flow from Operating Activities
For the Year Ended September 30, 1988

Net income	$205,000
Noncash revenues, expenses, gains, and losses included in net income:	
Gain on sale of land	(40,000)
Loss on sale of truck	3,000
Depreciation expense	25,000
Increase in accounts receivable	(30,000)
Increase in inventories	(7,000)
Decrease in prepaid insurance	5,000
Increase in accounts payable	5,000
Decrease in salaries payable	(3,000)
Decrease in income taxes payable	(20,000)
Net cash flow provided by operating activities	$143,000

Note that this reconciliation results in the same net cash flow from operating activities amount as calculated earlier using the direct method. To better understand the preceding reconciliation, we consider each of the three types of adjustments made.

Nonoperating Gains and Losses   Gains or losses, such as on the sale of noncurrent assets, affect reported net income. Cash is received as proceeds from the sale. However, the transaction is not considered to arise from normal operations. It is considered an investing activity rather than an operating activity.

These gains and losses are included in net income. To calculate cash flow from operating activities, however, they must be eliminated. Gains appear on the income statement as additions to income; to eliminate them on the reconciliation, they must be subtracted from net income. Similarly, losses appear as deductions from income; to eliminate them, they must be added back to net income on the reconciliation. Thus, the above reconciliation shows the subtraction of the $40,000 gain on the sale of land and the addition of the $3,000 loss on the sale of the truck.

Depreciation and Other Noncash Expenses   In the reconciliation of net income to cash flow from operating activities, depreciation is shown as an add-back to net income. Don't be fooled, however, by this addition of depreciation to net income in the calculation of cash flow from operations. Depreciation is *not* a source of cash because the entry does not affect the cash account.

Changes in Current Asset and Current Liability Balances   The third type of adjustment in preparing the reconciliation is needed for changes in the balance of current asset and current liability accounts. The analysis of these changes has already been presented. For example, in adjusting from sales to cash collections from customers, the increase in accounts receivable was subtracted. The impact of these changes may be summarized as follows:

To adjust net income to cash flow from operations:

> Add:
> > Decreases in current assets (accounts receivable, inventories, prepaid items)
> > Increases in current liabilities (accounts payable, taxes payable, salaries payable, and other accruals)
> Subtract:
> > Increases in current assets
> > Decreases in current liabilities

Only those current asset and current liability accounts that reflect operating transactions (sales, purchases, expenses) are included. Accounts that reflect investing activities (e.g., marketable securities) or financing activities (e.g., short-term bank loans) are not considered in adjusting net income to cash flow from operating activities.

Transactions Not Affecting Cash

One transaction that does not affect cash at all has already been discussed—the depreciation entry. Three other transactions of this type are analyzed below:

Transaction	Journal entry		
Conversion of preferred stock to common	Preferred Stock	5,000	
	Common Stock		1,000
	Paid-in Capital in Excess of Par		4,000
	To record conversion of preferred stock into common stock.		
Acquisition of building for long-term mortgage	Buildings	26,000	
	Mortgage Payable		26,000
	To record acquisition of building in exchange for long-term mortgage.		
Declaration and distribution of stock dividends	Stock Dividend Declared	700	
	Common Stock		100
	Paid-in Capital from Stock Dividends		600
	To record declaration and distribution of stock dividend.		

These transactions have no effect on cash. However, the first two transactions represent financing and/or investing activities. The first transaction involves a conversion from financing through preferred stock to financing by common stock. The second transaction involves an investment in buildings financed by a long-term mortgage. Since the statement of cash flows presents information on the firm's operating, investing, and financing activities, all financing and investing activities should be presented on the statement even though they do not affect cash. The third transaction, the declaration and distribution of a stock dividend, merely capitalizes some retained earnings. It is not a financing or investing activity, and therefore is not presented on the statement of cash flows.

An acceptable method of disclosing these noncash financing and investing activities is to present a separate list following the statement of cash flows. The above transactions would be presented as follows:

Schedule of Noncash Investing and Financing Activities

Common stock issued in conversion of preferred stock	$ 5,000
Retirement of preferred stock by conversion	(5,000)
Acquisition of building	$26,000
Long-term mortgage debt assumed	(26,000)

SUMMARY

The statement of cash flows summarizes a company's operating, investing, and financing activities. This statement provides information to financial statement readers to help them answer questions such as: What happened to profits, why is cash down while profits are up (or vice versa), what became of the proceeds from issuance of securities or sale of noncurrent assets, or where did the funds come from to acquire noncurrent assets or retire debt issues?

Learning Objective 1: Identify and calculate cash flows from operating activities.

Operating activities are a major source of cash. Cash flow from operating activities can be determined directly by converting operating transactions from the accrual basis used on the income statement to the cash basis. Cash flow from operating activities may also be determined indirectly by adjusting net income for (1) nonoperating gains and losses, (2) depreciation and other noncash revenues and expenses, and (3) changes in current asset and current liability account balances.

Learning Objective 2: Identify and calculate cash flows from investing activities.

Investing activities include the purchase and sale of assets (securities, land, buildings, equipment), lending money, and collecting repayment of loans.

Learning Objective 3: Identify and calculate cash flows from financing activities.

Financing activities include obtaining resources (and subsequently returning/re-paying them) from stockholders and from lenders, as well as paying dividends to stockholders.

Learning Objective 4: Prepare the statement of cash flows in good form.

The statement of cash flows contains separate sections showing net cash flows from operating activities, investing activities, and financing activities. A recon-ciliation of net income to cash flow from operating activities should also be presented. Noncash investing and financing activities should be reported in a separate schedule.

KEY TERMS

Cash flows

Direct method

Financing activities

Indirect method

Investing activities

Operating activities

Statement of cash flows

REVIEW QUESTIONS

1 What is the purpose of the statement of cash flows? Which of the other basic financial statements does it replace?

2 A broad, all-inclusive approach is required on the statement of cash flows. All financing and investing activities should be presented on the statement even though the transaction did not affect cash. Which of the following three transactions should be included on the statement: a) convertible bonds are converted into shares of common stock, b) land is acquired in exchange for issuance of a long-term mortgage, and c) a stock dividend is declared and distributed to common stockholders? Explain your answer.

3 When should a statement of cash flows be issued by a profit-oriented business?

   a As an alternative to the statement of income

b Only if the company showed a profit for the period

c Whenever annual financial statements are issued

d At the option of the company

(AICPA Adapted)

4 Describe activities that would appear in the cash flows from operating activities section of the statement of cash flows.

5 Describe activities that would appear in the cash flows from investing activities section of the statement of cash flows.

6 Describe activities that would appear in the cash flows from financing activities section of the statement of cash flows.

7 Is it possible for a company to be profitable and have positive cash flow from operating activities, and yet have its cash decrease during the period? Explain your answer.

8 Is it possible for a company to have suffered a net loss for the period and still have a positive net cash flow from operating activities? Explain.

9 Branton Co. sold a piano to a customer for $1,800. The sale was on account. The piano had cost Branton $1,100 when purchased. What effect will this transaction have on cash flow from operating activities?

10 Clarion Co. sold an old delivery truck for $2,000 cash. The sale resulted in a $400 gain. How would this transaction appear on the statement of cash flows?

11 Under the indirect method of calculating net cash flow from operating activities, depreciation expense is added to net income. Would increasing the depreciation expense increase the cash flow? Explain your answer.

12 Adding back depreciation expense to net income is sometimes used as a means of estimating cash flow from operations. Is the answer obtained by this technique likely to be an accurate determination of cash flow from operations? Explain your answer.

13 Carton Co.'s sales totaled $1,802,000 for the year. Twenty percent were cash sales, the remainder on account. Accounts receivable, which were $380,000 at the beginning of the year, were $540,000 at year end. How much cash was received from customers during the year?

14 Dragovits, Inc.'s salary expense for 1988 totaled $185,000. Salaries payable on January 1, 1988 were $4,000. At December 31, 1988 the company owed $2,300 of wages to its employees. Determine the cash outlay for salaries in 1988.

EXERCISES

E11-1 A list of transactions for F. Gordon, Inc. is presented below. Each transaction is to be analyzed to determine a) its effect on the amount of cash (i.e., increases, decreases, or no effect) and b) the type of activity (operating, investing, or financing). The first one is already done as an example.

1 Acquisition of new machine for cash

  a Decreases cash

  b Investing activity

2 Sale of long-term bonds at premium

3 Declaration and payment of cash dividend

4 Issuance of common stock at price in excess of par

5 Salaries expense of $48,000 for year ($2,000 balance in salaries payable at beginning of year and $1,000 unpaid at end of year)

6 Depreciation expense

7 Acquisition of land in exchange for long-term note payable

E11-2 Family Films Company, which operates several local movie theaters, is interested in determining the amount of cash provided by its operating activities. The company provides the following information:

Fees earned	$280,000
Film rental expense	160,000
Salaries expense	50,000
Depreciation expense	7,000
Insurance expense	3,000
Net income	60,000

Current accounts:

	Jan. 1	Dec. 31
Cash	$130,000	$120,000
Prepaid insurance	8,000	7,500
Accounts payable to film distributors	28,000	35,000
Salaries payable	3,000	1,000

Required:

Calculate cash flow from operating activities for the year, using the direct method.

E11-3 Quito Company's net income for 1988 was $4,200,000. Other information available for 1988 includes:

Cash dividends declared	$2,800,000
Depreciation on buildings and equipment	700,000
Cash proceeds from sale of land	108,000
Loss on sale of land	12,000
Acquisition of new equipment for cash and	
a short-term note payable	81,000

Required:

Calculate cash flow from operating activities, using the indirect method (i.e., reconcile from net income to net cash flows from operating activities by adjusting net income for noncash items and nonoperating gains and losses).

E11-4 Bragan, Inc. reveals the following selected information for 1988:

Sales	$820,000
Cost of goods sold	390,000
Selling, general, and administrative expenses	
(including $30,000 depreciation)	330,000
Changes in current accounts during year:	
Accounts receivable	+25,000
Inventory	-60,000
Accounts payable (to inventory suppliers)	-20,000

Required:

Calculate:

1 Cash received from customers during 1988

2 Cash paid out during 1988 for inventory purchases

3 Cash paid out for selling, general, and administrative expenses in 1988.

E11-5 Identify errors on the following statement of cash flows for Allentown, Inc. for 1988.

Allentown, Inc.
Statement of Cash Flows
December 31, 1988

Cash Flows from Operating Activities:		
Cash received from customers		$270,000
Cash dividend revenue collected		8,000
Cash interest collected on bond investments		5,000
Cash provided by operating activities		$283,000
Cash paid to suppliers	$190,000	
Cash dividends paid to stockholders	10,000	
Cash paid to employees	45,000	
Cash used by operating activities		245,000
Net cash flow provided by operating activities		$ 38,000
Cash Flows from Investing Activities:		
Sale of marketable securities investment	$ 85,000	
Purchase of land, net of sale of equipment	(120,000)	
Net cash flow used for investing activities		(35,000)
Cash Flows from Financing Activities:		
Purchase of treasury stock	$ 15,000	
Proceeds of bank loan	5,000	
Net cash flow provided by financing activities		20,000
Net Increase (Decrease) in Cash		$ 23,000

E11-6 Although net income of Herman, Inc. for 1989 was identical in amount to net income for 1988, the company's cash flow from operating activities increased significantly. Comparative information available shows:

	For 1988	For 1989
Net income	$180,000	$180,000
Depreciation expense	22,000	22,000
Change in accounts receivable	− 3,000	− 40,000
Change in inventory	+ 6,000	− 44,000
Change in accounts payable	− 5,000	+ 26,000
Cash flow from operations	194,000	312,000

Explain the significant improvement in the amount of cash from operations during 1989 in light of the identical net income amounts. Are similar increases in the amount of cash from operations likely to continue in the future with an unchanging net income?

E11-7 For each transaction below, complete the worksheet by placing an "X" in the appropriate column. The first one is done as an example.

	Transaction will		
Transactions	Increase cash	Decrease cash	Have no effect on amount of cash
1) Payment of an account payable		X	
2) Revenue from sale on account			
3) Cash sale of land at loss			
4) Depreciation expense			
5) Purchase of treasury stock			
6) Declaration of cash dividend			
7) Payment of cash dividend			
8) Sale of building at gain, 90-day note received from buyer for sales price			
9) Conversion of preferred stock into common stock			
10) Purchase of inventory, on account			

PROBLEMS

P11-1 *Preparing a Simple Statement of Cash Flows*
The following information is available relating to the 1988 operations of the Bower Company:
1 Net cash flow provided by operating activities was $16,000.
2 New equipment was purchased at a cost of $8,000.
3 Preferred stock was issued for $5,000.
4 Equipment having a book value of $3,000 was sold, resulting in a loss of $1,000.
5 In November, $5,950 was borrowed from the bank, repayable in 90 days.
6 Cash dividends of $4,000 were declared and paid during the year.
7 During 1988, the company reacquired 500 shares of its own common stock at a total cost of $9,000.

Required:
Prepare a statement of cash flows for the year ended December 31, 1988.

P11-2 *Finding Errors in Statement of Cash Flows*
The following is the statement of cash flows for Grog, Inc. for the year ended October 31, 1988. Grog has omitted two items from the statement: 1) conversion of preferred stock into common stock and 2) declaration and distribution of a stock dividend.

Grog, Inc.
Increase in Cash Statement
October 31, 1988

Cash Provided:

Net income	$ 8,000
Less expenses not requiring outlay of cash:	
Depreciation	(18,000)
Elimination of nonoperating gain:	
Gain on sale of equipment	(3,500)
Total Cash Provided	$22,500
Cash Used:	
Purchase of equipment, net of sales of equipment	$14,000
Cash dividends declared and paid	6,000
Total Cash Used	$20,000

Required:

List the errors and weaknesses in Grog's statement of cash flows.

P11-3 *Preparing a Statement of Cash Flows*

The following schedule shows net changes in balance sheet accounts at December 31, 1988, compared to December 31, 1987, for Lancaster Co.

	Net change increase (decrease)
Assets:	
Cash	$ 31,000
Accounts receivable	26,000
Inventories	(8,000)
Property, plant, and equipment, net	71,000
Total Assets	$120,000
Liabilities:	
Accounts payable	$ 24,000
Notes payable—due in 1992	40,000
Total Liabilities	$ 64,000
Stockholders' Equity:	
Common stock, $1 par	$ 4,000
Paid-in capital in excess of par	32,000
Retained earnings	20,000
Total Stockholders' Equity	$ 56,000
Total Liabilities and Stockholders' Equity	$120,000

Additional information:

1 Net income for the year ended December 31, 1988, was $30,000. The only change in the retained earnings account, other than for net income, was a deduction for cash dividends declared and paid.

2 During the year the company issued an additional 4,000 shares of common stock at $9 per share.

3 A comparison of property, plant, and equipment at the end of each year shows:

| | December 31 | | Increase |
	1987	1988	(decrease)
Cost of property, plant, and equipment	$280,000	$346,000	$66,000
Accumulated depreciation	62,000	57,000	(5,000)
Net property, plant, and equipment	$218,000	$289,000	$71,000

Equipment with an original cost of $15,000 and a current book value of $6,000 was sold during 1988 for $8,500. Equipment purchased during 1988 totaled $22,000. The remaining increase in property, plant, and equipment resulted from the purchase of land ($12,000 cost) and a factory building (? cost).

Required:

Prepare a statement of cash flows for Lancaster Co. for the year ended December 31, 1988. Use the indirect method to determine net cash flow provided by operating activities (i.e., reconcile from net income to net cash flow from operations by adjusting net income for noncash items, nonoperating gains and losses, and changes in current assets and current liabilities).

P11-4 *Preparation of Statement of Cash Flows*

Springer Co. has never presented a statement of cash flows. The company wants you to prepare this year's statement. The company provides you with the following data:

Springer Co.
Statement of Income
For the Year Ended August 31, 1988

Revenues:		
Fees Earned		$560,000
Gain on Sale of Equipment		4,500
Total Revenues		$564,500
Expenses:		
Salaries Expense	$462,000	
Rent Expense	41,500	
Depreciation Expense	3,000	
Insurance Expense	2,500	
Interest Expense	6,500	
Income Tax Expense	17,000	532,500
Net Income		$ 32,000

Springer Co.
Balance Sheets
August 31,

	1987	1988
Assets		
Current Assets:		
Cash	$ 51,000	$ 66,400
Accounts Receivable	38,000	63,100

	1987	1988
Prepaid Insurance	800	1,500
Total Current Assets	$ 89,800	$131,000
Equipment	91,000	73,000
Less Accumulated Depreciation	(18,000)	(14,000)
Total Assets	$162,800	$190,000

Liabilities and Stockholders' Equity

	1987	1988
Current Liabilities:		
Rent Payable	$ 1,900	$ 14,600
Salaries Payable	3,700	8,900
Income Taxes Payable	21,800	30,000
Total Current Liabilities	$ 27,400	$ 53,500
Bonds Payable	100,000	100,000
Total Liabilities	$127,400	$153,500
Stockholders' Equity:		
Common Stock, $1 par	$ 5,000	$ 5,400
Paid-in Capital in Excess of Par	14,800	16,000
Retained Earnings	15,600	15,100
Total Stockholders' Equity	$ 35,400	$ 36,500
Total Liabilities and Stockholders' Equity	$162,800	$190,000

Other information:

1 The only change in retained earnings for the year ended August 31, 1988, other than net income, is due to the declaration and payment of cash dividends.

2 During the year ended August 31, 1988, the company issued 400 shares of common stock at $4 per share.

3 There were no purchases of equipment in 1987 or 1988.

Required:

1 Prepare a schedule determining the cash flow from operating activities, using the direct method.

2 Prepare a statement of cash flows for the year ended August 31, 1988.

P11-5 *Cash from Operations*
Comparative balance sheets and an income statement for Rancocas Company are presented below and on the following page. Subtotals for current assets, current liabilities, and so on are omitted.

Rancocas Company
Balance Sheets
December 31,

	1987	1988
Assets		
Cash	$ 15,000	$103,000
Accounts Receivable	8,000	12,000
Inventories	26,000	22,000
Prepaid Assets—Insurance	7,000	3,000
Equipment	152,000	152,000
Accumulated Depreciation—Equipment	(48,000)	(68,000)
Total Assets	$160,000	$224,000

	1987	1988
Liabilities and Stockholders' Equity		
Accounts Payable (owed to inventory suppliers)	$ 18,000	$ 17,000
Interest Payable	-0-	400
Rent Payable	2,000	-0-
Notes Payable—due 1990	-0-	60,000
Total Liabilities	$ 20,000	$ 77,400
Common Stock, $5 par value	80,000	100,000
Paid-in Capital in Excess of Par	19,000	23,600
Retained Earnings	41,000	23,000
Total Liabilities and Stockholders' Equity	$160,000	$224,000

The company's income statement for 1988 shows:

Net Sales		$450,000
Cost of Goods Sold		300,000
Gross Profit		$150,000
Operating Expenses:		
Salaries Expense	$117,600	
Insurance Expense	4,000	
Rent Expense	24,000	
Depreciation Expense	20,000	
Interest Expense	2,400	168,000
Net Income (Loss)		$ (18,000)

Required:

1 Determine cash flow from operating activities for 1988, using the direct method.

2 Prepare a reconciliation of net income to net cash flow from operating activities.

P11-6 *Statement of Cash Flows*

The following are comparative balance sheets for Conversion Company as of December 31, 1987 and December 31, 1988. Also presented is the income statement for the year ended December 31, 1988.

Conversion Company
Balance Sheets
December 31,

	1987	1988
Assets		
Current Assets:		
Cash	$ 83,000	$ 102,000
Accounts Receivable	117,000	111,000
Inventory	160,000	180,000
Prepaid Insurance	18,000	25,000
Total Current Assets	$378,000	$ 418,000
Property, Plant, and Equipment:		
Land	$ 80,000	$ 210,000
Buildings	280,000	380,000
Equipment	60,000	60,000
Less Accumulated Depreciation	(48,000)	(68,000)
Total Property, Plant, and Equipment	$372,000	$ 582,000
Total Assets	$750,000	$1,000,000

	1987	1988
Liabilities and Stockholders' Equity		
Current Liabilities:		
Accounts Payable	$165,000	$ 200,000
Salaries Payable	38,000	30,000
Income Taxes Payable	17,000	23,000
Total Current Liabilities	$220,000	$ 253,000
Note Payable—due 1993	-0-	130,000
Total Liabilities	$220,000	$ 383,000
Stockholders' Equity:		
Common Stock, $10 par	$ 50,000	$ 50,000
Retained Earnings	480,000	580,000
Treasury Stock	-0-	(13,000)
Total Stockholders' Equity	$530,000	$ 617,000
Total Liabilities and Stockholders' Equity	$750,000	$1,000,000

Conversion Company
Statement of Income
For the Year Ended December 31, 1988

Net Sales	$2,400,000
Cost of Goods Sold	1,800,000
Gross Profit	$ 600,000
Other Expenses:	
Advertising	$ 54,000
Salaries	310,000
Depreciation	20,000
Insurance	24,000
Income Taxes	92,000
Total Other Expenses	$ 500,000
Net Income	$ 100,000

Additional information:

1 All accounts receivable arise from the sale of merchandise to creditors on account.

2 There were no sales of property, plant, or equipment during 1988.

3 Additional land was acquired on December 31, 1988 in exchange for a note due in 1993.

4 On July 1, 1988, the company reacquired 1,000 shares of its common stock for $13 per share. The shares are being held as treasury stock.

5 Accounts payable includes only amounts owed to inventory suppliers.

Required:

1 Prepare a schedule determining the cash flow from operating activities, using the direct method.

2 Prepare a statement of cash flows for the year.

P11-7 *Preparation of Statement of Cash Flows*

The following are comparative balance sheets of Shaburn Co. at December 31, 1989 and December 31, 1988. Also presented is the company's statement of income for the year ended December 31, 1989.

Shaburn Co.
Balance Sheets
December 31,

	1988	1989
Assets		
Current Assets:		
Cash	$ 50,000	$174,000
Accounts Receivable	80,000	112,000
Inventories	62,000	96,000
Total Current Assets	$192,000	$382,000
Property, Plant, and Equipment:		
Land	$ 80,000	$ 37,000
Buildings	125,000	125,000
Equipment	76,000	95,000
Accumulated Depreciation	(40,000)	(41,000)
Total Property, Plant, and Equipment	$241,000	$216,000
Total Assets	$433,000	$598,000
Liabilities and Stockholders' Equity		
Current Liabilities:		
Accounts Payable	$ 42,000	$ 64,000
Income Taxes Payable	20,000	50,000
Total Current Liabilities	$ 62,000	$114,000
Bonds Payable	100,000	100,000
Long-term Notes Payable	15,000	20,000
Total Liabilities	$177,000	$234,000
Stockholders' Equity:		
Preferred Stock, $10 par value	$ 80,000	$ 40,000
Common Stock, $5 par value	110,000	150,000
Paid-in Capital in Excess of Par—Common Stock	36,000	36,000
Retained Earnings	30,000	138,000
Total Stockholders' Equity	$256,000	$364,000
Total Liabilities and Stockholders' Equity	$433,000	$598,000

Shaburn Co.
Statement of Income
For the Year Ended December 31, 1989

Sales	$480,000
Gain on Sale of Land	10,000
Total Revenues	$490,000
Expenses:	
Cost of Goods Sold	$266,000
Depreciation	6,000
General and Administrative	45,000
Interest	8,000
Loss on Sale of Machine	3,000
Income Taxes	42,000
Total Expenses	$370,000
Net Income	$120,000

Additional information:

1 On January 1, 1989, the company's preferred stockholders converted 4,000 shares of preferred stock into common stock. Each share of preferred stock is convertible into two shares of common stock.

2 Land was sold during the year. The proceeds from the sale were $53,000.

3 A machine that had cost $21,000 when purchased in 1985 was sold during 1989 for $13,000. The book value of machine at time of sale was $16,000.

4 During 1989 the company purchased a new machine for $40,000.

Required:

1 Prepare a schedule determining the cash flow from operating activities, using the direct method.

2 Prepare the statement of cash flows for the year ended December 31, 1989.

P11-8 *Statement of Cash Flows*

Stockdale Company's management is confused over the apparently contradictory situation presented by their 1988 financial statements. The company's income statement for 1988 shows a $28,000 net loss. In addition, the company: a) declared and paid an $8,000 cash dividend, b) acquired a new rug-cleaning machine for $8,000 cash, and c) issued a 10 percent stock dividend during the year. However, comparative balance sheets indicate that the company's cash increased $14,000 during 1988.

You have been hired to explain to management how the apparently conflicting results above could have occurred. The company's management is concerned there may be errors in their income statement or balance sheets. In addition to the company's financial statements, which are reproduced below and on the following page, you are able to obtain the following information:

1 An old drape cleaner no longer needed by the company was sold during 1988 for $3,000. Accumulated depreciation on the old drape cleaner at time of sale was $6,000. The drape cleaner had cost $9,000 when originally purchased.

2 The 10 percent stock dividend occurred when the market value of the stock was $3 per share. Two thousand shares were distributed through the stock dividend. The remaining change in the common stock and paid-in capital accounts arose from the sale of shares for cash.

3 The bonds that were issued were sold at face.

Stockdale Company
Income Statement
For the Year Ended December 31, 1988

Cleaning Fees Earned		$ 55,000
Operating Expenses:		
Office Rent	$24,000	
Salaries	46,000	
Advertising	4,000	
Supplies	28,500	
Depreciation—Equipment	6,500	109,000
Income (Loss) Before Income Taxes		$(54,000)
Income Tax Refund		26,000
Net Income (Loss)		$(28,000)

Stockdale Company
Balance Sheets
December 31,

	1987	1988
Assets		
Current Assets:		
Cash	$ 8,000	$ 22,000
Accounts Receivable	17,000	12,000
Tax Refund Receivable	-0-	26,000
Supplies Inventory	21,000	4,000
Prepaid Rent	2,000	2,000
Total Current Assets	$48,000	$ 66,000
Equipment	61,000	60,000
Less Accumulated Depreciation	(18,500)	(19,000)
Total Assets	$90,500	$107,000
Liabilities and Stockholders' Equity		
Current Liabilities:		
Accounts Payable (owed to supplies vendors)	$16,000	$ 5,000
Salaries Payable	1,500	10,000
Income Taxes Payable	4,000	-0-
Total Current Liabilities	$21,500	$ 15,000
Long-term Liabilities:		
Bonds Payable	-0-	55,000
Total Liabilities	$21,500	$ 70,000
Stockholders' Equity:		
Common Stock, $1 par	$20,000	$ 23,500
Paid-in Capital in Excess of Par	6,500	13,000
Retained Earnings	42,500	500
Total Stockholders' Equity	$69,000	$ 37,000
Total Liabilities and Stockholders' Equity	$90,500	$107,000

Required:
Assist Stockdale's management in proving the accuracy of their financial statements and unraveling the confusion by preparing:
1 A schedule of cash flows from operating activities, using the direct method
2 A statement of cash flows

Business Decision Problem

Chen Engineering Company is a young and growing producer of electronic measuring instruments and technical equipment. You have been retained by Chen to advise in the preparation of a statement of cash flows. For the fiscal year ended October 31, 1988, you have obtained the following information concerning certain events and transactions of the company:

1 The amount of reported earnings for the year was $800,000.
2 Depreciation expense of $240,000 was included in the statement of income.
3 Uncollectible accounts receivable of $30,000 were written off against the allowance for uncollectible accounts.

4 A gain of $4,700 was realized on the sale of a machine; it originally cost $75,000, of which $25,000 was undepreciated at the time of sale.

5 On July 3, 1988, building and land were purchased for $600,000; Chen paid $100,000 in cash, issued stock having a market value of $200,000, and financed $300,000 by a long-term mortgage.

6 On August 3, 1988, $700,000 face value of Chen's 6 percent convertible bonds were converted into shares of common stock.

Required:

For each of the six preceding items, explain whether it is an inflow or outflow of cash, and what type of activity it represents. If the item did not affect cash, indicate the disclosure, if any, that should be made on the statement of cash flows.

12

FINANCIAL STATEMENT ANALYSIS

LEARNING OBJECTIVES

When you complete this chapter, you should be able to:

1 Prepare and evaluate a horizontal analysis of comparative financial statements.
2 Prepare and analyze common-sized financial statements.
3 Calculate and analyze ratios relating to current financial condition.
4 Calculate and analyze ratios relating to long-term financial condition.
5 Calculate and analyze ratios relating to profitability.
6 Describe required disclosures and the auditor's report that accompany the financial statements.

Financial statement analysis techniques will help statement readers identify a company's financial strengths and weaknesses. Financial statements often are complex documents with relevant information not immediately evident to the statement reader. Financial statement analysis attempts to simplify and reduce the statements to more understandable terms. Through simplification and rearrangement, financial statement analysis highlights important relationships among the items on the financial statements and points out significant trends that may be developing.

Financial statements cannot be analyzed in a vacuum. Analyzing financial statements requires a thorough understanding of the statements and what is behind the numbers that appear on them. An awareness of general economic and industry conditions influencing a company's operations and knowledge of the company's own particular policies, programs, and procedures are required.

There are a variety of different methods and procedures used in financial statement analysis. Analysis often takes the form of trend analysis—*intracompany* comparisons of a company's current financial statements with statements from prior years. Another popular analysis technique is *intercompany* comparisons, in which a company is compared with other companies in the industry and/or to an industry average.

Entire textbooks have been devoted to the topic of financial statement analysis. In this chapter the discussion will be limited to:

1 Comparative financial statements
2 Horizontal analysis emphasizing:
   a Increase or decrease in the absolute dollar balances between years
   b Percentage increase or decrease in the account balances between years
3 Common-sized financial statements where each component of a financial statement is expressed as a percentage of an important total appearing on the financial statement
4 Ratios emphasizing the relationship between key financial statement items
5 Disclosure of important financial information in notes to financial statements
6 Independent auditors' reports attesting to the fairness of the financial statements

COMPARATIVE FINANCIAL STATEMENTS

Virtually all large companies present comparative financial statements covering the current period and one or more preceding periods. Comparative financial statements allow the financial analyst to study changes in operating results and financial position. Analyzing comparative financial statements and appraising the direction and extent of changes occurring over time is one way of indicating company strengths and weaknesses.

Analyzing comparative statements requires some means of organizing the data for comparative purposes. The following sections discuss two such approaches: horizontal analysis and common-size analysis.

Horizontal Analysis

Exhibit 12-1 presents condensed financial statements (with horizontal analysis added) for Realquick, Inc. The horizontal analysis shows the dollar increase or decrease between 1987 and 1988 (Column A) and the percentage increase or decrease between 1987 and 1988 (Column B). Column A was computed by subtracting the 1987 dollar amount from the 1988 amount. Column B, showing the percentage change, was calculated by dividing the dollar change in Column A by the 1987 balance. Note that the percentages in Column B cannot be totaled; each is calculated using a different base (denominator).

Horizontal analysis highlights changes in account balances that the financial statement reader might otherwise overlook. Among the significant developments highlighted in Realquick's comparative statements in Exhibit 12-1 are:

1 Realquick's net sales decreased $437,000, or 4.8 percent between 1987 and 1988. Note that horizontal analysis does *not indicate why* total revenues decreased

EXHIBIT 12-1
Realquick, Inc.
Statements of Income and Retained Earnings
For the Years Ended December 31, 1987 and 1988

	(Dollars in thousands)		Horizontal analysis	
			Column A dollar increase (decrease)	Column B percentage increase (decrease)
	1988	1987		
Net Sales	$8,761	$9,198	$(437)	(4.8)%
Expenses:				
Cost of Goods Sold	$6,756	$7,160	$(404)	(5.6)
Selling and Administrative	1,354	1,328	26	2.0
Interest	191	230	(39)	(17.0)
Total Expenses	$8,301	$8,718	$(417)	(4.8)
Income Before Income Tax	$ 460	$ 480	$ (20)	(4.2)
Income Tax Expense	195	219	(24)	(11.0)
Net Income	$ 265	$ 261	$ 4	1.5
Retained Earnings, Jan. 1	2,187	2,019	168	8.3
Dividends Declared	103	93	10	10.8
Retained Earnings, Dec. 31	$2,349	$2,187	$ 162	7.4

Realquick, Inc.
Balance Sheets
December 31, 1987 and 1988

Assets

Current Assets	$2,029	$2,136	$(107)	(5.0)%
Property, Plant, and Equipment, net	3,130	3,000	130	4.3
Other Assets	35	18	17	94.4
Total Assets	$5,194	$5,154	$ 40	0.8

Liabilities and Stockholders' Equity

Current Liabilities	$1,174	$1,330	$(156)	(11.7)%
Long-term Debt	1,037	1,180	(143)	(12.1)
Total Liabilities	$2,211	$2,510	$(299)	(11.9)
Stockholders' Equity	2,983	2,644	339	12.8
Total Liabilities and Stockholders' Equity	$5,194	$5,154	$ 40	0.8

by $437,000. Is the revenue decrease the result of a) the discontinuance of some old product lines or sales territories, b) decreased sales volume from products and territories that are not being dropped, c) decreased selling prices, or d) some combination of these three? To answer these and other questions, the financial statement analyst needs more information than is provided by horizontal analysis. Management's discussion of operations in the annual report and selected financial statement ratios might be useful sources.

2 There was a significant decrease in Realquick's interest expense. Interest expense went down 17 percent (from $230,000 in 1987 to $191,000 in 1988). A plausible explanation would be a substantial reduction in Realquick's outstanding debt. A look at the horizontal analysis on the balance sheet confirms the significant debt reduction.

3 Another significant relationship for many financial statement analysts is dividends paid out in relation to net income. Net income increased 1.5 percent from 1987 to 1988, while dividends rose 10.8 percent. The effect this had on the dividend payout ratio will be examined later in the chapter.

In employing horizontal analysis, consider the absolute dollar change as well as the percentage increase or decrease. For example, on Realquick's balance sheet, the largest percentage change on the statement, a 94.4 percent increase in other assets, involved only a $17,000 absolute dollar increase—the smallest change on the statement. On the other hand, a decrease of only 4.8 percent in net sales on the income statement reflected a $437,000 dollar decrease—the largest dollar change on the statement.

Common-Sized Financial Statements

A *common-sized financial statement* expresses each item on the statement as a percentage of an important base amount on that statement. On the income statement, net sales is usually the base. On the balance sheet, each item is usually expressed as a percentage of total assets. Differences in the relative size of companies make intercompany comparisons of dollar amounts difficult. Common-sized statements, by expressing each component of the statement in percentage terms, makes intercompany analysis possible.

For example, Company B's net income is $10,000 for the year, while Company A, which is in the same industry, earned only $2,000 for the year. Are Company B's results of operations five times better than Company A's? Without some idea of the relative size of Company B versus Company A, it is impossible to make relevant comparisons of the two net income amounts. Consider for example the following condensed income statements for the companies:

Company B		Company A	
Net Sales	$200,000	Net Sales	$10,000
Expenses	190,000	Expenses	8,000
Net Income	$ 10,000	Net Income	$ 2,000

Conversion to common-sized statements yields:

Company B		Company A	
Net Sales	100%	Net Sales	100%
Expenses	95	Expenses	80
Net Income	5%	Net Income	20%

The common-sized income statements indicate Company B's performance is not five times better than Company A's. In fact, Company A's ability to maintain expenses at 80 percent of net sales (versus 95 percent for Company B) yields a profit margin of 20 percent. This is four times greater than the 5 percent of net sales earned by Company B. Another factor to consider is the effect of the size of each firm's total assets. The rate of return on total assets ratio to be discussed later in the chapter will include consideration of relative asset size.

Intercompany comparisons of common-sized financial statements only indicate where differences exist—the starting point of the analysis. Subsequent investigation is necessary to pinpoint the reasons for the difference.

In addition to financial statements, other sources of information available to the analyst include: the notes to the financial statements, the five-year summary of operations and financial data, and management's discussion and analysis of operations. All this information is available to the financial analyst in the company's annual report.

COMPUTER APPLICATION

Computerized data bases are very helpful in performing intercompany comparisons. The COMPUSTAT tapes, for example, contain financial statement data for a large number of publicly held companies. Use of computer programs to extract and analyze the data permits extensive intercompany comparisons to be done at low cost. Another important source is the National Automated Accounting Research System (NAARS), which contains annual reports of several thousand companies. Not only numerical data (e.g., financial statement numbers) but also verbal data (e.g., auditors' reports and notes to financial statements) may be accessed through this system.

It is crucial when performing intercompany comparisons that the companies be in the same business and that their financial statements be comparable. If the companies are not in the same line of business or they do not use the same methods to record revenue, value assets, and amortize expenses, then it is difficult, and in some cases impossible, to obtain valid comparisons. The preceding words of caution are applicable whether comparing common-sized financial statements as discussed in this section of the chapter or performing intercompany ratio analysis as discussed in the next section.[1]

RATIO ANALYSIS

A *ratio* is simply the relationship of one item to another. Ratio analysis of the financial statements focuses the analyst's attention on important relationships among financial statement items.

In performing ratio analysis, the student is advised to employ the following three-step approach.

---

[1]Average financial statement ratios for various industries are available from a number of sources (e.g., Dun & Bradstreet, Robert Morris Associates, Moody's, and Standard & Poor's).

First—select the ratios that are pertinent. Stockholders, creditors, management, potential investors, and others frequently use ratio analysis. The financial statement ratios that are relevant may vary due to the differing interests of the various statement readers.

Second—properly calculate the ratios that are relevant in the particular circumstances.

Third—remember the limitations of ratio analysis. Investigation is needed beyond the mere calculation of a ratio.

Current Financial Condition Ratios

Although of particular interest to short-term creditors and management, ratio analysis of a firm's current financial position is of value to almost all financial statement users. Ratio analysis of a company's current financial position can help provide answers to such questions as: Will the company be able to pay current debts as they become due? Is working capital sufficient to support operations without being excessive? Are the current assets maintained in the proper mix and are they being properly utilized by management? Is the company's current financial position improving, deteriorating, or unchanged from prior years?

Current Ratio (or Working Capital Ratio)   The *current ratio* is a measure of liquidity. It is a rough indicator of the ability of a company to pay its current obligations. The current ratio is computed as follows:

$$\text{Current Ratio} = \frac{\text{Current Assets}}{\text{Current Liabilities}}$$

The current ratio may provide a different perspective on liquidity than that obtained from merely comparing dollar amounts of working capital.[2] Consider the following two companies' current positions at the end of the accounting period.

	Previtz Co.	Mautz Co.
Current Assets	$16,000	$36,000
Current Liabilities	− 4,000	− 24,000
Working Capital	$12,000	$12,000
Current Ratio	4 to 1	1.5 to 1
	($16,000 ÷ $4,000)	($36,000 ÷ $24,000)

Both Previtz and Mautz have a $12,000 excess of current assets over current liabilities. However, the current ratios differ significantly. Previtz's 4 to 1 current ratio means the firm has $4 of current assets from which to realize funds necessary to pay off each dollar of current liabilities. Mautz with its 1.5 to 1 ratio has only $1.50 of current assets for each dollar of current liabilities.

In evaluating the adequacy of the current ratio it is important to consider the

---

[2]Working capital is the title given to the difference between current assets and current liabilities.

type of industry in which each company operates and the composition of the current assets. Perhaps Mautz's 1.5 current ratio is satisfactory because it is a restaurant with no receivables, a small inventory, and substantial cash available to pay obligations as they become due. Previtz, on the other hand, may be a manufacturer whose current assets are tied up in accounts receivable and inventories, with little cash available for short-term creditors. Or both companies could be in the same industry and Previtz's current ratio could be *too high,* rather than Mautz's being too low. Previtz may be holding unproductive cash balances and investments in receivables and inventory in excess of those needed to support regular operations.

At best the current ratio is only a crude measure of liquidity. The current ratio is particularly susceptible to window dressing, which decreases the usefulness of the ratio. *Window dressing* is the practice of executing certain transactions near the close of the accounting period for the purpose of presenting a more favorable financial statement ratio. Reconsider Mautz with its 1.5 to 1 current ratio. A payment of $18,000 to short-term creditors at year end would double its current ratio, without changing the company's $12,000 working capital total.

	Mautz before $18,000 payment	Mautz after $18,000 payment	
Current Assets	$36,000	$18,000	
Current Liabilities	− 24,000	− 6,000	
Working Capital	$12,000	$12,000	(Unchanged)
Current Ratio	1.5 to 1	3 to 1	(Doubled)
	($36,000 ÷ $24,000)	($18,000 ÷ $6,000)	

Has Mautz's liquidity position dramatically improved as indicated by the doubling of the current ratio? Based on the information presented, the answer is no. The doubling of the ratio is a window-dressing illusion.

Quick Ratio (or Acid Test Ratio) The *quick ratio* is another ratio used to measure liquidity. It often serves as a supplement to the current ratio.

$$\text{Quick Ratio} = \frac{\text{Cash} + \text{Marketable Securities} + \text{Accounts Receivable}}{\text{Current Liabilities}}$$

Only those assets (cash and marketable securities) currently available for paying liabilities, or those (accounts receivable) that will be available in the near future, are included in the quick ratio. Other current assets are excluded: inventories, because two or three steps (production, sale, and collection) are required before cash will be generated, and prepaid assets, which are not usually expected to be converted into cash.

In evaluating a firm's liquidity with either the quick ratio or the current ratio, the key factors are *when the cash will be available* and *how soon the current liabilities are due.* It's possible, for example, that an inventory item in demand by customers is more liquid than an overdue account receivable. The real significance of the liquidity ratios can be determined only by studying in detail the items that are included in the ratio calculations. A statement of cash flows may be more valuable in analyzing liquidity than either the quick ratio or the current ratio.

Average Collection Period The *average collection period* for accounts receivable serves as a measure of the liquidity of the receivables and also provides information on how efficiently management controls the firm's investment in receivables.

$$\text{Average Collection Period} = \frac{\text{Average Accounts Receivable (Net)}}{\text{Average Daily Sales}}$$

The numerator of the calculation usually is based on an *average* of the beginning and end of year net accounts receivable balances. *Average daily sales* is computed by dividing sales for the year by 360 days. If known, only credit sales (i.e., sales on account) should be used in determining average daily sales.

Consider the following data for Trown Co.:

Sales for the year (all credit sales)	$5,400,000
Average daily sales ($5,400,000 ÷ 360 days)	15,000
Net accounts receivable, beginning of year	850,000
Net accounts receivable, end of year	950,000
Average net receivables ($850,000 + $950,000) ÷ 2	900,000
Terms of sale	30 days

Trown's average accounts receivable is $900,000 and its average daily sales is $15,000.

$$\text{Average Collection Period} = \frac{\$900,000}{\$15,000} = 60 \text{ days}$$

On the average, 60 days elapse between the date of a sale by Trown and the time the cash is collected. Trown is taking twice the allowed 30-day term to collect its receivables. Further questions immediately come to mind: What was Trown's average collection period in the past? Has control over credit sales and collections deteriorated? Are there mitigating circumstances? Has Trown changed its credit terms recently? How does Trown's collection period compare to the average collection period for the industry?

Shortening the average collection period for a given sales level lowers the amount of working capital invested in accounts receivable. On the other hand, too stringent a credit policy and too forceful a collection effort may result in a significant decrease in sales and profits. The extreme case would be no credit sales—all sales for cash. The result would be a zero days average collection period and no funds invested in accounts receivable. However, a tremendous amount of sales would be lost from customers who are not willing or able to pay cash at date of sale. In today's economy, except for certain retail sales and professional services, the majority of sales are on account.

Average Number of Days' Supply in Inventory The *average number of days' supply in inventory* measures how quickly inventory is being sold. It can indicate whether a company has symptoms of excessive inventories or the possibility of lost sales from too little inventory. Generally, the smaller the supply of inventory on hand for a given level of sales, the better the job management is doing in handling the firm's investment in inventory. Preventing excess inventories from building up not only improves liquidity but also lowers the cost of carrying inventory. Working capital invested in inventories is minimized, inventory storage and insurance costs are reduced, and the risk of inventory obsolescence is lessened. Inventory levels should not be cut to the point where shortages occur frequently. Sales, customers, and profits will be lost if management fails to maintain adequate supplies of items demanded by customers.

The calculation of the ratio is:

$$\frac{\text{Average Number of Days'}}{\text{Supply in Inventory}} = \frac{\text{Average Inventory}}{\text{Average Daily Cost of Goods Sold}}$$

On the average, Jay Company has a 90-day supply of inventory on hand based on the following:

Cost of goods sold for the year	$2,880,000
Average daily cost of goods sold	
($2,880,000 ÷ 360 days)	8,000
Inventory, beginning of year	660,000
Inventory, end of year	780,000
Average inventory ($660,000 + $780,000) ÷ 2	720,000

$$\frac{\text{Average Number of Days'}}{\text{Supply in Inventory}} = \frac{\$720,000}{\$8,000} = 90 \text{ days}$$

Intracompany and intercompany comparisons would help put into perspective Jay's 90-day supply of inventory on hand. Physical volume, inventory prices, and inventory valuation methods (LIFO, FIFO, Weighted Average Cost) all can affect the calculation of the number of days' supply of inventory. In addition, if the information is available, the average number of days' inventory on hand should be determined for each separate product line and department in the company. Excessive inventories for some product lines or departments may be obscured in a single, overall calculation for the firm.

Long-Term Financial Condition Ratios

A company's long-term financial condition is of importance to both stockholders and long-term creditors. In addition to the horizontal and common-sized analysis techniques previously described, ratios are used by analysts to evaluate long-term financial strengths and weaknesses.

Ratio of Debt to Total Assets   The percentage of total assets provided by creditors is shown by the *ratio of debt to total assets*.

$$\text{Ratio of Debt to Total Assets} = \frac{\text{Total Debt}}{\text{Total Assets}}$$

Subtracting the ratio of debt to total assets from 100 percent yields the *ratio of stockholders' equity to total assets*. The two ratios show the relative importance of borrowed funds and owners' investment. From the creditors' standpoint, a large percentage of debt usually is viewed as an unfavorable financial condition. Consider Dee Company's financing:

Total Assets	$4,000,000
Total Liabilities	3,600,000
Total Stockholders' Equity	400,000

$$\text{Ratio of Debt to Total Assets} = \frac{\$3,600,000}{\$4,000,000} = 90\%$$

The high proportion of borrowed funds (90 percent) means Dee is already locked into significant fixed interest charges and faces the necessity of repaying the substantial amount of debt as it matures. If Dee is unable to meet its debt-related obligations, the company may be forced into bankruptcy. Although stockholders would absorb losses before creditors, the relatively small stockholders' investment in Dee provides very little cushion, or margin of safety. Losses totaling only 10 percent of net assets would wipe out the entire $400,000 stockholders' equity. After that, the creditors would be left holding the bag.

Owners view the relationship between debt and equity financing with mixed emotions. Relatively high amounts of debt increase the possibility the company will be forced into bankruptcy through inability to meet debt-payment obligations. Also, if additional financing is needed, the chances of the company borrowing the funds will be significantly reduced if it already is heavily in debt. On the other hand, if the majority of financing arises from borrowed funds, the owners have invested only a relatively small amount of their own funds. If the company is unsuccessful, the owners have minimized their potential losses. For example, the stockholders of Dee, with a book value investment of only $400,000, own a firm with total assets of $4,000,000—ten times the book value of their investment.

Another point stockholders and potential investors should consider is leverage. *Leverage* is the technique of borrowing funds at a fixed interest charge with the hope of earning more on the borrowed funds than their interest cost. That leverage can bring substantial benefits to the owners will be illustrated in the discussion of rate of return on stockholders' equity.

Times Interest Earned Ratio   If forced liquidation of the company is to be avoided, earnings must be sufficient to cover fixed interest costs on borrowed funds. The *times interest earned ratio* is an indicator to long-term creditors of the ability of the company to meet required interest payments. The times interest earned ratio is computed as follows:

$$\frac{\text{Times Interest}}{\text{Earned Ratio}} = \frac{\text{Operating Income}}{\text{Interest Expense}}$$

Note that operating income in the numerator of the ratio is net income plus interest expense and income tax expense. Since income taxes apply only to income remaining *after* deducting interest expense, a company's ability to cover interest costs is not directly affected by income taxes.

The calculation of the times interest earned ratio for Realquick, Inc. (see Exhibit 12-1) would be:

	1988	1987
Income before taxes (per Exhibit 12-1)	$460,000	$480,000
Interest expense (per Exhibit 12-1)	+ 191,000	+ 230,000
Operating income (before interest and income taxes)	$651,000	$710,000

[handwritten annotation: = net income + income tax expense]

For 1987,

$$\frac{\text{Times Interest}}{\text{Earned Ratio}} = \frac{\$710,000}{\$230,000} = 3.1$$

and for 1988

$$\frac{\text{Times Interest}}{\text{Earned Ratio}} = \frac{\$651,000}{\$191,000} = 3.4$$

One result of Realquick's previously discussed reduction in outstanding debt in 1988 (and consequent decrease in interest expense) was an improvement in the times interest earned ratio from 3.1 to 3.4. However, interest is not paid out of earnings. A company cannot mail to creditors slips of paper marked "earnings." Interest obligations to creditors must be paid in *cash*. The numerator of the times interest earned ratio is an earnings measure. It is *not* a measure of cash available for interest payments. To determine a company's ability to meet continuing interest payments, liquidity as well as adequacy of earnings must be analyzed.

Book Value per Share of Common Stock Financial statement analysts sometimes use book value per share, and changes in it from year to year, as a measure of a company's net worth. The book value per share of stock often is compared to market price per share to determine if the company's stock is selling for more or less than book value. In addition, legal contracts occasionally state that book value per share is to be used as the basis for valuing certain transactions. For example, book value per share may be used to value a company's stock when no market price is available.

If there is no preferred stock outstanding, the *book value per share of common stock* is computed by determining the ratio of total stockholders' equity recorded on the books to the number of common shares outstanding.

$$\text{Book Value per Share of Common Stock} = \frac{\text{Book Value of Common Stockholders' Equity}}{\text{Common Shares Outstanding}}$$

Recall that stockholders' equity is the residual amount after liabilities have been subtracted from total assets. Since most assets are recorded on the books at cost or depreciated cost (not current market value or liquidation value), *book value per share* does *not* indicate the current market value per share nor the amount per share that would be realized if the company actually were liquidated.

To calculate book value per common share when preferred stock also is outstanding, it is first necessary to determine the portion of total stockholders' equity belonging to the preferred stockholders. The portion will depend on the rights of the preferred stockholders: Is the preferred stock cumulative or noncumulative, is the preferred stock participating or nonparticipating, does the preferred stock have a redemption value greater than its par value?

For example, consider the following stockholders' equity for Neanderthal Corporation:

9% Preferred Stock; cumulative and nonparticipating; $100 par value; redeemable at $105 per share; authorized 100,000 shares, 20,000 shares issued and outstanding	$ 2,000,000
Common Stock; $10 par; 360,000 shares authorized, issued, and outstanding	3,600,000
Paid-in Capital in Excess of Par	5,520,000
Retained Earnings	7,180,000
Total Stockholders' Equity	$18,300,000

If the dividends on the cumulative preferred stock have not been paid for the current year and are in arrears for the prior two years, the portion of total equity assigned to preferred stock would be as follows:

Redemption value ($105 per share × 20,000 shares)	$2,100,000
Current year's dividend (9% × $100 par × 20,000 shares)	180,000
Two years' dividends in arrears ($180,000 × 2)	360,000
Equity allocated to preferred stock	$2,640,000

The remaining $15,660,000 ($18,300,000 total minus $2,640,000 allocated to preferred) of stockholders' equity is the equity of the common stockholders. Thus, the book value per share of common stock for Neanderthal Corporation would be computed as:

$$\text{Book Value per Share of Common Stock} = \frac{\$15,660,000 \text{ Book Value of Common Equity}}{360,000 \text{ Common Shares Outstanding}}$$

$$= \$43.50$$

Profitability Ratios

The generation of a satisfactory level of income is a major objective of an enterprise operated for profit. Profits are a key element in determining the return stockholders will earn on their investment. Thus, profitability is a crucial factor used by investors in evaluating management's effectiveness. There are a number of ratios available to measure a firm's profitability. We will discuss: rate of return on total assets, rate of return on common stockholders' equity, earnings per share, price-earnings ratio, and dividend payout.

Rate of Return on Total Assets Management is provided with resources (assets) to run the company. One measure of the effectiveness of management in utilizing the resources entrusted to it is the ratio of earnings to total assets (i.e., the rate of return on total assets).

Profit margin and asset turnover are the two components of *rate of return on total assets*. The *profit margin* indicates the percentage of each sales dollar remaining as earnings after all expenses, other than interest, have been deducted. The *asset turnover* measures the intensity with which assets are used during the period. In other words, asset turnover indicates the dollars of net sales generated per dollar of assets. Certain types of firms (e.g., furriers and jewelers) have a low asset turnover but a relatively high profit margin. Other firms (e.g., grocery stores) are characterized by very low profit margins but an extremely high asset turnover.

Combining the profit margin and asset turnover components yields the following calculation for rate of return on total assets:

$$\frac{\text{Rate of Return}}{\text{on Total Assets}} = \underbrace{\frac{\text{Net Income} + \text{Interest Expense}}{\text{Net Sales}}}_{\text{PROFIT MARGIN}} \times \underbrace{\frac{\text{Net Sales}}{\text{Average Assets}}}_{\text{ASSET TURNOVER}}$$

Note the add-back of interest expense to net income in the numerator of the profit margin calculation. The objective of the rate of return on total assets is to compare earnings on total assets (*before* deducting expenses related to the financing of those assets) to the amount of total assets. Interest expense is not an operating expense, but a financing cost associated with borrowed funds. Thus, to determine earnings before deduction of financing costs, interest expense must be added back to net income. Average assets in the denominator of the asset turnover computation normally is an average of the total assets at the beginning and the end of the year.

Based on the financial statement data in Exhibit 12-1, Realquick's rate of return on total assets for 1988 was 8.8 percent.

$$\frac{\text{Rate of Return}}{\text{on Total Assets}} = \frac{\text{Net Income} + \text{Interest Expense}}{\text{Sales}} \times \frac{\text{Net Sales}}{\text{Average Assets}}$$

$$= \frac{\$265,000 + \$191,000}{\$8,761,000} \times \frac{\$8,761,000}{\$5,174,000}$$

$$= 5.20\% \text{ profit margin } \times 1.69 \text{ asset turnover}$$
$$= 8.8\%$$

Realquick earned approximately five cents in income (before deducting interest expense) on each dollar of sales revenue in 1988. Each dollar of Realquick's average assets during 1988 generated $1.69 in net sales. Multiplying the 5.20 percent profit margin by the 1.69 asset turnover yields an 8.8 percent rate of return on total assets for Realquick in 1988.

Care should be exercised in using the rate of return on total assets to measure performance. The average assets amount used in the denominator of the ratio reflects the *book value* of a firm's assets, not the fair market value of the assets. Thus, accounting rates of return, if not properly interpreted, can be a misleading measure of performance.

Rate of Return on Common Stockholders' Equity The *rate of return on common stockholders' equity* compares income available for common stockholders to the book value of the common stockholders' equity. The ratio is calculated as follows:

$$\frac{\text{Rate of Return on}}{\text{Common Stockholders' Equity}} = \frac{\text{Net Income } - \text{ Preferred Dividends (if any)}}{\text{Average Common Stockholders' Equity}}$$

Note the ratio is based on book values—not current market prices nor the amount an individual shareholder paid to acquire shares of common stock. Again, one should exercise care in interpreting this return.

Due to *leverage*, the rate of return earned by common stockholders can differ significantly from the rate of return on total assets. Recall that leverage was defined as the practice of raising resources from creditors (or preferred stockholders) with the hope that the assets acquired with the borrowed money will earn enough to pay the fixed interest cost (or preferred dividend) and leave an excess, which accrues to the common stockholders. A company successfully employs leverage to the extent that the rate of return earned on the assets acquired is *more* than the fixed cost of the borrowed funds. However, leverage is a two-edged sword. If the rate of return earned is *less* than the fixed cost of the borrowed funds, the common stockholders will suffer.

For example, consider the following data for Zee Company:

Average assets for the year	$1,000,000
Average common stockholders' equity for the year	400,000
8% cumulative preferred stock, $100 par, 1,000 shares authorized, issued, and outstanding	100,000
Annual preferred dividends (8% × $100 par × 1,000 shares)	8,000
Total liabilities (6 percent interest cost)	500,000
Interest expense (6% × $500,000)	30,000
Net income	70,000

$$\begin{aligned}\text{Rate of Return} \atop \text{on Total Assets} &= \frac{\text{Net Income} + \text{Interest Expense}}{\text{Average Assets}} \\ &= \frac{\$70,000 + \$30,000}{\$1,000,000} = 10\%\end{aligned}$$

$$\begin{aligned}\text{Rate of Return on Common} \atop \text{Stockholders' Equity} &= \frac{\text{Net Income} - \text{Preferred Dividends}}{\text{Average Common Stockholders' Equity}} \\ &= \frac{\$70,000 - \$8,000}{\$400,000} = 15.5\%\end{aligned}$$

The use of leverage produced a 15.5 percent return for the common stockholders, even though the company earned only a 10 percent return on total assets.[3] The common stockholders benefited since Zee earned a higher return (10 percent) on the funds provided by the creditors and preferred stockholders than the 6 percent and 8 percent cost associated with the debt and preferred stock.

Earnings Per Share   *Earnings per share* is a measure that permits the individual stockholders (or any other interested party) to view the earnings of the firm in relationship to a single share of stock ownership. If a stockholder reading an income statement observes that the company's net income last year was $819,000, the stockholder may ask, "What is my share of those profits?" Thus, in addition to knowing net income on a total basis, it is desirable to know net income on a per share basis.

In its simplest form, earnings per share is determined as follows:

$$\text{Earnings per Share} = \frac{\text{Net Income for the Period,} \atop \text{minus Preferred Stock Dividends (if any)}}{\text{Weighted Average Number of Common Shares} \atop \text{Outstanding During the Period}}$$

The numerator of the earnings per share ratio is the *net earnings available for the common stockholders*. Because preferred stockholders must receive dividends before any dividends are paid to common stockholders, net earnings available for common stockholders is defined as net income minus preferred dividends. Net income for the period can be found on the income statement, and preferred stock dividends, if any, would be found on the statement of retained earnings. The denominator, the *weighted average number of common shares outstanding during the period,* weights shares by the portion of the year they were outstanding.

For example, assume Largay Co. earned $42,000 net income and paid preferred stock dividends of $12,000 during 1988. Net income available for common

---

[3]The rate of return on total assets formula used here is a simplified version of the one previously presented. Net sales, which appeared in both the denominator of the profit margin and in the numerator of the asset turnover, has been eliminated.

stockholders is $30,000 ($42,000 net income minus $12,000 preferred dividends). On January 1, 1988, 7,000 shares of common stock were outstanding, and an additional 9,000 shares were issued on September 1, 1988. The weighted average shares outstanding are calculated as follows:

Shares	×	Portion of year outstanding	=	Weighted average
7,000 outstanding for entire year	×	$\dfrac{12\text{ months}}{12\text{ months}}$	=	7,000
9,000 issued on September 1	×	$\dfrac{4\text{ months}}{12\text{ months}}$	=	3,000
Weighted average number of shares outstanding				10,000

$$\text{Earnings per Share} = \frac{\$30,000}{10,000} = \$3.00$$

The above earnings per share calculation was based on the weighted average number of common shares *actually outstanding*. Some companies also have *commitments* to issue common stock. One type of commitment is convertible securities. Convertible bonds, for example, give the bondholder the right to exchange the bonds for a specified number of common shares. If this conversion were to occur, the number of shares of common stock outstanding would increase. Earnings would also be affected as interest charges (and their tax effect) would be eliminated in the calculation of net income. Stock options are a second type of commitment for the future issuance of common shares. Options give the holder the right to purchase a given number of shares at a specified price. If a company has issued convertible securities or stock options in the past, it is commited to issue additional common shares if and when the holders of these commitments choose to exercise their rights. Where these commitments exist, two earnings per share figures may be required: one known as *primary earnings per share* and a second known as *fully diluted earnings per share*. These two measures give recognition to the *potentially outstanding* common shares related to the commitments, as well as to *actually outstanding* common shares. Details of these calculations are left for advanced courses.

Price-Earnings Ratio   The price-earnings ratio is calculated as follows:

$$\text{Price-Earnings Ratio} = \frac{\text{Market Price per Share of Common Stock}}{\text{Earnings per Share of Common Stock}}$$

The *price-earnings ratio* (P/E ratio) provides a means of expressing earnings per share in relation to *market price* per share. A company with earnings per share of $3 and a market price of $15 per share would have a price-earnings ratio of 5 ($15 divided by $3).

The average P/E ratio for all firms can fluctuate widely over time as general economic conditions change. Even at a given time, significant differences exist between the P/E ratios of individual firms. Given a choice between S Company with a price-earnings ratio of 10 and G Company with a P/E of 20, which company's stock should an investor purchase?

S Company requires an investment of $10 for each $1 of current earnings. On the other hand, it is necessary to invest $20 in G Company for each $1 of its current earnings. At first glance, S Company may appear to be the better investment alternative. However, that is not necessarily the correct choice. When acquiring stock, a person is investing in a company's future—not its past. One of the most important factors determining the current market price of a company's common stock is the expected *future* earnings. If an investor expects G Company's (Growth Company's) earnings to increase at a substantially faster rate than S Company's (Stable Company), an investor may be quite willing to buy G Company's stock—even though it has a comparatively high current P/E ratio. The projected substantial earnings growth for G Company (and accompanying expected increase in dividends and/or market price of the stock) may or may not actually occur.

Dividend Payout   There are two ways investors actually receive the return they earn on their investment: 1) cash dividends, and 2) selling the stock at a higher price than when it was originally acquired. The *dividend payout ratio* expresses the relationship between cash dividends and earnings.

The ratio is calculated as follows:

$$\text{Dividend Payout Ratio} = \frac{\text{Cash Dividends}}{\text{Net Income}}$$

Stockholders do not automatically receive cash dividends equal to their share of the company's earnings. A company's board of directors makes the determination of how much is to be paid as cash dividends. Among the factors the board of directors must evaluate in setting a cash dividend policy are: 1) investment opportunities for the earnings if the earnings are reinvested in the company, 2) amount of pressure by stockholders for current cash dividends, 3) cash available for dividends (remember *cash*, not earnings, is what is paid to stockholders), and 4) related income tax considerations.

Growth companies usually have low dividend payout ratios. Growth companies, which have extremely profitable investment opportunities for funds, tend to reinvest most of their earnings in the company rather than pay cash dividends. For stockholders interested primarily in company growth (and the expected accompanying increase in the market price of the company's stock), a low dividend payout ratio is acceptable. However, other stockholders may be dependent on periodic cash dividends. For them, only stocks with a high dividend payout are acceptable investments.

Realquick's dividend payout ratio for 1988 was 38.9 percent.

$$\text{Dividend Payout Ratio} = \frac{\$103,000 \text{ Cash Dividends (per Exhibit 12-1)}}{\$265,000 \text{ Net Income (per Exhibit 12-1)}}$$

$$= 38.9\%$$

Dividend yield is closely related to dividend payout; it expresses the current cash dividend as a percentage of market price of the stock. Dividend yield is calculated by dividing cash dividends per share by market price per share. Based on a market price of $35 per share on December 31, 1988 and $1.40 dividends per share, Realquick's dividend yield was 4 percent.

Summary of Financial Ratios

The ratios discussed in the preceding section of the chapter are summarized in Exhibit 12-2.

In using ratios to analyze a company's financial strengths and weaknesses, remember that:

1 Ratios can be influenced by management's selection among alternative accounting principles available in the circumstances.

2 Intercompany ratio comparisons are usually valid only among firms in the same industry.

3 Most ratios are based on book values, not current values. Book-value-based ratios may not be relevant information for some financial statement readers' decisions.

4 The single year and two-year comparisons illustrated in the chapter may be inadequate to identify intracompany trends. Computation of ratios for five years or more may be necessary to detect trends.

5 Ratios by product line, division, branch, geographic sales territory, and so on, may be more valuable than ratios for the total company.

6 Ratios are merely indicators of financial strengths and weaknesses. They point out significant relationships where further investigation of the underlying conditions may be warranted.

DISCLOSURE IN FINANCIAL REPORTING

Analysts need more information about a company than the dollar account balances appearing directly in the financial statements. Additional details about the financial statement amounts and descriptive information that cannot be expressed in numbers is presented by means of *supplemental schedules* (tables of data) and *notes*. This additional information may well cover more pages than the financial statements themselves.

Summary of Significant Accounting Policies

As its name implies, the summary of significant accounting policies discloses the accounting methods that the firm employs. Typical areas covered include the

EXHIBIT 12-2 Summary of Financial Ratios

Ratio	Formula for calculation	Primary significance
Current financial condition		
1. Current Ratio	$\dfrac{\text{Current assets}}{\text{Current liabilities}}$	Rough indicator of liquidity.
2. Quick Ratio	$\dfrac{\text{Cash} + \text{marketable securities} + \text{accounts receivable}}{\text{Current liabilities}}$	Comparison of current assets quickly convertible into cash with current debts.
3. Average Collection Period	$\dfrac{\text{Average accounts receivable (net)}}{\text{Average daily sales}}$	Indicates effectiveness of management's control over credit sales and collections.
4. Average Number of Days' Supply in Inventory	$\dfrac{\text{Average inventory}}{\text{Average daily cost of goods sold}}$	Indicates management's ability to control the investment in inventory.
Long-term financial condition		
5. Ratio of Debt to Total Assets	$\dfrac{\text{Total debt}}{\text{Total assets}}$	Indicates percentage of assets financed by creditors; it shows the extent to which leverage is being used.
6. Times Interest Earned	$\dfrac{\text{Operating income}}{\text{Interest expense}}$	Measures ability of company to cover required interest payments.
7. Book Value per Share of Common Stock	$\dfrac{\text{Book value of common stockholders' equity}}{\text{Common shares outstanding}}$	Expresses book value on a per share basis.
Profitability		
8. Rate of Return on Total Assets	$\dfrac{\text{Net income} + \text{interest expense}}{\text{Net sales}} \times \dfrac{\text{Net sales}}{\text{Average assets}}$	Measures management's ability to generate earnings on total assets.
9. Rate of Return on Common Stockholders' Equity	$\dfrac{\text{Net income} - \text{preferred dividends (if any)}}{\text{Average common stockholders' equity}}$	Compared to rate of return on total assets, it indicates if leverage was effectively utilized.
10. Earnings per Share	$\dfrac{\text{Net income for the period} - \text{preferred stock dividends (if any)}}{\text{Weighted average number of common shares outstanding during the period}}$	Expresses net income on a per share basis.
11. Price-Earnings Ratio	$\dfrac{\text{Market price per share of common stock}}{\text{Earnings per share of common stock}}$	Indicates investors' cost of acquiring each dollar of current earnings.
12. Dividend Payout	$\dfrac{\text{Cash dividends}}{\text{Net Income}}$	Measures percentage of earnings paid out in current dividends.

Handwritten annotation next to item 8: Profit after taxes + interest exp. / total assets methods of accounting for inventories, depreciation, income taxes, and so forth. The format is a brief paragraph discussing each item. An example appears in the Goodyear Tire and Rubber Company annual report in Appendix B at the end of the book.

Notes to the Financial Statements

The notes to the financial statements provide explanatory and descriptive information about the company and its financial activities. The notes include details on the components of inventory and property, plant, and equipment; interest rates, maturities, and security on long-term debt; information on pension plans and other employee benefit programs; and descriptions of major unusual transactions. The notes are a very important part of the financial report; an analyst must study the notes as well as the financial statements.

The topics covered in the notes vary somewhat among companies depending on the type of business and the complexity of the firm's financial activities. In the Goodyear report in Appendix B, notes cover subjects ranging from a discussion of the disposition of certain subsidiary companies to a discussion of contingent liabilities.

THE AUDITOR'S REPORT

The financial statements, and the notes and other disclosures that accompany them, are prepared by the management of the company. Readers of the financial statements are somewhat hesitant to accept as accurate statements prepared by the company's own management. To add credibility to the statements, most organizations hire independent auditors to perform an examination (an *audit*) of the statements and to reach a conclusion (known as an *auditor's opinion*) on whether the statements and accompanying notes fairly present the financial position of the company and the results of its operations. If the auditor concludes affirmatively, the auditor's report takes the form shown in Exhibit 12-3. The wording of this report is standard, and few variations will be seen.

Examine the auditor's report in Exhibit 12-3. Note first that it is addressed to the board of directors of the company. In the first paragraph of the letter, the auditor:

1 Identifies (in the first sentence) the name of the company, the financial statements involved, and the reporting period.

2 States (in the second sentence) that an audit was carried out, using professional auditing standards, based on the auditor's professional judgment as to the nature and extent of testing.

In the second paragraph, the auditor gives a professional opinion that:

1 The financial statements constitute a fair presentation of the company's

EXHIBIT 12-3 Auditor's Report

To the Board of Directors of American National Corporation:

We have examined the consolidated statement of condition of AMERICAN NATIONAL CORPORATION (a Delaware corporation) and subsidiaries as of December 31, 1986, and 1985, and the related consolidated statements of income, changes in stockholder's equity and changes in financial position for each of the three years in the period ended December 31, 1986. Our examinations were made in accordance with generally accepted auditing standards and, accordingly, included such tests of the accounting records and such other auditing procedures as we considered necessary in the circumstances.

In our opinion, the financial statements referred to above present fairly the financial position of American National Corporation and subsidiaries as of December 31, 1986, and 1985, and the results of their operations and the changes in their financial position for each of the three years in the period ended December 31, 1986, in conformity with generally accepted accounting principles applied on a consistent basis.

Arthur Andersen & Co.

Chicago, Illinois,
January 13, 1987

---

financial position, the results of its operations, and the changes in its financial position (cash flow).

2 Acceptable accounting methods have been used (". . .in conformity with generally accepted accounting principles").

3 The company has not changed its accounting methods ("applied on a consistent basis").

This is known as an *unqualified opinion*, which means that the auditor does not take exception to any significant item in the financial statements. In cases where the auditor does take exception to something, the format of the report changes; this is known as a *qualified opinion*.

SUMMARY

Financial statement analysis attempts to reduce complex financial statements to more understandable terms and to highlight important relationships among the items on the statements. In performing financial statement analysis it is important to select an analysis technique that will provide relevant input for the particular decision being made, properly perform the necessary computation, and understand the limitations of the method of analysis being employed. Financial statement analysis is only a tool. It represents one source of information for the decision maker. Financial statement analysis will not provide complete answers to all statement readers' questions. It is only a starting point for further investigation.

Learning Objective 1: Prepare and evaluate a horizontal analysis of comparative financial statements.

Horizontal analysis of comparative financial statements presents both dollar and percentage changes in each financial statement item. This analysis focuses on trends within the company and is a major tool for *intracompany* comparisons.

Learning Objective 2: Prepare and analyze common-sized financial statements.

Common-sized financial statements present each statement item as a percentage of an important base amount (such as net sales or total assets). The common-sized statements are useful for both *intracompany* and *intercompany* comparisons.

Learning Objective 3: Calculate and analyze ratios relating to current financial condition.

These ratios include the current ratio, quick ratio, average collection period, and average days' supply in inventory. They focus on the adequacy of current resources to meet current obligations and on the utilization of current assets in the firm's operations.

Learning Objective 4: Calculate and analyze ratios relating to long-term financial condition.

These ratios include the ratio of debt to total assets, the times interest earned ratio, and the book value per share of common stock. They focus on the firm's capital structure and ability to meet interest payments.

Learning Objective 5: Calculate and analyze ratios relating to profitability.

These ratios include the rate of return on total assets, rate of return on common stockholders' equity, earnings per share, price-earnings ratio, and dividend payout. They focus on the relationship of profits to assets, equity, and market price, and the distribution of profits to stockholders.

Learning Objective 6: Describe required disclosures and the auditor's report that accompany the financial statements.

More information is needed about a company than can be expressed directly by the financial statement account balances. Supplemental schedules and notes disclose details about financial statement amounts and descriptive information that can't be expressed in numbers. The independent auditor's report lends credibility to management-prepared financial statements.

KEY TERMS

Auditor's report	Price-earnings ratio
Average collection period	Quick ratio
Average days' supply in inventory	Rate of return on common
Book value per share of common stock	stockholders' equity
Common-sized financial statements	Rate of return on total assets
Current ratio	Ratio of debt to total assets
Dividend payout	Summary of significant accounting
Earnings per share	policies
Horizontal analysis	Times interest earned
Notes to the financial statements	

REVIEW QUESTIONS

1 "Financial statements present all the information needed by statement readers. Why is financial statement analysis necessary?" Comment on the preceding statements.

2 "Financial statement analysis is easy. To be a financial analyst all one needs is a list of formulas and a calculator to help with the computations." Do you agree with any parts of the preceding statements? Are there any parts of the preceding statements with which you disagree?

3 Distinguish between intracompany analysis and intercompany analysis.

4 When performing horizontal analysis of comparative financial statements, Simple Co. has adopted the policy that any percentage increase or decrease in excess of 5 percent must be further investigated and satisfactorily explained. Company policy calls for ignoring percentage increases or decreases of less than 5 percent. Comment on the wisdom of Simple's policy.

5 Bragadoseo Co.'s net income in 1988 of $1,000,000 is twice the $500,000 net income earned by Small Fry Co. in 1988. Both companies are in the same industry. Is Bragadoseo twice as profitable? What types of financial statement analyses would help you answer the question?

6 Some textbooks and financial analysts state "2 to 1" as the standard current ratio and "1 to 1" as the standard quick ratio. What dangers can you see in comparing a specific company's ratios against these two standards?

7 Is it possible for a transaction to change a company's current ratio without altering the company's dollar balance of working capital? If so, give an example.

8 Why is the quick ratio usually considered a better indicator of liquidity than the current ratio?

9 Joyce Bradford, manager in charge of credit and collections for TD Company, is responsible for maintaining a reasonable collection period for accounts receivable. What advantages are gained by shortening the average collection period? Are there any dangers in cutting the average collection period too drastically?

10 Teenpop Co. has 80 percent of its $1,000,000 total assets financed by interest-bearing long-term debt which matures proportionally over the next several years. As a banker would you be willing to grant an additional $300,000, three-year loan to Teenpop? Why or why not?

11 George H. Roller bought 100 shares of Pipe & Stem Company for $30 per share two years ago. During the past year the company issued a 2 for 1 stock split. The book value per share is now $20. George figures he has lost $10 per share on his investment. Comment on George's calculation.

12 Contrast the rate of return on total assets to the rate of return on common stockholders' equity. How is each ratio calculated? What is the purpose of each ratio?

13 "Leverage" often is described as a two-way street or double-edged sword. Define leverage. Why is the preceding description appropriate?

14 What is the purpose of the earnings per share measure? In its simplest form, how is earnings per share calculated?

15 Ojibway Industries is considered a growth company. Is Ojibway likely to have a price-earnings (P/E) ratio higher, lower, or equal to the average P/E ratio for all companies? Is Ojibway likely to have a relatively high or low dividend payout ratio? Explain your answers.

16 "The role of the independent auditor is to prepare the financial statements and accompanying notes." Evaluate this statement.

17 I. M. Boss, president of Thump Corporation, begins his discussion with the newly hired independent auditors with the following statement: "Here's how I want you to do the audit. . ." Based on the wording of the first paragraph of the auditor's report, how are the independent auditors likely to reply to the president's statement?

18   In the second paragraph of the auditor's report, the auditor states an opinion. In an unqualified report, what would be covered in the auditor's opinion?

EXERCISES

E12-1   George Ferguson and Ray Snyder are partners in the F & S Equipment Company. George supplied most of the funds when the company was formed and Ray serves as manager. Ray presents George with the condensed comparative statement of income shown below. George is impressed with the significant increase in sales and net income over the prior year. How would you view the comparative performance? Present horizontal analysis and common-sized statements to support your views.

F & S Equipment Company
Condensed Statement of Income
For the Years Ended December 31,

	1988	1987
Net Sales	$1,300,000	$820,000
Cost of Goods Sold	1,170,000	697,000
Gross Profit	$ 130,000	$123,000
Other Expenses	115,000	70,000
Income Before Extraordinary Item	$ 15,000	$ 53,000
Extraordinary Item—Excess of insurance proceeds over cost of inventory destroyed by flood	65,000	-0-
Net Income	$ 80,000	$ 53,000

E12-2   Karen Smith, owner of Engineering Supply Company, is comparing her company's comparative statements of income with those of Finegan Parts Company, a close competitor. Ms. Smith is well satisfied since her firm's sales and net income in both years are greater than her competitor's. In addition, the dollar increase in both sales and net income for Engineering Supply exceeds the dollar increases for Finegan Parts Company. The condensed comparative statements of income follow. Both companies use similar accounting methods for inventory, depreciation, and so on.

	Engineering Supply Company		Finegan Parts Company	
	This year	Last year	This year	Last year
Net Sales	$20,000,000	$18,000,000	$5,400,000	$5,000,000
Cost of Goods Sold	12,100,000	10,800,000	3,186,000	3,000,000
Gross Profit	$ 7,900,000	$ 7,200,000	$2,214,000	$2,000,000
Other Expenses	6,000,000	5,400,000	1,620,000	1,500,000
Net Income	$ 1,900,000	$ 1,800,000	$ 594,000	$ 500,000

Required:
Prepare common-sized statements of income for both companies for both years. Comment on the common-sized statements. To be able to better compare the two

companies' performances, what additional financial statement item would you like to know?

E12-3 The following information is available for D.D.E., Inc.:

	1989	1988
Accounts receivable (net)	$ 180,000	$ 150,000
Cost of goods sold	2,430,000	1,966,000
Current assets total (cash + receivables + inventory)	480,000	386,000
Income tax expense	100,000	80,000
Interest expense	30,000	30,000
Inventory	256,000	284,000
Net income	110,000	93,000
Net sales	2,970,000	2,428,000
Total current liabilities	160,000	174,000

Required:
For 1989, calculate the following ratios for D.D.E.:
1 Current ratio
2 Quick ratio
3 Average collection period (use a 360-day year)
4 Average number of days' supply in inventory (use a 360-day year)
5 Times interest earned

E12-4 Presented below are selected ratios for Reegan Co.:

	1989	1988	1987
Current ratio	3.2	3.0	2.9
Quick ratio	.4	.9	1.5
Average collection period for receivables	60 days	47 days	28 days
Number of days' supply in inventory	76 days	49 days	38 days
Debt to total assets ratio	85%	80%	70%
Number of times interest earned	2	4	7

The company's credit terms have been "net 30" for the last three years. Based only on the ratios presented, would you make a short-term loan to the company? Would you invest in the company's forthcoming ten-year bond issue? Discuss your answers.

E12-5 Comet Co. and Donner Co. both sell sleighs. Comet made a $48,000 special bargain purchase of inventory on December 28, 1988 from Rudolph Co., which was going out of business. Comet had no immediate need for the items acquired from Rudolph, but decided it couldn't pass up the ridiculously low purchase price. Comet uses the FIFO inventory valuation method. Donner Co. uses LIFO. Based on the following data, calculate and compare the number of days' supply of inventory on hand for the two companies. Be sure to comment on the appropriateness of your calculations.

	Comet Co.	Donner Co.
Inventory, Jan. 1, 1988	$ 80,000	$ 44,000
Inventory, Dec. 31, 1988	144,000	52,000
Cost of goods sold for 1988	1,440,000	1,728,000

E12-6 Presented below is the stockholders' equity for King Co. and Bracket, Inc. Compute the book value per common share for each company. Preferred dividends have not been declared by Bracket for the current year and are in arrears for the preceding three years.

	King Co.	Bracket, Inc.
8% Cumulative Nonparticipating Preferred Stock; $100 par, redeemable at par	$ -0-	$ 2,500,000
Common Stock; $10 par	6,100,000	8,000,000
Paid-in Capital in Excess of Par	4,850,000	1,275,000
Retained Earnings	12,230,000	26,725,000
Total Stockholders' Equity	$23,180,000	$38,500,000

E12-7 Selected data for two companies are as follows:

	Jan's Jewelers	Pete's Pizzeria
Net income	$ 160,000	$ 300,000
Interest expense	40,000	-0-
Net sales	1,200,000	15,000,000
Average assets	1,000,000	1,000,000

Which of the two companies had the higher rate of return on total assets? Is it due to a better profit margin, asset turnover, or both?

E12-8 Complete the chart below by filling in the amounts that should appear on the blank lines. Evaluate each company's success in employing leverage.

Company	Average assets	Average liabilities	Interest expense (8 percent)	Net income	Rate of return on total assets	Rate of return on stockholders' equity
True	$1,000,000	$750,000	$60,000	$100,000	_____%	_____%
Bore	1,000,000	-0-	-0-	100,000	_____	_____
Gold	1,000,000	500,000	40,000	20,000	_____	_____

E12-9 The following information is available for Flyer, Inc.:

Net income for 1988	$5,400,000
Cash dividends declared and paid on common stock during 1988	$ 135,000
Common shares outstanding Jan. 1, 1988	2,400,000 shares

Additional common shares issued on July 1, 1988	600,000 shares
Market price per share on December 31, 1988	$ 64.00

Required:
Calculate: 1) earnings per share, 2) price-earnings ratio, 3) dividend payout, and 4) dividend yield. Use the number of shares outstanding at December 31, 1988 to calculate the dividend yield. Use weighted average number of shares outstanding during the year to calculate earnings per share. Based upon your calculations, would you guess that Flyer is an established, stable company or a growth company?

PROBLEMS

 P12-1 *Horizontal Analysis and Common-Sized Statements*
Presented below are comparative statements of income for Morris Corporation:

Morris Corporation
Statement of Income
For the Years Ended August 31,

	1989	1988
Net Sales	$1,200,000	$1,000,000
Cost of Goods Sold	900,000	800,000
Gross Profit	$ 300,000	$ 200,000
Other Expenses:		
Depreciation	$ 32,000	$ 32,000
Advertising	80,000	40,000
Administrative & General	30,000	28,000
Income Tax	62,000	34,000
Total Other Expenses	$ 204,000	$ 134,000
Net Income	$ 96,000	$ 66,000
Earnings per Share	$ 4.00	$ 2.75

Required:
Prepare horizontal analysis columns (dollar and percentage) and common-sized statement columns. Comment on each item on the comparative statements of income and the results of your additional horizontal and common-sized statement analysis. Round all percentages to the nearest tenth of a percent (e.g., 45.58% = 45.6%).

P12-2 *Ratio Analysis*
The following is a condensed balance sheet for NBF Corporation. Net sales for the year totaled $270,000,000. The gross profit was $198,000,000. Accounts receivable (net) decreased $1,140,000 during the year. NBF's sales are all on account with terms of "net 30." The average inventory during the year was $56,000,000.

NBF Corporation
Condensed Balance Sheet
June 30, 1988

Current Assets:		Current Liabilities:	
Cash	$ 11,870,000	Accounts Payable	$ 16,000,000
Accounts Receivable		Income Taxes	
(net)	23,430,000	Payable	21,520,000
		Total Current	
Inventory	58,500,000	Liabilities	$ 37,520,000
Total Current Assets	$ 93,800,000	Long-term Debt	37,480,000
Property, Plant, &		Total Liabilities	$ 75,000,000
Equipment (net)	156,200,000		
		Stockholders' Equity	175,000,000
		Total Liabilities	
		and Stockholders'	
Total Assets	$250,000,000	Equity	$250,000,000

Required:

1 Calculate: a) the current ratio, b) quick ratio (to nearest hundredths, e.g., 1.782 = 1.78), c) average collection period for receivables, d) average number of days' supply in inventory, and e) debt to total assets ratio (to nearest tenth of a percent). Use a 360-day year.

2 If NBF reduces its accounts payable to $6,600,000 by paying $9,400,000 to creditors, which of the ratios calculated in requirement (1) would be affected? Recalculate the ratios that would be affected.

P12-3 *Analysis of Liquidity*

High Flyer, Inc. wants to obtain a short-term loan from the local bank. Management believes its chances of obtaining the loan would be increased if the company could improve the appearance of its liquidity position. Working capital accounts for High Flyer at December 18, 1988 are listed below. Also presented is a list of suggestions to improve the company's liquidity position.

Current Assets:	
Cash	$ 886,000
Marketable Securities	695,000
Accounts Receivable (net of	
$37,000 Allowance for	
Uncollectible Accounts)	949,000
Inventory	1,100,000
Prepaid Rent	50,000
Total Current Assets	$3,680,000
Current Liabilities:	
Accounts Payable	$1,469,000
Note Payable—due in 6 months	500,000
Income Taxes Payable	331,000
Total Current Liabilities	$2,300,000

Suggestions to improve liquidity position:

1 Sell marketable securities with carrying value on books of $130,000 for current market price of $210,000.

2 Pay $200,000 of accounts payable balance.
3 Hold special inventory clearance sale to sell $500,000 of inventory for $450,000.
4 Collect $400,000 of the accounts receivable balance.
5 Declare and distribute a 3 for 1 stock split.
6 Purchase $248,000 of inventory on account.
7 Write off a $6,000 account receivable deemed uncollectible.
8 Sell for cash some old unused machinery at a $22,000 loss.

Required:
1 Calculate as of December 18, 1988 the following: a) dollar amount of working capital, b) current ratio, and c) quick ratio.
2 Indicate the effect (increase, decrease, or no effect) each of the above suggestions would have on the three calculations in requirement (1). The first one is presented below as an example.

Suggestion number	Dollar amount of working capital	Current ratio	Quick ratio
1	Increase	Increase	Increase

P12-4 *Calculation of Various Ratios*

	Average assets	Average common stockholders' equity	Net sales	Interest expense	Net income
Case 1	$2,000,000	$2,000,000	$6,000,000	$ -0-	$180,000
Case 2	2,000,000	1,000,000	3,000,000	90,000	210,000
Case 3	2,000,000	500,000	4,000,000	120,000	60,000
Case 4	5,000,000	5,000,000	_____	-0-	_____
Case 5	_____	_____	7,000,000	_____	200,000

	Profit margin	Asset turnover	Rate of return on total assets	Rate of return on common stockholders' equity
Case 1	_____ %	_____ times	_____ %	_____ %
Case 2	_____	_____	_____	_____
Case 3	_____	_____	_____	_____
Case 4	2.0	_____	3.0	3.0
Case 5	_____	2 times	8.0	10.0

Required:
For each case above, fill in the blank lines. There are no preferred dividends.

P12-5 *Calculation of Various Ratios*
The following are the statement of income, statement of retained earnings, and balance sheet for Fantasy, Inc. Assume accounts receivable, inventories, total assets, and common stockholders' equity are unchanged from the previous year. The market price of Fantasy's common stock at the end of the year was $6.30 per share.

Fantasy, Inc.
Statement of Income
For the Year Ended December 31, 1988

Net Sales	$9,972,000
Cost of Goods Sold	7,200,000
Gross Profit	$2,772,000
Selling, Administrative, and General	
Expenses (excluding interest and taxes)	$2,028,000
Interest Expense	200,000
Income Tax Expense	245,400
Total Other Expenses	$2,473,400
Net Income	$ 298,600
Earnings per Share	$ .45

Fantasy, Inc.
Statement of Retained Earnings
For the Year Ended December 31, 1988

Retained Earnings,		
beginning of year		$1,081,240
Net Income		298,600
		$1,379,840
Less Cash Dividends:		
Preferred Stock	$ 16,000	
Common Stock	175,840	191,840
Retained Earnings,		
end of year		$1,188,000

Fantasy, Inc.
Balance Sheet
December 31, 1988

Current Assets:		Current Liabilities:	
Cash	$ 308,750	Accounts Payable	$1,897,300
Marketable Securities	730,000	Income Taxes Payable	180,200
Accounts Receivable (net)	831,000	Total Current Liabilities	$2,077,500
Inventory	1,600,000	Long-term Debt, Bonds Payable	2,500,000
Prepaid Assets	165,875	Total Liabilities	$4,577,500
Total Current Assets	$3,635,625	Stockholders' Equity:	
Property, Plant, & Equipment		8% Preferred Stock, $100 par	$ 200,000
(net of Accumulated Depr.)	4,674,375	Common Stock, $2.50 par	1,570,000
		Paid-in Capital in Excess of Par	774,500
		Retained Earnings	1,188,000
		Total Stockholders' Equity	$3,732,500
		Total Liabilities and	
Total Assets	$8,310,000	Stockholders' Equity	$8,310,000

(handwritten left margin: Quick assets — Cash, Marketable Securities, Accounts Receivable (net))

Required:
Calculate for Fantasy, Inc. each of the following for 1988:
1 Current ratio
2 Quick ratio
3 Average collection period (use 360-day year)

(handwritten right margin: common shares = 1,570,000 / 2.50)

    4 Average number of days' supply in inventory (use 360-day year)
    5 Ratio of debt to total assets (round to nearest tenth of a percent)
    6 Times interest earned
    7 Book value per share of common stock
    8 Rate of return on total assets
    9 Rate of return on common stockholders' equity (assuming total stockholders' equity is unchanged from the beginning of the year)
    10 Price-earnings ratio
    11 Dividend payout ratio, and dividend yield for common stockholders (round to nearest tenth of percent)

P12-6 *Calculation of Ratios*
Using the financial statements for Goodyear Tire and Rubber Company in Appendix B at the back of the book, calculate the ratios listed below for 1986. Round all percentages to the nearest tenth of a percent. Use a 360-day year.
1 Current ratio
2 Quick ratio
3 Average collection period for accounts and notes receivable
4 Average number of days' supply in inventory
5 Ratio of debt (including deferred taxes) to total assets
6 Rate of return on common stockholders' equity
7 Price-earnings ratio (use $36 market price per share)

P12-7 *Analysis of Earnings Performance*
Management of Build-Up Co. is concerned about the company's slow growth in net income. Most earnings are reinvested in the company. Thus, total assets have steadily increased over the last several years. However, with earnings remaining relatively stable, both the rate of return on total assets and the rate of return on common stockholders' equity are continually decreasing. Management believes the information presented below may help explain the company's disappointing performance:

	Accounts receivable	Inventory	Net sales	Cost of goods sold
1985	$199,920	$431,800	$3,022,750	$2,478,800
1986	280,000	548,200	3,085,200	2,520,000
1987	373,600	720,800	3,096,000	2,538,000
1988	453,600	834,400	3,168,000	2,592,000

Required:
1 Using only the information above, what tentative conclusions would you reach as to the possible cause of the company's disappointing results? Present appropriate ratios to support your conclusions. Use a 360-day year.
2 Considering your tentative conclusions in requirement (1), how would you proceed in your investigation? List several specific steps you would take to confirm your tentative conclusions.

P12-8 *Reconstruction of Financial Statements*
The partially completed statement of income and balance sheet for Brickville Sales, Inc. are presented on the following page:

Brickville Sales, Inc.
Statement of Income
For the Year Ended December 31, 1988

Net Sales		$? *750,000*
Cost of Goods Sold		? *580,000*
Gross Profit		$? *170,000*
Other Expenses,		
excluding interest	$110,000	
Interest Expense	15,000	125,000
Net Income		$? *45,000*
Earnings per Share		$ 4.90

Brickville Sales, Inc.
Balance Sheet
December 31, 1988

Current Assets:		
Cash		$? *125,000*
Accounts Receivable (net)		175,000
Inventory		? *150,000*
Total Current Assets		$ 450,000
Equipment	$? *700,000*	
Less Accumulated		
Depreciation	150,000	? *550,000*
Total Assets		$? *1,000,000*
Current Liabilities:		
Accounts Payable		$ 100,000
Accrued Liabilities		? *50,000*
Total Current Liabilities		$? *150,000*
Long-term Debt		? *250,000*
Stockholders' Equity:		
Common Stock	$200,000	
Retained Earnings	? *400,000*	? *600,000*
Total Liabilities and		
Stockholders' Equity		$1,000,000

(handwritten margin notes:
total assets = total liab. + stockholders' Equity
Asset turnover = Net sales / average total assets = .75 (1,000,000) = 750,000
net sales = .75 (1,000,000) = 750,000)

The following ratios are known for Brickville Sales:

1 Current ratio = 3 to 1
2 Quick ratio = 2 to 1
3 Ratio of total debt to assets = 40 percent
4 Profit margin = 8 percent
5 Rate of return on total assets = 6 percent
6 Asset turnover = .75

Assume the amount of total assets is unchanged from the previous year.

Required:

Solve for all the question marks on Brickville Sales' financial statements.

P12-9 *Reading an Annual Report*

The financial section of Goodyear's 1986 annual report is presented in Appendix B at the back of the book. Refer to the report and answer the following questions (assume questions apply to 1986 unless otherwise indicated):

1 What is the amount of earnings per share for income from continuing operations for the year?
2 Which inventory methods does the company use?
3 Did the auditors issue an unqualified opinion?
4 What lines of business is the company involved in?
5 Has net sales increased every year during the four-year period 1983–1986?
6 What was the earnings per share for income from continuing operations for the second quarter of the year?
7 What is the interest rate on the promissory notes due 1991–2000?
8 According to management, what caused the 60 percent decrease in worldwide income from continuing operations this year?
9 What line of business accounted for the largest portion of sales—tires; or industrial rubber, chemical, and plastic products?
10 Which depreciation method is used by the company?
11 What is the balance in the allowance for doubtful accounts at the end of the year?
12 What was the dollar amount of foreign taxes included in the provision for income taxes that is currently payable?
13 How much was rental expense for 1986?
14 What is the amount of cash dividends paid on common stock for the year?
15 How many shares of common stock are held in the treasury at year end?

Business Decision Problem

Presented in Exhibit 12-4 are financial statements of Get Rich Quick Co. and Fast Buck, Inc. Both companies operate in the same industry, and their common stock has a market price of $20 per share.

Required:
Using only the information given and the appropriate ratio calculations, discuss each of the questions below. Show ratio calculations to support each answer. Round all percentages to the nearest tenth of a percent. If averages are required in a ratio, assume the item has not changed over the year (i.e., use the ending balance as the average). Also assume a 360-day year.
1 Which of the two companies is in a more "liquid" position?
2 Which company probably has the better chance of successfully issuing a large additional amount of bonds payable? Assume both companies would offer the same interest rate.
3 If an investor is primarily concerned with receiving a high current yield, which common stock would seem to be the better investment?
4 Which company earned the higher rate of return on total assets? Was it due to profit margin, or asset turnover, or both?
5 Which company was more successful using leverage?

EXHIBIT 12-4
Financial Statements for Business Decision Problem

Statements of Income

	Get Rich Quick Co.	Fast Buck, Inc.
Net Sales	$29,376,000	$49,860,000
Cost of Goods Sold	22,932,000	36,855,000
Gross Profit	$ 6,444,000	$13,005,000
Selling, Administrative, and General		
Expense (excluding interest & taxes)	$ 2,443,920	$ 7,464,800
Interest Expense	350,000	1,000,000
Income Tax Expense	1,650,000	2,050,000
Total Other Expenses	$ 4,443,920	$10,514,800
Net Income	$ 2,000,080	$ 2,490,200
Earnings per Share	$ 2.00	$ 2.49

Statements of Retained Earnings

Retained Earnings, beginning of year	$ 7,341,520	$ 8,427,820
Net Income	2,000,080	2,490,200
Cash Dividends, $.40 and $1.50 per		
share, respectively	(400,000)	(1,500,000)
Retained Earnings, end of year	$ 8,941,600	$ 9,418,020

Balance Sheets

Assets

Current Assets:		
Cash	$ 1,000,000	$ 620,000
Marketable Securities	2,480,000	840,000
Accounts Receivable (net)	2,040,000	5,540,000
Inventory	3,503,500	8,190,000
Prepaid Assets	176,500	810,000
Total Current Assets	$ 9,200,000	$16,000,000
Property, Plant, and Equipment (net		
of Accumulated Depreciation)	10,384,000	19,614,285
Total Assets	$19,584,000	$35,614,285

Liabilities and stockholders' equity

Current Liabilities:		
Accounts Payable	$ 2,769,000	$ 8,721,000
Rent Payable	449,000	75,000
Income Taxes Payable	462,000	1,204,000
Total Current Liabilities	$ 3,680,000	$10,000,000
Long-term Debt, Bonds Payable	2,500,000	12,000,000
Total Liabilities	$ 6,180,000	$22,000,000
Common Stockholders' Equity	13,404,000	13,614,285
Total Liabilities and		
Stockholders' Equity	$19,584,000	$35,614,285

Condensed Statements of Cash Flow

Cash Provided:		
From Operations	$ 2,650,000	$ 1,148,000
Other	1,800,000	3,970,000
Total Cash Provided	$ 4,450,000	$ 5,118,000
Cash Used	2,990,000	5,250,000
Increase (Decrease) in Cash	$ 1,460,000	($ 132,000)

13

ISSUES IN
FINANCIAL REPORTING

LEARNING OBJECTIVES

When you complete this chapter, you should be able to:

1 Calculate and record income tax expense.
2 Explain the impact of timing differences on income tax expense.
3 Prepare an income statement that includes one or more special items (discontinued operations, extraordinary items, and the cumulative effect of a change in accounting principle).
4 Account for transactions with international customers and suppliers.
5 Present foreign assets and liabilities on a balance sheet.
6 Describe the concept of inflation and its impact on financial statements.
7 Differentiate between constant dollar and current value reporting.

Throughout the past several chapters we have discussed the accounting for a variety of routine transactions and their impact on revenues, expenses, assets, and liabilities. In this chapter, we consider the treatment of income taxes, the presentation of certain nonroutine transactions (including international transactions), and reporting the impact of inflation on financial statements. Each of these has been a controversial issue in accounting in recent years.

INCOME TAXES AND INCOME REPORTING

Income taxes are assessed on the taxable income of a corporation according to rates established by Congress. The tax laws have been modified frequently;

sometimes these changes involve corporate tax rates. At the time of this writing, federal corporate tax rates[1] are:

15 percent on taxable income up to $50,000
25 percent on taxable income from $50,001 to $75,000
34 percent on taxable income over $75,000

In a simple case, income tax expense is calculated by applying the rates to taxable income. For example, if a corporation has taxable income of $60,000, its income tax expense of $10,000 is calculated as follows:

$$
\begin{array}{lr}
\$50{,}000 \text{ at } 15\% = & \$\ 7{,}500 \\
\underline{10{,}000} \text{ at } 25\% = & \underline{\ 2{,}500} \\
\underline{\$60{,}000} & \underline{\$10{,}000}
\end{array}
$$

If the company's accounting income before taxes equals its taxable income, the entry to record income tax expense would be:

Income Tax Expense	10,000	
Income Taxes Payable		10,000
To record income taxes		
for the year.		

The determination and recording of income tax expense becomes more difficult when accounting income and taxable income are not equal.

Timing Differences

A difference between accounting income and taxable income will exist if different rules are used for these two income calculations. For example, management might choose to use straight line depreciation for accounting income and an accelerated method for taxable income. This will cause accounting income and taxable income to differ in a given year. An example is presented in Exhibit 13-1. The company has annual income, before depreciation and income tax, of $50,000. An asset costing $90,000, with estimated life of three years and zero salvage value, is purchased on January 2, 1988. Straight line depreciation is used for accounting purposes, while an accelerated method is used for income tax purposes. A corporate tax rate of 25 percent is assumed.

Note that, while there are annual differences between accounting depreciation and tax depreciation, the three-year totals are equal. This situation, where there are year-to-year differences but the same total, is called a *timing difference*. Observe that when timing differences exist, annual income tax expense (which is based on accounting income) differs from income taxes payable (which is based on taxable income). The difference, which may be positive or negative, is called *deferred*

---

[1]Many states also have a corporate tax. In many illustrations, exercises, and problems, a flat rate (such as 40%) is used for convenience, and may be assumed to reflect both federal and state taxes.

EXHIBIT 13-1
Depreciation Timing Differences

Accounting purposes

Year	Accounting income before depreciation and tax	Straight line depreciation	Accounting income before tax	Income tax expense (assuming 25% rate)
1988	$ 50,000	$30,000	$20,000	$ 5,000
1989	50,000	30,000	20,000	5,000
1990	50,000	30,000	20,000	5,000
	$150,000	$90,000	$60,000	$15,000

Tax purposes

Year	Taxable income before depreciation	Tax depreciation	Taxable income	Income taxes payable (assuming 25% rate)	Increase in deferred taxes (income tax expense minus income taxes payable)
1988	$ 50,000	$45,000	$ 5,000	$ 1,250	$3,750
1989	50,000	30,000	20,000	5,000	-0-
1990	50,000	15,000	35,000	8,750	(3,750)
	$150,000	$90,000	$60,000	$15,000	$ -0-

income tax; it is recorded in a balance sheet account. In the example in Exhibit 13-1, the company recorded $15,000 more depreciation on its tax return in 1988 than it showed on its books. This extra depreciation on the tax return reduced its income tax payable by $3,750 ($15,000 × 25% tax rate). However, recording more depreciation in 1988 means that the company will have less depreciation to record in 1989 and 1990. The $3,750 reduction in income tax payable in 1988 will catch up with the company in 1989 and 1990, when income tax payable will exceed the income taxes expense based on book income. Thus, the company has not permanently reduced its income tax by $3,750, but has only deferred it to the future. At December 31, 1988, the $3,750 is shown on the balance sheet as a deferred income tax credit, awaiting recognition on the income statement in future years.

The journal entries that follow from the example in Exhibit 13-1 are shown below:

	1988		1989		1990	
Account titles	Debit	Credit	Debit	Credit	Debit	Credit
Income Tax Expense	5,000		5,000		5,000	
Deferred Income Tax		3,750		-0-	3,750	
Income Taxes Payable		1,250		5,000		8,750

The journal entries demonstrate the temporary nature of the deferred tax. The $3,750 credit balance created in 1988 reverses in 1990, when income tax payable exceeds income tax expense, and the deferred income tax account is reduced by a debit entry. By the end of 1990, when total accounting depreciation equals total tax depreciation, the deferred income tax balance is zero.

In the above example, taxable income (and hence income taxes payable) originally was less than accounting income (and income tax expense). This led to an initial credit balance in deferred taxes, which would usually appear in the liability section on the balance sheet. This presentation causes controversy because deferred tax credits are not liabilities; there is, at present, no obligation to the government for this amount. In other examples, taxable income may initially be more than accounting income (meaning that income taxes payable would be initially more than income tax expense), leading to an initial debit balance in the deferred tax account. Deferred tax debits are usually shown in the other assets section of the balance sheet. The growing size of deferred tax amounts on the balance sheet is another concern. While deferred taxes reverse for individual transactions, as demonstrated in Exhibit 13-1, new transactions creating new timing differences may continue to occur. For many companies, deferred taxes have grown to a significant item on the balance sheet.

Timing differences occur with considerable frequency. Many of the accounting alternatives discussed in the last several chapters are also alternatives for tax purposes. For accounting purposes, the objective of income determination is to match costs and revenues so as to present the performance of the firm to outside parties. For tax purposes, the firm's objective may be to minimize the amount of income taxes currently payable to the government. Since different objectives exist, different accounting methods are often chosen.

SPECIAL ITEMS ON THE INCOME STATEMENT

Certain special components of income are shown separately on the income statement. We briefly discuss three of these. *Discontinued Operations* presents data on major segments of the business that have been sold or phased out. *Extraordinary Items* are gains and losses that are very unusual and are not expected to recur in the foreseeable future. *Cumulative Effect of Change in Accounting Principle* is the adjustment necessary when a company changes from one acceptable method of accounting to another (e.g., from straight line to declining balance depreciation). These items are presented separately so that their special nature is recognized when year-to-year comparisons are made. They are reported *net of tax*; that is, their tax effect is deducted. For example, if the tax rate is 30 percent, an extraordinary gain of $100,000 would be presented as:

Extraordinary gain, net of $30,000 tax $70,000

The gain is reduced by the $30,000 tax that would be due on this element of income. Losses are treated in a similar manner. An extraordinary loss of $50,000 would be shown as:

Extraordinary loss, net of $15,000 tax $35,000

Since deduction of the $50,000 loss on the tax return reduces income taxes by $15,000, the reduction in net income is only $35,000.

Discontinued Operations

Firms often sell or close down significant segments of their business. To facilitate year-to-year comparisons of income, the operating results and the gains or losses from disposition of the discontinued activity are shown as a separate item on the income statement. Assume that at the beginning of 1988, Sample Company had four divisions: book publishing, manufacture of business forms, office equipment repair services, and retail shoe stores. During 1988, management decides to sell all the shoe stores and to leave that line of business. Late in 1988, the shoe stores were sold to another company at a gain of $100,000 (before taxes). The shoe stores had 1988 operating income of $47,000 (before taxes) up to the time of sale. With a 40 percent tax rate, the amount reported as discontinued operations would be:

Operating income for shoe stores prior to sale	$ 47,000
Gain on sale of store assets	100,000
	$147,000
Tax effect, at 40%	(58,800)
Discontinued operations, net of tax	$ 88,200

By presenting discontinued operations separately, it will be easier to compare 1988 to later years, when the shoe stores will no longer be part of the company's activities.

Extraordinary Items

As the name suggests, extraordinary items are events or transactions that, for this particular firm, are unusual and are not expected to recur in the foreseeable future. These criteria should be applied in a way that considers the environment of the particular firm. For example, having a building damaged by a hurricane would be very unusual and infrequent for a firm located in Minnesota, but not so unusual for a firm located on the Florida coast. Thus, this loss would be an extraordinary item for the Minnesota firm, but not for the Florida firm.

Gains and losses from the sale of investments, buildings, equipment, and other assets are usually not considered extraordinary items because these are not unusual transactions for any firm. Gains and losses from destruction of property via casualty (fire, storm, accident) may or may not be extraordinary, depending on how unusual and infrequent the particular casualty is. Exact criteria for extraordinary items are difficult to establish; judgment must be made in each case.

Change in Accounting Principle

A change in accounting principle occurs if a company decides that a different way of accounting for some item (e.g., a different inventory method) would provide a better way of reporting information on its financial statements. A change also occurs if accounting standards are changed to eliminate a particular alternative or to mandate a particular treatment.

When a change of accounting principle occurs, the total past impact of the change, net of tax, is presented on the income statement for the year the change is made. For example, assume that in 1988, Sample Company decides to change its depreciation method for all its assets from declining balance to straight line. Depreciation expense for 1988 would be reported using the new (straight line) method. In addition, an adjustment must be recorded for the difference between past depreciation taken under the old declining balance method and the depreciation that would have been taken in past years under the new straight line method. Assume this comparison is as follows:

| | Depreciation expense | | |
Year	Declining balance	Straight line	Difference
1983	$155,000	$ 70,000	$ 85,000
1984	140,000	68,000	72,000
1985	134,000	77,000	57,000
1986	147,000	90,000	57,000
1987	140,000	86,000	54,000
Totals	$716,000	$391,000	$325,000

Under the straight line method, depreciation during 1983–87 would have been lower by $325,000. This past difference is reported, net of tax, as a special item on the income statement in the year of change. If we assume a 40 percent tax rate, the 1988 income statement would show:

Cumulative Effect of Change in Accounting Principle (net of tax of $130,000)	$195,000

Since the change to straight line involves a reduction of past expense (which is an increase of past income), showing the effect in the year of change increases 1988 income by $195,000.

Financial Statement Presentation

Exhibit 13-2 presents an income statement showing the three special items presented separately at the bottom of the statement, net of tax. Note that earnings per share is shown for each of these items.

EXHIBIT 13-2
Sample Company
Statement of Income
For the Year Ended December 31, 1988

Revenues:		
Sales		$870,000
Less: Sales Returns		8,800
Net Sales		$861,200
Cost of Goods Sold		444,500
Gross Profit		$416,700
Other Expenses:		
Selling	$149,300	
Office	21,600	
Interest	4,200	175,100
Income from Continuing Operations		
before Income Tax		$241,600
Income Tax Expense		96,200
Income from Continuing Operations		$145,400
Discontinued Operations (net of $58,800 tax)		88,200
Income before Extraordinary Items and		
Cumulative Effect of Accounting Changes		$233,600
Extraordinary Loss (net of $15,000 tax savings)	($35,000)	
Extraordinary Gain (net of $30,000 tax)	70,000	35,000
Cumulative Effect of Change in Accounting		
Principle (net of $130,000 tax)		195,000
Net Income		$463,600
Earnings per Share:*		
Income from Continuing Operations		$1.45
Discontinued Operations (net of tax)		.88
Income before Extraordinary Items and		
Cumulative Effect of Accounting Changes		$2.33
Extraordinary Items (net of tax)		.35
Cumulative Effect of Change in Accounting		
Principle (net of tax)		1.95
Net Income		$4.63

*Earnings per share amounts based on assumption of 100,000 shares of common stock outstanding throughout the year.

ACCOUNTING FOR INTERNATIONAL TRANSACTIONS

Accounting is an international language for communicating financial information. While the details of the language may vary from country to country, the main elements of accounting exist almost everywhere. Concern with international aspects of accounting is no longer limited to specialists in international affairs. Many U.S. companies have operations in foreign countries or deal in the import and export markets.

Exchange Rates

One complication in international accounting is the presence of different currencies. For example, when a U.S. firm imports goods from France, the bill may be payable in French currency (francs). To record the transaction, the U.S. firm must convert the francs into U.S. currency using the exchange rate between francs and dollars.

An *exchange rate* is the domestic price of one unit of foreign currency. For example, if the exchange rate for francs is quoted as $.15, this means that it costs $.15 to buy one franc. To convert a foreign currency amount into dollars, we multiply the foreign amount by the exchange rate for that currency. Thus, 10,000 francs would be converted into $1,500 (10,000 × $.15). Exhibit 13-3 presents exchange rates for various countries. Since exchange rates change over time, current rates may be different from those in Exhibit 13-3. Current rates can be found in the financial pages of your newspaper or in *The Wall Street Journal*.

Accounting for Import and Export Transactions

A U.S. company that engages in import or export transactions uses exchange rates to convert information from foreign currencies to dollars. Assume that on March 10, 1988 Western Importers purchases a shipment of Danish chocolate for

EXHIBIT 13-3 EXCHANGE RATES

Country	Name of currency	Exchange rate
Argentina	Austral	$1.09
Australia	Dollar	.61
Austria	Schilling	.07
Brazil	Cruzado	.07
Britain	Pound	1.49
Canada	Dollar	.72
China	Yuan	.27
Colombia	Peso	.005
Denmark	Krone	.13
Finland	Markka	.20
France	Franc	.15
Greece	Drachma	.007
India	Rupee	.08
Ireland	Punt	1.34
Israel	Shekel	.67
Italy	Lira	.0007
Japan	Yen	.006
Kuwait	Dinar	3.44
Mexico	Peso	.0015
Netherlands	Guilder	.43
Peru	Inti	.07
Saudi Arabia	Riyal	.27
South Korea	Won	.001
Spain	Peseta	.007
Switzerland	Franc	.60
West Germany	Mark	.48

18,500 krone (designated K18,500), payable on April 10. If the exchange rate for krone is $.13 on March 10, Western would record:

```
1988
Mar. 10      Inventory                          2,405
                 Accounts Payable                        2,405
             To record purchase of chocolate
             from supplier in Demark, at
             K18,500 × $.13.
```

When payment is due on April 10, Western will go to its bank and purchase 18,500 krone to send to the supplier in Denmark. The exchange rate for krone on April 10 may be different from the rate on March 10 when the transaction was recorded. Assume that the rate on April 10 is $.12. Acquisition of 18,500 krone will cost $2,220, and will be recorded as:

```
Apr. 10      Foreign Currency                   2,220
                 Cash                                    2,220
             To record purchase of foreign
             currency (K18,500 × $.12).
```

The K18,500 will now be remitted to the Danish supplier. This will satisfy the liability for the purchase. Note however that the current value of the foreign currency ($2,220) is less than the recorded amount of the liability ($2,405). The difference represents a gain to Western due to a favorable change in the exchange rate for Danish currency. The price of krone fell, and thus Western was able to discharge its liability at a lower cost. The entry to record payment and reflect the exchange gain would be:

```
Apr. 10      Accounts Payable                   2,405
                 Foreign Currency                        2,220
                 Exchange Gain                             185
             To record payment of K18,500
             to Danish supplier.
```

As another example, consider an export transaction. On December 1, 1988, Buffalo Electronics ships merchandise to a Swiss customer, billing them for 27,000 Swiss francs (denoted SF27,000), payable in 90 days. The exchange rate on December 1 is $.59. Buffalo Electronics records the sale as:

```
1988
Dec.  1      Accounts Receivable                15,930
                 Sales                                   15,930
             To record sale billed at SF27,000,
             current exchange rate $.59.
```

Payment is not due until March 1, 1989. At December 31, 1988, financial statements for the year are being prepared. The accounts receivable balance must be revalued to reflect the December 31 exchange rate, so that the balance sheet presents the current dollar equivalent of this asset. If the exchange rate for Swiss francs is $.60 on December 31, the receivable is adjusted for the $.01 difference, and an exchange gain is recorded:

Dec. 31	Accounts Receivable	270	
	Exchange Gain		270
	To adjust receivable to reflect exchange rate of $.60.		

If, at March 1, the exchange rate had fallen to $.57, the final settlement of the transaction would show an exchange loss. SF27,000, worth $15,390 (SF27,000 × $.57), would be received in settlement of a receivable currently recorded at $16,200 (the original $15,930 plus the $270 increase on December 31). A loss of $810 would be recorded on March 1:

1989			
Mar. 1	Foreign Currency	15,390	
	Exchange Loss	810	
	Accounts Receivable		16,200
	To record receipt of SF27,000, current exchange rate $.57.		
1	Cash	15,390	
	Foreign Currency		15,390
	To record conversion of SF27,000 into dollars.		

The entire transaction resulted in an exchange loss of $540, recorded as a $270 gain in 1988 and an $810 loss in 1989.

Forward Exchange Contracts

In the examples above, the firm bore a risk of gain or loss due to fluctuations in exchange rates over time. To avoid this risk, a firm engaging in international transactions may enter into a *forward contract* to buy or sell foreign currency at a future date. For example, an importer may need to buy foreign currency in order to pay a supplier's bill due in 90 days. By entering into a forward contract with a bank or foreign currency dealer, the importer agrees to buy the foreign currency in 90 days for a specified price; this price applies no matter what the current rate is 90 days from now.

When exchange rates are quoted, several rates may be quoted for a given currency: a current rate (called a *spot rate*) and one or more forward rates (perhaps for 30-day, 90-day, and 180-day futures). The forward rates may be higher or lower than the spot rate, depending on the expected movement of the exchange rate for that currency.

Reporting Foreign Assets and Liabilities

When a U.S. company maintains an office, branch, or subsidiary in a foreign country, accounting records may be maintained in foreign currency. This foreign accounting data must eventually be translated into dollars so that it can be incorporated into the U.S. firm's financial statements.

Current practice requires the conversion of foreign assets and liabilities at the current exchange rate. Stockholders' equity, however, is translated at historical exchange rates (the rates in effect when the particular component of stockholders' equity originated). Revenues and expenses are converted at the average exchange rate for the year.

Assume that American Exporters opens a sales office in the Netherlands. On January 3, the company sends $21,000 to its agent in Amsterdam to open a bank account. The agent converts the $21,000 into 50,000 guilders (denoted G50,000), reflecting an exchange rate of $.42. The agent uses this account to pay expenses during the year and submits the following report at December 31:

Beginning balance		G50,000
Payments:		
Office equipment	G 5,000	
Office rent	3,600	
Commissions	26,000	
Other expenses	5,400	40,000
Ending balance		G10,000

In other words, American Exporters' $21,000 (G50,000) advance to the agent in Amsterdam is now represented by two asset accounts and three expense accounts:

Assets:	
Cash on hand	G10,000
Office equipment	5,000
Expenses:	
Commissions	26,000
Office rent	3,600
Other expenses	5,400
	G50,000

If the average exchange rate for the year was $.43 and the year-end rate is $.44, the above list converts into dollars as follows:

Item	Amount (G)	Exchange rate	Amount ($)
Cash on hand	G10,000	$.44	$ 4,400
Office equipment	5,000	.44	2,200
Commissions	26,000	.43	11,180
Office rent	3,600	.43	1,548
Other expenses	5,400	.43	2,322
Total	G50,000		$21,650

Note that the total in dollars is $21,650, while American Exporters had advanced only $21,000. The $650 difference is an exchange gain, as the guilder became more valuable during the year.

INFLATION ACCOUNTING

For years, accountants have discussed the need to adjust conventional financial statements for the effects of inflation. To understand the impact of inflation on financial statements and the procedures advocated to adjust financial statements for its effects, it is appropriate to first review the concept of inflation.

Inflation

In the United States, the dollar is the unit of measurement used by accountants. The dollar's value arises from the amount of goods and services it can buy. Unlike other units of measurement (e.g., pounds, gallons, meters, and so on), which have a fixed physical value, the value of the dollar is not constant. The dollar's value, or *purchasing power*, varies over time.

The term *inflation* means that the purchasing power of the dollar has decreased. As the price level of goods and services increases, the quantity of goods and services that can be purchased per dollar decreases. During an inflationary period, an increasing number of dollars are needed to purchase a fixed quantity of goods and services.

As an illustration of the concept of inflation, consider the following situation. Assume items A through D are a representative sample of all goods and services in the economy.

	Prices	
	Year 1	Year 2
A (a refrigerator)	$ 500	$ 605
B (rental cost of one-bedroom apartment)	250	260
C (a visit to the dentist)	50	65
D (a set of graphite golf clubs)	200	170
	$1,000	$1,100

Year 2 would be characterized as inflationary. In Year 2, $1,100 would be needed to purchase the same package of goods and services that could have been purchased in Year 1 for $1,000. The general inflation rate for Year 2 is 10 percent, computed as follows:

$$\text{General Inflation Rate} = \frac{\text{Year 2 Costs} - \text{Year 1 Costs}}{\text{Year 1 Costs}}$$

$$= \frac{\$1,100 - \$1,000}{\$1,000}$$

$$= 10\%$$

A person holding $1,000 cash in Year 1 and maintaining that cash position through Year 2 would become poorer in *real terms* (i.e., in terms of goods and services that could be acquired with the cash). $1,000 would buy fewer goods and services in Year 2 than in Year 1.

It is important to realize that even relatively small increases in prices can have a significant cumulative effect. For example, the compounded effect of a 5 percent annual price increase is to double the price in 15 years, triple it in 23 years, and quadruple it in 29 years.

General Price Changes versus Specific Price Changes

Note in the previous example that the 10 percent rate of inflation was for changes in the *general purchasing power* of the dollar—the composite effect of changes in prices of all goods and services in the economy. The price change for an *individual* good or service may be more than, less than, or equal to the general price-level change. In the previous example, specific price changes were:

Item A	21%	[($605 − $500) ÷ $500]
Item B	4%	[($260 − $250) ÷ $250]
Item C	30%	[($ 65 − $ 50) ÷ $ 50]
Item D	(15)%	[($170 − $200) ÷ $200]

It is important to distinguish between general price-level changes and changes in the prices of specific goods or services. Adjusting financial statements for general price-level changes does not mean that the individual assets are presented at their current values. Similarly, adjusting individual assets to current value does not necessarily reflect changes in the general purchasing power of the dollar.

The Stable Monetary Concept

One of the basic concepts underlying accounting is that the dollar is a stable unit of measurement. However, over the last several decades the dollar has not always been stable. Thus, accountants have been adding together dollars using an elastic unit of measurement—one that has been frequently decreasing in value.

Ignoring changes in the purchasing power of the dollar can result in serious distortion of financial statements. Dollars expended years ago are combined with recent dollars, resulting in a mixture of dollars of different purchasing power. Assets, especially long-lived assets and inventories, are likely to be understated on the balance sheet. Depreciation and cost of goods sold are also likely to be understated on the income statement, resulting in an overstatement of net income. Purchasing power gains and losses are not recognized. Comparability over time and among companies can also be seriously affected.

As an example of some of the possible distortions caused by failure to adjust for inflation, consider the following:

1 Stewart Company purchased one building in 1962 for $100,000 and another in 1988 for $100,000. Financial statements based on unadjusted historical cost show buildings at $200,000 and base depreciation expense on this amount. However, the $200,000 amount defies economic logic. In terms of purchasing power at the time of each acquisition, the two buildings are significantly different. With an inflation rate of approximately 230% from 1962 to 1988, the 1962 purchase of $100,000 represents about $330,000 in terms of 1988 purchasing power. If presented in terms of 1988 purchasing power (the value of the dollar in 1988), the two buildings would be shown on the balance sheet at $430,000, not $200,000. Even if the $430,000 were reported, however, this would not necessarily represent the current value of the two buildings, as the change in the value of the 1962 building may be different than the change in the general price level from 1962 to 1988.

2 Comparato Company presents the following comparative data on its historical-cost financial statements:

	1974	1988
Cash	$250,000	$250,000
Inventory	600,000	600,000

The cash amounts are identical for both years. However, in terms of purchasing power, the $250,000 will buy only about half as much in goods and services in 1988 as it would in 1974. The inventory amounts are also identical, but because prices have doubled from 1974 to 1988, the physical quantity of goods on hand has dropped by one-half.

3 A major U.S. corporation reported that its sales increased by $27.4 billion over a recent five-year period, a 77% increase, and that its net income increased by 46% over the same period. Adjusted for inflation, the increase in sales is only 20%, and net income actually declined over the five years.

On a national level, the distortion can be staggering. For example, in a recent year, U.S. nonfinancial corporations reported after-tax income of $66 billion, a 74% apparent increase over the $38 billion reported nine years earlier. After adjusting for the effects of inflation on only two financial statement items (cost of sales and depreciation expense), after-tax income actually declined from $38 billion to $21 billion over the nine years, a 45% decrease. For a single recent year, an adjustment for inflation would have reduced the pre-tax earnings of U.S. companies by over $42 billion.

Illogical Decisions

As a result of the failure to reflect the effects of inflation on financial statements, it is possible that financial statement readers are using the distorted information and making illogical decisions. Consider, for example, the case of Conventional Co., which was formed on January 2, 1988. At that time, 50,000 shares of $10 par value stock were issued at par. The company immediately invested the $500,000 in a parcel of land. Late in December, 1988 the land is sold for $550,000.

With a 40 percent tax rate and a 100 percent dividend payout, the company's conventional statement of income and retained earnings would show:

Unadjusted Historical Cost Statement

Revenue	$550,000
Cost of Land Sold	500,000
Income before Tax	$ 50,000
Income Tax Expense	20,000
Net Income	$ 30,000
Less Cash Dividends	30,000
Ending Retained Earnings	$ -0-

The $30,000 net income represents a 6 percent return on stockholders' equity. However, if the rate of inflation during 1988 was 10 percent, what were the real earnings in terms of increase in the company's purchasing power? Adjusting the statement for inflation yields the following:

General Price-Level-Adjusted Statement

Revenue	$550,000	
Cost of Land Sold	550,000	($500,000 × 1.10)
Income before Tax	$ -0-	
Income Tax Expense	20,000	(based on unadjusted income)
Net Income (Loss)	$ (20,000)	
Less Cash Dividends	30,000	
Ending Retained Earnings	$ (50,000)	

Note that the $50,000 income before tax reported on the conventional statement was an illusion. The statement adjusted for general price-level changes shows a $20,000 net loss, and return on stockholders' equity was actually negative. The $20,000 income taxes paid to the government and the $30,000 dividends distributed to stockholders were paid out of invested capital, not out of earnings.

How many financial statement readers are misled by failure to report the effects of inflation? The answer is difficult to determine. The economic cost of illogical decisions arising from these statements also is immeasurable. Resources may be misallocated by management and by investors; employees may demand and receive significant wage increases; stockholders may receive larger dividends; tax payments may be required based on illusory profits; and business critics may attack "excessive corporate profits"—all these may follow from using financial statements that do not reflect the impact of inflation.

Techniques for adjusting financial statements for the effects of inflation are available. Because there are two types of price changes—general price-level changes and specific price changes—there are two approaches to adjusting financial statements for the impact of inflation:

1 Reporting in units of general purchasing power reflects general price-level changes (commonly called constant dollar reporting).

2 Reporting in units of current cost (commonly called current value) reflects specific price changes.

Constant Dollar Reporting

Constant dollar financial statements (also called general price-level-adjusted financial statements) explicitly take into account the changing purchasing power of the dollar. Financial statement amounts are expressed in units of current purchasing power. This process changes the units for measuring cost from nominal (historical) dollars to constant dollars, but the underlying cost principle is unaffected.

The techniques to restate financial statements into constant dollars are not difficult to apply. A key factor is to distinguish between monetary items and nonmonetray items, as each is treated differently in the adjustment process. In addition, purchasing power gains or losses (which appear on a constant dollar income statement) are based on the net monetary position during the period.

Monetary Items   *Monetary assets and liabilities* are fixed in terms of number of dollars, regardless of changes in prices. Cash, accounts receivable, notes receivable, and loans receivable are examples of monetary assets. These assets represent cash or a right to receive a fixed amount of cash that will not be affected by changing prices. Examples of monetary liabilities include accounts payable, notes payable, cash dividends payable, bonds payable, and other long-term debt. The amounts owed are fixed in terms of number of dollars to be paid, regardless of changes in prices. At the current balance sheet date, account balances for monetary items are by definition already expressed in terms of current purchasing power. Therefore, monetary items are not restated when the conventional balance sheet is converted to a constant dollar balance sheet. Thus, $10,000 of cash would be reported as $10,000 on both the conventional and constant dollar balance sheets.

Although monetary items are not restated, they do play an important role in the preparation of constant dollar financial statements. A *purchasing power gain or loss* results from holding monetary items during a period of change in the general price level. During periods of inflation, holders of monetary assets suffer a loss of purchasing power because the fixed dollars these assets represent will buy fewer goods and services. Those who owe monetary liabilities during an inflationary period have purchasing power gains. The fixed dollar amount of these liabilities can be repaid in dollars that represent less purchasing power than when the liabilities were incurred. Purchasing power gains and losses are presented in a constant dollar income statement, but are not shown in a conventional income statement.

An Example of Purchasing Power Gains and Losses   As an example of the purchasing power gain or loss from holding monetary items during a period of inflation, consider the following situation. On January 2, 1988, Lennon Co. acquires new machinery for $50,000, financed by a bank loan. The loan is due on December 31, 1988. If there is an 8 percent rate of inflation during 1988, Lennon would have a $4,000 purchasing power gain.

Monetary liability (loan payable) on January 2,1988	$50,000
Adjustment to reflect general rate of inflation during 1988	× ___1.08
Number of dollars at 12/31/88 that represent the same amount of purchasing power as was borrowed on 1/2/88	$54,000
Number of dollars actually needed to repay bank loan on 12/31/88	50,000
Purchasing Power Gain	$ 4,000

Lennon's purchasing power gain results from being able to repay the bank in cheaper dollars (dollars representing less purchasing power than the dollars borrowed).

The bank, which held a monetary asset (the loan receivable) during the year, suffered a $4,000 purchasing power loss. Lenders are aware of the risk of losing substantial purchasing power if inflation is significant during the period of the loan. Accordingly, lenders increase the interest rates they charge to compensate for the expected loss of purchasing power.

Nonmonetary Items All assets and liabilities other than those designated as monetary items, along with all components of stockholders' equity, are *nonmonetary items*. Nonmonetary items do not represent a right to receive or pay a fixed amount of cash. The price of a specific nonmonetary item can change over time. Examples of nonmonetary items include inventories; investments in stocks; property, plant, and equipment; intangible assets; and stockholders' equity accounts.

For constant dollar balance sheets, all nonmonetary items are restated in terms of current purchasing power. Restatement is also necessary for revenues and expenses on the income statement and for the components of the statement of retained earnings. The process of restatement involves multiplying the unadjusted historical cost of each nonmonetary item by a conversion ratio. The conversion ratio is the index of purchasing power at the end of the current period divided by the index of purchasing power at the date the nonmonetary item was received or incurred.

$$\begin{array}{c}\text{Nonmonetary Item} \\ \text{expressed in} \\ \text{Constant Dollars}\end{array} = \begin{array}{c}\text{Unadjusted} \\ \text{Historical Cost} \\ \text{of Nonmonetary Item}\end{array} \times \dfrac{\text{Index at End of Current Period}}{\begin{array}{c}\text{Index at Date} \\ \text{Nonmonetary Item was} \\ \text{Received or Incurred}\end{array}}$$

The formula for restatement is illustrated on the following page for three nonmonetary assets acquired in different years. The index of purchasing power at the end of the current period is 217.4.

Year asset acquired	Index for year acquired	Unadjusted historical cost of nonmonetary asset	Ratio of indexes	Cost in constant dollars
20 years ago	86.6	$100,000	217.4/ 86.6	$251,039
12 years ago	100.0	120,000	217.4/100.0	260,880
7 years ago	125.3	80,000	217.4/125.3	138,803
		$300,000		$650,722

Summary of Advantages and Disadvantages   The following list summarizes the principal arguments for and against presenting constant dollar financial statements:

Arguments for
1 The degree of inflation has at times been so significant that its effects on financial statements cannot be ignored. Constant dollar financial statements help the reader better evaluate a company's financial position and results of operations. As a result, financial trends, key financial ratios, intrafirm and interfirm comparisons, dividend policies, taxes, wage demands, and needs for funds may all be substantially revised.

2 Constant dollar statements are not a radical departure from current accounting principles. The historical cost basis is retained; only the unit of measurement is changed.

3 Constant dollar techniques are well defined and are not difficult to implement.

Arguments against
1 A second set of financial statements only confuses the readers as to which is the correct one. Confidence in financial reporting could be damaged.

2 The presentation of purchasing power gains and losses is especially misleading. For example, a purchasing power gain, while increasing net income and retained earnings, does not represent any cash inflow to the firm; this gain cannot be invested or distributed as dividends.

3 Constant dollar statements are not needed. LIFO and accelerated depreciation can be used within conventional accounting to reflect the impact of inflation.

4 If any change is needed, current value statements would be more useful than constant dollar statements.

Current Value Reporting

The objective of current value reporting (also called current cost reporting) is quite different from that of constant dollar reporting. Constant dollar statements adjust historical cost for changes in the measuring unit—the purchasing power of the dollar. Current value accounting abandons historical cost and reflects changes in the specific value of each nonmonetary item. Specific price changes reflect changes in supply and demand for that particular item, as well as technological changes.

As an illustration of the different financial statements resulting from constant dollar reporting versus current value reporting, consider the following example.

Information for Example Land was purchased at the end of Year 1 for $40,000. The market price of the land was $52,000 at the end of Year 2 and $68,000 at the end of Year 3. The land was sold at the beginning of Year 4 for $68,000. General price-level index:

End of Year 1	100
End of Year 2	110
End of Year 3	120
Beginning of Year 4	120

Balance Sheet Results The balance sheet presentation of the investment in land at the end of each of Years 1 through 3 would be:

	Unadjusted historical cost	Constant dollar	Current value
End of Year 1	$40,000	$40,000	$40,000
End of Year 2	40,000	44,000	52,000
End of Year 3	40,000	48,000	68,000

The constant dollar balance sheets report the land at historical cost restated for changes in the general price level:

End of Year 1 = $40,000 ($40,000 × 100/100)
End of Year 2 = $44,000 ($40,000 × 110/100)
End of Year 3 = $48,000 ($40,000 × 120/100)

The current value balance sheets show the land at its current market values of $40,000, $52,000, and $68,000 respectively.

Income Statement Results The income effects of holding the land, then selling it at the beginning of Year 4, would be:

	Unadjusted historical cost	Constant dollar	Current value
Year 1	$ -0-	$ -0-	$ -0-
Year 2	-0-	-0-	12,000
Year 3	-0-	-0-	16,000
Year 4	28,000	20,000	-0-
Total	$28,000	$20,000	$28,000

The historical cost gain of $28,000 in Year 4 is the difference between the $68,000 selling price of the land and the $40,000 original unadjusted historical cost. The $20,000 gain recognized on the constant dollar statement in Year 4 is the difference between the $68,000 selling price and the general-price-level adjusted cost of $48,000. The current value gains recognize the change in the land's market value during each period. Note that current value reporting changes the timing of recognition of the gain, but not the $28,000 total amount. Constant dollar statements recognize the gain in the same time period as historical cost statements, but change the amount to $20,000.

Summary of Advantages and Disadvantages   The following lists summarize the advantages and disadvantages of reporting on a current value basis:

Arguments for
1 Inflation does not affect every item in the same way. Current value reporting better reflects this fact by considering the current value of each asset and liability, rather than by multiplying historical cost by an average price index.
2 Current values give readers of financial statements a better idea of the cost to replace the company's assets, and thus reflect more accurately the investment of the company.

Arguments against
1 Current value abandons the conventional historical cost approach to accounting and substitutes an entirely different basis of valuation.
2 Current values are often very difficult to determine; preparing current value statements may be very time consuming.
3 Determination of current values often requires a good deal of judgment; this introduces a considerable element of subjectivity into financial statements.

Current Reporting Requirements

In recent years, when inflation was high, large companies were required to present supplemental information in the notes to the financial statements, showing the impact of inflation on major aspects of the company's operations. Both constant dollar and current value techniques were used. Currently, this disclosure is no longer required, although companies may voluntarily present this information.

SUMMARY

Learning Objective 1: Calculate and record income tax expense.
Federal income tax rates are applied to taxable income to calculate income tax payable. If accounting income equals taxable income, this amount is also recorded as income tax expense.

Learning Objective 2: Explain the impact of timing differences on income tax expense.
Accounting income may not equal taxable income because of timing differences. If timing differences exist, income tax expense will not equal income tax payable, and deferred taxes (which may be an asset or a liability) will exist.

Learning Objective 3: Prepare an income statement that includes one or more special items (discontinued operations, extraordinary items, and the cumulative effect of a change in accounting principle).

To help the financial statement reader understand the results of operations for the period and make comparison with the results of other periods, the format of the income statement is designed to disclose separately discontinued operations, extraordinary items, and the cumulative effect of a change in accounting principle. By presenting these items separately on the income statement (and showing them net of tax), these elements of income, which are not expected to recur, are highlighted.

Learning Objective 4: Account for transactions with international customers and suppliers.

Entries are normally needed twice—when the transaction occurs and when payment occurs. If exchange rates change between these two dates, exchange gains and losses may occur. The risk of exchange rate fluctuations may be minimized by entering into forward exchange contracts, which fix the price for the future purchase or sale of foreign currency.

Learning Objective 5: Present foreign assets and liabilities on a balance sheet.

To be presented on a U.S. balance sheet, foreign assets and liabilities must first be converted from foreign currency to dollars. The current exchange rate is used for assets and liabilities. A historical exchange rate is used for stockholders' equity accounts, and revenues and expenses are converted at the average exchange rate for the year.

Learning Objective 6: Describe the concept of inflation and its impact on financial statements.

The general purchasing power of the U.S. dollar varies, often substantially, over time. In periods of inflation, the value of the dollar declines, and so the amount of goods and services that can be purchased per dollar decreases. Conventional historical cost financial statements reflect neither the effects of changes in the general price level nor changes in specific prices (current values) of individual assets. As a result, assets are often understated and net income overstated.

Learning Objective 7: Differentiate between constant dollar and current value reporting.

Constant dollar reporting standardizes transactions that originally occurred at various times in terms of the current purchasing power of the dollar. By using an average price-level adjustment, constant dollar reporting ignores the fact that some price changes are above the average and others are below. Constant dollar reporting retains the historical cost basis; only the measuring unit (value of the dollar) is changed. Current value reporting departs from historical cost and recognizes specific price changes for each item.

KEY TERMS

Change in accounting principle

Constant dollar financial statements

Cumulative effect of a change in
accounting principle

Current value reporting

Deferred income taxes

Discontinued operations

Exchange rate

Extraordinary item

Forward exchange contract

Inflation

Monetary items

Net of tax

Nonmonetary items

Price index

Purchasing power

Purchasing power gain or loss

Timing difference

REVIEW QUESTIONS

1 Define timing differences and give an example.

2 Shaw Company's income statement shows income before taxes of $525,000. Income taxes currently payable are $160,000. $50,000 in taxes was deferred due to timing differences. The tax rate was 40%. Determine the amount of income tax expense for the year.

3 Mulligan Co. uses straight line depreciation to compute accounting income and uses an accelerated method to compute taxable income. Tax rates are assumed unchanged over the life of the asset. "Over the life of the asset, total depreciation and total income taxes will be the same for both accounting and tax return purposes, and thus no tax saving accrues to the firm." Evaluate the preceding statement.

4 What are deferred income taxes?

5 Growth, Inc.'s deferred tax liability account on its balance sheet has continually increased over the last three years. The company uses accelerated depreciation for tax purposes and straight line depreciation for accounting purposes. Deferred taxes are created in the year the company acquires a depreciable machine and reverse over the remaining two years of the machine's life. In view of the reversals of the deferred taxes in years two and three, how can you explain the continual growth in the company's deferred tax liability account?

6 Define extraordinary items. How are extraordinary items presented on the financial statements?

7 Pleasbemine Co., an Ohio firm that manufactures canned dog food, had the following events occur in 1988: (a) loss from the sale of one of the two marketable securities owned by the firm; (b) flood damage to inventory; (c) loss from discontinuing the operations of a segment of the business; (d) earthquake damage to the factory building; and (e) gain from the sale of an old machine. If floods and earthquakes are very rare in the area, which of the above items would be treated as extraordinary?

8 When is a cumulative effect adjustment required? How is it shown on the financial statements?

9 Why are items such as discontinued operations, extraordinary items, and cumulative effect adjustments shown separately on the income statement? Why aren't they presented as part of regular, continuing operations?

10 Why are the special items mentioned in Question 9 presented net of tax effect?

11 What is an exchange rate? Differentiate between a current exchange rate (spot rate) and a forward exchange rate.

12 How many U.S. dollars would be owed by a U.S. company that acquired goods costing 20,000 yen from a Japanese supplier? Use Exhibit 13-3 to find the exchange rate.

13 Kabs Co., a U.S. firm, recently imported several taxis from Japan when the exchange rate for yen was $.008. The supplier's invoice was for 2,500,000 yen. If the exchange rate for yen is $.01 when Kabs makes payment several months later, what will be the dollar amount of the exchange gain or loss incurred by Kabs?

14 In recent years, many businesses have reported record profits while simultaneously complaining that income taxes and dividends often are being paid out of invested capital, not earnings. How has accounting aided the existence of this apparent abnormality?

15 Differentiate between the constant dollar approach to dealing with inflation and the current value approach.

16 Imwon Co. invested $100,000 in 1956 to acquire five acres of land in what is now the hotel district surrounding Disney World in Florida. Four years earlier, in 1952, Metoo, Inc. invested $100,000 to acquire five acres of land in the desert area of New Mexico. The land was believed to contain oil, but none was ever found. It is December 31, 1989, and both companies still own their land investments. Assume the general price level has increased each year since 1952. What amount would each company show on its December 31, 1989 historical cost balance sheet as investment in land? Which company would show the larger amount of dollars invested in land on (a) constant dollar financial statements and (b) current value financial statements?

17 Differentiate monetary items from nonmonetary items. How is each treated in preparing constant dollar financial statements?

18 What is a purchasing power gain? Where on conventional historical cost financial statements are purchasing power gains disclosed?

19 During periods of inflation, interest rates tend to rise. Explain why this occurs.

20 Barnabee Co. speculates in land investments. Evaluate the following statement: "The timing of recognition of gains, but not the total amount of gains, will differ if current value accounting is used rather than conventional historical cost accounting."

EXERCISES

E13-1 Shaw Company's statement of income shows income before depreciation and taxes of $600,000. Depreciation for accounting purposes, using the straight line method, is $200,000. For tax purposes, depreciation is $250,000. Assuming the tax rate is 40 percent, calculate: 1) income tax expense, 2) income taxes currently payable, and 3) the amount of deferred income taxes.

E13-2 Pleco, Inc. has the following timing differences between accounting income and taxable income:

	Accounting income	Taxable income
Year 1	$80,000	$65,000
Year 2	90,000	85,000
Year 3	85,000	95,000

Assuming a 40 percent income tax rate for all years, present the journal entries for income taxes for each year.

E13-3 Identify where each item listed below would appear on an income statement and whether or not it should be presented net of tax effect:
1 Uninsured fire loss (this is the company's first loss from a fire in its twenty-year existence).
2 Loss from frost damage to citrus fruit trees in northern Florida (frost damage occurs every four or five years).
3 Gain on disposal of the insurance division of a manufacturing company.
4 Loss from operating the insurance division from January 1 through August 31 (the division was sold on September 1).
5 Gain on sale of a warehouse building (the company has over 40 warehouses throughout the country).
6 Change in method of accounting for inventory from FIFO to weighted average.

E13-4 Multison Products Co. has maintained three separate divisions for a number of years. During 1988 the company sold its pet food division at a before-tax loss of $942,000. Operating data for 1988 are as follows:

Division	Sales	Cost of goods sold	General expense
Hardware	$14,800,000	$ 7,965,000	$2,845,000
Paper Products	19,200,000	9,053,000	3,947,000
Pet Food	4,810,000	3,940,000	1,020,000
Totals	$38,810,000	$20,958,000	$7,812,000

Assuming a 45 percent tax rate, prepare a statement of income for Multison Products for the year ended December 31, 1988. Ignore earnings per share calculations.

E13-5 Changeover Co. began operations on January 2, 1984 and adopted straight line depreciation for its machinery. The machinery cost $100,000 and had an estimated life of ten years and an estimated salvage value of $10,000. Before preparing the financial statements for 1988, Changeover decides to change to the sum of years digits depreciation method for the machinery in order to better match revenues and expenses. Changeover's income tax rate is 40 percent from 1984 through 1988. Determine the cumulative effect of change in accounting principle to appear on the 1988 income statement. Will the change increase or decrease 1988 income? Calculate depreciation expense for 1988. Round all answers to the nearest dollar.

E13-6 On April 4, 1988, Snowdon Importers purchases 1,000 Swiss watches from a Swiss manufacturer. The invoice price is 225,000 Swiss francs, payable on May 31, 1988. The exchange rate on April 4 is $.44 per Swiss franc. On May 31, Snowdon purchases the 225,000 Swiss francs from an international currency dealer at the current exchange rate of $.45 and then pays the Swiss manufacturer. What is the amount of Snowdon's exchange gain or loss? Prepare the journal entries Snowdon Importers would record for (1) purchase of the watches on April 4, (2) acquisition of the Swiss francs from the currency dealer on May 31, and (3) payment to the Swiss manufacturer on May 31.

E13-7 George Crashly, Thailand agent for Wrecker Incorporated, sends the following list to Wrecker on December 31, 1988 as an accounting for the $60,000 advance he had received on January 2, 1988:

Item	Amount (Baht)
Commission expense	B 400,000
Currency on hand	368,000
Elephant rental expense	100,000
Office equipment	90,000
Other expense	242,000
	B1,200,000

Applicable exchange rates are: $.05 on January 2, $.046 on December 31, and $.04 average for 1988. Convert George's list to U.S. dollars using the appropriate exchange rates and indicate the exchange gain or loss for the year.

E13-8 In the mythical country of Harmony, there are only three goods and services that can be purchased. The three items and their respective prices, measured in dollars, during years 1 and 2 were as follows:

	Prices	
	Year 1	Year 2
Dragon burgers	$ 4.00	$ 5.60
Haircut	6.00	7.50
Nehru jackets	25.00	24.00
Total	$35.00	$37.10

Determine the general inflation rate for Year 2. Assume consumers buy equal quantities of each product. Calculate the percentage changes in the specific prices of the three goods and services. If a citizen of Harmony had $100 in Year 1, how many dollars would be needed in Year 2 to maintain the same purchasing power?

E13-9 On January 2, 1989, three companies were formed when stockholders invested $800,000 in each company. Solo Company invested its $800,000 in land and buildings. Duet Company lent its $800,000 to Trio Company. Trio Company invested its own $800,000, the $800,000 it borrowed from Duet, plus an additional $1,000,000 borrowed from the bank in marketable equity securities. The general price-level index on January 2, 1989 was 150. By December 31, 1989, the index had risen to 180. Calculate the purchasing power gain or loss for 1989 for each company.

E13-10 Perdie Company purchased marketable equity securities at a cost of $18,000 on January 2, 1988. The percentage invested in each company represents less than 20 percent of that company's outstanding shares. The aggregate market value of the investment was $20,000 on December 31, 1988 and $24,000 on December 31, 1989. The general price-level index was 110 on January 2, 1988; 115 on December 31, 1988; 120 on December 31, 1989; and 125 on December 31, 1990 (the date the investments were sold for $27,000). Indicate in the following tables how the investment would affect the financial statements under each of three reporting methods:

Balance Sheet

December 31	Unadjusted historical cost	Constant dollars	Current value
1988	$	$	$
1989			

Income Statement

Year ended December 31	Unadjusted historical cost	Constant dollars	Current value
1988	$	$	$
1989			
1990			
Total gains	$_____	$_____	$_____

PROBLEMS

P13-1 *Income Tax Accounting: Deferred Taxes*
Solve each of the following independent cases.

Case 1—Caddis, Inc. began business on January 3, 1986. The company sells household appliances. Most customers make a down payment and then pay the balance in monthly installments over a three-year period. For accounting purposes, income is recognized when the sale is made. For tax purposes, income is recognized only as cash payments are received from customers. The company's tax rate is 40 percent. Selected data from the company show:

Year	Accounting income	Taxable income
1986	$800,000	$400,000
1987	900,000	700,000
1988	600,000	700,000
1989	700,000	800,000

Required:
Present journal entries for income taxes for 1986 through 1989.

Case 2—Pupa, Inc. purchased $800,000 of machinery on January 2, 1986. The machinery has an estimated life of ten years and an estimated salvage value of $140,000. Straight line depreciation is selected for accounting purposes, while the company adopts 150 percent declining balance depreciation for tax purposes. Income before depreciation and income taxes is:

1986	$400,000
1987	500,000
1988	550,000

The income tax rate is 45 percent for all three years.

Required:
Calculate deferred income tax credits for each of the three years.

P13-2 *Prepare Statement of Income with Special Items*
Presented below is selected information for Fiber Co.:

1 The cumulative effect of switching in 1988 from straight line to sum of years digits depreciation is to decrease income by $18,000 (prior to tax effect)

2 Sales $520,000

3 Cost of goods sold $270,000

4 General and administrative expenses $60,000

5 Selling expenses $70,000

6 Dividends declared $8,000

7 Loss from earthquake damage to Chicago plant $40,000

8 Discontinued operations produced income before tax of $11,000 during 1988 (this $11,000 is not reflected in any of the above amounts)

9 With a 40 percent tax rate, total tax expense for 1988 is $29,200

10 10,000 shares of common stock were outstanding during 1988.

Required:
Prepare a statement of income for Fiber for the year ended December 31, 1988.

P13-3 *Cumulative Effect of Change in Accounting Principle*
Solve independently each of the following two cases involving changes in accounting principle:

Case 1—Nolan Co. began operations in 1984. It had been computing depreciation by an accelerated method until January 1, 1988, when a change to the straight line method was made. Depreciation computed by the accelerated method was reported as follows:

1984	$9,000	1986	$8,000
1985	8,000	1987	7,000

Had the straight line method been used, depreciation would have been as follows:

1984	$5,200	1986	$5,800
1985	5,200	1987	5,800

The change to straight line depreciation is effective as of January 1, 1988. Nolan's income tax rate has been 40 percent throughout the years 1984-88. Nolan's 1988 income before taxes and before the cumulative effect of the accounting change is $50,000.

Required:
1 Calculate the cumulative effect of the change in accounting principle.
2 Where on the income statement would the cumulative effect item be presented?
3 Determine net income for 1988.

Case 2—Prior to 1988, the Cougar Company used accelerated depreciation methods for plant equipment. In 1988 Cougar changed to the straight line method. At December 31, 1987 the book value of the plant equipment was $3,500,000. If the straight line method had previously been used, the book value at December 31, 1987 would have been $3,800,000. For 1988, depreciation expense was $120,000 under the straight line method; it would have amounted to $150,000 had accelerated depreciation methods still been used.

Required:

Assuming an income tax rate of 45 percent, calculate the cumulative effect of change in depreciation methods.

(AICPA Adapted)

P13-4 *Correct Errors in Presentation of Income Statement*

The statement of income for B. L. Under Company for 1988 is presented below:

B. L. Under Company
Statement of Income
December 31, 1988

Revenues:		
Net Sales		$8,972,000
Expenses:		
Cost of Sales	$5,615,000	
Selling, General, Administrative	3,112,000	
Condemnation Loss (extraordinary)	63,000	8,790,000
Income before Income Taxes		$ 182,000
Income Tax Expense		72,800
Net Income		$ 109,200

B. L. Under Company had 30,000 shares of common stock outstanding throughout the year. The income tax rate is 40 percent. Net sales includes $1,380,000 from the drug division of the company, whose operations were discontinued late in the year. Cost of sales of $965,000 and $635,000 of selling, general, and administrative expenses are attributable to the discontinued division, and are included in the amounts shown on the statement.

Required:

Prepare a corrected statement of income following the format of Exhibit 13-2 in the chapter.

P13-5 *Entries for Import Transactions*

Eastern Merchandise Co. imports a variety of items for resale to U.S. retailers. During one month, it made the following purchases:

Country	Invoice amount	Currency	Exchange rate at purchase	Exchange rate at payment
Australia	15,000	Aust. dollar	$1.10	$1.13
Finland	42,000	Markka	.26	.25
Turkey	80,000	Lira	.06	.06

Required:

1 Prepare journal entries to record each of the above inventory acquisitions on date of purchase.

2 Prepare journal entries to record acquisition of foreign currencies and payment to vendors on settlement dates.

P13-6 *Export Transaction*

Electro Co. sells to foreign customers. A recent sale to an Indian customer was billed at 1,380,000 Indian rupees. The current exchange rate on November 1,

1988 (the date of the sale) was $.10 per rupee. On January 31, 1989 payment is received from the customer; the exchange rate is $.105.

Required:

1 What is Electro's exchange gain or loss on the transaction?

2 If the exchange rate on December 31, 1988 (the last day of Electro's accounting year) is $.098, how much of the exchange gain or loss would be reported in 1988? In 1989?

3 Prepare journal entries to record (a) the sale on November 1, 1988; (b) the December 31, 1988 adjusting entry to revalue the receivable; and (c) the receipt of payment on January 31, 1989 and the conversion of the rupees to dollars.

P13-7 *Purchasing Power Gain or Loss*

Presented below are the January 1, 1988 balance sheets for two companies. Note that the companies have the same dollar amounts of current assets, current liabilities, and total assets.

	Steed, Inc.	Peal, Inc.
Current Assets:		
Cash	$ 150,000	$ 8,000
Marketable Equity Securities	10,000	109,000
Accounts Receivable,		
Net of Allowance	50,000	16,000
Inventory	30,000	107,000
Total Current Assets	$ 240,000	$ 240,000
Property, Plant, and Equipment:		
Land	$ 120,000	$ 160,000
Buildings, Net of Accumulated		
Depreciation	310,000	305,000
Equipment, Net of Accumulated		
Depreciation	170,000	295,000
Total Property, Plant,		
and Equipment	$ 600,000	$ 760,000
Investment—Cash Surrender Value		
of Officers' Life Insurance	160,000	-0-
Total Assets	$1,000,000	$1,000,000
Current Liabilities:		
Accounts Payable	$ 60,000	$ 80,000
Interest Payable	40,000	15,000
Income Taxes Payable	10,000	15,000
Total Current Liabilities	$ 110,000	$ 110,000
Long-term Debt:		
8% Bonds Payable	-0-	600,000
Total Liabilities	$ 110,000	$ 710,000
Stockholders' Equity	890,000	290,000
Total Liabilities and		
Stockholders' Equity	$1,000,000	$1,000,000

Required:

If there were no changes in the account balances during 1988 and the general rate of inflation was 10 percent, determine the purchasing power gain or loss for each company for 1988 (assume the Investment—Cash Surrender Value of Officers' Life Insurance is a monetary asset).

P13-8 *Transactions Under Conventional, Constant Dollar, and Current Value Approaches*

Clemens Corporation made the following purchases of assets:

January 2, 1988—$80,000 investment in land
July 1, 1989— $120,000 investment in marketable securities

On January 2, 1990, the land was sold for $118,000, and the marketable securities were sold for $122,000. Other information is as follows:

General price-level indexes:

January 2, 1988	100
December 31, 1988	120
July 1, 1989	135
December 31, 1989	140
January 2, 1990	140

Current values:

	Land	Securities
December 31, 1988	$ 93,000	$ -0-
December 31, 1989	118,000	122,000

Required:

Indicate in the tables below how the investments in land and marketable securities would affect the financial statements:

Balance Sheet

December 31	Conventional historical cost	Constant dollar	Current value
1988:			
Land	$	$	$
1989:			
Marketable Securities			
Land			

Income Statement

Year ended December 31	Conventional historical cost	Constant dollar	Current value
1988 gain from holding land	$	$	$
1989 gain from holding land			
1989 gain from holding marketable securities			
1990 gain from sale of land			
1990 gain (loss) from sale of marketable securities			
Total gains	$_____	$_____	$_____

P13-9 *Evaluation of Positions on Inflation Accounting*

Published financial statements of U.S. companies are currently prepared on a stable dollar assumption even though the purchasing power of the dollar has at times declined considerably. To account for the changing value of the dollar, many accountants suggest that financial statements should be adjusted for general price-level changes.

Three independent statements regarding constant dollar financial statements follow. Each contains some fallacious reasoning.

Statement I

The accounting profession has not seriously considered constant dollar financial statements because the rate of inflation from year to year usually has been so small that adjustments would be immaterial in amount. Constant dollar financial statements represent a departure from the historical cost basis of accounting.

Statement II

If financial statements were presented on a constant dollar basis, depreciation charges in the income statement would permit the recovery of dollars of current purchasing power and thereby equal the cost of new assets to replace the old ones. A constant dollar balance sheet would present amounts closely approximating current values.

Statement III

When preparing constant dollar financial statements, a distinction must be made between monetary and nonmonetary assets and liabilities that, under the historical cost basis of accounting, have been identified as "current" and "noncurrent." When using the historical cost basis of accounting, no purchasing power gain or loss is recognized in the accounting process, but when constant dollar financial statements are prepared, a purchasing power gain or loss will be recognized on monetary and nonmonetary items.

Required:

Evaluate each of the above statements. Identify the areas of fallacious reasoning in each and explain why the reasoning is incorrect.

(AICPA Adapted)

Business Decision Problem

Mr. Changer, president of Clothier, Inc., believes he is in danger of losing his job. Profits have been steadily decreasing over the last several years. In early December 1988, a projected income statement for 1988 shows:

Clothier, Inc.
Projected Statement of Income
For the Year Ended December 31, 1988

Net Sales		$52,000,000
Cost of Goods Sold		41,000,000
Gross Profit		$11,000,000
Other Expenses:		
Selling	$3,100,000	
Depreciation	900,000	
Office	2,000,000	
Interest	4,000,000	10,000,000
Income before Income Tax		$ 1,000,000

Income Tax Expense (40% rate)	400,000
Net Income	$ 600,000
Earnings per Common Share	
(1,000,000 shares outstanding)	$ .60

In an attempt to improve reported earnings and save his job, Mr. Changer has been considering doing the following in December, 1988:

1 Selling the company's profitable children's shoe division to another company late in December at a gain of $9,000,000 (before taxes). For 1988, the children's shoe segment of the business is expected to contribute $5,000,000 in sales revenue and incur expenses of $3,700,000 for cost of goods sold, $160,000 of selling expenses, and $40,000 of office expenses.

2 Repurchasing and retiring on December 31 the 8 percent bond issue currently outstanding. Mr. Changer plans to use most of the proceeds from a new $50,000,000 issue of 14 percent bonds to retire the old 8 percent bonds. The outstanding 8 percent bonds were issued at face, but can be repurchased at their current market value of $42,000,000. The new 14 percent bonds would be issued at face. Any gain or loss on the retirement of the old 8 percent bonds is presented on the income statement as an extraordinary item.

3 Changing from declining balance to straight line depreciation. The effects of the change are summarized in the following table:

	Declining balance	Straight line
1988	$ 900,000	$ 600,000
Prior to 1988	6,000,000	2,400,000

Assume a tax rate of 40 percent applies.

Required:

1 If Mr. Changer implements all three suggestions listed above, determine if he will be successful in increasing the reported net income for 1988. Prepare a revised projected income statement to support your answer.

2 Discuss whether the revised net income amount is a good indicator of expected future earnings.

14

INTRODUCTION TO MANAGERIAL ACCOUNTING

LEARNING OBJECTIVES

When you complete this chapter, you should be able to:

1 Describe and discuss the four major areas of managerial accounting.
2 Prepare journal entries for the flow of costs in a manufacturing operation.
3 Prepare a schedule of cost of goods manufactured and sold.
4 Distinguish fixed, variable, and semivariable costs.

We have seen that financial accounting is the language by which management communicates with outsiders concerning the overall performance of the firm. Similarly, *managerial accounting* is the language by which members of management communicate among themselves the financial and operational information needed to plan, administer, and evaluate the firm's activities.

Managers need operating information that is more detailed than that on external reports. They need specific information useful in making particular management decisions. The variety of purposes for which internal reports are used leads to a diversity of the form and content of these reports. The need for flexibility in presenting information outweighs the usefulness of established statement structures. The importance of common standards is also reduced. Whereas GAAP governs financial accounting, formal managerial accounting standards have generally not been developed.

MANAGERIAL ACCOUNTING REPORTS

Managerial accounting reports are used to help managers at all levels formulate plans for action, evaluate the success or failure of their past efforts, and communicate information to others. The following examples are typical of reports prepared for managerial accounting purposes:

Product Cost Reports. Detailed information regarding the cost to manufacture a certain product may be needed by management for pricing decisions, decisions to continue or discontinue that product, or evaluation of last month's production operations. A product cost report would present the several elements of cost involved in the manufacture of that product.

Budgets. Management requires formal financial plans (*budgets*) to serve as guides for future action and to serve as a basis for the evaluation of performance. For example, a cash budget presents a detailed plan of expected cash transactions for a future time period. It could be used to determine times of expected cash shortage (when a loan might be required) or expected cash excesses (when short-term investments might be made). At the end of the time period, actual cash transactions can be compared to the budget as a means of evaluating the firm's cash management activities.

Projected Financial Statements. Along with the preparation of budgets, projected financial statements may also be prepared. These aid management in forecasting future earnings and financial position.

Performance Reports. Cost and revenue data may be accumulated for each department within the firm to serve as a basis for evaluation of performance. For example, a performance report will indicate the amount of costs over which a department supervisor is expected to exercise some control—such as materials used, labor hours worked, and equipment maintenance.

Decision Analysis Reports. These reports present the data needed by management in analyzing and resolving specific decision problems. For a decision whether to manufacture a certain component or purchase it from an outside supplier, a decision analysis report comparing the costs of each alternative would be prepared. A decision to invest in new equipment would require a report that (a) analyzes the desirability of the investment in terms of future costs and revenues and (b) analyzes the effect of various methods of financing the purchase.

The information needs of management are diverse. The management accountant must therefore be flexible, able to analyze data, and able to present reports in ways appropriate to management needs. A good management accountant needs originality, creativity, and a thorough understanding of the firm's business activities. These qualities cannot be taught. What can be taught is a series of analytical tools and an analytical thought process that guides the selection of the tool to be used for a particular application.

In the study of managerial accounting, income measurement remains a central focus. Managers, as well as external users of financial data, are concerned with the firm's income. Profits are a central concern of the four major areas of managerial accounting: planning, control and performance evaluation, decision analysis, and product costing. This chapter introduces these topics; subsequent chapters further develop each topic.

PLANNING

One major function of the managerial accounting system is the provision of data for planning future costs and revenues. Projected data frequently take the form of a budget, a formally stated plan of activity for one or more future periods. The plan is usually expressed in financial terms. It may be very general or quite detailed. For example, a sales budget for next year may present only the estimated total sales for the year, or may present monthly estimates for each of the company's products. An example of the latter is shown in Exhibit 14-1.

The more detailed the budget, the more specific the estimates and assumptions that are required, and the more useful the budget is likely to be as a plan of action. Having sales estimates for each month and each product will aid management in planning production, advertising, sales efforts, cash flows and profits, and other operating activities. Of course, preparing a more detailed budget requires a greater investment of time and effort.

A specific budget, such as the sales budget shown in Exhibit 14-1, may be an individual, isolated document, or it may be part of a *comprehensive* (or master) *budget* for the firm. A comprehensive budget is an integrated plan of activity, which sets forth budgets for:

EXHIBIT 14-1
Marx Brewery, Inc.
Sales Budget
For the Year Ending December 31, 1988

Month	Standard beer		Premium beer	
	Cases	Revenue	Cases	Revenue
January	12,000	$ 81,600	6,000	$ 45,000
February	11,500	78,200	6,000	45,000
March	13,000	88,400	6,000	45,000
April	13,000	88,400	6,000	45,000
May	17,000	115,600	7,500	56,250
June	21,000	145,950	9,000	69,300
July	26,500	184,175	10,000	77,000
August	25,000	173,750	10,000	77,000
September	18,000	125,100	8,000	61,600
October	15,500	107,725	6,500	50,050
November	13,000	90,350	6,000	46,200
December	17,500	121,625	9,500	73,150
Totals	203,000	$1,400,875	90,500	$ 690,550
Total Sales				$2,091,425

Budgeted selling prices to distributors:
  Standard: $6.80 per case; $6.95 after June 1
  Premium: $7.50 per case; $7.70 after June 1

Sales
Production and inventory levels
Materials, labor, and overhead
Selling activities
Other activities (research, administration, and so forth)
Cash flow
Projected financial statements

Because budgets are *estimates of future activity*, they entail some degree of uncertainty. The subject of budgeting, and particularly comprehensive budgeting, will be further developed in Chapter 17.

CONTROL AND PERFORMANCE EVALUATION

A second major responsibility of management is the control and evaluation of performance. While budgeting occurs *prior* to the period of activity, control and evaluation occur *during* and *after* the period of activity. In the context of the sales budget in Exhibit 14-1, control and performance evaluation with respect to sales means that management should do the following:

1 Closely monitor sales during each month.

    a If sales occur approximately as budgeted, management's main task is to ensure that all other activities (production, shipping, collections, and so on) also proceed according to plan.

    b If sales substantially exceed budgeted levels, other activities will have to be adjusted as well. For example, production may need to be increased, which may in turn require hiring new employees, acquiring new equipment, and so on. Also, in light of the higher sales, the budget for the remainder of the year should be reconsidered and possibly revised.

    c If sales fall substantially short of budgeted levels, the cause must be sought so that corrective action can be taken. Perhaps the company's sales force is inadequate and requires some additional or replacement personnel. Perhaps competitive breweries have cut prices, requiring a cut by Marx Brewery. If no identifiable cause can be found, this leads to a conclusion that the budget was overly optimistic and should be revised.

2 Use sales data to evaluate the performance of individuals responsible for sales — the sales manager, advertising manager, individual salesmen, and distributors. For some purposes, such as the evaluation of individual salesmen and distributors, budgeted and actual sales data will be needed for specific territories. As a result of this evaluation, management will make decisions concerning retention of individual personnel, salary increases, and so forth.

The role of managerial accounting is to provide management with the data needed for its control and performance evaluation responsibilities. Depending on the particular circumstances, the data may take a variety of forms. The examples below show three different types of accounting data that may be employed.

1 *Profit and rate of return.* Assume that a large company is composed of several divisions. Each division is involved in the manufacture and sale of a certain line of products, and each divisional manager has considerable autonomy in operating the division. In these circumstances, each division is similar to an individual firm. Central management may evaluate the performance of each divisional manager according to overall profit criteria, such as net income and rate of return.

2 *Comparison of performance to budget.* Assume that the sales manager of a company is given budgets setting forth planned performance in areas under the sales manager's responsibility. The budgets may include (a) a sales budget detailing expected sales levels and (b) a selling expense budget detailing planned expenditures for sales salaries, commissions, travel, advertising, and so forth. The sales manager's performance is evaluated by comparing sales actually achieved with the sales budget and by comparing actual selling expenses with the selling expense budget.

3 *Comparison of performance to detailed standard costs.* Assume that a production supervisor is responsible for a particular operation in the production process. The company has carefully studied the requirements of this particular operation, and has developed *standard costs*—target figures of what the costs should be if the operation is efficient. It has been determined that each unit of product manufactured should require the following cost items:

Material A:	
3 pounds at $.80 per pound	$ 2.40
Material B:	
2 pounds at $1.70 per pound	3.40
Labor:	
0.5 hours at $7.50 per hour	3.75
Machine cost (based on machine hours):	
0.4 machine hours at $10.00 per hour	4.00
Standard cost of one unit of product	$13.55

It must next be determined who is responsible for each element of the standard cost. It may, for example, be concluded that the following cost responsibility exists:

Production Supervisor:	Quantity of materials used
	Hours of labor used
	Hours of machine time used
Plant Manager:	Wage rates
	Machine costs
Purchasing Agent:	Price paid per pound of materials

The performance evaluation of the production supervisor would compare actual performance to standard performance on those items for which the supervisor is responsible. This performance report is shown in Exhibit 14-2.

Note that the top part of the performance report presented in Exhibit 14-2 compares actual and standard performance in terms of physical units. That is, it

EXHIBIT 14-2 PERFORMANCE REPORT

Department ___2___   Month ___March 1988___
Operation ___7___   Units Produced ___7,200___
Supervisor M. Willis

In units

Cost item	Standard per unit	Standard for total production	Actual for total production	Difference over or (under) standard
Material A	3 lbs.	21,600 lbs.	22,200 lbs.	600 lbs.
Material B	2 lbs.	14,400 lbs.	14,250 lbs.	(150) lbs.
Labor hours	0.5 hrs.	3,600 hrs.	3,710 hrs.	110 hrs.
Machine hours	0.4 hrs.	2,880 hrs.	2,920 hrs.	40 hrs.

In dollars

Cost item	Standard per unit	Standard cost for total production	Actual cost for total production	Difference over or (under) standard
Material A	3 lb. @ $ .80	$17,280	$17,760	$ 480
Material B	2 lb. @ $ 1.70	24,480	24,225	(255)
Labor hours	0.5 hr. @ $ 7.50	27,000	27,825	825
Machine hours	0.4 hr. @ $10.00	28,800	29,200	400
Total		$97,560	$99,010	$1,450

indicates that the usage of material A exceeded the standard by 600 pounds, the usage of labor hours exceeded the standard by 110 hours, and so forth. The bottom section of Exhibit 14-2 analyzes performance in terms of *dollars* by multiplying each physical measure by its unit cost.

The subject of standard costs will be presented in Chapter 16. Further development of the topics of control and performance evaluation will appear in Chapter 18.

DECISION ANALYSIS

The third major function of the managerial accounting system is to provide data for the analysis of decisions. In this area, the applications are of a much less routine nature. Almost every situation is a special case. Some examples of decision analysis problems requiring data from the managerial accounting system are:

1 Company A currently manufactures a certain component that is used in several of its products. It is considering discontinuing production and buying the components from an outside supplier. An analysis must be made of the effect this decision would have on costs to the company. Certain manufacturing costs associated with the component would no longer be incurred. New costs associated with the purchase of components would be incurred. The analysis must indicate how the cost savings compare with the new costs to be incurred.

2 Company B is considering expanding its sales effort to a territory where it has not previously operated. An analysis is required to assess the effect of this decision on profits. What amount of new sales may be expected? What price can be charged? Will there be any effect on existing sales in other territories? What costs will be incurred to serve the new territory? Are the company's production facilities adequate to meet the increased demand? Data to answer these and other questions must be developed and presented in an analysis of expected revenues, costs, and profits.

3 Company C is considering the replacement of existing machinery with new equipment. An analysis is needed to determine if the new equipment will provide sufficient savings to justify its cost. Data must be developed regarding cost savings that would result, such as lower labor costs per unit (i.e., higher productivity), reduced repair and maintenance expense, less spoilage, and so forth. Since these savings may extend over several years, a present value may be calculated and compared to the cost of the new equipment.

As these cases show, each decision analysis is likely to have its own special characteristics. While some general approaches to analysis exist, attention must always be given to determining exactly what information will be relevant for a particular case. While general approaches can be studied in a textbook, skill in identifying relevant information comes mainly through experience. Decision analysis will be discussed in Chapters 19 and 20.

PRODUCT COSTING

A significant function of a manufacturing firm's managerial accounting system is to provide detailed records of product cost. Both external and internal reporting require product cost data. For external reports, product costs are needed to determine the amounts assigned to inventories and to cost of goods sold on the financial statements. For internal purposes, product cost data are needed for planning, control, and decision making. Costs not assigned to the product but expensed in the time period to which they relate are called *period costs*. Examples of period costs are selling and administrative expenses, insurance or depreciation on office buildings and equipment, and other nonmanufacturing costs.

Product costs represent sacrifices of the firm's resources in acquiring or making a product and readying it for sale. In the case of merchandising firms, the invoice cost of buying the product is the primary product cost. In the process of producing goods ready for sale, manufacturing firms incur three categories of product costs: direct materials, direct labor, and manufacturing overhead. Product costs are assigned to inventories and are reported as assets on the balance sheet. When the inventory is sold, the associated product cost is transferred to cost of goods sold expense on the income statement.

Direct materials are the materials employed in the production process that are identifiable in the final product. For example, the direct materials used in manufacturing a sofa are wood, upholstery fabric, and padding. Materials that are not identifiable in the final product, or are a very minor element, are called *indirect materials* and are considered to be part of manufacturing overhead. For example, the glue and nails used in the sofa are indirect materials.

Direct labor is the work clearly identified with producing the final product. For example, the wages of the person assembling a sofa are direct labor costs in a furniture manufacturing firm. Factory labor that is not directly traceable to a particular product is called *indirect labor*, and this cost is also included in manufacturing overhead. Examples of indirect labor costs are wages for factory maintenance and factory supervision.

The inputs of wood, fabric, padding, and labor are not sufficient to produce a sofa ready for sale. There must be a factory building with equipment. Costs such as electricity to run the equipment must be incurred to make the facilities operative. Goods must be inspected to ensure that company or government standards are met. These costs compose the third element of manufacturing costs — *manufacturing overhead*. Contrary to costs of direct materials and direct labor, these costs are not readily traceable to the individual product (e.g., a particular sofa). All costs, other than direct materials and direct labor, that are essential to the manufacturing activity are classified as manufacturing overhead.

Manufacturing overhead encompasses two aspects of production:

1 *Productive capacity*—the physical facilities essential to production and
2 *Production support*—the activities and minor materials necessary to make the capacity operative and the product ready for sale.

Typical costs of productive capacity are:

Depreciation of factory building
Depreciation of factory equipment
Property taxes on factory building and equipment
Insurance on factory building and equipment
Rental of factory building and equipment

Production support includes production-related costs for:
Heat, light, and power
Repairs and maintenance
Supervision
Materials handling and storage
Inspection of product
Supplies and minor materials used in production
Packaging and warehousing of product

The following sections illustrate the entries required in a simple cost accounting system for a manufacturing firm. Accounting procedures for each of the three categories of manufacturing cost — direct materials, direct labor, and manufacturing overhead—are discussed. As these costs move through the accounting system, they are debited to various inventory accounts. Direct materials are initially debited to Materials Inventory when purchased. Then, when materials, labor, and manufacturing overhead are used in production, these costs are debited to Work in Process Inventory. When production is complete, the costs are debited to Finished Goods Inventory. Finally, when the goods are sold and sales revenue is recorded, we recognize an expense (cost of goods sold). Thus, expenses of the sale are appropriately matched with revenues. Exhibit 14-3 shows the flow of costs in a manufacturing firm.

Accounting for Direct Materials

Accounting for direct materials in a manufacturing firm is similar to accounting for merchandise purchases. Instead of using a separate Purchases account, manufacturing firms normally record purchases of materials directly into the Materials Inventory account. During the period, the cost of materials used in production must be calculated and entered into the Work in Process Inventory account. One of the usual cost flow methods (FIFO, LIFO, weighted average cost) is employed. Because of the need to maintain up-to-date product cost records, perpetual rather than periodic inventory methods are used.

For example, assume that Cornell Corporation, a manufacturer of men's neckties, had an inventory of fabrics of $7,000 at January 1, 1988. During January the company purchased additional quantities of fabrics at a total cost (including

EXHIBIT 14-3   Flow of Costs in a Manufacturing Operation

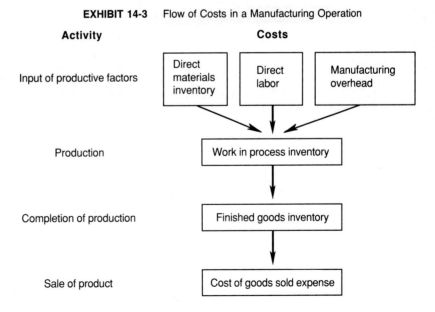

freight and import taxes) of $54,000. The entry[1] to record these purchases of direct materials would be:

```
1988
Jan. 31    Materials Inventory            54,000
               Accounts Payable                       54,000
           To record purchases of direct
             material on account.
```

Cornell Corporation, using the FIFO method, determines that the cost of direct materials used in production during January was $51,000. This amount would be debited to the Work in Process Inventory account, as follows:

```
Jan. 31    Work in Process Inventory      51,000
               Materials Inventory                     51,000
           To charge cost of direct materials
             used in production to work in
             process.
```

Thus, as direct materials are used in production, their cost is transferred from the Materials Inventory account into the Work in Process Inventory account. This entry updates the Materials Inventory account as of the end of the month, as shown in the T-account below:

Materials inventory

January 1 balance	7,000		
Direct materials purchased	54,000		
		51,000	Transfer direct materials used
	61,000	51,000	
		10,000	To balance
	61,000	61,000	
January 31 balance	10,000		

In this illustration costs are charged to production monthly. In practice it is not unusual for costs to be charged to production more frequently.

Accounting for Direct Labor

Accounting for direct labor is straightforward. As costs for direct labor are incurred, they are debited directly to the Work in Process Inventory account. Normally, direct labor cost means the gross earnings of individuals who are directly engaged in manufacturing the product. Although it would be possible to include the employees' fringe

---

[1]As a convenience, we will date all entries as of the last day of the month. In reality, entries might be made at any time during the month.

benefits in recording direct labor cost, it is more common and more convenient to treat fringe benefit costs as a part of manufacturing overhead.

For the tie manufacturing activity of the Cornell Corporation, direct labor costs (cutting fabric, operating sewing machines, and pressing) for January total $73,000. The entry would be:

Jan. 31	Work in Process Inventory	73,000	
	Wages Payable		73,000
	To charge earned but unpaid gross earnings by direct labor employees to work in process.		

Accounting for Manufacturing Overhead

As defined earlier, manufacturing overhead consists of all costs, other than direct materials and direct labor, associated with production. These costs include those associated with providing the production capacity and the necessary support services. As was the case with other inputs, these costs will be debited to work in process. However, it is often useful first to collect all manufacturing overhead costs in a single account. A second entry is then required to transfer manufacturing overhead to the Work in Process Inventory account.

Cornell Corporation determines that the following costs constitute its manufacturing overhead for January 1988:

Rent of factory building	$12,000
Depreciation of equipment used in manufacturing	7,700
Insurance on factory equipment	1,200
Repair and maintenance of factory building and equipment	6,200
Salary of production supervisors (indirect labor)	19,000
Utilities used in production	8,600
Wages of product inspectors (indirect labor)	9,000
Supplies (thread, labels, packing containers) used in production (indirect materials)	8,400
Fringe benefits for all production employees	15,900
Total actual manufacturing overhead cost	$88,000

All of the above costs (except depreciation) were paid in cash. The combined entry would be:

Jan. 31	Manufacturing Overhead	88,000	
	Cash		80,300
	Accumulated Depreciation		7,700
	To record various manufacturing overhead costs for the month.		

In more complex manufacturing cost systems, the next question would be: how much of this $88,000 of manufacturing overhead should be charged to work in process? For now, simply assume that *all* manufacturing overhead is debited to work in process, as in the following entry:

Jan. 31	Work in Process Inventory	88,000	
	Manufacturing Overhead		88,000
	To charge manufacturing overhead costs to work in process.		

At this point all the costs involved in January's manufacturing activities—direct materials, direct labor, and manufacturing overhead—have entered the accounting records. To parallel the production activity, the next accounting step entails transferring the cost of completed goods out of the Work in Process Inventory account.

Completion of Production

As products are completed, they must be reclassified from work in process to *finished goods*. The costs associated with the units completed during the period must be determined and transferred out of the Work in Process Inventory account to the Finished Goods Inventory account. This transfer of costs will result in an ending balance in the Work in Process Inventory account that represents the costs of products that are incomplete as of the end of the reporting period.

On January 1, 1988 the balance of Cornell Corporation's work in process inventory was $21,000. This represents the cost of ties that were in some stage of production but not yet complete on January 1. During January, costs of additional inputs were debited to work in process as described in the preceding sections. At this point we have:

Cost of beginning work in process inventory		$ 21,000
Current production costs:		
Direct materials	$51,000	
Direct labor	73,000	
Manufacturing overhead	88,000	212,000
Total manufacturing costs in process		$233,000

The total manufacturing costs of $233,000 relate to both ties completed during January and the partially completed ties on hand at January 31. Manufacturing costs associated with goods completed during the period are known as the *cost of goods manufactured*. Manufacturing costs related to partially completed goods on hand at the end of the period remain in the Work in Process Inventory account as the ending work in process inventory balance.

Cornell Corporation determines its cost of goods manufactured to be $206,000 and the cost of ending work in process inventory to be $27,000 (together these equal the $233,000 of total manufacturing costs). The following entry transfers the cost of goods manufactured to the finished goods inventory account:

Jan. 31	Finished Goods Inventory	206,000	
	Work in Process Inventory		206,000
	To transfer to finished goods the cost of ties completed during January.		

This entry also updates the Work in Process Inventory account as of the end of the month, as shown in the T-account below:

Work in process inventory

January 1 balance	21,000		
Direct materials	51,000		
Direct labor	73,000		
Manufacturing overhead	88,000		
		206,000	Transfer costs of finished goods
	233,000	206,000	
		27,000	To balance
	233,000	233,000	
January 31 balance	27,000		

The $27,000 balance is the cost of ties that are partially complete on January 31.

Cost of Goods Sold

When finished goods are sold, the costs of manufacturing the goods become an expense matched against the sales revenue. The final stage of cost flow, therefore, is the transfer of inventory costs to expense. Costs in the Finished Goods Inventory account must be transferred to the Cost of Goods Sold expense account when the goods are sold. Assume that on January 1, 1988, the balance in Cornell's finished goods inventory was $43,000. This means that at the beginning of the year completed ties with a cost of $43,000 were on hand.

During January, more ties were completed at a cost of $206,000. As shown earlier, this cost was transferred to the Finished Goods Inventory account. At this point we have:

Cost of beginning finished goods inventory	$ 43,000
Cost of goods manufactured during January	206,000
Total cost of goods available for sale	$249,000

At the end of the reporting period, the total cost of goods available for sale must be allocated between two categories: the ties sold during January and the completed ties still in the finished goods inventory. The costs relating to the ties sold must be recognized as cost of goods sold expense. Costs relating to completed ties on hand at year end comprise the ending inventory balance in the Finished Goods Inventory account.

Cornell Corporation determines the January cost of goods sold to be $214,000 and the cost of ending finished goods inventory to be $35,000 (together these equal the $249,000 cost of goods available for sale). The appropriate journal entry is:

Jan. 31	Cost of Goods Sold	214,000	
	Finished Goods Inventory		214,000
	To record cost of ties sold during January.		

Computation of the ending finished goods is demonstrated below:

Finished goods inventory

January 1 balance	43,000			
Transfer from work				
in process	206,000			
		214,000	Transfer cost of goods sold	
	249,000	214,000		
		35,000	To balance	
	249,000	249,000		
January 31 balance	35,000			

Flow of Manufacturing Costs Reviewed

As seen from Exhibit 14-3, the three input cost categories flow through the accounts representing the various stages of manufacturing activity. During production, costs of direct materials, direct labor, and manufacturing overhead are entered into the Work in Process Inventory account. When production is completed, costs are transferred to the Finished Goods Inventory account. Finally, when the product is sold to customers, costs are transferred to the Cost of Goods Sold expense account on the income statement.

As we consider this flow of costs for any given time period, observe that inventories will be present at several stages. At the beginning and end of each period, a manufacturing firm is likely to have (1) direct materials that have not yet been used in production (materials inventory); (2) goods in the process of being manufactured, but not yet completed (work in process inventory); and (3) goods that have been completed, but not yet sold (finished goods inventory).

Financial Statement Presentation

Since the determination of cost of goods sold in a manufacturing context is a rather complex task, a separate schedule is often prepared to explain its calculation. (In the language of accounting, a schedule is a detailed analysis supporting certain figures on one of the financial statements. In this case, the schedule will support

EXHIBIT 14-4
Cornell Corporation
Schedule of Cost of Goods Manufactured and Sold
For the Month Ended January 31, 1988

Beginning Inventory, Work in Process			$ 21,000
Current Manufacturing Costs:			
Direct Materials Used:			
Beginning Inventory	$ 7,000		
Purchases	54,000		
Available for Use	$61,000		
Less: Ending Inventory	10,000	$51,000	
Direct Labor		73,000	
Manufacturing Overhead		88,000	212,000
Total Manufacturing Costs in Process			$233,000
Less: Ending Inventory, Work in Process			27,000
Cost of Goods Manufactured			$206,000 ✓
Beginning Inventory, Finished Goods			43,000
Total Cost of Goods Available for Sale			$249,000
Less: Ending Inventory, Finished Goods			35,000
Cost of Goods Sold			$214,000 ✓

the cost of goods sold amount on the income statement.) Exhibit 14-4 presents a typical schedule of cost of goods manufactured and sold, based on the information accumulated for the Cornell Corporation.

The schedule in Exhibit 14-4 explains the $214,000 that will appear on Cornell Corporation's income statement as cost of goods sold. The difficult task in computing cost of goods sold is determining correct amounts of cost at each stage of the process. For example, the amount of manufacturing overhead to be debited to work in process must be determined. Also, the amount of cost to be associated with each inventory amount must be determined. Product costing is concerned with these tasks. Product costing will be discussed in more detail in Chapter 15.

COST BEHAVIOR

The four major areas of managerial accounting (planning, control and performance evaluation, decision analysis, and product costing) are all concerned with costs. Costs can be classified in many ways. In managerial accounting, different cost classifications will be required for different purposes. Categories of cost will be introduced and discussed as needed in future chapters. For the present, we shall consider only one classification—cost behavior—but one that is widely used for several managerial accounting purposes.

By the "behavior of costs" we mean the manner in which costs change when the level of activity changes. While the relationship of costs to activity levels may take many possible forms, it is convenient and useful to limit our consideration to a few patterns: fixed, variable, and semivariable costs. We assume that each cost element fits one of these patterns.

Fixed Costs

Cost items are classified as *fixed* when we assume that the total amount of the cost does not change when the level of activity changes. A company, for example, may employ one production manager at $2,000 salary each month, irrespective of the monthly level of production. The salary is a fixed cost—the total cost is $2,000 for any production level. This can be graphically represented as:

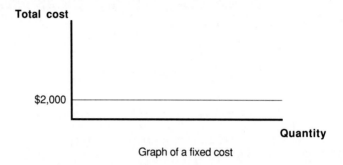

Graph of a fixed cost

Technically, the fixed cost assumption applies only to the range of activity where the company has experience (for example, 10,000 to 18,000 units per month). It would be reasonable to extend the assumption slightly beyond the range of experience. For example, if the company expects to produce 20,000 units next month, the fixed cost of $2,000 might be a valid assumption. Great care should be taken in extending the assumption far beyond the range of experience. If production levels are expected to jump to 40,000 per month (or drop to 2,000), we cannot automatically assume that the cost would continue to be $2,000 per month. Keeping in mind this limitation, we will classify a cost as fixed if we expect the total amount of the cost to remain constant as the level of activity changes.

Variable Costs

If the total cost of an item is assumed to change proportionately as the level of activity changes, it is a *variable* cost. For example, in the manufacture of its product, a company may use one unit of a certain material, costing $2, for each unit of product. Material cost would then be $2,000 for 1,000 units, $10,000 for 5,000 units, and so forth. Graphically, this appears as:

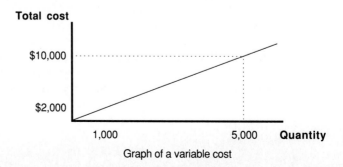

Graph of a variable cost

Semivariable Costs

The actual relationship of cost to activity may take numerous forms. For convenience of analysis, a few simple patterns are chosen to represent these relationships. The fixed and variable categories are two extreme cases—one indicating no total cost change as activity changes and the other indicating a proportionate change in total cost as activity changes. Many cost items are well represented by one of these patterns. Some costs are not easily classified as fixed or variable, because they exhibit characteristics of both. When a cost has both a fixed and variable component, it is called a *semivariable* or *mixed* cost. For example, assume a company leases a machine and pays a rental of $800 per month, plus $10 for each hour used. Assuming that 100 units can be produced per hour, the total cost at various levels of production is shown below:

Units produced per month	Machine hours	Rate per hour	Variable cost component	Fixed cost component	Total cost
-0-	-0-	$10	$ -0-	$800	$ 800
1,000	10	10	100	800	900
2,000	20	10	200	800	1,000
5,000	50	10	500	800	1,300

Graphically, this appears as:

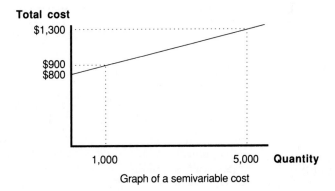

Graph of a semivariable cost

Other patterns of cost behavior could also be considered. For our purposes, however, these three will suffice. These cost behavior patterns—in particular, fixed and variable—will be employed in the next several chapters.

SUMMARY

Learning Objective 1: Describe and discuss the four major areas of managerial accounting.

Managerial accounting (internal reporting) is concerned with accounting data and reports prepared for parties within the firm. Managerial accounting can be functionally classified into the areas of: (1) planning, (2) control and performance evaluation, (3) decision analysis, and (4) product costing. Planning involves preparation of budgets, or estimates of future activities. While planning occurs prior to the period of activity, control and evaluation functions occur during and after the period of activity. Managerial accounting data and reports generated for control and evaluation purposes are intended to allow management to: (1) evaluate the performance of departments and key personnel, (2) revise unrealistic plans, or (3) take other necessary corrective action. Decision analysis, the third functional area of managerial accounting, provides data to management for the analysis of nonroutine problems such as adding a new sales territory, dropping an old product line, or leasing versus buying a new factory machine. In the product costing area of managerial accounting, the concern is the assignment of costs incurred to products.

Learning Objective 2: Prepare journal entries for the flow of costs in a manufacturing operation.

Direct materials, direct labor, and manufacturing overhead costs incurred in producing the product are recorded as work in process inventory. When units are completed, the cost of the completed items is removed from work in process inventory and transferred to finished goods inventory. Only when the finished items are sold to a customer (and thus the revenue recognized) is the cost removed from finished goods inventory and recorded as cost of goods sold expense.

Learning Objective 3: Prepare a schedule of cost of goods manufactured and sold.

This report reflects the flow of costs in manufacturing. Current manufacturing costs (direct materials, direct labor, and manufacturing overhead) are adjusted for changes in work in process inventory to yield cost of goods manufactured. This amount, adjusted for changes in finished goods inventory, yields cost of goods sold.

Learning Objective 4: Distinguish fixed, variable, and semivariable costs.

Managerial accounting necessitates classification of costs in various ways. A common classification of costs is according to the behavior of costs in relationship to changes in activity level. Total fixed costs remain constant as activity levels fluctuate. Total variable costs fluctuate proportionately to changes in the activity level. Semivariable costs contain both fixed and variable elements.

KEY TERMS

Budget	Fixed cost
Control	Managerial accounting
Decision analysis	Manufacturing overhead
Direct labor	Performance evaluation
Direct materials	Performance report
Finished goods inventory	Period cost

Planning	Semivariable cost
Product cost	Standard cost
Product costing	Variable cost
Schedule of cost of goods manufactured and sold	Work in process inventory

REVIEW QUESTIONS

1 Distinguish between financial accounting and managerial accounting.

2 Evaluate the following statement: "Managerial accounting reports solely illustrate the determination of inventory valuations and cost of goods sold."

3 The management of Brickle Manufacturing Co. has responsibilities for planning, controlling, and evaluating the operations of its three separate divisions. What role can managerial accounting play in providing data to management to help it meet its planning, controlling, and evaluation responsibilities?

4 What is the factor that most clearly differentiates decision analysis from the other major areas of managerial accounting?

5 A merchandising company purchases inventory from vendors and then resells the inventory to customers without further processing. Describe the operations of a manufacturing company.

6 "All material, labor, and overhead costs incurred by the manufacturing operations of the business during the current period should be reported as cost of goods sold expense for the current period." Evaluate the preceding statement.

7 For a manufacturing company, list the three categories of production costs and the three types of inventories on hand.

8 Distinguish between direct materials and indirect materials. Distinguish between direct labor and indirect labor.

9 Fernville Manufacturing Co. has the following labor costs during the period: sales salaries, assemblers' and finishers' factory wages, secretaries' salaries, and factory supervisor's salary. How would each of these labor costs be classified (i.e., direct labor; indirect factory labor; or selling and administrative expense)? Which labor costs are product costs and which are period costs?

10 Distinguish between productive capacity and production support. List three examples of each.

11 The president of Levin Manufacturing Company states: "All costs other than direct materials and direct labor are manufacturing overhead costs and should be added to work in process inventory." As head accountant of Levin Manufacturing, how would you respond to the president's statement?

12 "Factory-related depreciation, rent, salaries, and maintenance costs are not expensed when incurred by a manufacturing company. Instead these costs are recorded in an asset account." Evaluate the preceding statements. Include a discussion of the matching concept in your answer.

13 Racquet Manufacturing Company's beginning work in process inventory was $48,740,450. The company's ending work in process inventory was only $35,572,830. None of the work in process inventory was stolen. Why is the company's ending work in process inventory less than the beginning work in process inventory?

14 Concordia Manufacturing Co.'s beginning finished goods inventory totaled $13,200. If the cost of goods available for sale was $85,400, what was the cost

of goods manufactured for the period? If the ending inventory of finished goods totaled $19,800, what was the cost of goods sold for the period?

15 Define "cost of goods manufactured." Explain how it is calculated.

16 Can cost of goods sold exceed the cost of the goods available for sale? Can the cost of goods sold for a period exceed the cost of goods manufactured?

17 Sprendell Manufacturing Co. uses one gallon of X-16 in producing one unit of product Z-14. The cost of one gallon of X-16 is $3.50. Is X-16 a fixed or variable cost?

18 Catellet Trucking Co. leases its tractor-trailer trucks for $30,000 per year plus $.06 per mile. Catellet Trucking Co.'s truck-leasing expense represents what type of cost behavior pattern? If Catellet's trucks run 680,000 miles in a year, what is the company's total truck-leasing expense for the year?

19 Total fixed costs are fixed regardless of changes in the activity level. Evaluate the preceding statement.

20 "I don't plan on being an accountant; I'm going to be a manager. Why should I spend my time studying accounting?" How would you respond to the preceding comment?

EXERCISES

E14-1 Out-of-Line Co. uses a standard cost system. Each unit produced in Department AZ-10 requires 18 feet of lumber, 6 hours of direct labor, and 5 hours of machine time. Manufacturing overhead is based on machine hours. Standard costs are $1.20 per foot of lumber, $4.00 per direct labor hour, and $12.00 manufacturing overhead per machine hour. Out-of-Line Co.'s production in Department AZ-10 totaled 9,100 units during November, 1988. Actual production costs were $201,000 for lumber, $181,000 for direct labor, and $540,000 for manufacturing overhead. Prepare a performance report in dollar terms for Department AZ-10 for November, 1988. Follow the format shown in Exhibit 14-2.

E14-2 Presented below is a simple flow chart of the costs of a manufacturing operation. The rectangular boxes represent inventory. The arrows depict "flows." Complete the flow chart by identifying the items labeled (a), (b), (c), (d), (e), and (f).

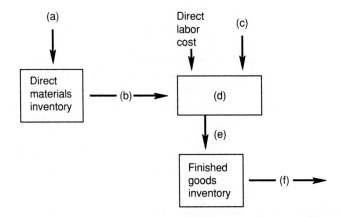

E14-3 The records of the Leonard Manufacturing Company contain the following accounts. Identify those accounts that should be included in "manufacturing overhead."
  1 Direct materials used
  2 Office supplies used
?**3** Production supplies used ✓ Supplies + minor materials used in production
  4 Labor—factory maintenance employees
✓**5** Labor—plant supervisors
  6 Labor—administrative staff
  7 Labor—sales staff
  8 Labor—design and engineering
  9 Labor—production employees
✓**10** Labor—warehouse employees
✓**11** Depreciation—factory and office building
✓**12** Depreciation—production equipment
  13 Depreciation—design and engineering equipment
  14 Depreciation—office equipment
✓**15** Employee fringe benefits
✓**16** Fire insurance on building and equipment
✓**17** Property taxes
  18 Telephone
  19 Travel expenses—salesmen
✓**20** Rental of production equipment

E14-4 Presented below is a series of incomplete accounting equations for Marvin's Manufacturing Company. Solve for the question mark (?) in each equation. The first one already is done as an example.
  1 Net Income = ? − Cost of Goods Sold − Other Expenses
    Answer: ? = Sales Revenue
  2 Cost of Goods Sold = Beginning Finished Goods Inventory + ? − Ending Finished Goods Inventory   *COG manuf.*
  3 Cost of Goods Manufactured = Beginning Work in Process Inventory + Current Manufacturing Costs − ? *W/P Ending Inventory*
  4 Current Period Manufacturing Costs = Direct Materials Used + ? + Manufacturing Overhead   *Direct Labor*
  5 Direct Materials Used = Beginning Direct Materials Inventory + ? − Ending Direct Materials Inventory   *Purchases*

E14-5 Todd Manufacturing Company had a beginning work in process inventory of $30,000 and a beginning finished goods inventory of $43,000. Other information available:
  1 Direct materials purchased on account, $130,000
  2 Direct materials used, $122,000
  3 Direct labor of $165,000, paid in cash
  4 Manufacturing overhead costs incurred $98,000, all paid in cash except for $12,000 depreciation
  5 Entire manufacturing overhead of $98,000 charged to work in process
  6 Cost of units completed in factory during period and transferred to finished goods was $320,000

7 Cost of goods sold was $338,000. Selling price to customers was $484,000—all sales on account.

Calculate:

1 Cost of goods manufactured
2 Ending work in process inventory
3 Cost of goods available for sale
4 Ending finished goods inventory

E14-6 An examination of the annual financial statements for Milroy Manufacturing Company shows the following information:

	12/31/88	12/31/89
Statement of Income:		
Cost of Goods Sold	$2,700,000	$3,100,000
Balance Sheet:		
Inventory—Materials	150,000	180,000
Inventory—Work in Process	312,000	288,000
Inventory—Finished Goods	515,000	643,000

Determine the following:

1 Current manufacturing costs during 1989
2 Cost of goods manufactured for 1989
3 Cost of goods available for sale during 1989

E14-7 Brockport Manufacturing Co. provides you with the information below. Prepare a schedule of cost of goods manufactured and sold for the year ended December 31, 1988, following the format of Exhibit 14-4.

Direct Materials:	
Inventory, January 1, 1988	$21,000
Purchases during 1988	63,000
Inventory, December 31, 1988	18,000
Direct Labor	59,000
Manufacturing Overhead	74,000
Work in Process:	
Inventory, January 1, 1988	30,000
Inventory, December 31, 1988	32,000
Finished Goods:	
Inventory, January 1, 1988	41,000
Inventory, December 31, 1988	44,000

E14-8 Given the following data for Merkle Manufacturing Co., prepare a schedule of cost of goods manufactured and sold for 1988, following the format of Exhibit 14-4.

1 Inventories:

	1/1/88	12/31/88
Direct Materials	$24,000	$18,000
Work in Process	15,000	25,000
Finished Goods	21,000	20,000

2 Direct materials purchased during 1988, $53,000

3 Direct labor cost for 1988, $80,000
4 Manufacturing overhead for 1988, $40,000

E14-9 Gownick Manufacturing Co. rents its factory for a fixed cost of $20,000 per month. Direct materials cost per unit is $1.00. Graphically illustrate cost behavior at 5,000, 10,000, 15,000 and 20,000 units of output per month for (1) total rent cost and (2) total direct materials cost.

PROBLEMS

P14-1 *Sales Budget and Performance Report*
Aero Shirts, Inc. is a manufacturer of men's shirts that are sold via mail order. Expected sales of the company's three lines of shirts for the next three months are as follows:

	April	May	June
Casual shirts	3,000	3,000	3,500
Economy dress shirts	2,000	2,000	4,000
Executive dress shirts	1,200	1,100	1,000

Current prices are $7 for the casual shirts, $8 for the economy dress shirts, and $11 for the executive dress shirts. In June, a special promotion of the economy dress shirts will be held, with the price dropping to $6. The price of executive dress shirts will be increased by $1 beginning May 1.
Required:
1 Prepare a sales budget for the three-month period.
2 Assume that sales during April were as follows:

Casual shirts	$22,505
Economy dress shirts	14,720
Executive dress shirts	11,473

If the expected prices were obtained, how did the unit sales of each line compare with the budgeted unit sales?

P14-2 *Performance Report*
Pretone Manufacturing Company uses standard costs to compare to actual costs in order to control and evaluate department managers' performance. Ron Smith, manager of Department #6, is worried about his performance report for July, 1988 when his department produced 116,000 units. Total standard costs for the 116,000 units are: Material A, $2,784,000; Material B, $4,176,000; Material C, $580,000; direct labor, $1,160,000; and $742,400 manufacturing overhead. The standard costs per pound are: Material A, $4; Material B, $9; and Material C, $1. Standard rates per hour are $10 per direct labor hour and $8 per machine hour. Manufacturing overhead is based on machine hours. During July, 1988 Department #6 had the following actual costs to produce the 116,000 units: Material A, $2,828,000; Material B, $4,190,000; Material C, $574,000; direct labor, $1,172,000; and manufacturing overhead, $731,300.

Required:

Prepare a performance report in dollar terms, following the format shown in Exhibit 14-2.

P14-3 *Classification of Manufacturing Costs*

Adams Furniture Company manufactures and sells sofas, chairs, and beds. Costs incurred during the year are as follows:

DL **a** Carpenters' salaries
MOH + PC **b** Rental of factory building
SG&A **c** Interest on bank loan
SG&A **d** Depreciation on office photocopy machine
DM **e** Lumber used
MOH+ PC **f** Depreciation on power saws and sanders
DM **g** Metal frames used
DL **h** Assemblers' salaries
SGA **i** Sales commissions
MOH+PS **j** Factory supervisor's salary
MOH+PS **k** Electricity used to run power saws and sanders
SG&A **l** Rental of office building
MOH+PS **m** Factory janitor's salary

Required:

Categorize each cost as: 1) direct material; 2) direct labor; 3) manufacturing overhead; or 4) selling, general, and administrative expense. If the item is a manufacturing overhead cost, also indicate whether it provides productive capacity or production support.

P14-4 *Journal Entries for Cost Flow*

The following is a summary of the manufacturing transactions for Wirth Manufacturing Company:

1 Purchased $118,000 of direct materials on account.
2 Transferred $102,000 of direct materials from the materials storeroom to the factory, where they were placed into production.
3 Wages earned by and paid to direct labor employees totaled $406,000.   reduce cash
4 Actual manufacturing overhead costs incurred totaled $283,000. Assume all of the $283,000 total (except $29,000 depreciation) was paid in cash.
5 The $283,000 manufacturing overhead is charged to work in process.
6 Products with a cost of $646,000 are completed and transferred from the factory into the finished goods showroom.
7 Finished goods costing $591,000 are sold to customers on account for $800,000.

Required:

Prepare journal entries to record the above transactions.

P14-5 *Cost Flow Journal Entries from Ledger Postings*

Presented below are selected general ledger accounts for Krissk Manufacturing Company:

Materials inventory		
Jan. 1 bal.	10,000	74,000
(1)	86,000	

Work in process inventory		
Jan. 1 bal.	18,000	199,000
(2)	74,000	
(3)	91,000	
	107,000	

Manufacturing overhead		
107,000	(4)	107,000

Finished goods inventory		
Jan. 1 bal.	46,000	(6) 202,000
(5)	199,000	

Cost of goods sold	
202,000	

Accounts payable		
81,000	Jan. 1 bal.	11,000
		86,000

Wages payable		
84,000	Jan. 1 bal.	4,000
		91,000

Required:

1 Recreate the journal entries in proper debit and credit form for items marked 1 through 6 in the above ledger accounts. The first one is done below to serve as an example.

(1)	Materials Inventory	86,000	
	Accounts Payable		86,000

To record purchases of direct materials on account.

2 Compute the ending ledger account balances for the three inventory accounts.

P14-6 *Schedule of Cost of Goods Manufactured and Sold* p. 437
Presented below is selected information for SUNY Manufacturing Co.:

Inventories, May 1, 1988:	
Direct Materials	$ 46,000
Work in Process	83,000
Finished Goods	106,000
Inventories, April 30, 1989:	
Direct Materials	42,000
Work in Process	88,000
Finished Goods	110,000
Direct materials purchased during year	230,000
Direct labor utilized during year	360,000
Manufacturing overhead utilized during year	540,000

Required:

Prepare a schedule of cost of goods manufactured and sold for the year ended April 30, 1989.

P14-7 *Schedule of Cost of Goods Manufactured and Sold*   437

Presented below are selected data, in alphabetical order, for Ventor Manufacturing Co. for the year ended December 31, 1988:

Accounts payable	$ 18,000
Accounts receivable	71,000
Accumulated depreciation	328,000
Allowance for uncollectible accounts	48,000
Beginning finished goods inventory	64,000
Beginning work in process inventory	52,000
Cash	26,000
Common stock	160,000
Depreciation expense—office equipment	4,000
Ending finished goods inventory	63,000
Ending work in process inventory	103,000
Labor utilized (direct)	209,000
Manufacturing overhead utilized	153,000
Materials utilized (direct)	34,000
Sales revenue, net	673,000
Selling expense	59,000

Required:

Prepare a schedule of cost of goods manufactured and sold for the year ended December 31, 1988.

P14-8 *Flow of Manufacturing Costs*

The Wolverine Manufacturing Company provides the following information:

Direct Materials Inventory:	
Inventory, beginning of period	$ 50,000
Purchases during period	380,000
Inventory, end of period	40,000
Direct Labor	200,000
Manufacturing Overhead	190,000
Work in Process Inventory:	
Inventory, beginning of period	80,000
Inventory, end of period	95,000
Finished Goods Inventory:	
Inventory, beginning of period	110,000
Inventory, end of period	90,000

Required:

Calculate each of the following:

1 Direct materials available for use

2 Direct materials used

3 Total manufacturing costs in process

4 Cost of goods manufactured

5 Cost of goods available for sale

6 Cost of goods sold

P14-9   *Flow of Manufacturing Costs: Missing Data*

	Situation 1	Situation 2	Situation 3
Direct materials inventory 1/1	$ 12,000	$ 40,000	$ G
Purchases of direct materials	40,000	D	600,000
Direct labor	70,000	70,000	70,000
Cost of goods manufactured	150,000	E	747,000
Direct materials inventory 12/31	A	35,000	60,000
Manufacturing overhead	B	80,000	140,000
Direct materials used	48,000	100,000	560,000
Cost of goods sold	C	265,000	777,000
Work in process inventory 1/1	10,000	15,000	H
Work in process inventory 12/31	10,000	10,000	85,000
Finished goods inventory 1/1	8,000	30,000	I
Finished goods inventory 12/31	13,000	F	45,000

Required:
For each situation above, solve for the unknowns.

Business Decision Problem

You are the vice-president in charge of operations for Rossman Manufacturing Co. A decision has been made to modernize production facilities. You are to make the final choice of which of two machine groups is to be purchased to replace existing equipment. Information about the two machine groups is as follows:

Machine Group A
$1,000,000 current investment cost
$250,000 annual cash savings from machine operations
Ten-year estimated life with zero estimated salvage value

Machine Group B
$1,800,000 current investment cost
$300,000 annual cash savings from machine operations
Fifteen-year estimated life with $260,000 estimated salvage value

The company's desired rate of return (interest) is 10 percent, compounded annually. Assume annual cash savings would be recognized at the end of each year.

Required:
1 Using present values and present value tables, determine which machine group is the preferable acquisition.
2 What other factors should be considered before making the final choice?

15

PRODUCT COSTING

LEARNING OBJECTIVES

When you complete this chapter, you should be able to:

1 Describe the characteristics of a job-order cost system and a process cost system.
2 Prepare journal entries for materials, labor, and overhead.
3 Calculate and apply a predetermined overhead rate.
4 Calculate equivalent units of product and costs per equivalent unit.
5 Prepare a production cost report.

Product costing is one of the important functions of a managerial accounting system. Product cost data are needed for external reporting to determine amounts assigned to inventory and cost of goods sold. Product cost data are also used in internal reporting for planning, control, and decision analysis.

The purpose of a product-costing system is to associate specific amounts of manufacturing cost (direct materials, direct labor, and manufacturing overhead) with the units being produced, and then to identify the units as either units sold or units remaining in inventory. While each manufacturing firm develops its product-costing system to fit its own circumstances, most product-costing systems can be classified as either a *job-order cost system* or a *process cost system*.

Job-order costing considers each unit of product to be distinct, unlike any other unit. The association of manufacturing costs with units of product must be done on an item-by-item basis. That is, the amounts of direct materials, direct labor, and manufacturing overhead to be associated with unit A will be different from the amounts associated with unit B, and so forth. To determine the amount of cost to be assigned to inventory and cost of goods sold, it is necessary to know *exactly which units* fall in each category.

Process costing considers each unit of product to be the same as any other unit. Thus, the association of manufacturing costs with units of product is done on an *average* basis. Each complete unit of product is assigned the same amount of cost, and each partially complete unit is assigned an appropriate portion of the cost of a complete unit. To determine the amount of cost to be assigned to inventory and cost of goods sold, it is only necessary to know *how many units* fall in each category.

The choice between these two systems depends primarily on the nature of the firm's manufacturing activities. A firm producing a single, standard product is likely to employ process costing. A firm producing diverse products will likely use job-order costing.

JOB-ORDER COSTING

Job-order costing is used by companies whose manufacturing process consists of jobs that are separately identifiable and significantly different from one another. Each job has unique, identifiable features causing the cost of production to vary from other jobs the company produces. A job may be a single item, a composite item (e.g., the construction of a building), or a batch of similar items (e.g., 100 chairs of a given type).

For example, consider a furniture manufacturer. A chair is easily differentiated from a sofa, love seat, or hassock, and the cost of manufacturing a batch of chairs varies significantly from the cost of making a batch of sofas, love seats, or hassocks. The furniture manufacturer using job-order costing would determine a separate cost for each different batch of production. Other types of manufacturers typically using job-order costing include shipbuilders, building contractors, aerospace manufacturers, and print shops.

Exhibit 15-1 illustrates the general operation of a job-order cost system. Manufacturing costs are assigned to individual jobs, which constitute the Work in Process Inventory. Costs of completed jobs are assigned to Finished Goods Inventory, and then, when the product is sold, to Cost of Goods Sold.

Exhibit 15-2 illustrates the flow of costs through the applicable general ledger accounts for a job-order cost system. Items to note include the use of three different inventory accounts, the inclusion of three costs of production (direct materials, direct labor, and manufacturing overhead), and the use of a predetermined rate to apply manufacturing overhead to production. Each of these important aspects of cost flow in a job-order cost system will be discussed in subsequent sections.

Work in Process Inventory

The central account in a job-order costing system is the *Work in Process Inventory* account. This account presents manufacturing costs for jobs that have been started

EXHIBIT 15-1 Operation of a Job-Order Cost System

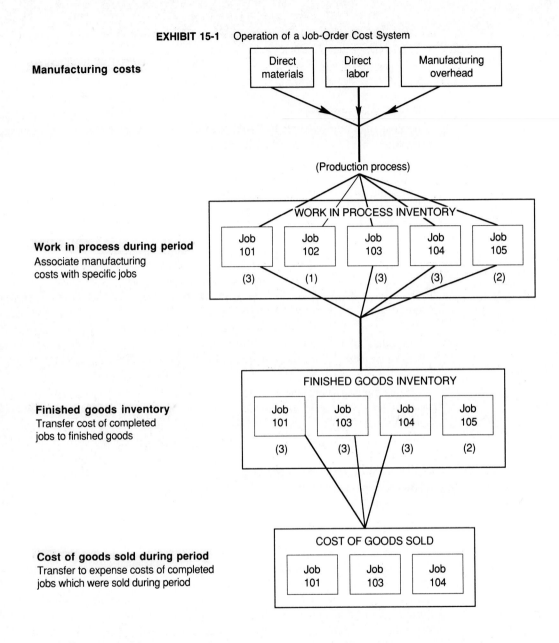

Manufacturing costs

Work in process during period
Associate manufacturing
costs with specific jobs

Finished goods inventory
Transfer cost of completed
jobs to finished goods

Cost of goods sold during period
Transfer to expense costs of completed
jobs which were sold during period

(1) At the end of the period, Job 102 was not yet completed. It remains in Work in Process Inventory.
(2) At the end of the perid, Job 105 was completed but not yet sold.
(3) Jobs 101, 103, and 104 were completed and sold during the period.

EXHIBIT 15-2   Accounts in a Job-Order Cost System

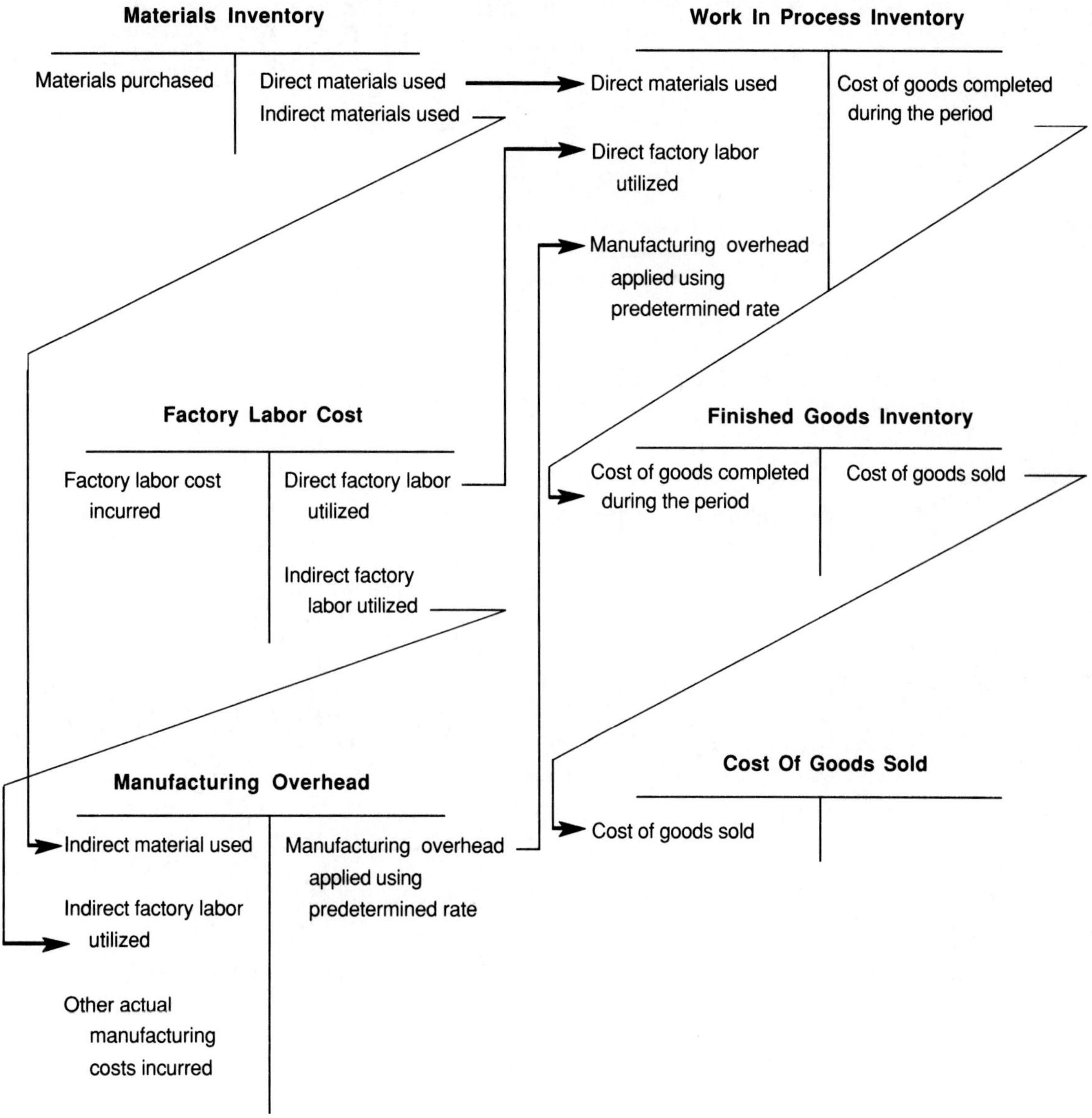

but have not yet been completed. The entry of costs into this account marks the point in the cost system where we begin to accumulate cost data by job.

The Work in Process Inventory account in the general ledger presents a summary of the following information:[1]

	1. Work in process inventory, beginning of period
Plus	2. Direct materials issued to production during the period
Plus	3. Direct labor utilized in production during the period
Plus	4. Manufacturing overhead applied to production during the period
Minus	5. Cost of goods completed during the period and transferred to finished goods
Equals	6. Work in process inventory, end of period

As indicated above, the three elements of manufacturing cost—direct materials, direct labor, and manufacturing overhead—are added to work in process. To understand the Work in Process account, we must first study these three cost elements.

Materials

The *Materials Inventory* general ledger account provides a summary of material purchases and usage:

	1. Materials inventory, beginning of period
Plus	2. Materials purchased during the period
Minus	3. Materials issued to production during the period
Equals	4. Materials inventory, end of period

When a vendor's invoice for materials is received, the cost is recorded in materials inventory. Assume that on January 8, 1988, $24,000 of materials were purchased by Croton Manufacturing Co.

```
1988
Jan.  8      Materials Inventory              24,000
                 Accounts Payable                          24,000
             To record purchase of materials on
                 account.
```

Materials issued from the materials inventory to production must be identified as either direct materials or indirect materials. *Direct materials* issued are those items that can be traced to specific jobs. The cost of direct materials used is debited to the Work in Process Inventory account. *Indirect materials*, on the other hand, cannot be traced to specific jobs. Or, they can only be identified with specific jobs at a very high cost for the relatively small dollar amounts of materials involved. For example, nails, glue, machine lubricant, and floor cleaners are often considered to be indirect materials. Indirect materials used are debited to the Manufacturing Overhead account.

---

[1]We assume no loss of inventory via theft, spoilage, and so on. This assumption applies to inventory accounts discussed throughout the chapter.

Croton Manufacturing's journal entry to record the January 14, 1988, issuance of materials from the materials storeroom into production is as follows:

Jan. 14	Work in Process Inventory *Direct*	4,916	
	Manufacturing Overhead *Indirect*	84	
	Materials Inventory		5,000

> To record direct and indirect mater-
> ials transferred out of the
> materials storeroom into the pro-
> duction departments.

The $4,916 cost of direct materials issued is debited to Work in Process Inventory. The $84 cost of indirect materials issued is debited to Manufacturing Overhead. The combined $5,000 cost of all materials (direct and indirect) issued to production is credited to Materials Inventory.

Labor

A second production cost is manufacturing labor. Since the cost of manufacturing labor is destined eventually for the Work in Process account, one possibility is to enter these costs to Work in Process as incurred. However, as cost assignment to products becomes more complex, it is convenient to record manufacturing labor costs first in a Factory Labor Cost account. Assume total factory employee earnings total $7,500 for Croton Manufacturing for the period January 1 through January 15. The following entry would be made:

Jan. 15	Factory Labor Cost	7,500	
	Salaries and Wages Payable		7,500

> To record earnings by manufactur-
> ing employees for the period
> Jan. 1 through Jan. 15.

The question of cost assignment can then be addressed. The total factory labor cost should be analyzed and categorized as direct and indirect labor costs. *Direct labor* represents wages earned by employees working directly on the job under production. Direct labor costs are debited to the Work in Process Inventory account. All other factory labor costs, not directly traceable to specific jobs, are *indirect labor*. Examples of indirect labor are supervisors' salaries and janitorial wages. Indirect labor costs are debited to Manufacturing Overhead.

The journal entry to distribute Croton's assumed factory labor costs for the period is:

Jan. 15	Work in Process Inventory *Direct*	6,000	
	Manufacturing Overhead *Indirect*	1,500	
	Factory Labor Cost		7,500

> To record direct and indirect labor cost
> for the period Jan. 1 through Jan.
> 15.

Note the similarity to the handling of materials utilized. Factory labor costs must be identified as either direct or indirect. Direct material and direct labor costs are added to the Work in Process Inventory account. Indirect materials and indirect labor costs are added to Manufacturing Overhead. These indirect costs will then become part of the manufacturing overhead applied to work in process using a predetermined rate.

Manufacturing Overhead

The third cost of production is manufacturing overhead. *Manufacturing overhead* consists of all costs necessary to manufacture the product, other than direct materials and direct labor. Two examples of manufacturing overhead costs—indirect materials and indirect labor—have already been discussed. Other manufacturing overhead costs include factory utilities, depreciation of factory buildings and equipment, factory repairs, and factory insurance. On the other hand, costs related to sales or administration of the firm (e.g., advertising, sales commissions, office salaries, depreciation of office equipment) are not included in manufacturing overhead.

The journal entries debiting the Manufacturing Overhead account for utilization of indirect materials and indirect labor were previously illustrated. Journal entries for other actual manufacturing overhead costs are recorded by debits to Manufacturing Overhead and credits to other accounts such as Cash or Accounts Payable (for factory utility bills, repairs, and so on), Accumulated Depreciation (for depreciation on factory buildings and machinery), and Prepaid Insurance (for expired factory insurance).

Most companies do not add *actual* manufacturing overhead to the Work in Process Inventory account. There are several reasons actual manufacturing overhead is not put into production cost (i.e., added to work in process). These reasons are:

1 *Timeliness.* As jobs are completed, all actual manufacturing overhead costs may not yet be known. Company officials may need a total cost amount, including manufacturing overhead, immediately upon completion of the job in order to help set a selling price or determine whether to repeat the job.

2 *Monthly variations.* Certain actual manufacturing overhead costs occur irregularly during the year. For example, heating bills are higher in January than June, or a major machine repair may occur in January. Adding these actual January heating and repair overhead costs to January's cost of production would produce unrealistically high, and noncomparable, costs for the jobs that happened to be scheduled during January. Also, actual production activity can vary significantly from month to month during the year, without a corresponding variation in actual manufacturing overhead costs. Consider the effect on a company that produces many units in September, few units in April, and assigns the stable, actual manufacturing overhead costs to units produced. Identical jobs scheduled in different months could be assigned significantly different costs.

3 *Nonallocability.* It is extremely difficult to allocate accurately a number of manufacturing overhead items to specific jobs. For example, if job #2843 happened to be in progress when a machine broke down, how should the cost of repairing the machine be allocated to various jobs?

Instead of adding *actual* manufacturing overhead costs to work in process, most companies apply manufacturing overhead to work in process using a *predetermined rate.* The use of a predetermined rate provides an *estimated* manufacturing overhead cost that alleviates the problems encountered when using actual manufacturing overhead. The amount of manufacturing overhead applied to production is found by (1) calculating a predetermined manufacturing overhead rate and (2) multiplying the predetermined rate times the volume of the application base for the period. Each of these steps is described below.

Manufacturing Overhead Rate   The predetermined manufacturing overhead rate is calculated at the beginning of the year. The rate is determined by dividing *expected manufacturing overhead costs* for the coming year by the *expected volume* of some *application base* (such as direct labor hours, direct labor dollars, or machine hours). Selecting an overhead application base is not an easy task. A base should be selected that is easy to measure and that provides a reasonable way of distinguishing among different jobs. Recall that manufacturing overhead represents the cost of providing the capacity and support for production activity. In one company, the amount of labor time (direct labor hours) spent on a job may be a reasonable way of estimating the job's share of overhead costs. In another company, direct labor dollars (direct labor cost) may be the most appropriate base for relating manufacturing overhead costs with jobs. In a highly mechanized company that uses robots in its production process, the number of machine hours used on each job might be an appropriate measure.

Croton Manufacturing chose direct labor hours as their overhead application base. The company believes that the overhead costs utilized in their production process vary proportionately to the number of direct labor hours worked on each job. Croton's predetermined manufacturing overhead rate of $4.60 per direct labor hour for the year was calculated at the beginning of the year using the following formula:

$$\text{Predetermined Manufacturing Overhead Rate} = \frac{\text{Estimated Manufacturing Overhead Costs for Coming Year}}{\text{Estimated Volume of Application Base for Coming Year}}$$

$$\$4.60 \text{ rate per direct labor hour} = \frac{\$184,000}{40,000 \text{ direct labor hours}}$$

Applied Manufacturing Overhead   Manufacturing overhead costs are applied to production by multiplying the *actual volume of the application base* for the period by the *predetermined manufacturing overhead rate* calculated in the preceding step. The amount of overhead applied can be expressed in equation form as:

$$\begin{array}{l} \text{Applied Manufacturing} \\ \text{Overhead} \end{array} = \begin{array}{c} \text{Predetermined Manufacturing Overhead Rate} \\ \text{times Actual Volume of} \\ \text{Application Base During the Period} \end{array}$$

If 2,800 direct labor hours were worked by Croton's factory employees during January, the applied manufacturing overhead for the month would be $12,880.

$$\begin{array}{l} \$12,880 \text{ applied} \\ \text{manufacturing overhead} \end{array} = \begin{array}{c} \$4.60 \text{ predetermined rate} \\ \text{times 2,800 direct labor hours} \\ \text{worked during January} \end{array}$$

The journal entry to apply manufacturing overhead to production for Croton for January would be:

Jan. 31	Work in Process Inventory	12,880	
	Manufacturing Overhead		12,880
	To record overhead costs applied to production by multiplying $4.60 predetermined manufacturing over- head rate by 2,800 direct labor hours worked during January.		

Information on the actual volume of the application base for the period is needed to calculate the amount of the above journal entry. It is also required on a job-by-job basis in order to apply manufacturing overhead to the individual jobs.

To summarize:

1 *Actual manufacturing overhead costs are debited to Manufacturing Overhead.* Credited are various accounts such as Materials Inventory (indirect materials), Factory Labor Cost (indirect labor), Cash or Accounts Payable (utilities, repairs, and so on), Accumulated Depreciation (depreciation), and Prepaid Insurance (expired insurance).

2 *Applied manufacturing overhead costs are debited to Work in Process Inventory and credited to Manufacturing Overhead.* The amount of overhead to apply is determined by multiplying the volume during the period of the selected application base (e.g., direct labor hours, or direct labor dollars, or machine hours) by the predetermined manufacturing overhead rate.

Many companies with several manufacturing departments would have separate Work in Process Inventory and Manufacturing Overhead accounts for each department. Similarly, each department could have its own predetermined manufacturing overhead rate. The application base selected might vary from department to department.

Completion of Jobs in Process

Upon completion, all jobs should have been charged with the appropriate amount of direct materials, direct labor, and applied manufacturing overhead. As jobs were transferred out of work in process and into finished goods inventory, Croton Manufacturing made the following journal entry:

Jan. 25	Finished Goods Inventory	17,720	
	Work in Process Inventory		17,720
	To record cost of jobs completed and		
	transferred to finished goods.		

Costs for uncompleted jobs remain in the Work in Process account.

Finished Goods Inventory and Cost of Goods Sold

The *Finished Goods Inventory* account presents the costs of completed jobs awaiting sale. Specifically, the account summarizes the following information:

	1. Finished goods inventory, beginning of period
Plus	2. Items completed and transferred to finished goods during the period
Minus	3. Items sold during the period
Equals	4. Finished goods inventory, end of period

To record the sale on January 29 of 140 units of product at a selling price of $160 each, Croton made two journal entries:

Jan. 29	Accounts Receivable	22,400	
	Sales		22,400
	To record sale on account of 140 units.		
29	Cost of Goods Sold	13,260	
	Finished Goods Inventory		13,260
	To record cost of units sold.		

Note that the debit to Accounts Receivable and credit to Sales is recorded at the *selling price* charged the customer. The debit to Cost of Goods Sold and credit to Finished Goods Inventory records the *cost* to the company of manufacturing the items sold. Until the time of sale, all manufacturing costs (direct materials, direct labor, and manufacturing overhead) utilized in production have been deferred as assets in one of the inventory accounts. Only upon sale of the item and recording of sales revenue are manufacturing costs released to the income statement as expenses (i.e., cost of goods sold). The *matching concept*, discussed earlier in the textbook, justifies deferring recognition of manufacturing costs as expenses until related sales revenue is recorded.

Underapplied or Overapplied Manufacturing Overhead

Recall that most companies debit Work in Process Inventory with applied manufacturing overhead according to a predetermined rate. Since the predetermined rate is based on *estimates* of both manufacturing overhead costs and the volume of the selected application base, it is almost certain that actual manufacturing overhead costs for the year will differ from the amount of manufacturing overhead costs applied.

Manufacturing overhead is *underapplied* if actual overhead costs *exceed* overhead applied to production. If actual overhead costs are *less* than overhead applied to production, then manufacturing overhead is *overapplied*. The existence of a difference between actual and applied overhead is seen by examining the Manufacturing Overhead account.

Manufacturing overhead

Debit for *actual* overhead costs incurred	Credit for overhead *applied* to jobs using predetermined rate

As a general rule, the debits will not equal the credits in this account, and thus a balance will remain. A debit balance indicates underapplied manufacturing overhead, while a credit balance indicates manufacturing overhead is overapplied.

At the end of the year, the underapplied or overapplied overhead in the Manufacturing Overhead account must be eliminated. Ideally, the Work in Process Inventory, Finished Goods Inventory, and Cost of Goods Sold accounts should be adjusted to reflect the actual overhead costs. However, an accurate adjustment of this nature requires a difficult, detailed analysis of the subsidiary records of work in process, finished goods, and cost of goods sold. As a practical alternative, many companies adjust the Cost of Goods Sold account for the entire difference between actual and applied manufacturing overhead.

If at December 31, 1988, Croton Manufacturing had a debit balance of $4,600 in its manufacturing overhead account, the entry to adjust underapplied overhead to cost of goods sold would be:

Dec. 31	Cost of Goods Sold	4,600	
	Manufacturing Overhead		4,600
	To record adjustment for underapplied manufacturing overhead for the year.		

If the Manufacturing Overhead account had been overapplied for the year by $4,600, the entry to adjust for the overapplied manufacturing overhead would have been:

Dec. 31	Manufacturing Overhead	4,600	
	Cost of Goods Sold		4,600
	To record adjustment for overapplied manufacturing overhead for the year.		

The practical expediency of adjusting for the entire difference between actual and applied manufacturing overhead solely through cost of goods sold can be supported if the dollar amount is immaterial. If material in amount, underapplied or overapplied manufacturing overhead should be allocated among work in process, finished goods, and cost of goods sold.

PROCESS COSTING

Process costing is used by companies such as canneries, petroleum refineries, and chemical producers whose manufacturing operations involve the continuous, mass production of identical units. Unlike job-order costing, process costing does not accumulate cost data and determine unit costs for individual jobs or batches of production. Items manufactured throughout the period in a process cost system are so similar in appearance and cost incurrence that calculation of an average unit cost per batch of production is not meaningful. One batch of production is not significantly different from another. Instead, *under process costing a unit cost of production for the period is computed for each manufacturing process or department*. The unit cost is then used to assign costs to completed goods and to ending work in process inventory.

The operation of a process cost system is shown in Exhibit 15-3. Note that costs are accumulated in each department and then transferred to the next department in the production process. By this means, all production costs are assigned to products by the time they enter finished goods inventory.

An example helps to clarify the flow of costs in a process cost system. Consider a cannery producing cans of tuna fish. A can of tuna fish manufactured at the end of the period is essentially the same as a can produced at the beginning of the period. Since all cans of tuna fish are indistinguishable, accumulating costs for each batch of production during the period is unnecessary. Therefore, a process cost system could be used by the cannery. Under this system, total production costs per department would be accumulated for the period. These manufacturing costs, when divided by the number of cans produced during the period, would yield production cost per can of tuna fish. The unit cost serves as the basis for determining departmental work in process inventories, finished goods inventory, and cost of goods sold.

Work in Process Inventory

The flow of costs in a process cost system closely parallels the cost flow illustrated earlier for a job-order cost system. The major differences lie in the treatment of accounts for work in process inventory. In a job-order system, *one* Work in Process Inventory account is generally maintained, along with individual job cost records. In a process cost system, *several* accounts for work in process inventories are normally used, one for each step in the manufacturing process. No individual job cost records are maintained with process costing since all items

EXHIBIT 15-3 Operation of a Process Cost System

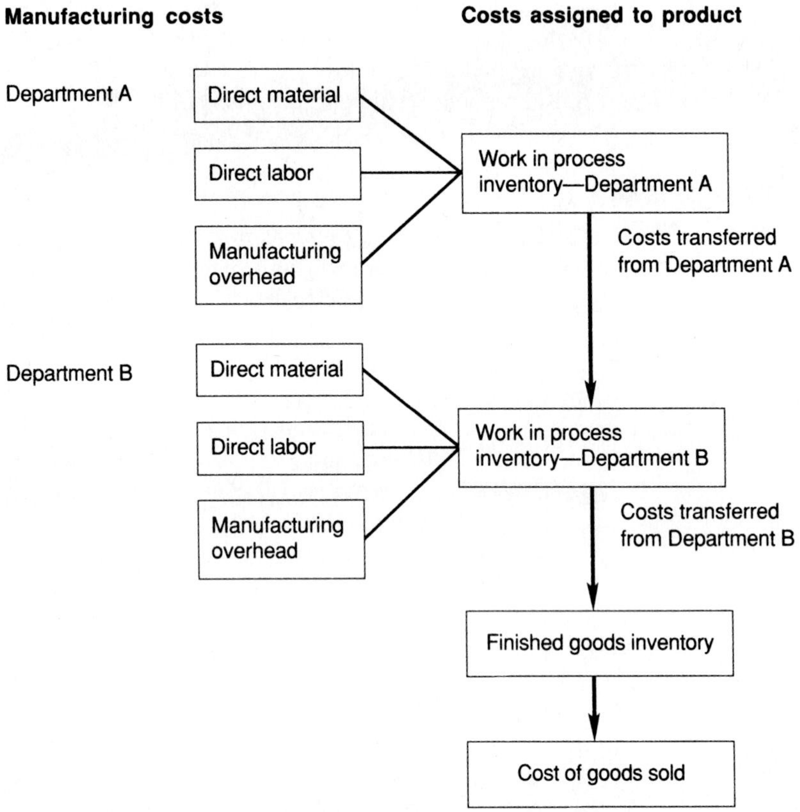

Manufacturing costs

Costs assigned to product

Department A

Direct material

Direct labor

Manufacturing overhead

Work in process inventory—Department A

Costs transferred from Department A

Department B

Direct material

Direct labor

Manufacturing overhead

Work in process inventory—Department B

Costs transferred from Department B

Finished goods inventory

Cost of goods sold

passing through the manufacturing process will be assigned the same amount of cost.

Compare the cost flow shown in Exhibit 15-4 for process costing with the job-order cost flow shown earlier (Exhibit 15-2). The significant differences in process cost flow are the use of multiple Work in Process Inventory accounts and the transfer of costs from one departmental Work in Process account to another. Process costing emphasizes the accumulation of costs by manufacturing department. A manufacturing department corresponds to a step in the production process. Each manufacturing department has its own ledger account for work in process inventory. In Exhibit 15-4, a separate Work in Process Inventory account is shown for each of the three manufacturing processes of the tuna fish cannery: cleaning, filleting, and packing.

To understand the role of the departmental account for work in process inventory, consider the account Work in Process Inventory—Packing Department for the tuna fish cannery. The account summarizes the following information:

EXHIBIT 15-4   Accounts in a Process Cost System

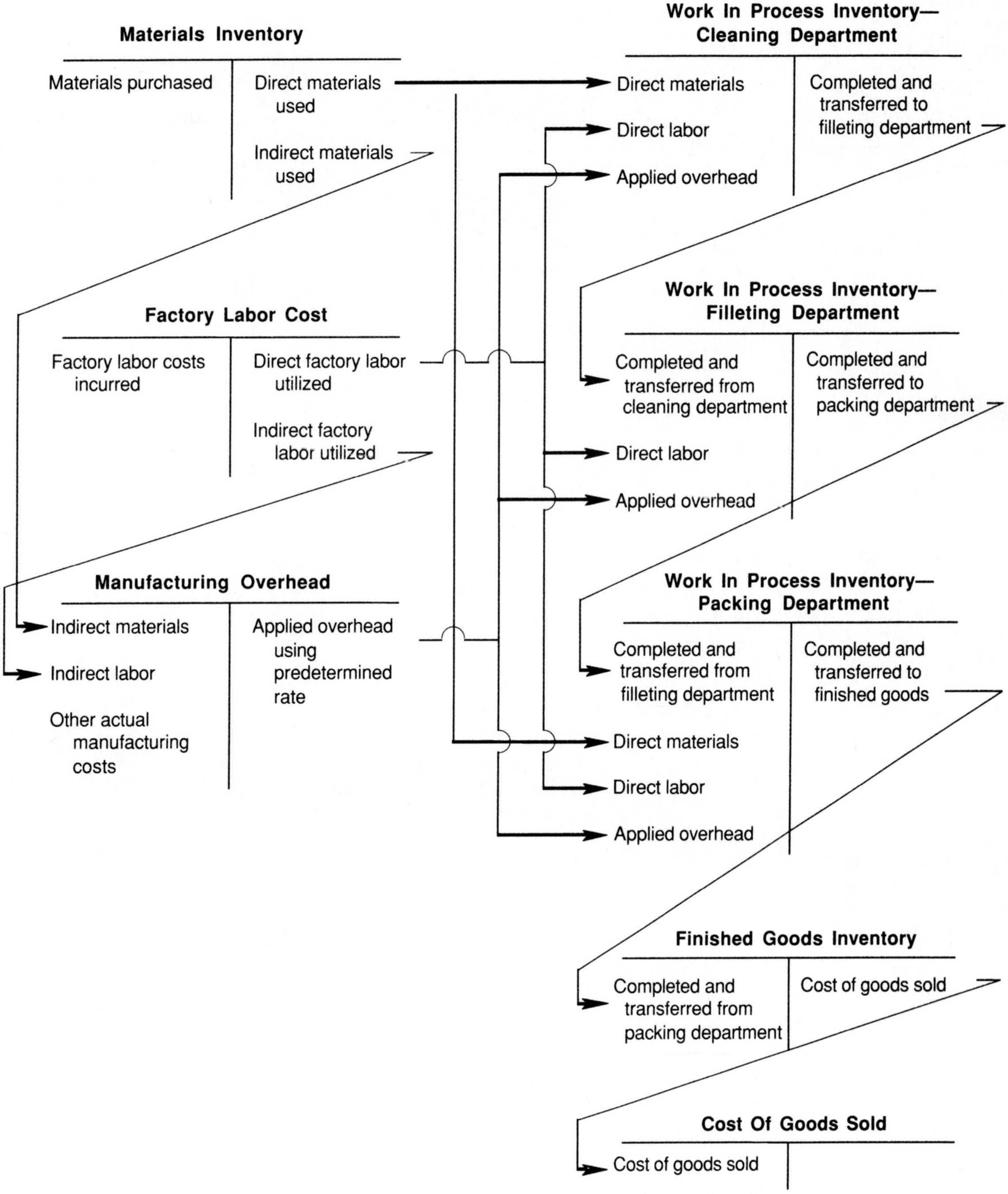

Materials Inventory

Materials purchased	Direct materials used
	Indirect materials used

Work In Process Inventory— Cleaning Department

Direct materials	Completed and transferred to filleting department
Direct labor	
Applied overhead	

Factory Labor Cost

Factory labor costs incurred	Direct factory labor utilized
	Indirect factory labor utilized

Work In Process Inventory— Filleting Department

Completed and transferred from cleaning department	Completed and transferred to packing department
Direct labor	
Applied overhead	

Manufacturing Overhead

Indirect materials	Applied overhead using predetermined rate
Indirect labor	
Other actual manufacturing costs	

Work In Process Inventory— Packing Department

Completed and transferred from filleting department	Completed and transferred to finished goods
Direct materials	
Direct labor	
Applied overhead	

Finished Goods Inventory

Completed and transferred from packing department	Cost of goods sold

Cost Of Goods Sold

Cost of goods sold	

	1. Departmental work in process inventory, beginning of period
Plus	2. Costs associated with units transferred to the packing department during the period
Plus	3. Direct materials issued to the packing department during the period
Plus	4. Direct labor utilized in the packing department during the period
Plus	5. Manufacturing overhead applied to the packing department during the period, based on a predetermined departmental rate
Minus	6. Costs associated with units packed and transferred to finished goods during the period
Equals	7. Departmental work in process inventory, end of period

Materials

The recording of materials purchases under process costing is identical to that previously described for job-order costing. A difference arises when materials are issued from the materials inventory and entered into production. Under process costing, when materials are being put into production, they are not assigned to particular jobs, but to specific *manufacturing departments*.

For example, when $2,000 of direct materials are transferred from the Ace Tuna Fish Cannery storeroom to the cleaning department on March 2, 1988, the following entry is made:

```
1988
Mar.  2        Work in Process Inventory—
                   Cleaning Department          2,000
                       Materials Inventory                    2,000
               To record the transfer of direct mate-
               rials to the cleaning department.
```

Note that the debit is to a particular Work in Process Inventory account, the one associated with the cleaning department.

The definitions of direct materials and indirect materials will also differ somewhat from those presented for job-order costing. Under process costing, *direct materials* are defined as materials directly traceable to a specific manufacturing department or process. *Indirect materials* are defined as materials used in the manufacturing operation that are not directly traceable (or, because of their small amount, are not worth tracing) to individual manufacturing departments. For example, Ace Tuna Fish Cannery considers frozen tuna issued from its storeroom freezers to the cleaning department to be direct materials. Sheets of metal, issued to the packing department for forming into cans, are also considered direct materials. On the other hand, the cannery considers materials such as maintenance supplies and machine oil to be indirect materials, as their use cannot be easily associated with specific departments. As in job-order costing, indirect materials are debited to manufacturing overhead when used.

Direct materials are not necessarily issued to all manufacturing departments. Many departments process items transferred from other departments without adding additional materials. In Exhibit 15-4, only the cleaning and packing departments received direct materials.

Labor

Direct labor costs under process costing are the wages of production workers that can be directly traced to a particular manufacturing department or process. If production line employees work for the entire period in the same department, their total wages for the period are treated as direct labor costs of the respective departments in which they worked. If the employees perform tasks in more than one department during the period, direct labor costs must be distributed among departments. For example, assume that $15,000 of direct labor costs are incurred by Ace Tuna Fish Cannery during March. The costs are incurred equally in the three production departments. The entry to transfer these costs from the factory labor cost account to the appropriate inventory accounts follows:

Mar. 31	Work in Process Inventory— Cleaning Department	5,000	
	Work in Process Inventory— Filleting Department	5,000	
	Work in Process Inventory— Packing Department	5,000	
	Factory Labor Cost		15,000
	To record direct labor cost for the three production departments for March.		

Indirect labor costs are not directly traceable (or not traceable at a reasonable cost) to a particular department but are associated with several departments. For example, Ace Tuna Fish Cannery includes wages of janitors, security personnel, and supervisors whose services are common to several departments as indirect labor. The cost of indirect labor is debited to manufacturing overhead.

Manufacturing Overhead

If levels of production and actual manufacturing overhead costs were constant from period to period, it would be possible to add actual overhead costs to work in process. However, since both quantities produced and actual overhead costs can vary significantly from period to period, manufacturing overhead is usually applied to production (i.e., added to work in process accounts) using a *predetermined rate*.

Under process costing, each department has a rate for assigning overhead costs to the departmental Work in Process Inventory account. For example, assume Ace Tuna Fish Cannery projects annual manufacturing overhead costs to be $100,000. Management estimates that 30 percent of these costs relate to the cleaning department, 56 percent to the filleting department, and 14 percent to the packing department. Direct labor hours are considered an appropriate measure of departmental activity for the cleaning and filleting departments. Machine hours serve as the application base for the packing department's manufacturing overhead. The following table shows the computation of departmental predetermined rates:

	Cleaning department	Filleting department	Packing department
A. Percentage of overhead costs	30%	56%	14%
B. Dollar amount of estimated overhead costs (A × $100,000)	$30,000	$56,000	$14,000
C. Expected activity of departmental application base (estimates based on experience and projected production)	15,000 direct labor hours	16,000 direct labor hours	2,800 machine hours
D. Department rate (B ÷ C)	$2.00 per direct labor hour	$3.50 per direct labor hour	$5.00 per machine hour

Assume that during March, 1,300 hours of direct labor were worked in the cleaning department and 1,400 hours in the filleting department. Machine hours in the packing department were 185, and actual overhead costs totaled $8,400. The entries for March to manufacturing overhead are summarized below:

Mar. 31	Manufacturing Overhead	8,400	
	Cash and Other Accounts		8,400
	To record actual manufacturing overhead costs as incurred.		
31	Work in Process Inventory— Cleaning Department	2,600	
	Manufacturing Overhead		2,600
	To apply overhead to work in process (1,300 direct labor hours × $2.00 per hour departmental rate).		
31	Work in Process Inventory— Filleting Department	4,900	
	Manufacturing Overhead		4,900
	To apply overhead to work in process (1,400 direct labor hours × $3.50 per hour departmental rate).		
31	Work in Process Inventory— Packing Department	925	
	Manufacturing Overhead		925
	To apply overhead to work in process (185 machine hours × $5.00 per hour departmental rate).		

As a result of the three preceding entries, the amount of manufacturing overhead applied to production is $8,425. Thus, manufacturing overhead for March has been overapplied by $25 ($8,425 applied vs. $8,400 actual). The end-of-year adjustment to reduce the Manufacturing Overhead account balance to zero under process costing is the same as the entry under a job-order system. If underapplied or overapplied overhead is immaterial, the adjustment to close Manufacturing Overhead can be made to the Cost of Goods Sold account. Ace Tuna Fish Cannery chose this procedure. To account for $1,500 of overapplied manufacturing overhead at year end, Ace made the following journal entry:

Dec. 31	Manufacturing Overhead	1,500	
	Cost of Goods Sold		1,500
	To record adjustment for overapplied manufacturing overhead for the year.		

If the amount is considered material, the various work in process inventories, finished goods inventories, and cost of goods sold should be adjusted for the underapplied or overapplied manufacturing overhead.

Interdepartmental Transfers

Manufacturing departments (other than the first department in the manufacturing process) must account for costs associated with units of product transferred into their department from other manufacturing departments. To determine total departmental manufacturing costs, the costs associated with units transferred into a departmental work in process account during the period must be combined with the department's own costs for direct materials, direct labor, and manufacturing overhead.

For example, assume that the packing department of Ace Tuna Fish Cannery receives 1,000 units of product from the filleting department on March 8. Each unit has an associated cost of $2.50, which represents the costs of direct materials, direct labor, and manufacturing overhead applicable to the cleaned and filleted tuna fish. The entry to record the interdepartmental transfer is:

Mar. 8	Work in Process Inventory— Packing Department	2,500	
	Work in Process Inventory— Filleting Department		2,500
	To record the transfer of 1,000 units from the filleting department to the packing department.		

Finished Goods Inventory and Cost of Goods Sold

The flow of costs from the final manufacturing department to finished goods inventory parallels the procedures used in job-order costing. Costs associated with completed products are credited to the departmental Work in Process Inventory account of the last department in the manufacturing process. Finished Goods Inventory is debited for the total product costs. For example, if a unit has a cost of $2.65 associated with it by the time it is packed and ready for sale, the following entry would record the transfer of 500 units to finished goods on March 23.

Mar. 23	Finished Goods Inventory	1,325	
	Work in Process Inventory—		
	Packing Department		1,325
	To record the transfer of 500 units from the packing department to finished goods.		

When 200 units are sold on account by Ace Tuna Fish Cannery on March 28 at $3.40 each, the following two entries are made:

Mar. 28	Accounts Receivable	680	
	Sales		680
	To record sales of 200 units at $3.40 each.		
28	Cost of Goods Sold	530	
	Finished Goods Inventory		530
	To record cost of goods sold (200 units × $2.65).		

Note that these entries are identical in form to those made under a job-order costing system.

Assignment of Cost to Product

The first major step in process costing is the assignment of direct materials, direct labor, and applied overhead costs to specific manufacturing departments. This procedure is fairly straightforward. The next step involves assigning costs to product. Recall that process costing is used when essentially identical units are being produced. Therefore, it is reasonable to assign an equal amount of cost to each unit. This is accomplished by averaging the total departmental costs over all the units produced during the period. In short:

$$\text{Cost per Unit} = \frac{\text{Total Departmental Costs for Period}}{\text{Total Units Produced during Period}}$$

If no beginning or ending work in process inventories exist in a department, calculation of cost per unit is very easy. Assume, for example, that during April a department incurs total cost (direct materials, direct labor, and applied overhead) of $1,700. Assume further that 850 units of product were started and completed during April and that no work in process inventories existed at either the beginning or end of the month. The cost per unit is simply:

$$\frac{\text{Total Cost}}{\text{Total Units}} = \frac{\$1,700}{850} = \$2.00$$

Complications arise when partially completed units (work in process inventories) are present. Most companies using process costing have work in process inventories both at the beginning and end of the period. Ordinarily, each manufacturing department (1) has some partially completed units in process at the beginning of the period, (2) adds inputs (costs) into production during the period, (3) completes and transfers units to the next department during the period, and (4) has some units still in process at the end of the period.

When beginning or ending inventories exist, consideration must be given to the selection of an inventory method. We consider only the weighted-average method. Under the *weighted-average* method, beginning inventory costs are combined with current-period costs to form an average. In effect, all production (including the beginning inventory) is treated as if it took place during the current period.

Beginning Inventories   The presence of beginning inventories poses no problems in calculating unit costs under the weighted-average cost flow method. For example, assume the following information for a particular department during April:

> Beginning inventories:
>   1,000 units, 40 percent complete
>   Cost of beginning inventory, $2,100
> Current-period activity:
>   7,000 units completed
>   Costs of direct materials, direct labor, and
>   overhead applied during April, $33,600
> Ending inventories:
>   None

Observe that the 7,000 units completed during April must include the 1,000 units in inventory at April 1. In other words, these 1,000 units were completed during April, and an additional 6,000 units were started and completed.

Under weighted-average costing, the beginning inventory cost is combined with the current-period cost in computing a cost per unit. For April the departmental cost per unit is:

$$\text{Cost per Unit} = \frac{\text{Total Departmental Costs for the Period}}{\text{Total Units Produced during the Period}}$$

$$= \frac{\$2,100 + \$33,600}{7,000}$$

$$= \$5.10$$

Ending Inventories   When ending inventories are present, the partially completed units must be expressed in terms of an *equivalent number of completed* *units.* This step is necessary in order to state properly the production activity during a period of time. For example, assume that on Monday the machining department started work on 200 units of product. By the end of the day, each unit was 25 percent finished. How can the department's production for the day be expressed? We cannot say that they produced 200 units, because there is much work still to be done before these units are finished. If we assume that all of the work done in the machining department is of the same basic nature, then we could say that performing 25 percent of the work on each of 200 units *is equivalent to* performing 100 percent of the work on 50 units (i.e., 25 percent of 200 equals 50). The machining department's production for Monday is expressed as *50 equivalent units* of product.

The equivalent units concept is used in process costing whenever ending inventories are present. For example, assume the following departmental data for July:

> Beginning inventories:
> 500 units, 60 percent complete
> Cost of beginning inventory, $3,300
> Current-period activity:
> 3,680 units completed (this includes comple-
> tion of the 500 units in beginning inventory)
> Costs of direct materials, direct labor, and
> overhead applied during July, $42,300
> Ending inventories:
> 800 units, 40 percent complete

To determine the *cost per equivalent unit*, the total departmental costs must be averaged over the number of units completed *plus* the equivalent number of units in the ending inventory. For July the departmental cost per equivalent unit is:

$$\text{Cost per Equivalent Unit} = \frac{\text{Total Departmental Costs for the Period}}{\text{Total Equivalent Units Produced during that Period}}$$

$$= \frac{\$3,300 + \$42,300}{3,680 + (40\% \times 800)}$$

$$= \frac{\$45,600}{3,680 + 320}$$

$$= \frac{\$45,600}{4,000}$$

$$= \$11.40$$

The cost per equivalent unit is used in assigning costs to the 3,680 completed units and to the 800 units in ending inventory.

Cost of 3,680 completed units:
    3,680 times $11.40 $41,952
Cost of 800 units in ending inventory:
    320 equivalent units times $11.40   +   3,648
Costs accounted for $45,600

Observe that the costs assigned to output must agree in total with the costs entering the department. Recall that costs entering the department (the "costs to account for") were:

Beginning inventory $ 3,300
Current-period costs   + 42,300
Costs to account for $45,600

In a process costing system, the "costs to account for" must always agree with "costs accounted for."

Use of Separate Component Costs   In many situations, it may not be possible to simply say "the ending inventory is X percent complete." Each component of input (direct materials, direct labor, and applied overhead) may have been added to product to a different extent. For example, the ending departmental work in process may include 80 percent of the materials included in completed units but only 30 percent of the direct labor and applied overhead required for completed units. This is expressed by saying, "The ending inventory is 80 percent complete as to direct materials and 30 percent complete as to direct labor and applied overhead."

Since the assignment of overhead is often based on direct labor, the completion percentage is frequently the same for both labor and overhead. These two inputs are sometimes called *conversion costs*.

For example, assume the following departmental data for March:

Beginning inventories:
    1,000 units, 100 percent complete as to direct materials and 60
       percent complete as to direct labor and applied overhead
    Cost of beginning inventory, $14,000 (direct materials, $4,800;
       direct labor, $3,700; applied overhead, $5,500)
Current-period activity:
    7,400 units completed
    Costs incurred during period, $141,250 (direct materials,
       $34,200; direct labor, $45,050; applied overhead, $62,000)
Ending inventories:
    500 units 80 percent complete as to direct materials and
       20 percent complete as to direct labor and applied overhead

A total cost per equivalent unit cannot be directly determined. A *cost per equivalent unit for each input* (direct materials, direct labor, and applied overhead) must first be found. The same general procedure as before is used, except the equivalent units produced for each input must be considered separately.

First, consider the direct materials component. The March production activity with respect to materials includes the units completed in March and the units partially completed in March. The calculation below shows the determination of total equivalent units with respect to direct materials, under the weighted-average method.

	Units		Percent complete with respect to direct materials		Equivalent units
Completed	7,400	×	100%	=	7,400
Ending Inventory	500	×	80%	=	400
					7,800

Next, the conversion cost component (direct labor and manufacturing overhead) is addressed:

	Units		Percent complete with respect to direct labor and manufacturing overhead		Equivalent units
Completed	7,400	×	100%	=	7,400
Ending Inventory	500	×	20%	=	100
					7,500

Once the equivalent units for each component are found, the *cost* per equivalent unit for each input can be calculated.

$$\frac{\text{Direct Materials Cost}}{\text{per Equivalent Unit}} = \frac{\$4,800 + \$34,200}{7,800}$$

$$= \frac{\$39,000}{7,800}$$

$$= \$5.00$$

$$\text{Conversion Costs per Equivalent Unit} = \frac{\overset{\text{Begin Labor}}{\$3,700} + \overset{\text{Direct labor during period}}{\$45,050} + \overset{\text{Begin OH}}{\$5,500} + \overset{\text{Applied OH during period}}{\$62,000}}{7,500}$$

$$= \frac{\$116,250}{7,500}$$

$$= \$15.50$$

Conversion costs include the costs of direct labor and applied manufacturing overhead. If labor and overhead have different completion percentages (e.g., if inventory is 20 percent complete as to direct labor and 30 percent complete as to applied manufacturing overhead), then separate calculations are required for labor and overhead equivalent units and costs per unit.

The assignment of cost to product now proceeds as previously described. First, note that total costs to account for are $155,250, as shown below:

Beginning inventory	$ 14,000
Current-period costs	+ 141,250
Costs to account for	$155,250

The equivalent units and costs per equivalent unit are used in assigning costs to completed units and ending inventory.

Cost of 7,400 completed units:
Direct materials 7,400 × $5.00 $ 37,000
Conversion costs 7,400 × $15.50 + 114,700 $151,700
Cost of 500 units in ending inventory:
Direct material 400 × $5.00 $ 2,000
Conversion costs 100 × $15.50 + 1,550   3,550
Costs accounted for $155,250

(handwritten: 400 = 500 × 80%)
(handwritten: 100 = 500 × 20%)

Note that the cost of the 7,400 completed units can be found by simply multiplying 7,400 units by the total cost per equivalent unit of $20.50 ($5.00 + $15.50). For the ending inventory, however, each component must be calculated separately, since the number of equivalent units is not the same for all cost components. Since there are 400 equivalent units of direct materials in ending inventory and only 100 equivalent units of direct labor and applied overhead, it is incorrect to make a single multiplication (using the $20.50 total cost per equivalent unit) to determine the cost of the ending work in process inventory.

The Production Cost Report

The key document in a process cost system is the production cost report which is prepared for each manufacturing department or process. A *production cost report* presents:

1 Production activity in actual physical units
2 Calculation of equivalent units of production
3 Manufacturing costs to account for
4 Unit cost(s) of manufacturing per equivalent unit
5 Assignment of costs to:
  a Units completed and transferred to subsequent manufacturing departments or finished goods and
  b Units in ending work in process.

Exhibit 15-5 presents Tory Manufacturing Co.'s production cost report for its assembly department. The report is for the month ended August 31, 1988, and is based on the weighted-average cost method of process costing. Each step in the preparation of a production cost report is discussed in the sections that follow.

Step 1. Units to Account For The physical number of units in production at the beginning of the period plus the number of units started into production during the period (or transferred in from another department) provide a total number of physical units to account for. This total serves as a control number that must be accounted for in completing the second step of the production cost report. Note the total units to account for is in terms of *physical units* only and ignores the fact that the units may be in various stages of completion. There are no equivalent unit calculations in the first step. The assembly department of Tory Manufacturing must account for 35,000 units of product.

EXHIBIT 15-5
Tory Manufacturing Co.
Assembly Department
Production Cost Report (Weighted-Average Cost Method)
For the Month Ended August 31, 1988

	Actual physical units		
1. Units to account for:			
Beginning work in process—assembly department	6,600		
Units started into production this month	28,400		
Total units to be accounted for	35,000		

2. Units accounted for:

		Equivalent units of production	
		Direct materials	Conversion costs: direct labor and overhead
Completed and transferred to finishing dept.	29,400	29,400	29,400
Ending work in process—assembly department (80% completed as to direct materials and 60% completed as to direct labor and overhead)	5,600	4,480 (80% × 5,600)	3,360 (60% × 5,600)
Total units accounted for	35,000	33,880	32,760

			Conversion costs	
3. Costs to account for:	Total	Direct materials	Direct labor	Applied overhead
Beginning work in process	$ 33,050	$14,300	$ 9,650	$ 9,100
Costs this month	153,614	62,946	46,697	43,971
Total costs to account for	$186,664	$77,246	$56,347	$53,071

4. Cost per equivalent unit

$5.62

$$\frac{\$77,246}{33,880} = \$2.28$$

$$\frac{\$56,347 + \$53,071}{32,760} = \$3.34$$

5. Total costs accounted for:

Completed and transferred to finishing department	$165,228	(29,400 equivalent units × $5.62 total cost per equivalent unit)
Ending work in process in assembly department:		
Direct materials	$ 10,214	(4,480 equivalent units × $2.28 direct materials cost per equivalent unit)
Direct labor and applied overhead	11,222	(3,360 equivalent units × $3.34 conversion costs per equivalent unit)
Ending work in process inventory	$ 21,436	
Total costs accounted for	$186,664	

Step 2. Units Accounted For The second step on a production cost report accomplishes two objectives. First, the total physical units to account for (as determined in Step 1) must be identified as either (a) completed during the period and transferred out or (b) remaining in ending work in process inventory. More complex cases where units are lost due to theft, evaporation, spoilage, and so forth, are found in advanced textbooks on cost accounting.

The other objective of Step 2 of the production cost report is to determine the equivalent units of production for the period. The assembly department of Tory Manufacturing must make separate equivalent units calculations for the components of ending inventory because direct materials and conversion costs (direct labor and overhead) have been added to ending inventory to a different extent. As shown in Step 2 of Exhibit 15-5, the assembly department's work in process at the end of August is 80 percent completed as to direct materials, but only 60 percent completed as to direct labor and overhead.

Step 3. Costs to Account For Costs associated with departmental work in process inventory at the beginning of the period plus manufacturing costs added in the department during the current period yield total departmental manufacturing costs to account for. This total provides a check figure for Step 5 of the production cost report, where the total departmental costs are accounted for by assignment either to (1) units completed and transferred out of the department during the period or (2) units remaining in work in process at the end of the period.

The production cost report for Tory Manufacturing shows the assembly department must account for total costs of $186,664. Breakdowns of the total costs into subtotals for direct materials, direct labor, and applied overhead are also presented on the production cost reports. These cost subtotals for each component of input will be needed in Step 4, where costs per equivalent unit are determined.

Step 4. Cost per Equivalent Unit The cost per equivalent unit for each factor of production is computed using the following formula:

$$\frac{\text{Cost per Equivalent}}{\text{Unit of Production}} = \frac{\text{Cost to Account For (per Step 3)}}{\text{Equivalent Units of Production (per Step 2)}}$$

Exhibit 15-5 shows the assembly department's cost per equivalent unit calculations for direct materials and conversion costs. The total cost per equivalent unit for the assembly department is determined as follows:

	Assembly department
Direct materials cost	$2.28
Conversion costs	+ 3.34
	$5.62

Under the weighted-average cost method, the calculations of cost per equivalent unit are actually *averages* combining prior data (from beginning work in process) and current-period production and costs. The calculation for equivalent units of production in Step 2 combined production work done last period (on units in the beginning inventory) with work done during the current period. Similarly, in Step 3, beginning inventory costs were combined with manufacturing costs incurred this period.

Step 5. Total Costs Accounted For The fifth and final step in completing a production cost report is to determine the allocation of total departmental costs between (a) items completed during the period and transferred out and (b) ending work in process inventory. Both equivalent units of production (per Step 2) and cost per equivalent unit (per Step 4) are used to allocate the total departmental production costs.

Under the weighted-average cost method of process costing, the cost of units completed and transferred out of a department is calculated by multiplying total cost per equivalent unit times the number of units completed and transferred. For example, the assembly department's production cost report for Tory Manufacturing (Exhibit 15-5) indicates $165,228 (29,400 equivalent units × $5.62 total cost per equivalent unit) as the cost of the 29,400 units actually completed during August in the assembly department and transferred to the finishing department.

Ending work in process inventory costs in a department can then be determined as:

	Total departmental costs to account for (per Step 3)
Less:	Costs associated with units completed in the department during the period and transferred out
Equals:	Costs of ending departmental work in process inventory

The ending work in process in the assembly department is $21,436 ($186,664 less $165,228).

The accuracy of the ending inventory amount obtained by subtraction can be verified by calculating the ending inventory using equivalent units data as shown on the production cost report. The production cost report shows the detailed calculations supporting the $21,436 ending departmental work in process inventory as follows:

Cost of 5,600 units in ending inventory:	
Direct materials (4,480 × $2.28)	$10,214
Direct labor and applied overhead	
(3,360 × $3.34)	+ 11,222
Assembly department—ending inventory	$21,436

When both the cost of units completed and transferred out and the cost of ending inventory are calculated directly, their total verifies that all costs have been assigned to product.

For the assembly department, the calculation is:

Cost of units completed and trans-	
ferred out	$165,228
Cost of ending inventory	+ 21,436
Total costs accounted for	$186,664

This total agrees with the total costs to account for in Step 3.

Use of Production Cost Reports   Based on the assembly department's production cost report, the following journal entry would be made by Tory Manufacturing:

		Debit	Credit
Aug. 31	Work in Process Inventory— Finishing Department	165,228	
	Work in Process Inventory— Assembly Department		165,228
	To record the costs associated with the 29,400 units completed dur- ing August in the assembly depart- ment and transferred to the finishing department—per assembly depart- ment's production cost report for August.		

Production cost reports are useful for purposes other than providing cost data for product-costing journal entries. These reports provide management with information by department on both units produced and costs incurred. Current-period equivalent cost per unit calculations, when compared with unit costs achieved in previous periods and with projected unit costs for the current period, serve to highlight differences that may need to be investigated and explained.

SUMMARY

Learning Objective 1: Describe the characteristics of a job-order cost system and a process cost system.

Process cost and job-order cost are the two principal product-costing systems used by manufacturers. Job-order costing is used by companies whose manufacturing process consists of single items or batches of production that are separately identifiable and significantly different from one another. Direct material, direct labor, and manufacturing overhead costs are accumulated for each job. The manufacturing overhead is applied to production using a predetermined rate. Unit costs of production are determined by dividing accumulated manufacturing costs for each separately identifiable job by the number of units produced for that job.

Process costing is used by companies whose manufacturing operations involve the continuous, mass production of identical units. Unlike job-order costing, process costing does not accumulate cost data for specific jobs or batches of production during the period. Rather, costs are averaged over all work completed during a period.

Learning Objective 2: Prepare journal entries for materials, labor, and overhead.

Each cost is initially recorded into a summary account (Materials Inventory, Factory Labor Cost, or Manufacturing Overhead). From these accounts, costs flow to Work in Process, then Finished Goods, and finally Cost of Goods Sold.

Under process costing, each department has a Work in Process account. Costs for direct materials, direct labor, manufacturing overhead, and costs transferred from other departments are accumulated in the departmental Work in Process account. Costs of completed product are transferred to the next department or to finished goods.

Learning Objective 3: Calculate and apply a predetermined overhead rate.

A predetermined overhead rate is calculated by dividing the estimated total overhead for the period by the estimated volume of the application base. This rate is then used to apply overhead costs to work in process. Applied overhead may not equal actual overhead. The underapplied or overapplied balance is usually an adjustment to cost of goods sold.

Learning Objective 4: Calculate equivalent units of product and costs per equivalent unit.

Production work accomplished during the period is determined by calculation of equivalent units of production. Dividing the accumulated departmental manufacturing costs for the period by the equivalent units of production yields equivalent cost per unit. The equivalent costs per unit and equivalent units of production serve as the basis in assigning departmental costs to items completed and transferred to the next department or to finished goods during the period and to ending work in process inventories.

Learning Objective 5: Prepare a production cost report.

The departmental production cost report is the key document in a process cost system. The production cost report presents for each manufacturing department (a) production activity in actual physical units, (b) calculation of equivalent units of production, (c) manufacturing costs to account for, (d) costs per equivalent unit, and (e) the assignment of costs between units completed and transferred to other manufacturing departments or finished goods and ending work in process inventory in the department. In addition to providing cost data for product-costing journal entries, the production cost report provides management with information helpful in controlling production activity and costs.

KEY TERMS

Applied manufacturing overhead	Indirect materials
Conversion cost	Job-order costing
Cost per equivalent unit	Manufacturing overhead
Costs to account for	Materials inventory
Departmental work in process	Overapplied manufacturing overhead
Direct labor	Predetermined overhead rate
Direct materials	Process costing
Equivalent unit of production	Production cost report
Finished goods inventory	Underapplied manufacturing overhead
Indirect labor	Work in process inventory

REVIEW QUESTIONS

1 Real-Built Construction Co. custom builds residential homes, stores, and small factories to buyers' specifications. What type of product-costing system would be most appropriate for Real-Built? Why?

2 Why do companies usually apply manufacturing overhead based on a predetermined annual rate, rather than adding actual manufacturing overhead to jobs in process?

3 Lipton Manufacturing Co. is trying to select between a) direct labor hours and b) machine hours as the basis for applying manufacturing overhead to jobs in process. What factors should Lipton Manufacturing consider in making its selection?

4 Evaluate the following statement: "In a manufacturing company, depreciation for the period can become either an asset or an expense."

5 "For both manufacturing firms and nonmanufacturing firms, all wages earned during the period are expenses of the period and should be deducted as salary expense on the income statement." Comment on the preceding statement.

6 Merkle Manufacturing Co. uses direct labor hours as the basis for applying manufacturing overhead to work in process. At the beginning of the year, Merkle Manufacturing estimated that 100,000 direct labor hours would be worked during the year. Actually, 94,000 direct labor hours were worked and resulted in $188,000 of manufacturing overhead applied to work in process. What was the predetermined manufacturing overhead rate used to apply manufacturing overhead to work in process? At the beginning of the year, what was the company's estimate of manufacturing overhead cost for the year?

7 Kresmen Manufacturing Co. actually incurred $1,420,000 of manufacturing overhead during the period. Using a predetermined rate, $1,394,000 of manufacturing overhead was applied to work in process. Kresmen's Manufacturing Overhead account would have a _____ (debit, credit) balance and would be $26,000 _____ (overapplied, underapplied). If the entire $26,000 account balance were closed to the Cost of Goods Sold account, it would _____ (increase, decrease) the Cost of Goods Sold account.

8 Which of the following situations would result in manufacturing overhead being overapplied? (The company uses direct labor hours as its basis for applying manufacturing overhead.)

   a Actual direct labor hours worked during the year exceeded the hours estimated by the company at the beginning of the year.

   b A major machine breakdown occurred in the factory during the period. The costly machine repairs had not been anticipated by the company.

   c The company fired three office secretaries during the year, thus significantly decreasing office salaries.

9 Simkar Co. is a new car manufacturer. The Company mass produces on its assembly line only one make and model of car—the "Huefder." What type of product-costing system would be most appropriate for Simkar? Why?

10 Distinguish between the definitions of direct materials and direct labor for a company using job-order costing and the definitions of direct materials and direct labor for a company employing process costing.

11 What are the basic differences in the journal entries for a process costing system versus a job-order cost system?

12 What is an "equivalent unit"?

13   Outsell Manufacturing Co. had no beginning work in process inventory. During the period, 5,000 units were started into production, of which 2,000 remained in ending work in process only 50 percent completed. If manufacturing costs for the period total $20,000, then a cost per unit of $4.00 ($20,000 ÷ 5,000 units) should be used to determine the cost of ending inventory and the cost of goods completed. Evaluate the preceding statement.

14   For Question 13 above, calculate the correct cost of ending work in process inventory and cost of goods completed.

15   The last section of Castleton Manufacturing Co.'s finishing department's production cost report shows:

Completed and transferred to packing dept.		$160,000	(40,000 × $4)
Ending work in process:			
Transferred from assembling dept. costs	$20,000		(10,000 × $2)
Direct materials—finishing dept.	12,000		(8,000 × $1.50)
Direct labor and overhead— finishing dept.	2,000		(4,000 × $ .50)
		34,000	
Total costs accounted for		$194,000	

What is the appropriate journal entry based on the preceding information? If there were 8,000 units in beginning inventory, how many units were transferred into the finishing department from the assembling department during the month?

16   Referring to the partial production cost report in Question 15, describe the ending inventory in terms of total units and status of completion. If the cost of direct materials in the beginning inventory was $15,000, what was the cost of direct materials added during the period?

EXERCISES

E15-1   Present journal entries to record the following transactions of Brighton Manufacturing Co. during its first year of operations. The company uses a job-order cost system. (Omit explanations)

1 Purchased materials on account for $186,000.

2 Materials used:

Job #1	$81,000
Job #2	16,000
Job #3	41,000
General factory supplies	18,000

3 Labor cost incurred but not yet paid:

Job #1	$18,000
Job #2	6,000
Job #3	14,000
Factory supervision	8,000
Office help	9,000
Sales salaries	13,000

E15-2   Presented below are data concerning three common bases on which manufacturing overhead can be applied to jobs in process:

	Direct labor hours	Machine hours	Direct labor cost
Estimated overhead costs	$250,000	$250,000	$250,000
Estimated volume of activity base:			
1. Direct labor hours	100,000		
2. Machine hours		50,000	
3. Direct labor cost			$500,000
Predetermined manufacturing over-head rate	?	?	?
Actual activity for period:			
1. Direct labor hours	115,000		
2. Machine hours		46,000	
3. Direct labor cost			$512,000
Actual manufacturing overhead	$236,000	$236,000	$236,000

Required:

1 Calculate the respective manufacturing overhead rate for each of the three possible bases.

2 Present for each situation the journal entry to apply manufacturing overhead to jobs in process.

3 Determine for each situation the overapplied or underapplied manufacturing overhead.

E15-3 The Carlo Company estimated manufacturing overhead costs at $255,000 for the period for Department A based on an estimated activity base volume of 100,000 direct labor hours. At the end of the period the manufacturing overhead account for Department A had $270,000 in debit entries. Actual direct labor hours were 105,000.

Required:

1 What was the amount of actual manufacturing overhead costs incurred during the period?

2 What was the amount of manufacturing overhead costs applied to production?

3 What was the overapplied or underapplied manufacturing overhead for the period?

(AICPA Adapted)

E15-4 Solidito Manufacturing Co.'s job-order cost system provides the following information:

Work in process: January 1		Finished goods: January 1	
Job #68	$24,000	Job #67	$31,000
Job #70	15,000	Job #69	22,000
Job #71	8,000		

	Job numbers				
	#68	**#70**	**#71**	**#72**	**#73**
Costs added during January	$2,000	$9,000	$4,000	$18,000	$6,000

Job status on January 31:
  In work in process—Jobs #71, #73
  In finished goods—Jobs #68, #69, #70, #72

Required:
1 Calculate cost of goods sold.
2 Calculate work in process inventory, January 31.
3 Calculate finished goods inventory, January 31.

E15-5 Tinelli Manufacturing Company used a job-order cost system. The following transactions occurred during May:
1 Purchased on account $120,000 of materials.
2 Issuance of $40,000 direct materials and $1,000 indirect materials.
3 Salaries of $125,000 were earned by factory employees: $105,000 in direct labor and $20,000 in indirect labor.
4 Factory overhead applied to production at a rate of $.50 per direct labor dollar.
5 Actual factory overhead costs (other than indirect materials and indirect labor) totaled $50,000. (All paid in cash)
6 Cost of goods completed and sent to finished goods totaled $60,000.
7 Sales revenue from sales on account totaled $40,000.
8 Cost of goods sold was $28,000.
9 Over- or underapplied manufacturing overhead is closed to cost of goods sold. Record the journal entries that correspond to the above transactions. (Omit explanations)

E15-6 For each situation below calculate the equivalent units of production during the period under the weighted-average cost method:
1 Number of units started during the period was 200,000, ending work in process consists of 80,000 units that are 40 percent complete. No beginning work in process.
2 Ending work in process inventory consists of 35,000 units that are 25 percent complete. Beginning work in process consisted of 18,000 units that were 40 percent complete as of the beginning of the period. During the period 50,000 units were completed.
3 Beginning work in process inventory consisted of 12,000 units that were 30 percent complete as of the beginning of the period. During the period 42,000 units were completed. No ending work in process inventory.
4 Beginning work in process inventory consisted of 4,600,000 units that were 95 percent complete as of the beginning of the period. During the period 18,200,000 units were completed. Ending work in process inventory consists of 6,400,000 units that are 45 percent complete.

E15-7 Calculate equivalent units of production using the weighted-average cost method for each of the following situations:
1 Situation 1
  a No beginning work in process
  b 14,000 units started into production during the period
  c 3,000 units in ending work in process; 60 percent completed
2 Situation 2
  a Beginning work in process, 4,000 units; 30 percent already completed
  b 26,000 units started into production during the period
  c 6,000 units in ending work in process; 60 percent completed
3 Situation 3
  a Beginning work in process, 24,000 units; 80 percent already completed

    b 87,000 units completed during the period

    c 8,000 units in ending work in process; 25 percent completed

E15-8 Hicksville Manufacturing Co. produces one product in its sole processing department. Direct materials, direct labor, and manufacturing overhead are added to production uniformly throughout the production process. Work in process as of the beginning of the period consisted of 35,000 units that were 65 percent complete. The Work in Process Inventory account at the beginning of the period had a $94,000 balance. During the current period, 54,000 units were started. Work in process at the end of the period consists of 10,000 units that are 70 percent complete. Direct materials, direct labor, and manufacturing overhead costs incurred during the period totaled $225,920.

Required:
1 Calculate equivalent units of production using the weighted-average cost method.
2 Calculate cost per equivalent unit.
3 Calculate cost of goods manufactured.
4 Calculate the work in process inventory balance at the end of the period.

E15-9 The Jorcano Manufacturing Co. uses a process cost system to account for the costs of its only product. Production begins in the fabrication department where units of raw materials are molded into various connecting parts. After fabrication is complete, the units are transferred to the assembly department. There is no material added in the assembly department. After assembly is complete, the units are transferred to a packaging department where packing material is placed around the units. After the units are ready for shipping, they are sent to the shipping area. At year end the following inventory of product D is on hand:
1 No unused raw material or packing material
2 Fabrication department: 300 units, 1/3 complete as to raw material and 1/2 complete as to direct labor
3 Assembly department: 1,000 units, 2/5 complete as to direct labor
4 Packaging department: 100 units, 3/4 complete as to packing material and 1/4 complete as to direct labor
5 Shipping department: 400 completed units

Required:
1 Calculate the number of equivalent units of packing material in all inventories at year end.
2 Calculate the number of equivalent units of raw material in all inventories at year end.
3 Calculate the number of equivalent units of fabrication department direct labor in *all* inventories at year end.

(AICPA Adapted)

E15-10 The equivalent units of production and manufacturing costs for Lapage Manufacturing Co. are presented below. The company produces one product in one department. All manufacturing costs are added uniformly to production throughout the manufacturing process. Lapage Manufacturing uses the weighted-average cost method of process costing. At the beginning of the period, 6,000 units were in process.

	Actual physical units	Equivalent units
Completed and transferred out	64,000	64,000
Ending work in process	20,000	2,500
	84,000	
Costs:		
Beginning work in process	$ 30,625	
Current-period costs	252,000	

Required:

Calculate each of the following:

1 Cost of ending work in process inventory.

2 Percent completion of ending work in process.

3 Cost of units completed and transferred out.

PROBLEMS

P15-1 *Journal Entries for Job-Order Costs*

Nicamica Furniture Co. manufactures tables, desks, chairs, and other office equipment items. Nicamica Furniture, which uses job-order costing, had job #3806 ($83,000 cost) in process on September 1, 1988. At the beginning of 1988, the company had estimated its annual manufacturing overhead would be $600,000. For the year, direct labor hours were estimated at 200,000. Nicamica Furniture applies manufacturing overhead to jobs in process based on direct labor hours. Transactions during September included:

1 Purchased $45,000 of materials, on account.

2 Issued materials to factory:

Job #3806	$11,000
Job #3807	38,000
Factory supplies	5,000

3 September wages earned:

	Hours	Cost
Job #3806	2,000	$12,000
Job #3807	6,300	37,000
Factory supervisors	450	4,400
Office secretary	160	1,000
		$54,400

4 Applied manufacturing overhead for September.

5 Depreciation on factory buildings and machinery totaled $8,000 for September.

6 September's unpaid factory heat, light, and power totals $4,000.

7 Job #3806 was completed during September and transferred to finished goods.

Required:

1 Prepare journal entries (omit explanations) for September's transactions.

2 Set up general ledger account for work in process inventory, enter beginning balance, and post September's transactions. Calculate balance in account on September 30, 1988.

3 Prepare for Job #3806 and Job #3807 cost summaries showing for each job: September 1, 1988 balance; plus direct materials, direct labor, and applied overhead for September; and total cost for the job.

P15-2 *Flow of Manufacturing Costs*
As of May 1, 1989, Brookhaven Manufacturing Co., which uses a job-order cost system, had the following inventory balances:

Direct materials		$120,000
Work in process		?
Finished goods:		
Job #106	$84,000	
Job #108	76,000	
Job #109	90,000	250,000

Manufacturing overhead is applied to jobs in process at $5.00 per direct labor hour. Beginning of the period work in process and manufacturing activity during May 1989 are summarized below by job. During May, Jobs #107 and #110 were completed and transferred to finished goods. Jobs #106, #107, and #109 were sold on account to customers for a total of $636,000.

Job #107

		Direct labor		Applied manufacturing
Date	Direct materials	Hours	Cost	overhead
Bal. 5/1/89	$61,000	11,000	$43,000	?
May 1989	33,000	8,000	31,000	?

Job #110

		Direct labor		Applied manufacturing
Date	Direct materials	Hours	Cost	overhead
Bal. 5/1/89	$26,000	4,000	$16,500	?
May 1989	81,000	12,000	47,500	?

Job #111

		Direct labor		Applied manufacturing
Date	Direct materials	Hours	Cost	overhead
Bal. 5/1/89	$ 3,000	400	$ 1,500	?
May 1989	54,000	10,000	38,500	?

Job #112

		Direct labor		Applied manufacturing
Date	Direct materials	Hours	Cost	overhead
May 1989	$31,000	4,500	$17,000	?

Job #113

Date	Direct materials	Direct labor Hours	Direct labor Cost	Applied manufacturing overhead
May 1989	$14,000	3,000	$12,000	?

Required:

1 Determine work in process inventory balance on May 1, 1989.

2 Prepare journal entries for May, 1989. Show calculations supporting the journal entries.

  a Direct materials used

  b Direct labor used

  c Manufacturing overhead applied

  d Cost of goods manufactured

  e Sales revenue

  f Cost of goods sold

3 Determine inventory balances on May 31, 1989 for direct materials, work in process, and finished goods. Show supporting detail by job for work in process and finished goods.

P15-3 *Incomplete Data: Flow of Costs*

Presented below are incomplete cost data for Valley Forge Foundry, Inc. as of December 31, 1988. The company uses a job-order cost system and applies manufacturing overhead to jobs in process using a predetermined rate of 70 percent of direct labor cost.

Materials inventory

Bal. 1/1/88	200,000	
	300,000	

Work in process inventory

Bal. 1/1/88	100,000	
Direct materials	115,000	
Direct labor	150,000	

Finished goods inventory

Bal. 1/1/88	90,000	

Factory labor cost

	225,000	225,000

Manufacturing overhead

Indirect materials	35,000	
Factory depreciation	12,000	

Cost of goods sold

	264,000

Additional information:

Cost of goods manufactured	$240,000
Salesperson's travel expense	23,800
Depreciation on office equipment	12,100

Required:

1 Calculate materials inventory, December 31, 1988.

2 Determine cost of indirect labor for 1988.

3 Calculate balance in manufacturing overhead account on December 31, 1988. Indicate amount and whether over- or underapplied.

4 Determine work in process inventory, December 31, 1988.

5 Determine finished goods inventory, December 31, 1988.

P15-4 *Comprehensive Job-Order Cost Problem*

The Broxite Print Shop uses a job-order cost system. On April 1, 1988, the Work in Process Inventory account had a balance of $8,800, composed of the following:

	Direct materials	Direct labor	Applied manufacturing overhead
Job #A 138	$2,400	$1,000	$1,130
Job #C 184	3,000	560	710

At the beginning of April, the materials inventory totaled $18,600. Finished goods inventory on April 1 was $17,800, consisting solely of Job #A 137. Broxite applies manufacturing overhead to jobs based on direct labor hours. At the beginning of 1988, Broxite estimated: 1) $60,000 of manufacturing overhead for the year and 2) 20,000 direct labor hours of activity for the year. During April, 1988, the following transactions occurred:

1 Purchased $26,400 of materials on account.

2 Materials were issued to:

Job #A 138	$ 420
Job #A 139	810
Job #A 140	6,000
Job #C 184	8,000
Job #C 185	11,000
Supplies for general factory use	3,000
Total	$29,230

3 Rent on the building of $120,000 had been paid for 1988 on January 2, 1988 and debited to an asset account, Prepaid Rent. The print shop utilizes 80 percent of the building, with a small office occupying the remaining space.

4 The printing press and other equipment used in the shop were purchased on July 1, 1987 for $58,000. The estimated life of the press and equipment is 15 years with a $4,000 salvage value. Broxite Print Shop uses straight line depreciation.

5 During April, $1,800 was paid to Press Service Co. for repair work done on the shop's printing press on March 24, 1988. The $1,800 had been set up as an account payable on March 31, 1988.

6 Wages earned:

	Hours	Cost
Job #A 138	800	$ 3,100
Job #A 139	1,200	4,900
Job #A 140	600 ₃₇₀₀	2,250
Job #C 184	850	3,000
Job #C 185	250	980
Factory supervisor	190	1,200
Office secretary	160	480
		$15,910

7 Manufacturing overhead was applied to jobs for April.

8 Jobs #A 138, #A 139, and #C 184 were completed and transferred to finished goods during April.

9 Jobs #A 137, #A 138, and #C 184 were sold, on account, to customers at invoice prices totaling $62,000.

Required:

1 Enter beginning inventory balances in general ledger accounts.

2 Prepare journal entries to record April's transactions.

3 Post April's transactions to general ledger inventory accounts (ignore postings to accounts other than inventories). Compute April 30, 1988 inventory balances.

4 Maintain a subsidiary record of the costs by job for each job. For each job, enter beginning of the month's balance and post April's transactions.

5 Prepare a schedule that summarizes the costs at April 30, 1988 for jobs still in process.

6 For April, calculate amount of overapplied or underapplied manufacturing overhead.

7 Prepare a schedule of cost of goods manufactured for April.

 P15-5 *Equivalent Units and Product Costs*

Presented below are data from the production cost report of Stroeham Manufacturing Co. for November 1988. Stroeham produces one product in one department.

Units completed during the period	12,000 units
Ending work in process	10,000 units
(80 percent complete as to direct materials, 60 percent complete as to direct labor and overhead)	
November 1, 1988 work in process inventory:	
Direct materials	$ 4,000
Direct labor	2,000
Applied manufacturing overhead	? 4,000
Manufacturing costs for November:	
Direct materials used in November	$38,000
Direct labor cost incurred in November	13,000
Applied manufacturing overhead in November	? 26,000

Manufacturing overhead is applied at the predetermined rate of 200 percent of direct labor cost.

Required:

Using the weighted-average cost method, calculate:

1 Cost per equivalent unit for: (a) direct materials and (b) direct labor and manufacturing overhead.

2 The dollar amount associated with <u>work in process inventory</u> on November 30, 1988.

3 The cost of units completed during November, 1988.

 P15-6 *Journal Entries for <u>Process Cost System</u>*
Squariton Manufacturing Co. has just completed its first month of operations. The company has two manufacturing departments that process the company's single product. The company uses a process cost system. Units completed in Dept. A are transferred to Dept. B. When completed in Dept. B, the units are transferred to finished goods. During the month the following occurred:

1 Purchased materials on account for $200,000.

2 Used materials: $110,000 directly traceable to Dept. A; $40,000 directly traceable to Dept. B; and $25,000 of indirect materials.

3 Factory wages earned:

Dept. A	$46,000
Dept. B	21,000
General factory	12,000
	$79,000

4 Manufacturing overhead is applied to work in process using a predetermined rate of $2.00 per direct labor <u>dollar</u>.

5 Actual manufacturing overhead costs incurred (other than indirect materials and indirect labor) totaled $150,000. All of these costs were paid in cash.

6 Production cost report for Dept. A shows $40,000 ending work in process inventory. *Interdepartmental transfer*

7 Production cost report for Dept. B shows $64,000 ending work in process inventory.

Required:
Prepare journal entries required for each of the above. (No entry is required to close out any balance in the Manufacturing Overhead account at the end of the month. The company will account for overapplied or underapplied overhead at the end of the year.)

P15-7 *Production Cost Report*
Romulas Manufacturing Co. produces one product in one department. All direct materials arc added at the very beginning of the production process. Cost data for October, 1990 show:

	Physical units	Percent complete as to direct labor and overhead
Work in process, October 1	100,000	25%
Units completed during October	860,000	–
Work in process, October 31	110,000	60%

	Costs	
	Direct materials	Labor and overhead
Work in process, October 1	$ 360,000	$ 287,000
Current-period costs for October	2,938,000	5,130,100

Required:
Prepare a 5-step production cost report for October using the weighted-average cost method. Follow the format of Exhibit 15-5.

 Process Costing: Two Departments

P15-8 Thrifty Manufacturing Co. has two production departments—Departments X and Z. The company uses the weighted-average cost method of process costing. A partially completed production cost report for Department Z, the final production department, is presented below. Department Z adds direct materials, direct labor, and manufacturing overhead uniformly to the units it receives from Department X.

Units Accounted For:

		Equivalent units of production	
	Actual physical units	Transferred from department X	Direct materials, direct labor, and manufacturing overhead
Completed and transferred out	47,000	47,000	47,000
Ending work in process	6,000	6,000	4,000
Total units accounted for	53,000	53,000	51,000

Costs to Account For:

	Total	Transferred from department X	Direct materials, direct labor, and manufacturing overhead
Beginning work in process	$ 630,791	$ 284,391	$ 346,400
Current-period costs	2,275,209	1,040,609	1,234,600
Total costs to account for	$2,906,000	$1,325,000	$1,581,000

Required:
1 Calculate for Department Z the cost per equivalent unit for: (a) transfers from Department X, and (b) direct materials, direct labor, and manufacturing overhead added in Department Z.
2 Calculate cost of units completed and transferred from Department Z to finished goods during the period. What is the journal entry for this transaction?
3 Calculate the cost of the work in process inventory in Department Z at the end of the period.

Business Decision Problem

Donaldson Manufacturing Company has recently begun operations. It produces a single product in one department. A completed production cost report at the end of the first month of operations shows:

1 *Units to Account For:*

	Actual physical units
Beginning work in process	-0-
Units started into production this month	40,000
Total units to be accounted for	40,000

2 *Units Accounted For:*

		Equivalent units of production	
	Actual physical units	Direct materials	Conversion costs: direct labor and overhead
Completed and transferred to finished goods	32,000	32,000	32,000
Ending work in process	8,000	5,600	4,800
(70 percent complete as to direct materials and 60 percent complete as to direct labor and overhead)			
Total units accounted for	40,000	37,600	36,800

3 *Costs to Account For:*

			Conversion costs	
	Total	Materials	Direct labor	Applied overhead
Beginning work in process	$ -0-	$ -0-	$ -0-	$ -0-
Costs this month	241,200	94,000	90,240	56,960
Total costs to account for	$241,200	$94,000	$90,240	$56,960

4 *Cost per Equivalent Unit:*

Direct materials $2.50 $= \dfrac{\$94,000}{37,600}$

Conversion costs $4.00 $= \dfrac{\$90,240 + \$56,960}{36,800}$

Total $6.50

5 *Total Costs Accounted For:*

Completed and transferred to finished goods	$208,000	(32,000 × $6.50)
Ending work in process:		
Direct materials	$ 14,000	(5,600 × $2.50)
Direct labor and applied overhead	19,200	(4,800 × $4.00)
Ending work in process inventory	$ 33,200	
Total costs accounted for	$241,200	≈ 208,000 + 33,200

The number of direct labor hours worked totaled 6,016. The applied manufacturing overhead rate is based on direct labor hours.

The president of Donaldson Manufacturing is considering ways of decreasing production costs. Two specific proposals are being considered:

1 Purchasing a cheaper grade of direct materials and reducing direct materials cost per equivalent unit to $2.00. However, the cheaper grade of materials would add 10 percent to the time required to produce the product.

2 Adding a new machine to the production process that would replace a production worker. This proposal would reduce direct labor hours worked by 5 percent. The machine would cost $360,000 and have an estimated life of 10 years and estimated salvage value of zero.

Required:
Analyze each of the two proposals in terms of their expected effect on total manufacturing costs. Consider each proposal separately.

16

STANDARD
COSTING

LEARNING OBJECTIVES

When you complete this chapter, you should be able to:

1 Define the concept of standard cost.
2 Apply costs to product using standard costs.
3 Analyze variances for performance evaluation and control purposes.

A *standard cost* is a target figure, an estimate of what costs *should be* under efficient operations. To merit the name standard, these costs must be more than haphazard estimates. Standard costs are intended to represent realistically the costs incurred by a firm that operates efficiently and correctly estimates the prices it will have to pay for materials, labor, and other goods and services. Standards must be carefully determined and regularly updated.

Normally, standard costs are viewed in the context of manufacturing costs— direct materials, direct labor, and manufacturing overhead. The concept can also be used in connection with shipping costs, clerical costs, sales costs, and so forth.

Developing and updating standards costs are not simple tasks. Extensive research involving accountants, engineers, personnel experts, economists, and management is often necessary. Studies must be made of the material specifications and the expected unit costs of materials. Standards of work performance for each operation must be developed, and this often involves the use of detailed time-and-motion studies. Expected wage rates must be forecast. Expected factory overhead costs must be projected. For a large company with complex production processes that are constantly and significantly affected by changing economic conditions, determination of standard costs can be a difficult, time-consuming, and expensive task. In addition, if the standards are to serve the purpose for which they were developed, they must be regularly reviewed and updated to reflect changing prices of cost inputs, changing technology, and the introduction of new products.

USES OF STANDARD COSTS

While standard costs are difficult to determine and keep up-to-date, many firms nonetheless use them because they serve several managerial purposes. The uses of standard costs are introduced below and then developed more fully in this and subsequent chapters.

Product Costing

In the product-costing systems discussed in Chapter 15, *actual* costs for direct labor and direct materials were assigned to products. These actual costs were charged to jobs in process under a job-order cost system and to departmental work in process under a process costing system. Because assigning actual manufacturing overhead is very difficult, a predetermined rate was used in Chapter 15. Although this predetermined rate was based on estimates of annual productive activity, it was *not* called a standard rate. The predetermined rate expressed what overhead costs and the application base were *expected to be*. No effort was made to determine what these costs and base levels *should be* under efficient operations.

Convenience in the assignment of costs to product is one advantage of using standard costs in a product-costing system. Standard costs can be determined for direct materials, direct labor, and manufacturing overhead. These standard costs, rather than actual costs, are then assigned to product. At the end of the accounting period, differences will exist between the standard costs assigned to product and the actual costs incurred for each of the three manufacturing cost elements. These differences (called *variances*) must then be assigned to production (cost of goods sold and/or inventory), as was the case for underapplied and overapplied overhead. The use of standard costs in a product-costing system will be discussed and illustrated later in the chapter.

If the only use of standard costs were to provide a convenient means of accounting, few firms would take the trouble to develop and maintain them. Standard costing systems also serve other important functions—planning, control, and performance evaluation.

Planning

One aspect of planning is the preparation of budgets. Budgets reflect estimates of production levels, revenues, costs, and so forth in a future period. Once production levels are estimated, standard costs of materials, labor, and overhead may be applied to determine what total production costs should be.

Standards may aid in planning beyond the preparation of formal budgets. Suppose, for example, that a restaurant must quote a price for a large banquet. Standard serving sizes, food costs, labor requirements, wage rates, and the like

EXHIBIT 16-1
Direct Costs for Banquet
(150 Dinners)

Food costs:

Soup—cup		$ .15	
Salad:			
Lettuce—6 salads/head	$.08		
Other ingredients	.06		
Dressing	.06	.20	
Rolls (average 2 per person)		.12	
Butter		.04	
Strip steak (12 oz., $4.40 per pound)		3.30	
Potatoes (1/3 lb. per serving)		.06	
Vegetable		.10	
Gravy, parsley, etc.		.05	
Ice cream and topping		.15	
Coffee (40 cups per pound; cost $4.60			
per pound incl. sugar and cream;			
2 cups per person)		.23	
Food cost per dinner		$4.40	
Total food cost for 150 dinners			$660.00

Labor costs:		
Chef: 6 hours at $8.00	$ 48.00	
Assistant cook: 4 hours at $5.00	20.00	
Kitchen help: 8 hours at $3.75	30.00	
Dishwasher: 4 hours at $3.75	15.00	
Service personnel: (1 for each 20–24		
people) 7, 4 hours each at $3.75	105.00	
Busboys: 3, 4 hours each at $3.75	45.00	
Total labor cost		263.00
Total Direct Cost		$923.00

could be employed. The restaurant manager's analysis might proceed as shown in Exhibit 16-1.

Beyond these direct food and labor costs, allowance must be made for overhead and profit in establishing a price for the banquet. These steps will not be explicitly considered in this chapter. The point to be noted here is the usefulness of standards to the manager's planning. For example, each waiter or waitress should be able to serve 20 to 24 people, each pound of potatoes yields three servings, and so forth. These established standards can be used regularly in the manager's planning.

Control and Performance Evaluation

A final major use of standard costs lies in the area of performance evaluation and control. Recall that standard costs are carefully determined estimates of what costs should be under efficient operations. Performance can therefore be evaluated by comparing what costs were (actual costs) with what they should have been (standard costs). This difference is known as a variance. In general, a variance is defined as

$$\text{Variance} \; = \; \text{Actual Cost minus Standard Cost}$$

Variances may be calculated for specific elements of cost, such as the price paid for materials, the amount of materials used in production, and so forth.

For example, suppose a charter bus company has planned its gasoline cost for a 2,000 mile trip as follows:

200 gallons (based on 10 miles per gallon) at $1.10 per gallon, total cost $220.

Suppose that at the conclusion of the trip (which was indeed 2,000 miles) the gasoline costs were found to be 250 gallons at a total cost of $300 (therefore averaging $1.20 per gallon).

The total variance—the total difference between the actual cost of gasoline ($300) and the standard or planned cost ($220) is $80. This variance could be further broken down by asking how much is due to the higher cost ($1.20 per gallon instead of the standard $1.10) and how much is due to the increased usage (250 gallons instead of 200). These computations are as follows:

Due to higher cost: an extra $.10 ($1.20−$1.10) was paid for each of the 250 gallons purchased, a total of	$25.00
Due to increased usage: an extra 50 gallons (250−200) were used, at a standard price of $1.10 per gallon[1]	55.00
Total variance	$80.00

For control purposes, if the amounts are significant enough to warrant concern, the causes of the variances should be investigated. Actions that can be taken to correct the situation should then be considered. With respect to the higher gasoline cost, possibly the driver is not sufficiently cost-conscious in selecting gasoline stops, or perhaps the price of gasoline has increased since the standard was established. The first cause can be corrected; the second suggests a change in standard is needed. Similar analysis can be applied to the increased gasoline consumption: perhaps the driver has bad driving habits, the bus's engine needs a tune-up, and so on. When causes are sought to explain variances and appropriate corrective action is initiated, standard costs are being used as a control tool.

PRODUCT COSTING WITH STANDARD COSTS

Standard costs are often used in product costing because they facilitate accounting. The previous chapter discussed two product-costing systems: job-order costing and process costing. It is important to note that standard costing is *not* a third, distinct type of product-costing system. Rather, it is a procedure to be used in conjunction with either job-order or process costing. The major feature of standard costing is the division of actual costs into two parts: standard costs and variances—the differences between actual and standard costs.

---

[1]The reason for using the standard cost of $1.10, rather than the actual cost of $1.20, will be discussed later in the chapter.

Seven events may be identified in the assignment of cost to product and the determination of cost of goods sold:

1 Purchase direct materials
2 Use direct materials in production
3 Purchase direct labor services
4 Use direct labor in production
5 Incur overhead costs and assign them to product
6 Complete production
7 Sell goods

Each event gives rise to an entry in the product-costing system. In the previous chapter, these events led to the assignment of actual costs to products. Under a standard costing system, standard costs (rather than actual costs) are assigned to products. The purpose of standard costing is to show product costs at amounts that should be incurred if the company is operating efficiently and paying expected prices. Any differences that appear between actual and standard costs (variances) indicate how much better or worse than anticipated is the firm's actual performance. In addition, using standard costs is a convenience at several steps in the product-costing system.

The effect of standard costing on each of the seven events listed above is now examined. In general, the procedures for standard costing are (1) calculate the standard cost for each event and (2) compare standard to actual costs to determine the variance. The first five events, which entail cost incurrence for and utilization of materials, labor, and overhead, account for all differences between actual and standard costs. In the final steps of completing production and selling goods, all costs will be at standard, and thus no variances will exist.

Purchase of Direct Materials

When materials are purchased, it is appropriate to ask: According to our standards, what should be the price per unit of these materials? This *standard price per unit of materials* would be revised periodically as conditions change. Of course, a separate standard price would exist for each type of material. At any time, the standard reflects an estimate of what price should be paid for the particular type of material purchased.

For example, assume that the Stand Company's current standards indicate a standard price for material B of $.68 per gallon. On June 1, 1988, the company buys 3,000 gallons at $.70 per gallon, a total *actual* purchase cost of $2,100. How should this purchase be recorded under a standard cost system?

First, calculate the *standard cost of the materials purchased,* as follows:

Quantity puchased	3,000 gallons
Standard price per gallon	×$ .68
Standard cost of materials purchased	$2,040

The $2,040 is the standard cost which should be entered in the materials inventory account. However, the company must pay the supplier $2,100 for these materials. The $60 difference between actual cost and standard cost is called a variance. It may be positive (a debit balance, often called "unfavorable") or negative (a credit balance, often called "favorable"). In this case, the materials price variance is a $60 debit (unfavorable) balance:

Actual cost of materials purchased	$2,100
Standard cost of materials purchased	− 2,040
Materials price variance	$ 60 Unfavorable

The difference is called a *materials price variance* because it arises from a difference between the actual unit price ($.70) and the standard price ($.68). This two-cents-per-gallon difference, on 3,000 gallons, amounts to a total of $60. The formula for the determination of the materials price variance can also be expressed as:

$$\text{Materials Price Variance} = \frac{(\text{Actual Price per Unit} - \text{Standard Price per Unit})}{\times \text{ Actual Quantity Purchased}}$$

Substituting for Stand Company:

$$\$60 = (\$.70 \text{ per gallon} - \$.68 \text{ per gallon}) \times 3,000 \text{ gallons}$$

The unit of materials in the formula is stated as gallons to coincide with the type of materials used by Stand Company. In other situations, the unit of materials could be pounds, feet, quarts, and so on.

Under a standard cost system, Stand's purchase on June 1, 1988, is journalized as:

1988			
June 1	Materials Inventory	2,040	
	Materials Price Variance	60	
	Accounts Payable		2,100
	To record the purchase of materials.		

Note that the materials inventory is recorded at the *standard* price of $.68 per unit. As materials are later withdrawn from the inventory and used in production, we must continue to use this standard price in journal entries. Note also that a new account enters the product-costing system—the materials price variance account. As other events occur, additional variance accounts will be created. The eventual treatment of these variance accounts will be discussed later in the chapter.

Use of Direct Materials in Production

When materials are used in production, it is appropriate to ask: What quantity of materials should be used to produce this quantity of goods? To answer this, we must have a *materials quantity standard*. Based on technical and engineering considerations, this standard would indicate the amount of materials necessary to produce one unit of product. When materials are placed in production, it is the standard quantity of materials, rather than the actual quantity, that enters the work in process inventory account.

Assume that Stand Company produces product XZ and has determined that each unit of XZ should require 2 gallons of material B. During June 1,200 units of product XZ are manufactured using 2,600 gallons of material B. First, the *standard cost of materials used* is calculated as follows:

Production of XZ	1,200
Standard quantity of materials per unit	× 2 gallons
Standard quantity of materials	2,400 gallons
Standard price per gallon	×$ .68
Standard cost of materials used	$1,632

This is the amount to be charged to the work in process inventory account as the standard cost of materials used in production. However, the amount removed from the materials inventory account, which we will call the recorded cost of materials used, is:

Actual quantity of materials used	2,600 gallons
Standard price per gallon	×$ .68
Recorded cost of materials used	$1,768

Note that the $.68 standard cost per gallon, not the $.70 actual cost paid per gallon, is used to determine the credit to the materials inventory account. Since the $.68 standard cost per gallon is debited to materials inventory when materials are purchased, the $.68 must also be used when materials are removed from materials inventory. This illustrates how standard costing simplifies the accounting process. A materials item may be purchased at various prices, but we account for all purchases and uses through the materials inventory account at *one* price (the standard). In a standard cost system, remember this rule: *Once a standard cost is determined, it is used in all subsequent accounting steps.*

COMPUTER APPLICATION

This feature makes a standard cost system well suited to computer application. The various standards can be stored in the computer. As actual transactions are recorded, appropriate standard costs can be automatically calculated and posted to the proper accounts. At the same time, variances are calculated by comparing actual and standard data. The system may be programmed to provide a dual set of records—actual cost records for financial reporting purposes, and standard cost records for managerial purposes.

To record the use of materials in production by Stand Company during June, the following entry is required:

June 30	Work in Process Inventory	1,632	
	Materials Quantity Variance	136	
	Materials Inventory		1,768
	To record use of materials.		

The *materials quantity variance* is the $136 difference between the recorded cost of materials used ($1,768) and the standard cost of materials used ($1,632). In formula format, the materials quantity variance can be expressed as:

$$\text{Materials Quantity Variance} = \begin{array}{c} \text{(Actual Units Used} - \text{Standard Units Allowed)} \\ \times \text{ Standard Price per Unit} \end{array}$$

Substituting for Stand Company:

$$\$136 = (2,600 \text{ gallons} - 2,400 \text{ gallons}) \times \$.68 \text{ per gallon}$$

Purchase of Direct Labor Services

In a standard cost system, it is convenient to view labor costs in the same manner as direct material costs. Even though materials can be inventoried before use and labor cannot, labor cost can be seen as having two distinct components: the *purchase* of labor services and the *use* of labor in production. From this perspective, standard costing for direct labor exactly parallels that for direct materials.

In considering the purchase of labor services, we ask: What is the rate per hour that should be paid for labor services? The *standard labor rate* will be based on the level of skill and experience required and on factors such as market conditions, union contracts, and the minimum wage. Separate rate standards may exist for the different classifications or categories of direct labor within a company.

For example, assume that for a certain production job the Stand Company had established a standard labor rate of $4.20 per hour. During June, 610 hours were worked and the employees received $2,440 (an average of $4.00 per hour). The *standard cost of labor services* would be:

Actual hours worked	610 hours
Standard rate per hour	×$ 4.20
Standard cost of labor services purchased	$2,562

This amount will be debited to the factory labor cost account as the standard cost of labor services purchased. The actual direct labor cost was only $2,440. The difference, the *labor rate variance,* is a $122 credit, or favorable balance, in this case and reflects the fact that actual cost was less than standard.

The entry to record the June purchases of labor services for Stand Company:

June 30	Factory Labor Cost	2,562	
	Labor Rate Variance		122
	Wages Payable		2,440

To record purchase of factory labor.

In formula format, the labor rate variance can be expressed as:

$$\text{Labor Rate Variance} = \begin{array}{c} (\text{Actual Rate per Hour} - \text{Standard Rate per Hour}) \\ \times \text{ Actual Hours Worked} \end{array}$$

Substituting for Stand Company:

$$\$122 = (\$4.00 \text{ per hour} - \$4.20 \text{ per hour}) \times 610 \text{ hours}$$

Use of Direct Labor in Production

When labor is used in production, we ask: How many hours of labor should be used to produce this quantity of goods? The answer, based again on technical considerations, is the *labor usage standard*. When labor costs are charged to inventory, it is the standard labor hours, rather than the actual hours worked, that enter the work in process inventory account.

Assume that for Stand Company the labor usage standard is determined to be one-half direct labor hour per unit of XZ produced. For the 1,200 units of XZ produced in June, Stand Company's *standard cost of labor used* is:

Production of XZ	1,200 units
Standard use of labor per unit	× .5 hours
Standard direct labor hours	600 hours
Standard rate per hour	×$ 4.20
Standard cost of labor used	$2,520

This $2,520 standard cost of labor used is entered in work in process inventory.

Recall that labor costs were recorded in the factory labor cost account at the standard labor rate, not the actual rate paid. Following the rule that a standard cost once determined must be used in all subsequent accounting steps, the transfer of labor costs out of the factory labor cost account must be at the previously calculated $2,562 standard cost of labor services purchased.

The entry to record the use of direct labor during June in Stand Company's manufacturing process is:

June 30	Work in Process Inventory	2,520	
	Labor Usage Variance	42	
	Factory Labor Cost		2,562

To record labor used in production.

Work in process inventory is debited for the standard cost of labor used. The factory labor cost account is credited for the recorded cost of labor services. The $42 *labor usage variance* (unfavorable) is the difference between the recorded cost of labor services purchased ($2,562) and the standard cost of labor services used ($2,520). The formula for direct computation of the labor usage variance is:

$$\text{Labor Usage Variance} = \frac{\text{(Actual Hours Worked} - \text{Standard Hours Allowed)}}{\times \text{ Standard Rate per Hour}}$$

For Stand Company:

$$\$42 = (610 \text{ hours} - 600 \text{ hours}) \times \$4.20 \text{ rate per hour}$$

The labor usage variance is sometimes referred to as the *labor efficiency variance*.

Manufacturing Overhead

In the previous chapter, manufacturing overhead costs were applied to products based on a predetermined overhead rate times the actual volume of the specified application base. Under a standard cost system, a *standard manufacturing overhead rate* is developed in a similar manner. The resulting rate is applied to the *standard volume* of the application base in assigning costs to product. The result is the *standard manufacturing overhead cost,* which is the amount charged to the work in process inventory account.

Assume the following for Stand Company:

1 The company's actual manufacturing overhead costs totaled $4,000 (depreciation of $1,200, cash payments of $2,400, and $400 accounts payable).

2 Stand Company's standard manufacturing overhead rate is $7.00 per direct labor hour.

3 Direct labor hours is the application base. The standard volume of the application base is 600 direct labor hours, based on the 1,200 units of product XZ produced.

The *standard manufacturing overhead cost* is determined as follows:

Standard volume of application base for units produced	600 hours
Standard overhead rate per hour	×$ 7.00
Standard manufacturing overhead cost	$4,200

Using the above data, journal entries for June are presented that illustrate (1) the recording of actual overhead, (2) the application of standard overhead to production, and (3) the closing of the overapplied manufacturing overhead account balance into the manufacturing overhead variance account.

June 30	Manufacturing Overhead	4,000	
	Accumulated Depreciation		1,200
	Cash		2,400
	Accounts Payable		400

To record actual manufacturing
overhead costs incurred.

| 30 | Work in Process Inventory | 4,200 | |
| | Manufacturing Overhead | | 4,200 |

To apply standard manufacturing
overhead costs to production.

30	Manufacturing Overhead	200	
	Manufacturing Overhead		
	Variance		200

To close overapplied manufacturing
overhead into manufacturing
overhead variance.

Because $4,200 in manufacturing overhead costs were applied to product but only $4,000 of costs were actually incurred, manufacturing overhead was overapplied by $200. This amount, which represents the difference between actual and standard costs, is the *manufacturing overhead variance*.

The formula for calculating the manufacturing overhead variance is:

$$\text{Manufacturing Overhead Variance} = \begin{array}{l}\text{Actual Overhead Costs Incurred} \\ - \text{(Standard Overhead Rate} \times \\ \text{Standard Volume of Application} \\ \text{Base for Units Produced)}\end{array}$$

For Stand Company:

$$\$200 = \$4,000 - (\$7.00 \text{ rate per hour} \times 600 \text{ standard hours})$$

In the Stand Company example, only one ledger account, manufacturing overhead variance, was used. Many companies divide this total manufacturing overhead variance into two, three, or four separate variances. The appendix to this chapter describes how the manufacturing overhead variance can be subdivided into four components.

Cost of Goods Manufactured and Sold

Of the seven events in the assignment of costs to product and the determination of cost of goods sold, five events have been discussed. The assignment of costs to finished goods and to cost of goods sold remains.

Under a standard costing system, all entries to the work in process inventory account are made using standard costs. Recall that all manufacturing costs are incorporated into the product by the time the product enters the finished goods inventory. There are no additional costs entering the product-costing system at this point. Transfers to the finished goods inventory account are simply determined by multiplying units completed times the standard cost per unit. Since all costs are at standard, there are no additional variances to be determined. Variances arise only when actual costs are compared to standards.

As goods are sold, costs are taken out of finished goods inventory and recorded as cost of goods sold using standard costs. Again, no variance exists. Only standard costs are used in recording the last two events in the product-costing system.

For example, in the previous entries, Stand Company's work in process inventory was debited with the following standard costs for the 1,200 units of Product XZ produced:

Direct materials	$1.36 per unit × 1,200 units = $1,632
Direct labor	2.10 per unit × 1,200 units = 2,520
Applied manufacturing overhead	3.50 per unit × 1,200 units = 4,200
Total	$6.96 per unit × 1,200 units = $8,352

With no beginning or ending work in process inventory, the journal entry to record cost of goods manufactured during June would be:

June 30	Finished Goods Inventory	8,352	
	Work in Process Inventory		8,352
	To record transfer of completed goods to finished goods inventory.		

Cost of goods sold under a standard cost system represents the standard cost of units sold during the period. Multiplying standard unit cost by units sold yields the standard cost to be removed from finished goods inventory and debited to cost of goods sold.

For example, if Stand Company sold on account 1,000 units of Product XZ on June 30 at a selling price of $9.00 per unit, the journal entries would be:

June 30	Accounts Receivable	9,000	
	Sales		9,000
	To record sales on account.		
30	Cost of Goods Sold	6,960	
	Finished Goods Inventory		6,960
	To record cost of sales.		

The sales amount of $9,000 is based on 1,000 units sold at $9.00 selling price per unit. The $6,960 debit to cost of goods sold is for the standard cost of the units sold ($6.96 standard cost per unit × 1,000 units).

Cost Flow in a Standard Cost System Reviewed

Recall that five events had standard costs associated with them. As each event was recorded, two cost elements were determined: a standard cost and a variance. This is summarized in the table below:

		Cost elements	
Event	Standard for this event	Standard cost	Variance
Purchase of Materials	Standard Price per Unit of Materials	Standard Cost of Materials Purchased	Materials Price Variance
Use of Materials in Production	Standard Quantity of Materials per Unit of Product	Standard Cost of Materials Used	Materials Quantity Variance
Purchase of Labor Services	Standard Rate per Hour of Labor	Standard Cost of Labor Services Purchased	Labor Rate Variance
Use of Labor in Production	Standard Hours of Labor per Unit of Product	Standard Cost of Labor Used	Labor Usage Variance
Assignment of Manufacturing Overhead	Standard Rate per Unit of Application Base	Standard Manufacturing Overhead Cost	Manufacturing Overhead Variance

Summary of Variance Calculations

The formulas for the five variances are summarized below:

$$\text{Materials Price Variance} = \begin{array}{c}(\text{Actual Price per Unit} - \text{Standard Price per Unit}) \\ \times \text{Actual Quantity Purchased}\end{array}$$

$$\text{Materials Quantity Variance} = \begin{array}{c}(\text{Actual Units Used} - \text{Standard Units Allowed}) \\ \times \text{Standard Price per Unit}\end{array}$$

$$\text{Labor Rate Variance} = \begin{array}{c}(\text{Actual Rate per Hour} - \text{Standard Rate per Hour}) \\ \times \text{Actual Hours Worked}\end{array}$$

$$\text{Labor Usage Variance} = \begin{array}{c}(\text{Actual Hours Worked} - \text{Standard Hours Allowed}) \\ \times \text{Standard Rate per Hour}\end{array}$$

$$\text{Manufacturing Overhead Variance} = \begin{array}{c}\text{Actual Overhead Costs Incurred} \\ - (\text{Standard Overhead Rate} \times \\ \text{Standard Volume of Application} \\ \text{Base for Units Produced})\end{array}$$

Disposition of Variances

Most companies using standard costing allow variances to accumulate during the year. If monthly statements are prepared, the variances appear on the balance sheet. Work in process and finished goods inventories are presented at standard cost on monthly statements. Materials inventory is shown at standard price but actual quantity. This presentation is in keeping with the status of the ledger accounts at month-end.

At the end of the fiscal year, a company using standard costs for product-costing purposes is faced with the task of disposing of the variance accounts. Ideally, the variances should be prorated among the inventory accounts and the cost of goods sold account. After the variances are prorated, the inventory balances and cost of goods sold reported on the financial statements would then represent actual costs, not standard costs. Recall that assets are typically reported at historical (actual) cost. However, in those situations where the variances are not significant, or the variances are due to extraordinary inefficiency, or the inventory levels are low, the variance accounts are usually closed solely to the cost of goods sold account.

After the journal entries presented in the chapter are recorded, the following variance account balances exist for Stand Company:

Materials price variance—unfavorable	$ 60	(debit)
Materials quantity variance—unfavorable	136	(debit)
Labor rate variance—favorable	122	(credit)
Labor usage variance—unfavorable	42	(debit)
Manufacturing overhead variance— favorable	200	(credit)

If it is the end of the fiscal year and variances are to be closed to the cost of goods sold account, the entry to dispose of the variances would be:

June 30	Labor Rate Variance	122	
	Manufacturing Overhead Variance	200	
	Materials Price Variance		60
	Materials Quantity Variance		136
	Labor Usage Variance		42
	Cost of Goods Sold		84
	To close variances to cost of goods sold.		

Note that the favorable variances serve to decrease cost of goods sold, while unfavorable variances increase cost of goods sold.

STANDARD COSTS FOR CONTROL

In the preceding section, a standard cost accounting system and the related variances were developed and illustrated. We discussed standard costing as part of the formal accounting system's valuation of inventories and determination of income, and emphasized the appropriate journal entries for a standard cost system. In this section, standard costs are examined from the standpoint of providing information to management for the purposes of controlling and evaluating performance.

Variances, the differences between actual and standard performance, can serve as red flags signaling management as to the location of potential problems. Determining the cause of the variance, the responsible individual, and the corrective action needed are important factors.

Actual costs may differ from standards for many reasons. When a manager's actions caused the variance, then examination of the actions is in order. It is important to keep in mind that the *standards themselves, not the actual results, may be the cause of variances*. If standards were developed without proper care or if they are outdated, then actual results will differ from standards. Another possibility is that uncontrollable factors, external to the firm, may cause variances. Actual results may be as good as possible under the circumstances. Only a knowledgeable investigation of a variance will reveal if objectives are being accomplished, if corrective action is needed to meet expected performance, or if standards are in need of revision.

Variance analysis can be an effective way for a firm to pinpoint problems and correct them. Variance analysis can also be useful in evaluating performance of employees. However, a warning is in order. Using the management accounting tool of variance analysis indiscriminately, without adequate understanding and necessary investigations, can do far more to harm an organization than to benefit it. Such indiscriminate use may cause unfair performance evaluation and seriously affect the morale and motivation of company employees.

Variance Analysis for Control—An Example

The example below relates to Rontoll Manufacturing Co. In the sections that follow, each variance is determined, the cause investigated, and the employee to be held responsible identified. Outlined below are Rontoll Manufacturing's production data for the month of July, 1988:

Budgeted production = 30,000 units
Standards per unit:

Direct materials—2 gallons @ $5.00 per gallon	$10.00	per unit
Direct labor—3 hours @ $6.00 per hour	18.00	per unit
Manufacturing overhead—		
$4.00 per direct labor hour	12.00	per unit
	$40.00	

Actual data for July, 1988:
  25,000 units produced
  45,000 gallons of direct materials purchased @ $4.50 per gallon
  54,000 gallons of direct materials used in production
  82,000 direct labor hours worked @ $5.80 per hour
  $377,200 actual total manufacturing overhead cost incurred

Materials Price Variance The materials price variance for Rontoll Manufacturing, based on the preceding data is a favorable $22,500, calculated as follows:

Actual cost per gallon	$ 4.50
Standard cost per gallon	− 5.00
Savings per gallon	$ .50
Gallons actually purchased	× 45,000
Materials price variance	$22,500 Favorable

Recall that a favorable variance is achieved when the actual cost element being considered is less than the standard. Rontoll Manufacturing's actual purchase cost per gallon was $.50 less than the standard cost per gallon. This yields a $22,500 total favorable materials price variance for the 45,000 gallons purchased.

Who is to be held responsible for the materials price variance? In all likelihood, the purchasing department is responsible for acquiring the desired quality of materials at the lowest delivered cost. The purchasing department probably has responsibility for the selection of vendors, determination of quantities to purchase per order (within limits imposed by production requirements and inventory carrying costs), and the arrangements for delivery of materials purchased. If the purchasing department has authority to control materials purchased, it should be held responsible for materials price variances. If the $5.00 standard cost per gallon accurately reflects current market conditions and the materials acquired are not substandard in quality, Rontoll Manufacturing's purchasing department is to be congratulated for locating the $4.50 per gallon bargain price.

Note that Rontoll Manufacturing determined the materials price variance based on actual quantities purchased. Isolating the materials price variance at the time of purchase, or possibly even at the time the order is placed, notifies management of materials price variances at the earliest possible time. Waiting until materials are used in production to determine the materials price variance would unnecessarily delay the discovery of valuable price variance information. Maintaining tight control over material purchase costs is as crucial to company profitability as is efficient operation of the factory.

In many cases, investigation may reveal that a materials price variance is caused by external factors such as unexpected market price changes that are not reflected in current material price standards. In such situations, the variance is noncontrollable. It is not fair to hold the purchasing department responsible for such a noncontrollable variance. The variance still may be important to management, however, as it indicates a revision is necessary to update the materials price standard. Also, if significant, management might consider the feasibility of using substitute materials or possibly raising the selling price of their own product to compensate for a price increase in a particular material.

Rontoll Manufacturing uses only one type of direct material in its production process. Therefore, a single materials price variance calculation sufficed. In many companies, detailed variance reports are necessary. These detailed reports can be designed to provide management with materials price variance data categorized by (1) type of material, (2) supplier, and (3) individual employee making the purchase.

Materials Quantity Variance   The materials quantity variance for Rontoll Manufacturing is an unfavorable $20,000, calculated as follows:

Actual gallons used	54,000
Standard gallons used	− 50,000
Extra gallons used	4,000
Standard cost per gallon	×$ 5.00
Materials quantity variance	$20,000 Unfavorable

The variance is unfavorable since the actual quantity of 54,000 gallons used in producing the 25,000 units was greater than the standard quantity allowed of 50,000 gallons (2 gallons per unit × 25,000 units).

Note the concept of *standard quantity allowed for units produced,* which is part of the materials quantity variance calculation. The 50,000 standard gallons allowed is based on the 25,000 units actually produced—not the 30,000 units that had been budgeted. The materials quantity variance is thus a good measure of efficiency (i.e., how well the actual output was produced in terms of materials usage). A separate measure of effectiveness, the failure to reach the budgeted 30,000 unit level of output, is not allowed to influence the materials quantity (efficiency) variance.

Who has responsibility for the quantities of materials used in production? In most cases, quantities of materials used are controllable by (and therefore the responsibility of) the production supervisor.[2] It is the supervisor's responsibility to see that raw materials are efficiently transformed into finished units. The standard quantity allowed usually permits a normal, expected amount of scrap or waste. However, excessive material usage due to improper employee handling, theft in the factory, or malfunctioning machinery is the responsibility of the production supervisor.

At first glance, it appears that the supervisor of Rontoll Manufacturing must take the blame for the $20,000 unfavorable materials quantity variance. However, consider the following. The favorable $22,500 materials price variance previously calculated could be due to the purchase of substandard materials. The result of that purchase of substandard materials may be excessive defective units and waste when the materials enter production. Is the production supervisor to be responsible for an unfavorable materials quantity variance under these circumstances? Perhaps Rontoll Manufacturing's management is satisfied with the trade-off between the favorable price variance and unfavorable quantity variance.

The point to be made is that there are a number of interrelationships among the variances. Although variances are typically labeled favorable or unfavorable and certain individuals are associated with specific variances, management must realize that variances are only the starting point. They pinpoint potential problems. Only a thorough investigation of the variance will lead to understanding its true cause.

---

[2]When we state a cost is "controllable by (and therefore the responsibility of)" an individual within the organization, we are implying that the individual has significant influence over that cost, not necessarily complete control.

Labor Rate Variance   The labor rate variance closely parallels the materials price variance. The labor rate variance indicates the difference between the standard and actual cost of labor. For Rontoll Manufacturing a favorable (actual less than standard) labor rate variance of $16,400 can be calculated.

Actual rate per hour	$ 5.80
Standard rate per hour	− 6.00
Savings per hour	$ .20
Hours actually worked	× 82,000
Labor rate variance	$16,400 Favorable

What caused the $.20 per hour labor rate variance? Who is responsible for the total favorable variance of $16,400? Merely calculating the labor rate variance will not answer these questions. An investigation might reveal the standard rate of $6.00 was set too high. Perhaps Rontoll's management expected a $6.00 per hour rate to be the final settlement reached in management and labor union bargaining. The $5.80 actual rate agreed upon (and resultant $.20 "savings" per hour) thus could reflect either management's skills at the bargaining table or management's overly pessimistic forecast of the $6.00 standard rate per hour. In either case, the standard rate should be revised to the $5.80 rate set by the union contract since $5.80 now better reflects the estimated labor rate.

While the preceding paragraph described a situation where a faulty standard was responsible for the labor rate variance, it is possible that the production supervisor is responsible for labor rate variances. It is the production supervisor's responsibility to assign each worker to the appropriate task. Assigning highly skilled and highly paid engineers to janitorial duties would result in an unfavorable labor rate variance for janitors' salaries. On the other hand, assigning relatively low-paid janitors to engineering jobs would result in a favorable labor rate variance for engineers' wages. Keep in mind, however, that the labor rate variance must be considered in conjunction with other variances. Misallocating workers will not only affect the labor rate variance but also the number of hours to do the assigned job and possibly the quantity of materials used. Thus, the labor usage variance, the materials quantity variance, and even the manufacturing overhead variance would need to be analyzed in conjunction with the labor rate variance. To repeat—*understanding the interrelationships among the variances is crucial to an intelligent analysis of the variances.*

Labor Usage Variance   The labor usage variance measures the productivity, or efficiency, of labor. It is generally considered to be one of the most important variances. As will be discussed in the appendix, labor efficiency not only influences the amount of labor cost but also the manufacturing overhead cost incurred. Management usually monitors labor usage quite closely because of its significant impact on production costs. Weekly, or even daily, reports of labor usage are often compiled for management. These reports, often expressed only in terms of standard hours allowed versus actual hours worked, promptly inform management of a particular department or specific job that is not conforming to standard labor usage. Prompt knowledge of off-standard performance notifies management that corrective action is necessary or that possibly the job cannot be completed within the standard hours set.

The calculation of the labor usage variance is similar to the computation of the materials quantity variance. In both instances, actual quantities used are compared to standard quantities allowed for the units produced. The quantity difference is then multiplied by the appropriate standard cost. The labor usage variance for Rontoll Manufacturing is an unfavorable $42,000, determined as follows:

Actual hours worked	82,000
Standard hours allowed	− 75,000
Excess hours worked	7,000
Standard cost per hour	×$ 6.00
Labor usage variance	$42,000 Unfavorable

The 75,000 standard hours allowed is based on the 25,000 units actually produced times the three standard hours allowed per unit. As was the case with the materials quantity variance, the 5,000 unit difference between actual and budgeted production (30,000 budgeted units versus 25,000 actual units) does not influence the labor usage variance calculation.

Labor usage standards normally make allowance for expected time lost for such things as set-up time, learning a new task, normal fatigue, machine breakdowns, and so forth. If the labor usage standard reflects reasonable allowances for such factors, the production supervisor is usually held responsible for controllable labor hour variances. Normally, the production supervisor has authority over the workers. Therefore, the supervisor should be responsible for how well the workers use their time.

Care must be used to make sure the production supervisor is not held responsible for uncontrollable labor usage variances. If the $42,000 unfavorable labor usage variance was caused by spending an abnormal amount of time trying to work on substandard materials acquired by the purchasing department, the purchasing department manager (not the production supervisor) should be held responsible. Again, merely calculating and reporting the variance would be insufficient. The causes of the variance must be determined before responsibility can be fixed.

Manufacturing Overhead Variance   The total manufacturing overhead variance for Rontoll Manufacturing shows:

Actual manufacturing overhead	$377,200
Applied manufacturing overhead	− 300,000
Manufacturing overhead variance	$ 77,200 Unfavorable

The $300,000 applied manufacturing overhead was determined by multiplying the $4.00 manufacturing overhead rate per direct labor hour times the 75,000 standard hours allowed for the 25,000 units actually produced.

What are the causes of the unfavorable $77,200 variance? Who is to be held responsible? The single manufacturing overhead variance computed above (and used earlier for inventory valuation purposes) is difficult to analyze for control and performance evaluation purposes. The appendix to this chapter will divide the manufacturing overhead variance into several components for purposes of analysis.

SUMMARY

Learning Objective 1: Define the concept of standard cost.

Standard costs are predetermined cost estimates that provide forecasts of what costs should be under efficient operating conditions and expected prices. Predetermined standard costs provide targets that management can use in planning or in evaluating performance. Direct materials, direct labor, and manufacturing overhead standards can be estimated only after extensive research and study of the production process. Standard costs can be integrated in the formal accounting system with either job-order or process costing systems.

Variances, representing differences between actual and standard costs, are important elements in standard costing systems. Five variances commonly encountered are: materials price variance, materials quantity variance, labor rate variance, labor usage variance, and manufacturing overhead variance.

Learning Objective 2: Apply costs to product using standard costs.

Under a standard cost system of product costing, standard amounts are assigned to work in process, and the several variances are recorded separately. At the end of the period, variances are often closed to cost of goods sold. Journal entries illustrating the effect standard costing has on the formal accounting system of a manufacturing company were presented in the chapter along with the procedures for calculating the respective variances.

Learning Objective 3: Analyze variances for performance evaluation and control purposes.

In addition to being used for product costing, variance analysis is used for evaluating performance and for control purposes. Actual cost is compared to standard for each element of manufacturing cost (the price paid for materials, the quantity of materials used, and so forth). Variances serve as red flags, signaling management of the location of potential problems. Investigation of variances is necessary to determine their causes, the person responsible, and any appropriate corrective action.

KEY TERMS

Fixed manufacturing overhead budget variance (Appendix)
Fixed manufacturing overhead volume variance (Appendix)
Labor rate variance
Labor usage variance
Manufacturing overhead variance
Materials price variance

Materials quantity variance
Standard cost
Variable manufacturing overhead efficiency variance (Appendix)
Variable manufacturing overhead spending variance (Appendix)
Variance

APPENDIX: Manufacturing Overhead Variances

The $77,200 manufacturing overhead variance determined for Rontoll Manufacturing in the chapter is difficult to analyze for control and evaluation purposes. It is necessary to divide the total manufacturing overhead variance into variable overhead variance components and fixed overhead variance components. The subdivision is necessary since variable manufacturing overhead costs behave differently than fixed manufacturing overhead costs. Recall that total variable costs change proportionately with changes in volume. Total fixed costs, on the other hand, remain constant as volume changes.

In order to perform the detailed analysis of Rontoll Manufacturing's $77,200 total manufacturing overhead variance, the following information is obtained:

> Standard direct labor hours per unit—3 hours
> Manufacturing overhead standards:
>   Variable rate—$3.50 per standard direct labor hour
>   Fixed rate—$.50 per standard direct labor hour
> Budgeted fixed manufacturing overhead costs = $45,000
> Actual variable manufacturing overhead costs incurred = $336,200
> Actual fixed manufacturing overhead costs incurred = $41,000
> Actual direct labor hours worked—82,000 hours
> Budgeted production—30,000 units
> Actual units produced—25,000 units
> Standard hours allowed for units produced—75,000 hours
>   (25,000 units × 3 hours per unit)

VARIABLE MANUFACTURING OVERHEAD VARIANCES

Rontoll Manufacturing's variable manufacturing overhead variance is an unfavorable $73,700.

Actual variable manufacturing overhead cost incurred	$336,200
Variable manufacturing overhead applied	
($3.50 standard rate per hour × 75,000 standard hours allowed)	− 262,500
Variable manufacturing overhead variance	$ 73,700 Unfavorable

The variable manufacturing overhead applied is determined by multiplying the $3.50 variable manufacturing overhead rate per direct labor hour times the 75,000 standard direct labor hours allowed for the 25,000 units produced. Applied variable overhead thus reflects standard hours allowed for *actual* production, not *budgeted* production.

In order to understand the causes of the variance, the variable manufacturing overhead variance typically is subdivided into a *spending* variance and an *efficiency* variance. The *spending variance* indicates the portion of the variable manufacturing overhead variance attributable to (1) price differences between the actual and standard prices of variable manufacturing overhead items and (2) inefficient usage of variable manufacturing overhead items other than that related to excess direct labor hours worked.

As an example of the price difference portion of the spending variance, consider a situation where the actual price per kilowatt hour of electricity differed from the standard cost forecasted. Price differences of this type may be uncontrollable. No one within the organization can be held responsible for the price change, and management should revise the standard cost per kilowatt hour for electricity. Perhaps management might also consider means of modifying the production process to minimize the use of electricity if the increase in price is significant. Also, management might consider the possibility of increasing the selling price of their product to cover the increase in the cost of electricity.

Inefficient usage of variable manufacturing overhead items, other than that due to excess direct labor hours worked, can be illustrated by considering the cost of leaving the windows open on cold winter nights when the factory is not operating or letting machinery run when not in use. The inefficient use of heat and power will increase the factory heat and power cost, but not because of any excess direct labor hours worked. The portion of the variable manufacturing overhead spending variance resulting from inefficient use of overhead items usually would be the responsibility of the supervisor or the supervisor's designated representative.

The spending variance portion of Rontoll Manufacturing's variable manufacturing overhead variance is an unfavorable $49,200, calculated as follows:

Actual variable overhead rate per direct labor hour ($336,200 ÷ 82,000 actual hours)	$ 4.10
Standard variable overhead rate per direct labor hour	− 3.50
Excess cost per direct labor hour	$ .60
Actual direct labor hours worked	× 82,000
Variable manufacturing overhead spending variance	$49,200 Unfavorable

To divide the spending variance causes between 1) price differences between actual and standard costs and 2) inefficiencies other than due to direct labor usage requires a detailed investigation of each individual variable manufacturing overhead item (e.g., indirect materials, indirect labor, factory heat, light, power, repairs, and so on).

The *efficiency variance* component of variable manufacturing overhead measures the extra cost (if the variance is unfavorable) or the cost savings (if the variance is favorable) due solely to the actual level of the application base differing from the standard level. If direct labor hours is selected as the basis for applying variable manufacturing overhead, it is assumed that the number of direct labor hours actually worked bears a direct relationship to the variable manufacturing overhead costs incurred. The variable manufacturing overhead efficiency variance thus is intended to spotlight the dollar impact of direct labor usage on variable manufacturing overhead costs.

For Rontoll Manufacturing, the variable manufacturing overhead efficiency variance is an unfavorable $24,500 calculated as follows:

Actual hours used	82,000
Standard hours allowed	− 75,000
Excess hours worked	7,000
Standard variable overhead rate per hour	×$ 3.50
Variable manufacturing overhead efficiency variance	$24,500 Unfavorable

Since there is an assumed relationship between direct labor hours worked and variable manufacturing overhead costs incurred, it is to be expected that the 7,000 excess hours worked would cause actual variable manufacturing overhead costs to exceed standard. The efficiency variance quantifies these added variable manufacturing overhead costs due to excess direct labor hours at $24,500 for Rontoll Manufacturing.

Who is to be held responsible for the variable manufacturing overhead efficiency variance? Since the efficiency variance is due to the hours worked in excess of the standard hours allowed, the person responsible for the labor usage variance (normally the production supervisor) also should be responsible for the subsequent variable manufacturing overhead efficiency variance.

FIXED MANUFACTURING OVERHEAD VARIANCES

Rontoll Manufacturing's fixed manufacturing overhead variance is an unfavorable $3,500, calculated as follows:

Actual fixed manufacturing overhead cost incurred	$41,000
Fixed manufacturing overhead applied ($.50 standard rate per hour ×75,000 standard hours allowed)	− 37,500
Fixed manufacturing overhead variance	$ 3,500 Unfavorable

The $37,500 applied fixed manufacturing overhead was computed by multiplying the $.50 rate per standard direct labor hour times the 75,000 standard direct labor hours allowed for the 25,000 units actually produced.

The behavior of fixed costs does not coincide with that of variable costs. Therefore, analysis of the fixed manufacturing overhead variance will differ somewhat from the analysis of direct materials, direct labor, and variable manufacturing overhead. To a large extent, the fixed manufacturing overhead variance may be uncontrollable.

Part of the variance may be due to price differences between actual and budgeted fixed manufacturing overhead costs. This portion of the fixed manufacturing overhead variance is referred to as the *budget variance*. Rontoll Manufacturing's fixed manufacturing overhead budget variance is a favorable $4,000, calculated as follows:

Actual fixed manufacturing overhead	$41,000
Budgeted fixed manufacturing overhead	− 45,000
Fixed manufacturing overhead budget variance	$ 4,000 Favorable

A second portion of the fixed manufacturing overhead variance arises from the failure of the planned volume of activity to agree with the standard hours allowed for the actual output produced. This part of the fixed manufacturing overhead variance is referred to as the *volume variance*. For Rontoll Manufacturing, the volume variance is an unfavorable $7,500, calculated as follows:

Budgeted activity level expressed in terms of direct labor hours (30,000 budgeted units×3 standard hours allowed per unit)	90,000 hours
Standard hours allowed for output actually produced (25,000 units ×3 hours)	− 75,000
Underutilization of plant capacity	15,000 hours
Fixed manufacturing overhead rate per hour	×$ .50
Fixed manufacturing overhead volume variance	$ 7,500 Unfavorable

In some cases, a volume variance may be caused by inability to produce at desired levels (due, perhaps, to lack of materials, machine breakdowns, labor problems, and so on). To some extent, these factors are controllable by the production supervisor. In other cases, the volume variance may be uncontrollable. Perhaps budgeting for 30,000 units was the result of an unrealistically optimistic forecast from the sales department. In reality, 25,000 units may be sufficient for actual sales orders received. If only 25,000 units were ultimately required, the production supervisor should not be held responsible for the volume variance. In this situation only the supervisor's ability to produce efficiently the 25,000 units actually needed should be judged. If anyone is to be held responsible for the volume variance, it would be the sales department for their failure to generate the sales level they projected. Even in this situation, a better measure of performance evaluation for the sales department would be the lost contribution margin (sales minus variable expenses) on the 5,000 units—not the $7,500 manufacturing overhead volume variance.

The four overhead variances discussed above are summarized in Exhibit 16-2. Note that direct labor hours has been assumed to be the application base. If a different application base is employed, the appropriate units of measure should be substituted for direct labor hours in the variance formulas.

REVIEW QUESTIONS

1 Define the term *standard costs*.
2 Mr. G. H. Groton, President of Fratin Industries, is considering the introduction of a standard cost accounting system. What advantages could Mr. Groton achieve through use of a standard cost accounting system?
3 Evaluate the following statement: "Although initially time consuming and expensive to compute, standards, once developed, do not require change."

EXHIBIT 16-2
Summary of Overhead Variances

Manufacturing overhead variance formulas (using direct labor hours as the application base)	Rontell Manufacturing Co. example

Variable manufacturing overhead

Spending Variance = (Actual variable overhead rate −Standard variable overhead rate) ×Actual direct labor hours	$49,200 Unfavorable
Efficiency Variance = (Actual direct labor hours −Standard hours allowed) ×Standard variable overhead rate	24,500 Unfavorable
Total variable manufacturing overhead variance	$73,700 Unfavorable

Fixed manufacturing overhead

Budget Variance = Actual fixed overhead −Budgeted fixed overhead	$ 4,000 Favorable
Volume Variance = (Budgeted direct labor hours −Standard hours allowed) ×Fixed overhead rate	7,500 Unfavorable
Total fixed manufacturing overhead variance	$ 3,500 Unfavorable
Total manufacturing overhead variance	$77,200 Unfavorable

4 Mrs. M. M. Smith, Vice-President for Finance for Trainor, Inc., is attempting to determine the proper product-costing system for making inventory valuations for the company's new petroleum-refining operations. Mrs. Smith is trying to select among: (1) job-order costing, (2) process costing, and (3) standard costing. Help Mrs. Smith make her decision.

5 When standard costs and variances are integrated into the basic accounting system, unfavorable variance accounts would have _____ (debit, credit) balances, while variance accounts with favorable balances would have _____ (debit, credit) balances.

6 If a company using standard costing and variance accounts as part of its basic accounting system records the direct materials price variance when materials are purchased, and records the direct materials quantity variance when materials are placed into production, the debit to materials inventory when direct materials are purchased would be composed of:
a Actual quantity purchased times actual price
b Actual quantity purchased times standard price
c Standard quantity used times actual price
d Standard quantity used times standard price

7 If a company using standard costing and variance accounts as part of its basic accounting system records the direct labor rate variance when labor services are purchased and the direct labor usage variance when labor is used, work in process reflects:
a Actual direct labor hours worked times actual direct labor rate per hour
b Actual direct labor hours worked times standard direct labor rate per hour
c Standard direct labor hours times actual direct labor rate per hour
d Standard direct labor hours times standard direct labor rate per hour

8 Woodwork, Inc. uses a standard cost system as part of its basic accounting system. The standard manufacturing overhead rate is $3.40 per standard direct labor hour. At standard, each unit should require three direct labor hours. If 1,300 units were produced using 4,000 actual direct labor hours, what is the amount of the debit to work in process for applied manufacturing overhead?

9 If the actual manufacturing overhead incurred by Woodwork, Inc. (see Question 8 above) was $13,500 during the period, what would be the proper journal entry to close the manufacturing overhead account and transfer the balance to the manufacturing overhead variance account?

10 "When standard costs and variances are integrated into the basic accounting system, both cost of goods manufactured and cost of goods sold are recorded at standard." Explain the preceding statement.

11 "Both the theoretical and practical means of disposing of variances at the end of the year is to close the variances to cost of goods sold." Evaluate the preceding statement.

12 Shoner Co. closes all variance accounts to cost of goods sold at the end of the year. Cost of goods sold before closing of the variances totaled $108,000. If Shoner Co.'s favorable variances total $4,100 and unfavorable variances total $4,600, what will be the cost of goods sold balance after the variance accounts are closed?

13 Which of the following variance accounts have favorable balances?

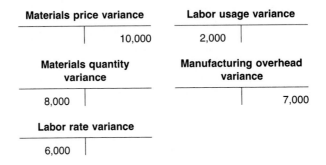

Materials price variance	Labor usage variance
10,000	2,000

Materials quantity variance	Manufacturing overhead variance
8,000	7,000

Labor rate variance
6,000

14 What role does variance analysis play in assisting management to perform its controlling and evaluation function?

15 A fellow accounting student suggests that companies' performance bonuses should automatically be correlated with variances. For example, unfavorable variances (actual exceeds standard) would eliminate any performance bonuses. Favorable variances (actual less than standard) would result in performance bonuses; the more favorable the variance, the larger the bonus. Evaluate the accounting student's suggestion.

16 If a variance proves to be caused by noncontrollable factors, is there any advantage to be gained from having calculated and analyzed the variance?

17 (Appendix) Is the variable manufacturing overhead spending variance due solely to price differences between the actual and standard prices of variable manufacturing overhead items?

18 (Appendix) Under what circumstance would it be possible to hold the purchasing department responsible for parts of the materials quantity variance, labor usage variance, and variable manufacturing overhead variance?

19 (Appendix) _____ and _____ are subdivisions of the total variable manufacturing overhead variance. The fixed manufacturing overhead variance is subdivided into the _____ variance and the _____ variance.

20 (Appendix) As indicated in Question 19, the manufacturing overhead variance is subdivided into variable and fixed components. Why aren't the direct materials variance and direct labor variance similarly subdivided into variable and fixed components?

EXERCISES

E16-1 Cachet, Inc. uses a standard cost system. The quantity of direct materials purchased was 8,000 pounds at $26 per pound. The actual quantity of direct materials used was 7,900 pounds. Standard quantity of direct materials that should have been used for the output produced was 8,400 pounds at $28 standard price per pound.

Calculate direct materials price variance and quantity variance. Indicate amounts and whether favorable or unfavorable. Also prepare journal entries to record the purchase of direct materials and the usage of direct materials.

E16-2 Norton Co. uses a standard cost system. During the period, 670 actual direct labor hours at $6 per hour were worked. The standard direct labor rate is $6 per hour. During the period 1,300 units were produced. The standard time allowed for each unit produced is one-half hour.

Calculate direct labor rate variance and usage variance. Indicate amounts and whether favorable or unfavorable. Also prepare the journal entries to record the purchase and use of direct labor services.

E16-3 Actual manufacturing overhead incurred by Gages, Inc. totaled $135,000 for the period. The standard manufacturing overhead rate per standard direct labor hour is $5. The actual direct labor hours worked during the period equaled 30,000. The standard direct labor hours that should have been worked based on the output produced totaled 29,000 hours.

Prepare journal entries to: (1) record actual manufacturing overhead incurred (credit: Various Accounts), (2) apply standard manufacturing overhead to production (i.e., work in process inventory), and (3) close the manufacturing overhead account balance into the manufacturing overhead variance account.

E16-4 During the period, Traiton, Incorporated produced 14,000 units at a standard cost per unit of $23. Traiton sold 12,000 units to customers on account at a selling price of $30 each.

Assuming Traiton uses standard costing as part of its accounting system, prepare journal entries to record: (1) transfer of cost of 14,000 units from work in process to finished goods, (2) sales to customers, and (3) cost of goods sold.

E16-5 Flagent Co. has the following variance account balances at the end of the year:

Materials price variance	$1,300 Favorable
Materials quantity variance	1,900 Unfavorable
Labor rate variance	300 Favorable
Labor usage variance	1,100 Favorable
Manufacturing overhead variance	2,400 Unfavorable

Assuming Flagent closes its variance accounts to cost of goods sold, prepare the closing journal entry for the variance accounts.

E16-6 There are two materials variances and two labor variances described in the chapter. List the calculation formula for each of the four variances. Assuming the standards represent realistic, efficient performance and that no noncontrollable events occurred, state whom you would hold responsible for each variance and why.

E16-7 (Appendix) The personnel department of Zanzer Co. has responsibility for hiring properly qualified employees to work on the factory's assembly line. In order to reduce the factory payroll cost, the personnel department hires untrained, unqualified employees at $2 per hour less than the standard labor rate for properly qualified employees. What variance (or variances) could be affected? Support your answer(s) by specifying which part or parts of the variance calculation(s) could be affected.

E16-8 (Appendix) Some of the variance calculations presented below are not in agreement with those described in the chapter. Identify which ones are incorrect and explain why they are incorrect and how they should be corrected.
1 Materials quantity variance = (Actual quantity used − Standard quantity allowed) × Actual price
2 Labor rate variance = (Actual rate per hour − Standard rate per hour) × Standard hours that should have been worked
3 Fixed manufacturing overhead budget variance = Actual fixed manufacturing overhead − Budgeted fixed manufacturing overhead

E16-9 (Appendix) Each statement below gives a clue as to the identification of one of the variances. Identify each variance based on the clue presented.
1 Based on excess hours worked above standard, but does not involve actual or standard labor rate.
2 Usually the responsibility of the purchasing agent.
3 Includes manufacturing overhead inefficiencies, but is not the efficiency variance.
4 Indicates effectiveness in reaching forecasted volume.
5 Hiring untrained, unskilled employees at lower wage rates for skilled jobs makes this variance favorable.
6 Based on quantity of materials purchased, not quantity used.

PROBLEMS

P16-1 *Simple Variance Calculations*
The Raliton Co. manufactures Glyoxide, a product used in the chemical industry. Data on standards:

	Per unit
Direct materials per unit, 4 lbs. @ $1.10 per lb.	$ 4.40
Direct labor per unit, 6 hrs. @ $3.50 per hr.	21.00
Manufacturing overhead per unit, 6 hrs. @ $6.90 per hr.	41.40
Standard cost per unit	$66.80

Costs for September:

> Direct materials purchased and used, 4,700 lbs. at $1.15 per lb.
> Direct labor, 7,400 hrs. @ $3.55 per hr.
> Actual manufacturing overhead costs incurred $51,634
> Raliton Co. produced 1,200 units of Glyoxide in September.

Required:

Calculate the five variances defined and illustrated in the chapter. Indicate favorable or unfavorable for each variance.

(AICPA Adapted)

P16-2 *Material and Labor Variances and Journal Entries*
The Repak Co. incorporates standard costing in its accounting system. The company's standards for the 8,000 units produced during the period were:

> 24,000 ft. of direct material @ $.16 per ft.
> 85,000 hrs. of direct labor @ $4.80 per hr.

During the year, Repak Co. purchased 27,000 feet of direct materials @ $.14 per foot, used in production 25,000 feet of direct materials, and used in production 84,000 direct labor hours @ $5.00 per hour.

Required:

1 Calculate the two variances for direct materials and the two variances for direct labor. Indicate amounts and whether favorable or unfavorable.
2 Prepare journal entries to record the following (show supporting calculations):
  a Purchase of direct materials
  b Usage of direct materials
  c Purchase and usage of direct labor services

P16-3 *Standards and Variances: Missing Data*
Bob Johnson, an accountant for J. D. Dougherty Manufacturing Co., took work home with him in order to complete some reports that were needed for a board of directors meeting the following day. Unfortunately, the next morning on his way to work, Bob left his briefcase containing the finished reports and supporting calculations on the subway train. From scratch papers in his office wastebasket, Bob is able to determine the following information:
1 Manufacturing overhead variance is $18,000 unfavorable
2 Standard direct labor rate per hour is $3.50
3 The standard time allowed for each unit is 4 hours
4 Units produced during period, 33,000
5 Actual manufacturing overhead is $240,000
6 Actual direct materials used is 100,000 pounds
7 Standard for direct materials per unit, 3 pounds at $8.00 per pound.
To compile the remaining information needed for his report to the board of directors, Bob must determine the four items listed below.

Required:

Help Bob by calculating the following:

1 Manufacturing overhead applied to work in process inventory.
2 Standard manufacturing overhead rate per *unit*.
3 Direct labor debited to work in process inventory.
4 Direct materials quantity variance (Indicate amount and whether favorable or unfavorable).

P16-4 *Product Costing with Standard Costs: Journal Entries*
Tolbert Manufacturing uses a standard cost system in accounting for the cost of production of its only product, Product A. The standards for the production of one unit of Product A are as follows:

	Per unit
Direct materials:	
10 ft. of item #1 @ $.75 per ft.	$ 7.50
3 ft. of item #2 @ $1.00 per ft.	3.00
Direct labor:	
4 hrs. @ $3.50 per hr.	14.00
Manufacturing overhead:	
150% of standard direct labor cost	21.00
Standard cost per unit	$45.50

No inventories are on hand at the beginning of July. There is no work in process at the end of July. During July, 8,000 units of Product A were manufactured. Also during July, the following events happened:

100,000 ft. of item #1 purchased @ $.78 per ft.
78,000 ft. of item #1 used in production
30,000 ft. of item #2 purchased @ $.90 per ft.
26,000 ft. of item #2 used in production
31,000 direct labor hrs. worked @ $3.60 per hr.

Required:
1 Assuming actual manufacturing overhead incurred during July was $173,000, determine the overapplied (or underapplied) manufacturing overhead. Would the Manufacturing Overhead Variance account for Tolbert Manufacturing have a debit or credit balance after the overapplied (or underapplied) overhead is transferred into the variance account?
2 Prepare journal entries to record the following (show supporting calculations):
  a Purchase of item #1
  b Usage of item #1
  c Purchase of item #2
  d Usage of item #2
  e Purchase and usage of direct labor services
  f Manufacturing overhead applied
  g Transfer of 8,000 completed units from work in process to finished goods
  (AICPA Adapted)

P16-5 *Product Costing: Variances and Journal Entries*
The Groomer Company manufactures Florimene, a product used in the plastics industry.
Data on standards:

	Per unit
Direct materials per unit, 3 lbs. @ $1 per lb.	$ 3.00
Direct labor per unit, 5 hrs. @ $3 per hr.	15.00
Manufacturing overhead per unit, 5 hrs. @ $6.80 per hr.	34.00
Standard cost per unit	$52.00

Costs for September:

> Direct materials purchased and used, 3,100 lbs. at $.90 per lb.
> Direct labor, 4,900 hrs. at $2.95 per hr.
> Actual manufacturing overhead costs incurred, $37,100.
> There are no beginning or ending inventories.
> Groomer Company produced and sold 1,000 units of Florimene in September.

Required:

1 Calculate the five variances defined and illustrated in the chapter. Indicate favorable or unfavorable.
2 Prepare journal entries to record the following (show supporting calculations):
   a Purchase of direct materials
   b Usage of direct materials
   c Purchase and usage of direct labor services
   d Applied manufacturing overhead
   e Actual manufacturing overhead incurred (Credit: Various Accounts)
   f Transfer 1,000 completed units from work in process to finished goods
   g Sale on account of 1,000 units at $65 per unit
   h Cost of goods sold at standard
   i Transfer of overapplied or underapplied manufacturing overhead to variance account
   j Close all variances to cost of goods sold

(AICPA Adapted)

P16-6 *Standards and Variances: Missing Data*
As part of the course requirements in Advanced Accounting at Wissahocken University, students are required to develop problems to be submitted to the American Institute of Certified Public Accountants (AICPA) for possible use as future CPA exam problems. One of the students in the class, George Berkowitz, submitted the following problem without providing the solutions. Provide solutions for the requirements listed at the conclusion of George's problem.

The Crandell Co. uses standard costs in accounting for the cost of producing its sole product. Information furnished to you by the company includes:

1 Actual direct labor rate per hour is $.10 less than standard direct labor rate per hour
2 Actual direct labor cost is $168,200
3 Standard direct labor cost is $180,000; 60,000 standard hours allowed for output produced
4 Manufacturing overhead variance is $3,000 favorable
5 Standard manufacturing overhead rate is $6 per standard direct labor hour
6 Units produced during period, 30,000
7 Standard quantity of direct materials per unit is 3 gallons

8 Actual quantity of direct materials purchased is 100,000 gallons
9 Material price variance is unfavorable by $.20 per gallon
10 Material quantity variance is $10,000 favorable
11 Actual quantity of direct materials used is 80,000 gallons

Required:
Calculate the following:
1 Standard cost per gallon of direct materials
2 Actual cost per gallon of direct materials
3 Standard direct labor rate per hour
4 Actual number of direct labor hours worked
5 Direct labor usage variance (Indicate amount and whether favorable or unfavorable)
6 Actual manufacturing overhead incurred

P16-7 *Standard Costs for Planning*
This problem builds on the banquet planning data presented in the chapter.

Required:
Answer each of the following questions.
1 Assume that the manager arrived at his price by the following process:
  a Standard direct costs for food and labor, as calculated in the chapter,
  b Add 25 percent of labor cost to cover fringe benefits,
  c Add $200 to cover other overhead expenses,
  d Add $100 profit,
  e Divide by planned number of dinners and round to next highest $.50 (e.g., $7.15 becomes $7.50).
  What price per dinner did the manager quote?
2 Assume that by the time the banquet took place the cost of steak was $4.60 per pound, the cost of potatoes was $.18 per pound, and the cost of lettuce was $.54 per head. Determine the food cost variance per meal.
3 In planning for the banquet, the manager neglected to include six hours of clean-up work (at $2.50 per hour). Also, by the time of the banquet, the chef and assistant cook had each negotiated a $.50 per hour raise. Determine the actual total labor cost (exclude fringe benefits).
4 Given the costs in (2) and (3), and assuming food costs are incurred only for the actual number of dinners served, prepare brief statements of income if the number of people attending the banquet is:
  a 125
  b 150
  c 175
  Assume that fringe benefits are 25 percent of actual labor costs, and overhead is $200. Assume further that no changes in the number of personnel occurred as a result of variations in the number of people attending, and that a 135 guaranteed minimum exists.

P16-8 (Appendix) *Manufacturing Overhead Variances*
Starburst Manufacturing Co. has both a variable and a fixed component as part of its manufacturing overhead. The company applies manufacturing overhead using direct labor hours as a base. Selected data are presented below.

Required:

Calculate the four manufacturing overhead variances described in the appendix. Also, state what the purpose of calculating each variance is and who would normally be held responsible for each variance.

Budgeted production—60,000 units
Budgeted fixed manufacturing overhead—$90,000
Actual direct labor hours worked—50,000 hours at $7
Actual fixed manufacturing overhead cost—$91,380
Actual variable manufacturing overhead cost—$201,500
Actual number of units produced—64,000
Standards per unit:
   Direct materials—4.5 pounds at $8 per pound
   Direct labor—.75 hour at $7 per hour
   Manufacturing overhead—$6 per standard labor hour
     ($4 variable + $2 fixed)

P16-9 (Appendix) *Calculation of Eight Variances*

The Wilkerson Manufacturing Co. uses a standard cost system. Selected data follow:

Data on standard manufacturing costs:

	Per unit
Direct materials, 6 pounds at $1.10 per pound =	$ 6.60
Direct labor 4 hours at $7.50 per hour =	30.00
Variable overhead, $3.00 per direct labor hour =	12.00
Fixed overhead, $2.00 per direct labor hour =	8.00
Standard cost per unit	$56.60

Budgeted production for current month:

1,200 units (or 4,800 direct labor hours)

Actual results for current month:

6,300 pounds of direct materials acquired at $1.15 per pound
6,100 pounds of direct materials used in production
4,750 direct labor hours worked at $7.50 per hour
$14,012.50 variable overhead cost incurred
$10,000 fixed overhead cost incurred
1,000 units produced (no beginning or ending work in
   process inventories)

Required:

Calculate the following eight variances. Show amount of variance and label as favorable or unfavorable.

1 Direct materials price variance

2 Direct materials quantity variance

3 Direct labor rate variance

4 Direct labor usage variance

5 Variable overhead spending variance

6 Variable overhead efficiency variance

7 Fixed overhead budget variance

8 Fixed overhead volume variance

P16-10   (Appendix) *Relevant Variances for Control Problems*

The management of Noncontrel Manufacturing Co. is disturbed by the poor results of operations over the last few years. Along with other possible ideas, management is considering implementing a standard cost system and associated variance analysis. Direct labor hours are to be the base used for applying manufacturing overhead to work in process.

Required:

If standards are established by Noncontrel that reflect current efficient operations, which variance(s) would be relevant in analyzing the performance in question?

1 Management believes the purchasing agent for the company has arranged with a major supplier to make purchases at higher than the normal market price in return for a 5 percent kickback payment.

2 Management believes the factory supervisor may be submitting time cards for fictitious employees and then personally cashing the payroll checks issued for the fictitious employees.

3 Management believes the personnel department may be hiring unskilled workers for skilled jobs and agreeing to pay them regular wages of skilled employees in return for a 10 percent kickback of their gross wages to the personnel manager.

4 Management believes substantial quantities of materials are being stolen from goods in process in the factory.

5 Management feels the factory supervisor is not being effective in terms of achieving budgeted production levels.

Business Decision Problem

Brightube TV Manufacturing Co. is currently suffering from poor economic conditions in the consumer durable goods industry. As a cost savings maneuver, the company has decided to cut back on the size of its current labor force. However, the company's union contract specifies procedures on how layoffs are to be handled. Included in these procedures are complex "bumping" rules that provide that the electronic engineers (the employees with the longest seniority) are transferred to factory production jobs and current assembly line workers (with the least seniority) are the first to be laid off. The transferred engineers continue to receive their regular engineers' salaries upon transfer to the assembly line. None of the engineers has ever worked in the production area.

The assembly line supervisor for Brightube is concerned about the potential impact of the transfers on his own performance evaluation. The supervisor knows that top management holds him responsible for all variances except the materials price variance. The company uses direct labor hours as the basis for applying manufacturing overhead to work in process.

Required:

Why should the assembly line supervisor be concerned? What do you envision happening if management bases its evaluation on the dollar amounts of the variances without adequate investigation of the underlying reasons for the variances? Be specific. Discuss individual variances.

17

BUDGETING FOR PLANNING— COMPREHENSIVE BUDGETS

LEARNING OBJECTIVES

When you complete this chapter, you should be able to:
1 Discuss the various managerial uses of budgeting.
2 Prepare a comprehensive budget for planning future operations.

In the last several chapters, the product-costing function of a managerial accounting system has been emphasized. In the job-order costing, process costing, and standard costing chapters, the focus was on calculation of a manufacturing company's product cost data for external reporting. Specifically, product-cost information was used to determine the amounts assigned to inventories and to cost of goods sold on financial statements.

In addition to product costing, major functions of managerial accounting are planning, control, and evaluation of performance. This chapter examines the managerial accounting tool that is the key to effective planning—the budget. In particular, numerous considerations involved in formulating a budget are addressed. The process of preparing a comprehensive master budget will be illustrated. A discussion of the control and evaluation aspects of the budgeting process will also be presented.

INTRODUCTION TO BUDGETING

Budgets are formal financial plans that management uses as guides for future action and for the evaluation of performance. "Management" can be taken quite literally to include the management of any type of organization, not just profit oriented businesses. Virtually all organizations are faced with questions on *what* resources to acquire and use, *how many* (what amount) to acquire and use, and *when*. Budgeting provides a formal plan of action to identify the resources needed, the appropriate quantities, and the proper timing.

Budgeting ranges from the weekly household budget of an average family trying to make ends meet to the complex, multi-billion dollar annual budget of the U.S. Government (which also is trying to make ends meet). Local governments, colleges, churches, and hospitals are among the myriad of nonprofit organizations that spend considerable time and effort in the preparation, approval, and implementation of the annual budget. Similarly, most successful profit-oriented businesses devote substantial time and effort to planning. Lack of success of an organization, whether profit or nonprofit, can often be traced to the lack of proper planning.

An organization should prepare budgets for many reasons, such as:

1 To better understand the structure of the organization
2 To identify problem areas in advance
3 To coordinate, communicate, and authorize action
4 To aid in the control and evaluation of performance.

These benefits of budgeting are discussed in the following sections.

Budgets: An Aid to Understanding the Organization

The budgeting process forces management to study its own organizational structure and interactions. To develop a realistic and detailed budget, management must be thoroughly familiar with patterns of interaction among the company's divisions, departments, and employees. The relationship of the company with the world outside and the impact of external forces on company operations must also be studied. Understanding these internal and external interactions fosters better decision making.

The complexities of an organization should not be underestimated. Even small organizations may in reality be more complex than appears at first glance. If budgeting is to be an effective planning tool, the complexities of an organization must be thoroughly understood. For example, consider the ramifications of a proposed change in product selling price. How will competitors react to the price change? How will customers react? Will quantities sold be affected? Will production levels need to be revised? Will labor and material needs be altered? How will the amount and timing of cash inflows and outflows be affected? These are only some of the questions that need to be answered.

Budgets present *estimates of future activity* and thus necessarily contain a degree of uncertainty. Budgeted financial statements are only as good as the assumptions on which they are based.

COMPUTER APPLICATION

A number of companies have built *computer simulation models* of their firms to aid in budgeting. These computer simulations are a set of mathematical equations that express the complex interrelationships of the firm's internal functions and external relationships. With such a model of the firm, all expected ramifications of a planned change (such as a change in product selling price) are systematically considered. Revised projected financial statements incorporating the expected impact of all the interrelated changes are available in seconds with the use of a high-speed computer to solve the mathematical equations.

Budgets: Identifiers of Problem Areas

Budgeting forces management not only to understand the workings of its present organization but also to plan ahead—to look at the future. The budgeting process may reveal specific problems the organization is expected to encounter. With the advance identification of problem areas, management may have sufficient time to act toward alleviating expected problems or minimizing their undesirable impact.

For example, a cash budget may reveal expected cash flow problems by presenting a detailed plan of expected cash transactions for a future time period. Periods of expected cash shortages (when a loan might be required) or periods of expected cash excesses (when short-term investments might be made) are identified in advance. The warning of a potential cash shortage is certainly preferable to an unanticipated crisis resulting from insufficient cash available to cover required payments.

Consider another example relating to sales, production, inventory, and material purchases. Assume forecasted sales and related production levels indicate that an unusually large quantity of a crucial raw material will be needed to maintain production. The present inventory level of this raw material is not large enough to meet the production requirement. The regular supplier requires several weeks notice before delivering the raw material. If management does not budget, the firm may face a future inventory stockout of this particular material. The result could be a major interruption in the production process. Or, if another supplier can be located, the firm may be forced to place an expensive, emergency rush order for the crucial material. A coordinated sales, production, inventory, and materials purchasing budget could identify this problem well in advance. Management could acquire sufficient supplies of the crucial raw material by ordering in advance through normal channels.

The advantage of budgeting in early identification of problem areas also can be generalized to encompass budgeted financial statements. Perhaps projected net income, earnings per share, financial position, or some other item on the budgeted financial statements is unacceptable to management. Management may believe that budgeted results are not satisfying the organization's goals and objectives. When the budgeting process forewarns of unacceptable results, management has time to revise its strategies and formulate a plan that can achieve acceptable results. In many cases, a change in management decisions will alter budgeted results. Computer simulation models provide a quick, convenient way of producing projected financial statements for a multitude of possible strategy revisions.

Budgets: Guidelines to Action

Budgets are guidelines that (1) inform people of the resources expected to be available for use and (2) inform people of the level of performance that is expected of them. A budget communicates information, provides direction, and authorizes action.

Budget planning can offer an excellent opportunity for the various components of a business (e.g., sales, production, research, personnel, finance) to communicate with each other and to appreciate the necessity of coordinating their activities. When department managers are allowed to participate in formulating the organization's budget, they become more aware of the effects of departmental activities on the organization as a whole. Knowledge of organizational interrelationships, coupled with an understanding of overall company goals and strategies, is intended to foster coordination and cooperation and lessen departmental conflict and empire-building tendencies.

Involving department managers directly in the budget formulation process can yield other positive behavioral effects. By being invited to participate in budget preparation, managers are likely to feel their talents and knowledge are being recognized. Participation also promotes acceptance of the budget as a legitimate, realistic guideline of expected performance and as a fair basis for subsequent performance evaluation. On the other hand, if top management imposes budgets without departmental participation, the reaction of department managers is often negative. Managers who are not allowed to participate in budget formulation are more likely to perceive the budget as a restrictive or unfair set of rules.

Another advantage of *participative budgeting* is the expert advice often obtained. In many instances, department managers are in the best position to forecast future developments accurately. Any bias or narrow departmental viewpoint can be tempered by top-level management reevaluation of departmental estimates. Top-level management plays other roles in a participative budgeting scheme. Often utilizing the managerial accounting staff's expertise, top management must (1) coordinate the individual departmental forecasts into a consolidated master plan, (2) implement the budget, (3) record subsequent actual performance, (4) compare actual performance to budgeted, (5) analyze significant differences between actual and budget, and (6) take appropriate follow-up action.

The benefits of budgeting are many. However, when budgets are imposed from the top rather than developed with departmental participation, there may be negative results. Valuable inputs from department managers may be lost. Interdepartmental communication and coordination may suffer. The most damaging effect may be the negative attitude, poor morale, and resultant substandard performance that can be fostered. The problems that can be created when those who will be affected by a budget are not allowed to participate in its formulation may far outweigh the benefits of budgeting.

Budgets: Performance Evaluation and Control

Budgets represent plans for future action. They are a base against which management can compare subsequent actual results. If the budget was carefully and properly formulated and revised as changed conditions warranted, then reports on budgeted versus actual results should be a valuable tool in evaluating performance and identifying areas that may need corrective action.

Choosing a Budget Period

The time horizon of budgets can range from the next hour to several decades. For example, how have you budgeted your time over the next sixty minutes? How much time will you devote to studying your accounting textbook, watching television, or getting a snack to eat? On the other extreme of the time scale are capital expenditure budgets of some organizations that extend ten, twenty, or more years into the future. The long-range capital budgets notify management of expected major cash needs well in advance. As time passes, the forecasted capital expenditure budget is modified and refined.

Although time spans of budgets vary greatly, the budgeting horizon is often one year. An annual budget, supplemented by a long-range capital expenditure plan, is typical for most organizations. Often the annual budget is further divided into quarters. The first quarter is often subdivided into detailed monthly budgets. As each quarter of the year passes, the budget for the succeeding quarter can be subdivided into detailed monthly budgets.

To constantly maintain a planning horizon of one year, many companies have adopted continuous budgeting. *Continuous budgeting* requires management to add a new month to the budget as each current month passes. For example, at the end of January, 1988, forecasted results for January, 1989 would be added to the budget. At any one time, the budget covers the next twelve-month period. While continuous budgeting entails considerable time and effort, many companies believe the advantages of maintaining a constant twelve-month planning horizon far outweigh the costs.

Having discussed at some length the importance of budgeting in managerial accounting, we now turn to the topic of formulating a budget.

COMPREHENSIVE BUDGETING

Budgeting procedures and details will vary among organizations of different complexity and with different goals and objectives. For example, the budget for a large university will differ significantly from the budget of a small print shop. Some budgets may be quite general, while others are very detailed. A specific budget may be presented as an individual, isolated plan, or it may be part of a comprehensive (master) budget.

In this section of the chapter, comprehensive budgeting for a manufacturing company will be illustrated. A *comprehensive* or *master budget* is an integrated plan of activity for the organization that (1) includes separate budgets for sales, production, manufacturing costs, selling and administrative activities, and cash flow and (2) culminates in projected financial statements.

A comprehensive budget will be developed for More Manufacturing Co., a small company that produces and sells only one product. Exhibit 17-1 shows the network of interrelationships among the individual budgets comprising More Manufacturing's master budget. Specifically, the individual budgets to be developed are:

Sales budget	Exhibit A
Production budget—units	Exhibit B
Direct materials purchases budget	Exhibit C
Direct labor budget—hours and dollars	Exhibit D
Manufacturing overhead cost budget	Exhibit E
Projected schedule of cost of goods manufactured and sold	Exhibit F
Selling and administrative expenses budget	Exhibit G
Chronological cash budget	Exhibit H
Projected income statement	Exhibit I
Projected balance sheet	Exhibit J

COMPUTER APPLICATION

Because budgets are plans for the future, they involve many estimates and assumptions. In the course of planning, some estimates and assumptions may be changed by management. Or, management may ask: What would be the impact if a certain change occurred (e.g., if sales increased by 10 percent)? We see from Exhibit 17-1 how the individual budgets are interrelated in the master budget. A change in one budget might mean a change in several others. For example, if a change were made in the sales budget, virtually every other budget would be affected.

Computer programs such as electronic spreadsheets are a great aid in budgeting, because when a change is made in one component of a budget, all other affected components are immediately and automatically revised. This enables management to quickly answer questions concerning the impact of a change in a particular estimate or assumption.

The ten individual budgets comprising More Manufacturing's comprehensive budget for January, 1990 are based on the trial balance and additional information that follow.

EXHIBIT 17-1 Diagram of Master Budget Interrelationships

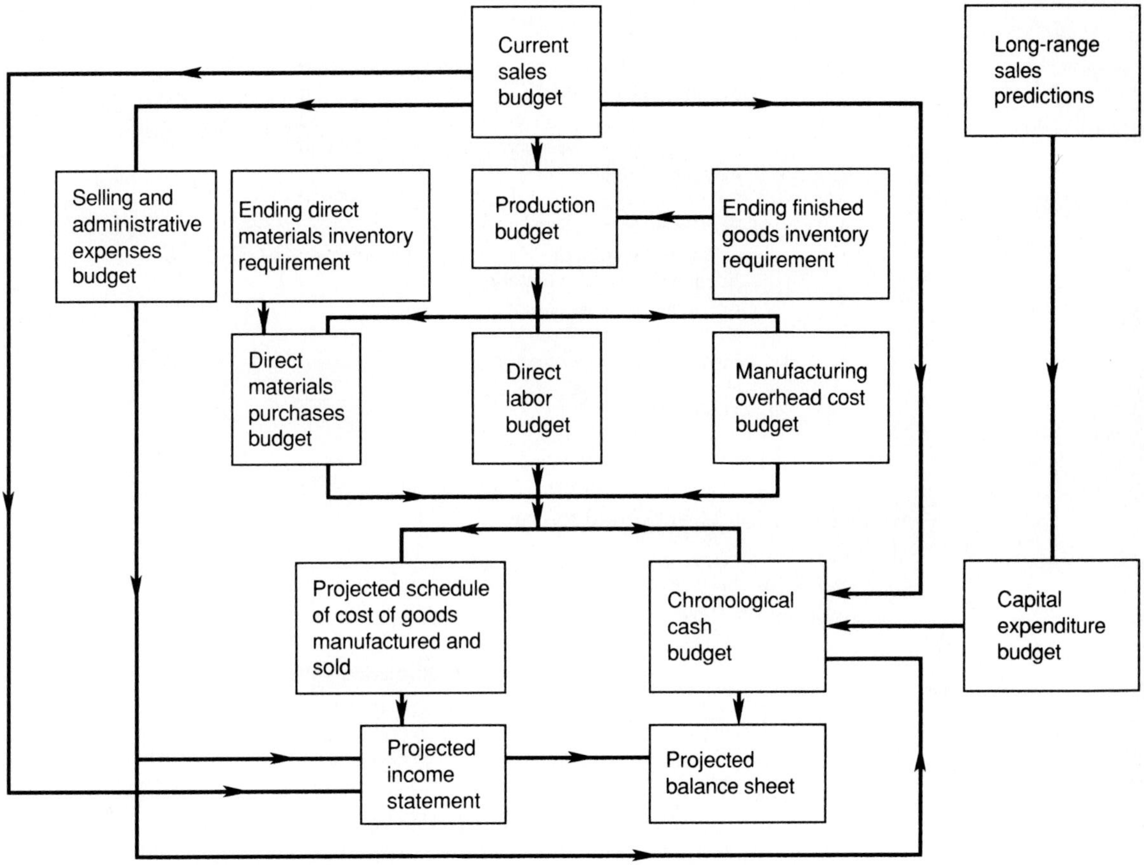

More Manufacturing Co.
Trial Balance
December 31, 1989

Cash	$ 7,200	
Accounts receivable	85,000	
Direct materials inventory	10,750	
Finished goods inventory	26,400	
Investment in land	24,000	
Factory equipment	85,250	
Accumulated depreciation—		
factory equipment		$ 11,080
Accounts payable—materials		33,650
Accounts payable—other		24,050
Common stock, $1 par		10,000
Paid-in capital in excess of par		45,000
Retained earnings		114,820
Totals	$238,600	$238,600

Other data for More Manufacturing:

1 Sales for the company's sole product are budgeted as follows for the first three months of 1990:

Month	Budgeted sales
January	40,000 units
February	50,000 units
March	30,000 units

2 The company plans to maintain its sales price at $4 per unit.

3 All sales are made on account and are evenly distributed throughout the month. Sales are billed to customers and recorded by the company on the fifteenth and on the last day of the month. No cash discounts are allowed.

4 Experience indicates:
   a 40 percent of customers pay their accounts ten days after being billed
   b The remaining 60 percent pay their accounts one month after being billed.

5 No allowance is made for doubtful accounts. In those rare instances when a customer's account is deemed uncollectible, the receivable is written off directly to expense. No customer accounts are expected to be written off during January or February.

6 During December, 1989, there were 26,500 units sold. Sales billed during December, 1989:

December 15	$ 53,000
December 31	53,000
	$106,000

7 The finished goods inventory on December 31 consists of 12,000 units at a cost of $2.20 each. The company maintains a month-end finished goods

inventory equal to 30 percent of forecasted unit sales for the next month. The FIFO method is used for finished goods inventory.

8 There is no work in process at the end of any month.

9 The direct materials inventory on December 31 consists of 21,500 pounds at a $.50 cost per pound. Two pounds of direct materials are required for each finished unit manufactured. The company maintains a month-end direct materials inventory equal to 25 percent of the budgeted production requirements for the next month. More Manufacturing does not use a standard costing system.

10 Direct materials are purchased on account (credited to Accounts Payable—Materials). The liability is paid, without cash discount, on the fifteenth of the month following purchase.

11 The purchase cost of direct materials is expected to remain at $.50 per pound during January and February.

12 Direct labor employees produce ten units per hour. The direct labor employees are paid on the last day of each month for hours worked during the month. The direct labor rate is expected to remain at $5 per hour in January and February.

13 Manufacturing overhead costs budgeted for January and February are $34,400 and $34,990 respectively. Each of these amounts includes $3,000 depreciation on factory equipment. Manufacturing overhead costs, other than depreciation, are credited when incurred to Accounts Payable—Other. They are paid on the twentieth day of the following month. No cash discounts are allowed.

14 Selling and administrative expenses each month are expected to average 15 percent of the monthly revenue. All selling and administrative expenses are paid on the last day of the month in which they are incurred. No cash discounts are allowed.

15 The company's long-range capital investment plans call for the purchase of an additional factory machine. The machine, which will cost $20,000, is scheduled for delivery on January 20, 1990. The seller demands cash on delivery.

16 Combined federal and state income taxes are accrued at a rate of 40 percent.

Preparation of the budgets comprising More Manufacturing's master budget for January, 1990 is straightforward. The difficult part of budgeting is the development of the sales estimates, pricing decisions, the establishment of desired inventory levels, and the formulation of other necessary assumptions. Often, the budget first formulated is revised many times before acceptance. For example, examine the chronological cash budget for More Manufacturing in Exhibit H. Can you identify a problem that may force More Manufacturing's management to revise their plans?

Sales Budget

Exhibit A presents the sales budget for January, 1990 for More Manufacturing. Because the company sells only one product at one price, the calculation of total

EXHIBIT A
More Manufacturing Co.
Sales Budget
For the Month Ending January 31, 1990

Forecasted sales in units	40,000
Forecasted selling price per unit	× $4
Budgeted sales revenue	$160,000

Billed $80,000 on January 15 and $80,000 on January 31.

sales revenue in Exhibit A is quite simple. However, the substantial effort often expended in developing the unit sales forecast and the importance of the sales forecast on virtually all other budgets should not be overshadowed by the apparent simplicity of the sales budget.

Companies employ a number of techniques in forecasting sales. Forecasted sales quantities can be estimated based on market surveys, current backlog of orders, predictions made by sales agents and/or sales department managers, extension of historic sales trends into the future, and results of econometric forecasting models. These models forecast sales based on economic factors such as the level of inflation, the condition of the economy, competition in the industry, and so forth. In forecasting sales, the projected economic conditions for the general economy and the particular industry in which the firm operates must be considered. Planned pricing and promotional policies, operating capacity, and expected actions of customers and competitors are other important factors. For large conglomerates involved in a number of different industries, sales forecasting can be a complex task.

A close examination of the master budget interrelationships in Exhibit 17-1 clearly reveals the sales budget as the first budget to prepare. All other budgets for More Manufacturing are affected by the sales budget. Production activity (including direct materials, direct labor, manufacturing overhead, and required inventory levels) is determined from projected unit sales. The required production activity, in turn, will significantly influence the cash budget and the projected financial statements. Budgeted sales also directly affect revenues on the projected income statement and accounts receivable and cash shown on the projected balance sheet. In addition, the budget for selling and administrative expenses fluctuates with budgeted sales. Even the capital expenditure budget is formulated based on long-range forecasted sales. If sales are incorrectly forecast, errors automatically will be incorporated into all other parts of the master budget.

Production Budget—Units

The production budget for More Manufacturing is presented in Exhibit B. A close examination of the production budget reveals it to be a rearrangement (using units instead of dollars) of the familiar calculation for cost of goods sold:

EXHIBIT B
More Manufacturing Co.
Production Budget—Units
For the Month Ending January 31, 1990

Budgeted sales in units for January (per Exh. A)	40,000
Plus: Finished goods inventory in units required at end of January (30% × 50,000 units forecasted February sales)	15,000
Total finished goods units needed	55,000
Less: Finished goods inventory in units available at the beginning of January	12,000
Budgeted production in units	43,000

$$\text{Units Sold} = \text{Beginning Finished Goods Inventory}$$
$$+ \text{Units Produced During Period}$$
$$- \text{Ending Finished Goods Inventory}$$

Substituting budgeted for actual figures and rearranging terms yields:

$$\begin{aligned} \text{Budgeted Production} & = \text{Units to be Sold} \\ \text{in Units} \quad & \quad + \text{Desired Ending Finished Goods Inventory} \\ & \quad - \text{Available Beginning Finished Goods Inventory} \end{aligned}$$

The sales forecast specified the units to be sold. The desired ending inventory of 30 percent of next month's forecasted sales is based on a cost-minimization policy established by management. By carrying excessive inventory, a firm incurs unnecessary costs. Not carrying sufficient inventory can be costly in terms of stockouts.

Direct Materials Purchases Budget

The direct materials purchases budget is a rearrangement of the calculation for the cost of direct materials used:

$$\text{Direct Materials Used} = \text{Beginning Direct Materials Inventory}$$
$$+ \text{Direct Materials Purchased}$$
$$- \text{Ending Direct Materials Inventory}$$

Substituting budgeted for actual figures and rearranging terms yields:

$$\begin{aligned} \text{Budgeted Direct} & = \text{Direct Materials to be Used} \\ \text{Materials Purchases} & \quad + \text{Desired Ending Direct Materials Inventory} \\ & \quad - \text{Available Beginning Direct Materials Inventory} \end{aligned}$$

EXHIBIT C
More Manufacturing Co.
Direct Materials Purchases Budget
For the Month Ending January 31, 1990

	Pounds	Cost at $.50 per lb.
Budgeted production in units for January (per Exh. B)	43,000	
Number of pounds required per unit	× 2	
Needed for January production	86,000 lb.	$43,000
Plus: Direct materials inventory required at end of January (see calculation below)	22,000	11,000
Total direct materials needs	108,000 lb.	$54,000
Less: Direct materials inventory available at beginning of January	21,500	10,750
Budgeted direct materials to be purchased	86,500 lb.	$43,250

Determination of Required Direct
Materials Inventory at End of January

Forecasted sales in units for February	50,000	units
Plus: Required ending February finished goods inventory in units (30% × 30,000 March sales)	9,000	
Total finished goods inventory needs during February	59,000	units
Less: Finished goods inventory in units available beginning of February (per Exh. B)	15,000	
Budgeted February production in units	44,000	units
Pounds required per unit	× 2	
Budgeted February production needs in pounds	88,000	lb.
Ending materials inventory requirement	× 25	%
Direct materials inventory required at end of January	22,000	lb.

The direct materials purchases budget for More Manufacturing is presented in Exhibit C. Note the dual-column format that expresses the budget in both pounds and dollars. Desired beginning and ending direct materials inventory levels have been set by management at 25 percent of materials production requirements for the upcoming month. As illustrated at the bottom of Exhibit C, the calculation of ending direct materials inventory for January necessitates the prior determination of February's production needs for materials.

Direct Labor Budget

The direct labor budget for More Manufacturing in both hours and dollars is presented in Exhibit D.

The important factors affecting the direct labor budget are budgeted production

EXHIBIT D
More Manufacturing Co.
Direct Labor Budget—Hours and Dollars
For the Month Ending January 31, 1990

Budgeted production in units for January (per Exh. B.)	43,000 units
Units produced per direct labor hour	÷ 10
Budgeted direct labor hours for January production	4,300 hours
Forecasted cost per direct labor hour	× $5
Budgeted cost of direct labor	$21,500

in units, units expected to be completed per hour, and cost of direct labor per hour. If direct labor employees are salaried, productive activity should ideally be scheduled in a manner that will minimize both overtime and idle time. In addition, the direct labor budget may aid in forecasting the need to hire, lay off, or reassign employees.

Manufacturing Overhead Budget

In preparing a manufacturing overhead budget, cost behavior patterns should be considered. Many manufacturing overhead items are variable costs whose total amount will change as production varies. Other manufacturing overhead costs remain unchanged in total regardless of changes in predicted production (these are fixed costs).

The manufacturing overhead cost budget for More Manufacturing is presented in Exhibit E. Factory rent and depreciation on factory equipment are fixed costs. The remaining manufacturing overhead costs of More Manufacturing are classified as variable.

After the production budget (Exhibit B), the direct materials purchases budget (Exhibit C), the direct labor budget (Exhibit D), and the manufacturing overhead cost budget (Exhibit E) have been completed, it is possible to prepare a projected

EXHIBIT E
More Manufacturing Co.
Manufacturing Overhead Cost Budget
For the Month Ending January 31, 1990

Factory rent—fixed	$ 6,000
Factory supplies—variable	5,000
Indirect labor—variable	4,000
Factory maintenance and repairs—variable	10,400
Factory heat, light, and power—variable	6,000
Depreciation on factory equipment—fixed	3,000
Budgeted manufacturing overhead cost	$34,400

EXHIBIT F
More Manufacturing Co.
Projected Schedule of Cost of Goods Manufactured and Sold
For the Month Ending January 31, 1990

Beginning inventory, work in process			$ -0-
Current manufacturing costs:			
Direct materials used (Exh. C):			
Beginning inventory	$10,750		
Purchases	43,250		
Available for use	$54,000		
Less: Ending inventory	11,000	$43,000	
Direct labor (Exh. D)		21,500	
Manufacturing overhead (Exh. E)		34,400	98,900
Total manufacturing costs in process			$ 98,900
Less: Ending inventory, work in process			-0-
Cost of goods manufactured			$ 98,900
Beginning inventory, finished goods			26,400
Total cost of goods available for sale			$125,300
Less: Ending inventory, finished goods			34,500*
Cost of goods sold			$ 90,800

*Calculation of ending inventory—finished goods:

Beginning inventory   12,000 units at $2.20
Goods manufactured during January 43,000 units at $2.30 ($98,900 ÷ 43,000)
Under FIFO, ending inventory of finished goods (15,000 units) is valued at $2.30 per unit, for a total of $34,500.

schedule of cost of goods manufactured and sold. This schedule is presented in Exhibit F.

All amounts appearing on More Manufacturing's projected schedule of cost of goods manufactured and sold, except ending finished goods inventory, were either (1) stated in the information provided at the beginning of the problem or (2) carried forward from other budgets already discussed. The calculation of the ending finished goods inventory under the FIFO cost assumption is shown at the bottom of Exhibit F.

Selling and Administrative Expenses Budget

More Manufacturing's selling and administrative expenses budget is presented in Exhibit G. For simplicity, it has been assumed that selling and administrative expenses are expected to be 15 percent of sales revenue. In reality, a number of selling and administrative expenses are fixed, while others may vary proportionally with a base other than sales revenue.

Chronological Cash Budget

A chronological cash budget can now be prepared. This budget is based on the budgets previously discussed and on information regarding the timing of cash

EXHIBIT G
More Manufacturing Co.
Selling and Administrative Expenses Budget
For the Month Ending January 31, 1990

Forecasted sales revenue for January (per Exh. A)	$160,000
Forecasted selling and administrative expenses as a percent of sales revenue	× 15%
Budgeted selling and administrative expenses	$ 24,000

receipts and disbursements (given early in the example). Exhibit H presents More Manufacturing's chronological cash budget for January, 1990. The cash budget indicates projected cash inflows, cash outflows, and the balance after each transaction during the period.

Note the advantages of detailing cash receipts and disbursements chronologically. A temporary cash shortage of $17,500 is projected on January 20

EXHIBIT H
More Manufacturing Co.
Chronological Cash Budget
For the Month Ending January 31, 1990

	Receipts	Disbursements	Balance
Cash balance, December 31, 1989			$ 7,200
January 10:			
Collect 40% of $53,000 sales from 12/31/89	$ 21,200		28,400
January 15:			
Collect 60% of $53,000 sales from 12/15/89	31,800		60,200
Pay for December direct materials purchases (Accounts payable—materials)		$ 33,650	26,550
January 20:			
Pay for December manufacturing overhead (accounts payable—other)		24,050	2,500
Pay for additional factory machine		20,000	(17,500)
January 25:			
Collect 40% of $80,000 sales from 1/15/90	32,000		14,500
January 31:			
Collect 60% of $53,000 sales from 12/31/89	31,800		46,300
Pay for January direct labor (per Exh. D)		21,500	24,800
Pay for January selling and administrative expenses (per Exh. G)		24,000	800
Total cash receipts and disbursements	$116,800	$123,200	

EXHIBIT I
More Manufacturing Co.
Projected Income Statement
For the Month Ending January 31, 1990

Sales	$160,000	(per Exh. A)
Cost of goods sold	90,800	(per Exh. F)
Gross profit	$ 69,200	
Selling and administrative expenses	24,000	(per Exh. G)
Income before taxes	$ 45,200	
Income tax expense	18,080	(at 40%)
Projected net income	$ 27,120	
Earnings per share	$2.71*	

*Assuming 10,000 shares of common stock outstanding throughout the month.

because of the required payment for the new machine. With a detailed chronological cash budget, management is aware in advance of the forthcoming problem. Sufficient warning allows management time to plan and implement appropriate action to remedy the situation. A short-term loan can be arranged, or perhaps delivery of the machine can be rescheduled. If cash receipts and disbursements had simply been presented as monthly totals, without chronological details, the projected cash shortage would not have been revealed.

Projected Income Statement

The format of a projected income statement is identical to that of one based on actual, historical data. The projected income statement for More Manufacturing is presented in Exhibit I. Amounts, other than the income tax expense and earnings per share, are taken from other budgets. If the projected income statement indicates results unacceptable to management, strategies must be reexamined and revised in an attempt to produce satisfactory results.

Projected Balance Sheet

The format of a projected balance sheet parallels that of an actual statement based on historical data. As was the case with the projected income statement, if the projected balance sheet indicates an unsatisfactory financial position, management may consider adjusting its plans in an attempt to alleviate the situation.

The projected balance sheet for More Manufacturing as of January 31, 1990 is presented in Exhibit J. Several account balances are unchanged from the December, 1989 trial balance given at the start of the example. Other amounts appearing on the projected balance sheet are carried forward from other budgets.

Using Budgets for Performance Evaluation and Control

The formulation of plans does not automatically assure that actual results will coincide with predicted results. Plans must be implemented, the actual results measured, and these results analyzed for performance evaluation and control.

EXHIBIT J
More Manufacturing Co.
Projected Balance Sheet
January 31, 1990

Assets

Current assets:

Cash (per Exh. H)		$ 800
Accounts receivable (see calculation below)		128,200
Direct materials inventory (per Exh. F)		11,000
Finished goods inventory (per Exh. F)		34,500
Total current assets		$174,500
Investment in land		24,000*
Factory equipment ($85,250* + $20,000 new machine)	$105,250	
Less accumulated depreciation ($11,080* + $3,000)	14,080	91,170
Total assets		$289,670

Liabilities and Stockholders' Equity

Current liabilities:

Accounts payable—materials (per Exh. C)		$ 43,250
Accounts payable—other (see calculation below)		31,400
Income taxes payable (per Exh. I)		18,080
Total current liabilities		$ 92,730
Stockholders' equity:		
Common stock, $1 par	$ 10,000*	
Paid-in capital in excess of par	45,000*	
Retained earnings ($114,820* + $27,120 net income, per Exh. I)	141,940	196,940
Total liabilities and stockholders' equity		$289,670

* From 12/31/89 trial balance

Calculation of accounts receivable balance
Accounts receivable: $85,000 beginning balance plus $160,000 January sales (per Exh. A) minus $116,800 January cash receipts (per Exh. H).

Calculation of accounts payable—other
Beginning balance $24,050 minus payment of $24,050 on January 20 (per Exh. H) plus $31,400 January manufacturing costs, other than depreciation (per Exh. E).

Control and performance evaluation procedures are necessary to detect and rectify situations where actual performance that deviates from planned results is hindering an organization's attempt to reach its goals and objectives. Positively stated, control and performance evaluation is a means to assure goal-directed performance. The control and performance evaluation aspects of budgeting are discussed in the first several sections of the next chapter.

SUMMARY

Learning Objective 1: Discuss the various managerial uses of budgeting.

A crucial component of an organization's success is proper planning. A key to effective planning is effective use of the budget. Budgeting allows management to better understand the structure of the organization; to identify problem areas in advance; to coordinate, communicate, and authorize action; and to aid the control and evaluation of performance.

Learning Objective 2: Prepare a comprehensive budget for planning future operations.

A comprehensive budget is an integrated plan of activity for an organization that includes separate budgets for sales, production, manufacturing costs, general and administrative expenses, cash flows, and projected financial statements. The key to the master budget is the sales forecast. All other budgets are affected by the sales budget. To the extent sales are incorrectly forecast, errors automatically will be incorporated into all other parts of the master budget. The actual preparation of the comprehensive budget is a highly mechanical process that can present a false sense of accuracy. Budgets are only as good as the estimates and assumptions on which they are based.

KEY TERMS

Budget
Budgeting
Cash budget
Comprehensive budget
Continuous budgeting

Participative budgeting
Production budget
Projected financial statements
Sales budget

REVIEW QUESTIONS

1 A budget is an important tool used by management in planning for the future. What is a budget; what questions does a budget help answer?

2 George Trofa, secretary-treasurer of Hartsville's Chamber of Commerce states: "We are not a profit-making organization; therefore, we do not need to develop a budget for the coming year." Evaluate Mr. Trofa's statement.

3 Mr. Emerson, head of the Hardware Division of Rariton Co., appreciates budgeting since it provides him as a manager with a base with which to compare the actual performance of his departmental managers. What other advantages should Mr. Emerson be realizing from the budgeting process?

4 What are computer simulation models? How can these models aid companies in planning future operations?

5 Brockton Manufacturing Co.'s operating budget is determined solely by the company's top management (i.e., president; vice-presidents of sales, manufacturing, and finance; and controller). Individual department managers are not consulted. What advantages might be gained by involving the department managers in the budget formulation process?

6 What is continuous budgeting?

7 How can the familiar cost of goods sold calculation for a manufacturing company (i.e., Beginning Finished Goods Inventory + Cost of Goods Manufactured − Ending Finished Goods Inventory = Cost of Goods Sold) be rearranged to yield a method of determining the budgeted production in units?

8 What is a comprehensive (master) budget?

 9 How can the familiar cost of direct materials used calculation for a manufacturing company (i.e., Beginning Direct Materials Inventory + Direct Materials Purchased − Ending Direct Materials Inventory = Cost of Direct Materials Used) be rearranged to produce a means of calculating budgeted direct materials purchases?

10 "All budgeted manufacturing overhead costs (as well as budgeted selling, general, and administrative expenses) will require cash expenditures during the current budget period." Evaluate the preceding statement.

11 Ralph Cramden, president of Choman, Inc., is interested in forecasted total cash receipts and total cash disbursements. Why might a detailed chronological list of projected cash receipts and disbursements be more informative than merely a list of total forecasted receipts and disbursements?

12 "The hardest part of comprehensive budgeting is the mechanical preparation of the various individual budgets that comprise the master budget." Evaluate the preceding statement.

EXERCISES

E17-1 Fish Bait, Inc. forecasts sales of 90,000 worms in each of February and March. The forecasted selling price is $.12 per worm. Management's policy is to maintain inventories at the end of each month equal to 40 percent of the following month's forecasted sales. On December 31, the desired inventory of 32,000 worms was on hand. Calculate:
1 Forecasted sales for January, in units
2 Purchases budgeted for January

E17-2 Using the following information, calculate how many gallons of direct materials should be budgeted for purchase during January.

> Budgeted January production = 15,000 barrels
> Budgeted February production = 12,000 barrels
> Six gallons of direct materials are needed to produce one barrel of finished goods
> Desired ending direct materials inventory is 20 percent of the following month's budgeted production needs
> 18,000 gallons of direct materials are in inventory on January 1

E17-3 Given below is selected information for Speider Manufacturing Co.:

Forecasted sales for May, 1988	30,000 barrels
May 1, 1988 finished goods inventory	9,000 barrels
Desired May 31, 1988 finished goods inventory	8,000 barrels
Gallons of raw materials needed to produce one barrel of finished goods	5 gallons
May 1, 1988 raw materials inventory	40,000 gallons
Desired May 31, 1988 raw materials inventory	50,000 gallons

Calculate:
1 Barrels of finished goods to be produced in May
2 Gallons of raw materials to be purchased in May

E17-4 Tomlinson Drug Stores, Inc. seeks your assistance in determining the number of bottles of aspirin to purchase during July for its chain of 108 drug stores. Projected sales are 12,000 bottles in July and 12,200 bottles in August. Each month's ending inventory is to be 130 percent of the next month's units of sales. Calculate July's budgeted purchases of aspirin bottles.

(AICPA Adapted)

E17-5 Kugler, Inc. operates a chain of stores in area shopping centers that specialize in selling deluxe transistor radios at discount. The company is trying to determine budgeted cash disbursements for June, 1989. The following forecasted information is available:

Month	Sales revenue	Inventory purchases
May 1989	$357,000	11,250 units
June 1989	342,000	12,180 units

Each radio is expected to cost $20. Selling, general, and administrative expenses (including $2,000 depreciation) are projected to total 15 percent of current month's sales revenue. Fifty-four percent of all purchases of inventory and selling, general, and administrative expenses are paid in the month incurred. The remaining 46 percent are paid in the following month. Calculate forecasted cash disbursements for June 1989.

(AICPA Adapted)

E17-6 Prepare a cash budget for August, 1988 for Certoon Co. based on the following data:
1 Cash balance August 1, 1988, $187,000.
2 Sales forecast for August is $800,000. All sales are on account. Sixty percent of sales are collected in month of sale, 30 percent in next month, and 10 percent in third month. June sales totaled $580,000, and July sales were $600,000. No cash discounts are allowed.
3 Inventory purchases for August are forecasted at $484,000. Purchases of inventory are paid for in full in the month following purchase.
4 Depreciation expense is forecasted at $10,000 for August.
5 A two-year insurance policy for $12,000 is scheduled for payment in August.
6 August 1, 1988 balances:

Accounts payable (July inventory purchases)	$ 390,000
Accounts receivable	298,000
Machinery	2,140,000

E17-7 The Bardot Manufacturing Co. is the world's largest producer of mannequins. The company has forecasted sales for 1988 of 300,000 mannequins. Projected manufacturing costs per mannequin are: $180 for direct materials, $85 for direct labor, $120 for manufacturing overhead (including $40 per mannequin for depreciation). Selling, general, and administrative expenses are forecasted to be $100 per mannequin sold (including $16 per mannequin for depreciation). The finished goods inventory on January 1, 1988 totals $28,800,000 (80,000 mannequins at $360). Ending finished goods inventory is budgeted for 100,000 mannequins on December 31, 1988. Bardot uses the FIFO cost method. Direct materials and work in process inventories are immaterial at the beginning and end of the year. Prepare projected schedule of cost of goods manufactured and sold for Bardot for 1988.

E17-8 Dilly Co. sells all of its harmonicas to wholesalers on account. Terms for sales on account are 2/10; net 30. Fifty percent of each month's sales are collected during the month of sale, 45 percent are collected in the succeeding month, and the remainder are usually uncollectible. Seventy percent of the collections in the month of sale qualify for the cash discount while 10 percent of the collections in the succeeding month are subject to discount.

Projected sales data indicate:

Month	Projected gross sales on account
January	$1,500,000
February	1,700,000

Calculate budgeted cash collections for February.

(AICPA Adapted)

PROBLEMS

P17-1 *Production and Cost of Goods Sold Budgets*

The Krist Manufacturing Company manufactures and sells flashlights. The company prepares monthly operating and financial budgets. Estimates of sales (in units—a unit equals one flashlight) are made for each month. Production is scheduled at a level high enough to meet current needs and to carry into each month a finished goods inventory equal to one-half of that month's unit sales. Direct materials, direct labor, and variable manufacturing overhead are estimated at $1, $2, and $.50 per flashlight respectively. Fixed manufacturing overhead is budgeted at $77,000 per month. Sales for April, May, and June are estimated at 50,000, 60,000, and 80,000 flashlights. Inventory at April 1 consists of 25,000 units with a cost of $4.10 per flashlight. Raw materials and work in process inventories are immaterial.

Required:

1 Prepare a schedule showing budgeted production in units for April and May.
2 Prepare a schedule showing budgeted cost of goods sold for April. Assume the FIFO method is used for inventories.

P17-2 *Cash Receipts Budget*

Garrison Corp. sells ball-point pens on account at a sales price of $2 per pen. Sales are billed and recorded by the company on the fifteenth and last day of each month. The terms of sale are 2/10; net 30. Experience indicates sales are even throughout the month and 50 percent of the customers pay the billed amount within the discount period. The remainder pay at the end of 30 days, except for uncollectible accounts, which average 1/2 percent of gross sales.

Sales are budgeted at 120,000 pens for October, 1988 and 90,000 pens for November, 1988.

Required:

Prepare a chronological schedule of projected cash receipts for November, 1988. Use the following headings in your solution.

November collection dates	Collection from sales billed on	Gross amount of original sales billed	Amount collected on indicated November collection date

(AICPA Adapted)

P17-3 *Cash Disbursements Budget*

Barney's Bagels, Inc. bakes bagels. Production involves six direct materials. The following data are available for April, 1988.

1 Direct materials are purchased on account (credited to Accounts Payable—Materials). Direct materials are delivered on the first day of each month and the liability is paid on the ninth day of each month. Budgeted direct materials purchases for April are as follows:

	Amount	Terms
Direct material #1	$ 2,389	2/10; net/30
Direct material #2	3,075	net/30
Direct material #3	2,990	2/10; net/30
Direct material #4	500	2/15; net/30
Direct material #5	205	net/30
Direct material #6	1,079	net/30
	$10,238	

2 Direct labor employees are paid $5.75 per hour. Payment is made to employees on the fifteenth and the last day of each month. Each employee can produce 4,000 bagels in 40 hours. Direct labor is incurred evenly throughout the month. Budgeted production is 84,000 bagels.

3 Other expenses budgeted for April are:

	Amount	Payment date
Selling and administrative	$9,200	4/20
Manufacturing overhead	3,000	4/30
Insurance	500	4/15
Delivery—incurred evenly	200	4/15, 4/30

Required:

Prepare a chronological schedule of projected cash payments for April, 1988. Use the following headings in your solution.

April payment dates	Description of payment	Gross amount of original bill	Amount paid on April payment date

P17-4 *Production and Materials Budgets*

Dougherty Manufacturing Co.'s inventory of finished goods on October 1, 1988 is 24,000 units. Sales are forecasted as follows:

October 1988	120,000 units
November 1988	90,000 units
December 1988	120,000 units
January 1989	120,000 units

The finished goods inventory is to be maintained at 20 percent of sales anticipated in the following month. There is no work in process inventory at the end of a month.

Each finished unit produced requires 1/2 pound of direct materials. The inventory of direct materials on October 1, 1988 was 22,800 pounds. At the end of each month, the direct materials inventory is to be maintained at 40 percent of anticipated production requirements for the following month.

Required:
1 Prepare a production budget in units for October, November, and December. (Follow the format of Exhibit B in the chapter.)
2 Prepare a direct materials purchases budget in pounds for October and November. (Follow the format of Exhibit C in the chapter.)

(AICPA Adapted)

P17-5   *Budgeted Revenues and Expenses: Comparison of Alternatives*
Thorne Transit, Inc. has decided to inaugurate express bus service between its headquarters city and a nearby suburb (one-way fare $.50) and is considering the purchase of either 32- or 52-passenger buses, on which pertinent estimates are as follows:

	32 passenger bus	52 passenger bus
Number of each to be purchased	6	4
Useful life	8 years	8 years
Purchase price of each bus (paid on delivery)	$80,000	$110,000
Mileage per gallon	10	7.5
Salvage value per bus	$ 6,000	$ 7,000
Drivers' hourly wage	6.50	7.20
Price per gallon of gasoline	1.50	1.50
Other annual cash expenses	90,000	100,000

During the four daily rush hours, all buses would be in service and are expected to operate at full capacity (state law prohibits standees) in both directions of the route, each bus covering the route twelve times (six round trips) during that period. During the remainder of the 16-hour day, 500 passengers would be carried and Thorne would operate only four buses on the route. Part-time drivers would be employed to drive the extra hours during the rush hours. A bus traveling the route all day would go 480 miles, and one traveling only during rush hours would go 120 miles a day during the 260-day year.

Required:
1 Prepare a schedule showing the computation of estimated annual revenue of the new route for both alternatives.
2 Prepare a schedule showing the computation of estimated annual drivers' wages for both alternatives.
3 Prepare a schedule showing the computation of estimated annual cost of gasoline for both alternatives.

(AICPA Adapted)

P17-6   *Comprehensive Budget*
DeMars College has asked your assistance in developing its budget for the 1988-89 academic year. You are supplied with the following data for the 1987–88 year:

	Lower division (freshman–sophomore)	Upper division (junior–senior)
Average number of students per class	25	20
Average salary of faculty member	$24,000	$24,000
Average number of credit hours carried each year per student	33	30
Enrollment including scholarship students	2,000	1,360
Average faculty teaching load in credit hours per year (8 classes of 3 credit hours)	24	24

1 For 1988-89, lower division enrollment is expected to increase by 10 percent, while the upper division's enrollment is expected to remain stable. Faculty salaries will be increased by a standard 8 percent, and additional merit increases to be awarded to individual faculty members will be $150,000 for the lower division and $135,000 for the upper division.

2 The current budget is $384,000 for operation and maintenance of plant and equipment; this includes $180,000 for salaries and wages. Experience of the past three months suggests that the current budget is realistic, but that expected increases for 1988-89 are 8 percent in salaries and wages and $18,000 in other expenditures for operation and maintenance of plant and equipment.

3 The budget for the remaining expenditures for 1988-89 is as follows:

Administrative and general	$280,000
Library	220,000
Health and recreation	150,000
Athletics	240,000
Insurance and retirement	330,000
Interest	96,000

4 The college expects to award 15 tuition-free scholarships to lower division students and 10 to upper division students. Tuition is $44 per credit hour and no other fees are charged.

5 Budgeted revenues for 1988-89 are as follows:

Endowments	$340,000
Net income from auxiliary services	500,000
Athletics	460,000

The college's remaining source of revenue is an annual support campaign held during the spring.

Required:
1 Prepare a schedule for 1988–89 computing by division (a) the expected enrollment, (b) the total credit hours to be carried, and (c) the number of faculty members needed.
2 Prepare the budget for faculty salaries by division for 1988-89.
3 Prepare the tuition revenue budget by division for 1988-89.
4 Prepare a schedule that determines the amount that must be raised during the annual support campaign in order to cover the 1988-89 expenditures budget.

(AICPA Adapted)

P17-7 *Comprehensive Budget and Projected Financial Statements*

In the chapter, ten individual budgets comprising More Manufacturing Co.'s master budget for January, 1990 were illustrated based on the company's December 31, 1989 trial balance and other data given. Budgeted sales for April, 1990 are 40,000 units. The other data given in the chapter can be used to prepare budgets for February, 1990, as well as the January, 1990 budgets shown in the chapter.

Required:

For More Manufacturing Co. prepare the February, 1990 budgets listed below. For each budget follow the format of the appropriate exhibit in the chapter.

1 Sales budget
2 Production budget—units
3 Direct materials purchases budget—pounds and dollars
4 Direct labor budget—hours and dollars
5 Manufacturing overhead cost budget (Include the following variable costs: $5,116, factory supplies; $4,093, indirect labor; $10,642, maintenance and repairs; and $6,139, heat, light, and power. February's fixed cost of factory rent and factory equipment depreciation are unchanged from their January amounts.)
6 Projected schedule of cost of goods manufactured and sold
7 Selling and administrative expenses budget
8 Chronological cash budget
9 Projected income statement
10 Projected balance sheet

Business Decision Problem

Kristen Barnes is planning to open a retail office supplies store in a local shopping mall. She has developed the following estimates of activity for the first two years, and she asks your help in preparing a cash budget for each year and in identifying any potential cash problems.

1 Store rent, including all maintenance and utilities, will be $1,500 per month over a two-year lease, plus 3 percent of annual sales in excess of $100,000. The base rent is payable monthly, and the override is payable at year end.
2 An initial inventory costing $35,000 will be needed, and it is expected that the inventory will be maintained at a constant level throughout the first two years.
3 Merchandise will be sold at a markup of 50 percent over cost (that is, an item costing $10 to purchases will be sold for $15). On average, one month's purchases will be unpaid as of year end.
4 Barnes projects sales of $180,000 the first year and $360,000 the second year. All sales will be for cash.
5 Projected annual expenses for the first year are $27,000 for clerks, $10,000 for advertising, and $8,000 for other operating expenses. These are expected to increase by 10 percent in the second year. These expenses will be paid as incurred.
6 Barnes hopes to draw an annual salary of $30,000, although she is willing to receive only half that amount the first year so that the early cash demands on the business will be lessened.
7 Barnes plans to invest $40,000 to start the business.

18

RESPONSIBILITY ACCOUNTING, PERFORMANCE EVALUATION, AND CONTROL

LEARNING OBJECTIVES

When you complete this chapter, you should be able to:

1 Discuss the basic concepts of control.
2 Prepare performance reports for cost centers using flexible budgeting.
3 Calculate income under both direct costing and absorption costing.
4 Discuss the arguments for and against direct costing.
5 Analyze departmental performance in terms of contribution toward indirect expenses and profit.
6 Calculate and analyze rate of return.
7 Discuss the problems inherent in measuring and using rate of return for performance evaluation.

In addition to planning for the future, management must evaluate and control actual performance, that is, analyze how well the plans are being implemented. The question to answer is: Are people doing the job expected of them? In the standard costing chapter, this question was addressed via variance analysis. In this chapter, additional accounting procedures and managerial accounting reports for performance evaluation and control are illustrated. Discussions are not limited to a narrow use of the word control, such as merely identifying areas in need of corrective action. Measuring the performance of persons assigned the authority and the responsibility for meeting standards and achieving planned results is examined. Topics covered include the information feedback system, responsibility accounting, flexible budgeting, direct costing, contribution toward indirect expenses, and rate of return analysis.

BASIC CONCEPTS OF CONTROL

Through the accounting and reporting system, top management exercises control over the firm's operations. Because top-level management cannot practically make every decision regarding the firm, decision making is delegated to various levels throughout the organization. Top-level managers maintain overall control, monitoring whether the decisions made follow the goals, objectives, policies, and plans for the firm.

Two concepts are central to retaining this control. First, there must be a feedback system that provides management with the proper information about decisions made and the results of those decisions. Next, the information must be presented in terms of the organizational component responsible for making the decisions.

Information Feedback System

To effectively control and evaluate performance, it is necessary to know what the actual performance was. Actual results can then be compared to projected (budgeted) results to determine if the company's plans are being met. The process of providing management with reports comparing actual performance to planned results often is referred to as *feedback*. Feedback allows management to determine if plans are being executed as formulated. If not, action may be required to improve actual performance or to revise the plans.

The circular nature of the planning, control, and evaluation process is shown in the diagram in Exhibit 18-1. Note the crucial role played by feedback in controlling and evaluating performance.

Reports detailing variances under a standard cost system are a type of feedback. The report of an unfavorable materials price variance, for example, would be investigated to determine the cause of the excess amount paid for materials over the projected price. One possible finding is that the purchasing agent is not adhering to company policies requiring price comparisons among suppliers. Steps could then be taken to ensure that such policies are followed in the future. In the scheme of Exhibit 18-1, the feedback information would lead to modifying the methods of implementing the plan.

Responsibility Accounting

Responsibility accounting is a management accounting system specifically designed to accumulate and report accounting information for various segments of the organization. Under this system, top management can evaluate the performance of each organizational segment as distinct from that of other segments. The manager in charge of each organizational segment can be held responsible for the performance of that segment. Responsibility accounting thus serves to personalize performance of an organization's various subdivisions.

The key to an effective responsibility accounting system is to hold a manager responsible only for those items that the manager was authorized to control.

EXHIBIT 18-1   Planning, Control, and Evaluation Process

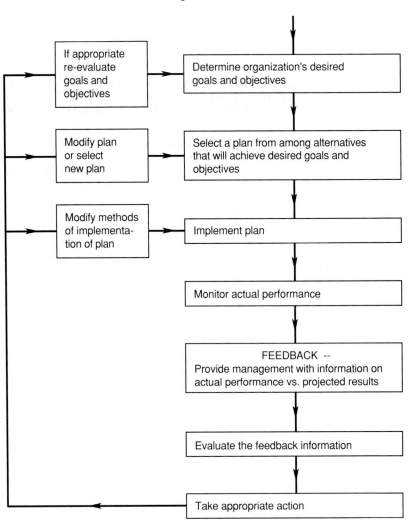

Allocation of noncontrollable items leads to inappropriate, unfair evaluation of performance. A person should not be held responsible for something beyond the individual's control. Responsibility should parallel authority.

For example, consider the manager of the men's clothing department at the local department store. Assume the profit generated by the department for the current year is substantially less than that of previous years and less than the budgeted profit for the current year. Is the department manager to be held responsible? The answer depends upon whether the substantial profit decrease for the current year is attributable to factors under the manager's control. What if the profit decrease is due to a large inventory loss caused by a write-down for obsolete items? The authority for selecting clothing styles rests with the purchasing agent, not the manager of the men's clothing department. If the department manager made a reasonable attempt to sell the obsolete styles, the obsolescence loss appears to be entirely noncontrollable from this manager's perspective. Under an effective responsibility accounting system, the obsolescence loss should not influence evaluation of the performance of the men's clothing department manager.

The higher the level of the segment within the organization, the wider the degree of authority and responsibility, and hence the greater the range of control. Exhibit 18-2 presents an organizational structure with four responsibility accounting levels. The manager at each level should be provided with performance reports for all levels of the organization over which that manager has control. Note that the degree of control broadens in the upper levels of the organizational structure.

The type of segment for which responsibility accounting information is accumulated and reported varies widely. In some cases, the segments will be *cost centers,* which incur costs but do not directly generate revenues. Many examples exist, such as a maintenance department, a payroll department, or a power department. For these segments, performance can be assessed by comparing actual costs with planned costs, using either flexible budget analysis or standard costs and variance analysis.

In addition to cost centers, responsibility accounting segments may be categorized as profit centers and investment centers. *Profit centers* are segments that

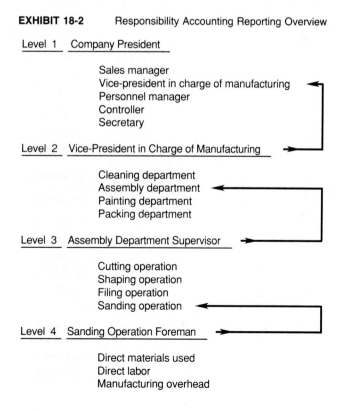

EXHIBIT 18-2   Responsibility Accounting Reporting Overview

Level 1   Company President

                   Sales manager
                   Vice-president in charge of manufacturing
                   Personnel manager
                   Controller
                   Secretary

Level 2   Vice-President in Charge of Manufacturing

                   Cleaning department
                   Assembly department
                   Painting department
                   Packing department

Level 3   Assembly Department Supervisor

                   Cutting operation
                   Shaping operation
                   Filing operation
                   Sanding operation

Level 4   Sanding Operation Foreman

                   Direct materials used
                   Direct labor
                   Manufacturing overhead

not only incur costs but also directly generate revenues. Examples include the prescriptions department of a drug store, the meat department of a supermarket, and the Ohio sales territory of an auto parts firm. Since profit centers incur costs, the methods for evaluating cost center performance are applicable. In addition, since profit centers generate revenues, income measures serve as a further device for the evaluation and control of performance. This chapter considers two additional procedures for evaluation and control—direct costing and the contribution towards indirect expenses.

Investment centers have the same characteristics as profit centers (that is, they incur costs and generate revenues), and in addition they are charged with a substantial asset investment. By this means, the responsibility of the manager is broadened. The manager is evaluated on the segment's ability to generate profits *and* on the efficiency of utilization of the segment's assets. Examples of investment centers include the games division of a toy manufacturer and the St. Louis plant of a multiplant firm.

The designation of an organizational segment as either a profit center or an investment center is made by top management. If asset acquisitions are determined by top management, then the segment will likely be classified as a profit center. If the segment manager has authority over and responsibility for selection of assets, then the segment may be designated an investment center. Evaluating the performance of an investment center involves cost comparisons and income measures. Also, a rate-of-return calculation relates income to assets and measures performance regarding asset utilization. Rate-of-return analysis for an investment center is considered in the final section of this chapter.

FLEXIBLE BUDGETING

Care must be taken to ensure that the comparison of a cost center's actual costs to budgeted costs is a valid one. In particular, it is necessary to compare costs based on *equal levels of output*. This process is known as flexible budgeting.

Exhibit 18-3 presents a performance report for the assembly department of Ranzone Manufacturing Co. for July, 1988. Note that actual results for the month are compared to budgeted results and the last column shows the actual versus budgeted cost difference. How would you evaluate the performance of the assembly department and its supervisor, Mr. Johnson? In four out of six cases, actual costs were less than budgeted. Is Mr. Johnson to be congratulated? Does he deserve a salary increase, bonus, or promotion?

Before forming an opinion, reexamine Exhibit 18-3. The top section of the performance report indicates that 9,000 units were produced in the assembly department during July, 1988. The "actual cost" column discloses actual costs incurred to produce the *9,000 units*. However, carefully note that the "budgeted cost" column represents budgeted costs for the *10,000 units* that were planned for July production. How does this fact affect your evaluation of the assembly department's performance?

EXHIBIT 18-3
Ranzone Manufacturing Co.
Performance Report—Static Budgeting

Department Assembly   Month July 1988
Supervisor Mr. Johnson   Units Produced 9,000

Cost item	Actual cost	Budgeted cost for 10,000 forecasted units	Actual cost over (under) budget
Material A	$28,000	$30,000	($2,000)
Material B	9,125	10,000	(875)
Direct labor	35,000	42,000	(7,000)
Indirect materials	980	1,000	(20)
Factory rent	2,000	2,000	-0-
Factory supervisor	1,100	1,000	100
	$76,205	$86,000	($9,795)

Static Budgeting—Apples versus Oranges

A *static budget* reflects forecasted costs for a *single* expected level of activity. The amounts shown in the budgeted cost column in Exhibit 18-3 were developed for a forecasted activity level of 10,000 units of production. The static budget creates problems when the actual activity level differs from the expected level. In the assembly department case, actual costs relate to 9,000 units, whereas budgeted costs relate to 10,000 units.

With a static budget it is impossible to make an accurate analysis of most of the cost items shown on a performance report. Except for fixed cost items, trying to compare actual costs to produce 9,000 units with budgeted costs for 10,000 expected units of production is as meaningless as the proverbial "apples versus oranges" comparison. To accurately analyze performance, it is necessary to compare actual costs for the number of units produced to budgeted costs for the *same* production level. With static budgeting, this would only be possible on the rare occasions when the actual production level equaled the forecasted production level.

Flexible Budgeting—A Dynamic Approach

Flexible budgeting formulates budgets for a series of activity levels within the normal production range—not just a single forecasted activity level. In addition, if the series of flexible budgets initially prepared does not contain a budget exactly matching the actual production level achieved, a budget can be tailor-made *after the fact* to correspond with the actual activity level.

Cost Behavior Patterns To develop a flexible budget, costs must be classified according to their cost behavior pattern. Recall that in Chapter 14 costs were classified as either fixed, variable, or semivariable. A cost is classified as *fixed* if it is assumed that the total cost does not change when the level of activity changes within some limited, relevant range. A cost is classified as *variable* if the total cost is assumed to change proportionately with changes in the activity level. When a cost has both a fixed and a variable component, it is classified as a semivariable cost.

Variable Costs per Unit—The Key to Flexible Budgets   For variable costs, the cost per unit is constant while the total costs vary depending on volume. For example, if variable cost per unit is $10, then total variable cost is $30 for three units, $60 for six units, and so on. Multiplying variable cost per unit times each forecasted activity level will produce different total variable costs for each activity level. Thus variable costs (and the variable portion of semivariable costs) are what inject a dynamic element into flexible budgeting. Variable costs per unit are the building blocks for preparation of flexible budgets.

Review the cost items and budgeted amounts shown in Exhibit 18-3 for Ranzone Manufacturing's assembly department. Assume that the first four cost items listed (i.e., material A, material B, direct labor, and indirect materials) are variable costs. By dividing the respective budgeted cost amounts for these four items by the 10,000 forecasted units of production, the following variable costs per unit can be determined for the assembly department:

Material A	$3.00	($30,000 ÷ 10,000)
Material B	1.00	($10,000 ÷ 10,000)
Direct labor	4.20	($42,000 ÷ 10,000)
Indirect materials	.10	($ 1,000 ÷ 10,000)
Total variable costs per unit	$8.30	

Remember that within the relevant range, it is assumed that variable costs per unit remain unchanged. Total budgeted cost for each variable cost item will vary proportionately with changes in volume.

The last two assembly department cost items shown in Exhibit 18-3 (i.e., $2,000 factory rent and $1,000 factory supervision) are assumed to be fixed costs. Recall that budgeted fixed costs remain unchanged in total as volume varies. By combining the fixed cost and variable cost components, total budgeted cost for any relevant production volume in the assembly department can be calculated as follows:

$$\text{Total Budgeted Cost} = \begin{array}{l} \$3,000 \text{ Budgeted Fixed Costs} \\ + [\$8.30 \text{ Budgeted Variable Cost per Unit} \\ \times \text{ Number of Units Forecasted}] \end{array}$$

Flexible Budgeting—An Example

Exhibit 18-4 presents flexible budgets for Ranzone Manufacturing's assembly department for 8,000, 9,000, 10,000, and 11,000 units of production. Note that budgeted dollar amounts for the variable cost items change as the forecasted level of activity changes. Each budgeted variable cost amount in Exhibit

EXHIBIT 18-4
Ranzone Manufacturing Co.
Assembly Department—Flexible Budgets
For the Month of July 1988

Cost item	Variable cost per unit	Budgeted costs at various production levels			
		8,000	9,000	10,000	11,000
Material A	$3.00	$24,000	$27,000	$30,000	$33,000
Material B	1.00	8,000	9,000	10,000	11,000
Direct labor	4.20	33,600	37,800	42,000	46,200
Indirect materials	.10	800	900	1,000	1,100
Total variable cost	$8.30	$66,400	$74,700	$83,000	$91,300
Factory rent	Fixed cost	2,000	2,000	2,000	2,000
Factory supervision	Fixed cost	1,000	1,000	1,000	1,000
Total budgeted costs		$69,400	$77,700	$86,000	$94,300

18-4 was determined by multiplying the constant variable cost per unit previously calculated by the respective production levels. For example, the budgeted variable cost amounts in Exhibit 18-4 for material A were determined as follows:

Variable cost per unit for material A	Forecasted production level	Total budgeted variable cost for material A
$3.00	8,000 units	$24,000
3.00	9,000	27,000
3.00	10,000	30,000
3.00	11,000	33,000

The total budgeted variable costs for material B, direct labor, and indirect materials were determined in a similar manner.

Note in Exhibit 18-4 that total budgeted costs for factory rent and factory supervision do not fluctuate as volume varies from 8,000 to 11,000 units. Budgeted factory rent is $2,000 and budgeted factory supervision is $1,000, regardless of fluctuations in the number of units forecasted for production. Recall that both factory rent and factory supervision were classified as fixed costs for the assembly department. By definition, these budgeted cost totals remain unaffected by variations in the forecasted production level over the relevant range of activity.

Flexible budgeting permits calculation of budgeted costs for any production level within the relevant range. Although Exhibit 18-4 shows budgeted costs for only four possible production levels, other flexible budgets can easily be calculated. If actual units produced do not correspond to one of the four projected levels (e.g., if the assembly department output is 8,600 units), a budget can be prepared after the fact to match the actual production level obtained.

Flexible Budgeting and Performance Reports

A performance report based on flexible budgeting for Ranzone Manufacturing's assembly department is presented in Exhibit 18-5. The budgeted dollar amounts are taken from the 9,000 unit flexible budget production level shown in Exhibit

EXHIBIT 18-5

Ranzone Manufacturing Co.

Performance Report—Flexible Budgeting

Department Assembly   Month July 1988
Supervisor Mr. Johnson   Units Produced 9,000

Cost item	Actual cost	Flexible budget cost for 9,000 units	Actual cost over (under) budget
Material A	$28,000	$27,000	$1,000
Material B	9,125	9,000	125
Direct labor	35,000	37,800	(2,800)
Indirect materials	980	900	80
Factory rent	2,000	2,000	-0-
Factory supervisor	1,100	1,000	100
	$76,205	$77,700	($1,495)

18-4. The assembly department's flexible-budgeting performance report thus compares actual costs to produce 9,000 units with budgeted costs for 9,000 units. Since both actual costs and budgeted costs are associated with the same production level (i.e., 9,000 units), the "actual cost over (under) budget" column in Exhibit 18-5 is the result of a meaningful comparison.

Note that the comparison column of Exhibit 18-5 portrays a different story than that of the performance report based on static budgeting (Exhibit 18-3). According to the static budget, four variances appeared to be favorable in that actual costs were less than budgeted costs. When a flexible budget comparison is made, three of those four variances are unfavorable.

Recall that under responsibility accounting, department managers should be held accountable only for costs they have the authority to control. Although the flexible budget comparison indicates primarily unfavorable results for the assembly department, care should be taken in evaluating Mr. Johnson (the supervisor) based on this information. Costs not under his control should be ignored in evaluating his performance.

DIRECT COSTING

For manufacturing firms, changes in the number of units in inventory can affect the measurement of income. If the manufacturing segment is a profit center, then the manager's evaluation is based on income. The influence of inventory quantities on income limits the usefulness of income as a measure of performance. For instance, a manager could manipulate income by ordering inventory build-ups or depletions that are not in the best interest of the company as a whole. The problem arises from the treatment of fixed manufacturing overhead. Since these costs are fixed in total, the greater the level of production, the lower the costs per unit. For example, assume that fixed manufacturing overhead for a period of time is $100,000. The effect of the level of production on per-unit fixed manufacturing overhead cost is shown on the following page:

Level of production	Fixed manufacturing overhead per unit		
10,000	$10.00	($100,000 ÷	10,000 units)
20,000	5.00	($100,000 ÷	20,000 units)
40,000	2.50	($100,000 ÷	40,000 units)
80,000	1.25	($100,000 ÷	80,000 units)
100,000	1.00	($100,000 ÷	100,000 units)
200,000	.50	($100,000 ÷	200,000 units)

If virtually all units produced are sold during the period, no great difficulty arises in evaluating performance. However, assume that substantial increases in ending inventory quantities occur. The fixed costs applied to the product are inventoried; they will not flow through the income statement until the products are sold. The result is that income for the period of inventory build-up is distorted from the perspective of performance evaluation. It appears higher than the production performance justifies. A decline in inventory quantities will create the opposite effect. To resolve this problem for performance evaluation purposes, direct costing is often employed.

Direct Costing versus Absorption Costing

In simple terms, the issue is whether fixed manufacturing overhead should be deducted as an expense in the period the unit is produced or in the period the unit is sold. *Direct costing* (also called *variable costing*) includes only *variable* manufacturing costs in determining work in process inventory, finished goods inventory, and cost of goods sold. Thus, inventoriable costs under direct costing include direct materials, direct labor, and variable manufacturing overhead— all the variable manufacturing costs of production. With direct costing, fixed manufacturing overhead is deducted as an expense in the period incurred and never becomes part of the cost of the product. Direct costing is frequently used for internal management information purposes.

Absorption costing (also called *full costing*) includes *all* manufacturing costs as part of the cost of work in process inventory, finished goods inventory, and cost of goods sold. With absorption costing, fixed manufacturing overhead is included along with the variable manufacturing costs as part of product cost. Absorption costing is required by both generally accepted accounting principles and the Internal Revenue Service. Direct costing is not permitted for external reporting. The differing treatment of fixed manufacturing overhead under direct and absorption costing is summarized in Exhibit 18-6.

Direct Costing versus Absorption Costing—An Example

The following example illustrates the effect on net income of treating fixed manufacturing overhead costs differently under the two costing methods. Note that a significant portion of total manufacturing costs is assumed to be fixed manufacturing overhead and that inventory quantities fluctuate significantly from

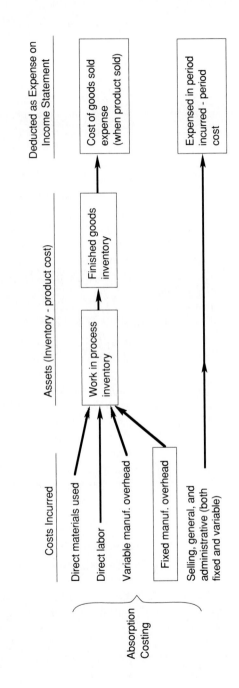

EXHIBIT 18-6 Flow of Costs - Direct Versus Absorption Costing

period to period. Both of these assumptions serve to magnify the differences in net income caused by the two costing methods.

	Direct costing	Absorption costing
Production costs per unit:		
Direct materials	$1.00	$1.00
Direct labor	.50	.50
Variable manufacturing overhead	.50	.50
Fixed manufacturing overhead	—	3.00
Total product cost	$2.00	$5.00
Selling price per unit		$ 8.50
Fixed manufacturing overhead per year		600,000
Selling, general, and administrative expenses per year (assumed to be fixed)		400,000
Work in process inventories are assumed to be zero at the beginning and end of each year. Income taxes are ignored.		

	Year 1	Year 2
Units in beginning finished goods inventory	-0-	40,000
Units produced	200,000	200,000
Units sold	160,000	230,000
Units in ending finished goods inventory	40,000	10,000

Exhibit 18-7 presents income statements under both direct costing and absorption costing for the two years. Why does net income each year differ between direct and absorption costing? Remember there is no change in selling price, manufacturing costs, or selling, general, and administrative expenses between Years 1 and 2.

Changes in inventory quantities are the key to determining net income effects. If the number of units produced differs from the number of units sold, the change in inventory quantity (times the fixed manufacturing overhead cost per unit) quickly indicates the net income difference between direct and absorption costing. In equation form:

$$\begin{matrix} \text{Difference in Net Income} \\ \text{between Direct Costing} \\ \text{and Absorption Costing} \end{matrix} = \begin{matrix} \text{Change in Inventory Quantity during Period} \\ \times \text{ Fixed Manufacturing Overhead Cost per Unit} \end{matrix}$$

Utilizing the equation and the information presented in the preceding example yields:

$$\begin{matrix} \text{Year 1 difference} \\ \text{in net income} \end{matrix} = \begin{matrix} \text{40,000 } \textit{Increase} \text{ in units in inventory} \\ \times \$3 \text{ fixed manufacturing overhead cost per unit} \end{matrix}$$

$$= \begin{matrix} \$120,000 \text{ (\$160,000 absorption costing net} \\ \text{income versus \$40,000 direct costing net income)} \end{matrix}$$

EXHIBIT 18-7
Direct versus Absorption Costing
Comparative Income Statements

	Year 1		Year 2	
	Direct costing	**Absorption costing**	**Direct costing**	**Absorption costing**
Sales	$1,360,000	$1,360,000	$1,955,000	$1,955,000
	(160,000×$8.50)	(160,000×$8.50)	(230,000×$8.50)	(230,000×$8.50)
Cost of Goods Sold:				
Beginning Finished Goods Inventory	$ -0-	$ -0-	$ 80,000	$ 200,000
				[Ending inventory for year 1]
Cost of Goods Manufactured	400,000	1,000,000	400,000	1,000,000
	(200,000×$2)	(200,000×$5)	(200,000×$2)	(200,000×$5)
Available for Sale	$ 400,000	$1,000,000	$ 480,000	$1,200,000
Less Ending Finished Goods Inventory	80,000	200,000	20,000	50,000
	(40,000×$2)	(40,000×$5)	(10,000×$2)	(10,000×$5)
Cost of Goods Sold	$ 320,000	$ 800,000	$ 460,000	$1,150,000
Gross Profit	$1,040,000	$ 560,000	$1,495,000	$ 805,000
Other Expenses:				
Fixed Manufacturing Overhead	$ 600,000	$ -0-	$ 600,000	$ -0-
Selling, General, and Administrative Expenses	400,000	400,000	400,000	400,000
Total Other Expenses	$1,000,000	$ 400,000	$1,000,000	$ 400,000
Net Income	$ 40,000	$ 160,000	$ 495,000	$ 405,000

$120,000 Difference $90,000 Difference

$$\begin{array}{ll}\text{Year 2 difference} \\ \text{in net income}\end{array} = \begin{array}{l} \text{30,000 } \textit{Decrease} \text{ in units in inventory} \\ \times \$3 \text{ fixed manufacturing overhead cost per unit}\end{array}$$

$$= \begin{array}{l}\$90,000 \ (\$405,000 \text{ absorption costing net} \\ \text{income versus } \$495,000 \text{ direct costing net income})\end{array}$$

When inventory quantities increase (as in Year 1), absorption costing will yield a higher net income than direct costing. The higher net income under absorption costing arises since the fixed manufacturing overhead costs associated with Year 1's inventory build-up ($120,000, or 40,000 units × $3) are not included as an expense in the income statement for Year 1. On the other hand, when inventory quantities decrease (as in Year 2), absorption costing will yield a lower net income than direct costing since the cost of goods sold expense includes not only the current period's fixed manufacturing costs, but also the fixed manufacturing costs from the prior year that are associated with the inventory decrease ($90,000, or 30,000 unit decrease × $3).

Consider which method is more useful in evaluating performance of the manufacturing segment or manager. If the number of units produced equals the number of units sold during the period, total expenses and net income will be the same under either direct or absorption costing. In the long run, production and sales have to be approximately equal. You cannot sell more than you produce. Similarly, in the long run it makes no sense to produce more than can be sold. While net income may differ between direct and absorption costing in the short run, over a long period of time the total profits under both methods should be equal. However, because performance evaluation is usually carried out on a month-by-month, or year-by-year, basis, the short-run measurement of income becomes very important. Direct costing is often used when assessing the performance of profit centers because it results in an income measure unaffected by inventory fluctuations.

The question of direct versus absorption costing for various accounting purposes continues to be controversial. The following two sections briefly summarize the arguments on both sides of this issue.

The Case for Direct Costing

Direct costing's treatment of fixed manufacturing overhead as a single deduction on the income statement in the period incurred properly reflects the nature of fixed manufacturing overhead. Total fixed manufacturing overhead is unresponsive to changes in volume. Fixed manufacturing overhead is related to providing the capacity to produce and cannot be identified readily with units produced. Absorption costing confuses the relationship between costs and volume by including in the cost of a unit a fixed manufacturing overhead component.

Direct costing eliminates the possibility of management's manipulation of inventory quantities in order to influence net income. Under absorption costing, increasing inventory will increase reported net income.

Direct costing presents information in a format that is more useful to management when making various decisions. For example, the fixed versus variable distinction highlighted by direct costing is valuable in planning (e.g., preparing flexible budgets or determining selling prices for special orders). Control and performance evaluation decisions also are aided by direct costing information. For example, a contribution margin that relies on direct costing data is valuable in analyzing cost-volume-profit relationships and in evaluating performance of various segments of the organization.

The Case for Absorption Costing

Absorption costing includes all costs necessary to manufacture the product. Fixed manufacturing overhead is a cost necessary to produce the product and therefore is properly included as a cost of the product. Direct costing's exclusion of fixed manufacturing overhead from work in process and finished goods inventories improperly understates asset cost.

In the long run, sales must exceed all costs—fixed as well as variable. Absorption costing makes this point clearer by including fixed manufacturing costs (as well as variable) in determining product costs.

Generally accepted accounting principles and Internal Revenue Service rules currently permit only absorption costing for *external* reporting.

CONTRIBUTION TOWARD INDIRECT EXPENSES

The measurement of profit center income is complicated by the difficulty of allocating a firm's common costs to various profit centers. Consider, for example, a supermarket. Profit centers may include the meat, produce, dairy, frozen food, baked goods, and general grocery departments. For each of these, the sales revenue can be determined. Some costs can be easily associated with each department, such as the cost of employees assigned specifically to that department. However, there are other costs that are incurred to serve all departments simultaneously, such as check-out cashiers, the store manager, heating and lighting, and so forth. How are these common costs to be treated in evaluating the performance of each department? One approach is to differentiate between *direct* and *indirect* expenses and to formulate an income measure based on direct expenses only.

Direct versus Indirect Expenses

Direct expenses are specifically related and traceable to a particular segment of the organization. If the particular segment of the organization were eliminated, the direct expenses of that segment would be eliminated. *Indirect expenses,* on the other hand, are not directly traceable to a particular segment of the organization. Indirect expenses are common costs incurred for the continued existence of the organization as a whole. For some purposes, such as inventory valuation, indirect costs may be allocated among the various segments of the business. However, the indirect expenses allocated to a particular segment of the organization would not be eliminated if the particular organization segment were discontinued. This is an important fact to remember when attempting to evaluate performance.

An Illustration

Presented below is the condensed income statement for Dirty Shirt Laundry Company. Note that the income statement also includes information on profitability of the two profit center segments (i.e., shirts and diapers) that comprise Dirty Shirt Laundry's total business.

Dirty Shirt Laundry Company
Income Statement
For the Year Ended June 30, 1988

| | Total | Profit centers | |
		Shirt cleaning	Diaper cleaning
Sales	$1,120,000	$640,000	$480,000
Expenses	1,050,000	550,000	500,000
Net Income (Loss)	$ 70,000	$ 90,000	($ 20,000)

As manager of the Dirty Shirt Laundry, how would you evaluate the company's performance? Should the diaper-cleaning operation be discontinued? What would happen to total profits for the firm if the diaper-cleaning operation were discontinued?

It is impossible to answer these questions based on the traditional income statement presented above. The expenses must be subdivided into direct and indirect expenses for a meaningful evaluation of operations to be made. Recall that direct expenses are directly traceable to a particular segment of the organization and would be eliminated if that segment of the organization were discontinued. Included among the direct expenses for Dirty Shirt Laundry are the detergent, hot water, electricity, and washing machine rental fees directly traceable to the respective shirt-cleaning and diaper-cleaning operations. Indirect expenses for Dirty Shirt Laundry include the manager's salary, real estate taxes, and depreciation on the building. While the traditional income statement allocated indirect expenses between the two cleaning operations, these expenses are incurred for the existence of the business as a whole. It is assumed they would remain unchanged in amount, even if one of the two operations were discontinued.

Assume the total expenses for Dirty Shirt Laundry can be segregated as follows:

		Profit centers	
	Total	Shirt cleaning	Diaper cleaning
Direct expenses	$ 890,000	$470,000	$420,000
Indirect expenses	160,000*	80,000*	80,000*
Total expenses	$1,050,000	$550,000	$500,000

* The total indirect expenses of $160,000 were arbitrarily allocated between the two cleaning operations on a 50-50 basis.

A Revised Income Statement

With the segregation of expenses into direct and indirect components, it is possible to prepare the following revised income statement. The statement is designed to assist management in evaluating the performance of the two cleaning operations.

Dirty Shirt Laundry Company
Income Statement—
Showing Contribution Toward Indirect Expense and Profit
For the Year Ended June 30, 1988

		Profit centers	
	Total	Shirt cleaning	Diaper cleaning
Sales	$1,120,000	$640,000	$480,000
Direct Expenses	890,000	470,000	420,000
Contribution toward Indirect Expenses and Profit	$ 230,000	$170,000	$ 60,000
Indirect Expenses	160,000	80,000	80,000
Net Income (Loss)	$ 70,000	$ 90,000	($ 20,000)

What would happen if management of Dirty Shirt Laundry discontinues the diaper-cleaning operations? The diaper cleaning's $480,000 of sales revenue and $420,000 of direct expenses would be eliminated, but the total indirect expenses for the company would be unaltered. Eliminating the diaper-cleaning segment of the business would cause a decrease in profits of $60,000 ($480,000 lost revenue versus only $420,000 decrease in expenses). Total profit of Dirty Shirt Laundry would become $10,000 instead of the current $70,000 if the diaper-cleaning operations were discontinued.

With discontinuance of the diaper-cleaning operation, Dirty Shirt Laundry's income statement would appear as:

Dirty Shirt Laundry Company
Projected Income Statement—
Assuming Discontinuance of Diaper-Cleaning Operation
For the Year Ended June 30, 1988

	Total	Profit centers Shirt cleaning	Diaper cleaning
Sales	$640,000	$640,000	$ -0-
Direct Expenses	470,000	470,000	-0-
Contribution toward Indirect Expenses and Profit	$170,000	$170,000	$ -0-
Indirect Expenses	160,000	160,000	-0-
Net Income	$ 10,000	$ 10,000	$ -0-

This example illustrates that when indirect expenses have been allocated among profit centers, net income becomes a poor indicator of performance. Using the $20,000 loss as a measurement of the diaper-cleaning operations's performance can lead to the incorrect decision of discontinuing the diaper cleaning. Total firm profits would suffer a $60,000 decrease from such a decision. Clearly, some other measure of performance is needed. The contribution of a profit center towards indirect expenses and profit of the company as a whole is a more appropriate measure of performance. *Contribution toward indirect expenses and profit* indicates the excess of sales revenue over direct expenses for a segment of the business. If the only alternatives are to continue to operate the profit center or to discontinue operations, the rule becomes:

Positive Contribution: Revenues > direct expenses
Decision: Continue operating the profit center.

Negative Contribution: Direct expenses > revenues
Decision: Discontinue operating the profit center.

Many accountants prefer not to analyze profit center operations beyond the determination of each segment's contribution toward indirect expenses and profit.

They argue that analysis beyond the determination of the segment's contribution only serves to confuse the statement reader. Following this position, statements would show neither allocation of indirect expense among profit centers of the business nor any net income amount for each center.

In real life, rarely is the decision process as simple as indicated by the rule given above and as illustrated for Dirty Shirt Laundry. Difficulties arise in real-life situations in identifying and segregating direct versus indirect expenses. Also, a decision is rarely as simple as "continue operations exactly as currently in effect" or "discontinue operations entirely." Efforts may be made to increase revenues or decrease expenses. Interrelationships among the various segments of the business must also be considered. In the Dirty Shirt Laundry example, the following questions might be asked: Would discontinuing diaper cleaning allow a profitable expansion of the shirt-cleaning operation? Or, would shirt-cleaning sales diminish as customers transfer to firms that continue to offer both shirt- and diaper-cleaning facilities? What other uses could be made of the diaper-cleaning area of the building if the diaper-cleaning operations were discontinued? These and other questions would have to be answered in a real-life situation before making decisions concerning the improvement of performance.

RATE OF RETURN ANALYSIS

In large, decentralized companies, the authority and responsibility delegated to managers of the various segments of the company include not only control over selling activities and costs but also the authority and responsibility to control asset investment. The operating divisions or branches of the company where the manager controls revenues, expenses, and the asset investment base are called investment centers. It is difficult to select a measure of performance that encompasses all the factors under the control of an investment center manager. In addition, it is extremely difficult to quantify such factors as an investment center's ongoing research and development endeavors, employee training efforts, and development of customer goodwill.

The principal performance measure for investment centers is the rate of return on asset investment. Although it is used by many companies, there is considerable disagreement over how the rate of return is to be calculated and how it is to be used to control operations and measure performance.

Calculation of Rate of Return

The rate-of-return ratio compares a measure of income with a measure of the investment necessary to achieve that income. The words "income" and "investment" in the ratio can take on different meanings, depending on the context in which the rate-of-return ratio is being used. The context in this chapter is the evaluation of the performance of company segments designated as investment centers. For this purpose, the rate of return is formulated as:

$$\text{Rate of Return} = \frac{\text{Profit}}{\text{Sales}} \times \frac{\text{Sales}}{\text{Assets}}$$

(Profit   (Asset
Margin)   Turnover)

Dividing the rate of return into two components (profit margin and asset turn-over) aids in the evaluation of performance since it relates earnings, sales revenue, and the investment in assets. The profit margin component, which indicates profit earned on each dollar of sales, reflects the ability of an investment center manager to control costs. The asset turnover component reflects the skill exhibited in selecting the proper type and amount of assets to acquire and the skill in using those assets to generate revenue. Too high an investment in less productive assets (e.g., cash or inventories) is an important fact that management should know. The asset turnover component of the rate-of-return measure highlights this factor.

Profit margin and asset turnover figures vary significantly among industries. For example, grocery stores would be expected to have a lower profit margin (profit per dollar of sales) than stores selling mink coats. The compensating factor is the respective asset turnovers of these two industries. The grocery store's asset turnover (amount of sales generated per dollar of assets) should greatly exceed the turnover for the mink coat store. Overall rate of return can be increased by improving the profit margin, or the asset turnover, or both.

Rate of Return and Performance Evaluation

Using rate-of-return measures for performance evaluation does present some difficulties. Briefly discussed below are some of the problems encountered in using the rate-of-return measure to control operations and evaluate performance.

How is "profit" to be defined? If management is trying to determine which investment centers are contributing the most to overall company income, profit should be contribution towards indirect expenses. Contributions toward indirect expenses would indicate the change in overall company profit if the investment center were discontinued. In reality, many companies allocate indirect expenses to the various investment centers. For these companies, the rate-of-return measure would be viewed with skepticism since contribution towards indirect expenses is not used as the profit measure.

What assets are to be included in the asset investment base? Some companies include only assets that can be directly traced to specific investment centers. Other companies allocate common assets (e.g., central headquarters cash and property) to investment centers. Because such allocation must be somewhat arbitrary, rate of return where common assets are allocated is a less valid measure of investment center performance.

How are the assets included in the asset investment base to be valued? Original cost, depreciated cost, and replacement cost are three possibilities. The method selected not only affects the rate-of-return measure directly, but also can lead to suboptimal decisions by investment center managers. For example, a policy of not replacing aging assets, coupled with the depreciated cost method of valuing assets, results in a smaller and smaller asset investment base each year. Investment center managers might be tempted in the short run to postpone needed asset replacements. The small (but outdated) asset base would inflate the rate-of-return measure for their investment center.

How should transfer prices be set? *Transfer prices* are the prices set for goods that are transferred from one segment of the company to another. The price set is revenue to the selling division and an inventory cost (which eventually becomes cost of goods sold expense) to the buying division. Thus, profit and the rate-of-return measure are influenced by the interdivisional transfer price. Transfer prices can be based on (a) current market price, if available; (b) price negotiations among divisions; or (c) some measure of cost. The objective in setting a transfer price is to motivate investment center managers to make decisions that simultaneously will improve their own performance evaluation and also lead to maximization of profits for the firm as a whole. This is a complex subject, which is covered in detail in advanced courses in managerial accounting.

What should be the basis for evaluating an investment center's rate-of-return measure? Inefficient operations in previous years and changed conditions over time can make previous years' rate-of-return calculations a relatively poor basis for evaluating current period rate of return. Differences in industry conditions may make it unfair to compare the rate of return for one segment of a company to the rate of return for another segment of the company in a different industry. For example, one investment center manager in a depressed industry may be performing exceptionally well considering the depressed economic conditions in the industry. The segment's rate of return, however, could be significantly lower than the rate of return achieved by an inefficient manager fortunate enough to manage an investment center engaged in an industry enjoying good economic conditions. Comparing rate-of-return measurements for these two investment centers would not provide an equitable basis to evaluate the managers' performances.

Perhaps the best way of utilizing rate-of-return measurements to evaluate an investment center's performance is to compare the actual rate of return obtained to a predetermined goal or standard that was developed for that individual investment center. The standard should reflect current economic conditions in the industry and be based on attainable results under efficient operations. Comparing an investment center's rate of return to that achieved by a competitor would also be valuable, if both ratios are comparable (i.e., profit and asset investment are determined in a similar fashion) and the competitor's ratio is available for comparison.

Rate of Return—An Illustration

The following is information on General Motors Corporation's foreign operations for two recent years, which we will designate as Year 2 and Year 1.

**Attributable to Operations Outside
the United States and Canada
(In Millions of Dollars)**

	December 31	
	Year 2	Year 1
Assets:		
Total current assets	$2,768.8	$2,716.6
Real estate, plants and equipment	3,009.8	2,911.2
Accumulated depreciation	(2,021.3)	(1,941.0)
Special tools, less amortization	300.0	222.0
Other assets	240.5	209.5
Total assets	$4,297.8	$4,118.3
Liabilities:		
Loan payable	$ 610.3	$ 737.1
Other current liabilities	1,211.5	1,035.5
Total current liabilities	$1,821.8	$1,772.6
Long-term debt of subsidiaries	337.6	407.0
Other liabilities and deferred credits	449.6	416.5
Total liabilities	$2,609.0	$2,596.1
Owners' equity	$1,688.8	$1,522.2
Net sales	$7,495.2	$7,227.3
Net income	$ 357.2	$ 72.4

The rate of return on foreign operations for the two years (showing both profit margin and asset turnover) is determined as follows:

$$\text{Rate of Return} = \text{Profit Margin x Asset Turnover}$$

$$\text{Rate of Return} = \frac{\text{Profit}}{\text{Sales}} \times \frac{\text{Sales}}{\text{Assets}}$$

$$\text{Year 1's Rate of Return} = \frac{\$72.4}{\$7,227.3} \times \frac{\$7,227.3}{\$4,118.3}$$
$$= .01 \times 1.75$$
$$= .018$$

$$\text{Year 2's Rate of Return} = \frac{\$357.2}{\$7,495.2} \times \frac{\$7,495.2}{\$4,297.8}$$
$$= .048 \times 1.74$$
$$= .084$$

As can be seen, General Motors significantly improved its rate of return on foreign operations from less than 2 percent in Year 1 to over 8 percent in Year 2. All of the improvement was in the profit margin component, as it increased from 1 percent to nearly 5 percent. Asset turnover, in fact, decreased slightly from 1.75 to 1.74.

How should the improved foreign operation's performance be evaluated? On the surface, Year 2 would certainly appear to be a good year. However, if Year

1 was an unusually bad year, it would be a poor basis for evaluating Year 2's rate of return. The predetermined rate-of-return goal for Year 2 is not revealed in the annual report for comparison. A word of caution does appear in the annual report:

> Any determination of income by areas of operations is necessarily arbitrary because of the allocation and reallocation of costs, including corporate costs.

Clearly, the foreign operations's net income includes indirect expenses. Because profit is not defined as contribution towards indirect expenses, the rate-of-return measurements must be evaluated accordingly.

SUMMARY

Learning Objective 1: Discuss the basic concepts of control.

Control and performance evaluation is a necessary follow-up to planning. Control and performance evaluation allows management to determine if plans and people are performing as expected. Feedback of actual results to compare to planned performance is necessary. Designing the accounting system so that feedback is segregated by various segments of the organization is known as responsibility accounting. The key to an effective responsibility accounting system is to hold an organizational segment and its manager responsible only for the costs, sales, and asset investment that it has the authority to control. Allocating noncontrollable items can lead to an inappropriate, unfair evaluation of performance.

Learning Objective 2: Prepare performance reports for cost centers using flexible budgeting.

Cost centers are segments within a firm that incur costs but do not generate revenues. To evaluate and control the performance of such segments, detailed analyses of costs are required, comparing actual costs with expected costs. Flexible budgeting compares actual costs with budgeted costs adjusted to the level of actual activity.

Learning Objective 3: Calculate income under both direct costing and absorption costing.

Profit centers directly generate revenues as well as incur costs. For profit centers in a manufacturing firm, an absorption costing treatment of fixed manufacturing overhead as a part of the cost of the product, when coupled with changes in inventory levels, can influence the measurement of income (and hence the evaluation of performance). Direct costing, an alternative technique employed for performance evaluation purposes, treats fixed manufacturing overhead as an expense in the period incurred—not as a cost of the product.

Learning Objective 4: Discuss the arguments for and against direct costing.

The possibility of manipulating production quantities and inventory levels to influence income measurement is eliminated with direct costing. Fixed manufacturing overhead is expensed as incurred. Maintaining the fixed-variable distinction is consistent with other areas of managerial accounting. On the other hand, fixed manufacturing cost is no less important than variable costs; all costs must be recovered via sales revenue in order for a firm to succeed.

Learning Objective 5: Analyze departmental performance in terms of contribution toward indirect expenses and profit.

Performance evaluation for profit centers can be influenced by the treatment of direct and indirect expenses. Direct expenses are specifically related and traceable to a particular segment of the organization. Indirect expenses, however, are costs incurred to serve all organizational segments. Allocating indirect expenses among a firm's profit centers and subsequently evaluating the profit centers' performances based on net income can lead to erroneous conclusions. Contribution toward indirect expenses and profit (revenues minus direct expenses) is preferable to net income for the evaluation and control of profit centers.

Learning Objective 6: Calculate and analyze rate of return.

Investment centers are charged with a substantial asset investment, as well as with responsibility for directly generating revenues and controlling costs. Rate of return (profit margin $\times$ asset turnover) is a common measure used for evaluation and control of an investment center's performance.

Learning Objective 7: Discuss the problems inherent in measuring and using rate of return for performance evaluation.

Difficulties to overcome in utilizing the rate-of-return measure include determining how income is to be defined, what assets are to be included in the investment base and how they are to be valued, how transfer prices are to be set, and what basis should be adopted for evaluating the rate of return calculated.

KEY TERMS

Absorption costing
Contribution toward indirect
  expenses and profit
Cost center
Direct costing
Direct expenses
Feedback
Flexible budget
Full costing

Indirect expenses
Investment center
Performance evaluation
Profit center
Rate of return for investment center
Responsibility accounting
Static budget
Transfer prices
Variable costing

REVIEW QUESTIONS

1 What benefits are to be reaped from performance evaluation and control?
2 Define feedback. Based on feedback, what decisions may management elect to make?
3 Define responsibility accounting. What is the key to an effective responsibility accounting system?

4   Differentiate among the following three terms: cost center, profit center, and investment center.

5   Differentiate static budgeting and flexible budgeting.

6   What provides the "flex" in flexible budgeting?

7   Evaluate the following statement: "Within the relevant range, variable costs per unit and total fixed costs remain unchanged as the volume of activity fluctuates."

8   For a given volume of activity within the relevant range, complete the following flexible budgeting formula:

$$\text{Total Budgeted Cost} = ? + (? \times ?)$$

9   Direct costing is a performance evaluation technique employed in measuring the income of profit centers of manufacturing firms. How does direct costing differ from absorption costing? What is the advantage of using direct costing for performance evaluation?

10   "All variable costs under direct costing are considered to be part of the cost of the goods manufactured, while all fixed costs incurred are treated as expenses in the period used." Evaluate the preceding statement.

11   "If sales exceed production during the period (and if fixed manufacturing overhead cost per unit is unchanged from the preceding period), direct costing will produce a higher profit than absorption costing." Evaluate the preceding statement.

12   Pronton Co.'s income statement using absorption costing has $12,000 as income before taxes. If the level of finished goods inventory increased by 4,000 units during the year and the fixed manufacturing overhead cost is $2 per unit, what would be the income before taxes using direct costing?

13   Distinguish between "direct expenses" and "indirect expenses."

14   In deciding whether to continue or discontinue operations of a particular segment of the business, what is the quantitative criterion or rule for making the decision?

15   The Sponge Division of Mop Up Company reported a $19,000 net loss last year. It is the second year in succession the division's income statement indicated a loss. What factors should be considered in deciding whether or not to discontinue operations of the sponge division?

16   The rate-of-return ratio for investment centers that was used in the chapter had two elements: a profit margin and an asset turnover. How is each element computed and what information revealed by each element assists top management in evaluating investment center performance?

17   What difficulties can be encountered in using rate of return on asset investment as a performance evaluation measure?

18   At a cocktail party, Mr. Brag and Mr. Orr were discussing the profit margin each had attained for the previous year. Mr. Brag boasted that his profit margin was 25 percent. Mr. Orr admitted his operations only earned a 5-cent profit on each dollar of sales. Is Mr. Brag's performance five times superior to Mr. Orr's?

19   Define a transfer price. How can transfer prices affect an investment center's rate of return on asset investment?

EXERCISES

E18-1   Listed below are various expenses appearing on the income statement of the Bronton Manufacturing Division of Mertle, Inc. The manager of the Bronton Division has been given the responsibility and authority to control variable manufacturing costs, and is solely responsible for generating and collecting sales. Productive capacity, plus machinery and office furniture and fixtures, is determined by management at Mertle's corporate headquarters. Administrative and general services are provided by corporate headquarters. Each division of Mertle is allocated a portion of corporate headquarter's cost based on relative sales revenue.

Required:

Indicate which expense accounts of the Bronton Division are controllable and which expense accounts are noncontrollable at the division level.

1 Administrative and general expense
2 Advertising expense
3 Depreciation expense—office furniture and fixtures
4 Salespersons' salary expense
5 Bad debts expense
6 Cost of goods sold:
  a Variable manufacturing costs
  b Factory rent
  c Depreciation on factory machinery

E18-2 Presented below is the performance report for the 12,000 units produced during December, 1988 in the finishing department of Carlton, Inc. The company president is very dissatisfied that the department was over budget for three of the four cost items. If performance does not improve significantly, the president has threatened to fire J.M. Fields, the current department manager, and "hire someone who can stay under budget." Do you agree with the president's assessment of the department's performance? How could you "stay under budget"?

Cost item	Actual cost	Budgeted cost for 10,000 forecasted units	Actual cost over or (under) budget
Indirect materials	$ 49,800	$ 42,000	$ 7,800
Direct labor	75,000	64,000	11,000
Factory depreciation (units of output method)	12,000	10,000	2,000
Factory rent	20,000	20,000	-0-
	$156,800	$136,000	$20,800

E18-3 The following partially completed flexible budget is presented for Baker Manufacturing Co. Fill in the missing amounts for the 150,000 and 200,000 units columns.

	100,000 units	150,000 units	200,000 units
Manufacturing costs:			
Variable	$300,000	-?-	-?-
Fixed	200,000	-?-	-?-
Selling and other costs:			
Variable	200,000	-?-	-?-
Fixed	160,000	-?-	-?-
Total	$860,000	$ -?-	$ -?-

(AICPA Adapted)

E18-4 Gyro Gear Company produces a special gear used in automatic transmissions. Variable unit cost data, which are unchanged from last year, show:

Direct materials	$6.00
Direct labor	5.00
Manufacturing overhead	2.00
Selling and administrative	4.00

Production is forecasted to remain unchanged from last year's level of 8,000 units per month. Annual fixed costs also are expected to continue at last year's amounts of $672,000 for manufacturing overhead and $288,000 for selling and administrative costs.

Required:
1 Calculate cost per unit for inventory under direct costing.
2 Calculate cost per unit for inventory under absorption costing.
3 If inventory increased by 10,000 units during the period, calculate the difference in income before taxes between direct costing and absorption costing. (Indicate both the amount of net income difference and which method would produce the larger net income.)

(AICPA Adapted)

E18-5 The following information is available for Keller Corporation's new product line:

Selling price per unit	$ 15
Variable manufacturing costs per unit produced	8
Total annual fixed manufacturing costs	25,000
Variable general and administrative costs per unit produced	3
Total annual fixed general and administrative expenses	15,000

There was no beginning inventory. During the year 12,500 units were produced and 10,000 units were sold.

Required:
1 Calculate ending inventory using direct costing.
2 Calculate ending inventory using absorption costing.
3 Calculate total variable costs that would be included as expense (including cost of goods sold) during the year, assuming direct costing.
4 Calculate total variable costs that would be included as expense (including cost of goods sold) during the year, assuming absorption costing.
5 Calculate the total fixed costs that would be included as expense (including cost of goods sold) during the year, assuming absorption costing.
6 Calculate the total fixed costs that would be included as expense (including cost of goods sold) during the year, assuming direct costing.

E18-6 Mink, Inc.'s top-level management is considering dropping product #1 since it showed a loss on the company's statement of income presented below. As controller of Mink, you investigate the matter and find that a total of $4,000 of indirect costs have been included in the cost of goods sold and other expenses classifications for product #1.

Mink, Inc.
Statement of Income
For the Year Ended December 31, 1988

	Product #1	Product #2	Total
Sales	$25,000	$47,000	$72,000
Cost of Goods Sold	14,000	23,000	37,000
Gross Profit	$11,000	$24,000	$35,000
Other Expenses	14,000	18,000	32,000
Net Income (Loss)	($ 3,000)	$ 6,000	$ 3,000

Required:
As controller, would you advise management to discontinue product #1? Consider quantitative factors only. Support your answer by calculating the effect on overall company net income of dropping product #1.

E18-7 The chief executive officer of Gleason Company is reviewing the profitability of the company's products and considering discontinuing one of the products in order to increase total company profit. The following information is available:

	Product C	Product J
Sales	$8,200	$10,500
Cost of Goods Sold	9,300	5,500
Gross Profit	($1,100)	$ 5,000
Other Expenses	928	2,410
Net Income (Loss)	($2,028)	$ 2,590
Units sold	6,560	4,200
Sale price per unit	$ 1.25	$ 2.50
Direct cost of manufacturing per unit	1.00	1.00
Direct selling and administrative cost per unit	.30	.25

Required:
1 If product C were discontinued, what would the effect on income be?
2 If the sale price of product C was increased to $1.75 and the number of units sold decreased to 6,300, determine product C's contribution toward indirect expenses.

E18-8 The following information is available for Sodus, Inc. at December 31, 1989:

Current assets	$125,000
Property, plant, and equipment	900,000
Current liabilities	80,000
Long-term liabilities	620,000
Stockholders' equity	325,000

The income statement for the year ended December 31, 1989 shows sales of $2,000,000 and net income of $200,000. Determine:
1 The rate of return in terms of the two components of profit margin and asset turnover.

2 What the effect would be on the rate of return if sales revenues were expected to increase by 25 percent while expenses increased only by 10 percent.

E18-9 In calculating a division's rate of return on investment, Mills, Inc. defines profit as "contribution towards indirect expenses." Asset investment for a specific division is defined by Mills as "assets directly traceable to the division." The condensed statement of income for the appliance division is shown below. Total division assets of $1,000,000 includes $200,000 of central headquarters' cash that has been allocated to the appliance division's investment base.

Mills, Inc.—Appliance Division
Condensed Statement of Income
For the Year Ended December 31, 1988

Sales	$1,200,000
Cost of Goods Sold	700,000
Gross Profit	$ 500,000
Other Expenses:	
Advertising Expense	$ 40,000
Depreciation Expense	80,000
Corporate Executive Salary Expense	
(allocated from corporate headquarters)	35,000
Headquarters' Administrative and General	
Expense (allocated)	25,000
Salaries Expense—Appliance Division	200,000
Total Other Expenses	$ 380,000
Income before Income Taxes	$ 120,000

Required:

Ignoring income taxes, calculate the appliance division's rate of return on asset investment.

PROBLEMS

P18-1 *Performance Reports: Static vs. Flexible Budgets*

Clay Manufacturing Co.'s partially completed static-budgeting performance report for its packaging department is shown below.

Clay Manufacturing Co.
Static-Budgeting Performance Report

Department   Packaging   Month   October 1988
Supervisor   Ms. Smith   Units Produced   22,000

Cost item	Actual cost	Budgeted cost for 20,000 forecasted units	Actual cost over (under) budget
Cartons—variable	$ 4,200	$4,000	$
Direct labor—variable	2,300	2,000	
Supervisor's salary—fixed	2,000	2,000	
Factory rent—fixed	1,100	1,000	
Depreciation on			
machinery—fixed	500	500	
	$10,100	$9,500	$

Required:

1 Complete the "actual cost over (under) budget" column on the static-budgeting performance report.

2 Evaluate the packaging department's performance for October as indicated by the static-budgeting performance report.

3 Prepare for Clay Manufacturing's packaging department a flexible-budgeting performance report. Also state the total cost-estimating equation (i.e., flexible-budgeting formula) that would indicate total budgeted cost for any activity level within the relevant range.

P18-2 *Preparation of Flexible Budgets*

Kelly Manufacturing Corp. has budgeted the following costs for October 1988 in its assembly department based upon forecasted production of 40,000 units:

Variable costs:	
Direct materials	$ 60,000
Direct labor	120,000
Variable manufacturing costs	80,000
Variable selling and	
administrative costs	40,000
Fixed costs:	
Manufacturing costs	90,000
Selling and administrative costs	50,000

Required:

1 Prepare budgets for 30,000, 35,000, and 45,000 units.

2 State the total cost-estimating equation (i.e., flexible-budgeting formula) that would indicate total budgeted cost for any activity level within the relevant range.

P18-3 *Absorption and Direct Costing*

The following information is available for Swerson, Inc. for its first year of operations, ending March 31, 1989:

Sales price per unit	$ 90
Direct materials cost per unit	20
Direct labor cost per unit	5
Variable manufacturing overhead cost per unit	5
Variable selling cost per unit sold	6
Total fixed manufacturing costs	140,000
Administrative and general costs (all fixed)	120,000
Units produced during first year	10,000 units
Units in ending finished goods inventory	3,000 units
Ending work in process inventory	-0- units

Ignore income taxes.

Required:

1 Prepare an income statement using absorption costing.

2 Prepare an income statement using direct costing.

3 Prepare a reconciliation between the two income figures in steps (1) and (2) using the equation presented in the chapter.

4 Calculate the "contribution per unit towards indirect expenses" (assuming all variable costs are direct and all fixed costs are indirect).

P18-4 *Absorption and Direct Costing*

The following data relate to the year ended June 30, 1989 for Patsy Corporation:

	Units
Beginning inventory	30,000
Production	+120,000
Available for sale	150,000
Sales	−110,000
Ending inventory	40,000

	Per unit
Selling price	$5.00
Variable manufacturing cost	1.00
Variable selling cost	2.00
Fixed manufacturing cost	.25

	Total
Total fixed manufacturing costs	$30,000
Total fixed selling costs	65,000

Required:

1 Using the equation in the chapter, calculate the net income difference between direct costing and absorption costing. Ignore income taxes.

2 Prepare for the year ended June 30, 1989 (a) an income statement using direct costing and (b) an income statement using absorption costing. Ignore income taxes. (In computing beginning inventories, use the current year's per unit amounts.)

(AICPA Adapted)

P18-5 *Analysis of Performance Using Direct Costing and Absorption Costing*

The owner of Rising Sales, Inc. is completely flabbergasted at the $310,000 loss reported on the company's statement of income during 1988. During 1987, the company earned a profit of $50,000. With sales volume increasing by 10 percent (from 100,000 to 110,000 units) in 1988, the owner expected earnings to increase. Comparative information for the two years, including statements of income (income taxes ignored), show:

	1987	1988
Sales volume in units	100,000	110,000
Sales price per unit	$ 5	$ 5
Variable manufacturing cost per unit	$ 1	$ 1
Fixed manufacturing overhead costs	$400,000	$400,000
Selling, general, administrative costs (all fixed)	$150,000	$150,000
Beginning inventory in units	-0-	100,000
Units produced	200,000	10,000
Ending inventory in units	100,000	-0-

Rising Sales, Inc.
Statement of Income
For the years ended December 31

	1987		1988	
Sales		$500,000		$550,000
Cost of Goods Sold:				
Beginning Inventory	$ -0-		$300,000	
Cost of Goods				
Manufactured	600,000 (A)		410,000 (C)	
Cost of Goods				
Available for Sale	$600,000		$710,000	
Ending Inventory	300,000 (B)		-0-	
Cost of Goods Sold		300,000		710,000
Gross Profit		$200,000		($160,000)
Less Selling, General, and				
Administrative Expenses		150,000		150,000
Net Income (Loss)		$ 50,000		($310,000)

(A) $600,000 = $200,000 variable manufacturing costs + $400,000 fixed manufacturing overhead cost
(B) $300,000 = 100,000 units × $3 full manufacturing cost per unit ($1 variable + $2 fixed)
(C) $410,000 = $10,000 variable manufacturing costs + $400,000 fixed manufacturing overhead cost

Required:

1 Explain to the owner of Rising Sales why the $50,000 profit in 1987 became a $310,000 loss in 1988. (Remember sales volume increased; selling price per unit and variable costs per unit were unchanged; total fixed manufacturing overhead cost and total selling, general, and administrative costs were unchanged.)
2 Prepare income statements for 1987 and 1988 using direct costing. Ignore income taxes.

P18-6 *Contribution Toward Indirect Expenses*

Prestomatic Corporation's top management is analyzing the past year's results of operations for their several sales territories. In particular, they are seriously considering discontinuing operations in the Northern and Western sales territories. Considering quantitative factors only, and ignoring income taxes, complete the requirements listed below.

Prestomatic Corporation
Statement of Income
For the Year Ended August 31, 1988

	Total	Eastern territory	Southern territory	Northern territory	Western territory
Sales	$348,000	$120,000	$90,000	$90,000	$48,000
Cost of Goods Sold	298,000	88,000	68,000	96,000	46,000
Gross Profit	$ 50,000	$ 32,000	$22,000	($ 6,000)	$ 2,000
Other Expenses	40,000	14,000	8,000	6,000	12,000
Net Income (Loss)	$ 10,000	$ 18,000	$14,000	($12,000)	($10,000)

Indirect costs included above:

		Eastern	Southern	Northern	Western
Cost of goods sold		$22,000	$18,000	$18,000	$7,000
Other expenses		4,000	3,000	2,000	1,000

Required:

1 Calculate the "contribution toward indirect expenses" for both the Northern Territory and the Western Territory. Determine if they should be discontinued. Calculate the effect on total company income if each was discontinued.

2 Prepare a statement of income for Prestomatic using a format that will: (a) show the contribution toward indirect expenses for each sales territory, but (b) not allocate indirect costs among sales territories (i.e., indirect cost amounts are listed only for the company as a total).

P18-7 *Analysis of Product Line Changes*

The officers of Bradshaw Company are reviewing the profitability of the company's products and considering possible changes in products R and Q. Selected information shows:

	Product R	Product Q
Sales	$12,600	$18,000
Cost of Goods Sold	13,968	7,056
Gross Profit	($ 1,368)	$10,944
Other Expenses	2,826	2,976
Net Income (Loss)	($ 4,194)	$ 7,968
Units sold	1,800	1,200
Sales price per unit	$ 7.00	$ 15.00
Direct cost of manufacturing per unit	6.50	3.00
Direct selling and administrative cost per unit	1.00	1.25

Ignore income taxes, and consider each case below separately.

Required:

1 If product R is discontinued, determine the effect on total firm income.

2 If the sales price of product R is increased to $8 with a decrease in the number of units sold to 1,500, determine product R's contribution toward indirect expenses.

3 If product R is discontinued and a consequent loss of customers causes a decrease of 200 units in sales of product Q, determine the total effect on income.

4 Production of product Q can be doubled by adding a second shift, which requires higher wages for the additional units. The higher wages would increase the direct cost of manufacturing per unit to $4 for each of the additional units only. If the 1,200 additional units can be sold at $15 each, determine the effect on income of running the second shift.

(AICPA Adapted)

P18-8 *Rate of Return Analysis*

The balance sheet of Hassler, Inc. at December 31, 1989 shows the following:

Current assets	$100,000
Fixed assets	700,000
Current liabilities	40,000
Long-term liabilities	360,000
Stockholders' equity	400,000

The statement of income for the year ended December 31, 1989 shows sales of $1,000,000 and net income of $100,000.

Required:

1 Determine the rate of return in terms of the two components of profit margin and asset turnover.

2 Management is considering several actions to improve its performance. Determine the effect on rate of return of each of the following (consider each independently and ignore taxes):

    a A price increase on the company's product: sales revenues would be expected to increase by 20 percent, and total expenses would be unchanged.

    b A cost reduction program: total expenses would decrease by $50,000.

    c The price increase and cost reduction program combined.

    d Disposal of vacant land with a book value of $70,000. Assume that $20,000 of cash would be received.

    e Build a new warehouse, at a cost of $400,000 (all financed by borrowing), so as to be able to serve a new territory. Sales would be expected to increase by $400,000, and total expenses by $360,000.

P18-9 *Rate of Return and Performance Evaluation*

Respond, Inc. is attempting to initiate a system of measuring the performance of their divisional managers. They have elected to include among their evaluating tools a divisional rate of return on asset investment. The rate-of-return calculation for Respond is designed to include only items controllable at the individual divisional level. Thus, for purposes of calculating divisional rate of return on asset investment, both profit and asset investment are to include only items controlled at the divisional level.

Information available for two of Respond's five divisions is presented below. Twenty percent and 30 percent respectively of division X and division Y's cost of goods sold represents depreciation on factory machinery (straight line depreciation, 10-year life, no salvage value). Factory machinery is purchased by corporate headquarters, who assigns it to the divisions. The divisions have no control over the investment in machinery. Factory rent of $200,000 and $250,000 respectively is included in division X and division Y's cost of goods sold. Corporate headquarters negotiated the rental agreement and pays the rent when due. The total corporate rent cost of $1,800,000 is allocated among the divisions based on square footage of space assigned to each division by corporate headquarters. The corporate headquarters' $200,000 annual advertising expenditure is allocated evenly among the five divisions. Each division also is permitted to advertise on its own. Each division is charged 10 percent of its sales as an administrative expense by corporate headquarters.

Corporate headquarters' cash is allocated among the divisions, and interest at the rate of 5 percent is charged to each division by corporate headquarters based on the cash allocated to that division. The principal amount of cash charged to each division is unchanged during the year. In addition, corporate headquarters' property is allocated among the divisions. $100,000 and $130,000 of the cost of corporate headquarters' property has been allocated to division X and division Y's asset investment respectively. Other than indicated above, all revenues, expenses, and investment in assets are controllable at the division level.

	Division X	Division Y
Total asset investment (including factory machinery and corporate headquarters' cash and property which is noncontrollable at the divisional level)	$10,200,000	$12,950,000
Sales	1,500,000	1,800,000
Cost of goods sold	700,000	900,000
Advertising expense	85,000	40,000
Administrative expense	170,000	200,000
Sales salaries expense	205,000	170,000
Interest expense	10,000	6,000
Miscellaneous expense	20,000	30,000

Required:
Ignoring income taxes and assuming inventories are unchanged during the year, calculate for both divisions their rate of return on asset investment, including only controllable items in both profit and asset investment.

Business Decision Problem

Mendel Department Store uses a responsibility accounting system to evaluate supervisors and as a basis for computing bonuses. The following information is available for the toy department for the past two years:

	1987	1988
Sales	$1,200,000	$1,440,000
Cost of goods sold	794,000	974,000
Gross profit	$ 406,000	$ 466,000
Other expenses:		
Administrative	$ 20,000	$ 30,000
Depreciation—building	80,000	140,000
Salespersons' salaries	121,000	150,000
Supplies	5,000	6,000
Total other expenses	$ 226,000	$ 326,000
Income before income tax	$ 180,000	$ 140,000
Supervisor's bonus: 10 percent of income before income tax	$ 18,000	$ 14,000

Each department supervisor has complete control over all purchasing and sales-related activities. Store space is allocated by top management. There was no change in this allocation during the year, although the store's controller switched from straight line depreciation to sum of the years digits depreciation. Administrative costs are incurred at the store level and allocated equally to all departments. As supervisor of the toy department, would you be happy with your 1988 bonus? Why?

19

SHORT-TERM
DECISION ANALYSIS

LEARNING OBJECTIVES

When you complete this chapter, you should be able to:

1 Describe and apply the fixed and variable cost concepts.

2 Calculate contribution margin in both dollar and percentage terms.

3 Apply cost-volume-profit analysis by both graphic and formula methods.

4 Distinguish relevant and irrelevant items in the context of incremental analysis.

5 Describe and apply the concept of opportunity cost.

6 Apply incremental analysis to nonroutine decision problems.

As a member of management, you might face questions such as:

1 What will happen if we increase our product's selling price by 10 percent?

2 Should we increase our advertising budget by $2,000,000 if, as a result, sales would increase by 180,000 units?

3 Should we expand to new markets?

4 Should we purchase a new machine that will replace three production workers?

These are a sample of the many questions that management must answer when planning for the future.

The preparation of detailed budgets, discussed previously, assists management in planning for the future. In this chapter, other aids to decision making are discussed. Specifically, cost-volume-profit analysis and incremental analysis are presented as short-run, quantitative tools for projecting the outcomes of contemplated actions such as the four listed above. Chapter 20 will cover the use of discounted cash flow analysis as a tool for long-run decision making.

COST-VOLUME-PROFIT (CVP) ANALYSIS

In many decision problems, the manager's concern is with profits. For example, increased advertising expenditures must be translated into the effect on profit of (1) the additional advertising costs, (2) the additional revenue from increased sales, and (3) the additional production costs incurred in making more units of product. The relationships among costs, volume, and profit are crucial to this analysis.

Cost Behavior

Costs can be defined and classified in a number of ways, depending on the purpose for which the cost data are used. For cost-volume-profit analysis, all costs are considered—whether direct or indirect, manufacturing or nonmanufacturing, product or period. The critical distinction is *fixed versus variable* costs.

Recall that a cost item is defined as fixed if we assume that the total amount of the cost does not change when the level of activity varies. This definition is usually qualified as applying only in the short run and only within some limited relevant range of activity. Examples of fixed costs include rent expense, depreciation expense, and property taxes.

If the total cost of an item is assumed to change proportionately as the level of activity changes, it is called a variable cost. The assumption that variable costs are exactly proportional to volume is a simplification. For example, within some normal ordering range, a firm can expect material prices per unit to remain constant. If orders increase drastically, the material may be in short supply, and the per unit cost may increase; or alternatively, the per unit cost may decrease because of quantity discounts on the larger orders. While total costs would vary with volume in each case, the relationship would not be exactly proportional. Nonetheless, the assumption that variable costs are proportional to volume is generally reasonable and in most cases gives a good approximation of the actual relationship of cost to volume.

Contribution Margin

The concept of a contribution margin is essential in cost-volume-profit analysis and in other areas of managerial accounting. The *contribution margin* is defined as the difference between selling price and variable cost. For example, assume the Banner Corporation has classified all its costs into fixed and variable categories as follows:

Fixed costs (per month):	
Manufacturing	$56,292
Selling	18,300
Administrative	24,000
Total	$98,592
Variable costs (per unit):	
Manufacturing	$ 26.90
Selling	14.50
Administrative	3.00
Total	$ 44.40

Banner sells its product for $60 per unit. The contribution margin may be expressed in dollars or percent:

	Dollars	Percent
Selling price	$60.00	100.0%
Variable cost	− 44.40	− 74.0
Contribution margin	$15.60	26.0%

These figures may be interpreted as follows. Each unit that is sold brings the company $60.00 in revenue and costs $44.40 in variable manufacturing, selling, and administrative expenses. For each unit sold, $15.60 is available toward meeting the monthly fixed costs of $98,592 and toward providing a profit. On a percentage basis, from each dollar of revenue, 74 percent goes to cover variable costs and 26 percent is available to cover fixed costs and provide profit. Thus, we say that Banner has a contribution margin of $15.60 per unit, or 26 percent.

CVP Analysis—Graphic Solution

Cost-volume-profit analysis is well suited to graphic presentation. Assume that the management of Razorby Co. is trying to determine what sales level (in units and in sales dollars) must be obtained next month to earn $150,000 profit. Analysis of last month's operations reveals that 10,000 units were sold at $60 each, variable cost per unit was $25, and total fixed costs were $300,000. Razorby operates in a competitive market and management anticipates no change in unit selling price during the coming month. Variable costs are expected to increase by $5 per unit due to higher costs for raw materials and labor, but fixed costs are expected to remain at $300,000.

A cost-volume-profit graph shows quantity on the horizontal axis and dollar amounts of costs and revenue on the vertical axis. To construct a graph that will visually indicate the sales volume necessary to earn the desired $150,000 income, the following steps are needed:

1 Plot quantity (in units) along the horizontal axis of the graph and draw a 45 degree diagonal line sloping upward from the origin, as shown in Figure 19-1. Label it the sales revenue line. Sales revenue is directly proportional to the number of units sold. While this relationship can be expressed with lines drawn at

FIGURE 19-1

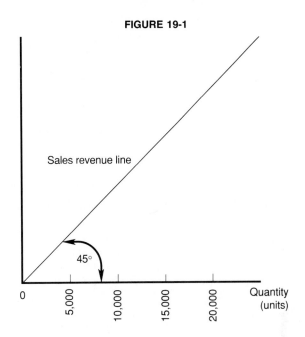

angles other than 45 degrees, this graphical construction facilitates the CVP analysis.

2 Plot total sales dollar amounts on the vertical axis, corresponding to the quantities on the horizontal axis, as shown in Figure 19-2. For the Razorby example, the total sales dollar amounts are determined by multiplying each quantity by the unit sales price of $60. This gives:

FIGURE 19-2

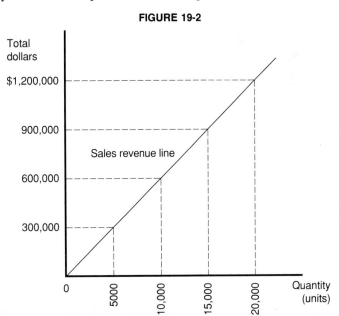

Quantity	×	Selling price per unit	=	Total sales revenue
5,000	×	$60	=	$ 300,000
10,000	×	60	=	600,000
15,000	×	60	=	900,000
20,000	×	60	=	1,200,000

3 Plot (a) the variable cost line and (b) the total cost line (which combines both variable and fixed costs). For the Razorby example, the variable cost amounts are determined by multiplying each quantity by the unit variable cost of $30. The total cost line is then determined by adding the $300,000 fixed cost to the variable costs for each volume level. This gives the following:

Quantity	Variable costs	+	Fixed costs	=	Total costs
5,000	$150,000		$300,000		$450,000
10,000	300,000		300,000		600,000
15,000	450,000		300,000		750,000
20,000	600,000		300,000		900,000

The cost-volume-profit graph drawn in Figure 19-3 is based on the assumption that the relevant range for Razorby is 2,000 to 21,000 units. The relationships are assumed to be valid only within this range.

Analyzing a CVP Graph

The graph shown in Exhibit 19-1 is identical to Figure 19-3 except that areas have been labeled. The area below the variable cost line equals the total variable cost for each quantity. This area increases proportionately as volume increases. The area between the total cost line and the variable cost line represents fixed

FIGURE 19-3

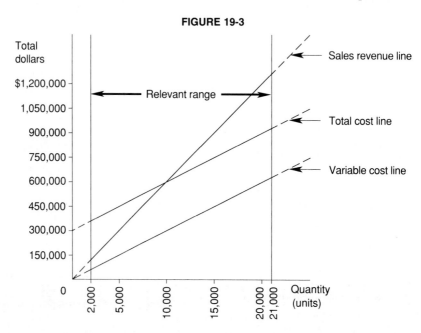

EXHIBIT 19-1
Razorby Co.
Projected Cost-Volume-Profit (CVP) Graph

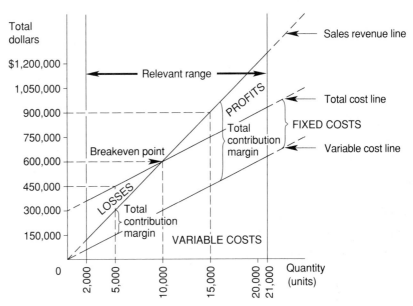

costs. Notice that the distance separating these two lines remains at a constant amount ($300,000) as volume increases.

For each item sold, Razorby's contribution margin is $30 ($60 selling price less $30 variable cost). In Exhibit 19-1, the contribution margin in total dollars (the area between the sales revenue line and the variable cost line) increases at a constant rate of $30 per unit as volume increases.

Profit or loss for any particular volume level can be read directly from the graph. The profit or loss is indicated by the distance between the sales revenue line and the total cost line at the particular volume level selected. To the left of the 10,000 unit volume level, total costs exceed sales revenue; this area is marked "losses" in the exhibit. To the right of the 10,000 unit volume level, "profits" are indicated since sales revenue exceeds total costs.

Razorby was attempting to determine the sales level needed to earn a $150,000 profit. To find the answer using the graph in Exhibit 19-1, find the quantity on the horizontal axis where the distance between the sales revenue line and the total cost line measures $150,000 on the vertical axis. This distance should be found at 15,000 units. The solution is proven by:

Sales (15,000 units at $60)	$900,000
Less:	
Variable costs (15,000 units at $30)	(450,000)
Fixed costs	(300,000)
Net income	$150,000

What would happen if sales volume next month dropped to 5,000 units?

Exhibit 19-1 indicates a loss of $150,000 ($450,000 total cost versus $300,000 sales revenue) at 5,000 units. Does this mean that Razorby should discontinue operations if only 5,000 units can be sold? Examining Exhibit 19-1 again, we see that at the 5,000 unit level there is a positive contribution margin of $150,000 ($300,000 sales revenue minus $150,000 variable costs). This amount contributes toward meeting the $300,000 of fixed costs. It is reasonable to assume that most, if not all, fixed costs would continue despite a temporary plant closing. If this is true, Razorby would have a $300,000 loss if the plant is closed, but only a $150,000 loss if the plant operates at the 5,000 unit level.

Finally, examine Exhibit 19-1 to determine Razorby's *breakeven point*—where the firm earns no profits and incurs no losses. For Razorby, the breakeven point is sales of $600,000, or 10,000 units. At that level, sales revenue of $600,000 equals total costs of $600,000, and profit is zero. Management is interested in the breakeven point because it represents the minimum level of sales that must be maintained to avoid losses.

CVP Equation with Unit Data

Graphic analysis of cost-volume-profit relationships may be cumbersome. A formula approach is often preferred. We begin with the basic revenue-cost-profit relationship:

$$\text{Sales Revenue} - \text{Variable Costs} - \text{Fixed Costs} = \text{Profit}$$

For convenience, let:

$$S = \text{selling price per unit}$$
$$V = \text{variable cost per unit}$$
$$F = \text{fixed costs for the period}$$
$$Q = \text{quantity produced and sold during the period}$$
$$NI = \text{net income}$$

Using these symbols, the revenue-cost-profit relationship is expressed as:

$$SQ - VQ - F = NI$$

To find the number of units that must be sold to achieve a stated net income, solve the equation for Q:

$$Q = (F + NI) \div (S - V)$$

Since $(S - V)$, selling price per unit less variable cost per unit, equals the contribution margin per unit (denoted CM($)), the cost-volume-profit equation can be written as:

$$Q = (F + NI) \div CM(\$)$$

Expressed in words, this equation says that the sales in units needed to reach the desired net income equals total fixed costs plus the desired net income, divided by the contribution margin in dollars per unit.

In the Razorby example earlier, we had

$$S = \$60$$
$$V = \$30$$
$$CM(\$) = S - V = \$30$$
$$F = \$300,000$$
$$NI = \$150,000$$

Using the above formula, we get:

$$Q = (F + NI) \div CM(\$)$$
$$= (\$300,000 + \$150,000) \div \$30$$
$$= 15,000 \text{ units}$$

which is the same result produced by the graphic analysis.

To solve for Razorby's breakeven point, we use NI = \$0 in the formula. We get:

$$Q = (F + NI) \div CM(\$)$$
$$= (\$300,000 + \$0) \div \$30$$
$$= 10,000 \text{ units}$$

The cost-volume-profit equation can be adapted to solve for any component of the equation, so long as the remaining components are known. For example, consider each of the following situations for Razorby Co.:

1 What would Razorby's net income be next month if fixed costs increase to \$350,000, sales are 15,000 units, selling price is \$60 per unit, and variable cost is \$30 per unit? Solution:

$$Q = (F + NI) \div CM(\$)$$
$$15,000 = (\$350,000 + NI) \div \$30$$
$$\$450,000 = \$350,000 + NI$$
$$\$100,000 = NI$$

2 What would the unit selling price have to be next month if fixed costs increase to \$400,000, 15,000 units are sold, variable cost per unit is \$30, and Razorby desires a net income of \$200,000? Solution:

$$Q = (F + NI) \div (S - V)$$
$$15,000 = (\$400,000 + \$200,000) \div (S - \$30)$$
$$15,000 \ S - \$450,000 = \$600,000$$
$$15,000S = \$1,050,000$$
$$S = \$70$$

3 What variable cost per unit must be achieved next month to earn $160,000 net income if 18,000 units will be sold, the unit selling price is $60, and fixed costs are $560,000? Solution:

$$Q = (F + NI) \div (S - V)$$
$$18,000 = (\$560,000 + \$160,000) \div (\$60 - V)$$
$$\$1,080,000 - 18,000V = \$720,000$$
$$-18,000V = -\$360,000$$
$$V = \$20$$

4 What total fixed cost amount must be maintained next month to earn $160,000 net income if 18,000 units are sold, the unit selling price is $60, and variable cost per unit is $35? Solution:

$$Q = (F + NI) \div CM(\$)$$
$$18,000 = (F + \$160,000) \div (\$60 - \$35)$$
$$\$450,000 = F + \$160,000$$
$$\$290,000 = F$$

CVP Equation with Total Revenue Data

When per unit data are known, the total sales revenue, total variable cost, and total contribution margin can be found by multiplying the respective per unit data by Q (the quantity to be produced and sold during the period). In some CVP problems, per unit data are not available. In these cases, variable costs and contribution margin are typically expressed as a percentage of sales. Often the information requested is the total sales revenue needed to achieve a specified profit. To formulate the problem in terms of dollars rather than units, use the following notations:

$$SQ = \text{sales revenue desired}$$
$$CM(\%) = \text{contribution margin expressed as a percentage of sales}$$
$$\text{(this equals } (S - V) \div S)$$
$$VC(\%) = \text{variable costs expressed as a percentage of sales (this}$$
$$\text{equals } V \div S)$$

The cost-volume-profit equation is now expressed as:

$$SQ = (F + NI) \div CM(\%)$$

For example, assume the following information for Gyro Company for the past month:

Sales	$1,000,000
Variable costs	600,000
Fixed costs	300,000
Net income	100,000

Variable cost as a percentage of sales [VC(%)] is 60 percent ($600,000 ÷ $1,000,000). The contribution margin in total dollars is $400,000 ($1,000,000 minus $600,000). Expressed as a percentage of sales [CM(%)], the contribution margin is 40 percent ($400,000 ÷ $1,000,000). If Gyro's management predicts that fixed costs will increase to $360,000 next month while the variable cost percentage remains unchanged, the sales revenue needed to earn $120,000 net income is:

$$SQ = (F + NI) \div CM(\%)$$
$$= (\$360,000 + \$120,000) \div 40\%$$
$$= \$1,200,000$$

This is verified by:

Sales revenue	$1,200,000
Variable costs	
(60% × $1,200,000)	(720,000)
Contribution margin (40% × $1,200,000)	$ 480,000
Fixed costs	(360,000)
Net income	$ 120,000

As was illustrated earlier, variations of the formula can be used to solve a variety of problems.

Margin of Safety

An important consideration for management, both in analyzing current operations and in evaluating possible future actions, is the amount by which sales can decline before losses are incurred. This measure is called the *margin of safety*. In absolute dollar terms, the margin of safety is the difference between the current sales level and the breakeven level:

$$\text{Margin of Safety (dollars)} = \text{Current Sales} - \text{Breakeven Sales}$$

The margin of safety can also be expressed as a percentage, indicating the percent that sales can decline before losses occur. The margin of safety percentage is expressed as:

$$\text{Margin of Safety Percentage} = \frac{\text{Current Sales} - \text{Breakeven Sales}}{\text{Current Sales}}$$

For example, assume that current sales are $5,500,000 and that breakeven sales are $4,400,000. We calculate:

$$\text{Margin of Safety Percentage} = \frac{\$5,500,000 - \$4,400,000}{\$5,500,000}$$
$$= 20\%$$

Sales revenue can decrease by $1,100,000, or 20 percent, from current levels before losses will be incurred.

Limitations of CVP Analysis

Cost-volume-profit analysis is a convenient tool for analyzing decision problems. When using this tool, its limitations should be kept in mind. CVP analysis is based on a number of simplifying assumptions that facilitate the analysis, but may result in distortions of reality. The user must evaluate the extent to which the CVP analysis adequately reflects real business conditions.

One important assumption underlying CVP analysis is that all costs may be classified as either fixed or variable. In reality, costs cannot be so easily classified, nor do they behave in exact patterns. Factors such as start-up costs, overtime, and economies of scale influence the true behavior of costs. It may, however, be difficult and expensive to develop cost estimates that take proper account of these factors.

CVP analysis also assumes that the selling price remains constant. In reality, price reductions may be necessary to achieve increased sales volume, and factors such as discounts and bad debts may reduce the true selling price.

In CVP analysis, changes in inventory levels are ignored; formulas are based on the assumption that the quantity produced equals the quantity sold. In reality, firms build up or deplete inventories. Despite these limitations, we often conclude that, within the relevant range, the approximations made by CVP analysis are reasonable. Moreover, the additional costs involved in obtaining more realistic data may far exceed the benefit gained.

INCREMENTAL ANALYSIS

Cost-volume-profit analysis is one of several techniques available to aid management in planning future operations. Another quantitative decision-making tool is *incremental analysis*. One distinguishing factor between the two techniques is that cost-volume-profit analysis is geared towards examining *recurring, routine operations,* while incremental analysis is designed to aid management in making *special, nonroutine decisions* such as entering a new sales territory. Through incremental analysis, the expected revenue and cost differentials for possible alternative solutions to a particular problem are determined and compared.

Understanding incremental analysis requires familiarity with several additional cost concepts. Before examining three specific incremental analysis situations (special order, make or buy, and equipment replacement), some terminology that is encountered frequently in problems of this type is introduced.

Relevant versus Irrelevant Costs and Revenues

In an effort to achieve a desired objective, often management must select one strategy from a number of possible alternative courses of action. Management needs expected cost and/or revenue data for all alternatives under consideration to make the correct decision. *Relevant items* are current or future revenues or expenses that are expected to *differ* among the alternatives being considered. Relevant revenues and costs are often referred to as *incremental* or *differential* revenues and costs. *Irrelevant items,* on the other hand, are current or future revenues or expenses that are *not expected to differ* among the alternatives being considered. Some accountants elect to show irrelevant items as part of their incremental analysis. In instances where irrelevant items are included in the formal analysis presented to management, they should be properly identified as irrelevant (or common to all alternatives). It should also be made clear that the irrelevant items could have been omitted from the presentation without affecting the relative desirability of the alternatives under consideration.

Consider the problem facing Cordair Manufacturing Co. The company is trying to decide whether to provide free delivery service to customers on all units sold. Incremental analysis based on projected production and sales of 20,000 units, including irrelevant and relevant items, shows:

Cordair Manufacturing Co.
Incremental Analysis to Determine Effects of
Free Delivery Policy on Income before Taxes
at 20,000 Unit Volume Level

	Cordair pays for delivery	Customer pays for delivery	Difference
Irrelevant items:			
Sales ($18 × 20,000)	$360,000	$360,000	$ -0-
Manufacturing cost $11 × 20,000	$220,000	$220,000	$ -0-
Administrative expenses	40,000	40,000	-0-
Relevant item:			
Delivery cost	20,000	-0-	20,000
	$280,000	$260,000	$20,000
Income before taxes	$ 80,000	$100,000	($20,000)

This simple illustration serves to differentiate between relevant items and irrelevant items. The relevant item is the expected $20,000 delivery cost—the item that differs between the two alternatives. It was assumed that expected sales revenue, manufacturing costs, and administrative expenses would be identical for both alternatives; they are, therefore, irrelevant to the decision. In this case, the expected irrelevant items are shown in the analysis. Notice, however, that they have been clearly labeled as irrelevant and do not affect the projected income difference between the two alternatives. If the irrelevant items had been excluded from the analysis, the projected income differential between the two alternatives would have remained at $20,000. If it were assumed that free delivery would result in increased sales, then additional items—sales revenue and manufacturing cost—would become relevant.

Sunk Cost

A *sunk cost* represents an expenditure that has been made in the past; it cannot be changed. If we ignore tax effects, a sunk cost will not affect any subsequent decisions and thus is an irrelevant cost in decision analysis. For example, assume

Halpern Quarry Co. is considering either (1) using some of its excess land as a site for constructing a new office building or (2) purchasing additional land to serve as the site for the office building. The company believes the excess land it currently owns, and is considering using for the office building site, has no other use and little or no resale value. All features of the two sites are assumed identical except as indicated below:

Original cost of owned land	$110,000
Cost to prepare owned land for construction of an office building	30,000
Cost to purchase additional land	120,000
Cost to prepare additional land for construction of an office building	5,000

What are the relevant costs of each of the two alternatives? The total relevant cost of purchasing and preparing additional land is $125,000 ($120,000 cost to purchase additional land plus $5,000 to prepare it for construction). The total relevant cost of using the land currently owned is $30,000. The $110,000 original cost of this property is an irrelevant sunk cost. The $110,000 expenditure has already been made. Regardless of which alternative course of action is selected now, the $110,000 previous expenditure is unchanged. [1]

Presented below is the incremental analysis concerning Halpern's office building site. Again, both relevant and irrelevant costs have been shown. Note, however, that using the property currently owned is preferable by $95,000, whether or not the irrelevant sunk cost is included in the analysis.

Halpern Quarry Co.
Analysis for Choice of Office Building Site

	Purchase additional land	Use land currently owned	Difference
Relevant costs:			
Purchase additional land	$120,000	$ -0-	$120,000
Prepare land for use as site for office building	5,000	30,000	(25,000)
Total relevant costs	$125,000	$ 30,000	$ 95,000
Irrelevant cost:			
Sunk cost—original cost of owned land	110,000	110,000	-0-
Total costs	$235,000	$140,000	$ 95,000

Opportunity Cost

An opportunity cost is not a "cost" in the usual sense of the word. That is, it does not reflect an outlay of resources. Rather, *opportunity cost* refers to the value that is lost by using a resource for one purpose rather than for its best alternative

[1] Recall in this example we are assuming that the excess land has no alternative use and that the potential proceeds from sale of the land are immaterial. Income taxes also are ignored.

purpose. Although not usually a part of the formal accounting records, and thus not always readily apparent, opportunity costs must be carefully analyzed and included in any comparison of alternatives.

Reconsider the previous Halpern Quarry Co. example. We originally assumed that the excess land currently owned had no alternative use other than as a building site and had little or no market value. Now assume that the excess property was believed to contain iron ore worth $180,000. The net value of the ore deposits (after deducting an estimated $80,000 for mining, processing, selling and delivery costs) is $100,000. Also assume the land (with the ore deposits) could be sold for an estimated $130,000.

If we ignore income taxes, is the original choice to use this property as the office building site still the correct decision? The modified analysis would show:

Halpern Quarry Co.
Modified Analysis for Choice of Office Building Site

	Purchase additional land	Use land currently owned	Difference
Relevant costs:			
Purchase additional land	$120,000	$ -0-	$120,000
Prepare land for use as site for			
office building	5,000	30,000	(25,000)
Opportunity cost—forgone pro-			
ceeds from sale of owned land	-0-	130,000	(130,000)
Total relevant costs	$125,000	$160,000	($ 35,000)
Irrelevant costs:			
Sunk cost—original cost of owned			
property	110,000	110,000	-0-
Total costs	$235,000	$270,000	($ 35,000)

The analysis now indicates that purchasing additional land is the preferable alternative, resulting in a $35,000 cost savings.

Note in particular the inclusion of the opportunity cost—the best alternative use forgone (the $130,000 sales proceeds of the owned land)—as a relevant cost in the "use land currently owned" column. An acceptable alternative would have been to show the $130,000 opportunity cost as a deduction (cash receipt) in the "purchase additional land" column. The other alternative use of the owned property, the $100,000 net value of extracting the iron ore deposits, is not included in the formal analysis since it is not the *best* alternative use of the property.

NONROUTINE DECISIONS

From time to time, many companies face one or more of the following problems: whether to accept a special order, whether to make or buy a production component, and whether to replace equipment. In each case, incremental analysis is an aid to the managers' decision-making process. The next sections discuss and illustrate each case.

The Special Order

Companies are occasionally confronted with the opportunity for an additional, special sales order at a price less than their normal selling price. For example, Mendenow Co. has been approached by a potential customer in another part of the country. The potential customer offers to buy 10,000 units of Mendenow's product at $6 per unit. Mendenow's regular sales price is $8.50 per unit, and the company has computed its cost per unit at $6.25. Would you accept the customer's offer? Would you accept a $6 sales price per unit when you have computed a $6.25 cost per unit?

The answer is not as obvious as it may seem. Recall the previous discussions on relevant versus irrelevant costs. Assume the $6.25 cost per unit was computed by management in the following way:

Variable cost per unit:	
Manufacturing	$4.00
Selling	.60
Administrative and general	.22
Total variable cost per unit	$4.82
Fixed costs per unit based on normal,	
expected volume of 100,000 units	
(excluding 10,000 units special order):	
Manufacturing ($88,000 ÷ 100,000)	.88
Selling ($44,000 ÷ 100,000)	.44
Administrative and general	
($11,000 ÷ 100,000)	.11
Total cost per unit	$6.25

If the special order is accepted, management expects the following cost changes:

1 Decrease in variable manufacturing costs of $.02 per unit (on additional 10,000 units only), resulting from purchasing raw materials in larger quantities and thus taking advantage of quantity discounts.

2 Increase of $4,000 in fixed selling costs due to sales commission on special order.

With the information above, should management accept the special order? Isolating only relevant, incremental items, the analysis would appear as:

Mendenow Co.
Special Sales Order Analysis—Relevant Items Only

Sales price per unit for special order	$ 6.00
Less variable cost per unit for special order	4.80
Contribution margin per unit for special order	$ 1.20
Units involved in special order	× 10,000
Dollar contribution margin for special order	$12,000
Less additional fixed selling cost for special order	4,000
Increase in pre-tax income from special order	$ 8,000

Based on this analysis, the special order is an attractive opportunity. Note that the regular $8.50 sales price per unit and the variable and fixed costs projected for the 100,000 normal volume level are irrelevant and were ignored in the analysis. Only incremental revenues and costs associated with the special order are relevant. An alternative presentation of the solution, including relevant and irrelevant items, is presented below. The alternative solution provides complete income statements, both with and without the special order. The final answer, however, is the same as previously indicated—accept the special offer because an $8,000 increase in pre-tax income is expected.

Mendenow Co.
Projected Income Statement

	With special order	Without special order	Difference
Sales:			
100,000 × $8.50	$850,000	$850,000	$ -0-
10,000 × $6.00	60,000	-0-	60,000
Total sales revenue	$910,000	$850,000	$60,000
Variable expenses:			
100,000 × $4.82	$482,000	$482,000	$ -0-
10,000 × $4.80	48,000	-0-	48,000
Fixed expenses:			
Manufacturing	88,000	88,000	-0-
Selling	48,000	44,000	4,000
Administrative and general	11,000	11,000	-0-
Total expenses	$677,000	$625,000	$52,000
Income before taxes	$233,000	$225,000	$ 8,000

In this example, note that when volume increased, variable costs did not increase proportionately and one of the fixed costs increased. The usual assumptions that total variable costs vary proportionately with volume changes and that fixed costs remain constant did not hold. Thus, it is dangerous to assume automatically that all variable costs are relevant and all fixed costs irrelevant for incremental analysis.

In real life, there are often a number of other considerations applicable to the special-order decision. For instance, the company must consider whether selling at a reduced price will damage the company's regular sales. If regular customers learn of the special price, they may demand price reductions. Another concern is whether the provisions of the Robinson–Patman Act would be violated. This law forbids selling at different prices to different customers, unless justified by varying costs associated with serving the different customer groups.

Make-or-Buy Decisions

Some companies produce a product by assembling a number of components into a finished unit. Often the company manufactures some of the components itself, while purchasing other components from outside suppliers. When faced with excess production capacity, a company may decide it would be more advantageous to start manufacturing some components that previously the company had purchased. The quantitative factors affecting a make-or-buy decision are considered in the following example.

All-Wet Manufacturing Co., a manufacturer of weather forecasting instruments, has excess capacity. There is unused space and equipment available. Also, the direct labor force, which is paid by the hour, is not working a full 40-hour week. The management of All-Wet Manufacturing is considering the use of excess capacity and available labor to manufacture hydrometer components. In the past, the hydrometer components were always purchased from an outside supplier for $185 each. Management calculates the following expected annual manufacturing costs to produce the 20,000 components needed:

Cost to Manufacture 20,000 Hydrometer Components

	Per unit	Total
Direct materials (sub-components)	$ 70	$1,400,000
Direct labor	40	800,000
Variable manufacturing overhead (150% of direct labor cost)	60	1,200,000
Fixed manufacturing overhead applied (75% of direct labor cost)	30	600,000
	$200	$4,000,000

Should the company continue to purchase components from the outside supplier at $185 each, or should it manufacture the components at a unit cost of $200? By now you should realize that the correct answer is not determinable based on the information as presented. Some elements of the $200 unit cost may not be relevant. What is needed are the incremental costs that are projected to occur if the hydrometer components are produced by All-Wet Manufacturing. In management's calculations above, assume projected direct materials, direct labor, and variable manufacturing overhead are relevant, *incremental* costs associated with manufacturing the hydrometer components. Next, consider the *applied* fixed manufacturing overhead. The rate of $30 per unit was computed by management at the beginning of the year based on budgeted fixed manufacturing overhead and budgeted direct labor cost. The rate of $30 per unit is irrelevant for the particular decision currently facing management. What is relevant is the incremental fixed cost expenditure, if any, expected to be incurred by All-Wet Manufacturing if the decision is made to manufacture rather than to buy the hydrometer components.

If total fixed manufacturing costs are expected to increase by only $200,000 (not the $600,000 indicated by using the predetermined $30 fixed overhead rate), the make-or-buy incremental analysis in per unit and total cost terms is:

All-Wet Manufacturing Co.
Make-or-Buy Analysis
For Next Year

Relevant Costs for 20,000 Hydrometer Components

	Per unit		Total cost	
	Make	**Buy**	**Make**	**Buy**
Direct materials	$ 70	$ -0-	$1,400,000	$ -0-
Direct labor	40	-0-	800,000	-0-
Variable manufacturing overhead	60	-0-	1,200,000	-0-
Fixed manufacturing overhead	10	-0-	200,000	-0-
Purchase cost	-0-	185	-0-	3,700,000
	$180	$185	$3,600,000	$3,700,000
		− 180		− 3,600,000
Difference in cost		$ 5		$ 100,000

The quantitative analysis above indicates a $5 per unit (or $100,000 annual total) cost savings realized by making, rather than buying, the components. Before the decision is finalized, some factors that were excluded from the incremental analysis must be addressed. First, the quality of the component is important. Will the internally manufactured hydrometer components be equal, inferior, or superior in quality to the components currently being purchased? Second, consider the company's relationship with the present supplier. The necessity of maintaining a guaranteed, long-run supply of other components from this supplier may nullify the short-run $5 per unit advantage of internally manufacturing the components.

Possible alternative uses for the excess capacity should also be considered. There may be opportunity costs associated with the make-or-buy decision. The make-or-buy analysis is actually an involved process of determining the best use of existing facilities, which in turn requires including opportunity cost considerations in the analysis.

The various elements in a make-or-buy decision are subject to change over time. New alternative opportunities for using excess capacity may arise. Or, if output increases, productive capacity may be fully utilized (i.e., there would be no excess capacity). Internal costs and suppliers' prices are also subject to change over time. Because any of these changes could occur gradually or rapidly, the make-or-buy decision should be re-evaluated periodically.

Equipment Replacement

Management of Padturn Co. is faced with the following dilemma. The sanding machine used in the manufacturing department has broken down. The company does not know whether to pay to repair the broken machine, purchase a new machine, or hire three additional workers to manually perform the sanding job. Regardless of the choice made, the decision will only affect the next year. One year from now the entire sanding operation is scheduled to be contracted out to another company.

Information gathered by Padturn's management about the alternatives indicates:

1 The sanding machine, which is now broken, was purchased two years ago for $60,000. Its life was then estimated at three years with no salvage value. Straight line depreciation is used. Current market value of the machine in its broken state is $4,000. The cost to repair is $36,000.

2 A new sanding machine will cost $50,000 and have a projected salvage value at the end of the year of $12,000.

3 Three additional workers can be hired at a cost of $15,000 for each worker for the year.

4 Regardless of which alternative is chosen, revenues are assumed to be unaffected.

5 Income taxes are ignored, and since all relevant amounts to be paid or received occur within one year, the time value of money (interest) also is ignored. [2]

Based on the above information, and including relevant items only, the incremental analysis of the equipment replacement decision should appear as:

Padturn Co.
Equipment Replacement Analysis—Relevant Items Only

	Repair old broken machine	Sell old machine and purchase new machine	Sell old machine and hire three more workers
Cost to repair old machine	$36,000	$ -0-	$ -0-
Current market value of old machine*	-0-	(4,000)	(4,000)
Net cost of new machine**	-0-	38,000	-0-
Cost of three additional workers	-0-	-0-	45,000
Total relevant costs	$36,000	$34,000	$41,000

*Alternatively the $4,000 could have been presented as an opportunity cost in the "Repair old broken machine" column.
**Purchase cost of $50,000 less $12,000 estimated salvage value.

The incremental analysis indicates that selling the old machine and purchasing a new one is the best alternative (i.e., the $34,000 total relevant cost of the new machine is less than the $36,000 and $41,000 totals associated with the other alternatives).

It is important to understand why the incremental analysis *excludes* three items representing irrelevant, sunk costs:

1 The original cost of the old machine
2 The depreciation on the old machine if the old machine is kept

---

[2]Both of these considerations (income taxes and time value of money) will be discussed in Chapter 20.

3 The $16,000 loss if the old machine is sold ($20,000 book value less $4,000 market price).

The $60,000 original cost of the old machine is an irrelevant, sunk cost because it has already been spent. Regardless of the alternative now chosen, the $60,000 cost cannot be avoided; it does not affect the replacement decision. Similarly, if the old machine is kept for one more year, the $20,000 depreciation on the old machine is irrelevant (ignoring taxes) to the replacement decision. Recording depreciation merely assigns the remaining one-third of the $60,000 sunk cost of the old machine to expense.

If the old machine is sold, the $20,000 book value would be written off immediately. With a market value of only $4,000, a $16,000 loss on disposal would be created. This $16,000 loss, the third item listed above, is equally irrelevant (ignoring taxes) to the replacement decision. The $16,000 loss would merely represent the portion of the $60,000 sunk cost not previously depreciated or recoverable as scrap value. It does not represent a current or future expenditure. Only the $4,000 current market value and $36,000 repair cost are relevant considerations for the old machine. They, along with the expected $38,000 net cost of the new machine and $45,000 incremental labor cost, represent differential, relevant factors for the alternatives being considered.

As with the preceding incremental analysis examples, Padturn probably would consider other factors in making its decision. Many of these factors could prove difficult, if not impossible, to quantify as part of the analysis. For example, will all three alternatives result in equally efficient performance in the sanding operation? Will the projected $12,000 estimated salvage value of the new machine and zero estimated salvage value for the old machine actually be the amounts realized one year from now? Will union contractual agreements permit the discharging of the three additional workers at the end of the year when they are no longer needed? What would happen to morale of the remaining employees, if their three co-workers were discharged? Management must consider these and other factors in reaching a final decision.

SUMMARY

Learning Objective 1: Describe and apply the fixed and variable cost concepts.
   Total fixed costs remain constant over a range of activity levels, while total variable costs change proportionately as activity level changes. These concepts are widely used in managerial accounting.

Learning Objective 2: Calculate contribution margin in both dollar and percentage terms.
   Contribution margin is selling price minus variable costs. This may be expressed in total dollars, dollars per unit of product, or percentage terms. This concept is also widely used in managerial accounting.

Learning Objective 3: Apply cost-volume-profit analysis by both graphic and formula methods.

Cost-volume-profit analysis attempts to determine the expected effects of revenue and costs on profits at various volume levels. The analysis can take the form of either a graphic approach or equation computations. Among the assumptions underlying cost-volume-profit analysis is linear behavior for sales revenue and total costs. While this and other underlying assumptions may be reasonable in many instances, management must be aware that cost-volume-profit analysis involves simplifications of reality.

Learning Objective 4: Distinguish relevant and irrelevant items in the context of incremental analysis.

Incremental analysis attempts to determine expected revenue and cost differentials for possible alternative solutions to a particular nonroutine decision problem. Only incremental current or future revenues and expenditures are relevant to choosing among the alternatives. Sunk costs (expenditures already made) are irrelevant, as is any other item that affects all alternatives equally.

Learning Objective 5: Describe and apply the concept of opportunity cost.

Opportunity cost, the value of the resource if used for the best available alternative, is an important aspect of incremental analysis that is often overlooked. The cost of not pursuing other alternatives must be considered in reaching a decision.

Learning Objective 6: Apply incremental analysis to nonroutine decision problems.

Special order, make-or-buy, and equipment replacement analyses were presented in the chapter as examples of short-run incremental analysis problems. While the presentation of these analyses may make the technique appear relatively simple, the necessity of accurately identifying and quantifying all relevant factors makes incremental analysis a difficult and challenging endeavor.

KEY TERMS

Breakeven point	Make or buy
Contribution margin	Margin of safety
Cost-volume-profit analysis	Opportunity cost
Differential analysis	Relevant items
Fixed cost	Special order
Incremental analysis	Sunk costs
Irrelevant items	Variable cost

REVIEW QUESTIONS

1 Identify the two cost-per-unit graphs on the following page as representing either fixed cost or variable cost behavior.

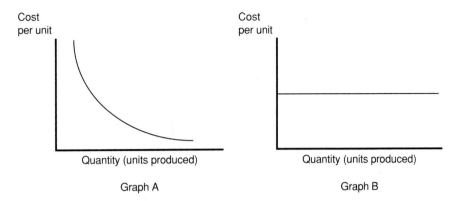

Graph A   Graph B

2 Violane, Incorporated sells its sole product for $.80 per unit. Variable cost per unit is $.56. What is the contribution margin per unit (1) in dollars and (2) in percent?

3 If Violane, Incorporated (see Question 2) has fixed costs of $360,000 per year, calculate the breakeven sales level (1) in units and (2) in sales revenue.

4 The breakeven formula is $SQ - VQ - F = Zero$, where S = selling price per unit, V = variable cost per unit, F = total fixed costs for the period, and Q = quantity to be produced and sold during the period. What modifications are necessary to convert the breakeven formula to a more general cost-volume-profit formula?

5 On a cost-volume-profit graph, what area (i.e., between which two lines) indicates (1) losses, (2) total contribution margin, and (3) fixed costs?

6 Boozer, Inc. is currently operating at a volume level to the left of the breakeven point and thus is incurring losses. Would you recommend that the company cease operations?

7 One-Shot, Inc. sells items at 150 percent of variable cost. If the company's variable cost per unit is $3 and fixed costs per month total $900,000, how many units must be sold each month (1) to break even, and (2) to earn $300,000 net income?

8 What is the contribution margin per unit for One-Shot, Inc. in Question 7? What is the contribution margin percentage? If fixed costs increase by $150,000 per month, by how much must sales increase in units and sales dollars to maintain the previous net income level?

9 Random, Inc.'s current sales level of $1,500,000 generates a $150,000 net income. Variable costs currently total $1,050,000. Determine Random's dollar margin of safety and margin of safety percentage.

10 In an incremental analysis situation, what is a relevant item? What is an irrelevant item?

11 Grendell Company's management is involved in a make-or-buy decision for heating coil components for its toasters. Data compiled indicate it will take one direct labor hour to produce each heating coil. The standard cost of production is $9.80 ($.20 direct materials, $5.60 direct labor, and $4.00 factory overhead). Factory overhead is applied at $4.00 per direct labor hour. Seventy percent of the applied overhead is fixed and will not be affected by the make-or-buy decision. For the make-or-buy decision, calculate the relevant production cost per heating coil.

12 If the heating coil components (see Question 11 above) are purchased, they would cost $8 each. Should Grendell make or buy the heating coils? Provide quantitative analysis to support your decision. What qualitative factors also should be considered?

13 "To choose among alternative courses of action, management needs to consider only relevant items and can ignore irrelevant items." Explain and evaluate the preceding statement.

14 Define the term "sunk cost." Is a sunk cost a relevant or irrelevant item?

15 George Wisecrack, a fellow accounting student, quips, "A sunk cost is money down the drain." Is there an element of truth to George's statement?

16 Define the term "opportunity cost." Is an opportunity cost a relevant or irrelevant item? Are opportunity costs readily determinable by looking at the accounting records?

17 In deciding which of two new machines to purchase to replace an old machine, the management of Ashworth Company should consider as relevant:
a Historical costs associated with the old machine
b Future costs that will be classified as variable rather than fixed
c Future costs that will be different under the two alternatives
d Future costs that will be classified as fixed rather than variable

(AICPA Adapted)

18 As part of the data presented in support of a proposal for production of a special order of clock-radios, the sales manager of Wittman Electronics reported the total additional cost required for the proposed special order. The increase in total cost is known as:
a Controllable cost
b Incremental cost
c Opportunity cost
d Sunk cost

(AICPA Adapted)

19 The Lantern Corporation has 1,000 obsolete lanterns that are carried in inventory at a manufacturing cost of $20,000. If the lanterns are remachined for $5,000, they could be sold for $9,000. If the lanterns are scrapped, they could be sold for $1,000. Which alternative is more desirable and what are the total relevant costs for that alternative?
a Remachine and $5,000
b Remachine and $25,000
c Scrap and $20,000
d Neither, as there is an overall loss under either alternative

(AICPA Adapted)

20 Greedy, Inc. has been approached by a potential foreign customer. The customer offers to buy 4,500 units at a price of $82 per unit. Up until now, Greedy has sold only to domestic customers. Greedy's cost for each unit is $94.70 (including $18.70 of allocated fixed costs). Greedy's domestic sales price is $105 per unit. Total fixed costs are not expected to change if Greedy accepts the foreign sales order. The company has no other alternative use for the idle capacity. Should Greedy accept the foreign sales order? Show calculations to support your answer.

EXERCISES

E19-1 Compute sales revenue needed in the current month (a) to break even and (b) to earn a $22,500 net income, for each of the following situations:

1 Holly Co. computed last month's variable costs at $30,000 and fixed costs at $67,500. Last month, 20,000 units were sold at $6 per unit.

2 Quest, Inc. suffered a $20,000 net loss last month on sales of $600,000; fixed costs are $140,000.

E19-2 Refer to the cost-volume-profit graph in Exhibit 19-1 and answer the following true-false questions:

1 The relevant range is from 2,000 to 21,000 units.

2 The contribution margin to the left of the breakeven point is negative.

3 At 5,000 units, total costs are $450,000.

4 At 10,000 units, total revenue and total costs are $600,000.

5 Total fixed costs increase as volume increases.

6 At zero volume, total costs would definitely be $300,000.

E19-3 The cost-volume-profit graph presented in Exhibit 19-2 is structured differently from the graph presented in Exhibit 19-1.

Required:

1 What basic feature differentiates the cost-volume-profit graph in Exhibit 19-2 from the graph presented in Exhibit 19-1?

2 Label the lines and areas designated (1) through (8) shown on the graph in Exhibit 19-2.

3 What advantage can you see for the graph in Exhibit 19-1 versus the graph in Exhibit 19-2?

EXHIBIT 19-2

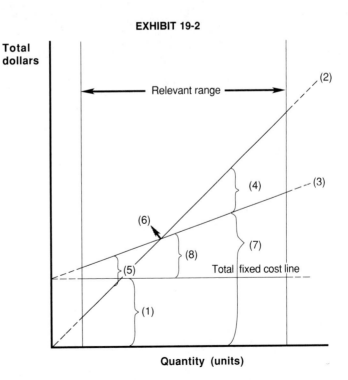

Quantity (units)

E19-4 Solve for the unknowns in each situation below:

	Sales	Variable costs	Contribution margin percent	Contribution margin	Fixed costs	Net income
1.	$200,000	?	?	$ 50,000	?	$10,000
2.	?	$300,000	?	100,000	?	40,000
3.	800,000	?	20%	?	$ 48,000	?
4.	?	?	30	?	160,000	50,000

E19-5 Solve for the unknowns in each situation below:

	(1)	(2)	(3)	(4)
Sales in units	100,000	?	?	150,000
Sales price per unit	$25	$50	?	?
Variable cost per unit	18	?	$30	$1.50
Contribution margin per unit	?	10	15	?
Contribution margin	?	150,000	?	?
Fixed costs	300,000	?	170,000	220,000
Net income	?	88,000	25,000	80,000

E19-6 The Walker Company sells its product for $14 per unit. Variable costs for this product are $8 per unit. Fixed costs are $300,000 per month.

Required:
1 How many units must be sold monthly to break even?
2 Last month Walker reported a profit of $72,000. How many units must be sold this month to achieve the same profit?
3 Calculate Walker's margin of safety amount and margin of safety percentage for last month.

E19-7 Relay Corporation manufactures batons. The company can manufacture 300,000 batons a year at a variable cost of $750,000 and a fixed cost of $450,000. Based on Relay's predictions, 240,000 batons will be sold at the regular price of $5 each. In addition, a special order was received for 60,000 batons to be sold at a 40 percent discount off the regular price. By what amount would income before income taxes be increased or decreased as a result of the special order.

(AICPA Adapted)

E19-8 Pratfall, Inc., a single product firm, plans to sell 185,000 units to its regular customers at $16 each. Standard cost per unit is projected to be:

Variable manufacturing costs	$ 3.20
Fixed manufacturing costs	.80*
Variable selling costs	5.40
Fixed selling costs	2.10*
Total standard cost per unit	$11.50

*Fixed costs per unit are based on planned production of 185,000 units.

Total fixed costs remain unchanged within the relevant range of 110,000 to capacity of 260,000 units. Company management has received a special order for an additional 15,000 units. If the selling price per unit is $10 for the special order, should the company accept the order? Support your decision with the appropriate calculations. Would your answer differ if the special order were for 150,000 units?

E19-9 Randolph, Inc. is considering replacing its completely worn-out polishing machine with either (1) a new $11,000 deluxe model (no trade-in required) or (2) a new $15,000 super deluxe model (trade-in required). Randolph can sell their old worn-out polishing machine to a scrap dealer for $500. The old polishing machine was purchased four years ago for $10,000. It is now fully depreciated. Considering relevant items only, present an analysis of the relevant costs, including any opportunity costs. Ignore any tax effects.

E19-10 Cramdom Co. is trying to determine whether to purchase a new delivery truck to replace their old run-down truck. The new truck will cost $7,000. The old truck cost $6,000 when purchased four years ago. It is being depreciated over six years by the straight line method with zero estimated salvage value. The old truck can be sold currently for $900. If the new truck is not purchased, Cramdom will invest the $7,000 in a bank savings certificate earning 8 percent compounded annually. Identify relevant, irrelevant, opportunity, and sunk costs for Cramdom's delivery truck decision if income taxes are ignored.

PROBLEMS

P19-1 *Cost-Volume-Profit Graph and Equation*
Pronton, Inc.'s analysis of operations for last month indicates:

Sales revenue	$380,000
Variable costs	285,000
Fixed costs	?
Net income	45,000
Units produced and sold 38,000	
Relevant range is from 5,000 to 55,000 units	

Required:
1 Prepare a cost-volume-profit graph for Pronton following the format of Exhibit 19-1. Label all lines on the graph and indicate the monthly volume in units and in sales dollars (a) to break even and (b) to earn $50,000 net income.
2 Using the cost-volume-profit equation, compute the monthly volume in units and in sales dollars (a) to break even and (b) to earn $50,000 net income.

P19-2 *Breakeven Analysis*
Swann Inc.'s manufacturing, selling, general, and administrative fixed costs total $184,000 per year. Variable costs per unit are:

Manufacturing	$25
Selling	10
Administrative	5

Swann sells its product for $50 per unit.

Required:

1 Calculate breakeven sales in units and in sales revenue based on the above data.

2 Assuming fixed costs increase to $200,000, calculate breakeven sales in units and in sales revenue if there are no changes in selling price or variable cost per unit.

3 Assuming fixed costs increase to $250,000 and variable cost per unit increases 10 percent, determine (a) contribution margin per unit in dollars, (b) the contribution margin percent, and (c) the decrease in the contribution margin percent resulting from the 10 percent increase in variable costs.

4 If Swann expects to break even next year by selling 28,400 units at $65 each, what are budgeted fixed costs for next year if variable cost per unit is $46?

P19-3 *Cost-Volume-Profit Analysis*

Freedom, Inc.'s management has performed cost studies and has projected the following annual costs based on 40,000 units of production and sales:

	Total annual costs	Percent of total annual cost that is variable
Direct materials	$ 400,000	100%
Direct labor	360,000	75
Manufacturing overhead	300,000	40
Selling, general, and administra-		
tive expenses	200,000	25
Total	$1,260,000	

Required:

1 Compute Freedom's unit selling price that will yield a projected $140,000 profit if sales are 40,000 units.

2 Assume management selects a selling price of $30 per unit. Compute Freedom's dollar sales that will yield a projected 10 percent profit on sales.

(AICPA Adapted)

P19-4 *Cost-Volume-Profit Analysis and Margin of Safety*

Breakneck, Inc. has decided to rent a new milling machine. The machine is expected to increase production and sales by 10,000 units per month. Last month's data showed a sales price of $18 per unit, variable cost of $14 per unit, fixed costs of $128,000, and net income of $32,000 on sales of 40,000 units.

Required:

1 Calculate last month's margin of safety amount and margin of safety percentage.

2 If the milling machine can be rented for a fixed monthly rental, determine the rental cost that will allow a $42,000 net income per month. Sales price and unit variable cost are assumed unaffected.

3 If the milling machine can be rented based on a charge per unit milled, calculate the rental fee per unit that will allow a $42,000 net income per month. Sales price and total fixed costs are assumed unchanged. All units will be milled on the new machine.

P19-5 *Special Order*

Nubo Manufacturing, Inc. is presently operating at 50 percent of practical capacity producing about 50,000 units annually of a patented electronic component. Nubo recently received a special offer from a company in Yokohama, Japan, to purchase 30,000 components at $6 per unit. Nubo has not previously sold components in Japan. Budgeted production costs for 50,000 and 80,000 units of output follow:

	50,000 units	80,000 units
Costs:		
Direct materials	$ 75,000	$120,000
Direct labor	75,000	120,000
Factory overhead	200,000	260,000
Total costs	$350,000	$500,000
Cost per unit	$7.00	$6.25

The sales manager thinks the order should be accepted, even if it results in a loss of $1 per unit, because he feels sales may build up in the future in Japan. The production manager does not wish to have the order accepted primarily because the order would show a loss of $.25 per unit ($6 sales price vs. $6.25 cost). The treasurer has made a quick computation indicating that accepting the order will actually increase gross profit.

Required:

1 Explain what apparently caused the drop in cost per unit from $7 to $6.25 when budgeted production is increased from 50,000 to 80,000 units. Show supporting calculations. (Hint: Calculate cost per unit for direct materials, direct labor, variable overhead, and fixed overhead at both 50,000 and 80,000 units of production.)

2 a Explain whether (either or both) the production manager or the treasurer is correct in their reasoning.

b Explain why the conclusions of the production manager and the treasurer differ.

3 Explain why the likelihood of repeat special sales orders and/or all sales to be made at $6 may affect the decision to accept or reject the special order.

P19-6 *Make or Buy*

Kinney Products Co. manufactures a single product that sells for $10 per unit. Variable costs are $6 per unit and fixed costs are $1,200,000 per year. Due to expected increases in material and labor costs, the company expects its variable costs to increase by $1 per unit, and its fixed costs to increase by $10,000 per month. Sales prices cannot be raised due to competitor pricing. In view of the expected cost increases, the company is considering subcontracting some of its manufacturing operations. If this is done, expected costs next year would be:

Subcontract, per unit	$2.50
Other variable costs, per unit	5.00
Annual fixed cost	1,000,000

Required:

1 Determine whether the company should subcontract if next year's expected volume is 420,000 units. Support your answer by calculating pre-tax income (or loss) if: (a) the company does subcontract vs. (b) the company does not subcontract.

2 Repeat requirement (1), except assume that next year's expected volume is 800,000 units.

P19-7 *Analysis of Special Order*

George Jackson operates a small machine shop. He manufactures one standard product available from many other similar businesses and he also manufactures products to customer order. His accountant prepared the annual income statement shown below:

	Custom sales	Standard sales	Total
Sales revenue	$50,000	$25,000	$75,000
Materials	$10,000	$ 8,000	$18,000
Labor	20,000	9,000	29,000
Depreciation	6,300	3,600	9,900
Power	700	400	1,100
Rent	6,000	1,000	7,000
Heat and light	600	100	700
Other	400	900	1,300
	$44,000	$23,000	$67,000
Net income	$ 6,000	$ 2,000	$ 8,000

The depreciation charges are for machines used in the respective product lines. The power charge is apportioned on the estimate of power consumed. The rent is for the building space, which has been leased for 10 years at $7,000 per year. The rent and heat and light are apportioned to the product lines based on amount of floor space occupied. All other costs are variable current expenses identified with the product line causing them.

A valued custom parts customer has asked Mr. Jackson if he would manufacture 5,000 special units for him. Mr. Jackson is working at capacity and would have to give up some other business in order to take this business. He can't renege on customer orders already agreed to, but he could reduce the output of his standard product by about one-half for one year while producing the specially requested custom part. The customer is willing to pay $7 for each part. The material cost will be about $2 per unit and the labor will be $3.60 per unit. Mr. Jackson will have to spend $2,000 for a special device that will be discarded when the job is done.

Required:

1 Calculate and present the following costs related to the 5,000 unit custom order:
a The incremental cost of the order.
b The full cost of the order including irrelevant costs.
c The opportunity cost of taking the order.
2 Should Mr. Jackson take the order? Explain your answer.

(CMA Adapted)

P19-8 *Incremental Analysis: Three Alternatives*

Ten years ago Noxin Company spent $800,000 to purchase a patent granting Noxin the exclusive right to produce and sell product Dee. An additional $75,000 has been spent during the last ten years for legal fees to defend the patent against infringement suits. Since the non-renewable patent expires at the end of the next year, Noxin is considering three alternative courses of action for next year:

Alternative A—sell the patent to Moroy Co. for $30,000 cash. This cash would be invested to earn an 8 percent return. Noxin would cease production and sale of product Dee for the next year.

Alternative B—allow a group of five other companies to produce and sell product Dee for 10 percent royalties on their sales of product Dee. A combined minimum guarantee of $31,000 is assured. Royalty payments would be received at the end of the year. Noxin would cease production and sale of product Dee for the next year.

Alternative C—continue to be the exclusive producer and seller of product Dee for the next year. The contribution margin on product Dee is $4.20 per unit with company sales of the product forecasted at 9,000 units for the coming year. On Noxin's product-line income statement, $33,000 fixed costs are deducted from product Dee's contribution margin. Thirty percent of these fixed costs would be eliminated if production of product Dee is discontinued.

Required:

1 Prepare an incremental analysis of the three alternatives. Include only relevant items in your analysis. Ignore income taxes.

2 Regardless of your decision in part (1), the exclusive rights enjoyed by Noxin will soon expire. List other points of consideration that Noxin should be taking into account as it plans for the end of its exclusive rights under the patent.

P19-9 *Incremental Analysis: Unprofitable Product Line*

Norton Manufacturing Company manufactures and sells three different products— Ex, Why, and Zee. Projected income statements by product line for the year ended December 31, 1988 are presented below:

	Ex	Why	Zee	Total
Unit sales	10,000	500,000	125,000	635,000
Revenues	$925,000	$1,000,000	$575,000	$2,500,000
Cost of Goods Sold:				
Variable	$285,000	$ 350,000	$150,000	$ 785,000
Fixed	304,200	289,000	166,800	760,000
Total Cost of Goods Sold	$589,200	$ 639,000	$316,800	$1,545,000
Gross Profit	$335,800	$ 361,000	$258,200	$ 955,000
General and Administrative Expenses:				
Variable	$270,000	$ 200,000	$ 80,000	$ 550,000
Fixed	125,800	136,000	78,200	340,000
Total General and Administrative Expenses	$395,800	$ 336,000	$158,200	$ 890,000
Income (Loss) before Tax	($ 60,000)	$ 25,000	$100,000	$ 65,000

Norton Manufacturing is concerned about the loss for product Ex and is considering two alternative courses of corrective action.

Alternative A—Norton Manufacturing would purchase some new machinery for the production of product Ex. This new machinery would increase total fixed costs allocated to product Ex to $480,000 per year. No additional fixed costs would be allocated to products Why or Zee. Management expects that the new machinery would reduce variable production costs of product Ex so that total variable costs (cost of goods sold and general and administrative expenses) for product Ex would be 52 percent of product Ex's revenues.

Alternative B—Norton Manufacturing would discontinue production of product Ex. Selling prices of products Why and Zee would remain constant. However, management believes production and revenues of product Zee would increase by 50 percent. Some of the present machinery devoted to product Ex could be sold at scrap value equal to its removal cost (i.e., zero net cash proceeds). The removal of this machinery would reduce the fixed costs allocated to product Ex by $30,000 per year. Remaining fixed cost allocated to product Ex includes $155,000 of rent expense per year. This space used for product Ex can be rented to an outside organization for $157,500 per year.

Required:
1 Prepare an incremental analysis of Alternative A's effect on total company income before tax. Include only relevant items in your analysis.
2 Prepare an incremental analysis of Alternative B's effect on total company income before tax. Include only relevant items in your analysis.

(AICPA Adapted)

P19-10 *Disposal of Equipment*

Itsock Co. is trying to decide how to dispose of a piece of equipment no longer needed in the production process. The machine cost Itsock $42,000 when purchased three years ago. Itsock is depreciating the machine over a four-year estimated life using straight line depreciation and an estimated salvage value of $1,800.

Itsock has two offers for the machine. Offer A is a straight cash sale for $8,000 less the $500 freight cost to be paid by Itsock for transporting the machine to the new owners.

Offer B involves a one-year leasing arrangement with monthly lease payments of $500. For Offer B, the new owners will pay transportation charges, but Itsock must pay repairs, insurance, and property taxes estimated to total $700 for the year. Under Offer B, the machine reverts to Itsock after the one-year lease expires. The estimated salvage value of the machine in one year is $2,000.

Required:
1 Prepare an incremental analysis of the sell vs. lease alternatives. Include only relevant items in your analysis. (Ignore the time value of money and income taxes for requirement (1).)
2 In view of your answer to requirement (1), would you expect your decision to be different if the time value of money was considered? Explain.

Business Decision Problem

Motor Company manufactures 10,000 units of Part M-1 for use in its production annually. The following costs are reported:

Direct materials	$ 20,000
Direct labor	55,000
Variable overhead	45,000
Fixed overhead	70,000
	$190,000

Valve Company has offered to sell Motor 10,000 units of Part M-1 for $18 per unit. If Motor accepts the offer, some of the facilities presently used to manufacture part M-1 could be rented to a third party at an annual rental of $15,000. Additionally, $4 per unit of fixed overhead applied to part M-1 would be totally eliminated.

Required:
1 Prepare an incremental analysis of the make vs. buy alternatives. Include only relevant items in your analysis. Provide per unit and total cost amounts.
2 Considering only your answer to (1), do you think Motor should accept Valve's offer?
3 Regardless of your decision in (2), list other points of consideration that are excluded from the incremental analysis that should also be addressed.

(AICPA Adapted)

20

CAPITAL INVESTMENT ANALYSIS

LEARNING OBJECTIVES

When you complete this chapter, you should be able to:

1 Identify cash inflows and outflows relating to a capital investment project.
2 Apply the payback, accounting rate-of-return, and internal rate-of-return methods.
3 Compare capital investment alternatives using net present value.
4 Calculate cash flows on an after-tax basis.
5 Compare lease and buy alternatives.

Planning is one of management's important responsibilities. Planning involves not only the establishment of goals, but also the choice of actions necessary to accomplish those goals. Accounting's role in planning is to provide data for decision analysis. Decisions may be short-run in nature, such as special order pricing and make-or-buy analysis. Techniques for developing accounting data relevant to these decisions were discussed in the preceding chapter. This chapter covers analysis for long-run decisions, those affecting the next several years. While various types of long-run decisions confront management, we shall focus on one type—the investment in capital assets.

In developing accounting data relevant for long-run decisions, a number of points must be noted. First, *long-run analysis is concerned with cash flows rather than income*. Throughout most of the book, the determination of *income* has been a central theme. Capital investment analysis focuses primarily on the amount of *cash* being received and spent each period. This shift in emphasis is due in part to the use of time-value-of-money techniques in long-run analysis.

Present value calculations involve the discounting of future cash flows rather than income. Another reason for the emphasis on cash is that long-run decisions affect the company's resources. When considering a capital investment project, management asks the following questions:

How much capital must be invested?
How much return will the investment generate?
When will these investments and receipts occur?

To answer these questions, we must use cash flow data.

A second point to consider is that *long-run decisions involve cash flows over several periods of time*. For example, suppose management is considering the following investment projects:

	Project I	Project II
Amount to be invested in:		
1988	$75,000	$50,000
1990	-0-	10,000
Amount expected to be received:		
1989	$25,000	$20,000
1990	35,000	20,000
1991	30,000	35,000
1992	15,000	10,000
1993	10,000	-0-

Because evaluating or comparing several items of data simultaneously is difficult, capital investment analysis summarizes the data for each project into a single figure. One simple way of summarizing the projects is to calculate the net cash received, as follows:

Project I		Project II	
Total to be received	$115,000	Total to be received	$85,000
Total to be invested	75,000	Total to be invested	60,000
Net cash received	$ 40,000	Net cash received	$25,000

On this basis, comparing the projects is easy. Project I appears to be superior in that it generates net cash of $40,000 compared to $25,000 from Project II. While a single-figure comparison simplifies the decision making, the technique for summarizing data into a single figure is crucial. The procedure, just illustrated, of adding all cash inflows and subtracting all cash outflows is *not* a useful analysis technique. No consideration has been given to the time value of money. From the perspective of a decision made in 1988, a dollar to be received in 1989 is worth more than a dollar to be received in 1991.

This chapter describes and illustrates four techniques for summarizing project data into a single figure. This figure can then be evaluated by comparing it to some standard. Or, it can be used as a basis for comparison with other projects. The techniques for capital investment analysis are:

1 Payback period
2 Accounting rate of return
3 Internal rate of return
4 Net present value

These techniques vary in their degree of sophistication and their consideration of the time value of money. Our discussion of the first three methods of capital investment analysis is limited. Courses in finance and advanced managerial accounting cover these methods in more detail. This chapter emphasizes the fourth technique—the net present value.

THE PAYBACK PERIOD

The *payback period* is the number of years needed to recover the cost of a capital investment. For example, if a company invests $21,000 today in a project that is expected to generate $7,000 in each of the next six years, the payback period is three years.

$$\text{Payback Period} = \frac{\text{Investment Cost}}{\text{Annual Cash Inflow}}$$
$$= \frac{\$21,000}{\$7,000}$$
$$= 3 \text{ years}$$

For a capital investment project with *unequal* annual cash inflows, the payback period is determined by simply adding the annual cash inflows until the cumulative cash inflows equal the investment cost. For example, if a project costs $400,000 and has expected cash inflows of $160,000 in Year 1, $130,000 in Year 2, $70,000 in Year 3, $40,000 in Year 4, and $20,000 in Year 5, the payback period is four years.

	Annual cash inflows	Cumulative cash inflows
Year 1	$160,000	$160,000
Year 2	130,000	290,000
Year 3	70,000	360,000
Year 4	40,000	400,000 = Investment Cost

The payback-period method is a simple, widely used technique for summarizing multiperiod data into a single figure. It also provides a simple decision rule. Management is interested in minimizing the risk involved in committing funds for long-term investment projects. A project that rapidly recovers its cost may be judged to be relatively less risky. Hence, the shorter the payback period, the more desirable the project. Many companies adopt a simple cutoff rule regarding payback. For instance, a company with a three-year cutoff rule would accept capital investments with a payback period of less than three years and reject projects with a payback period exceeding three years.

Although simple to calculate and frequently used in the real world, the payback-period technique has several serious deficiencies. In particular, this method ignores cash inflows occurring after the payback period and fails to adjust for the time value of money. Both of these deficiencies can lead to management not selecting the best capital investment alternative.

THE ACCOUNTING RATE OF RETURN

The *accounting rate of return* is a percentage determined by dividing a project's average annual accounting income by its investment cost. For example, consider the following two mutually-exclusive capital investment opportunities. ("Mutually exclusive" means that one or the other, but not both, of the alternatives will be selected.)

	Project A	Project B
Investment cost	$1,000,000	$500,000
Forecasted income:		
Year 1	$ 300,000	$ 50,000
Year 2	300,000	70,000
Year 3	300,000	155,000
Year 4	300,000	250,000
Year 5	300,000	350,000
Total	$1,500,000	$875,000
Average annual income		
(total income ÷ 5 years)	$ 300,000	$175,000

The respective accounting rates of return for Projects A and B would be 30 percent and 35 percent, calculated as follows:

$$\text{Accounting Rate of Return} = \frac{\text{Average Annual Income}}{\text{Investment Cost}}$$

$$\text{Project A} = \frac{\$300,000}{\$1,000,000} = 30\%$$

$$\text{Project B} = \frac{\$175,000}{\$500,000} = 35\%$$

Project B, with the higher accounting rate of return, would be preferable. If a single project is being evaluated, comparison would be made to the company's existing rate of return to determine if the proposed project would improve it.

Unlike the other techniques for capital investment analysis, the accounting rate of return is typically based on accounting income rather than cash flows. Because income is dependent on the accounting methods employed, it is important that income from all projects being compared be calculated according to the same accounting principles. Otherwise the results of accounting rate-of-return analysis could be misleading.

Note also that this technique (like the payback-period method) fails to consider the time value of money. The fact that the majority of Project B's income is not realized until the later years of the project's life is ignored by the accounting rate of return method. Conceivably, this could result in the wrong project being accepted.

INTERNAL RATE OF RETURN

The *internal rate-of-return* method calculates the discount rate that, when applied to expected cash inflows, will produce a present value equal to the current investment cost. The discount rate calculated indicates the rate of return earned on the project and includes the time value of money. The higher the rate of return, the more desirable the project. Many companies set a minimum acceptable internal rate of return. The minimum acceptable rate is often the company's *cost of capital* (i.e., the average cost to the company of obtaining investment funds). Capital investment projects yielding an internal rate of return higher than the minimum rate would be accepted, while those yielding less than the minimum rate would be rejected.

Consider the planned expansion of the R.M. Company. The expansion project would currently cost $54,200 and is expected to generate net cash inflows of $10,000 annually for the next twelve years. On a time-line diagram the expansion project's net cash flows would appear as follows (it is assumed that the $10,000 cash will be received at the end of each year):

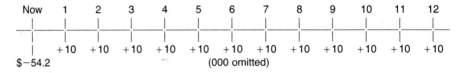

The internal rate of return is the discount rate that, when applied to the series of twelve $10,000 net cash inflows, will yield a present value of $54,200. Recall the present value of an annuity formula:

$$P_A = A \times (\text{present value of annuity factor, } n \text{ periods, } r \text{ percent})$$

In this equation,

P_A denotes the present value of an annuity A (a *series of equal periodic amounts* to be received or spent in the future).

n denotes the number of time periods over which the cash flows will occur.

r denotes the rate of interest to use when discounting future amounts to the present.

To find the internal rate of return (1) solve for the unknown factor in the above equation and then (2) check Table III (in Appendix A at the back of the book) to find r (the interest rate) corresponding to the factor found in step (1). The r found in the table is the internal rate of return for the investment project.

For the R.M. Company expansion project:

$$P_A = A \times \text{(present value of annuity factor, n periods, r percent)}$$
$$\$54,200 = \$10,000 \times \text{(present value of an annuity factor,}$$
$$\text{12 periods, r percent)}$$
$$5.42 = \text{factor for 12 periods at r percent}$$

Reading across the 12-period row in Table III, we find the factor 5.42 in the 15 percent column. Thus, the project's internal rate of return is 15 percent. If 15 percent exceeds the minimum acceptable rate, and no alternative project has a higher rate, then this project should be accepted.

Determining the internal rate of return when the forecasted cash inflows vary in amount from period to period requires a trial-and-error approach. Finding the internal rate of return without the aid of a computer can become quite tedious. In evaluating capital investment projects, another technique that usually produces similar results to the internal rate-of-return method is the net-present-value method. This method is better suited to handling capital investment projects with unequal cash flows.

NET PRESENT VALUE

The *net-present-value* (NPV) technique compares the present value of all cash inflows and all cash outflows for a capital investment project. If the net present value is positive (that is, the present value of the cash inflows exceeds the present value of the cash outflows), then the project is acceptable. If the net present value is negative (that is, the present value of the cash outflows exceeds the present value of the cash inflows), then the project should be rejected. When analyzing mutually-exclusive capital investment projects with approximately the same investment cost, the one with the greater net present value should be chosen. If a company has a limited amount of funds to invest, a ranking of projects according to their net present values provides a basis for allocating the limited funds.

Present Value Formulas

Recall that present value calculations apply to two situations:

1 A series of equal cash flows occurring at the end of each time period. This is known as an *annuity*.

2 A single sum of money to be paid or received at some future date.

Each situation requires the use of a particular present value formula and a particular present value table. In the case of an annuity, Table III is employed when using the formula:

$$P_A = A \times \text{(present value of annuity factor, n periods, r percent)}$$

This formula was reviewed in the previous section covering the internal rate of return.

In the case of a single sum of money, the following formula is used:

$$P = F \times (\text{present value factor, n periods, r percent})$$

where P denotes the present value of F (a *single amount* to be received or spent in the future). Table II is used for this calculation.

The rate of interest (r) in the present value formulas, when used in conjunction with the net-present-value technique, should be the cost of capital for the company. Recall that a firm's cost of capital is the average cost to the company of obtaining investment funds. By using the firm's cost of capital as the interest rate, only projects that yield a return higher than the cost of capital will show a positive net present value. Projects yielding less than the cost of capital will result in a negative net present value and should be rejected. Intuitively, this rule is reasonable. We accept projects that return more than the cost of obtaining funds to invest in the project (i.e., have positive NPVs). We reject projects that fail to yield a return that is large enough to cover the cost of raising investment funds (i.e., have negative NPVs).

Purchasing Equipment—A Simple NPV Example

Consider the following situation confronting Marjoe Manufacturing Co. The company is trying to decide whether to make a $20,000 investment to purchase a cutting machine. It is estimated that the machine will (1) generate incremental after-tax cash inflows of $5,730 per year for five years and (2) be sold at the end of five years for an after-tax cash inflow of $3,000. If expected cash inflows occur at the end of each year and the $20,000 purchase cost is a current cash outlay, the capital investment project can be portrayed on a time-line diagram as:

Adding the five $5,730 cash inflows plus the $3,000 disposal value would yield $31,650 in after-tax cash inflows. However, it would be meaningless to compare this figure to the $20,000 after-tax investment cost. The $31,650 total fails to take into account the time value of money. The $20,000 cash outlay represents a current expenditure. The expected future cash receipts are not currently available for the company to use; they will be available only in future years. The net-present-value method accounts for the time value of money by *discounting* these future expected cash flows to the present. If Marjoe Manufacturing's discount rate (i.e., its cost of capital) is 8 percent, the present value of the future cash inflows is $24,920 as determined below.

Present value of the equal periodic receipts:

$$P_A = A \times (\text{present value of annuity factor, n periods, r percent})$$
$$= \$5,730 \times (\text{present value of annuity factor, 5 periods, 8 percent})$$

$$= \$5,730 \times 3.9927 \text{ (from Table III)}$$
$$= \$22,878$$

Present value of the disposal value:

$$P = F \times \text{ (present value factor, n periods, r percent)}$$
$$= \$3,000 \times \text{ (present value factor, 5 periods, 8 percent)}$$
$$= \$3,000 \times .6806 \text{ (from Table II)}$$
$$= \$2,042$$

Summary of project's discounted cash flows:

Periodic receipts	$22,878
Disposal value	+ 2,042
Present value of cash inflows	$24,920
Less present cash outlay[1]	20,000
Net present value	$ 4,920

If there are capital investment funds available and no alternative projects to analyze, Marjoe Manufacturing should purchase the cutting machine since the project has a positive net present value of $4,920.

Summary of Methods

The following table summarizes the data required and the basis for project evaluation under each of the capital investment analysis techniques:

Method	Data required	Basis for evaluation of single project	Basis for comparison of several projects
Payback	Investment; Annual cash flows	Payback less than pre-established cutoff	Fastest payback
Accounting Rate of Return	Investment; Annual accounting income	Project's rate of return higher than existing rate of return	Highest rate of return
Internal Rate of Return	Investment; Annual cash flows	Project's rate of return higher than cost of capital	Highest rate of return
Net Present Value	Investment; Annual cash flows; Discount rate	Net present value greater than zero	Largest net present value per dollar invested

ESTIMATING CASH FLOWS

The capital investment analysis techniques for net-present-value, internal rate-of-return, and payback methods require estimations of all incremental cash inflows

---

[1]No discounting of the $20,000 is needed as it represents a current expenditure.

and outflows for each capital investment project being analyzed. In general, project analysis may be approached by considering four elements of cash flow:

1 After-tax acquisition cost
2 After-tax operating cash receipts and payments
3 Tax savings from depreciation
4 After-tax disposal value

It should be recognized that many cash flow figures are *estimates,* and thus are subject to uncertainty. Acquisition cost and the related tax savings from depreciation may be fairly easy to estimate. Future operating cash flows and disposal values, on the other hand, are much more difficult to estimate. Care should be taken not to let the presence of formal analysis obscure the fact that the underlying cash flows are estimates. It is tempting to believe that a formally calculated net present value is precise. The answer, however, can be no more precise than the underlying data.

The Impact of Income Taxes

Observe from the above list that a consideration of the impact of income taxes is an essential part of cash flow analysis. Three of the above four items require *after-tax inflows* or *after-tax outflows* of cash. For example, the receipt of $1,000 additional taxable revenue will require the payment of additional income taxes. If there is no change in expenses and an income tax rate of 40 percent, the after-tax cash inflow is calculated as:

Cash inflow	$1,000
Less: Cash outflow for additional income taxes ($1,000 × 40%)	400
After-tax inflow	$ 600

As a short cut, the after-tax inflow is calculated by multiplying the cash inflow by (1 − tax rate) as follows:

$$\text{After-tax inflow} = \$1,000 \times (1 - .40)$$
$$= \$1,000 \times .60$$
$$= \$600$$

Cash outflows net of tax are determined in a similar manner. A payment of $900 for expense will reduce taxable income and, as a result, the amount of income taxes payable. The resulting after-tax outflow is:

Cash outflow	$900
Less: Reduction in cash outflow for income taxes ($900 × 40%)	360
After-tax outflow	$540

Again, the same result can be found by multiplying the cash outflow by (1 − tax rate).

The treatment of depreciation is slightly different. Depreciation is an expense that does *not* require a current outlay of cash. The outlay occurred when the assets were originally purchased; depreciation is not a cash flow. Depreciation is, however, a deductible expense in calculating income taxes. Additional depreciation will reduce taxable income, and hence will reduce the cash outflow for income taxes. The only cash flow connected with depreciation is the tax savings that result. The tax savings from depreciation is calculated by multiplying the depreciation by the tax rate. If the tax rate is again 40 percent, depreciation of $2,000 would result in a tax savings of $800 ($2,000 times 40 percent).

In summary, income taxes enter the cash flow analysis as follows:

$$\text{After-tax Inflow} = \text{Cash Inflow} \times (1 - \text{Tax Rate})$$
$$\text{After-tax Outflow} = \text{Cash Outflow} \times (1 - \text{Tax Rate})$$
$$\text{Tax Savings from Depreciation} = \text{Depreciation} \times \text{Tax Rate}$$

Other Factors in Cash Flow Analysis

In addition to income taxes, other tax effects may enter the determination of a project's cash flows. Periodically, tax law has permitted companies that acquire certain assets to deduct an investment tax credit from their income tax liability. The investment tax credit reduces taxes in the year of asset acquisition by an amount equal to a percentage of the asset's cost. In capital investment analysis, the cash outflow related to a purchase is reduced by the amount of an investment tax credit. In essence, the government helps finance the new asset by reducing taxes otherwise payable.[2]

Another tax consideration relates to taxes due upon disposition of an asset. Taxes are calculated on the *gain* on disposal, not on the *proceeds*. The after-tax cash inflow from asset disposition is equal to the proceeds from disposal less taxes on the gain.

In addition to tax effects, the *timing* of cash flows is important to proper application of discounting techniques. Some cash flows, such as acquisition expenditures, may occur immediately and thus require no discounting. Other cash flows may occur in one or more future years. For convenience of discounting, we usually assume that cash flows relating to operations, tax savings from depreciation, and disposal values all occur at a *year-end*. It is also convenient to assume that the tax effects occur at the same time as the transaction to which they relate.

To illustrate the various factors involved in estimating cash flows from a proposed project, let us examine the previous example for Marjoe Manufacturing Co. in more detail. Recall that Marjoe Manufacturing is considering a $20,000 investment in a cutting machine that is expected to generate $5,730 annually for five years and to be sold for $3,000 (after tax) at the end of the five-year period. The company's cost of capital is 8 percent. The procedures for estimating the cash flows related to the cutting machine are discussed in the following sections.

---

[2]The Tax Reform Act of 1986 repealed the investment tax credit. The investment tax credit has been repealed and then later reinserted into the tax laws on several occasions. If Congress believes that it needs to stimulate the economy in the future by encouraging business investment, it is very possible the investment tax credit will again be reinserted into the tax law.

Acquisition Cost

Determination of the after-tax, initial investment outlay may be more difficult than first appears. The difficulty arises in identifying all relevant costs, including opportunity costs. For example, what costs may have been included in the $20,000 after-tax cash outlay in Marjoe Manufacturing's equipment purchase? Assume the following *before-tax cash flows*:

$18,620	Purchase price of cutting machine
500	Freight charge for delivery of machine
1,500	Charge to install machine
1,000	Cost to train employees to operate the machine
1,700	Cash inflow from sale of old cutting machine
	(book value of old machine equals $500)

Assume that current tax laws provide (1) no investment tax credit and (2) a 40 percent combined federal and state income tax on all income, including the gain from the sale of the old cutting machine. The after-tax cash outflow for the equipment purchase is $20,000 as calculated in Exhibit 20-1.

Note in Exhibit 20-1 the tax effects of the various items comprising acquisition cost. The $500 freight charge and $1,500 installation cost are added to the $18,620 purchase price of the machine to determine its $20,620 cost. The $1,000 cost of training employees to run the new machine is a deductible expense on the current year's tax return. The $1,000 increase in training expense will *reduce* the current cash outlay for taxes by $400 (40 percent of the $1,000 expense). With the tax savings, the after-tax cash outlay for training is only $600. Also note in Exhibit 20-1 the $1,220 reduction in acquisition cost resulting from disposal of the old cutting machine. While the disposal of the old cutting machine provides a $1,700 cash inflow, note that taxes *reduce* this cash inflow. Forty percent, or $480, of the $1,200 *gain* (not of the $1,700 selling price) must be paid in *increased* current taxes. The after-tax cash inflow of $1,220 from selling the old cutting machine serves to finance some of the acquisition cost of the new machine.

EXHIBIT 20-1
Calculation of After-Tax Acquisition Cash Outlay

Item	Pre-tax cash flow	Income tax effect	After-tax cash flow
Machine cost, delivered and installed	($20,620)	None	($20,620)
Cost of training employees to operate the machine	(1,000)	$400 (40% × $1,000) tax savings due to deduction of this cost	(600)
Disposal of old machine	1,700	$480 tax on gain*	1,220
		Total after-tax cash outflow	($20,000)

*Calculation of tax due on sale of old machine:

Sales price of old machine	$1,700
Book value of old machine	500
Taxable gain	$1,200
Tax rate	× 40%
Increased tax due	$ 480

Since the cash flows in Exhibit 20-1 all occur at the present, no discounting is necessary. These after-tax cash flows are already present values. However, if a capital investment project requires cash outlays subsequent to the initial acquisition cost, discounting of those after-tax cash outlays would be necessary.

Operating Cash Receipts and Payments

In estimating operating cash flows from its proposed investment in the new cutting machine, Marjoe Manufacturing has projected the following incremental receipts and payments:

1 It will be possible to manufacture (and sell) 1,000 additional units of product annually with the new machine. The contribution margin per unit (before taxes) is $2.60.

2 One machine operator, who earns $7,000 per year, will no longer be needed.

3 Payroll fringe benefits of 25 percent on the reduced wages will be saved.

4 Repairs and maintenance are expected to increase by $4,550 annually.

Exhibit 20-2 presents the calculation of the present value of the after-tax cash flows from operating the machine. It is assumed (1) that all operating revenues and expenses other than depreciation are cash transactions and (2) that all cash receipts and payments occur at the end of each year. Depreciation effects and expected proceeds from sale of the machine after five years are discussed in subsequent sections.

Note the treatment of the four incremental cash flows from operations in Exhibit 20-2. The $2,600 increased contribution margin ($2.60 per unit × 1,000 additional units) would increase taxable income and thus increase taxes. With a tax rate of 40 percent, $1,040 of the $2,600 will be paid to the government in increased taxes. The *after-tax cash inflow* is only $1,560.

The next two items in Exhibit 20-2 (the lower labor cost for wages and related fringe benefits) represent *cash savings*. Since both cost items will be reduced if the machine is acquired, the cost savings are treated as additional *cash inflows* in Exhibit 20-2. (Reducing cash outflows is equivalent to having increased cash inflows.) However, with less expense for wages ($7,000) and fringe benefits ($1,750), income taxes will increase by $2,800 and $700 respectively. To understand the tax effects, consider the following:

When there are less expenses to deduct, pre-tax income is increased.
When pre-tax income is increased, income taxes are increased.
When income taxes are increased, the after-tax cash savings are reduced.

For Marjoe Manufacturing's savings in wages, the incremental after-tax cash inflow is $4,200. For the related reduction in fringe benefits, the after-tax cash inflow is $1,050.

The final item in Exhibit 20-2, the increased expenditures for repairs and maintenance, represents an incremental *cash outflow* of $4,550 before taxes. However, the increased expense will decrease taxes by $1,820 and result in a net after-tax cash outflow of only $2,730 for the additional repairs and maintenance

EXHIBIT 20-2
Calculation of Present Value of After-Tax Cash
Flows From Operations

Item	Annual pre-tax cash flow	Income tax effect	Annual after-tax cash flow
Contribution margin on increased output	$2,600	$1,040 (40% × $2,600) tax on additional income	$ 1,560
Lower total wages paid	7,000	$2,800 (40% × $7,000) tax on additional income due to decrease in labor cost	4,200
Lower fringe benefits due to reduced wages	1,750	$700 (40% × $1,750) tax on additional income due to decrease in fringe benefits	1,050
Increased repairs and maintenance cost	(4,550)	$1,820 (40% × $4,550) tax reduction due to increased expense	(2,730)
Incremental annual net cash inflow from operations			$ 4,080
Present value of an annuity factor, 5 periods, 8 percent			× 3.9927
Present value of after-tax cash flows from operations			$16,290

cost. Note that for each item in Exhibit 20-2 (and, in general, for all operating receipts and payments) the after-tax cash flow can be calculated by multiplying the pre-tax cash flow by (1 − tax rate).

Investing in the cutting machine yields a net annual after-tax cash inflow from operations of $4,080 as computed in Exhibit 20-2. As this amount is expected to be received at the end of *each* of the next five years, it is necessary to determine the present value of these future net cash inflows. Multiplying the annual projected $4,080 after-tax cash inflows by 3.9927 (present value of an annuity factor, 5 periods, 8 percent) produces a discounted present value of $16,290.

Depreciation

Depreciation is *not* a cash inflow or outflow. Depreciation is the assignment of the cost of an asset to expense in a systematic and rational manner over the asset's useful life. The cash flow occurs when the asset is purchased, not later when that cost is periodically assigned to expense. However, depreciation ˋxpense is deductible in determining taxable income and therefore decreases annual cash needs for tax payments. Indirectly then, through its tax-savings effect, depreciation does affect cash flow.

Depreciation calculations for tax and for external reporting can differ. For income tax purposes, Marjoe Manufacturing ignored salvage value in calculating depreciation. (Recall that the new cutting machine does have an estimated disposal value.) Using straight line depreciation for taxes, the company calculates annual depreciation to be $4,124.

$$\text{Annual Depreciation} = \frac{\text{Cost minus Salvage Value}}{\text{Estimated Useful Life}}$$

$$= \frac{\$20,620 - \$0}{5 \text{ years}}$$
$$= \$4,124$$

With a tax rate of 40 percent, the depreciation expense will yield an incremental cash savings in taxes per year of $1,650.

Depreciation Expense Deducted for Tax Purposes per Year	×	Income Tax Rate	=	Incremental Increase in Annual Cash Flow due to Depreciation's Tax Effect
$4,124	×	40%	=	$1,650

Since the $1,650 tax savings will exist at the end of *each* of the next five years, it is necessary to calculate the present value of the cash flows.

Annual reduction in cash outflow for taxes due to tax deductibility of depreciation	$1,650
Present value of an annuity factor, 5 periods, 8 percent	× 3.9927
Present value of reduced cash outflow for taxes resulting from tax deductibility of depreciation expense	$6,588

Disposal Value

The final incremental cash flow to consider for the cutting machine investment is the present value of the anticipated after-tax cash flow when the new cutting machine is ultimately sold. Although the company used a zero salvage value in determining periodic depreciation for tax purposes, it expects to sell the cutting machine to a small machine shop for $5,000 at the end of its five-year life. The present value of the after-tax cash inflow involves (1) determining the tax on the gain (using the income tax rate of 40 percent), (2) finding the after-tax cash inflow, and (3) calculating the present value of the after-tax cash inflow.

(1)	Estimated disposal value after five years	$5,000
	Less book value (per taxes) after five years	-0-
	Taxable gain on disposal	$5,000
	Tax rate	× 40%
	Increase in income taxes	$2,000
(2)	Estimated disposal value after five years	$5,000
	Less tax	2,000
	After-tax cash inflow upon disposal	$3,000

(3)	After-tax cash inflow upon disposal	$3,000
	Present value factor, 5 periods,	
	8 percent (Table II)	× .6806
	Present value of after-tax cash	
	inflow from disposal of machine	$2,042

Exhibit 20-3 presents a summary of the capital investment analysis performed by Marjoe Manufacturing concerning the proposed acquisition of the new cutting machine. All aspects of the analysis have already been discussed. However, Exhibit 20-3 is a comprehensive overview of the analytical process and also indicates the investment's overall net present value. Since the net present value is positive (+$4,920), the purchase of the cutting machine is recommended. The format of Exhibit 20-3 should prove useful in analyzing a variety of capital investment problems, including problems at the end of the chapter.

LEASE-VERSUS-BUY DECISION

A part of many capital investment decisions is determining how to finance the acquisition—lease or buy. The lease-or-buy decision will affect both the amounts and timing of cash flows of a capital investment. The relative ranking of capital investment projects competing for limited funds may be affected by the method of financing chosen.

Consider the following information concerning Shero Services, Inc.'s proposed investment in a computer:

Lease computer	Buy computer
1. Noncancellable five-year lease; $44,000 annual rent	1. $150,000 cost, delivered and installed
2. Repairs, maintenance, and other incidental cost to be paid by company owning the computer	2. Estimated annual cash outflow of $10,000 for repairs, maintenance, and other incidental costs
3. Increased annual labor cost (including fringe benefits) for computer programmer and operator will be $25,000	3. Increased annual labor cost (including fringe benefits) for computer programmer and operator will be $25,000
	4. 5-year estimated life
	5. $10,000 estimated disposal value
	6. Depreciation for tax purposes (with zero salvage value) will be:[3]
	Year 1 $60,000
	Year 2 36,000
	Year 3 21,600
	Year 4 16,200
	Year 5 16,200

---

[3]We ignore the tax requirement that one-half year's depreciation be taken in the year of acquisition and the other one-half year's depreciation be taken in year 6.

EXHIBIT 20-3
Cash Flow Summary for Cutting Machine Investment

Time	Item	Col. 1 Pre-tax acquisition and disposal cash flow	Col. 2 Pre-tax operating cash flow	Col. 3 Tax depreciation	Col. 4 Income tax effect	Col. 5 After-tax cash flow	Col. 6 8% present value factor	Col. 7 (Col. 5 × Col. 6) Present value of after-tax cash flow
Now	Machine cost, delivered and installed	($20,620)			$ -0-	($20,620)	—	($20,620)
Now	Cost of training	(1,000)			400*	(600)	—	(600)
Now	Disposal of old machine	1,700			480**	1,220	—	1,220
End of years 1 through 5	Contribution margin		$2,600		1,040*	1,560	3.9927	$ 6,229
End of years 1 through 5	Lower total wages paid		7,000		2,800*	4,200	3.9927	16,769
End of years 1 through 5	Lower fringe benefits		1,750		700*	1,050	3.9927	4,192
End of years 1 through 5	Increased repairs and maintenance		(4,550)		1,820*	(2,730)	3.9927	(10,900)
End of years 1 through 5	Depreciation			$4,124	1,650*	1,650	3.9927	6,588
End of year 5	Disposal value of new machine	5,000			2,000**	3,000	.6806	2,042
							Net Present Value of Investment	$ 4,920

*40% of Col. 1, 2, or 3
**40% of gain on disposal of machine

If Shero Services has already decided the computer is needed, which method (lease or buy) should be used? *If taxes and the time value of money are ignored,* buying would clearly be the preferable financing technique:

Lease:		
Lease rentals	(5 × $44,000)	$220,000
Labor cost	(5 × $25,000)	125,000
Cost to Lease		$345,000
Buy:		
Computer cost		$150,000
Labor cost	(5 × $25,000)	125,000
Repairs, etc.	(5 × $10,000)	50,000
Disposal value		(10,000)
Cost to Buy		$315,000

However, Exhibit 20-4 indicates that when a 40 percent tax rate is assumed and a 10 percent discount rate is applied to after-tax cash flows, leasing (not buying) is the less expensive financing method ($156,939 cost to lease versus $177,224 cost to buy).

Note in Exhibit 20-4 the $25,000 pre-tax annual labor cost included under both lease and buy. This item has the same $56,862 after-tax present value for both financing methods. Thus, for comparing the lease and buy alternatives, the labor cost is irrelevant. It could have been omitted from the calculations in Exhibit 20-4 without changing the $20,285 relative advantage of leasing over buying.

PERFORMANCE EVALUATION

Planning is an important preliminary step in making short-term decisions and in investing in long-range projects. A firm benefits more fully from planning when the outcome of a decision is reviewed and evaluated. Comparison of subsequent actual performance with anticipated results provides evidence of the reliability and accuracy of the original decision. It also may indicate when plans or projects need modification in order to meet their objectives. In addition, performance evaluation may reveal errors or weaknesses in the planning process itself. The planning process can then be revised to prevent similar errors or weaknesses from contaminating future plans.

A follow-up evaluation is particularly complex for capital investment projects. When numerous factors are interrelated, it is difficult to identify the specific reason for incremental cash flows. For example, it is very hard to isolate the effects of one new machine on operating cash flows for an entire manufacturing operation. Thus, evaluating the performance of the new machine in terms of incremental cash flows, as well as evaluating the original cash flow predictions, is extremely difficult. In addition, the long-range nature of capital investment planning is inherently less exact than short-run annual budgeting. Usually the further one predicts into the future, the greater the degree of error to be expected (and tolerated) in evaluating performance.

Regardless of the difficulties encountered in evaluating performance for long-run capital investment projects, evaluation is not only desirable but necessary. The evaluation process often detects flaws in the organization's capital invest-

EXHIBIT 20-4
Lease vs. Buy Analysis

Time	Item	Col. 1 Pre-tax acquisition and disposal cash flow	Col. 2 Pre-tax operating cash flow	Col. 3 Tax depreciation	Col. 4 Income tax effect	Col. 5 After-tax cash flow	Col. 6 10% present value factor	Col. 7 (Col. 5 × Col. 6) Present value of after-tax cash flow
Lease								
End of years 1 through 5	Annual lease payment		($44,000)		$17,600*	($26,400)	3.7908	($100,077)
End of years 1 through 5	Annual labor cost		(25,000)		10,000*	(15,000)	3.7908	(56,862)
					Present Value of Cost of Leasing Computer			($156,939)
Buy								
Now	Computer cost	($150,000)			-0-	(150,000)	—	($150,000)
End of years 1 through 5	Annual labor cost		(25,000)		10,000*	(15,000)	3.7908	(56,862)
End of years 1 through 5	Repairs, maintenance costs		(10,000)		4,000*	(6,000)	3.7908	(22,745)
End of year 1	Depreciation			$60,000	24,000*	24,000	.9091	21,818
End of year 2	Depreciation			36,000	14,400*	14,400	.8264	11,900
End of year 3	Depreciation			21,600	8,640*	8,640	.7513	6,491
End of year 4	Depreciation			16,200	6,480*	6,480	.6830	4,426
End of year 5	Depreciation			16,200	6,480*	6,480	.6209	4,023
End of year 5	Disposal value of computer	10,000			4,000**	6,000	.6209	3,725
					Present Value of Cost of Buying Computer			($177,224)

*40% of Col. 2 or 3
**40% of gain on disposal

ment analysis process or identifies ongoing projects that should be scrapped or modified.

SUMMARY

Learning Objective 1: Identify cash inflows and outflows relating to a capital investment project.

Capital investment analysis is characterized by long-term multiperiod problems. Capital investment problems usually are concerned with measuring the amount and timing of cash flows rather than income. Relevant cash flows include acquisition outlay and annual operating inflows and outflows. Depreciation is not a cash flow, but it does affect the cash outflow for income taxes.

Learning Objective 2: Apply the payback, accounting rate-of-return, and internal rate-of-return methods.

The payback-period method and accounting rate of return are two frequently used techniques employed in capital investment analysis. Both techniques are seriously deficient since they fail to consider the time value of money in their calculations. This deficiency, coupled with other deficiencies in the two methods, can result in the selection of suboptimal capital investment projects.

The internal rate-of-return method calculates the discount (interest) rate that when applied to expected cash inflows from a capital investment project will produce a present value equal to the present value of the project's cost. The higher the internal rate of return, the more desirable the project. Many firms set as a minimum acceptable rate the firm's cost of capital.

Learning Objective 3: Compare capital investment alternatives using net present value.

The net-present-value technique calculates the present value of all cash inflows and outflows for a capital investment project. Projects with positive net present values are acceptable. The larger the net present value, the more desirable the project.

Learning Objective 4: Calculate cash flows on an after-tax basis.

After-tax cash flows are used in net-present-value analysis. Most inflows and outflows are converted to an after-tax basis by multiplying the cash flow by one minus the tax rate. The tax saving from depreciation is calculated by multiplying depreciation for tax purposes times the tax rate.

Learning Objective 5: Compare lease and buy alternatives.

The decision to lease or buy equipment can be analyzed by the net-present-value method. Each alternative provides different amounts and timing of after-tax cash flows.

KEY TERMS

Accounting rate of return	Internal rate of return
After-tax cash flows	Net present value
Cost of capital	Payback period

REVIEW QUESTIONS

1 What are the major differences between analyzing a capital investment project in this chapter and the cost-volume-profit and incremental analyses of the previous chapter?

2 Valery Slipknee is negotiating a new contract with the Hoboken Hockey Team. The hockey team has made two contract offers: (1) $2,500,000 payable in equal installments at the end of each of the next five years or (2) $2,000,000 for the next five years, payable immediately. Valery is willing to accept either contract offer. Why would the hockey team offer to invest $2,500,000 in Valery's contract when they can get him to sign a contract for $2,000,000? Ignore taxes.

3 List three specific reasons why a person would prefer to receive $1,000 today, rather than a promise to receive $1,000 two years from today.

4 Hairpiece Heaven, Inc. uses the payback method to evaluate capital investment projects. A new toupee-weaving machine would cost $148,000. The company believes the machine would generate incremental annual after-tax cash inflows of $32,000 for four years, and then $20,000 increased annual after-tax cash inflows for the next six years. Calculate the payback period. What weaknesses are inherent in the use of the payback method?

5 Sunkiss Citrus Co. is considering the acquisition of a new seed-removing machine. The machine would cost $246,000, and the company believes that it would increase income by $26,000 for each of the next three years, and then by $24,000 for each of the remaining seven years of the machine's life. Calculate the accounting rate of return. Does the accounting rate of return have the same deficiencies as the payback method?

6 "For many companies, the minimum acceptable internal rate of return is the firm's cost of capital." Evaluate the preceding statement, including definitions of internal rate of return and cost of capital in your answer. Also, relate the above statement to the breakeven concept discussed in the preceding chapter.

7 Brundone Corporation is considering the purchase of a new automatic dipping machine. The machine has a current after-tax cost of $88,000 and is expected to generate $18,462 in annual after-tax cash inflows (including tax savings from depreciation) at the end of each of the next six years. Brundone wants all capital investment projects to earn an internal rate of return equal to (or greater than) the company's 9 percent cost of capital. Is the new dipping machine an acceptable investment? Ignore any salvage value.

8 Nettie P. Valyou, financial vice-president of Butler, Inc., has decided to acquire a new crimping machine because of the following capital investment analysis she performed: "Acquire new machine since the sum of the five equal yearly cash inflows of $22,300 generated by the machine plus its $16,000 salvage value at the end of the fifth year exceed the current $112,500 investment cost." Evaluate Nettie's analysis procedures.

9 There are two time-value-of-money formulas that often are utilized in net-present-value analysis. State the formulas and indicate when each should be used.

10 Zipmart, Inc. is considering the acquisition of a new forklift truck. The forklift will cost $6,800 plus $150 delivery charge. Determine the present value of the acquisition cost of the forklift.

11 If Zipmart, Inc. (see Question 10 above) had an old forklift truck with a $3,000 book value that could be sold for $5,000, what would be the present value of the acquisition cost of the new forklift? (Assume a 40 percent tax rate applies.)

12 Loch Nessie Co. is planning to acquire a new lathe. With the new lathe the

company expects to increase annual sales by $4,000. Repairs and maintenance on the new machine are expected to be $300 yearly. Assume all revenues are received in cash at the end of the year and all expenses are paid in cash at the end of the year. The tax rate is assumed to be 40 percent. What is the annual net after-tax cash flow from operations (excluding tax savings from depreciation)? What is the present value of the net after-tax cash flows from operations (excluding tax savings from depreciation).

13 "Depreciation is a cash outflow that reduces the cash flow from operations." Evaluate the preceding statement.

14 For a machine that cost $50,400, has a zero estimated salvage value, and an estimated life of six years; calculate the annual cash savings (tax reduction) caused by depreciation. Assume a 40 percent tax rate and straight line depreciation.

15 "Depreciation over the life of an asset is the same regardless of the depreciation method selected. Therefore, for capital investment analysis purposes, the choice of depreciation method is irrelevant." Evaluate the preceding statements.

16 Mr. G. Howie Quakes, capital investment analyst of Trembles, Inc., is interviewing you for a job as his assistant. Mr. Quakes asks you what effect, if any, might the estimated disposal value of a prospective capital investment project have on a net-present-value analysis. Be specific in your answer to Mr. Quakes.

17 The cost of outright purchase of a tractor-trailer with a ten-year life is $58,000. The cost to lease the truck for five years would be $13,000 annually. Should the truck be purchased or leased?

18 Exacto Company prides itself on the small variances between budgeted annual operations and actual results of operations each year. Exacto also is hoping to obtain small variances when evaluating actual results of its capital investment projects. What is Exacto likely to encounter when it attempts to evaluate actual performance of capital investment projects?

EXERCISES

E20-1 Fill in each blank with either "larger" or "smaller." Acquiring the new machine will eliminate two machinists from the payroll. Thus expenses will be _____, income will be _____, income taxes will be _____, and after-tax cash savings from the reduced labor cost will be _____than pre-tax cash savings from the reduced payroll. Depreciation, per se, is not a cash inflow or outflow. Deducting depreciation on a tax return makes taxable income _____, which in turn makes the cash outflow for taxes _____. Acquiring a new machine will allow the old machine to be sold. The after-tax proceeds from sale of the old machine will make the acquisition cost of the new machine _____.

E20-2 For each statement below, list the capital investment technique(s) (i.e., payback period, accounting rate of return, internal rate of return, or net present value) to which the statement applies.

1 Has rule, "Accept if positive, reject if negative."

2 Ignores "time value of money."

3 Compared to cost of capital to determine if capital investment project is acceptable.

4 Ignores cash flows in later years of capital investment project's life.

5 Uses cost of capital as discount rate.

6 Often uses "income" instead of cash flows.

7 Involves discounting of forecasted after-tax cash flows.

8 Measures number of years it will take to recover cost of capital investment project.

9 Calculates discount rate that equates present value of future cash inflows with current investment cost.

E20-3 Izzy Goodenough, controller of Ghoul, Inc., is planning a major expansion project that is forecasted to have a current cost of $272,436. Incremental after-tax cash inflows of $40,000 at the end of each of the next fifteen years are forecasted if the expansion project is undertaken. What is the expansion project's internal rate of return? Using a 15 percent discount rate would yield a present value of $233,896 for the after-tax cash inflows. With the 15 percent discount rate, how much would have to be trimmed from the project's cost to yield a positive net present value of $35,000?

E20-4 Plimpton Company is planning to acquire a new machine that will cost $25,000. The estimated life of the machine is ten years, and estimated disposal value is zero. Plimpton estimates annual pre-tax cash savings (ignoring the tax savings from depreciation) of $10,000 from the new machine. The company's income tax rate is 40 percent and its cost of capital is 10 percent. Calculate: (1) the annual after-tax cash inflow from operations (excluding tax savings from depreciation) to be generated by the new machine, (2) the tax reduction from depreciation, and (3) the net present value of the investment in the new machine (rounded to the nearest dollar). The company uses straight line depreciation.

E20-5 Presston, Inc. is analyzing the proposed acquisition of a new piece of factory equipment. The vendor's invoice price is $162,000. Freight charges will cost Presston $2,500. An electrician will charge $2,000 to install the complex wiring for the equipment. An old piece of factory equipment with a book value of $4,000 will no longer be needed. It can be sold for $16,000. Current tax laws provide a 40 percent tax rate on the gain on sale of the old equipment. After-tax income over the life of the new equipment is forecasted to increase by an average of $15,530 per year. Calculate the after-tax, acquisition cash outlay. What is the accounting rate of return?

E20-6 Leeton Freezer Foods is considering the purchase of a new refrigerated delivery truck for $12,000. Estimated life of the truck is five years, after which the disposal value is estimated at $2,000. With the new delivery truck, sales and production are expected to increase by 2,200 boxes per year. Each box sells for $13.40 and has a variable production and selling cost of $4.90. Annual fixed expenses are forecasted to increase by $12,200. Assume an income tax rate of 40 percent. Also assume all revenues are received in cash at the end of each year and all expenses, except depreciation, are paid in cash at the end of each year. Determine: (1) the annual after-tax net cash flow from operations (excluding tax savings from depreciation), (2) the annual tax savings from depreciation if the straight line method is used with a zero salvage value, and (3) the after-tax cash inflow from disposal of the delivery truck after five years.

E20-7 Apex Company is evaluating a capital investment proposal for the current year. The initial investment would have an acquisition cost of $30,000. It would be depreciated on a straight line basis over six years with no salvage value. The annual cash inflow (and income) due to this investment is $10,000 before deducting depreciation and taxes. The company's income tax rate is 40 percent and the firm's cost of capital is 15 percent. Annual cash flows occur at year end.

Required:

1 Calculate the after-tax accounting rate of return (using net income) on Apex's capital investment proposal.
2 Calculate the payback period using after-tax cash flows.
3 Calculate the net present value of Apex's proposed investment.

(AICPA Adapted)

E20-8 Tricina Company wishes to purchase a machine costing $5,800. The machine has a useful life of five years and is depreciated on a straight line basis. After five years the machine will have a salvage value of zero. Annual after-tax cash inflows, including tax savings from depreciation, are $2,000. The company's cost of capital is 10 percent. Determine:

1 The payback period.
2 The internal rate of return (round to the nearest percent).
3 The net present value.

PROBLEMS

P20-1 *Payback, Internal Rate of Return, and Net Present Value*

Wareton Co. is considering the acquisition of a new well-drilling machine. The delivered cost of the drilling machine would be $65,623. The drilling machine is expected to have a useful life of ten years, after which its estimated disposal value will be zero.

Incremental cash inflows of $14,425 per year are projected if the new drilling machine is acquired (excluding tax savings from depreciation). Incremental cash outlays associated with the new well driller are forecasted to be $1,000.

Wareton has an 8 percent cost of capital. The company depreciates all its assets using the straight line method. The tax rate is 40 percent. Round all dollar amounts to nearest dollar and all percentages to nearest tenth of a percent.

Required:

1 Assuming all cash flows occur at the end of the year, calculate the internal rate of return using after-tax cash flows. If the company accepts capital investment projects with internal rates of return greater than the firm's cost of capital, would the well-drilling machine be acceptable?
2 Calculate the payback period, using after-tax cash flows. If the company accepts capital investment projects with a payback period of five years or less, would the well-drilling machine be acceptable?
3 Calculate the net present value using after-tax cash flows. If the company accepts only capital investment projects with positive net present values, is the well-drilling machine acceptable?

P20-2 *Determination of After-Tax Cash Flows*

Preytell Corporation is considering the acquisition of an automatic window-washing machine to clean windows at its corporate headquarters. The machine would cost $32,200. The machine has an estimated life of seven years and an estimated disposal value of $3,000. For tax purposes, the salvage value will be zero, and straight line depreciation will be used.

Acquiring the automatic window washer will allow Preytell Corporation to fire an employee who had cleaned the windows using a semiautomatic machine. The annual salary and fringe benefits of the the worker totaled $14,480. The old semiautomatic machine, which has been depreciated to an estimated $2,000 salvage value, will no longer be needed. Its current disposal value is $5,000.

Preytell's tax rate is 40 percent. Assume all expenses (other than depreciation) represent cash outflows at the end of the year.

Required:
1 Calculate the after-tax acquisition cash outlay for the automatic window-washing machine.
2 Calculate the annual after-tax cash savings for the automatic window washer. (Include labor cost and tax savings from depreciation.)
3 Calculate the after-tax cash flow at the end of the seventh year from projected disposal value of the new automatic window washer.
4 Present a time-line diagram of the after-tax cash flows determined for requirements (1), (2), and (3).

P20-3 *Net-Present-Value Calculations for Machine Purchase*
Madisons, Inc. has decided to acquire a new piece of equipment. It may do so by an outright cash purchase at $25,000 or by a leasing alternative of $6,000 per year for the life of the machine. Other relevant information follows:

Estimated useful life of machine	5 years
Estimated disposal value if purchased	$5,000
Annual cost of maintenance contract to be acquired with either lease or purchase	500
Assume a 40 percent tax rate	

Assume straight line depreciation and a zero
  salvage value for tax purposes if the
  machine is purchased	

All annual cash flows occur at the end of the year	
Madisons' cost of capital is 10 percent	

Required:
1 Calculate the present value of the after-tax, cash purchase price of the machine.
2 Under the purchase alternative, determine the present value of the estimated disposal value.
3 Under the purchase alternative, determine the annual cash savings (tax reduction) related to depreciation.
4 Under the purchase alternative, determine the annual after-tax cash outflow for maintenance.

(AICPA Adapted)

P20-4 *Lease vs. Buy*
Using the data for Madisons, Inc. in Problem 3, prepare an analysis of whether the new machine should be acquired by outright cash purchase or through leasing.

Present your analysis in a format similar to that shown in Exhibit 20-4 in the chapter.

P20-5 *Net Present Value*

The following information is available for a new machine that Tier Company is evaluating:

Annual operating costs (excluding depreciation)	$ 2,000
Annual operating savings	10,000
Disposal value in 5 years	600
Machine cost	39,800
Delivery cost	800
Sale price of old machine	
(book value of $1,000)	1,200
Tax rate	40%
Cost of capital	12%
Depreciation for taxes: Straight line, zero salvage value	

Required:

Determine the net present value of the investment. Present your analysis in a format similar to that shown in Exhibit 20-3 in the chapter.

P20-6 *Comparison of Three Projects*

Sandy Claws Co. is evaluating the following three proposed capital investment projects:

Project A

1 $108,000 initial investment cost.

2 Estimated useful life, six years.

3 Estimated disposal value of $7,800. However, for tax depreciation purposes, salvage value is assumed to be zero.

4 Incremental annual cash inflows of $26,000.

5 Incremental annual cash outlays of $6,933.

6 Straight line depreciation to be used.

Project AA

1 $72,000 initial investment cost.

2 Estimated useful life, six years.

3 Estimated disposal value and salvage value of zero.

4 $39,600 additional investment cost at end of year 3. Estimated useful life of additional investment is three years (years 4, 5, and 6) with zero estimated disposal and salvage value.

5 Incremental annual cash inflows of $39,867.

6 Incremental annual cash outlays of $20,800.

7 Straight line depreciation to be used.

Project AAA

1 $90,000 initial investment cost.

2 Estimated useful life, six years.

3 Estimated disposal value of $4,333. However, for tax depreciation purposes, salvage value is assumed to be zero.

4 $39,867 incremental annual cash inflows for years 1 through 4, $30,333 for year 5, and $26,000 for year 6.

5 Incremental annual cash outlays of $13,867.

6 Straight line depreciation to be used.

Assume all annual cash inflows and outlays are year-end cash flows. The income tax rate is 40 percent. The company's cost of capital is 5 percent.

Required:

Calculate the net present value of all three capital investment projects. (Round all amounts to nearest dollar.) Which projects are acceptable? Use a format similar to Exhibit 20-3 for calculation of net present values.

P20-7 *Net Present Value Analysis*

The Dino Sour Toy Company's research department has just perfected a new doll called the "Sabre-Tooth Tarantula" (STT, for short). The marketing department believes the STT doll will be a big success.

To produce the doll on a large scale, new production equipment will be needed. The delivered and installed cost of the new equipment would be $1,200,000. Physically the new equipment will last ten years. However, the Dino Sour Toy Company plans to sell the new equipment after five years when the market for the STT doll should be exhausted. The estimated value of the equipment after five years is $65,000.

A sales price of $10.50 per doll has been set. Variable costs of $6.50 per doll are expected. Other than depreciation of the new equipment, there are no incremental fixed costs expected in producing or selling the STT. The tax rate is assumed to be 40 percent. The company's cost of capital is 7 percent. The marketing department predicts sales of 260,000; 177,332; 69,334; 34,670; and 8,667 dolls respectively over the next five years.

Tax depreciation will be $480,000 in year 1, $288,000 in year 2, $172,800 in year 3, and $129,600 in years 4 and 5.

Required:

Prepare an analysis of the net present value of the after-tax cash flows involved in the STT project. Round all amounts to the nearest dollar. Assume the contribution margin generated by sales of the dolls represents cash inflow at the end of each year. Use Exhibit 20-3 in the chapter as a guide for the format of your analysis.

Business Decision Problem

Beta Corporation, a manufacturer of office equipment, recently learned of a patent on the production of a semiautomatic paper collator that can be obtained at a cost of $60,000 cash. The semiautomatic model is vastly superior to the manual model that the corporation now produces. At a cost of $40,000, present equipment could be modified to accommodate the production of the new model. Such modifications would not affect the remaining useful life of four years. Variable costs, however, would increase by $1.00 per unit. Fixed costs, other than amortization and depreciation charges, would not be affected. If the equipment is modified, the manual model cannot be produced.

The current statement of income relative to the manual collator appears as follows:

Sales (100,000 units @ $4)		$400,000
Variable costs	$180,000	
Fixed costs*	120,000	300,000
Income before income taxes		$100,000
Income taxes (40%)		40,000
Net income		$ 60,000

*All fixed costs are directly related to the production of the manual collator and include depreciation on equipment of $20,000, calculated by the straight line method using a useful life of ten years.

Market research has disclosed three important findings relative to the new semiautomatic model. First, a particular competitor will certainly purchase the patent if Beta does not. If this were to happen, Beta's sales of the manual collator would fall to 70,000 units per year. Second, if no increase is made in the selling price, Beta could sell approximately 190,000 units per year of the semiautomatic model. Third, because of advances being made in technology, the patent and machines used to produce the collator will be worthless at the end of four years.

Required:

1 Prepare an analysis which shows the net present value of the after-tax cash flows for the two alternatives. Assume Beta will use the sum of years digits method for depreciating the equipment modification costs. Beta's cost of capital is 15 percent. Assume the contribution margin and the fixed costs (except depreciation and amortization) represent cash flows at the end of the year. Use Exhibit 20-3 as a guide for the format of your analysis. Include in your analysis for each alternative: sales revenue, variable costs, fixed costs (except depreciation and amortization), depreciation, and patent amortization. Round all answers to the nearest dollar.

2 What concerns would you have about using the information given in the problem to reach a decision in this case?

(CMA Adapted)

GLOSSARY

absorption costing Also called full costing; includes all manufacturing costs as part of the cost of work in process inventory, finished goods inventory, and cost of goods sold. This is the required method of costing inventory for financial reporting and income tax purposes.

accelerated depreciation Methods of depreciation that provide for a systematic write-off of depreciable costs in progressively smaller annual amounts.

accountant's worksheet An informal, specially designed columnar sheet of paper that is often used by the accountant at the end of the accounting period as a test of the accuracy of the end-of-period accounting work prior to making formal entries in the accounting records.

accounting The process of recording, classifying, summarizing, and reporting financial information for the purpose of aiding decision makers.

accounting concepts General rules (sometimes called postulates or conventions) that provide a foundation for generally accepted accounting principles and procedures.

accounting equation Expressed as Assets = Liabilities + Stockholders' Equity. Because each asset must be financed by either creditors or owners, the total liabilities plus stockholders' equity must equal total assets.

accounting income Income determined in accordance with "generally accepted accounting principles" as set forth by the Financial Accounting Standards Board and other sources.

accounting periods concept Requires that the continuing activities of a firm be broken into periods for the purpose of issuing financial statements.

accounting rate of return The percentage determined by dividing a project's average annual income by its investment cost.

$$\text{Accounting Rate of Return} = \frac{\text{Average Annual Income}}{\text{Investment Cost}}$$

accounts payable   Obligations to those who have provided goods or services to a firm on credit.

accounts payable subsidiary ledger   A listing in alphabetical order of all vendor accounts. Each individual vendor account shows the past purchases on account, subsequent cash payments, and current balance owed.

accounts receivable   Represents customers' promises to pay amounts due as a result of a prior sale on credit.

accounts receivable subsidiary ledger   A listing in alphabetical order of all customer accounts. Each individual customer account provides a complete history of the customer's purchases on account, subsequent cash collections, and balance due.

accrual accounting   Provides for the recognition of revenue when a product is sold or services are rendered; provides for recognition of expenses in the period in which goods and services were consumed to generate the revenue.

accumulated depreciation   The total amount of plant and equipment cost expensed to date. This is a contra asset account.

acid-test ratio   See Quick Ratio.

acquisition cost   The after-tax cash outlay made for an investment after all relevant costs of the investment are considered.

activity base   A reasonable and easily measured basis used in the process of allocating overhead costs. Some common activity bases are direct labor hours, direct labor dollars, or machine hours.

adjusted bank balance   The bank statement balance adjusted for transactions recorded by the company but not yet recorded by the bank and corrections of any errors made by the bank. This balance must equal the adjusted book balance on a bank reconciliation.

adjusted book balance   The book balance adjusted for transactions recorded by the bank but not yet recorded on the books and corrections of any errors made by the company. This balance must equal the adjusted bank balance on a bank reconciliation.

adjusted trial balance   A trial balance taken after adjusting entries have been journalized and posted to the general ledger accounts.

adjusting journal entries   Journal entries commonly required at the end of a reporting period: (a) to record events that have occurred but have not yet been recorded, (b) to record a change in an item since it was originally recorded, or (c) to correct errors.

after-closing trial balance   A trial balance after the closing entries have been journalized and posted to the general ledger accounts.

after-tax cash flows   The net cash flows used in capital investment analysis after the tax impact is considered.

aging the accounts   Determining how long each individual customer account receivable balance has been outstanding. Used as a means of estimating the balance required in the allowance for uncollectible accounts.

allowance for uncollectible accounts   A contra asset account that reduces accounts receivable to net realizable value. The allowance account signifies that a reduction in accounts receivable is expected due to uncollectibility, but specific accounts and amounts are not yet known.

allowance for unrealized loss   A contra asset account that reduces marketable equity securities by the difference between the total cost of the securities and the total market value of the securities at the balance sheet date.

allowance method for uncollectible accounts   Method of recognizing and recording estimated bad debts expense in the same period the related sales revenue is recorded. Also designed to present accounts receivable at net realizable value on the balance sheet.

amortization   The charging to expense of the cost of an intangible asset over its estimated useful life using the straight line method. Amortization also refers to the process of adjusting bond interest expense due to the writing off of bond discount or bond premium.

amortization table   Shows the amortization of bond discount/premium, interest, and carrying value of bond for the life of the bond.

annuity   A series of equal cash flows occurring at the end of each of a sequence of time periods.

applied manufacturing overhead   Applied Manufacturing Overhead = Predetermined Manufacturing Overhead Rate × Volume of Activity Base During the Period.

appropriated retained earnings   The amount of retained earnings that is legally restricted by contract agreements or by voluntary action taken by the board of directors.

articles of incorporation   See Corporate Charter.

asset turnover   Ratio that measures the intensity with which assets are used during the period (i.e., it indicates the dollars of net sales generated per dollar of assets).

$$\text{Asset Turnover} = \frac{\text{Net Sales}}{\text{Average Assets}}$$

assets   Items of value owned or controlled by the firm that are expected to provide future benefits for the firm.

auditor's report   Contains the opinion of an independent certified public accountant regarding the fairness of the client's financial statements in conformity with generally accepted accounting principles, and a statement of the scope of the auditor's examination.

average collection period   Indicates the average number of days it takes to collect accounts receivable. It serves as a measure of the liquidity of the receivables and also provides information on how efficiently management controls the firm's investment in receivables.

$$\text{Average Collection Period} = \frac{\text{Average Accounts Receivable (net)}}{\text{Average Daily Sales}}$$

average number of days' supply in inventory   Measures how quickly inventory is being sold. It serves as an indication of how efficiently management controls the firm's investment in inventory.

$$\text{Average Number of Days' Supply in Inventory} = \frac{\text{Average Inventory}}{\text{Average Daily Cost of Goods Sold}}$$

bad debt   An account receivable or note receivable determined to be uncollectible after collection efforts have proven unsuccessful.

bad debt expense   Deduction on income statement for portion of sales revenue that is believed to be uncollectible.

balance sheet   A summarized report of a firm's assets, liabilities, and stockholders' equity as of a given date.

bank overdraft   The amount by which a company has overdrawn its bank balance (i.e., has a negative cash balance in the bank account). This is considered a loan by the bank to the company and therefore should be reported as a current liability.

bank reconciliation   The process of reconciling the bank statement balance with the company's general ledger cash account balance.

bank service charge   Fee charged by a bank to its customers for services performed.

bank statement   A bank-produced document that summarizes all transactions occurring in a bank account during the period.

board of directors   Responsible for promoting and protecting the stockholders' interests. The Board determines corporate goals and strategies, approves major contracts, authorizes dividends, and evaluates corporate officers' performance.

bond discount   The excess of the face value of the bonds over the amount of cash received from the issuance of the bonds. Bonds are issued at a discount when the current market rate of interest is higher than the coupon interest rate. The bond discount account is a contra liability.

bond premium   The excess of the cash received from the issuance of bonds over the face value of the bonds. Bonds are issued at a premium when the current market rate of interest is less than the coupon interest rate.

bonds   Legal obligation on the part of the issuer to make periodic interest payments and repay the face amount at maturity.

bonds payable   A long-term debt incurred by a company as a result of issuing bonds. The issuing corporation is required to make periodic interest payments and repay the face amount at maturity.

book value   Cost minus accumulated depreciation; the amount at which long-lived assets (e.g., buildings and equipment) are presented on the balance sheet. Also known as Net Book Value.

book value per share of common stock   A technique sometimes used to evaluate a company's net worth.

$$\frac{\text{Book Value per Share}}{\text{of Common Stock}} = \frac{\text{Book Value of Common Stockholders' Equity}}{\text{Common Shares Outstanding}}$$

breakeven point   The level of activity where total revenues equal total expenses and net income is thus zero.

budget   Formal financial plan that serves as a guide for future action, and also serves as a basis for the evaluation of performance. Budgets are estimates of future activity and therefore have some degree of uncertainty.

budget period   The time a budget covers. A budget period can range from the next hour to several decades, although most budgets cover a year.

budgeted direct material purchases   = Direct Materials to be Used + Desired Ending Direct Materials Inventory − Available Beginning Direct Materials Inventory.

budgeted production in units   = Units to be Sold + Desired Ending Finished Goods Inventory − Available Beginning Finished Goods Inventory.

budgeting   The process of providing for a designated time period a formal plan of action to identify the resources needed, the appropriate quantities, and the proper timing.

bulk purchase   Acquiring several assets in one purchase transaction.

business documents   Documents which present data concerning business transactions; used as evidence that the transactions in fact occurred.

callable bonds   Bonds that may be retired (called) before maturity at the option of the issuing corporation.

callable preferred stock   Preferred stock that the issuing corporation has the option to call (i.e., redeem) at a specified price.

capital   The amount invested in an entity by its owners; net assets.

capital investment analysis   Characterized by long-run, multiperiod alternatives where decisions are based on the amount and timing of after-tax cash flows rather than income.

capital stock   Stockholders' equity arising from direct investment by the stockholders.

capitalization of retained earnings   The transferral of a portion of the retained earnings account balance to invested capital accounts (common stock and paid-in capital) in the recording of a stock dividend.

capitalize   Debit to an asset account. Costs are capitalized if it is expected that they will not be entirely consumed in the current period.

capitalized lease   A lease agreement treated essentially as the purchase of an asset financed by a long-term installment debt. The present value of the lease payments is recognized as both an asset and a liability.

carrying value of bonds   Face value of outstanding bonds plus the unamortized premium or minus the unamortized discount.

cash basis of revenue recognition   Recognizes revenue only when cash is received. The cash basis is acceptable only if collection is a significant (nonroutine) element in the process of making a sale and the occurrence of collection is quite uncertain.

cash budget   A detailed plan of expected cash transactions for a future time period.

cash disbursements journal   A special journal restricted solely to cash payment transactions.

cash discount   An inducement for prompt payment that takes the form of a price reduction if payment is made within a specified period.

cash dividends   Payment of a specified amount of cash on each share of stock.

cash dividends payable   A legal liability of a corporation that results from the formal declaration of the cash dividend by the corporation's board of directors.

cash flows   Increases or decreases in cash classified as being from operating activities, investing activities, or financing activities.

cash from operations   Determined by adjusting net income to 1) convert from accrual basis to cash basis and 2) to eliminate any items not from *normal* operations.

cash in bank   Money on deposit in the company's name in a bank.

cash on hand   Coins, currency, or customers' checks physically on the company's premises.

cash receipts journal   The special journal restricted solely to all cash receipts transactions.

cash sale   The customer pays for the product or service immediately upon delivery.

change in accounting estimate   An ongoing process of revising accounting estimates based on newly available information or changed conditions; revisions are handled prospectively—only the current and future years are affected.

change in accounting principle   See Cumulative Effect of Change in Accounting Principle.

chart of accounts   Lists a company's ledger accounts and their assigned account numbers.

chronological cash budget   Presents projected cash receipts, cash disbursements, and cash balance on a day-to-day basis.

closing entry   Journal entry transferring revenue, expense, and dividends declared ledger account balances for the period to retained earnings.

commitments to issue common stock   A company's promise to issue common stock at some future date. Examples of commitments include: convertible securities, stock options, and warrants.

common-sized financial statements   A financial statement that expresses each item on the statement as a percentage of an important base amount on that statement. On the income statement, net sales is usually the base. On the balance sheet, total assets is usually the base.

common stock   Residual ownership interest in a corporation. Rights of common stockholders include the right to vote, the right to receive a proportionate share of assets upon liquidation, the right to receive a proportionate share of dividends declared, and the right to purchase a proportionate percentage of additional shares of common stock issued by the corporation.

comparative financial statements   Presentation of both the current period's and preceding period's financial statements.

compound interest   Interest calculated on the principal plus interest earned from previous periods.

compound journal entry   A journal entry that involves more than one debit and/or credit.

compounding   Moving from a known present value to an unknown future value using compound interest.

comprehensive budget   An integrated plan of activity that sets forth budgets for: sales; production and inventory levels; materials, labor, and overhead; selling activities; other activities (research, administrative); cash flow; and projected financial statements.

computer simulation models   A set of mathematical equations that express the complex interrelationships of a firm's internal functions and external relationships.

conservatism   Accounting concept that suggests that estimates/judgments be made cautiously. Unrealized probable losses or decreases in asset values are usually recognized, but probable gains or increases in asset values are not recognized until they actually occur (such as by sale of the asset).

consistency concept   Accounting concept that requires the same principles be used from one reporting period to the next in order to assure comparability of the financial statements.

constant dollar financial statements   Financial statements that adjust historical cost statements to reflect the change in the purchasing power of the dollar; only nonmonetary financial statement items are restated.

contingent liability   Potential obligation; existence of an actual liability depends upon the occurrence of a future event.

continuing operations   Section of the income statement containing the normal recurring revenues and expenses of the company.

continuous budgeting   Management maintains a constant planning horizon by adding a new month to the budget as each current month passes.

contra account   An account whose balance is subtracted from a related account on the financial statements. Examples include: accumulated depreciation, allowance for uncollectible accounts, sales returns, and bond discount.

contra asset   An account whose balance is subtracted from the related asset account on the balance sheet. For example: allowance for uncollectible accounts subtracted from accounts receivable.

contra liability An account whose balance is subtracted from the related liability account on the balance sheet. For example: bond discount subtracted from bonds payable face amount.

contribution margin The difference between sales revenue and variable cost. Contribution margin can be expressed in total dollars, dollars per unit, or as a percentage of sales.

contribution toward indirect expenses and profit Indicates the excess of sales revenue over direct expenses for a segment of the business.

control and performance evaluation One of the four major areas of managerial accounting; uses income, rate of return, budget comparisons, and cost comparisons to assess the results during and after the period.

conversion cost The cost of direct labor and applied manufacturing overhead applied to units of production.

conversion of bonds See Convertible Security.

conversion ratio The index of purchasing power at the end of the current period divided by the index of purchasing power at the date the nonmonetary item was received or incurred; used to restate nonmonetary items on constant dollar financial statements.

convertible preferred stock See Convertible Security.

convertible security A security (convertible bond or preferred stock) that the holder may exchange for a given amount of common stock.

copyrights Legal rights to literary and artistic works.

corporate charter Document that specifies the powers and restrictions imposed by the state in which the company incorporates.

corporation Legal entity that has an existence separate from that of its owners. A corporation can, in its own name, own property, enter into contracts, sue and be sued, and engage in any other business transactions permitted by the corporate charter.

cost A measure of the amount the firm has given up to acquire goods and services.

cost center A segment of an organization that incurs costs but does not generate revenues.

cost method Valuing assets (such as investments in bonds, inventories, nonmarketable-nonsignificant investments in stocks) at cost on the balance sheet.

cost of capital The average cost to the company of obtaining investment funds.

cost of goods available for sale The sum of the beginning inventory plus purchases. It indicates the cost of all the merchandise that the firm had available for sale during the period. This cost also must equal the cost of goods that were sold plus the cost of goods that were not sold (ending inventory).

cost of goods manufactured Manufacturing costs associated with goods completed during the period.

cost of goods sold The expense account showing the cost of goods that were sold to customers during the period. Cost of Goods Sold = Beginning Inventory + Purchases − Ending Inventory.

cost of operations Cost of services provided to the customers of service firms. Analogous to the merchandising or manufacturing firm's cost of goods sold.

cost of sales See Cost of Goods Sold.

cost per equivalent unit Requires averaging the total departmental costs over the number of units completed plus the equivalent number of units in the ending inventory.

$$\text{Cost Per Equivalent Unit} = \frac{\text{Total Departmental Costs for the Period}}{\text{Total Equivalent Units Produced During the Period}}$$

costs accounted for The costs assigned to output in a process costing system; must always agree with "costs to account for."

costs to account for The costs entering a department in a process costing system; must always agree with "costs accounted for."

cost-volume-profit analysis (CVP) Mathematical and/or graphical examination of projected profits at various levels of activity. Projections must be made for fixed costs, variable costs, and the sales price.

cost-volume-profit equations

(a) Unit volume data:

$$\text{Sales in Units to Reach Desired Net Income} = \frac{\text{Total Fixed Costs} + \text{Desired Net Income}}{\text{Contribution Margin (dollars)}}$$

(b) Total revenue data:

$$\text{Desired Total Sales Revenue} = \frac{\text{Total Fixed Costs} + \text{Desired Net Income}}{\text{Contribution Margin (percentage of sales)}}$$

coupon rate Stated interest rate appearing on bonds. Multiplying the coupon rate times the face value of the bonds determines the annual cash interest payment. The coupon rate is also known as the face rate, cash rate, nominal rate, and stated rate.

credit (cr.) An entry on the right side. Credits represent decreases in assets and increases in liabilities and stockholders' equity.

cumulative effect of change in accounting principle Special item on the income statement in the year a company changes from one acceptable method of accounting to another. The cumulative effect adjustment is the total past impact of the change shown net of tax effects.

cumulative preferred stock A preferred stock issue on which undeclared dividends accumulate and must be paid before any dividends can be paid to common stockholders. The accumulated preferred dividends are referred to as "preferred dividends in arrears."

current assets Defined as cash, or assets expected to be converted to cash or sold or consumed through normal operations within one year or the normal operating cycle, whichever is longer.

current liabilities Obligations that the firm expects to satisfy within a relatively short period of time (usually one year or less).

current portion of long-term debt Installment payments of long-term debt that are due within one year and are classified as a current liability on the balance sheet.

current ratio A measure of liquidity that is a rough indicator of the ability of a company to pay its current obligations.

$$\text{Current Ratio} = \frac{\text{Current Assets}}{\text{Current Liabilities}}$$

current value accounting Reports changes in the specific value of each nonmonetary item, not changes in the measuring unit (i.e., the dollar).

date of declaration Date on which a dividend is formally declared by the board of directors. Cash dividends become a current liability on this date.

date of payment Date on which a cash dividend is distributed.

date of record Date used to determine those individuals who are entitled to receive a corporation's dividend; persons listed on a corporation's records as owning the stock on this date will be paid the dividend even if they sell their shares of stock prior to the date of payment.

debit (dr.) An entry on the left side. Debits represent increases in assets and decreases in liabilities and stockholders' equity.

decision analysis One of the four main areas of managerial accounting. It concerns analyzing data to determine the effects of possible actions on projected revenues, expenses, and profits.

declining balance method A depreciation method in which depreciation expense is determined by multiplying a constant rate times a decreasing base (cost − accumulated depreciation).

deferred income taxes The difference between income tax expense recorded for accounting purposes and income taxes currently payable. Deferred income tax is due to timing differences.

deflation An economic state in which the purchasing power of the dollar increases (i.e., the price level decreases).

departmental work in process A separate work in process inventory account used for each manufacturing process to accumulate costs by department.

depletion Method of charging to expense over time the cost of land purchased for the extraction of natural resources. A units of production method is used for the calculation of depletion for each period.

deposit in transit Cash collected (and recorded) by the company and sent to the bank for deposit, but which has not yet been recorded as a deposit by the bank.

depreciation The allocation of the cost of a long-lived asset (e.g., building, equipment) to expense over its estimated useful life.

differential analysis See Incremental Analysis.

direct costing Method by which only variable manufacturing costs are included in the cost of work in process inventory, finished goods inventory, and cost of goods sold. Fixed manufacturing costs are expensed in the period incurred. Direct costing (also known as variable costing) is not a generally acceptable accounting method of valuing inventory for financial reporting or income tax purposes, but may be used for internal reporting.

direct expenses Expenses specifically related and traceable to a particular segment of the organization.

direct labor Wages for those factory employees directly engaged in the manufacture of the product.

direct labor budget Forecasted direct labor hours and dollars based on budgeted production in units for a period of time. It aids in forecasting the need to hire, lay off, or reassign employees, or to schedule production in a manner that will minimize overtime and idle time.

direct materials Raw material employed directly in the production process that is identifiable in the final product.

direct materials purchases budget Forecasted quantity and cost of direct materials to be purchased based on budgeted production in units and required inventory levels.

direct materials used = Beginning Direct Materials Inventory + Direct Materials Purchased − Ending Direct Materials Inventory.

direct method Determining cash flow from operations by analyzing each item on the income statement to determine if it represents an operating activity and, if so, converting it from an accrual measure to a cash flow.

direct write-off method for uncollectible accounts   Method of recognizing and recording an individual account receivable as a bad debt expense when the specific individual account is deemed uncollectible.

disclosure   Presenting additional, descriptive information that is relevant to the financial statements by means of notes, parenthetical expressions, and supplemental schedules.

discontinued operations   Special item on the income statement that presents (net of tax) the operating income and gain or loss on disposal of a discontinued segment of the company.

discount   See Bond Discount.

discount on common stock   The excess of par value over the issuance price of common stock.

discounting   Finding the present value of future amount(s).

discounting a note receivable   The process of selling a note to a bank or finance company in order to obtain cash prior to the note's maturity date.

dishonored notes receivable   An asset showing a holder's claim against the maker of a note who has failed to pay the note on its maturity date.

disposal value   The anticipated selling price of a long-lived asset at the end of its estimated useful life. The present value of the anticipated after-tax cash inflow from disposal is an element in a capital investment analysis.

dividend payout   Expresses the relationship between cash dividends and earnings.

$$\text{Dividend Payout Ratio} = \frac{\text{Cash Dividends}}{\text{Net Income}}$$

dividend yield   Expresses the cash dividends as a percentage of market price of the stock.

$$\text{Dividend Yield} = \frac{\text{Cash Dividends per Share}}{\text{Market Price per Share}}$$

dividends   Distributions of assets earned by profitable operations to stockholders. Also, see Stock Dividend.

dividends in arrears   See Cumulative Preferred Stock.

double taxation   Disadvantage of the corporate form of organization due to corporate income being taxed once when earned by the corporation and again when distributed to the stockholders in the form of dividends.

earnings per share   A measure of a firm's performance in relation to a single share of stock ownership.

$$\text{Earnings Per Share} = \frac{\text{Net Income Less Preferred Dividends, If Any}}{\text{Weighted Average Number of Common Shares Outstanding}}$$

effective interest method of amortization   Multiplies the market rate of interest at the date of issuance/purchase of a bond times the carrying value of the bond to determine the interest expense/revenue.

effective interest rate True interest rate being incurred by issuing corporation (and received by bond investors) when bonds are sold at a discount or premium.

entity concept An accounting concept that requires the focus of accounting to be on the company—not on the owners of the company.

equity method Valuing long-term, significant stock investments at cost, adjusted for percentage share of investee's net income and percentage share of dividends declared by investee.

equivalent units of production A concept used in process costing that requires partially completed units to be re-expressed in terms of completed units.

exchange gain or loss The difference between the amount initially recorded for a foreign transaction and the amount at which the transaction is ultimately settled. The difference is attributable to a change in the exchange rate between the time the transaction originated and the time it was settled.

exchange rate The conversion price from one country's currency to that of another country's. U.S. Amount = Foreign Amount × Exchange Rate.

expenses The cost of the goods and services that have been consumed in earning the revenues of the period.

extraordinary item Presented (net of tax) as a special item on the income statement. Extraordinary items are gains and losses that are very unusual and not expected to recur in the foreseeable future.

face value The dollar amount printed on a note or bond certificate. For a bond the face amount also is known as the maturity amount.

fair market value The current market price of an asset.

favorable variance Results from standard costs being greater than actual costs. This implies that either operations have been more efficient than expected or the standards were set too leniently.

federal income tax Tax levied by the federal government on the taxable income of corporations and individuals.

feedback Process of providing management with reports on actual performance. Feedback allows management to determine if plans are being executed as formulated.

fidelity bonds Insurance protection for a company against losses through employee dishonesty.

financial accounting The process of providing information, often in the form of financial statements, to stockholders, potential investors, creditors, government agencies, and other outside users.

Financial Accounting Standards Board (FASB) An independent agency whose task is to set generally accepted accounting principles.

financing activities Debt and equity transactions that result in an inflow or outflow of cash.

finished goods inventory Goods that have been completed in production but not yet sold.

first-in, first-out method (FIFO) Inventory cost flow method that assumes that the cost of the first unit purchased is the first cost to be charged to cost of goods sold.

fiscal period The accounting period used for reporting purposes by a company, usually a 12-month period.

fixed cost Assumption that total cost does not change (remains "fixed") when the level of activity varies within a relevant range.

fixed manufacturing overhead budget variance Attributable to price differences between actual and budgeted fixed manufacturing overhead costs. Fixed Manufacturing Overhead Budget Variance = Actual Fixed Overhead − Budgeted Fixed Overhead.

fixed manufacturing overhead volume variance Arises from failure to operate at the planned production level. Fixed Manufacturing Overhead Volume Variance = (Budgeted Direct Labor Hours − Standard Hours Allowed) × Fixed Overhead Rate.

flexible budget A series of budgets prepared for various production levels. A flexible budget prepared for the production level actually achieved should be used to evaluate performance.

flow chart A diagram, or graphic representation, using specified symbols.

footnotes See Notes to the Financial Statements.

foreign currency A ledger account stating in U.S. dollars the foreign currency held by a firm involved in international transactions.

forward exchange contract A contract that can be purchased for conversion of currency at a future date at a specified rate called a "forward rate."

forward rate The specified exchange rate of a forward exchange contract.

franchises Contractual rights to carry on a certain business operation in a particular area.

full costing See Absorption Costing.

future value The amount of money to be accumulated as of some future date.

general journal Book of original entry used to record transactions that do not fit into any of the special journals.

general price level adjusted financial statements See Constant Dollar Financial Statements.

general price level changes Composite effect of changes in prices of all goods and services in the economy.

generally accepted accounting principles Accounting principles that have been formally established by standard-setting organizations (currently the Financial Accounting Standards Board) or that have obtained acceptance through continued use over years.

going-concern concept The assumption that a firm will continue its business operations for a period of time sufficient to utilize its assets through normal operations.

goodwill The amount paid by the buyer of a business in excess of the total current market value of the individual assets acquired, net of any liabilities assumed.

gross margin See Gross Profit.

gross price method for cash discounts Commonly used method of accounting for discounts by which sales revenue is initially recorded at the full invoice price and then adjusted to record discounts at the time of collection. (Also applicable to purchases.)

gross profit The amount by which the selling price of a company's products exceeds the cost of buying or producing them (i.e., sales revenue less the cost of goods sold).

gross profit method A method of estimating cost of goods sold and ending inventory using historical gross profit percentages.

historical cost The original cost, unadjusted for subsequent changes in value, at which many assets are presented on the balance sheet.

horizontal analysis Technique that analyzes changes in dollar amounts and percentage changes for comparative financial statements.

income from continuing operations See Continuing Operations.

income statement Report of a firm's profitability for a period of time. Revenues, expenses, and the difference between the two (net income or net loss) are presented.

income summary account An account used by some accountants in the closing process.

Revenue and expense are closed into the income summary account and then the balance of the income summary account (net income or net loss) is closed into retained earnings.

income tax expense   Tax expense based on pre-tax accounting income.

income taxes payable   Calculated by applying the current tax rates to taxable income.

incremental analysis   A quantitative decision-making tool that analyzes special, non-routine decisions. Expected revenues and cost differentials for possible alternatives are determined and compared.

indirect expenses   Expenses incurred for the continued existence of the organization as a whole and not directly traceable to a particular segment of the organization.

indirect labor   Factory labor that is not directly traceable to a particular product or job. Indirect labor is included in manufacturing overhead.

indirect materials   Raw materials that are not identifiable in the final product or job or are a very minor element. Indirect materials are a part of manufacturing overhead.

indirect method   Presenting the cash flow from operations in the form of a reconciliation between net income and net cash flow provided by operating activities.

inflation   An economic state in which the purchasing power of the dollar has decreased, or, in other words, the price level of goods and services has increased.

installment notes   Notes that provide for periodic payments of both interest and principal.

installment sales method   Cash-basis recognition method used for installment sales if there is a high degree of uncertainty that the sales price will be collected. A portion of sales revenue is recognized each time an installment payment is collected.

intangible asset   A long-lived, nonphysical asset. Intangible assets derive their value from the exclusive rights or economic advantages they provide to the firm. Examples are patents, copyrights, goodwill, and trademarks.

intercompany comparisons   An analysis technique that compares a company with other companies in the industry and/or to an industry average.

interdepartmental transfers   Those partially completed units that are transferred from one manufacturing department to another. The cost of the units transferred in from another manufacturing department must be accounted for by the receiving department along with the receiving department's own direct materials, direct labor, and manufacturing overhead.

interest   The cost of borrowing money.

internal control   A company's plan of organization and the methods and procedures it uses to safeguard assets, achieve accuracy of accounting data, encourage and measure compliance with company policies, and evaluate the efficiency of all operations.

internal rate of return   The discount rate that, when applied to expected cash inflows for a capital investment project, will produce a present value equal to the current investment cost.

intracompany comparison   See Trend Analysis.

inventory   An asset; raw materials on hand, goods being manufactured, and finished goods being held for resale to customers.

inventory cost-flow assumption   The pattern of assigning costs to inventory and cost of goods sold. Some of the methods are: specific identification; last-in, first-out; first-in, first-out; and weighted average.

invested capital   Direct stockholder investment in a corporation. Represented by capital stock and paid-in capital accounts.

investing activities   Purchase or sale of investments; property, plant, and equipment; and other nonoperating assets that result in an inflow or outflow of cash.

investment center   A segment of an organization that in addition to generating revenues and expenses is also charged with a substantial asset investment and is responsible for earning the desired return on that investment.

investment tax credit A direct reduction in the amount of income taxes payable for firms that invest in new productive equipment.

irrelevant items Current or future revenues and expenses that are not expected to differ among the alternatives being considered and thus can be ignored when choosing among the alternatives.

job-order costing A product costing method that accumulates manufacturing costs for each job or batch of production. Job-order costing is used by companies whose manufacturing process consists of batches of production that are separately identifiable and significantly different from one another.

journal A record of transactions presented in chronological sequence.

journal entry Shows the accounts affected, amount of the change in the account balances, and an explanation of the transaction.

labor efficiency variance See Labor Usage Variance.

labor rate variance The difference between the actual direct labor cost and the standard direct labor cost for the hours actually worked. Labor Rate Variance = (Actual Direct Labor Rate Per Hour − Standard Direct Labor Rate Per Hour) × Actual Direct Labor Hours.

labor usage standard The standard that indicates the number of direct labor hours that "should be used" at standard to produce the output.

labor usage variance The difference between the standard cost for the direct labor hours actually worked and the standard cost for the direct labor hours that should have been used to produce the output. Labor Usage Variance = (Actual Direct Labor Hours − Standard Direct Labor Hours) × Standard Direct Labor Rate Per Hour.

last-in, first-out method (LIFO) Inventory cost flow method that assumes that the cost of the last unit purchased is the first cost to be charged to cost of goods sold.

lease A contract under which the owner of the asset (lessor) allows an asset to be used by the lessee for an agreed upon fee and period of time.

lease or buy The financing alternatives for many capital investment decisions.

ledger account A record of the debits, credits, and balance for any asset, liability, or stockholders' equity item.

legal capital Minimum amount of total stockholders' equity that must be kept in the corporation for creditors' protection. In many states the par value of common stock represents the legal capital of the corporation.

lessee One who is allowed to use for a period of time an asset legally owned by another party (the lessor) in exchange for lease rental payments.

lessor One who legally owns an asset but allows another party to use the asset for a period of time in exchange for lease rental payments.

leverage Raising funds from creditors or preferred stockholders with the hope that the assets acquired with the borrowed funds will earn enough to pay the fixed interest cost (or preferred dividends) and leave an excess that accrues to the common stockholders.

liabilities Debts or obligations owed to others.

limited liability Characteristic of a corporation whereby creditors of the corporation have a claim against the corporation's assets, but do not have any claim against the stockholders' personal assets.

liquidity A measure of an asset's nearness to cash.

long-term debt Liability whose payment date is more than one year from the balance sheet date.

long-term investments Stock and bond investments that are not readily marketable, or that management intends to hold for a long period of time as an income-producing asset or for purposes of maintaining a significant influence in the other company.

lower of cost or market Conservative valuation method used for marketable equity securities and inventories. Decreases in market value below cost are recorded but increases in market value above cost are not recorded.

make or buy A nonroutine decision on whether to manufacture components needed for the finished product or to purchase the components from an outside supplier.

managerial accounting Concerned with accounting data and reports prepared for users within the firm—managers and other employees. Managerial accounting is useful in planning, control and performance evaluation, decision analysis, and product costing.

manufacturing firm A firm that buys materials and, by the use of factory labor, machines, and other costs of carrying on the production activity, creates new products for sale to others.

manufacturing overhead All factory costs incurred in carrying on the manufacturing activity (except direct labor and direct materials). Manufacturing overhead provides the productive capacity and productive environment necessary to manufacture the product.

manufacturing overhead budget Forecast of manufacturing overhead costs based on cost behavior patterns (i.e., fixed and variable) and forecasted production levels.

manufacturing overhead variance The difference between actual manufacturing overhead and applied manufacturing overhead. This manufacturing overhead variance is subdivided into a variable overhead variance component and a fixed overhead variance component. Manufacturing Overhead Variance = Actual Manufacturing Overhead Cost − Standard Manufacturing Overhead Cost.

margin of safety The amount by which sales can decline before losses are incurred. In absolute dollar terms, it is the excess of the current or projected sales level over the breakeven sales level.

margin of safety percentage Indicates the percent that actual sales can decline before losses occur. The margin of safety percentage is equal to sales minus breakeven sales divided by sales.

marketable debt securities See Marketable Securities.

marketable equity securities See Marketable Securities.

marketable securities Securities with a readily available means of being bought and sold (i.e., listed on a stock exchange or actively traded by a securities dealer). These securities may either be debt securities (corporate or government bonds) or equity securities (common or preferred stocks).

master budget See Comprehensive Budget.

matching rule Requirement that expenses incurred in generating revenue be recorded as an expense in the same time period as the related revenue.

materiality concept Concept that suggests that the dollar size and significance of an item must be evaluated to determine the acceptable accounting treatment.

materials inventory Materials on hand that have not yet been used in production.

materials issued Materials that are taken from materials inventory and transferred to production.

materials price variance The difference between the actual cost of the materials purchased and the standard cost of the materials purchased. Materials Price Variance = (Actual Price per Unit − Standard Price per Unit) × Actual Quantity Purchased.

materials quantity standard The standard that indicates the quantity of materials that "should be used" at standard to produce the output.

materials quantity variance The difference between the standard cost of the direct materials actually used in production and the standard cost for the direct materials that should have been used to produce the output. Materials Quantity Variance = (Actual Quantity of Materials Used − Standard Quantity of Materials Allowed) × Standard Price per Unit of Material.

maturity date The date on which a note or bond is due.

maturity value The amount due on the maturity date.

merchandise inventory The cost of goods acquired for resale to customers.

merchandising firm A firm that buys goods and resells them to others, with little or no additional processing of the goods.

mixed cost See Semivariable Cost.

monetary items Those assets and liabilities that are fixed in terms of number of dollars regardless of changes in purchasing power of the dollar (e.g., cash, accounts receivable, notes receivable, bonds payable).

mutually exclusive Selection of one alternative automatically means rejection of all other alternatives.

natural resources Land from which minerals of some kind (coal, oil, and so on) are extracted by mining, drilling, excavation, and so forth.

net book value See Book Value.

net earnings available for common stockholders The numerator of the earnings per share calculation.

net income (loss) The bottom line on the income statement indicating for the period the excess of total revenue over total expenses (or for a net loss, the excess of expenses over revenue).

net of tax The tax effects associated with special income statement items (discontinued operations, extraordinary items, and change in accounting principles) are netted against the item itself rather than included in income tax expense.

net present value (NPV) Capital investment analysis technique that compares the present value of all cash inflows and outflows for a capital investment project. Net Present Value = Present Value of Cash Inflows − Present Value of Cash Outflows.

net price method for cash discounts The method to record inventory purchases (and the related accounts payable) at the net price—the gross invoice price minus the cash discount offered.

net realizable value The amount of cash a company expects to collect from its receivables. Net Realizable Value = Accounts Receivable − Allowance for Uncollectible Accounts.

non-interest-bearing note A note that does not specify a rate of interest (or specifies an unreasonably low rate). In recording such a note, accountants recognize the "implicit" interest included in the note.

nonmonetary items Those assets, liabilities, and stockholders' equity accounts that do not represent a right to receive or pay a fixed amount of cash. The price of a nonmonetary item can change over time. Nonmonetary items are restated on both constant dollar and current value financial statements.

note A formal written promise to pay a debt. Notes are usually interest bearing and have a maturity date.

notes receivable Receivables evidenced by formal written promises to pay.

notes to the financial statements An important component of the financial statements that provides explanatory and descriptive information about the company and its financial activities.

NSF check Customer check that has been deposited in the bank but is being charged back by the bank due to insufficient funds in the customer's bank account.

objectivity concept   Concept requiring that, to the greatest extent possible, financial statement data be substantiated by evidence and be subject to verification by others.

operating activities   Income-producing activities (the sale and delivery of goods and services) that result in an inflow or outflow of cash.

operating cycle   The average time period to complete the conversion of cash into inventory, the sale of inventory to customers, and the collection of cash from the customers.

operating lease   Classification for leases that do not meet one of the four capitalization criteria. Periodic lease payments are recorded as lease expense when the payments are made.

opportunity cost   The value that is lost by using a resource for one purpose rather than its best alternative use.

options   Commitments that give a holder the right to purchase for a period of time a given number of shares of stock at an established price. Outstanding stock options may affect the earnings per share calculation.

outstanding check   Check written and recorded as cash disbursement on the company's books but not yet presented to the bank for payment.

overapplied manufacturing overhead   The amount by which applied manufacturing overhead exceeds actual manufacturing overhead costs for the period.

paid-in capital in excess of par   Excess of amount received upon issuance of stock over par value of stock.

par value   Amount entered in capital stock account when shares of stock are issued. Par value is not intended to indicate the market value of the shares.

participating preferred stock   A preferred stock issue granting the preferred stockholders the opportunity to receive dividends in excess of the basic preferred dividend rate.

participative budgeting   Involving department managers directly in the budget formulation process.

partnership   An unincorporated business owned by two or more persons.

patents   Legal rights to inventions, product designs, or manufacturing processes. Patents are an intangible asset.

payback period   The number of years needed to recover the initial cost of a capital investment.

$$\text{Payback Period} = \frac{\text{Investment Cost}}{\text{Annual Cash Inflow}}$$

percentage of completion   Recognizes revenue and expenses from construction contracts as the construction is occurring.

performance evaluation   See Control and Performance Evaluation.

performance report   Cost and revenue data that are collected and reported according to specific departments or managers and used as a basis for evaluation of performance.

period cost   A cost not related to the manufacturing process. Period costs are expensed in the time period in which they occur.

periodic inventory system   Inventory system that does not update the inventory account for purchases and sales of inventory during the period. A physical count of the inventory on hand at the end of the period is necessary to determine the ending inventory and cost of goods sold for the period.

permanent accounts   Accounts whose balances reflect the cumulative balance since the origin of the firm. These accounts are not "closed out" in the closing entry process.

perpetual inventory system   Maintains a continuous record of inventory and cost of goods sold during the period, updating after each purchase and sale transaction.

petty cash fund   A fund maintained to pay small amounts due in cash where it is impractical to pay by check.

petty cash voucher   A document serving as evidence of a payment from the petty cash fund.

physical inventory   The process of counting and listing the inventory on hand at the end of the reporting period. A physical inventory is necessary under the periodic inventory method to determine the ending inventory and cost of goods sold for the period.

planning   One of the four major areas of managerial accounting. Planning involves selecting a future course of action designed to achieve organizational objectives.

posting   The process of transferring the debit and credit amounts recorded in the journal to the respective ledger accounts.

posting reference   A cross-reference between entries in the journal and ledger.

predetermined overhead rate   Used to apply manufacturing overhead cost to work in process. The rate is calculated at the beginning of the period by dividing expected manufacturing overhead costs by the expected volume of the activity base.

preferred stock   A type of stock that gives its holders preference over the holders of common stock in receiving dividends and in receipt of assets when the corporation is liquidated.

premium   See Bond Premium.

premium on common stock   See Paid-In Capital in Excess of Par.

prepaid assets   Items for which payment is made in one time period, but that are consumed (charged to expense) in a later time period (e.g., prepaid rent and prepaid insurance).

present value   The amount of money that is needed now in order to produce a specified future cash flow at a specified date at a stated interest rate.

price-earnings ratio   A profitability measure indicating the cost of acquiring each dollar of current earnings.

$$\text{Price-Earnings Ratio} = \frac{\text{Market Price per Share of Common Stock}}{\text{Earnings per Share of Common Stock}}$$

price index   Conversion ratio used to restate nonmonetary items to account for the effects of inflation.

prior period adjustment   An adjustment to the retained earnings balance at the beginning of the period because of the discovery of an accounting error made in a previous period.

process costing   A product-costing technique that does not differentiate one batch of production from another. Each complete unit of production is assigned the same amount of cost.

product cost   A cost related to a firm's manufacturing process. Product costs (direct labor, direct materials, and manufacturing overhead) are included in the cost of inventory.

product costing   One of the four major areas of managerial accounting. Product costing provides detailed records of product cost for both external reporting of inventory and cost of goods sold and for internal planning, control, and decision making.

production basis of revenue recognition   Allows the construction industry to recognize revenue as production is completed since construction represents completion of all the major earnings functions of the firm.

production budget   Shows units of scheduled production based on the sales budget and desired inventory levels.

production cost report   Summarizes cost and production activity for each manufacturing department for a firm that uses process costing.

production support   The auxiliary services necessary to support production and make the productive capacity operative (e.g., factory utilities and factory maintenance).

productive capacity   The physical facilities (e.g., factory building and equipment) necessary to manufacture a product.

profit center   A segment of an organization that incurs costs and generates revenues.

profit margin   Indicates the percentage of each sales dollar remaining as earnings after all expenses, other than interest, have been deducted.

$$\text{Profit Margin} = \frac{\text{Net Income} + \text{Interest Expense}}{\text{Net Sales}}$$

profitability   Refers to a firm's success in generating revenue in excess of expenses.

projected financial statements   Forecasted statements resulting from the comprehensive budgeting process.

property, plant, and equipment   Noncurrent, tangible assets used in the business.

proprietorship   An unincorporated business entirely owned by one individual. For accounting purposes the proprietorship is treated as a separate entity and should not reflect the personal dealings of the owner.

purchase discount   See Cash Discount.

purchase returns and allowances   An adjustment to purchases to reflect the cost of inventory returned to suppliers or price reductions granted by suppliers.

purchases account   Record of the cost of inventory bought during the period.

purchases journal   A special journal for recording purchases of inventory on account.

purchasing power   The value of a dollar arising from the amount of goods and services it can buy.

purchasing power gain or loss   A gain or loss resulting from holding monetary items during a period of change in the general price level.

quick ratio   Ratio used to measure liquidity, as a supplement to the current ratio.

$$\text{Quick Ratio} = \frac{\text{Cash} + \text{Marketable Securities} + \text{Accounts Receivable}}{\text{Current Liabilities}}$$

rate of return for investment center   A measure of the ability of an investment center manager to earn profits on each dollar of revenue and to select and utilize assets that generate revenues.

rate of return on common stockholders' equity   A comparison of income available for common stockholders to the book value of the common stockholders' equity.

$$\frac{\text{Rate of Return on Common}}{\text{Stockholders' Equity}} = \frac{\text{Net Income} - \text{Preferred Stock Dividends (if any)}}{\text{Average Common Stockholders' Equity}}$$

rate of return on total assets   A measure of the effectiveness of management in utilizing the entity's resources.

$$\frac{\text{Rate of Return}}{\text{on Total Assets}} = \underbrace{\frac{\text{Net Income} + \text{Interest Expense}}{\text{Net Sales}}}_{\text{(Profit Margin)}} \times \underbrace{\frac{\text{Net Sales}}{\text{Average Assets}}}_{\text{(Asset Turnover)}}$$

ratio The relationship of one financial statement item to another.

ratio analysis The analysis of important relationships among financial statement items.

ratio of debt to total assets An indication of the percentage of total assets provided by creditors.

$$\text{Ratio of Debt to Total Assets} = \frac{\text{Total Debt}}{\text{Total Assets}}$$

ratio of stockholders' equity to total assets Ratio that indicates the percentage of total assets provided by stockholders. Ratio of Stockholders' Equity to Total Assets = One Hundred Percent minus the Ratio of Debt to Total Assets.

realization rule Revenue is recorded when it is realized. Realization is said to occur when (1) the earning process is substantially complete, and (2) any remaining events and activities are capable of estimation with reasonable accuracy.

relevant items Current or future revenues or expenses that are expected to differ among courses of action being considered by management. They are also referred to as "incremental" or "differential" revenues or expenses.

responsibility accounting The accumulation and reporting of accounting information for various segments of the organization. Responsibility accounting aids in evaluating segment performance.

retail method A method of estimating the cost of ending inventory and cost of goods sold by using the actual retail value of inventory.

retained earnings The cumulative net increase in assets earned by a corporation's operations that have been retained in the firm. Retained earnings represents total net income (minus any net losses) minus total dividends since the corporation was formed.

retained earnings deficit A debit balance in the retained earnings account.

retirement of bonds Elimination of bond liability prior to maturity due to call, conversion, or repurchase in the bond market.

revenues Selling price of goods sold or services rendered to customers. Revenues are gross increases in the retained earnings component of stockholders' equity from a company's profit-directed activities.

sales budget Forecasted sales based on market surveys, current backlog of orders, sales departments' predictions, historic sales trends, and/or econometric forecasting models.

sales discount See Cash Discount.

sales journal A special journal for recording sales on account.

sales returns An adjustment to sales revenue when customer is granted credit (or a cash refund) because the product was defective or damaged. The sales return account is shown as a contra revenue account on the income statement.

sales tax A tax imposed by governmental units (states or municipalities) on certain sales transactions. Sales taxes collected are a liability to the seller until remitted to the government. Sales taxes paid by the buyer should be added to the cost of the item purchased.

salvage value The expected value of the asset at the end of its useful life. Salvage value is used in the computation of depreciation expense.

schedule of cost of goods manufactured and sold A formal presentation of the cost of materials inventory purchased; direct materials, direct labor, and manufacturing overhead transferred to work in process and finished goods inventories; and the cost of goods sold for a manufacturing firm.

selling and administrative expenses budget Forecasted selling and administrative costs based on budgeted sales and other management projections.

selling, general, and administrative expenses   Costs of carrying on a firm's basic business activities.

semivariable cost   Cost having both a fixed and variable component. Also called a mixed cost.

separation of duties   Division of custodial and record-keeping functions among several persons to provide a system of checks and balances within a firm's internal control system.

serially numbered documents   Business documents that have been sequentially prenumbered for purposes of internal control.

service firms   A firm that sells its customers a service rather than a product.

short-term investments   Temporary investment of excess cash in marketable securities of other companies.

simple interest   Interest calculated on original principal only. Interest earned during previous periods is not added to the principal.

solvency   The ability to pay debts owed when the debts become due.

special items   Discontinued operations, extraordinary items, and cumulative effect of changes in accounting principle presented in their own sections of the income statement.

special journals   Journals designed to record only certain types of transactions. For example, sales journal, purchases journal, cash receipts journal, and cash disbursements journal.

special order   A nonroutine decision analysis requiring evaluation of a sales order at a price less than the normal selling price.

specific identification   Inventory cost method in which the cost of each specific inventory item sold is determined and charged to cost of goods sold.

specific price changes   Changes in the prices of individual goods and services.

spot rates   Current exchange rates for foreign currency.

stable monetary concept   Assumes the dollar is essentially stable in value over time and thus any change in the purchasing power of the dollar will be immaterial and can be ignored.

standard cost   Target figures of expected costs if the firm has efficient operations and prices for labor, materials, and overhead were accurately forecasted.

stated value   A corporation's board of directors may establish a stated value per share for no par common stock. The stated value is credited to the common stock account when the shares are issued. Stated value is not intended to represent the market value per share.

statement of cash flow   Report of the cash flows from operating, financing, and investing activities of a company for a period of time.

statement of financial position   See Balance Sheet.

statement of income   See Income Statement.

statement of retained earnings   A reconciliation of the difference between the retained earnings balance at the beginning of the period and the balance at the end of the period. Typical reconciling items on the statement include net income (or net loss) and dividends declared.

static budget   Forecasted costs for a single expected level of activity. It is inappropriate to use a static budget to evaluate efficiency of operations if the actual activity level for the period differs from that predicted.

stock dividend   A dividend in the form of a proportionate distribution of additional shares of a corporation's own stock to the company's current stockholders.

stock split   An increase in the number of shares outstanding accompanied by a corresponding reduction in the par value per share.

stockholders' equity   The portion of the assets financed by the owners. Stockholders' equity arises from direct investments and from accumulated earnings retained by the corporation.

straight line method   A depreciation method whereby an equal amount of the asset's depreciable base (cost − salvage value) is expensed for each year of the asset's estimated useful life.

straight line method of amortization   Method of amortizing bond premium or discount where equal amounts are amortized each period.

subsidiary ledger   A listing of the individual accounts that compose the main (control) account in the general ledger.

sum of years digits method   An accelerated method of depreciation in which depreciation expense is determined by multiplying a decreasing fraction times the asset's depreciable base (cost − salvage value).

summary of significant accounting policies   Section of the annual report disclosing the accounting methods that a firm employs.

sunk cost   An expenditure that has been made in the past, cannot be revoked, and if tax effects are ignored, is an irrelevant cost in decision analysis.

T-account   A form of ledger account shaped like a T. The left side is the debit side and the right side is the credit side.

taxable income   Income determined in accordance with the Internal Revenue Code established by Congress.

temporary accounts   Revenue, expense, and dividends declared accounts that accumulate amounts only for the current period. At the end of the period, closing entries transfer the balance from the temporary accounts to retained earnings.

three-column, running balance account   A form of ledger account that has three dollar columns—a debit, a credit, and a running balance.

time-line diagram   A visual presentation of time value of money problems.

time value of money   The idea that a dollar received today is worth more than a dollar to be received at some future time.

times interest earned   Indicator to long-term creditors of the ability of the company to meet required interest payments.

$$\frac{\text{Times Interest}}{\text{Earned}} = \frac{\text{Operating Income (Income Before Deducting Interest and Income Taxes)}}{\text{Interest Expense}}$$

timing difference   Revenues and expenses recognized on the tax return in a different period than recognized for financial reporting purposes. Timing differences result in the recording of deferred taxes.

total costs accounted for   See Costs Accounted For.

trade-in   An exchange of assets. An old asset, plus cash, is given up to acquire a new asset.

trademarks   An intangible asset granting the holder exclusive legal rights to product names and symbols.

transaction   An exchange of goods or services between parties that has financial significance (that is, it affects a company's assets, liabilities, or stockholders' equity).

transaction worksheet   A technique used to introduce the basics of the recording, classifying, and summarizing phases of the accounting process.

transfer prices   Prices set for goods that are transferred from one segment of a firm to another.

treasury stock   Shares of a corporation's own stock that have been issued, reacquired, and not formally retired.

trend analysis   Intracompany comparisons of a company's current financial statements with statements from prior year(s).

trial balance   A list of the individual ledger accounts and their respective debit or credit balances.

trial balance of subsidiary ledger   A list of the individual customer/creditor accounts (accounts receivable/accounts payable) and their respective debit/credit balances.

uncollectible accounts expense   See Bad Debt Expense.

underapplied manufacturing overhead   The amount by which actual manufacturing overhead costs exceed applied manufacturing overhead.

unfavorable variance   Results from actual costs being greater than standard costs. This implies that operations were either less efficient than expected or standards were set too stringently.

units accounted for   The units completed in a process costing system and transferred out during the period plus those remaining in ending work in process inventory; must agree with "units to account for."

units of production method   A depreciation method in which depreciation expense is determined by multiplying a rate per unit times actual usage for the period.

$$\text{Rate per Unit} = \frac{\text{Cost} - \text{Salvage Value}}{\text{Estimated Useful Life in Production Units}}$$

units to account for   The number of units in a process costing system in production at the beginning of the period plus the number of units started into production (or transferred in from another department) during the period; must agree with "units accounted for."

unqualified opinion   An auditor's report accompanying the firm's financial statements that does not take exception to any significant item in the financial statements.

unrealized loss   Income statement deduction for portion of decline in market value below cost occurring during the period on investments in short-term marketable securities. Unrealized loss from writing down to market long-term stock investments is shown as negative stockholders' equity on the balance sheet.

useful life   The estimated period of time a firm expects to use a long-lived asset in its operations.

variable cost   Assumption that total cost changes proportionately when the level of activity varies within a relevant range.

variable costing   See Direct Costing.

variable manufacturing overhead efficiency variance   Measurement of the extra cost (if the variance is unfavorable) or the cost savings (if the variance is favorable) in variable manufacturing overhead costs due solely to the actual level of the activity base differing from the standard level. Variable Manufacturing Overhead Efficiency Variance = (Actual Direct Labor Hours − Standard Hours Allowed) × Standard Variable Overhead Rate.

variable manufacturing overhead spending variance   Variance attributable to a combination of: 1) price differences between actual and standard costs and 2) inefficiencies other than those related to the activity base. Variable Manufacturing Overhead Variance = (Actual Variable Overhead Rate − Standard Variable Overhead Rate) × Actual Direct Labor Hours.

variance   Difference between standard or budgeted and actual.

warranty   Guarantee to the buyer that a product or service will be satisfactory.

weighted average method   Inventory cost flow method that uses a weighted average cost per unit to determine cost of goods sold and inventory.

weighted average shares outstanding   Denominator in basic earnings per share calculation.

window dressing   Executing certain transactions near the close of the accounting period with the purpose of presenting more favorable financial statement ratios.

working capital   The excess of total current assets over total current liabilities.

working capital ratio   See Current Ratio.

work in process inventory   Goods or jobs in the process of being manufactured, but not yet completed.

worksheet   See Accountant's Worksheet and Transaction Worksheet.

PRESENT VALUE AND FUTURE VALUE TABLES

This appendix contains the future value and present value tables necessary to solve compounding and discounting problems. These topics are covered primarily in Chapters 8, 9, and 20.

The following tables are provided:

Table I: Future Value of $1

$$F = P \times (\text{future value factor, n periods, r percent})$$

Table II: Present Value of $1

$$P = F \times (\text{present value factor, n periods, r percent})$$

Table III: Present Value of an Annuity of $1

$$P_A = A \times (\text{present value of annuity factor, n periods, r percent})$$

TABLE I   FUTURE VALUE OF $1

Rate / Periods	1%	2%	2.5%	3%	4%	5%	6%
1	1.0100	1.0200	1.0250	1.0300	1.0400	1.0500	1.0600
2	1.0201	1.0404	1.0506	1.0609	1.0816	1.1025	1.1236
3	1.0303	1.0612	1.0769	1.0927	1.1249	1.1576	1.1910
4	1.0406	1.0824	1.1038	1.1255	1.1699	1.2155	1.2625
5	1.0510	1.1041	1.1314	1.1593	1.2167	1.2763	1.3382
6	1.0615	1.1262	1.1597	1.1941	1.2653	1.3401	1.4185
7	1.0721	1.1487	1.1887	1.2299	1.3159	1.4071	1.5036
8	1.0829	1.1717	1.2184	1.2668	1.3686	1.4775	1.5938
9	1.0937	1.1951	1.2489	1.3048	1.4233	1.5513	1.6894
10	1.1046	1.2190	1.2801	1.3439	1.4802	1.6289	1.7908
11	1.1157	1.2434	1.3121	1.3842	1.5395	1.7103	1.8983
12	1.1268	1.2682	1.3449	1.4258	1.6010	1.7959	2.0122
13	1.1381	1.2936	1.3785	1.4685	1.6651	1.8856	2.1329
14	1.1495	1.3195	1.4130	1.5126	1.7317	1.9799	2.2609
15	1.1610	1.3459	1.4483	1.5580	1.8009	2.0789	2.3966
16	1.1726	1.3728	1.4845	1.6047	1.8730	2.1829	2.5404
17	1.1843	1.4002	1.5216	1.6528	1.9479	2.2920	2.6928
18	1.1961	1.4282	1.5597	1.7024	2.0258	2.4066	2.8543
19	1.2081	1.4568	1.5987	1.7535	2.1068	2.5270	3.0256
20	1.2202	1.4859	1.6386	1.8061	2.1911	2.6533	3.2071
21	1.2324	1.5157	1.6796	1.8603	2.2788	2.7860	3.3996
22	1.2447	1.5460	1.7216	1.9161	2.3699	2.9253	3.6035
23	1.2572	1.5769	1.7646	1.9736	2.4647	3.0715	3.8197
24	1.2697	1.6084	1.8087	2.0328	2.5633	3.2251	4.0489
25	1.2824	1.6406	1.8539	2.0938	2.6658	3.3864	4.2919
30	1.3478	1.8114	2.0976	2.4273	3.2434	4.3219	5.7435
35	1.4166	1.9999	2.3732	2.8139	3.9461	5.5160	7.6861
40	1.4889	2.2080	2.6851	3.2620	4.8010	7.0400	10.2857
50	1.6446	2.6916	3.4371	4.3839	7.1067	11.4674	18.4202
60	1.8167	3.2810	4.3998	5.8916	10.5196	18.6792	32.9877

7%	8%	9%	10%	12%	15%	20%	Rate
							Periods
1.0700	1.0800	1.0900	1.1000	1.1200	1.1500	1.2000	1
1.1449	1.1664	1.1881	1.2100	1.2544	1.3225	1.4400	2
1.2250	1.2597	1.2950	1.3310	1.4049	1.5209	1.7280	3
1.3108	1.3605	1.4116	1.4641	1.5735	1.7490	2.0736	4
1.4026	1.4693	1.5386	1.6105	1.7623	2.0114	2.4883	5
1.5007	1.5869	1.6771	1.7716	1.9738	2.3131	2.9860	6
1.6058	1.7138	1.8280	1.9487	2.2107	2.6600	3.5832	7
1.7182	1.8509	1.9926	2.1436	2.4760	3.0590	4.2998	8
1.8385	1.9990	2.1719	2.3579	2.7731	3.5179	5.1598	9
1.9672	2.1589	2.3674	2.5937	3.1058	4.0456	6.1917	10
2.1049	2.3316	2.5804	2.8531	3.4785	4.6524	7.4301	11
2.2522	2.5182	2.8127	3.1384	3.8960	5.3502	8.9161	12
2.4098	2.7196	3.0658	3.4523	4.3635	6.1528	10.6993	13
2.5785	2.9372	3.3417	3.7975	4.8871	7.0757	12.8392	14
2.7590	3.1722	3.6425	4.1772	5.4736	8.1371	15.4070	15
2.9522	3.4259	3.9703	4.5950	6.1304	9.3576	18.4884	16
3.1589	3.7000	4.3276	5.0545	6.8660	10.7613	22.1861	17
3.3799	3.9960	4.7171	5.5599	7.6900	12.3755	26.6233	18
3.6165	4.3157	5.1417	6.1159	8.6128	14.2318	31.9480	19
3.8697	4.6610	5.6044	6.7275	9.6463	16.3665	38.3376	20
4.1406	5.0338	6.1088	7.4002	10.8038	18.8215	46.0051	21
4.4304	5.4365	6.6586	8.1403	12.1003	21.6447	55.2061	22
4.7405	5.8715	7.2579	8.9543	13.5523	24.8914	66.2474	23
5.0724	6.3412	7.9111	9.8497	15.1786	28.6252	79.4968	24
5.4274	6.8485	8.6231	10.8347	17.0001	32.9189	95.3962	25
7.6123	10.0627	13.2677	17.4494	29.9599	66.2117	237.3762	30
10.6766	14.7853	20.4140	28.1024	52.7996	133.1754	590.6680	35
14.9745	21.7245	31.4094	45.2593	93.0510	267.8633	1469.7710	40
29.4570	46.9016	74.3575	117.3909	289.0022	1083.656	9100.4320	50
57.9464	101.2571	176.0313	304.4816	897.5969	4383.994	56347.4700	60

TABLE II   PRESENT VALUE OF $1

Rate Periods	1%	2%	2.5%	3%	4%	5%	6%
1	0.9901	0.9804	0.9756	0.9709	0.9615	0.9524	0.9434
2	0.9803	0.9612	0.9518	0.9426	0.9246	0.9070	0.8900
3	0.9706	0.9423	0.9286	0.9151	0.8890	0.8638	0.8396
4	0.9610	0.9238	0.9060	0.8885	0.8548	0.8227	0.7921
5	0.9515	0.9057	0.8839	0.8626	0.8219	0.7835	0.7473
6	0.9420	0.8880	0.8623	0.8375	0.7903	0.7462	0.7050
7	0.9327	0.8706	0.8413	0.8131	0.7599	0.7107	0.6651
8	0.9235	0.8535	0.8207	0.7894	0.7307	0.6768	0.6274
9	0.9143	0.8368	0.8007	0.7664	0.7026	0.6446	0.5919
10	0.9053	0.8203	0.7812	0.7441	0.6756	0.6139	0.5584
11	0.8963	0.8043	0.7621	0.7224	0.6496	0.5847	0.5268
12	0.8874	0.7885	0.7436	0.7014	0.6246	0.5568	0.4970
13	0.8787	0.7730	0.7254	0.6810	0.6006	0.5303	0.4688
14	0.8700	0.7579	0.7077	0.6611	0.5775	0.5051	0.4423
15	0.8613	0.7430	0.6905	0.6419	0.5553	0.4810	0.4173
16	0.8528	0.7284	0.6736	0.6232	0.5339	0.4581	0.3936
17	0.8444	0.7142	0.6572	0.6050	0.5134	0.4363	0.3714
18	0.8360	0.7002	0.6412	0.5874	0.4936	0.4155	0.3503
19	0.8277	0.6864	0.6255	0.5703	0.4746	0.3957	0.3305
20	0.8195	0.6730	0.6103	0.5537	0.4564	0.3769	0.3118
21	0.8114	0.6598	0.5954	0.5375	0.4388	0.3589	0.2942
22	0.8034	0.6468	0.5809	0.5219	0.4220	0.3418	0.2775
23	0.7954	0.6342	0.5667	0.5067	0.4057	0.3256	0.2618
24	0.7876	0.6217	0.5529	0.4919	0.3901	0.3101	0.2470
25	0.7798	0.6095	0.5394	0.4776	0.3751	0.2953	0.2330
30	0.7419	0.5521	0.4767	0.4120	0.3083	0.2314	0.1741
35	0.7059	0.5000	0.4214	0.3554	0.2534	0.1813	0.1301
40	0.6717	0.4529	0.3724	0.3066	0.2083	0.1420	0.0972
50	0.6080	0.3715	0.2909	0.2281	0.1407	0.0872	0.0543
60	0.5504	0.3048	0.2273	0.1697	0.0951	0.0535	0.0303

7%	8%	9%	10%	12%	15%	20%	Rate
							Periods
0.9346	0.9259	0.9174	0.9091	0.8929	0.8696	0.8333	1
0.8734	0.8573	0.8417	0.8264	0.7972	0.7561	0.6944	2
0.8163	0.7938	0.7722	0.7513	0.7118	0.6575	0.5787	3
0.7629	0.7350	0.7084	0.6830	0.6355	0.5718	0.4823	4
0.7130	0.6806	0.6499	0.6209	0.5674	0.4972	0.4019	5
0.6663	0.6302	0.5963	0.5645	0.5066	0.4323	0.3349	6
0.6227	0.5835	0.5470	0.5132	0.4523	0.3759	0.2791	7
0.5820	0.5403	0.5019	0.4665	0.4039	0.3269	0.2326	8
0.5439	0.5002	0.4604	0.4241	0.3606	0.2843	0.1938	9
0.5083	0.4632	0.4224	0.3855	0.3220	0.2472	0.1615	10
0.4751	0.4289	0.3875	0.3505	0.2875	0.2149	0.1346	11
0.4440	0.3971	0.3555	0.3186	0.2567	0.1869	0.1122	12
0.4150	0.3677	0.3262	0.2897	0.2292	0.1625	0.0935	13
0.3878	0.3405	0.2992	0.2633	0.2046	0.1413	0.0779	14
0.3624	0.3152	0.2745	0.2394	0.1827	0.1229	0.0649	15
0.3387	0.2919	0.2519	0.2176	0.1631	0.1069	0.0541	16
0.3166	0.2703	0.2311	0.1978	0.1456	0.0929	0.0451	17
0.2959	0.2502	0.2120	0.1799	0.1300	0.0808	0.0376	18
0.2765	0.2317	0.1945	0.1635	0.1161	0.0703	0.0313	19
0.2584	0.2145	0.1784	0.1486	0.1037	0.0611	0.0261	20
0.2415	0.1987	0.1637	0.1351	0.0926	0.0531	0.0217	21
0.2257	0.1839	0.1502	0.1228	0.0826	0.0462	0.0181	22
0.2109	0.1703	0.1378	0.1117	0.0738	0.0402	0.0151	23
0.1971	0.1577	0.1264	0.1015	0.0659	0.0349	0.0126	24
0.1842	0.1460	0.1160	0.0923	0.0588	0.0304	0.0105	25
0.1314	0.0994	0.0754	0.0573	0.0334	0.0151	0.0042	30
0.0937	0.0676	0.0490	0.0356	0.0189	0.0075	0.0017	35
0.0668	0.0460	0.0318	0.0221	0.0107	0.0037	0.0007	40
0.0339	0.0213	0.0134	0.0085	0.0035	0.0009	0.0001	50
0.0173	0.0099	0.0057	0.0033	0.0011	0.0002	0.0000	60

TABLE III   PRESENT VALUE OF AN ANNUITY OF $1

Rate Periods	1%	2%	2.5%	3%	4%	5%	6%
1	0.9901	0.9804	0.9756	0.9709	0.9615	0.9524	0.9434
2	1.9704	1.9416	1.9274	1.9135	1.8861	1.8594	1.8334
3	2.9410	2.8839	2.8560	2.8286	2.7751	2.7232	2.6730
4	3.9020	3.8077	3.7620	3.7171	3.6299	3.5460	3.4651
5	4.8534	4.7135	4.6458	4.5797	4.4518	4.3295	4.2124
6	5.7955	5.6014	5.5081	5.4172	5.2421	5.0757	4.9173
7	6.7282	6.4720	6.3494	6.2303	6.0021	5.7864	5.5824
8	7.6517	7.3255	7.1701	7.0197	6.7327	6.4632	6.2098
9	8.5660	8.1622	7.9709	7.7861	7.4353	7.1078	6.8017
10	9.4713	8.9826	8.7521	8.5302	8.1109	7.7217	7.3601
11	10.3676	9.7868	9.5142	9.2526	8.7605	8.3064	7.8869
12	11.2551	10.5753	10.2578	9.9540	9.3851	8.8633	8.3838
13	12.1337	11.3484	10.9832	10.6350	9.9856	9.3936	8.8527
14	13.0037	12.1062	11.6909	11.2961	10.5631	9.8986	9.2950
15	13.8651	12.8493	12.3814	11.9379	11.1184	10.3797	9.7122
16	14.7179	13.5777	13.0550	12.5611	11.6523	10.8378	10.1059
17	15.5623	14.2919	13.7121	13.1661	12.1657	11.2741	10.4773
18	16.3983	14.9920	14.3534	13.7535	12.6593	11.6896	10.8276
19	17.2260	15.6785	14.9789	14.3238	13.1339	12.0853	11.1581
20	18.0456	16.3514	15.5892	14.8775	13.5903	12.4622	11.4699
21	18.8570	17.0112	16.1845	15.4150	14.0292	12.8212	11.7641
22	19.6604	17.6580	16.7654	15.9369	14.4511	13.1630	12.0416
23	20.4558	18.2922	17.3321	16.4436	14.8568	13.4886	12.3034
24	21.2434	18.9139	17.8850	16.9355	15.2470	13.7986	12.5504
25	22.0232	19.5235	18.4244	17.4131	15.6221	14.0939	12.7834
30	25.8077	22.3965	20.9303	19.6004	17.2920	15.3725	13.7648
35	29.4086	24.9986	23.1452	21.4872	18.6646	16.3742	14.4982
40	32.8347	27.3555	25.1028	23.1148	19.7928	17.1591	15.0463
50	39.1961	31.4236	28.3623	25.7298	21.4822	18.2559	15.7619
60	44.9550	34.7609	30.9087	27.6756	22.6235	18.9293	16.1614

7%	8%	9%	10%	12%	15%	20%	Rate
							Periods
0.9346	0.9259	0.9174	0.9091	0.8929	0.8696	0.8333	1
1.8080	1.7833	1.7591	1.7355	1.6901	1.6257	1.5278	2
2.6243	2.5771	2.5313	2.4869	2.4018	2.2832	2.1065	3
3.3872	3.3121	3.2397	3.1699	3.0373	2.8550	2.5887	4
4.1002	3.9927	3.8897	3.7908	3.6048	3.3522	2.9906	5
4.7665	4.6229	4.4859	4.3553	4.1114	3.7845	3.3255	6
5.3893	5.2064	5.0330	4.8684	4.5638	4.1604	3.6046	7
5.9713	5.7466	5.5348	5.3349	4.9676	4.4873	3.8372	8
6.5152	6.2469	5.9952	5.7590	5.3282	4.7716	4.0310	9
7.0236	6.7101	6.4177	6.1446	5.6502	5.0188	4.1925	10
7.4987	7.1390	6.8052	6.4951	5.9377	5.2337	4.3271	11
7.9427	7.5361	7.1607	6.8137	6.1944	5.4206	4.4392	12
8.3577	7.9038	7.4869	7.1034	6.4235	5.5831	4.5327	13
8.7455	8.2442	7.7862	7.3667	6.6282	5.7245	4.6106	14
9.1079	8.5595	8.0607	7.6061	6.8109	5.8474	4.6755	15
9.4466	8.8514	8.3126	7.8237	6.9740	5.9542	4.7296	16
9.7632	9.1216	8.5436	8.0216	7.1196	6.0472	4.7746	17
10.0591	9.3719	8.7556	8.2014	7.2497	6.1280	4.8122	18
10.3356	9.6036	8.9501	8.3649	7.3658	6.1982	4.8435	19
10.5940	9.8181	9.1285	8.5136	7.4694	6.2593	4.8696	20
10.8355	10.0168	9.2922	8.6487	7.5620	6.3125	4.8913	21
11.0612	10.2007	9.4424	8.7715	7.6446	6.3587	4.9094	22
11.2722	10.3711	9.5802	8.8832	7.7184	6.3988	4.9245	23
11.4693	10.5288	9.7066	8.9847	7.7843	6.4338	4.9371	24
11.6536	10.6748	9.8226	9.0770	7.8431	6.4641	4.9476	25
12.4090	11.2578	10.2736	9.4269	8.0552	6.5660	4.9789	30
12.9477	11.6546	10.5668	9.6442	8.1755	6.6166	4.9915	35
13.3317	11.9246	10.7574	9.7791	8.2438	6.6418	4.9966	40
13.8007	12.2335	10.9617	9.9148	8.3045	6.6605	4.9995	50
14.0392	12.3766	11.0480	9.9672	8.3240	6.6653	4.9999	60

FINANCIAL STATEMENTS

This appendix contains financial statements, notes, and other items from the 1986 annual report of the Goodyear Tire and Rubber Company. For convenience, the sequence of items has been rearranged, and some notes have been omitted. The contents are presented as follows:

Consolidated Statement of Income
The Goodyear Tire & Rubber Company and Subsidiaries

(Dollars in millions, except per share)	Year Ended December 31,		
	1986	1985	1984
Net Sales	**$9,103.1**	$8,377.7	$8,494.9
Other Income	**121.6**	114.2	82.9
	9,224.7	8,491.9	8,577.8
Cost and Expenses:			
Cost of goods sold	**6,993.9**	6,574.0	6,586.7
Selling, administrative and general expense	**1,601.3**	1,384.4	1,303.4
Interest and amortization of debt discount and expense	**134.4**	100.6	112.2
Unusual items:			
Restructuring costs	**334.9**	28.5	16.7
Pension settlement	**(304.4)**	—	—
Oil and gas write-down	**214.8**	—	—
Sale of facilities	**(17.0)**	(7.2)	(10.1)
Foreign currency exchange	**18.8**	33.8	46.9
Minority interest in net income of subsidiaries	**9.6**	6.6	6.5
	8,986.3	8,120.7	8,062.3
Income from continuing operations before income taxes	**238.4**	371.2	515.5
United States and foreign taxes on income	**137.7**	119.7	211.7
Income from continuing operations	**100.7**	251.5	303.8
Discontinued operations	**23.4**	160.9	107.2
Net Income	**$ 124.1**	$ 412.4	$ 411.0
Per Share of Common Stock:			
Income from continuing operations	**$ .94**	$2.34	$2.86
Discontinued operations	**.22**	1.50	1.01
Net Income	**$1.16**	$3.84	$3.87

The accompanying accounting policies and notes are an integral part of this financial statement.

Consolidated Statement of Shareholders' Equity
The Goodyear Tire & Rubber Company and Subsidiaries

(Dollars in millions, except per share)

	Common Stock Shares	Common Stock Amount	Capital Surplus	Retained Earnings	Foreign Currency Translation Adjustment
Balance at December 31, 1983					
after deducting 1,219,698 treasury shares	105,425,079	$91.5	$589.4	$2,678.8	$(343.5)
Net income for 1984				411.0	
Cash dividends paid in 1984—					
$1.50 per share				(158.7)	
Common stock purchased for treasury	(250,001)	(.3)	(6.8)		
Common stock issued (including 46,220					
treasury shares)	1,317,631	1.3	31.0		
Foreign currency translation adjustment . . .					(122.4)
Balance at December 31, 1984					
after deducting 1,423,479 treasury shares	106,492,709	92.5	613.6	2,931.1	(465.9)
Net income for 1985				412.4	
Cash dividends paid in 1985—					
$1.60 per share				(171.3)	
Common stock issued (including 102,750					
treasury shares)	1,617,376	1.6	41.8		
Foreign currency translation adjustment . . .					51.6
Balance at December 31, 1985					
after deducting 1,320,729 treasury shares	108,110,085	94.1	655.4	3,172.2	(414.3)
Net income for 1986				124.1	
Cash dividends paid in 1986 —					
$1.60 per share				(174.1)	
Common stock purchased for treasury	(13,130,805)	(13.1)	(601.1)		
Adjustment of stated capital to					
$1.00 per share		14.0	(14.0)		
Common stock issued (including 547,196					
treasury shares)	2,101,202	2.1	63.9		
Foreign currency translation adjustment . . .					93.4
Balance at December 31, 1986					
after deducting 13,904,338 treasury shares . . .	97,080,482	$97.1	$104.2	$3,122.2	$(320.9)

The accompanying accounting policies and notes are an integral part of this financial statement.

Consolidated Balance Sheet

The Goodyear Tire & Rubber Company and Subsidiaries

(Dollars in millions)	December 31, 1986	1985
ASSETS		
Current Assets:		
Cash and short term securities	$ 130.5	$ 139.0
Accounts and notes receivable	1,367.2	957.4
Inventories	1,352.2	1,378.5
Prepaid expenses	82.7	83.3
Net assets held for sale	107.8	—
Total Current Assets	3,040.4	2,558.2
Other Assets:		
Investments in nonconsolidated subsidiaries and affiliates, at equity	222.4	181.3
Long term accounts and notes receivable	240.0	126.8
Investments and miscellaneous assets, at cost	34.4	30.6
Deferred pension plan cost	320.2	—
Deferred charges	72.1	31.6
Net assets held for sale	96.6	—
	985.7	370.3
Properties and Plants	4,583.4	4,025.0
	$8,609.5	$6,953.5
LIABILITIES AND SHAREHOLDERS' EQUITY		
Current Liabilities:		
Accounts payable—trade	$ 749.5	$ 657.4
Accrued payrolls and other compensation	337.1	347.4
Other current liabilities	405.0	219.1
United States and foreign taxes:		
Current	168.0	173.2
Deferred	—	58.8
Notes payable to banks and overdrafts	304.2	116.3
Long term debt due within one year	44.4	35.2
Deferred gain on sale of assets	134.7	—
Total Current Liabilities	2,142.9	1,607.4
Long Term Debt and Capital Leases	2,487.5	997.5
Other Long Term Liabilities	317.5	301.6
Deferred Income Taxes	586.4	475.3
Minority Equity in Subsidiaries	72.6	64.3
Shareholders' Equity:		
Preferred stock, no par value:		
Authorized, 50,000,000 shares		
Outstanding shares, none	—	—
Common stock, no par value:		
Authorized, 150,000,000 shares		
Outstanding shares, 97,080,482 (108,110,085 in 1985)	97.1	94.1
Capital surplus	104.2	655.4
Retained earnings	3,122.2	3,172.2
	3,323.5	3,921.7
Foreign currency translation adjustment	(320.9)	(414.3)
Total Shareholders' Equity	3,002.6	3,507.4
	$8,609.5	$6,953.5

The accompanying accounting policies and notes are an integral part of this financial statement.

Consolidated Statement of Changes in Financial Position
The Goodyear Tire & Rubber Company and Subsidiaries

(Dollars in millions)	Year Ended December 31,		
	1986	1985	1984
Funds provided from operations:			
Income from continuing operations	$ **100.7**	$ 251.5	$ 303.8
Non-cash items:			
Depreciation and depletion	**378.6**	277.7	270.8
Restructuring costs	**262.3**	28.5	16.7
Pension settlement	(**304.4)**	—	—
Oil and gas write-down	**214.8**	—	—
Accounts and notes receivable (increase) reduction	(**409.8)**	412.7	157.3
Inventories (increase) reduction	**26.3**	(45.1)	(114.5)
Net assets held for sale—current (increase)	(**107.8)**	—	—
Long term accounts and notes receivable (increase) reduction	(**113.2)**	(87.2)	11.1
Deferred charges (increase) reduction	(**40.5)**	2.2	(14.4)
Net assets held for sale—long term (increase)	(**96.6)**	—	—
Deferred income increase	**134.7**	—	—
Other items increase	**35.3**	81.7	84.4
	80.4	922.0	715.2
Income from discontinued operations	**23.4**	160.9	107.2
	103.8	1,082.9	822.4
Funds provided from financing:			
Notes payable to banks and overdrafts increase (reduction)	**187.9**	(41.1)	2.8
Long term debt and capital lease reduction	(**79.6)**	(234.7)	(112.4)
Long term debt and capital lease increase	**1,578.8**	571.8	101.1
Common stock issued	**66.0**	43.4	32.3
Common stock acquired	(**614.2)**	—	(7.1)
	1,138.9	339.4	16.7
Funds used for investment:			
Capital expenditures	(**1,337.8)**	(1,623.3)	(585.6)
Property and plant dispositions	**210.8**	415.9	37.0
Other transactions	(**43.5)**	(99.6)	22.9
	(**1,170.5)**	(1,307.0)	(525.7)
Dividends paid	(**174.1)**	(171.3)	(158.7)
Foreign currency translation adjustment (increase) reduction	**93.4**	51.6	(122.4)
Cash and short term securities increase (reduction)	$(**8.5)**	$(4.4)	$ 32.3

The accompanying accounting policies and notes are an integral part of this financial statement.

A summary of the significant accounting policies used in the preparation of the accompanying financial statements follows:

Principles of Consolidation

The consolidated financial statements include the accounts of all majority owned subsidiaries except for Goodyear Financial Corporation. All significant intercompany transactions have been eliminated.

The Company's investments in Goodyear Financial Corporation and in 20% to 50% owned companies in which it has the ability to exercise significant influence over operating and financial policies are accounted for on the equity method. Accordingly, the Company's share of the earnings of these companies is included in consolidated net income. Investments in other companies are carried at cost.

Inventory Pricing

Inventories are stated at the lower of cost or market. Cost is determined using the last-in, first-out (LIFO) method for substantially all domestic inventories and average cost or standard cost approximating average cost for all other inventories.

Properties and Plants

Properties and plants are stated at cost, including oil and gas exploration and development properties under the full cost method. Under the full cost method all exploration and development costs relating to oil and gas reserves are capitalized, including the cost of non-productive drilling, surrendered acreage and delay rentals.

Depreciation is computed on the straight line method. Accelerated depreciation is used for income tax purposes, where permitted. Depletion is computed using the unit-of-production method.

Pensions

The Company adopted Statement of Financial Accounting Standards No. 87 (SFAS No. 87), ''Employers' Accounting for Pensions'' for all domestic and certain foreign pension plans in 1986.

Income Taxes

Income taxes are recognized during the year in which transactions enter into the determination of financial statement income with deferred taxes being provided for timing differences. United States investment tax credit is recorded, using the flow-through method, as a reduction of the current tax provision.

Reclassification

Certain items previously reported in specific financial statement captions have been reclassified to conform with the 1986 presentation.

Accounts and Notes Receivable

(In millions)	1986	1985
Accounts and notes receivable	**$1,689.6**	$1,743.4
Notes receivable on properties sold	**289.8**	—
Less:		
Allowance for doubtful accounts	**36.8**	36.5
Receivables sold to Goodyear Financial Corporation, less 5% holdback	**575.4**	749.5
	$1,367.2	$ 957.4

The Company sold with limited recourse domestic accounts receivable and certain foreign accounts and notes receivable, subject to recourse provisions, totaling approximately $823.6 million, $338.3 million and $201.2 million for 1986, 1985 and 1984, respectively. At December 31, 1986 and 1985 the balances of the uncollected portion of these receivables were $170.3 million and $55.0 million, respectively.

Inventories

(In millions)	1986	1985
Raw materials and supplies	**$ 377.2**	$ 431.9
Work in process	**83.4**	123.5
Finished product	**891.6**	823.1
	$1,352.2	$1,378.5

The approximate current cost of inventories priced using the last-in, first-out (LIFO) method (approximately 36% of consolidated inventories above in 1986 and 40% in 1985) exceeded the LIFO cost by $290.0 million at December 31, 1986 and $397.3 million at December 31, 1985.

The amount of progress payments applied against inventory by Goodyear Aerospace Corporation relating to long term contracts was $149.7 million at December 31, 1985.

Properties and Plants

(In millions)	1986			1985		
	Owned	Capital Leases	Total	Owned	Capital Leases	Total
Land and improvements	**$ 256.7**	**$ 9.0**	**$ 265.7**	$ 234.2	$ 9.0	$ 243.2
Buildings	**960.0**	**82.2**	**1,042.2**	932.4	88.7	1,021.1
Machinery and equipment ...	**4,102.4**	**119.4**	**4,221.8**	3,995.9	121.2	4,117.1
Oil and gas exploration and development properties ..	**762.1**	**—**	**762.1**	774.8	—	774.8
Construction in progress	**1,290.4**	**—**	**1,290.4**	763.2	—	763.2
Properties and plants, at cost	**7,371.6**	**210.6**	**7,582.2**	6,700.5	218.9	6,919.4
Less accumulated depreciation and depletion ...	**2,873.9**	**124.9**	**2,998.8**	2,767.6	126.8	2,894.4
	$4,497.7	**$ 85.7**	**$4,583.4**	$3,932.9	$ 92.1	$4,025.0

The amortization for capital leases included in the depreciation provision for 1986, 1985 and 1984 was $11.6 million, $11.5 million and $12.3 million, respectively.

Notes to Financial Statements
(Continued)

Foreign Operations

Net income from foreign operations (including export sales) and dividends received by the Company and domestic subsidiaries during the three years ended December 31, 1986 follow:

(In millions)	1986	1985	1984
Net Income	**$62.9**	$26.7	$69.5
Dividends	**85.2**	71.7	44.0

Net foreign assets were $1,157.2 million at December 31, 1986 ($1,287.6 million at December 31, 1985) after deducting minority shareholders' equity.

Credit Arrangements

Short Term Debt and Credit Lines

Effective April 1, 1986, the Company cancelled short term domestic bank lines aggregating $155.0 million which were also available to GFC. These cancelled credit lines were replaced with non-cancellable revolving credit agreements. In connection with domestic credit lines, the Company maintained average collected balances at banks of approximately $1.9 million during 1986 and $9.8 million during 1985. Foreign subsidiaries had short term credit lines and overdraft arrangements totaling $836.3 million of which $514.0 million were unused at December 31, 1986.

Long Term Debt and Capital Leases

(In millions)	1986	1985
Sinking fund debentures:		
8.60% due 1988-1994	$ 52.5	$ 52.5
7.35% due 1992-1997	38.9	38.9
Promissory notes:		
11.90% due 1994-1999	50.0	50.0
12.15% due 1991-2000	50.0	50.0
Yen bonds:		
6.875% due 1994	78.6	62.2
7.125% due 1995	157.2	124.4
6.625% due 1996	62.9	—
Swiss Franc bonds:		
5.375% due 2000	146.1	115.5
5.375% due 2006	122.8	—
Celeron pipeline facility	650.0	—
Other domestic debt	469.3	164.6
Foreign subsidiary debt	531.6	245.0
Capital lease obligations:		
Industrial revenue bonds	93.7	97.3
Other	28.3	32.3
	2,531.9	1,032.7
Less portion due within one year	44.4	35.2
	$2,487.5	$ 997.5

Refer to note on Leased Assets for additional information on capital lease obligations.

The Celeron pipeline facility is a term loan bank facility arranged with a group of 13 banks. The loan bears interest at specified rates over LIBOR or a defined Certificate of Deposit rate as selected by the Company. The loan provides for scheduled reductions starting in 1987 and ending in 1994.

Credit Arrangements
(continued)

The Yen denominated bonds due in 1994, 1995 and 1996 and the Swiss Franc denominated bonds due in 2000 and 2006 are completely hedged by contract against future fluctuations in the U.S. dollar value of those currencies. At December 31, 1986, $168.9 million associated with these hedge contracts is recorded in long term accounts and notes receivable on the Consolidated Balance Sheet.

The Company has interest rate swap agreements, amounting to $1,407.0 million at December 31, 1986, in effect to convert floating interest rates to fixed rates on the Celeron Pipeline Company debt and other variable rate debt instruments.

At December 31, 1986 there were non-cancellable revolving credit agreements totaling $4,018.0 million whereby the Company or GFC could borrow $2,270.0 million from major domestic banks and $1,748.0 million in various Euro-currencies from major foreign banks (GFC had access to $1,548.0 million of the $1,748.0 million Euro-currency revolving credits). Commitment fees were paid on the unused portions of the credit lines. These credit agreements also provided support for Goodyear and GFC outstanding commercial paper and a demand note payable to the trust department of a commercial bank. Foreign subsidiaries have credit facilities for $1,140.2 million under non-cancellable revolving credit agreements or unused term loan agreements which terminate subsequent to 1987.

Certain domestic and foreign subsidiary obligations amounting to $351.6 million and $331.4 million, respectively, which by their terms are due within one year, are classified as long term where the obligations are incurred under or supported by non-cancellable long term credit agreements and it is the Company's intent to maintain them as long term.

The annual aggregate maturities of long term debt for the five years subsequent to 1986 are presented below. Maturities of debt incurred under or supported by revolving credit agreements have been reported on the basis that these agreements will not be renewed or replaced.

(In millions)	1987	1988	1989	1990	1991
Debt incurred under or supported by revolving credit agreements	$ —	$ —	$ 87.3	$ —	$ —
Other	37.0	337.7	148.3	159.2	154.5
	$37.0	$337.7	$235.6	$159.2	$154.5

In January 1987, the Company terminated the $4,018.0 million non-cancellable revolving credit agreements. The terminated revolving credit agreements were replaced with a $4,000.0 million Credit Facility consisting of a $2,250.0 million three-year amortizing term loan and a $1,750.0 million seven-year amortizing revolving credit line. The Credit Facility was used to complete the Company's tender offer and refinance amounts outstanding under certain existing bank credit arrangements with the balance available for working capital purposes. To reduce a portion of this debt, the Company is committed to use at least 80 percent of the net proceeds from sales of significant assets.

The term loan provides for scheduled reductions of $650.0 million, $800.0 million and $800.0 million in January of 1988, 1989 and 1990, respectively, and the revolving credit line provides for $100.0 million and $150.0 million reductions in January 1991 and 1992, respectively.

The Credit Facility agreement includes certain covenants which, among other things, establish limits for interest coverage ratios, current ratios, net worth and debt.

The term loan bears interest at rates of not more than LIBOR plus 1 1/8 percent or a defined Certificate of Deposit rate plus 1 1/4 percent as selected by the Company. The revolving credit line bears interest at rates of not more than LIBOR plus 7/8 percent or the Certificate of Deposit rate plus 1 percent as selected by the Company. The interest rate premiums over LIBOR or Certificate of Deposit rates will be reduced as outstanding balances or total debt are reduced.

Notes to Financial Statements
(Continued)

Leased Assets

Certain manufacturing, retail store, transportation, data processing and other facilities and equipment are held under leases which generally expire within ten years but may be renewed by the Company. Many of the leases provide that the Company will pay taxes assessed against leased property and the cost of insurance and maintenance.

Minimum lease commitments follow:

(In millions)	Capital Leases	Operating Leases
1987	$ 17.3	$131.4
1988	20.5	108.2
1989	19.4	84.8
1990	18.4	57.7
1991	17.4	39.0
1992 and thereafter	116.8	144.3
Total minimum lease payments	209.8	$565.4
Less estimated executory costs	1.9	
Net minimum lease payments	207.9	
Less amounts estimated to represent interest	85.9	
Present value of net minimum lease obligations	122.0	
Less portion due within one year	7.3	
	$114.7	

Total rental expense charged to income and contingent rentals included therein follow:

(In millions)	1986	1985	1984
Minimum rentals	$169.7	$134.1	$124.5
Contingent rentals	1.3	1.1	.5
Less sublease rentals	30.0	23.8	19.5
Rental expense	$141.0	$111.4	$105.5

Stock Options

The Company's 1972 and 1982 Employees' Stock Option Plans provide for the granting of stock options and related stock appreciation rights (SARs). For options previously granted with related SARs, the exercise of an SAR cancels the stock option; conversely, the exercise of the stock option cancels the SAR and, in either instance, the share is no longer available for further granting of options.

The 1972 and 1982 Plans expired on December 31, 1981 and 1986, respectively, except for options and SARs then outstanding. Celeron also had a stock option plan which was terminated at the time of the merger and then outstanding options were converted to options for Goodyear common stock.

At January 1, 1985, there were 1,818,996 shares of common stock subject to outstanding options and 1,277,300 shares were available for the granting of additional options. During 1985, options for 780,650 shares, of which 32,800 had related SARs, were granted; options and SARs were exercised for 163,628 shares and options expired for 103,439 shares. During 1986, options for 559,750 shares, of which 66,500 had related SARs, were granted; options and SARs were exercised for 1,711,396 shares and options expired for 30,450 shares. At December 31, 1986, there were 1,150,483 shares subject to outstanding options exercisable at prices ranging from $12.00 to $35.50.

Notes to Financial Statements
(Continued)

Common and Preferred Stock

Details of certain common shares issued and purchased for treasury follow:

	1986	1985	1984
Dividend reinvestment and stock purchase plan	1,554,006	1,514,626	1,271,411
Stock option plans	507,393	68,828	3,710
Incentive profit sharing plan	39,803	33,922	42,510
Common shares issued	2,101,202	1,617,376	1,317,631
Shares acquired from General Oriental Group	12,549,400	—	—
Other acquired shares	581,405	—	250,001
Common shares purchased for treasury	13,130,805	—	250,001

The Company authorized 3,000,000 shares of Series A $10.00 Preferred Stock ("Series A Preferred") issuable only upon the exercise of rights ("Rights") issued under the Preferred Stock Purchase Rights Plan adopted in July 1986. Each share of Series A Preferred issued would be non-redeemable, non-voting and entitled to cumulative quarterly dividends equal to the greater of $10.00 or, subject to adjustment, 100 times the per share amount of dividends declared on Goodyear common stock during the preceding quarter, and would also be entitled to a liquidation preference.

Under the Rights Plan, each shareholder of record on July 28, 1986 received a dividend of one Right per share of Goodyear common stock. When exercisable, each Right entitles the holder to buy one one-hundredth of a share of Series A Preferred at an exercise price of $100. The Rights will be exercisable only after 10 days following the earlier of a public announcement that a person or group has acquired 20 percent or more of Goodyear common stock or the commencement of a tender offer for 20 percent or more of Goodyear common stock by a person or group. The Rights are non-voting and may be redeemed by the Company at $.05 per Right under certain circumstances. If not redeemed or exercised, the Rights will expire on July 28, 1996. If a person or group accumulates 35 percent or more of Goodyear common stock, or a merger takes place with an acquiring person or group and the Company is the surviving corporation, or an acquiring person or group engages in certain self-dealing transactions, each Right (except those held by such acquiring person or group) will entitle the holder to purchase Goodyear common stock having a market value then equal to two times the exercise price. If the Company is acquired or a sale or transfer of 50 percent or more of the Company's assets or earning power is made, each Right (except those held by the acquiring person or group) will entitle the holder to purchase common stock of the acquiring entity having a market value then equal to two times the exercise price.

Interest Expense

Total interest less amounts capitalized follows:

(In millions)	1986	1985	1984
Total interest	$269.4	$140.5	$126.5
Capitalized interest	135.0	39.9	14.3
Interest and amortization of debt discount and expense	$134.4	$100.6	$112.2

Income Taxes

The components of income from continuing operations before income taxes follow:

(In millions)	1986	1985	1984
Domestic operations	$126.1	$316.5	$414.0
Foreign operations.......................................	112.3	54.7	101.5
Total	$238.4	$371.2	$515.5

Notes to Financial Statements
(Continued)

Income Taxes
(continued)

The effective income tax rate information follows:

	1986	1985	1984
U.S. Federal statutory income tax rate	46.0%	46.0%	46.0%
Investment tax credit less tax effect of applicable			
asset basis reduction	(11.6)	(16.3)	(4.0)
Difference applicable to foreign operations	(1.7)	2.5	(1.0)
State and local taxes	4.6	.7	1.8
Restructuring costs	18.8	1.2	.1
Other items	(.6)	(2.4)	(2.4)
Effective rate on income from continuing operations			
before income taxes and minority interest	55.5	31.7	40.5
Discontinued operations	(1.2)	.2	(1.3)
Effective rate reflecting discontinued operations	54.3%	31.9%	39.2%

The investment tax credit, less the tax effect of the applicable asset basis reduction, included in income from continuing operations for 1986, 1985 and 1984 was $28.9 million, $61.7 million and $21.2 million, respectively.

The components of the provision for income taxes by taxing jurisdiction follow:

(In millions)	1986	1985	1984
Currently payable:			
Federal	$ (75.7)	$ (47.4)	$ 25.4
Foreign	104.5	109.8	98.9
State	37.6	6.8	19.2
	66.4	69.2	143.5
Deferred:			
Federal	83.6	39.4	53.4
Foreign	(5.6)	9.9	13.3
State	(6.7)	1.2	1.5
	71.3	50.5	68.2
United States and foreign taxes on income from			
continuing operations	$137.7	$119.7	$211.7

Prepaid and deferred taxes relating to timing differences in the recognition of revenues and expenses for tax and financial reporting purposes follow:

(In millions)	1986	1985	1984
Depreciation	$ 49.7	$63.2	$47.8
Exploration and development costs	31.3	(7.6)	17.8
Plant closures	(12.5)	3.1	11.3
Capitalized interest	53.4	14.9	3.8
Restructuring costs	(47.1)	—	—
Pensions	155.6	3.1	4.1
Oil and gas write-down	(104.0)	—	—
Sale of facilities.......................................	(62.0)	—	—
Other items...	6.9	(26.2)	(16.6)
	$ 71.3	$50.5	$68.2

No provision for Federal income tax or foreign withholding tax on retained earnings of foreign subsidiaries of $981.5 million is required because this amount has been reinvested in properties and plants and working capital.

Notes to Financial Statements
(Continued)

**Net Income
Per Share**

Net income per share has been computed based on the average number of common shares outstanding, including for this purpose only those treasury shares allocated for distribution under the incentive profit sharing plan; and for 1986, 1985 and 1984 was 107,092,197, 107,369,517 and 106,138,171, respectively.

**Commitments
and Contingent
Liabilities**

At December 31, 1986, the Company had binding commitments for investments in land, buildings, equipment, oil and gas exploration and production and the oil pipeline aggregating $294.9 million.

Various legal actions, claims and governmental investigations and proceedings covering a wide range of matters are pending against the Company and its subsidiaries. In the opinion of management, after reviewing such matters and consulting with the Company's General Counsel, any liability which may ultimately be incurred would not materially affect the consolidated financial position of the Company, although an adverse final determination in certain instances could materially affect the Company's consolidated net income for the period in which such determination occurs.

**Business
Segments**

As described in the note on discontinued operations, the Company has disposed of various operations during 1986. The sale of Motor Wheel Corporation and related assets affected the Tires and Related Transportation Products segment while the sale of Goodyear Aerospace Corporation and related assets affected the Aerospace segment, which has been eliminated.

Goodyear's principal industry segment is the development, manufacture, distribution and sale of Tires and Related Transportation Products. These products include tires, tubes, retreads, automotive belts and hose, automotive molded parts and foam cushioning accessories, auto repair services and merchandise purchased for resale. The Industrial Rubber, Chemical and Plastic Products segment includes various kinds of hose and belting products, hose couplings, tank tracks, organic chemicals used in rubber and plastic processing, synthetic rubber and rubber latices, polyester resins, films, vinyl products, roofing membrane, shoe products and graphic products. The Oil and Gas industry segment includes exploration, development and production of oil and gas reserves and a crude oil pipeline. The remaining revenues and income were derived from diverse businesses.

Operating income for each industry and geographic segment consists of total revenues less applicable costs and expenses related to those revenues. Transfers between industry segments were insignificant. A portion of the previously described restructuring costs have been included for presentation of the operating income of both the industry and geographic segments. Restructuring costs of $182.4 million, $26.3 million and $3.4 million have been assigned to the Tires and Related Transportation Products, Industrial Rubber, Chemical and Plastic Products and Oil and Gas segments, respectively. Geographically, $125.1 million, $20.7 million, $1.0 million, $25.5 million, $1.9 million and $37.9 million are attributable to the United States, Europe, Mediterranean-Africa, Latin America, Asia-Pacific and Canada segments. Inter-geographic sales were at cost plus a negotiated mark up. The following items have been excluded from the determination of operating income: interest and amortization of debt discount and expense, foreign currency exchange, equity in net income of affiliated companies, minority interest in net income of subsidiaries, general corporate revenues and expenses, income taxes, discontinued operations, the pension settlement and restructuring costs not related directly to the segments.

General corporate revenues and expenses were those items not identifiable with the operations of a segment. General corporate revenues were primarily from interest income, certain royalty and technical agreements and nonrecurring gains from the sale of assets. General corporate expenses were primarily central administrative office expenses.

Assets of industry and geographic segments represent those assets that were identified with the operations of each segment. Corporate assets consist of cash and short term securities, prepaid expenses, certain investments and miscellaneous assets, deferred charges and the assets of discontinued operations.

Notes to Financial Statements
(Continued)

Industry Segments

(In millions)	1986	1985	1984
Sales to Unaffiliated Customers			
Tires	$6,629.9	$6,190.2	$6,237.5
Related transportation products	1,214.0	985.5	995.2
Tires and related transportation products............	7,843.9	7,175.7	7,232.7
Industrial rubber, chemical and plastic products	1,136.4	1,102.0	1,137.9
Oil and gas	63.2	36.5	49.1
Other products and services	59.6	63.5	75.2
Net sales	$9,103.1	$8,377.7	$8,494.9
Income			
Tires and related transportation products	$ 305.2	$ 452.0	$ 591.5
Industrial rubber, chemical and plastic products	110.5	82.7	91.5
Oil and gas	(212.2)	7.9	13.9
Other products and services	23.2	15.1	21.0
Total operating income...........................	226.7	557.7	717.9
Interest and amortization of debt discount and expense ...	(134.4)	(100.6)	(112.2)
Foreign currency exchange...........................	(18.8)	(33.8)	(46.9)
Equity in net income of affiliated companies	8.3	2.6	2.8
Minority interest in net income	(9.6)	(6.6)	(6.5)
Corporate revenues and expenses	166.2	(48.1)	(39.6)
Income from continuing operations before income taxes	$ 238.4	$ 371.2	$ 515.5
Assets			
Tires and related transportation products	$4,882.9	$4,258.8	$4,134.0
Industrial rubber, chemical and plastic products	548.0	464.3	479.2
Oil and gas	1,755.3	1,296.1	430.0
Other products and services	237.0	101.0	100.1
Total identifiable assets	7,423.2	6,120.2	5,143.3
Corporate assets...................................	963.9	652.0	892.8
Investments in affiliated companies	222.4	181.3	158.2
Assets at December 31	$8,609.5	$6,953.5	$6,194.3
Capital Expenditures			
Tires and related transportation products	$ 532.1	$ 570.7	$ 431.1
Industrial rubber, chemical and plastic products	50.3	48.5	34.0
Oil and gas	737.1	992.4	113.5
Other products and services	18.3	11.7	7.0
For the year	$1,337.8	$1,623.3	$ 585.6
Depreciation and Depletion			
Tires and related transportation products	$ 311.3	$ 238.9	$ 228.4
Industrial rubber, chemical and plastic products	28.7	26.8	20.7
Oil and gas	30.9	9.4	19.4
Other products and services	7.7	2.6	2.3
For the year	$ 378.6	$ 277.7	$ 270.8

Notes to Financial Statements
(Continued)

Geographic Segments

(In millions)	1986	1985	1984
Sales to Unaffiliated Customers			
United States	$5,653.1	$5,338.8	$5,445.3
Europe	1,355.3	1,027.8	944.5
Mediterranean-Africa	419.5	325.5	338.2
Latin America	817.8	893.4	925.0
Asia-Pacific	428.4	383.8	435.9
Canada	429.0	408.4	406.0
Net sales	$9,103.1	$8,377.7	$8,494.9
Inter-Geographic Sales			
United States	$ 168.9	$ 153.8	$ 134.6
Europe	91.5	67.5	56.8
Mediterranean-Africa	4.7	2.8	2.2
Latin America	50.4	45.0	44.3
Asia-Pacific	24.9	16.0	17.4
Canada	59.2	50.7	77.9
Total	$ 399.6	$ 335.8	$ 333.2
Revenue			
United States	$5,822.0	$5,492.6	$5,579.9
Europe	1,446.8	1,095.3	1,001.3
Mediterranean-Africa	424.2	328.3	340.4
Latin America	868.2	938.4	969.3
Asia-Pacific	453.3	399.8	453.3
Canada	488.2	459.1	483.9
Adjustments and eliminations	(399.6)	(335.8)	(333.2)
Total	$9,103.1	$8,377.7	$8,494.9
Operating Income			
United States	$ 97.7	$ 397.1	$ 489.3
Europe	54.5	1.6	22.9
Mediterranean-Africa	36.7	25.8	28.9
Latin America	59.4	154.3	141.8
Asia-Pacific	13.0	(11.1)	22.7
Canada	(35.7)	(13.8)	10.2
Adjustments and eliminations	1.1	3.8	2.1
Total	$ 226.7	$ 557.7	$ 717.9
Assets			
United States	$5,739.5	$4,462.1	$3,896.7
Europe	1,067.9	849.4	649.7
Mediterranean-Africa	272.9	202.8	195.5
Latin America	729.7	723.3	729.5
Asia-Pacific	298.5	275.1	285.3
Canada	289.3	269.1	285.2
Adjustments and eliminations	(10.7)	(9.6)	(5.8)
Total identifiable assets	8,387.1	6,772.2	6,036.1
Investments in affiliated companies	222.4	181.3	158.2
Assets at December 31	$8,609.5	$6,953.5	$6,194.3

The financial statements of The Goodyear Tire & Rubber Company and subsidiaries were prepared in conformity with generally accepted accounting principles. The Company is responsible for selection of appropriate accounting principles and the objectivity and integrity of the data, estimates and judgments which are the basis for the financial statements.

Goodyear has established and maintains a system of internal controls designed to provide reasonable assurance that the books and records reflect the transactions of the companies and that its established policies and procedures are carefully followed. This system is based upon written procedures, policies and guidelines, organizational structures that provide an appropriate division of responsibility, a program of internal audit and the careful selection and training of qualified personnel.

Price Waterhouse, independent accountants, examined the financial statements and their report is presented on the following page. Their opinion is based on an examination which provides an independent, objective review of the way Goodyear fulfills its responsibility to publish statements which present fairly the financial position and operating results. They obtain and maintain an understanding of the Company's accounting and reporting controls, test transactions and perform related auditing procedures as they consider necessary to arrive at an opinion on the fairness of the financial statements. While the auditors make extensive reviews of procedures, it is neither practicable nor necessary for them to test a large portion of the daily transactions.

The Board of Directors pursues its oversight responsibility for the financial statements through its Audit Committee, composed of Directors who are not employees of the Company. The Committee meets periodically with the independent accountants, representatives of management and internal auditors to assure that all are carrying out their responsibilities. To assure independence, Price Waterhouse and the internal auditors have full and free access to the Audit Committee, without Company representatives present, to discuss the results of their examinations and their opinions on the adequacy of internal controls and the quality of financial reporting.

Robert E. Mercer
Chairman of the Board
and Chief Executive Officer

James R. Glass
Executive Vice President
and Chief Financial Officer

Report of Independent Accountants

Price Waterhouse

To the Board of Directors and Shareholders of
The Goodyear Tire & Rubber Company

In our opinion, the accompanying consolidated balance sheet and the related consolidated statements of income, shareholders' equity and changes in financial position present fairly the financial position of The Goodyear Tire & Rubber Company and subsidiaries at December 31, 1986 and 1985, and the results of their operations and the changes in their financial position for each of the three years in the period ended December 31, 1986, in conformity with generally accepted accounting principles consistently applied during the period except for the change, with which we concur, in the method of accounting for pension costs as described in the notes to financial statements. Our examinations of these statements were made in accordance with generally accepted auditing standards and accordingly included such tests of the accounting records and such other auditing procedures as we considered necessary in the circumstances.

Price Waterhouse

Cleveland, Ohio
February 18, 1987

Management's Discussion and
Analysis of Financial Condition and Results of Operations
The Goodyear Tire & Rubber Company and Subsidiaries

The Company has undertaken a restructuring program intended to enhance both near-term and long-term shareholder values. The program involves the sale of various subsidiary companies and certain other assets, the purchase of a significant portion of the Company's outstanding common stock, the closing of noncompetitive plants, employee reductions and other cost containment measures.

The Company entered into an agreement for the sale of Motor Wheel Corporation and related assets in December 1986 and reached an agreement in January 1987 for the sale of Goodyear Aerospace Corporation and related assets. Income and expenses related to those operations have been classified as discontinued operations (see note on Discontinued Operations). Accordingly, the accompanying financial information has been restated where required to reflect the effects of these transactions. In December 1986 certain properties in Arizona were sold (see note on Sale of Facilities). The Company is also offering for sale its oil and gas segment which includes a crude oil pipeline and oil and gas reserves.

In October 1986, General Oriental (Bermuda I) Limited Partnership and General Oriental (Delaware I) Limited Partnership (General Oriental Group), both represented by James Goldsmith, publicly announced that they had acquired 11.5 percent of the Company's outstanding common stock and were considering various other actions, among them, seeking control of the Company. On November 20, 1986, as part of the Company's restructuring program, the Company acquired all of the 12,549,400 shares of the Company's common stock then held by the General Oriental Group at a price of $49.50 per share. The Company also reimbursed certain expenses of $37.6 million, which has been charged against 1986 income. The General Oriental Group agreed not to acquire any of the Company's voting securities for five years and to use its best efforts to make certain of its banking facilities available to the Company. In addition, because the market price of the shares during the time of purchase was less than the amount paid, $34.5 million was charged against 1986 income. Such market price of the shares was recorded as the cost of treasury shares (see note on Restructuring Costs).

As part of the restructuring program the Company also announced its plans to make a tender offer for up to 40 million shares of its common stock at $50 net per share in cash (see note on Subsequent Event).

After completion of the restructuring program, the Company expects to remain a global leader in those areas representing its core business.

Results of Operations

The 1986 worldwide sales of $9.1 billion increased 8.7 percent from 1985 and rose 7.2 percent above 1984 levels. Worldwide income from continuing operations of $100.7 million was down 60.0 percent from $251.5 million recorded in 1985 and was down 66.9 percent from $303.8 million recorded in the 1984 period.

Impacting 1986 income from continuing operations were the following items:

· After tax charges of $224.6 million associated with the Company's restructuring program. Included are the closing of the Cumberland, Maryland and New Toronto, Ontario, Canada tire plants and the Windsor, Vermont shoe products plant, which were not competitive in the global marketplace. Also included were the implementation of special employee reduction programs, expenses related to the November 20, 1986 purchase of 12,549,400 shares of its common stock, the disposition of assets no longer required, the incurrence of certain contractual costs and other additional nonrecurring restructuring costs and fees. The Company expects that as a result of these structural changes, substantial reductions in operating expenses will occur in future periods. After tax charges of $20.4 million and $9.5 million were incurred for employee reductions in 1985 and 1984, respectively (see note on Restructuring Costs).

· An after tax charge of $110.8 million for the write-down of the Celeron Oil and Gas subsidiary's proved oil and gas reserves, as a result of a substantial decline in oil prices during the first quarter.

693

Management's Discussion and
Analysis of Financial Condition and Results of Operations
(Continued)

**Results of
Operations**
(continued)

· An after tax gain of $8.0 million from the sale of the assets of two Arizona subsidiaries which were involved in agricultural products, real estate development and a resort hotel. These sales were accounted for on an installment basis with the balance of the gain ($134.7 million before tax) to be recognized in 1987 (see note on Sale of Facilities).

· An after tax gain of $152.0 million from the settlement of a significant portion of the Company's pension obligation (see note on Pensions).

· The Company adopted, in the third quarter of 1986, Statement of Financial Accounting Standards No. 87, "Employers' Accounting for Pensions" for all domestic and certain foreign pension plans, retroactive to January 1, 1986. This change increased net income by $21.6 million for the year.

The 1986 net income of $124.1 million included earnings of $23.4 million from discontinued operations. The Company expects to realize a gain in 1987 upon completion of the sale of· Goodyear Aerospace Corporation and related assets.

Income from continuing operations for 1985 of $251.5 million included an $11.4 million after tax benefit associated with a change in the rate of recognition of investment gains and losses for domestic pension plans and an investment tax credit of $32.9 million associated with the oil pipeline project as compared to $22.8 million in 1986.

Net income for 1985 of $412.4 million included income of $160.9 million from the discontinued operations of Motor Wheel Corporation, Goodyear Aerospace Corporation, certain companies within the Celeron group and the gain from the sale of those Celeron operations in 1985.

Net income for 1984 of $411.0 million included income of $107.2 million from discontinued operations of the Celeron group, Motor Wheel Corporation and Goodyear Aerospace Corporation.

Sales in the U.S. for 1986 of $5.7 billion compare with $5.3 billion in 1985 and $5.4 billion in 1984, an increase of 5.9 percent and 3.8 percent, respectively. Operating income of $97.7 million decreased 75.4 percent from the $397.1 million recorded in 1985 and 80.0 percent from the $489.3 million of 1984, primarily due to the $214.8 million before tax write-down of the proved oil and gas reserves and nonrecurring restructuring charges of $125.1 million, which have been classified as operating expenses. Domestic tire unit sales increased 3.5 percent from 1985 and remained relatively unchanged from 1984.

Foreign sales of $3.4 billion in 1986 exceeded the $3.1 billion of 1985 by 13.5 percent and the $3.1 billion of 1984 by 13.1 percent. Foreign operating income of $127.9 million compares with $156.8 million from last year and $226.5 million of 1984, a decrease of 18.4 percent and 43.5 percent, respectively. Operating income for 1986 includes the effects of $87.0 million of restructuring charges attributable to foreign operations. Foreign sales were aided by tire unit sales increases of 6.3 percent over 1985 and 8.2 percent over 1984, and by strengthening foreign currencies.

Sales of tires and related transportation products were up 9.3 percent from 1985 and 8.5 percent from 1984 while operating income for that segment of the business was down 32.5 percent from 1985 and 48.4 percent from 1984 due to nonrecurring restructuring costs of $182.4 million that were charged to the segment.

In the industrial rubber, chemical and plastic products segment, sales were up 3.1 percent from 1985 and down slightly from 1984, while operating income was up 33.6 percent and 20.7 percent from 1985 and 1984, respectively, despite restructuring costs of $26.3 million related to the segment. Income gains came primarily from chemical products.

Management's Discussion and
Analysis of Financial Condition and Results of Operations
(Continued)

**Results of
Operations**
(continued)

The note on Business Segments provides further details of industry and geographic segments.

The Company has not provided supplementary data on Financial Reporting and Changing Prices, as the impact of inflation on the Company's net sales and income from continuing operations was minimal.

**Liquidity and
Capital Resources**

Consolidated debt, including capital lease obligations, increased from $1,149.0 million at December 31, 1985 to $2,836.1 million at December 31, 1986. The debt of Goodyear Financial Corporation decreased from $580.6 million at December 31, 1985 to $427.4 million at December 31, 1986. The net increase of consolidated and Goodyear Financial Corporation debt totaled $1,533.9 million and at December 31, 1986, debt was 52.1 percent of debt and shareholders' equity.

The increase in debt was primarily from the drawdown of the $650.0 million credit facility available to the Celeron Pipeline Company for the crude oil pipeline project and $658.8 million related to the November 20, 1986 purchase of the Company's common stock from the General Oriental Group.

The Company has interest rate swap agreements, amounting to $1,407.0 million at December 31, 1986, in effect to convert floating interest rates to fixed rates on the Celeron Pipeline Company debt and other variable rate debt instruments.

During the first quarter, the Company issued 6.625 percent Yen denominated bonds, due 1996, and 5.375 percent Swiss Franc denominated bonds, due 2006, net proceeds of which amounted to $50.0 million and $98.2 million, respectively. All Yen and Swiss Franc bond issues are hedged by contract to protect against changes in the value of the U.S. dollar versus the Japanese and Swiss currencies. Long term debt associated with the Yen and Swiss Franc bond issues increased as a result of revaluation of those currencies by $117.3 million during 1986 and was offset by a similar amount recorded in long term accounts and notes receivable.

Also during the first quarter the Company sold, with limited recourse, $100.0 million of domestic accounts receivable. As the receivables were collected, new amounts were sold under the agreement in order to maintain a level of approximately $100.0 million. Accounts receivable sold during the year under this and other agreements totaled approximately $823.6 million.

Substantial credit sources are available to the Company throughout the world under normal commercial practices. The Company's worldwide credit sources totaled $5,909.2 million at December 31, 1986, of which $4,200.6 million or 71.1 percent were unused. In January 1987, the Company terminated $4,018.0 million of the above credit lines and replaced them with a new $4,000.0 million Credit Facility consisting of a $2,250.0 million term loan and a $1,750.0 million revolving credit line.

The Company used the entire term loan and $950.0 million from the revolving credit line to purchase Company common stock pursuant to the tender offer and to refinance other borrowings (see note on Subsequent Event).

The Company is required to reduce portions of the term loan in the amounts of $650.0 million by January 1988 and $800.0 million by January 1989 and 1990, respectively. The Company is not required to reduce the outstanding balance of the revolving credit line until 1991. To reduce a portion of this debt, the Company is committed to use at least 80 percent of the net proceeds from sales of significant assets.

At December 31, 1986, the Company had binding commitments for investments in land, buildings, equipment, oil and gas exploration and production and the oil pipeline totaling $294.9 million.

The Company anticipates that funds available will be sufficient to meet liquidity needs into the foreseeable future.

Quarterly Data
and Market Price
Information

(In millions, except per share)

1986	First	Second	Third	Fourth	Year
Net sales	$2,063.3	$2,358.5	$2,316.3	$2,365.0	$9,103.1
Gross profit	437.8	557.3	540.5	573.6	2,109.2
Income from continuing operations	(64.0)	98.0	174.5	(107.8)	100.7
Discontinued operations	10.6	10.0	7.8	(5.0)	23.4
Net income	$ (53.4)	$ 108.0	$ 182.3	$ (112.8)	$ 124.1
Per share of common stock:					
Income from continuing operations	$ (.59)	$ .89	$ 1.61	$ (1.04)	$ .94
Discontinued operations	.10	.10	.07	(.05)	.22
Net income	$ (.49)	$ .99	$ 1.68	$ (1.09)	$ 1.16
Price Range*					
High	$ 36-3/4	$ 35-7/8	$ 35-1/8	$ 50	$ 50
Low	30	29	29-3/4	33-1/4	29
Dividends paid	.40	.40	.40	.40	1.60

1985	First	Second	Third	Fourth	Year
Net sales	$1,999.4	$2,161.2	$2,085.6	$2,131.5	$8,377.7
Gross profit	442.3	477.3	427.3	456.8	1,803.7
Income from continuing operations	65.0	68.5	46.1	71.9	251.5
Discontinued operations	21.7	18.2	108.4	12.6	160.9
Net income	$ 86.7	$ 86.7	$ 154.5	$ 84.5	$ 412.4
Per share of common stock:					
Income from continuing operations	$ .61	$ .64	$ .43	$ .66	$ 2.34
Discontinued operations	.20	.17	1.01	.12	1.50
Net income	$ .81	$ .81	$ 1.44	$ .78	$ 3.84
Price Range*					
High	$ 29-1/8	$ 30-1/4	$ 30-1/4	$ 31-1/4	$ 31-1/4
Low	25-5/8	25-1/2	26-7/8	25-1/8	25-1/8
Dividends paid	.40	.40	.40	.40	1.60

*New York Stock Exchange—Composite Transactions

Quarterly data has been restated to reflect the discontinued operations of Goodyear Aerospace Corporation and Motor Wheel Corporation. The first and second quarters of 1986 have been restated for the adoption of SFAS No. 87.

The 1986 first quarter includes charges of $110.8 million ($1.02 per share) for the write-down of the Celeron Oil and Gas subsidiary's proved oil and gas reserves.

The 1986 third quarter included a gain of $152.0 million ($1.39 per share) for the pension settlement and charges of $41.2 million ($.38 per share) related to restructuring.

The 1986 fourth quarter includes a charge of $183.4 million ($1.78 per share) for corporate restructuring and a gain of $8.0 million ($.08 per share) from sale of facilities.

The 1985 first quarter includes a gain of $5.7 million or $.05 per share ($3.7 million or $.03 per share adjusted) from the sale of Duo-Therm.

The 1985 third quarter includes charges of $17.3 million ($.16 per share) for conversion of the Tyler, Texas plant to radial production and various restructuring programs.

The 1985 fourth quarter includes a gain of $11.4 million ($.11 per share) from a change in the rate of recognition of investment gains and losses for domestic pension plans. The 1985 fourth quarter also includes investment tax credit of $21.7 million ($.20 per share) associated with the oil pipeline project.

Comparison with Prior Years
The Goodyear Tire & Rubber Company and Subsidiaries

(Dollars in millions, except per share)	1986	1985	1984	1983	1982
Net Sales	$9,103.1	$8,377.7	$8,494.9	$8,074.4	$8,004.1
Income from continuing operations					
before extraordinary item	100.7	251.5	303.8	189.9	232.4
Discontinued operations	23.4	160.9	107.2	80.5	80.2
Extraordinary item:					
Gain on long term debt retired	—	—	—	35.1	17.2
Net Income	124.1	412.4	411.0	305.5	329.8
Net Income per dollar of sales	1.4¢	4.9¢	4.8¢	3.8¢	4.1¢
Depreciation and depletion	$ 378.6	$ 277.7	$ 270.8	$ 260.0	$ 232.0
Capital Expenditures	1,337.8	1,623.3	585.6	455.2	364.7
Properties and Plants—Net	4,583.4	4,025.0	3,036.7	2,819.2	2,718.2
Total Assets	$8,609.5	$6,953.5	$6,194.3	$5,985.5	$5,885.9
Long Term Debt and Capital Leases	2,487.5	997.5	656.8	665.2	1,174.5
Shareholders' Equity	3,002.6	3,507.4	3,171.3	3,016.2	2,777.2
Per Share of Common Stock:					
Income from continuing operations					
before extraordinary item	$ .94	$ 2.34	$ 2.86	$ 1.90	$ 2.35
Discontinued operations	.22	1.50	1.01	.81	.81
Extraordinary item:					
Gain on long term debt retired	—	—	—	.35	.18
Net Income*	1.16	3.84	3.87	3.06	3.34
Dividends**	1.60	1.60	1.50	1.40	1.40
Book Value—on shares outstanding					
at December 31	30.93	32.44	29.78	28.61	28.09
Price Range:					
High	50	31-1/4	31-1/2	36-3/8	36-7/8
Low...........................	29	25-1/8	23	27	17-7/8
Employees:					
Average during the year	121,586	123,231	123,104	119,732	123,030
Total compensation for the year	$2,562.8	$2,337.1	$2,272.3	$2,158.1	$2,125.7
Shareholders of record***	62,007	72,582	75,619	76,014	83,915
Common Shares:					
Outstanding at December 31	97,080,482	108,110,085	106,492,709	105,425,079	98,866,612
Average outstanding	107,092,197	107,369,517	106,138,171	99,907,522	98,794,352

*Based on average shares outstanding—see note on Net Income Per Share.

**Dividends are the historical dividends paid by The Goodyear Tire & Rubber Company.

***Includes shareholders of record of Celeron for periods prior to the merger.

The method of accounting for pensions was changed in 1986 (SFAS No. 87).

Financial information for 1982 has been restated to include Celeron on a pooling of interests basis, 1982-1985 financial information was restated where necessary to reflect the discontinued operations of Motor Wheel Corporation and related assets, Goodyear Aerospace Corporation and related assets and the discontinued operations of the Celeron group in 1985—see note on Discontinued Operations.

INDEX